THE JEWS IN LUKE-ACTS

JACK T. SANDERS

THE JEWS IN
LUKE-ACTS

Fortress Press   Philadelphia

Library of Congress Cataloging-in-Publication Data

Sanders, Jack T.
  The Jews in Luke-Acts.

  Bibliography: p.
  Includes index.
  1. Jews in the New Testament.   2. Bible.   N.T.
Luke—Criticism, interpretation, etc.   3. Bible.
N.T. Acts—Criticism, interpretation, etc.
I. Title.
BS2545.J44S258   1987   226'.4'0089924   84–45926
  ISBN 0–8006–1969–2

2670K86   Printed in the United Kingdom   1–1969

This volume is dedicated
with much love
to my wife
Susan Elizabeth Plass

Contents

PART TWO: SYSTEMATIC ANALYSIS

PART THREE: CONCLUDING EVALUATION

Abbreviations

AB	Anchor Bible
AnBib	Analecta biblica
ASNU	Acta seminarii neotestamentici upsaliensis
BBB	Bonner biblische Beiträge
BETL	Bibliotheca ephemeridum theologicarum lovaniensium
BHT	Beiträge zur historischen Theologie
Bib	*Biblica*
BJRL	*Bulletin of the John Rylands University Library of Manchester*
BNTC	Black's NT Commentaries
BVC	*Bible et vie chrétienne*
BWANT	Beiträge zur Wissenschaft vom Alten und Neuen Testament
BZ	*Biblische Zeitschrift*
BZNW	Beihefte zur *ZNW*
CBQ	*Catholic Biblical Quarterly*
CIJ	*Corpus inscriptionum judaicarum*
EBib	Études bibliques
EncJud	*Encyclopaedia judaica* (1971)
EstBib	*Estudios biblicos*
EvT	*Evangelische Theologie*
ExpTim	*Expository Times*
FBBS	Facet Books, Biblical Series
FRLANT	Forschungen zur Religion und Literatur des Alten und Neuen Testaments
HKNT	Handkommentar zum Neuen Testament
HNT	Handbuch zum Neuen Testament
HNTC	Harper's NT Commentaries
HTKNT	Herders theologischer Kommentar zum Neuen Testament

HTR	*Harvard Theological Review*
HUCA	*Hebrew Union College Annual*
IB	*Interpreter's Bible*
ICC	International Critical Commentary
IDB	G. A. Buttrick (ed.), *Interpreter's Dictionary of the Bible*
Int	*Interpretation*
JBL	*Journal of Biblical Literature*
JES	*Journal of Ecumenical Studies*
JSJ	*Journal for the Study of Judaism in the Persian, Hellenistic and Roman Period*
JSNT	*Journal for the Study of the New Testament*
JTS	*Journal of Theological Studies*
KNT	*Kommentar zum NT*
LD	Lectio divina
MeyerK	H. A. W. Meyer, Kritisch-exegetischer Kommentar über das Neue Testament
MNTC	Moffatt NT Commentary
NF	Neue Folge
NICNT	New International Commentary on the New Testament
NovT	*Novum Testamentum*
NovTSup	*Novum Testamentum*, Supplements
NS	New Series
NTAbh	Neutestamentliche Abhandlungen
NTD	Das Neue Testament Deutsch
NTS	*New Testament Studies*
OBO	Orbis biblicus et orientalis
OCD	*Oxford Classical Dictionary*
ÖTNT	Ökumenischer Taschenbuchkommentar zum Neuen Testament
PTMS	Pittsburgh Theological Monograph Series
RAC	*Reallexikon für Antike und Christentum*
RB	*Revue biblique*
RevExp	*Review and Expositor*
RevQ	*Revue de Qumran*
RGG	*Die Religion in Geschichte und Gegenwart*
RivB	*Rivista biblica*
RNT	Regensburger Neues Testament
RSR	*Recherches de science religieuse*
SANT	Studien zum Alten und Neuen Testament
SB	Sources bibliques

SBLDS	SBL Dissertation Series
SBLMS	SBL Monograph Series
SBS	Stuttgarter Bibelstudien
SBT	Studies in Biblical Theology
SNTSMS	Society for New Testament Studies Monograph Series
SPB	Studia postbiblica
ST	*Studia theologica*
TBü	Theologische Bücherei
TDNT	G. Kittel and G. Friedrich (eds.), *Theological Dictionary of the New Testament*
TF	Theologische Forschung
THKNT	Theologischer Handkommentar zum Neuen Testament
TLZ	*Theologische Literaturzeitung*
TQ	*Theologische Quartalschrift*
TRu	*Theologische Rundschau*
TS	*Theological Studies*
TU	Texte und Untersuchungen
TV	*Theologia Viatorum*
TWNT	G. Kittel and G. Friedrich (eds.), *Theologisches Wörterbuch zum Neuen Testament*
TZ	*Theologische Zeitschrift*
UUÅ	Uppsala universitetsårsskrift
VS	*Verbum salutis*
WMANT	Wissenschaftliche Monographien zum Alten und Neuen Testament
WUNT	Wissenschaftliche Untersuchungen zum Neuen Testament
ZKG	*Zeitschrift für Kirchengeschichte*
ZNW	*Zeitschrift für die neutestamentliche Wissenschaft*
ZTK	*Zeitschrift für Theologie und Kirche*

Preface

The purpose of this volume is to make as clear as possible how the author of Luke-Acts portrays the Jews, *in toto* and *in partibus*, and to try to explain why he portrays them as he does. It is a historical study, prompted in part by the voluminous scholarly literature that has dealt with the subject in one way or another in the last decade or so without producing anything like a consensus on the author's attitude toward Jews, and in part by what seems, at first reading, to be confusion in the mind of the author of Luke-Acts as to whether he is friendly or hostile to Jews. This apparent confusion is especially noticeable in parts of Acts, where Christian speakers seem sometimes first to condemn Jews as vile and hopeless, and then to attempt to persuade Jews to be converted to Christianity.

Any historical study, however, is likely at the same time to be rooted somehow in a contemporary issue or issues, and this one no less so, for antisemitism – and with it Christian antisemitism – is one of the more pressing social issues of our day. Most Christians are opposed to antisemitism, and many are willing to expend effort to try to keep Christianity free of such prejudices; but those Christians who are interested in opposing Christian antisemitism and in talking with Jews about problems between the two religions – and I assume that most Christians are so interested – cannot ignore the support that parts of the New Testament give to anti-Jewish sentiment among Christians. Luke-Acts is a major such part.

If the following study is successful, therefore, in laying out just what the author of Luke-Acts intended in portraying the Jews as he did, and if the conclusions are convincing, we shall have succeeded, on the historical side, in settling that matter and, on the social-issue side, in defining a perspective for Christian introspection and for Jewish-Christian dialogue.

It will be advisable to present at this point a brief discussion of the

terms 'antisemitism' and 'antisemitic' as they are used here. Franz
Overbeck accused the author of Acts of a 'national anti-Judaism',
while Adolf von Harnack called Acts the first stage of developing
early Christian antisemitism (the second stage was the Gospel of
John, and the third was the Apologists); and Christian scholars are
still not entirely sure which term to apply to parts of the New
Testament. Many resist the term 'antisemitism', maintaining that
to call any pre-nineteenth-century attitude 'antisemitic' is anachron-
istic, or that Luke's attitude is not preeminently *racial*. There is a
very good discussion of the use of the two terms in modern scholarship
in John Gager's *The Origins of Anti-Semitism*, pp. 3–35, and there is
no need to repeat that discussion here, but several aspects and
conclusions of Gager's study do need to be emphasized. One is that
it is a mistake to think that modern antisemitism has no relation to
antiquity, for in fact it goes back to the early days of Christian
theological reflection (Gager's Part III, cf. esp. pp. 267–9). Another
is that it is a mistake to think that early Christian polemic against
the Jews is merely against the Jewish religion, or only against those
who practise the Jewish religion, and not against the Jewish people
as such. Gager puts his finger on this distinction as early as p. 18 of
his study as having become 'a standard apologetic device for refuting
the charge that the New Testament contains the seeds of anti-
Semitism'. I endorse that judgment. Gager may not have found as
many such seeds in Luke-Acts as are unearthed in this study, but I
am in principle in agreement that it is misleading to avoid labelling
as 'antisemitic' a work that vigorously opposes Jews as such. Gager's
definition of antisemitism is 'a fundamental and systematic hostility
toward Jews' (p. 17; he is agreeing with Marcel Simon), and he
correctly sees that, whether or not Christian writers cringe at
applying the term 'antisemitism' to part of the New Testament, we
must realize that it is that hostility that we are describing.

It may be that Luke's hostility toward Jews was not exactly racial
in the way in which we think of racial hatred today, but it was
something very close to it. At the least, it was a 'national' hostility
(Overbeck). That the author of Luke-Acts consistently and routinely
exhibits such hostility is what this study now shows, and to recognize
that is more important than the choice of terms – as Gager rightly
emphasizes. When I note Harnack's use of the term 'antisemitism';
when I recall the title of Samuel Sandmel's book, *Anti-Semitism in the
New Testament?*; when I see Gager's title; and when I then see that

Luke finds Jews who are not converted to Christianity just as guilty of the sentence of death as those other Jews who supposedly killed Jesus (Acts 18.6), or that he calls down the sentence, 'Slaughter them!' on those Jews who refuse to accept Christ as their ruler (Luke 19.27), I do not know what to call that hostility if not antisemitism. Perhaps the reader who blanches at that term is the one who needs to read this book most carefully of all.

All this, of course, anticipates the following pages, and I apologize for seeming to put the conclusions first. This study, naturally, includes many more findings than merely a justification of the use of the word 'antisemitism'; but readers of this study are invited to ask themselves this question as they read: whereas Luke regularly condemns 'the Jews' for killing Christ and for various other things, does he ever equally condemn any other non-Christians? What is one to make of such a negative portrait?

The bulk of this study is divided into two parts (a third section, a discussion of Luke's possible motives, follows them), which I have chosen to call a 'thematic investigation' and a 'systematic analysis'. The first attempts to clarify Luke's portrayal of various groups: the Jewish leaders, Jerusalem, the Jewish people, the Pharisees, and the outcasts and other peripheral elements in Jewish society. This is necessary in order to understand the overall portrait, but it may not entirely clarify that portrait. To be sure that the overall portrait is made clear, the systematic analysis proceeds, 'commentary-like', through Luke-Acts, tracing the interplay of the various themes discussed in Part One. Such a procedure makes this work rather longer than some other monographs, but the study seemed less than complete without both approaches. I have, in fact, often thought of this study as a single-issue commentary with a long introduction; the length of the 'commentary' reveals with what a prominent issue in Luke-Acts we are dealing here. One may also hope that Part Two will give this work a more enduring value for the future student of Luke-Acts, who may want information about how Luke portrays the Jews in one or another passage of his two-volume work.

The bulk of research for and about half the writing of this book were done during a sabbatical year, 1983–84, in Cambridge, Massachusetts. Since my return to Oregon from Cambridge, however, it has not been possible to be certain that I have examined every latest book and article related to the subject of the study, and research must be considered to have stopped with works available for use in the Andover Harvard Library on 1 June 1984. Given that *terminus*, I am naturally responsible for any oversights. All translations from works in foreign languages, including the Bible, are my own. An abbreviated form of Chapter 4 has already been published separately as 'The Pharisees in Luke-Acts', in *The Living Text. Essays in Honor of Ernest W. Saunders*, ed. D. E. Groh and R. Jewett, Lanham, New York and London: University Press of America 1985, pp. 141–88.

The sabbatical year was made possible by a sabbatical leave with part salary, for which I take this opportunity to thank the University of Oregon and the Oregon State Board of Higher Education, and by a National Endowment for the Humanities Senior Fellowship for Independent Study and Research, for which I take this opportunity to thank the Endowment. My work in Cambridge was eased by the faculty of the Harvard Divinity School, which was kind enough to make me a Visiting Scholar for the academic year, for which status I am also grateful. In this connection, I wish also to thank the librarians of the Andover Harvard Library and of the Episcopal Divinity School/Weston School of Theology Library for their ever-friendly help and assistance in response to my numerous and frequent queries. Yet not all my research was done in Cambridge, and therefore I should like here, as on other occasions, to thank University of Oregon Interlibrary Loan Librarian Joanne Halgren and her staff for much help efficiently and courteously given. I am also grateful to the Revd Dr John Bowden for accepting the MS for publication, and to Professor E. P. Sanders for reading the MS and for making a number of valuable suggestions. The typists who have laboured over my often illegible copy deserve some kind of special merit award, and I am grateful to them: Judy Gall, Jennifer Fox, Hac Do, and Sandy Livingston; and I should also like to thank my wife, Susan E. Plass, very much for having willingly interrupted her own career in order to accompany me to Cambridge and to assume complete domestic duties (not normally her role) in order to allow me to be able to work full-time on this study. Finally, I should like to thank Professors Robert M. Grant and Harry M. Orlinsky and Bishop Krister Stendahl for reasons which they will understand; and Professor Helmut Koester and his colleagues in the Harvard New Testament Department for their numerous expressions of hospitality so warmly and generously given.

Veritas! That is our goal.

Part One

THEMATIC INVESTIGATION

1

THE JEWISH LEADERS

The Jewish religious leaders in Luke-Acts are enemies of Jesus and the church. The point hardly even needs documentation. Thus Luke follows the Gospel tradition that the Jewish religious leaders in Jerusalem were responsible for the death of Jesus;[1] they plot his death, denounce him to the temporal authorities, and oversee his execution. Even so, Luke introduces certain modifications. It is true that he begins the passion narrative with the plot at Passover, to that degree following the Gospel of Mark ('The chief priests and the scribes sought a means for doing away with him', Luke 22.2), and that the means is found immediately when, again as in Mark (Luke 22.3–4), the traitor Judas offers to 'deliver' Jesus. Yet Luke has it that Jesus is to be delivered to the 'chief priests and captains' (cf. Mark 14.10, where only chief priests are mentioned).[2] Those who come to arrest Jesus, then (v. 52), are these same chief priests and captains – here called 'of the Temple' and substituted for the scribes of Mark 14.43 – as well as 'elders'; and Jesus is taken to 'the house of the high priest' (v. 54) for a preliminary hearing. Thus, in addition to his substitution of captains for scribes, Luke has altered the tradition in another way, for Mark and Matthew record that a 'crowd' from the authorities arrested Jesus, whereas Luke has the authorities themselves do the arresting. After Jesus' captors beat and mock him (vv. 63–64; Luke has changed the order of events), he is led by the presbyterium, composed of chief priests and scribes, to the Sanhedrin (v. 66). Luke has thus divided the Marcan and Matthaean account of the hearing before Jewish authorities into two. The effect of this reorganizing of the account is that the hearing before Jewish authorities takes on a more deliberate aspect; and the responsibility of the Jewish authorities for the death of Jesus is thereby heightened.

Sanhedrin

It is also an interesting question what relationship Luke intends between the presbyterium and the Sanhedrin. Wellhausen, joined by Klostermann and Hauck,[3] proposes that Luke thinks of only one group, which he calls the presbyterium, a term familiar to Gentile readers, and that he uses the term 'Sanhedrin' to refer to the court. Weiss, however, thinks that the presbyterium is intended to be, not the entire Sanhedrin (which cannot be a place), but the 'corporation of the *presbyteroi*',[4] and he refers to Luke 20.1, where the elders appear alongside the chief priests and the scribes. Grundmann also refers to 20.1 and sees three groups both there and in 22.66,[5] but it is unclear whether he takes Luke to mean that the Sanhedrin is identical with those three groups or whether he thinks that the term 'Sanhedrin' means a larger group. Montefiore discusses all the possibilities,[6] as well as the variant reading (also discussed by some of the other authors just mentioned), 'the presbyterium of the people *and* chief priests and scribes', and concludes by observing that 'the composition of the two verses [i.e., vv. 66–67] is very clumsy'. Whatever Luke meant exactly, his characterization of the organization of the Jewish religious leaders here in any case raises historical questions. Weiss objects to the apparent designation of the Sanhedrin as a place and argues that Luke must mean that Jesus was conducted to the full assembly of the Sanhedrin.[7] Klostermann expresses the same opinion and observes further that to suggest that the presbyterium was made up of chief priests and scribes involves 'an incorrect designation'.[8] If we clearly separate, however, what really happened from Luke's description of it, and if we rigorously pursue the latter question, we should be able to gain a clear view of Luke's portrait.

While Luke 22.66 is the only place in the Gospel of Luke where the word 'Sanhedrin' appears, the term occurs with some frequency in Acts, and an examination of Luke's use of the term in his second volume will perhaps make the issue clearer. Here one sees that, while Luke is capable of using the term 'Sanhedrin' to refer to an assembled body, he normally does use it to mean a place[9] – specifically, for Luke, the place where Christians are tried. In Acts 5.27; 6.12; 23.20, 28 Christians are 'led', as is Jesus in Luke 22.66, to or into the Sanhedrin. Further, in Acts 4.15; 5.34; 6.15; 23.6; 24.20, people are said to be outside the Sanhedrin or seated or standing in the Sanhedrin or merely in the Sanhedrin. In a minority of instances the term seems to refer to an assembled body: Acts 5.21; 22.30; 23.1, 15; and in Acts 5.41 the chastized and released Christians 'went out rejoicing from the presence of the Sanhedrin', a use of the term that might be taken to mean either a place or an assembled body. It thus seems that Luke in fact intends to say, in Luke 22.66, that the assembled religious leaders 'led [Jesus] away into [a place called] their Sanhedrin'.[10] Why Luke thinks of the Sanhedrin primarily as a place is not clear, but this is certainly not the first time that someone has noticed that Luke sometimes misunderstands Palestinian affairs.[11] In order to produce the wording of 22.66, Luke apparently reasoned in this way: Mark had referred (Mark 15.1) to a 'council' of 'chief priests with the elders and scribes, and the whole Sanhedrin' that turned Jesus over to Pilate; but the Sanhedrin is the place where Jesus was condemned, and the term 'presbyterium' is readily understandable as a designation of the group conducting the hearing; thus Mark's 'chief priests, with the elders and scribes' must become a 'presbyterium of the people, chief priests and scribes'; and the Sanhedrin, which in Mark's reading could possibly be taken as a group separate from the chief priests, elders and scribes, becomes the place of destination,[12] the court*room*.

The indictment against Jesus

In the Sanhedrin, then, Jesus' own words condemn him, although Luke's account is no clearer about why that is so than is Mark's or Matthew's. In fact, the scene as described by Luke in Luke 22.67–71 is more puzzling than it is in Mark and Matthew, since Luke omits the charge of blasphemy, which Mark and Matthew report.[13] Luke has doubtless suppressed that charge, however, in order not to confuse the issue of the indictment, since he then (alone of all the Gospel authors) immediately presents a political indictment in Luke 23.2. When the entire body (23.1) conducts Jesus to Pilate, it charges Jesus (v. 2) with three counts: disturbing the peace, counselling non-payment of the imperial tax,[14] and proclaiming himself 'Messiah' (i.e., King). Luke apparently expects his readers to understand that all the counts of this indictment are patently false.[15] The nearest that Jesus could have come to disturbing the peace, in the Gospel of Luke, was when he entered Jerusalem; but Luke there (19.37) reduced the body of those hailing Jesus from the large crowd of the other three Gospels to 'the multitude of disciples'. The second count flies in the face of Jesus' counsel in Luke 20.25, 'Remit what is Caesar's to

Caesar'.[16] The third count has the most credibility, since, on the occasion of the 'triumphal entry', the disciples did praise Jesus with the words, 'Blessed is he who is coming, the king in the name of the Lord' (Luke 19.38), and since Jesus rejected the Pharisaic counsel to rebuke the disciples (vv. 39–40); nevertheless, Luke continued the praise in the mouths of the disciples with the further words, drawn from Luke 2.14, 'Peace on earth and glory on high', thereby under-scoring the theme that any 'reign' attributed to Jesus must be understood as peaceful and heavenly.[17] If, therefore, any historical accuracy should lie behind the indictment of Luke 23.2, it is pure accident, since Luke's intent here is to show that the Jewish religious leaders turned Jesus over to Pilate on charges that had not surfaced in their own hearing, that would be recognized by any reader of the Gospel to this point as false charges,[18] but that might be reasonable charges to present to the Roman procurator, who would, if he found for the prosecution, order Jesus' execution.[19]

Daryl Schmidt has presented an interesting contradictory argument.[20] Schmidt gives attention to the first count of the indictment, which is repeated, with variations, in 23.5, 14 and then attempts to show that Luke has in fact presented abundant evidence for the truth of this charge throughout the Gospel.[21] The evidence hinges on the version of the first count given in 23.5, that Jesus 'stirs up the people, teaching throughout all Judaea, and beginning from Galilee to here'. Schmidt connects this charge with the frequent accounts in Luke of Jesus' attracting large crowds, and especially with the Temple authorities' fear that they would be stoned by the people if they opposed Jesus (19.48; 20.6, 19).[22] Thus 'Luke is not presenting a deliberate lie, but a realistic appraisal of the effect of Jesus' teaching on the people, as experienced by the chief priests and scribes'.[23] Schmidt then takes the 'Remit what is Caesar's to Caesar' saying to support the second count, since 'the chief priests and scribes interpret Jesus' refusal to singularly endorse Caesar as an act of defiance'; and the third charge is likewise true because 'the crowds call him king when he approaches Jerusalem'.[24]

The reason for Pilate's pronunciation of innocence in Luke is, then, according to Schmidt, not the obvious falsity of the charges, but scripture. The Servant in Isa. 53.11 is likewise innocent (δίκαιος).[25] Thus the centurion (Luke 23.47), Stephen (Acts 7.52) and Paul (Acts 22.14) all call Jesus innocent. If, however, Luke wanted to emphasize Jesus' innocence, then the obvious question is, 'Why did [he] present political charges . . . that have some plausibility?'[26] Schmidt's answer is that Luke wants to make the martyrdom of Jesus conform to that of Paul, who is represented in Acts as stirring up the people, but even more that Luke again relies on scriptural typology related to his theme of Jesus as prophet. Thus, Schmidt notes, Pharaoh accuses Moses in Exod.5.4 of 'perverting' the people, and King Ahab says the same thing of Elijah in I Kings 18.17. The same verb διαστρέφω is used in both LXX statements and in Luke 23.2; and Luke 23.14 employs a near equivalent, ἀποστρέφω.[27] Thus 'both the accusation and the declaration [of innocence] must be seen in the light of Luke's scriptural apologetic'.[28]

Now, to be sure, Luke views Jesus as a prophet, as everyone recognizes;[29] and he certainly makes Acts parallel to the Gospel in many ways, the parallels being especially marked in his accounts of the martyrdoms.[30] Yet the only real evidence that Schmidt can cite to show that the Gospel account has prepared the way for the charge in Luke 23.5 is that Jesus taught from Galilee to Jerusalem, attracting crowds, and that the Temple authorities feared the crowds because of Jesus' (and John's) popularity with them. This is hardly 'stirring up' the people. When Schmidt comes to the matter of reliance on scripture, however, he has fingered an important feature but has misunderstood his evidence;[31] for the Pharaoh and the Ahab who level such a charge at Moses and Elijah respectively are evil men at cross-purposes with the will of God. Moses and Elijah are carrying out God's will! Only the evil rulers consider their activity sedition ('perverting' the people), whereas from God's point of view they are righteous and innocent. This is exactly the case with Luke's first count of the indictment against Jesus. The evil Temple authorities may think of Jesus as perverting the people, but the charge is intended to be patently false to Luke's readers, because both God and Luke know that Jesus has been doing God's will and that the real evildoers are the Temple authorities.[32]

That Jesus' acclaim at the triumphal entry into Jerusalem does not make him guilty of the third count has already been explained above; Schmidt's explanation that the 'Remit what is Caesar's to Caesar' saying justifies the second count is, in my opinion, fantasy, inasmuch as such an explanation involves making opposites equal. In a word, it is Luke's purpose to show that the Jewish religious leaders turned Jesus over to the temporal authorities on false charges likely to result in his death.

The issue that has occupied the attention of Winter, Blinzler, Catchpole[33] and others – namely the historical reasons for Jesus' execution – must be passed over here, however important that issue may be in general. Our purpose here is to limit ourselves to an analysis of the way in which Luke describes that execution and the events that led up to it, particularly of those aspects of the description that are peculiarly Lucan – that is, of those changes introduced by Luke into the tradition. Even if, as noted above, there is a possibility that he has stumbled on to historical accuracy, what is important for us to remember here is that he portrays the Jewish religious leaders as presenting *obviously* false political charges to Pilate, charges the falsehood of which is immediately clear to any reader of the Gospel who has been paying attention. In the Gospel of Luke, the Jewish religious leaders are a cohesive group capable of manipulating the Roman authorities towards the end of getting rid of Jesus for very murky reasons.[34]

Trials and acquittals

According to Luke (and Luke only), Pilate quickly determined that there was no evidence of Jesus' guilt (Luke 23.4), but that the issue probably really fell under Herod's jurisdiction, and so he sent Jesus to Herod for trial. We shall return below to Luke's use of various Herods as judges both here and in Acts, but for the moment it is sufficient to note that Luke, consistent with his characterization of the Jewish religious leaders as Jesus' accusers, again states that it was the chief priests and scribes (Luke 23.10) who accused Jesus before Herod. The indictment is not given; apparently we are to understand that the indictment of 23.2 is simply repeated, since only the venue has been changed, while the accusers and the prisoner remain the same. Thus, even when Luke departs from his sources and invents a trial scene, his characterization of the Jewish religious leaders is constant.

Following the trial before Herod, Luke returns to the account of Mark and Matthew and brings Jesus back before Pilate. Here we see the failure of Luke's inventiveness, for no adequate reason is given for Herod's returning Jesus to Pilate. If the procurator had actually decided that the case fell under Herod's jurisdiction, then Herod would have decided the case and would have punished or released Jesus according to his decision. According to Luke, however, Herod first acquits Jesus (23.9), then abuses him (v. 11), and finally 'he sent him back to Pilate' (v. 11). Thus Herod's court, which started out (v. 6) as apparently the court designated by the procurator as the proper court for the trial of Jesus, is then portrayed as only something like an American grand jury, making pre-trial findings about guilt or innocence. But the 'grand jury' explanation is also inadequate to explain the return to Pilate. What is reported in v. 9 should have been the end of the matter: Herod 'put him on the witness stand at some length (ἐπήρωτα δὲ αὐτὸν ἐν λόγοις ἱκανοῖς)', but he evidently found him not guilty. No evidence of guilt, no trial.[35] The account of the trial or hearing before Herod, then, serves primarily the function of emphasizing that it was *only* because of the 'vigorous accusation' of the chief priests and scribes (v. 10) that Jesus was taken back to Pilate and put to death. Luke has emphasized the guilt of these people beyond the account of it in Mark and Matthew.

The doomed Jesus then appears once again before Pilate, who immediately (Luke 23.14) repeats his acquittal from v. 4, this time directly refuting the charges brought by Jesus' accusers against him: 'I here hand down my decision in your presence. I find no evidence in this person of the charges that you have brought against him'; and he repeats Herod's finding of insufficient evidence. The 'whole multitude', then, immediately begins to demand Barabbas's release, and Pilate for the third time – and Luke reminds us that it *is* the third time – declares Jesus 'not guilty' (v. 22). Luke has thus underscored the attempts of the legitimate authorities to release Jesus much more than has Mark or Matthew,[36] who do not go beyond having Pilate ask for further evidence (Matt. 27.23; the Gospel tradition is uniform, of course, in representing Pilate as attempting to release Jesus instead of Barabbas). By this heightening of the secular authorities' attempt to release Jesus, Luke has also heightened the role of the Jews in bringing about his death.[37] Were it not for the adamant, stiff-necked, irrational and perverse insistence of the chief priests and the scribes, Jesus would have been released. On the Temple authorities, then, not on the temporal, lies the entire burden of Jesus' wrongful death.[38]

Execution

It should not now be surprising that it is actually Jewish executioners who put Jesus to death in Luke, not Roman.[39] That some modern scholars do not recognize this fact is a matter of some amazement.[40] Nearly everyone observes, of course, that Luke omits the scourging scene of Mark 15.16–20 and moves directly from 'He delivered Jesus to their will' (Luke 23.25) to 'And as they led him away . . .' (v. 26) – that is, the normal reading of *Luke*, if we forget what we know from Matthew and Mark, is that those to whose will Jesus was delivered led him away to be crucified; but the explanations vary. Lagrange thinks that the appearance that it was actually Jews and not Romans who conducted Jesus to his death is purely accidental ('a vague plural'), and Wellhausen finds Luke's omission simply unfathomable.[41] Similarly, Grundmann, Hauck, Gilmour, Ernst and Klostermann note the appearance of Jewish participation but cannot quite believe that Luke really intended to give that impression.[42] Even Loisy thinks of Roman soldiers.[43] Schmid, Caird, Leaney, Harrington, Rengstorf, Bundy and Talbert insist that the Romans crucified Jesus,[44] even in Luke, and Schneider takes the half-way position that both Jews and Romans took part in the crucifixion of Jesus.[45] Montefiore sees the nuance, although he does not emphasize it and notes, regarding v. 25, '. . . as if the Jews, and not the Romans, were the real authors of the crucifixion'.[46]

There seem to be three reasons why some readers of Luke might not agree with the assessment that Luke has intended to represent the Jewish religious leaders, not the Roman authorities, as Jesus' executioners. The first is that everyone already knows that it was the Romans who did the crucifying, since not only do we know that crucifixion was a Roman and not a Jewish method of execution, but also we have the account of Mark and Matthew.[47] Here, however, the scholar must be very careful; for it is one thing to examine the historical question of Jesus' crucifixion, but it is another to try to determine just exactly what Luke would like us to understand.[48] If we focus our attention on the latter question alone, then Luke's alterations in the Gospel tradition become highly significant for understanding his purpose, and we cannot help but be struck by his omission of the Marcan and Matthaean scourging scene, thus giving the *impression*, in any case, that the Jewish accusers led Jesus to the cross. Who else could have done this? The procurator, in Luke, has moved earth, if not heaven, to release Jesus. Only the unwavering pressure of the unrelenting Jewish religious authorities has led him not to release Jesus outright; so, 'he deliver[s] Jesus to their will'. When the risen Jesus confronts some disciples, then, and feigns ignorance of his passion, the disciples tell him that it was the Jewish 'chief priests and rulers' who 'crucified him' (Luke 24.20).[49] Surely that is Luke's meaning.[50]

Evidence from Acts confirms this judgment. In Acts 2.23 Peter accuses his Jewish audience with these words: '. . . him . . . you nailed up and did away with, by the hand of lawless persons.' While the word ἄνομοι, 'lawless persons', may refer here, as many think,[51] to some role of the Roman authorities, such a meaning for ἄνομοι is by no means certain in view of the similar phrase in Luke 24.7, '. . . into the hands of sinful persons (ἄνθρωποι ἁμαρτωλοί)', which seems to refer to the Jewish authorities. Furthermore the 'you nailed up (προσπήξαντες)' is entirely clear. Acts 3.15 does not refer to such ἄνομοι and is unambiguous: 'You killed the Prince (ἀρχηγός) of life';[52] and the same is true of 4.10, '. . . whom you crucified', and 5.30, '. . . whom you apprehended and hanged on a tree'. The phrasing of this last accusation in fact coincides, as Fitzmyer has shown, with acceptable pre-Christian Jewish usage for Jewish crucifixion! Apparently, once crucifixion as a form of execution was known in Judah, it was possible to interpret Deut. 21.22 ('If a man is guilty of a capital offence and is killed, and you hang him on a tree. . .') as allowing such an execution.[53] Surely Luke intends his readers to have the impression that Jews, not Romans, put Jesus to death.

The soldiers

But what, in the second case, of the presence of soldiers in Luke's account? Does not their role in Luke's version of the crucifixion show that he really understood that it was Roman soldiers who crucified Jesus, not Jews?[54] According to such an understanding, the apparent indication of Luke 23.25–26 that Jews led Jesus to his crucifixion would be only some kind of accident, as Lagrange claimed. Surely Luke does not mean his readers to understand that there were *Jewish* soldiers who crucified Jesus? This argument, which I have found nowhere stated just in these terms but which is widely implied, the implicators apparently assuming that the burden of proof would lie with those who maintain that Luke represents Jews as the executioners of Jesus, will not stand up under an analysis of Luke-Acts. The soldiers in Luke 23.36 are Jewish soldiers.[55] Luke has given no indication that they are not and every indication that they are. In the first place, there is the matter of the captains. We have already had occasion to note Luke's insertion of Temple captains into his account of the arrest of Jesus (Luke 22.4, 52).[56] These captains appear only in Luke-Acts, nowhere in the rest of the New Testament, and, just as they arrest Jesus in the Gospel, so they arrest the apostles in Acts.

There is no difference between Luke and Acts in this regard; whereas 'captains' assist the chief priests in arresting Jesus, 'the captain' assists them in arresting the apostles in Acts 4.1; 5.26 (so also the reference to 'the captain' in 5.24). It is possible that Luke discovered, between the time that he finished the Gospel and the time that he wrote Acts, that there was one captain in charge of Temple security and that the officers under him were also called captains. Gealy surmises that Luke is either 'uninformed' or 'indifferent' to the distinction, or that he 'used the plurals' in the Gospel 'to be impressive, and without entertaining the possibility of confusion between the captain and his subordinate captains.'[57] What is clear is that Luke thinks of the Temple στρατηγοί, 'captains', not as the Temple security force but as a police force with the authority to go out into the city and arrest people.[58] In Acts 5.26 the captain who arrests the apostles is said to do so specifically with the aid of sergeants.[59] In this capacity the captains are, in Luke's thinking, just like the secular στρατηγοί of a Roman provincial city, the praetors (RSV: 'magistrates'). These στρατηγοί or praetors appear in Acts 16.19–40, where they exercise police authority in Philippi. Just as the Temple captains (στρατηγοί) joined in the beating of Jesus in Luke 22.63, so these Philippian praetors (στρατηγοί) order the beating of Paul and Silas (Acts 16.22). The Philippian praetors, furthermore, command police – ῥαβδοῦχοι, lictors – who inflict the punishment that the praetors decree (Acts 16.35,38; the ῥαβδοῦχοι are also implied in v. 22, where the praetors 'ordered a beating [ἐκέλευον ῥαβδίζειν]' for Paul and Silas). Luke thus constructs a parallel between Temple and secular police, both under the command of στρατηγοί.[60] If the secular στρατηγοί, however, have lictors under them who can carry out the commands of corporal punishment, then the Temple στρατηγοί must have comparable persons under their command, and they are called sergeants or, apparently, 'soldiers (στρατιῶται, στρατευόμενοι)'.[61]

The soldiers who respond to John's preaching in Luke 3.14 can only be Jewish soldiers,[62] and the soldiers who mock Jesus in Luke 23.36 will, then, also have to be Jewish. Luke, it will be noted, has imported these soldiers into the mocking scene at the cross.[63] They do not appear in the account of Mark and Matthew, who portray the chief priests, scribes, and (Matthew) elders as the ones who mock Jesus (Mark 15.31; Matt. 27.41). Luke has also sketched a Jewish mocking crowd, but with different designators: 'people' watching and 'rulers' nose-thumbing (Luke 23.35).[64] When, in the next verse, 'soldiers' join in mocking Jesus, they are not Roman soldiers, they are Jews.[65]

While soldiers appear frequently in Acts either as Roman or as Herodian soldiers (never in the service of the Temple), the function alloted them in Acts reinforces the judgment that the soldiers of Luke 23.36 are Jewish soldiers involved in the crucifixion of Jesus, since in Acts 'soldiers' appear almost exclusively as persons who arrest people at someone else's command.[66] That is what soldiers in Acts do – in other words, they do not make war, go on marches, or drill; they perform the same function as do the sergeants in Acts 5.26. If one asks under whose command the soldiers of Luke 23.36 are, then the answer is clear. They cannot be under Herod's or Pilate's command, since both those sought to release Jesus. They can only be under the command of those to whose will Pilate delivered Jesus, and that group includes captains. Luke thus seems to intend his readers to understand that the Temple authorities carried out the crucifixion of Jesus (allowed, grudgingly, by Pilate), and that they possessed the personnel so to do, captains and soldiers.

Roman complicity?

In spite, however, of Luke's apparent attempt to describe the crucifixion of Jesus as having been carried out by Jewish religious leaders and military, there are still, in the third place, some passages in Luke-Acts where the Romans seem to be fingered as the perpetrators of that calumny. First there is the third announcement of the passion, Luke 18.31–34. Here Jesus says of the Son of man that 'he will be delivered to the Gentiles and will be mocked and will be maltreated and will be spat upon, and they will flog and kill him'.[67] Luke, by shifting the three verbs that follow the word 'Gentiles' from the active to the passive, has made the saying even less clear than it is in Mark. When he then returns to the active voice, 'They will flog and kill him,' he apparently thinks that he has confused this recognizedly necessary saying beyond comprehension, so that the reader cannot tell who the subjects of those verbs are.[68] In fact, that is exactly what Luke says, for he adds v. 34 (not in Mark or Matthew): 'And they understood nothing of these, and this saying was hidden from them, and they did not know what was said.' Luke's heavy-handedness here is comical – or pitiful. He has told us how he wants his muddled form of the saying understood – that is, not understood. He does *not* intend to have Jesus prophesy his death at the hands of Gentiles.[69]

A somewhat similar explanation is likely for the quotation of Ps. 2.1–2 in Acts 4.25–26 and the brief exegesis given in vv. 27–28. It is widely recognized that Luke has taken the 'Gentiles' and 'peoples' of Ps.2.1 to mean 'Gentiles and people of Israel' (Acts 4.27), and that he has applied the 'kings' and 'rulers' of Ps. 2.2 to Herod and Pilate in Acts 4.27.[70] Luke has, further, brought down the word συνήχθησαν, 'were gathered together', from Ps. 2.2 into his exegesis in Acts 4.27, in order to say that both Herod and Pilate, both Gentiles and Israelites were grouped together . . . to what purpose? Here Luke begins to be less clear than his source again. The last line of Ps. 2.2 had said plainly, '. . . against the Lord and against his Christ', but Luke writes, in Acts 4.27, that the four entities were gathered ἐπὶ . . . Ἰησοῦν. Now while ἐπὶ + accusative *can* mean 'against', its normal meaning is 'at'; i.e. the construction is normally a designation of place (or time). Luke seems thus to have made some effort not to use the unambiguous κατά, 'against', of the psalm and to have substituted for it an ambiguous construction. To be sure, Schneider has shown that Luke elsewhere uses ἐπὶ + accus. to mean 'against', and that this is one of Luke's 'Septuagintalisms'.[71] Yet one must not overlook that Luke many, many times uses the construction in Acts in its normal meaning, location in space or time. Thus to pick up the preposition ἐπὶ from the phrase ἐπὶ τὸ αὐτό, 'in the same place', in Ps. 2.2 and to use it instead of κατά in the exegesis, when κατά was the word that was in the psalm, is to introduce a note of ambiguity into the meaning of the exegesis. However that may be, Luke goes on to emphasize that this all happened according to the divine will (Acts 4.28), and he does not say here what any of the parties mentioned did to Jesus. This passage could thus hardly be cited as evidence that Luke intended to designate the Romans and not the Jews as the executioners of Jesus.[72]

Finally, in Acts 13.28, Pilate is mentioned again in Paul's sermon at Antioch in a discussion of Jesus' death. Here also, however, Luke is careful to keep the blame on the Jewish religious leaders in Jerusalem and off Pilate. It is 'those dwelling in Jerusalem and their rulers' (v. 27) who tried Jesus and found him innocent, but who nevertheless 'asked Pilate to do away with him'. Rather than letting Pilate be culpable, however, Luke gives no indication that Pilate acceded to this request; rather, Luke returns to the presentation given in the Gospel and to the accusations of the speeches in the earlier part of Acts and has Paul continue in v. 29: 'When they had fulfilled all that had been written about him . . .' 'They', not Pilate, are guilty of executing Jesus.[73]

Nowhere, therefore, does Luke stray from his consistent portrayal of the Jewish religious authorities as those who plotted and *carried out* the crucifixion of Jesus, and who continued the same pattern of hostility against the leaders of the church.[74]

Finally, in order to describe Luke's compositional activity on this point entirely correctly, we need to return to Montefiore's statement, quoted above, that Luke describes the crucifixion scene '*as if* the Jews, and not the Romans, were the real authors of the crucifixion' (emphasis mine).[75] Luke has stopped a little short of explicitness in his accusation of the Jewish leaders in the crucifixion scene itself. While he gives the *appearance* that Jews carried out the actual crucifixion, he avoids saying so explicitly in the crucifixion scene. Also, the soldiers who mock Jesus in Luke 23.37 sound as if they might be Gentiles: 'If you are the King of the Jews . . .'; and many might read 23.47, where a *Roman* centurion declares Jesus innocent, to mean that the soldiers involved in the crucifixion are Romans, not Jews. Still Luke has provided indicators to lead the reader away from such associations. The mocking statement of the soldiers in 23.37 is followed by the explanation (v. 38) that 'there was indeed an epigraph on him, "This is the King of the Jews"' (thus implying that the 'Gentileness' of the soldiers' mocking statement derives from their reading the label, not from their natural disposition to talk that way); and Luke may intend to keep the centurion separate from the soldiers, since his only role is to declare Jesus 'innocent' (or, 'righteous').[76] Nevertheless, as soon as the reader progresses beyond the crucifixion scene to the Emmaus Road account, the accusations against the Jewish authorities become explicit and remain so throughout Acts. Why this difference? Why does Luke avoid coming right out and saying, in the crucifixion scene itself, that it was Jews and not Romans who 'did away with' Jesus? Why does he formulate his account of the crucifixion scene more or less in the traditional way, providing only strong hints that those who carry out the crucifixion are Jews, whereas thereafter he accuses the Jews directly? The reference to the 'traditional' passion narrative probably points the way to the answer to these questions; for Luke seems to have felt that he could not entirely alter the tradition if he wanted to maintain credibility. Better, in the passion narrative, to do just enough rewriting to emphasize Gentile innocence and to imply Jewish guilt.[77] Thereafter, in his freer compositions, he could accuse the Jews directly and explicitly.

A special Lucan source for the passion narrative?

In presenting his account of the crucifixion of Jesus, Luke has, of course, departed exceedingly from the account in Mark and Matthew. Perhaps he merely has an alternative source? This explanation of the variances in the Lucan passion narrative, which was quite in vogue a few years ago,[78] receded somewhat after the publication of Conzelmann's work,[79] because of the focussing of interest there on the intentions of the author of Luke-Acts himself;

but it is still often brought forward.[80] While it is not the purpose of this volume to discuss the source or sources of Luke's account, but rather to describe the way in which the Jews are portrayed in Luke-Acts, the issue of the sources, nevertheless, needs to be addressed briefly here. Two points need to be made. One is that, whatever Luke's sources were other than Mark and Q (or Matthew), the final product is his. (This point thus agrees with that of Conzelmann and of the bulk of scholarly works on Luke-Acts since the publication of Conzelmann's monograph.)[81] Luke could have repeated the account of the trial and crucifixion as it appeared in Mark, yet he chose to alter that account and to present a narrative in which the Jewish religious authorities, with their Temple police, actually carried out the crucifixion of Jesus. These authorities are also even more persistent in their demand for Jesus' execution and even more deliberate in their attempt to bring it about than they are in Mark and Matthew. Even if this version of the crucifixion narrative could be conclusively shown to have derived from some source, still the choice to use this version and not Mark's was Luke's choice.[82]

In the second place, however, Luke's version of the trial and crucifixion narrative coincides perfectly, as will become increasingly clear, with his portrayal of the Jews throughout his two-volume work. It is thus more likely to be the result of his attempt to portray the Jews always in as bad a light as possible than to derive from some source or sources.[83] As Loisy noted à propos of Acts, 'The Jews are the authors of all evil.'[84] In this vein, Stephen says of the Jews in Acts 7.51 that they 'always thrust against the Holy Spirit', and Acts concludes with the summary judgment, quoted from Isaiah 6, that 'the heart of this people has become dulled' (Acts 28.27). Jesus' public ministry in Luke in fact opens with a two-sided rejection: Jesus announces that God's salvation is intended for Gentiles, and his Jewish audience seeks to execute him for his views (Luke 4.16–30). The heightening of Jewish guilt in the execution of Jesus that we see in Luke, in this case the guilt of the religious authorities in Jerusalem, must therefore be seen as entirely in keeping with Luke's overall plan. The portrayal is his; it is deliberate.

Similar persecution of the church in Acts

If we now turn to Acts and examine the accounts of the arrests, trials and, in one case, execution of the apostles and other leaders of the early church, we are struck by a sensation of *déjà vu*, for here again we find the Temple authorities, with their police capability, arresting, trying and executing the Christian leaders. This situation is not the result of historical accident but is rather the consequence of Luke's making the narrative in Acts conform to that in the Gospel.[85] This 'architectonic'[86] parallelism between Luke and Acts has been demonstrated in great detail in the studies of Morgenthaler, Goulder, Talbert, Muhlack and Radl and does not need to be repeated here.[87] Throughout this volume, where Acts is discussed, we shall have occasion to refer to their works.[88]

At the beginning of Acts 4, Peter and John are arrested by 'the priests and captain of the Temple and the Sadducees' and are tried by 'the rulers and elders and scribes and some of the chief priests'. Here, no one is condemned to death, but the ruling of the court is that the preaching of the Christians must cease (Acts 4.17). When the order is not followed the apostles are arrested again and jailed (Acts 5.17) by 'the high priest and all his colleagues, who belonged to the sect of the Sadducees'. Then 'the high priest and his colleagues conven[e] the Sanhedrin and the entire senate (γερουσία, instead of the 'presbyterium' of Luke 22.66)' for the trial (v. 21) and, when the apostles are found to have escaped, the 'captain of the Temple and the chief priests' are the ones who are alarmed (v. 24). 'The captain and the sergeants' (ὑπηρέται) then arrest the apostles again, and the trial is conducted in the Sanhedrin with the high priest presiding (vv. 26–27). Only the friendly counsel of the Pharisee Gamaliel prevents the court's 'doing away with them' (vv. 33–34).[89] The role of the Jewish religious authorities in Jerusalem in Acts 4 and 5 is thus exactly the same as their role at the end of Luke in arresting, trying and executing Jesus, with one major and one minor exception. The major exception is that there are no Roman authorities – and no Herod's court and soldiers – in the picture. We therefore see that Luke views the Jewish leaders as having the legal authority to arrest, try and execute (Acts 5.33: 'They wanted to do away with them') persons for religious crimes, and as being opposed to the spread of the gospel in the same way in which they were formerly opposed to Jesus. The minor exception is that the authorities do not actually 'do away with' the apostles; but then, Jesus is nearly done away with by a group of Jews early in the Gospel, in Luke 4.29, but the execution there also does not come off.[90]

When Stephen is arrested, it is because the 'elders and scribes' (as well as 'the people') are aroused, and he is brought to the

Sanhedrin for trial (Acts 6.12). After his lengthy defence (or harangue) he is put to death in the Jewish manner, by stoning (7.58). The scholarly discussion as to whether the death of Stephen was by official action or by lynching, and as to whether there may therefore be two accounts of the execution of Stephen woven together here,[91] while interesting in the historical sense, is irrelevant for discovering Luke's purpose. What Luke describes is a trial in the Sanhedrin with a resulting Jewish execution.[92] If Luke does not again expressly mention here his normal entire list of Jewish religious leaders (priests and captains are notably absent), that can hardly be because he wanted his readers to understand that only elders and scribes were responsible for the death of Stephen. More likely, when Luke describes the trial as being 'in the Sanhedrin', he means his readers to understand that the court is constituted in the same way in which it was constituted for the several other trials that he has described as being held there.

In the complex of scenes at the end of Acts that make up Paul's trial, the Jewish religious leaders tend to be replaced by the mob as those who bring charges against Paul before Herod and the procurators and who seek his death.[93] Nevertheless, most of the familiar *dramatis personae* are present in some way in their familiar roles. In Acts 22.30 the tribune who had arrested Paul (for his own safety) sends him to 'the chief priests and all the Sanhedrin' for what looks like a preliminary hearing – the tribune wanted 'to know the exact nature of the charges brought by the Jews' – just as Jesus had to have a preliminary hearing in the Sanhedrin before being turned over to Pilate.[94] In 24.1, then, it is 'the high priest with some elders' who bring charges against Paul before the procurator Felix; and, when this action results only in Paul's languishing in prison until a change of procurators and not in his death, it is 'the chief priests and the leaders of the Jews' (25.1) who bring renewed charges before Festus and who also plot an ambush to 'do away with' Paul (v. 3).[95]

We have now seen that Luke consistently portrays the Jewish high priest (ἀρχιερεύς), chief priests (ἀρχιερεῖς), elders, senate, scribes, Sanhedrin, captains, sergeants and soldiers as maliciously opposed to Jesus and to the church, especially to its leaders.[96] They repeatedly seek to 'do away with' Jesus and the leaders of the church, bring false charges against them before the Roman authorities, and in fact execute Jesus and Stephen and almost succeed in executing Paul. As we have already had occasion to observe, Luke's altering the received tradition of the passion narrative in the direction of greater Jewish culpability in the death of Jesus represents more a theological tendency than any historical tradition. Furthermore, the fact that the same Jewish religious leaders appear so routinely in Acts rather woodenly working the same mischief on the church that they worked on Jesus casts a thick shadow of doubt on the historicity of those accounts. It seems likely that Luke's portrayal of the Jewish religious leaders throughout Acts is based at least as much on his theological notion of symmetry between Jesus and the church as it is on any sources or historical tradition. Now we must see if all the references in Luke-Acts to the Jewish religious leaders fit this pattern.

Further characterizations of the religious leaders

There is only one appearance in Luke and one in Acts of the high priest/chief priests in which they are not involved in persecution of Jesus or of the church. In Luke 3.2 there is a mere chronological designation, '. . . during the high priesthood of Annas and Caiaphas . . .', and Acts 19.14 makes Sceva, who had seven exorcist sons, a high priest.[97] Otherwise they are uniformly hostile. In addition to the portions of Luke-Acts that have already been discussed, the chief priests appear in the first announcement of the passion, Luke 9.22 (as in Mark), where Jesus prophesies that he will 'be rejected by the elders and chief priests and scribes'; and, in Acts 9, it is the high priest/chief priests (in Acts 22.5 the high priest and the presbyterium) who send the pre-Christian Paul out to persecute the church. Luke has also made sure that the parable of the Wicked Tenants, whatever its original meaning, is directed at the chief priests and their associates by rewriting Mark in Luke 20.19: 'The scribes and the chief priests . . . knew that he told this parable at them' (cf. Mark 12.2).[98] The Jewish elders also have no other role in Luke-Acts. Acts, of course, knows of Christian elders as well; and the word πρεσβύτερος further appears in Luke 7.3, where it only means 'embassy'.[99] Finally, we should note Acts 14.5, where Paul and Barnabas are the victims of combined Gentile and Jewish persecution. Luke says here that the missionaries are victims of the 'wrath of the Gentiles and of the Jews with their leaders'. Thus the hostile pressure of the Jewish 'leaders' is felt even in the Diaspora mission.

The place of the scribes in Luke-Acts is rather puzzling, but this only repeats the situation in Mark. We have seen that the scribes are regularly associated with the chief priests and elders as the opponents of Jesus and the church, and in this, as far as the Gospel is concerned, Luke is simply following Mark. Mark also, however, frequently associates the scribes with the Pharisees instead of with the chief priests, and Luke again simply follows. Whether the scribes who are reviled in Mark 12.37b–40 are to be associated with the Pharisees or with the chief priests Mark does not say, and Luke is content to let the ambiguity remain (Luke 20.45–47). When the (unassociated) scribes approve Jesus' answer to a baiting question (Luke 20.39, a Lucan addition to the Marcan pericope), it is unclear whether Luke means them to appear as friendly, hence to be associated with the Pharisees,[100] or as merely capitulating, since Luke had made 'the scribes and the chief priests' the ones who began the baiting (Luke 20.19–20; contrast Mark 12.12, which is indefinite). The Gospel tradition seems never to have the scribes clearly in focus, and Luke makes no attempt to improve the focus. Scribes are to be associated either with chief priests or with Pharisees, never with both at once. The three appearances of the scribes in Acts (4.5; 6.12; 23.9) also follow this pattern.[101]

Thus we see that, with the exception of the two unrelated references to chief priests, Luke has consistently portrayed the chief priests and elders of the Jews, with their various associates (including the scribes when they are associated with the chief priests) and functionaries, as actively opposing Jesus and the church, killing Jesus and the leaders of the church when they can get away with it. '*Ce sont les juifs qui ont tout fait.*'[102] In so characterizing the Jewish religious leaders Luke has not simply followed historical tradition; he has altered and expanded upon it so as to make the religious leaders more uniformly hostile to Jesus and to the church than the tradition had given one reason to believe they were. Before proceeding from this observation, however, to a discussion of the ways in which Luke has characterized the Jewish people and country generally, one more aspect of Jewish leadership needs to be examined. We must look briefly at the role of 'Herod' in Luke-Acts.

Herod

Four Herods appear in Luke's work. Herod I (called by Luke 'Herod the King') stands dimly in the background, serving only to designate the time when Jesus was born (Luke 1.5) and as a place name (Acts 23.35). Herod Antipas (called by Luke 'Herod the Tetrarch') appears throughout the Gospel and is mentioned in Acts

4.27 and, indirectly, in Acts 13.1. In Luke 3 this Herod arrests John the Baptist; in 9.7–9 he expresses a desire to see Jesus; in 13.31 he is reported to want to kill Jesus; and in ch. 23 he takes the role that has been described above. Except for the persecution of John, all these aspects of Antipas's attitude and behaviour are found only in Luke among the Synoptic Gospels. Since Herod Antipas is delighted, in 23.8, finally to see Jesus, and since he then acquits him, the question must arise whether his desire to see Jesus in 9.9 is in fact a desire to persecute Jesus, as might appear from the context there and from 13.31.[103] The warning of 13.31 is, indeed, difficult to understand in view of the acquittal in ch. 23. This Herod became, according to Luke 23.12, a friend of Pilate, and Acts 4.27 repeats the theme of their cooperation.[104] The third Herod is Agrippa I (called by Luke, again, 'Herod the King'), who persecutes the church in Acts 12; and the fourth Herod, finally, is Agrippa II (called by Luke 'Agrippa'), who figures in Paul's trials in Acts 25–26.

Luke seems at pains to distinguish the four Herods clearly so that they do not become confused in the reader's mind. In addition to using different names and titles for the three who actually figure in his narrative, he is also careful to introduce the title tetrarch, not found in Mark, into his account in Luke 3.1, 19; 9.7. If we ignore, however, the use of the name Herod in time and place designations and its other incidental occurrences (e.g., Luke 8.3), and if we set aside, for the moment, the warning to Jesus in Luke 13.31 and Antipas's desire to see him in 9.9, then we are left with a clear 'Herodian' pattern of behavior, according to which it is irrelevant which Herod is active in the narrative at the time. In this sense, there is only one Herod in Luke's account.

The pattern is this: first a persecution – of John in the Gospel and of the apostles in Acts – and then an acquittal – of Jesus in the Gospel and of Paul in Acts.[105] Why does Luke present this scheme? Why is it that some Herod or other, left to his own devices, persecutes the apostles and the forerunner, whereas some Herod or other (in the Gospel the same as the persecutor) acquits Jesus and then Paul when he stands in some association with the Roman procurator? The question has provided the answer. Herod, the Jewish *temporal* authority – who has no association whatever with the Jewish religious authorities[106] – follows what are for Luke his normal Jewish inclinations and persecutes and puts to death John and the leaders of the church. In this respect, then, Jewish temporal authorities and Jewish religious authorities take a uniform stance towards Christianity. Herod, however, unlike the chief priests and their associates, is an ally of Rome, 'friends' (Luke 23.12); and this alliance or friendship with Roman temporal authority leads to the Herodian acquittals. To the degree that Herod is Jewish he is hostile to the purposes of God. When he embraces Rome, however, he also embraces the Roman attitude towards Jesus and the church: acquittal. Conzelmann almost recognized this when he wrote of the Herod of the passion narrative, 'In a sense he occupies an intermediate position.'[107]

If this attempt to explain the behaviour of the Herods in Luke-Acts has anything to commend it, then it also allows us to make sense out of the desire expressed in 9.9 to 'see' Jesus and out of the warning of 13.31. Since both fall prior to Herod's association with the Roman procurator, they should be seen as expressions of Herodian hostility.[108] This will present no difficulty for 13.31, since it means that we may read it as a straightforward and unambiguous statement of the situation: Herod wanted to kill Jesus; in ch. 23 he comes into contact with Pilate and consequently decides for acquittal. As for the desire to 'see' Jesus in 9.9, we may recall that the context (a possible association of Jesus with the Baptist) would lead the reader to assume that this 'seeing' would be for foul purposes. Herod has done away with John, Jesus is acting like John, Herod wants to 'see' Jesus, and, in 13.31, Herod wants to kill Jesus. The problem with reading 9.9 as expressing a hostile desire is that the same word, 'see', is used again in the acquittal context, Luke 23.8. Can 'seeing' Jesus be meant in a hostile way in 9.9 and in a friendly way in 23.8? There seems to be no serious reason why the two references to Herod's desire to see Jesus and to his seeing Jesus may not so be understood, and the architectonic parallelism between Luke and Acts with regard to (the) Herod(s) would seem to require it.[109] Indeed, when we hold fast to the parallel pattern as the key to understanding Herod, then Luke's use of 'seeing' in the two places makes good sense: while for Herod to see Jesus before coming into association with Pilate would have implied a hostile act, his seeing Jesus after becoming associated with Pilate is a friendly act.[110]

The question of Luke's rationale(s)

We have seen that the Jewish authorities, as represented in Luke-Acts, are uniformly hostile to Jesus and the church and kill the leaders when they can. Only the Jewish secular authority escapes this pattern by conversion to 'Gentilism'. No good reason is ever given for the hostility, and we have seen ample ground for doubting its complete historicity. (Luke has, clearly, distorted the passion narrative tradition;[111] and the narrative in Acts conforms to that in the Gospel in an often wooden architectonic parallelism.) Why would Luke portray the Jewish leaders in such fashion if the portrayal is not historically accurate? Was he just giving expression to antisemitic prejudices, or did he have good – or, at least, understandable – reasons for representing the Jewish authorities as such villains? Did Luke, for example, have 'in view . . . oppressions that threatened the Hellenistic congregations from the synagogue quarter, brought about by Jewish accusation of Christians before pagan authorities';[112] or did he characterize the Jewish religious leaders as he did in response to an identity problem within Gentile Christianity?[113] Inasmuch as we know that Luke's portrayal of Roman persecution of Christianity (i.e., he gives no such portrayal) is theologically motivated, in order to promote the idea of official Roman friendliness toward Christianity, it would seem likely that his portrayal of Jewish persecution of Christianity is likewise theologically motivated; and so we would have to incline to the 'identity problem' explanation. But this issue can only adequately be taken up after we have the complete picture before us, and so we turn now to a further consideration of the evidence.

2

JERUSALEM

While earlier authors certainly noted that Jerusalem occupies a place
of prominence in Luke-Acts – something that could hardly be
overlooked in the light of the statement in Acts 1.8 and the ecclesiastical 'incubation period' in the first five chapters of Acts – it was
Hans Conzelmann who focused the attention of the most recent
generation of scholars on the important role that Jerusalem plays in
the *theological geography* of Luke-Acts. In Conzelmann's analysis, the
career of Jesus in Luke is divided into three periods – the Galilean
itinerary, the journey toward Jerusalem, and the ministry in Jerusalem culminating in his death.[1] While Jerusalem is the goal of the
journey, however (Luke 9.51), the journey concludes with Jesus'
correcting an eschatological misapprehension, namely that the
kingdom of God would 'appear' when he reached the city (Luke
19.11). In connection with Jerusalem, then, Luke shows (according
to Conzelmann) that 'Jerusalem has nothing to do with the Parousia,
though it has with the Resurrection'.[2] After the resurrection, 'the
Church . . . break[s] away from Jerusalem; . . . Church history is
[therefore] a development'.[3]

Four Jerusalem scenes

While Conzelmann's explanation of the Lucan eschatology has
been much discussed – accepted, rejected, and modified – no one
has tried to demonstrate that Jerusalem does not have an important
theological significance for Luke. That it has is seen even more clearly
when one takes Luke 1–2 into account, which Conzelmann did not.[4]
That this prehistory does belong to the Lucan account, however,
and that it is precisely the importance of Jerusalem in the prehistory
that shows the connection to the rest of Luke-Acts had already been
demonstrated, a few years before Conzelmann's work appeared, in

an often overlooked Bern dissertation by Robert Morgenthaler.[5] In his work, Morgenthaler called attention to the fact that both Luke and Acts have two large Jerusalem scenes, one at the beginning and one at the end (in the case of Acts, near the end) of each, and that these scenes have many elements in common.[6] Morgenthaler damaged his case by finding some parallels that are less than obvious to anyone else,[7] yet his emphasis on the place of the Temple in all four scenes is surely correct,[8] and one can hardly deny that something like what he, in conclusion,[9] called 'the unity of scene and the uniformity of treatment' does indeed tie the four scenes together.

What is it that Luke wants to show by his emphasis on Jerusalem at the beginning and end of the Gospel and at the beginning and end of Acts? Without entering here into a detailed discussion of Luke's eschatology and ecclesiology, which do not directly concern us, we may say that Jerusalem is, without any doubt, *the* geographical pivot in the divine plan of salvation.[10] In Luke 9.51 Jesus 'set [his] countenance to journey to Jerusalem'; and he explains exactly why in 13.33: 'It is not possible for a prophet to perish outside Jerusalem.' In other words, Jesus, whom Luke regularly designates as a prophet, must go to Jerusalem in order to perish there. The Gospel then concludes with Jesus' passion, death and resurrection in Jerusalem. When Acts opens, Jesus lays down the geographical pattern of the expansion of the church (Acts 1.8: Jerusalem, Judaea and Samaria, and to the end of the earth), and from then on Acts follows that prescribed pattern fairly closely. The church enjoys success in Jerusalem in the first five chapters; then the events of chs. 6–7 become the indirect cause of expansion beyond Jerusalem into, especially, Judaea and Samaria; and then the Gentile mission begins in earnest in ch. 13. Before Paul reaches Rome, however, there must be a last impetus from Jerusalem. Paul's arrest there provides the opportunity for him to journey to Rome.

Behind all this, of course, lies the divine plan. Jesus *must* perish in Jerusalem, and the gospel *must* then go to the Gentiles (cf. the conclusion drawn by the Jerusalem apostles after Peter's report of the conversion of Cornelius and his household, Acts 11.18: 'So God has given repentance unto life to the Gentiles also!'). In addition to Acts 1.8, we may also note the Lucan version of the great commission in Luke 24.46–48:[11] The risen Jesus 'said to them, "Thus it is written that the Messiah would suffer and rise from the dead on the third day, and that repentance and forgiveness of sins would be proclaimed in his name to all the Gentiles. Beginning from Jerusalem, you are witnesses of these things.'"[12] 'Jerusalem was the centre of St Luke's theological universe.'[13]

But it is not simply that history turns on the pivot of Jerusalem; not only that Jesus takes the message of the Kingdom of God to Jerusalem and that the apostles take the gospel out; not only that this geographical progression is theologically determined. For there is a darker side to that perspective, and Luke gives it full play in his two-volume work. That darker side is that Jesus must perish in Jerusalem because Jerusalem always kills the prophets, and that the gospel must proceed out from Jerusalem because Jerusalem always rejects the word of God.[14] In Luke-Acts, Jerusalem is not only 'the centre of St Luke's theological universe'; it is the *locus classicus* of hostility to God, to his purposes, to his messengers.[15] O'Neill has emphasized this two-sided picture of Jerusalem in Luke-Acts, noting that Jerusalem 'is at the same time the city which God redeems (Luke 2.38) and the city where he is rejected. It becomes the centre of the mission to the Gentiles, but it rejects the gospel for itself. Jerusalem is both the Heavenly City and the Earthly City.'[16] O'Neill combines this observation with the awareness of Jerusalem's place in the geographical scheme of Luke-Acts and concludes that Jesus' approach to Jerusalem in the Gospel involves an offering of salvation to the city, but that the city's rejection of salvation leads to the Gentile mission, which proceeds out from Jerusalem.[17] Stephen's martyrdom is the turning point in the progression. His death is a 'lynching' (not an official execution) and therefore in a certain sense carried out by the entire city. 'Stephen's arrest and trial and lynching mark the final failure of the mission to the capital'; therefore, from this point on, 'the mission to Jerusalem is no longer the concern of the author'.[18]

Morgenthaler had similarly noted the way in which the geographical significance of Jerusalem in Luke-Acts points to a theological principle: from the Jews to the Gentiles. Morgenthaler went even further. 'If anything is clear, then it is this, . . . that salvation is going over from the Jews to the Gentiles – figuratively expressed, from Jerusalem to Rome. This and only this is the key to the riddle of the construction of the Lucan work.'[19] Morgenthaler, however, understood Jerusalem's rejection of salvation to be present not only in the geographical progression of Luke-Acts, but in each of the four Jerusalem scenes independently; however, in order to make that explanation work, he had to include the account of John's baptism (with the hostility expressed by some to this activity) and imprisonment as part of the first Jerusalem episode. That is casting the net of 'Jerusalem' pretty wide, since Luke associates John with the Jordan, not with Jerusalem (Luke 3.33), and makes plain that the Herod into whose clutches John fell was 'Tetrarch of Galilee' (v. 1). The relation of Jerusalem in Luke 1–2 to the Lucan divine plan resides rather in that Luke begins his narrative with a scene of harmony between God and his city and then shows, at the end of the Gospel, how Jerusalem rejects God. The tableau of cosiness in Acts 2.46–47 is then the result of Luke's architectonic paralleling; as with Jesus, so with the apostles.

Yet Morgenthaler was correct in drawing attention away from a simple geographical explanation of the Jerusalem hostility, since the final Jerusalem scene does not fit the geographical pattern, just as the element of hostility is not really present in the first Jerusalem scene. Jerusalem as the place where the Messiah is killed and where, in the first part of Acts, the church is persecuted, which persecution gives the Gentile mission its start, fits the geographical pattern neatly; but the final Jerusalem scene, in which Paul is arrested and gets sent to Rome, falls outside the pattern. This last Jerusalem scene has the effect of giving renewed emphasis to the Gentile mission, of giving a last necessary thrust needed to throw Paul into the wider orbit that carries him to Rome[20] – as if the rejection in the first part of Acts was sufficient to get the gospel to Asia Minor and Greece but no farther.[21] Paul's address to Jerusalem in Acts 22.1–21 is, furthermore, not a 'last chance' for Jerusalem,[22] since Paul here makes no appeal for conversion and since his speech concludes with the reaffirmation that God sent him, even at the outset (v. 18), to the Gentiles. The 'last chance' had been offered before Stephen's martyrdom, as O'Neill stated.[23] Consequently it is the entire city, ἡ πόλις ὅλη, that turns on Paul in the Temple in 21.30.[24] Some further analysis of the place of hostility and rejection in the four Jerusalem scenes seems to be in order.

The place of hostility

While Luke 1–2 present no animosity between Jesus and Jerusalem, there is nevertheless a hint of what is to come in that the conclusion of ch. 2, and the climax of the prehistory, place Jesus in certain respects in the same relation to the Temple in which the passion narrative finds him – that is, he teaches the Temple authorities. Thus, although Jesus, according to Luke 2.46, is described first only as 'listening' and 'asking questions', he is then immediately (v. 47) also said to be giving 'answers'; and it is these answers and his 'understanding' that cause all who heard him to be 'astonished' (RSV: literally 'ecstatic, ἐξίσταντο'). The similarities and differences between Luke 2.46–47 and 19.47–48 are instructive. In 19.47, as in 2.47–48, Jesus is teaching in the Temple; and if 2.47–48 stop just short of saying that he was 'teaching', at least he comes as close to doing so there as might be expected of a twelve-year-old. Furthermore, just as 'all who heard him' were 'ecstatic' in 2.47, so the entire people of 19.48 'hung on his every word' (ἐξεκρέματο αὐτοῦ ἀκούων). Jesus in the Temple in the passion narrative, therefore, closely resembles Jesus in the Temple in the prehistory.[25] A significant difference, however, distances 19.47–48 from 2.46–47, and that is that, in the second Jerusalem scene, there is a division between leaders and people. Here, instead of the 'all' of 2.47, we have 'the chief priests and the scribes, as well as the leaders of the people [seeking] a way to destroy him'. Thus the first Jerusalem scene does not refer to the later hostility between Jerusalem and Jesus and between Jerusalem and Christianity but only presents Jesus' superiority to the Jerusalem 'teachers',[26] whereby the condition necessary for that later hostility is nevertheless given: Jesus' superiority over the old order. The second Jerusalem scene includes the hostility. (We shall return to the matter of the division between leaders and people below in ch. 3.)

If the first Jerusalem scene, then, provides only the precondition for the later hostility, the other three Jerusalem scenes express it. In scene 2 Jesus is killed, in scene 3 Stephen is killed, and in scene 4 Paul comes as close to being killed as possible without actually losing his life. Jerusalem is thus the city 'that kills the prophets and stones those who are sent to her', and she incurs the judgment, 'Behold, Your house is forsaken to you' (Luke 13.34–35).[27]

That the martyrdoms of Jesus and Stephen and the near martyrdom of Paul are parallel in many ways has been emphasized especially by Radl and Goulder.[28] All three come into some connection with the Temple (Jesus teaches in it, Stephen denounces it, and Paul is accused of denouncing and defiling it), all three are tried in the Sanhedrin, Stephen and Jesus have similar parting words,[29] and the various trials and hearings of Jesus and Paul before different authorities are highly similar.[30] Conzelmann understood the martyrdom of Jesus to mark the end of Period II (the time of Jesus) in his chronological division and the martyrdom of Stephen to mark the end of the first stage of Period III (the time of the church), the second stage of which still continues[31] – after all, Paul was *not* martyred and the church still exists. More recent authors have responded, some rather strongly, to Conzelmann's attempt to determine what outline Luke had in mind for God's plan in history, and nearly everyone has proposed an outline that is in some way different. While it would be beside the point to take up that issue in detail here, we may note, nevertheless, that Conzelmann's outline falls in neatly with the scenes of Jerusalemite hostility. When an underlying outline is proposed that ignores the importance of the four Jerusalem scenes, then the analysis is not as satisfying. This is the case, for example, with Goulder's study.

Goulder divided Acts itself into four sections – the 'Apostolic', the 'Diaconal', the 'Petrine' and the 'Pauline'[32] – and closed the sections with, respectively, the persecution of the apostles, the martyrdom of Stephen, the arrest of Peter in Acts 12.3 and the arrest and trials of Paul. Goulder connected these periods ending in persecution or martyrdom with the geographical plan of Acts 1.8 and referred to the similarities as belonging to 'a spiral, always moving on and out into new territory, into deeper trials, into new communities, like a series of waves breaking higher and higher on the sea-shore'.[33] While there is much to be said for his analysis, especially his emphasizing that Conzelmann's keeping all events from Acts 1 on in one period does not do adequate justice to Luke's periodicizing, it does seem that he has also overlooked an important factor, and that is Jerusalem itself. In the Gospel there is movement *towards* Jerusalem concluding in martyrdom; in Acts 1–7 there is activity *in* Jerusalem concluding in martyrdom; and in the rest of Acts there is movement *away from* Jerusalem concluding in near-martyrdom, which near-martyrdom must nevertheless *take place in Jerusalem*.[34] Jerusalem is thus both the pivot for Luke's geographical theology and the *locus classicus* of hostility to Jesus and the church.

Goulder was correct, of course, to point to other hostile actions against Christians in Jerusalem in the early part of Acts, but these persecutions are probably better seen as instances of increasing hostility leading up to Stephen's martyrdom. The martyrdom of James and the arrest of Peter in Acts 12.1–3 do not, it seems to me, close a 'Petrine' section of Acts. The end of the Jerusalem period of the church and the beginning of expansion begin immediately after Stephen's martyrdom; the persecution of Acts 12.1–3 (carried out by Herod and not by the religious authorities, unrelated to the Temple, not specifically related to Jerusalem, and narrated in the briefest summary) serves only as a transition to Paul's Gentile mission, which transition is more a shift of personnel than a move to a new period of the church. The Gentile mission, in Acts, begins after 7.60 and before 12.1.[35]

We see that it is not possible to discuss the Jerusalemite hostility to God, to Jesus, and to the apostles without reference to the city's role as pivot in the divine plan. Nevertheless, the hostility factor is also present in other ways as well. While there is persecution of Paul and his colleagues in the Diaspora, that persecution does not take place until after a persecution of Diaspora Christians has been initiated by the Jerusalem religious authorities. At the beginning of Acts 9 it is the pre-Christian Paul who carries authority from Jerusalem to persecute Christians as far removed as Damascus. Unlike the persecution of 12.1–3, here Jerusalem is specifically indicated as the *locus* of hostility: Paul is to bring Damascus Christians 'bound to Jerusalem' (9.3). Thus, while Jerusalem is not the only place where Jesus and the church experience hostility, and while portions of the populace of Jerusalem can be represented as friendly rather than as hostile to Jesus and the church (Luke 19.48; Acts 2.47; 5.13; 23.9),[36] Jerusalem remains the centre of hostility to the purposes of God. If Luke had had any real concept of theological dualism, he would have said that Jerusalem, with its temple, was Satan's capital.[37]

Pronouncements of judgment

When the uniformly hostile position of the Lucan Jerusalem towards the purposes of God is recognized, then Jesus' judgments on the city present no problem. We have already had occasion to note the lament in 13.33–35: 'It is not possible for a prophet to perish outside Jerusalem. Jerusalem, Jerusalem! killing the prophets and stoning those who have been sent to her. How often I have wanted to gather up your children as a hen her own brood under wings, and you did not wish it! Behold, your house is forsaken to you.'[38] To this saying one may add Jesus' prophecies about Jerusalem's coming destruction in 19.41–44 and 21.20–24, and his speech of woe to the women of Jerusalem in 23.28–31: 'Daughters of Jerusalem, cry not for me; but cry for yourselves and for your children; for behold the days are coming when you will say, "Fortunate are the barren and the wombs that have not given birth and breasts that have not given nourishment." Then they will begin to say to the mountains, "Fall on us!" and to the hills, "Hide us!" If they do these things when the wood is green, what will happen when it is dry?' 'The doom of the nation is now scheduled on the divine calendar.'[39]

Some authors wish to read these sayings against Jerusalem as calls to repentance, as offerings to Jerusalem of the opportunity of salvation. Thus Schweizer emphasizes the similarity of 13.33–35 to the classic prophetic threat and concludes that 'the warning of the judgment to come is also God's urgent invitation';[40] and he states, regarding the doom saying in ch. 23, that 'Jesus . . . seeks not pity but repentance'.[41]

Now it is indeed true that the prophetic threat, in its classical development, was intended to motivate change (*tešūbāh*); this point is best made by the Book of Jonah. Yet whether the threat continued to be so understood up through the development of apocalyptic and into the time of the Roman period and beyond is open to question. That is not, however, our issue, nor is it our purpose here to pursue the intent of the 'historical Jesus' in uttering these or similar sayings. Our task here is to try to understand Luke's meaning, the significance of the saying within the overall context of the Lucan portrayal of Jerusalem. In this regard, G. Schneider seems better to have grasped the meaning of these sayings when he writes, regarding 13.33–35, that 'Jesus is killed not only *in* Jerusalem, but *by* Jerusalem';[42] and, regarding 23.28–31, 'In the Lucan context, the reference is to the guilty inhabitants of Jerusalem.'[43]

Neyrey has gone into this issue in some detail, and it will be helpful now to give attention to his discussion.[44] After offering the contextual observation that 'there tends to be a negative portrayal of Jerusalem' in Luke-Acts, Neyrey then notes that Jesus' address in Luke 23.28 is to daughters of *Jerusalem*, not of *Israel*;[45] thus Luke 23.27–31 is an address to the hostile Jerusalem, not to all of Israel.[46] Furthermore, it is a mistake to read the introduction to the saying (v. 28), which says that Jesus 'turned . . . and said', as implying some positive kind of turning,[47] since Luke uses the same word in Acts 7.42 to indicate God's judgment on those who rejected the leadership of Moses.[48] Furthermore, in the apocalyptic discourse in Luke 21, 'the ruin of Jerusalem is the catastrophe of 70 A.D., seen as divine retribution', when that catastrophe is referred to as 'days of punishment' (ἡμέραι ἐκδικήσεως)' (v. 22).[49] The greater likelihood is therefore that 23.28–31 intend judgment.[50]

When the address to the daughters of Jerusalem is thus understood as a pronouncement of judgment, then it blends in with Luke's other statements about Jerusalem. The lament in Luke 13 has the effect of making the point that 'it is not Herod who will kill Jesus but . . . Jerusalem', since that lament follows the warning to Jesus that Herod seeks to kill him (v. 31);[51] and the lament in Luke 19.41–44 'allude[s] to Scriptural material from earlier traditions concerning Jerusalem's ruin, which now function as support for the verdict on the city as divine judgment'.[52] It should then be clear that, 'alongside Lk. 13.34–35 and 19.41–44,[53] the address to Jerusalem in 23.27–31 should be understood as another example of the prophetic oracle of judgment against Jerusalem, together with the more descriptive approach to this material in 21.20–24'.[54] We are therefore left with a consistent portrayal of

Jerusalem throughout Luke-Acts. While, in terms of salvation history, it is the pivot in the divine plan of salvation for the Gentiles, it is, even more than that, the *locus classicus* of evil, of hostility to Jesus, to the church, to the purposes of God. Consequently, it must be destroyed.[55]

If *Jerusalem*, therefore, has incurred the guilt of rejecting God's emissaries, including Jesus, then it is no longer merely the leaders who are guilty. As Paul says, according to Acts 13.27–28, 'The inhabitants of Jerusalem *and* their rulers' brought about Jesus' death. Thus, immediately Jesus sets foot in Jerusalem, he pronounces the judgment of 19.41–44;[56] and, shortly thereafter, he tells the parable of the Wicked Tenants, which, in its Lucan setting, may refer not only to the leaders' but also to Jerusalem's repeated 'killing [of] the prophets and stoning [of] those who have been sent to her' (13.34), since in 20.15 the tenants kill the last emissary and heir. That the Jerusalemite hearers understand that the judgment of the parable is pronounced on them is shown by their exclamation (v. 16, Luke only), 'God forbid (μὴ γένοιτο)'.[57] In the apocalyptic discourse of ch. 21, then, it is Luke (v. 20) who says explicitly that Jerusalem will be 'surrounded by armies', that 'its desolation [will have] come', and, what is of even greater significance for the issues that we are considering, that the forthcoming siege and destruction will be 'days of punishment' (v. 22).[58] Jerusalem, in Luke-Acts, is characterized primarily by enmity towards God and his purposes and messengers, by judgment, and by destruction.[59]

We shall do well to remember that, in Luke-Acts, Jerusalem's evil character is more basic than its role as pivot; it is not the other way round.[60] The several condemnations of the city in the Gospel and the presence of the concluding Jerusalem scene in Acts allow us to see that. For Luke, Jerusalem was not seen as hostile to the purposes of God because it was the pivot in the plan of salvation. The uniformly evil portrait of the city is unnecessary for such a point. Rather, it easily becomes the pivot in the divine plan because it is the place quintessentially opposed to God and his will.[61]

But if Luke's salvation-history scheme is not the reason for his portrayal of Jerusalem as evil and as meriting destruction, what is the reason? At this point no better answer to that question seems to suggest itself than that proposed in ch. 1, to which suggestion one will, of course, have to add that the destruction of Jerusalem had already occurred when Luke wrote, so that he had the advantage of being able to interpret an event after the fact.[62] Whether the answer suggested in ch. 1 can continue to carry the weight of Luke's portrayal of the Jews, we shall later have to inquire.

The Temple

What is true of Jerusalem in Luke-Acts is even more true of its temple, for the Temple is the heart of Jerusalem.[63] The youth Jesus teaches in the Temple, as does the prophet Jesus of the passion narrative. (The Jesus of the Lucan passion narrative, as a matter of fact, hardly leaves the Temple.)[64] Jesus, further, is martyred because of his Temple activity, and the near-martyrdom of Paul is likewise Temple-related; and, while Stephen is not arrested because of any Temple activity, he condemns the Temple in his defence speech (Acts 7:44–50). Thus the Temple is integrally involved in the Jerusalemite hostility.[65] If it is related to Jerusalem in this way, however, then it is also inseparably related to Jerusalem in its role as pivot in the divine plan of salvation, and for the same reasons.

Yet another aspect of the Lucan portrayal of the Temple, which goes beyond but is related to its role as pivot in the divine plan, is that Jesus and the apostles exhibit their traditional Jewish piety there.[66] Both the Gospel and Acts begin with, respectively, Jesus and the apostles devotedly serving God in the Temple; as Lohfink says, with a 'Jerusalem springtime'.[67] By emphasizing that connection, Luke makes two points for his Gentile readership: one, that Christianity has not broken with the ancient Israelite religion, and that, rather, a direct line of continuity runs from Moses and the Prophets to the church;[68] and, two, that it is not Christianity that has rejected Judaism, but Judaism that has rejected Christianity.[69]

Bihler has discussed these aspects of the Temple in Luke-Acts in some detail and has reached a somewhat different conclusion.[70] According to him, the Temple of the first Jerusalem scene is thoroughly Jewish,[71] but then the portrayal of the Temple shifts toward a Christian understanding in the body of the Gospel, i.e., it becomes a place of prayer (19.46) and the place where Jesus teaches.[72] This understanding of the Temple as a Christian place is then continued in Acts 1–5.[73] With the Stephen episode, however, the way in which the Temple is portrayed shifts again,[74] so that, from Stephen on (according to Bihler), criticisms of the Temple and references to its destruction occur, and Christianity separates itself from the Temple. Thus, 'with the aid of this organization of Temple motifs, Luke is able to present the distancing from the Jews in Acts 6–7, whereas, in Acts 1–5, he underlines the church's *heilsgeschichtliche* connection with Judaism'.[75] Bihler has, in this analysis, adequately isolated the relevant evidence – except for Luke 21.6 – and his concluding statement just quoted appears to be entirely correct. The contrast between the Temple in the first Jerusalem scene, however, and the Temple in the second Jerusalem scene, as Bihler has explained the matter, is not quite correct, inasmuch as, on the one hand, Jesus teaches in the Temple in both scenes, there being therefore in this respect no difference between Luke's portrayal of the Temple in Luke 2 and his portrayal of the Temple in Luke 20–21; whereas, on the other hand, the destruction of the Temple is foretold in the second Jerusalem scene (Luke 21.6)! This prophecy coincides with the judgments pronounced on Jerusalem in the second Jerusalem scene, not with an understanding of the Temple as a Christian place. It seems better, therefore, not to understand Luke as attempting to portray the Temple as a Christian place of worship in the second and third Jerusalem scenes, but rather to see him as attempting to show that Jesus and the disciples remain loyal to the most important Jewish religious place until they are ejected.

Finally, a peculiar part of Luke's attitude towards the Temple is that it is inherently perverse because it was χειροποίητος, 'made by hand'. That this judgment on the Temple is not merely some remnant of Samaritan theology that comes from the source or sources of Stephen's speech (Acts 7.48) is shown by the repetition of the term in Acts 17.24.[76] Here, in Paul's sermon on Athens's Mars Hill, there can be no question of a Samaritan background, since the Lucan Paul makes the connection that the 'unknown god' of the Athenians is worshipped in a temple that is not 'hand-made'; in other words, a distinguishing characteristic of the Christian god is that he does not have a physical temple.[77] Thus whereas, on the one hand, the Temple receives in a certain sense a positive evaluation as the place where the traditionally devout Jesus and apostles display their piety and their loyalty to tradition, it is in the final analysis viewed negatively, because it is the beating heart of the hostility to God and because it is, in any case, a perverse place, due to its having been 'made by hand', and therefore inherently a false temple. It is thus no accident that, in the Temple-cleansing scene (Luke 19.46), Luke omits the words 'for all the Gentiles' in the Isaiah quotation, although they appear in Mark 11.17. For Luke, the Temple was certainly not 'a house of prayer for all the Gentiles'.[78]

A minor point should not go unmentioned, and that is that Luke's portrayal of Jerusalem is also related to his theme that the gospel is going to the Gentiles. While that theme is not our concern here, nevertheless we should at least note that the themes of the Jewish rejection of salvation and of the continuity between Christianity and 'biblical' Israel have a lot to do with Gentile salvation, with which

Luke is vitally concerned, and that he pursues these themes, as we have seen, in connection with his portrayal of Jerusalem.[79]

Two spellings of Jerusalem

One of the more puzzling aspects of Luke's portrayal of Jerusalem is the way in which, especially in Acts, two different spellings occur, Ἰερουσαλήμ and Ἰεροσόλυμα, the former a reasonably accurate transliteration of the Aramaic pronunciation, the latter a Hellenized spelling that gives the impression that the name of the city is 'sacred' something.[80] Two authors, Bachmann and de la Potterie, have made considerable efforts to solve the puzzle, and we turn our attention now to their discussions.[81]

It is de la Potterie's position that Luke's purpose in employing these different *nomina* is theological: Ἰεροσόλυμα is the profane city meriting destruction, Ἰερουσαλήμ the sacred city where 'the messianic revelation and . . . the work of salvation' take place.[82] Thus, for example, Luke uses Ἰερουσαλήμ in the introduction to the parable of the Pounds, 19.11, because the context is the Kingdom of God. At the conclusion of the parable, however, destruction has been pronounced on the city, hence Ἰεροσόλυμα is the appropriate spelling in v. 28.[83] The appearance of the two terms in Acts is then also schematized according to this pattern. After the opening use of Ἰεροσόλυμα in 1.4, where Luke designates the city apart from its religious significance, only Ἰερουσαλήμ appears until the end of ch. 7, since in this section the salvation of the city is taking place. In chs. 8–19, then, Luke's usage alternates according to the aforementioned principle; in chs. 20–24 Ἰερουσαλήμ 'predominates' because of Paul's sojourn there; but from 25.7 on only Ἰεροσόλυμα occurs.[84]

While this analysis, however, probably correctly indicates the dual aspect under which Luke views Jerusalem, as we have already noted in some detail, there are some problems with de la Potterie's explanation of Luke's use of the two spellings for Jerusalem. In regard to the appearance of both spellings in connection with the parable of the Pounds, one may wonder whether de la Potterie's explanation of the occurrence of Ἰεροσόλυμα in Luke 19.28 is entirely to the point, inasmuch as Jesus' journey may be thought of as having a dual aspect, since Jesus goes there not only to die but also to teach. Furthermore, if Jesus' approach to the city thus requires the use of the profane spelling, then it is much less than clear why Paul's comparable approach to Jerusalem in Acts then requires the sacred spelling in Acts 20–24, when that section then also recounts Paul's arrest. For these reasons, the explanation of Bachmann, that the Lucan usage in this regard is a matter of *verisimilitude*, not of *theology*, seems more plausible.

Bachmann notes that the use of Ἰεροσόλυμα grows from the beginning of Luke to the end of Acts, while the use of Ἰερουσαλήμ diminishes. Thus Ἰεροσόλυμα appears only four times in Luke but six times in Acts 1–14, seven times in Acts 15–24, and ten times in Acts 25–28, whereas Ἰερουσαλήμ appears twenty-six times in Luke and twenty-four times in Acts 1–14, but only eleven times in Acts 15–24 and once in Acts 25–28.[85] Furthermore, Ἰεροσόλυμα never occurs in speech – only in narrative – before Acts 25.[86] Thus Bachmann sees two tendencies at work. One is simply that Luke shifts more and more, in the narrative portions, towards the spelling of his preference as he proceeds through his two-volume work;[87] the other is that he avoids having any speaker use the Hellenized version of the name of the city until finally, in Acts 25.9, Festus employs it. From this point on, Ἱεροσόλυμα occurs seven more times in speech. Luke's rationale, according to Bachmann, is that he puts Ἱερουσαλήμ on his speakers' tongues 'if the audience is composed primarily of Jews or of persons who are somehow closely related to Judaism as Judaism.'[88] In other cases, i.e. from Acts 25.9 on, the Hellenized spelling appears. The one apparent exception to this principle is Acts 28.17, where Paul uses Ἱεροσόλυμα when addressing Roman Jews; but this use is explained by its being the last occurrence of the name of the city in Luke-Acts – thus Luke's preference takes precedence – and by the fact that the terminology of the sentence in which it appears ('I was delivered a prisoner [δέσμιος . . . παρεδόθην]') smacks of Roman legal usage, so that the stated principle of choice in speech is not really missing here.[89]

Luke's variant spellings for Jerusalem do not, in and of themselves, provide much additional information about how he thought of the city. The fact that the key to understanding his usage, however, is the distinguishing of speech from narrative is an important insight, to which we shall shortly have to return.

3

THE JEWISH PEOPLE

The problem

We now come to the issue of the Jewish people as such, of 'the Jews' as a collective entity; and this is the sticky wicket. The issues that have been addressed in the first two chapters have been the easiest, for it is quite plain that, in Luke-Acts, the chief priests are the enemies of Jesus and the church and that Jerusalem plays a pivotal role in the author's geographical theology while being at the same time the city condemned to destruction as punishment for the murder of Jesus. Some readers may find a point here and there in the preceding chapters to quibble over, but the main issues are obvious and are almost universally agreed upon already. But when we ask what Luke thinks of the Jewish people we do not receive back such an easy answer; for sometimes it seems that only the religious leaders are guilty of having executed Jesus, and sometimes it seems that all the inhabitants of Jerusalem – or even all Jews everywhere – share in the guilt; and the accusations of hostility to the purposes of God seem sometimes to be directed specifically at the religious authorities and at other times to be thrown around indiscriminately at all Jews in sight. Thus it is clear that Temple authorities arrested Jesus and that Temple soldiers crucified him (in Luke), but Paul says, in Acts 13.27, that 'those dwelling in Jerusalem *and* their rulers' did it, and the conclusion of Stephen's speech seems to involve all Jews, since it accuses, without qualification, all descendants of the ancient Israelites: 'Whom of the prophets did your fathers not persecute? And they killed those who proclaimed beforehand the coming of the Righteous One, whose deliverers and murderers now you have become' (Acts 7.52). When Stephen then (v. 53) refers to these deliverers and murderers as those who had 'received the Law', this seems even more to indicate all Jews, or at least all religious ones, than to refer only to the chief priests.

This same passage may be cited again as an example of the way in which Luke sometimes seems to indicate all the Jewish people as those hostile to the divine purpose; and we may also note in this connection the repeated and, after a time, predictable – although not universal – hostility to Paul's preaching in the Diaspora synagogues. Otherwise, however, Luke 19.48 explains that the fact that 'the entire people (ὁ λαὸς ἅπας)' was 'hanging on [Jesus'] every word' was what at first prevented the Temple authorities from arresting Jesus; and Acts 2.47 claims that the apostles were 'standing in good stead with the whole people (ὅλος ὁ λαός)'.

And what are we to make of the fact that, in Antioch, in Corinth, and in Rome, Paul 'persuades' (πείθω, 13.43; 18.4; 28.23) Jews in his audience but then each time condemns them in quite general terms and announces that the gospel is to be taken to the Gentiles? If one explains that, of course, Jewish opposition to Paul developed after his successful 'persuasion' in Antioch and Corinth, prompting Paul's condemnation, then the inquirer will be forced to respond in turn that the pattern of persuasion followed by condemnation and rejection is repeated in the final scene in Acts *without* the benefit of that hostility.

These inconsistencies show that the Lucan portrait of 'the Jews' is done not in vividly contrasting colours but in subtle shades. What *does* Luke think of the Jewish people? Of course, I am here as before not thinking of such items as whether they are rich or poor, or what their table manners were. I am thinking of the issues that I have raised previously. Does Luke see the Jewish people as guilty in the death of Jesus or not, as irredeemably opposed to the will of God or not, as recipients of the salvation of God or not? Inasmuch as these issues have received no small discussion in modern scholarly writing, we may perhaps be helped on our way by some examination of the contributions made by other scholars to this discussion.

While several different opinions are current, there are nevertheless, in the main and broadly speaking, only two choices. (We shall deal with variations within the two options as we go along.) Either Luke intends to distinguish between those Jews who accept the gospel and become Christians and those who do not, in which case he hardly separates the latter group from their religious leaders and condemns them together, or he does not make this distinction and condemns all the Jewish people collectively for their obstinacy in the face of the divine proffering of salvation and for their participation in the execution of Jesus. The former view is today often connected with the name of Jacob Jervell, and the latter is probably most normally associated with the name of Ernst Haenchen, although it is certainly more widely held, so much so that Jervell referred to it as a 'common opinion'.[1] We proceed to a brief consideration of these two possibilities and then to a further analysis of the Lucan portrayal of 'the Jews', in the course of which analysis we shall, so we hope, be able to open up some new possibilities of interpretation. First, the 'common opinion'.

The view that all Jews are incorrigible

The view that Luke condemns 'the Jews' – that is, the Jewish people considered together as a group, without any distinctions among them – and 'writes them off'[2] is almost as old as critical New Testament scholarship. Franz Overbeck, in rejecting the explanation of Acts given by the Tübingen school (that the purpose of Acts was to reconcile apostolic Jewish Christianity and Pauline Gentile Christianity),[3] insisted that the 'conciliatory' explanation could not be reconciled with the obvious and emphatic '*nationale Antijudaismus* of Acts'.[4]

This book makes the development of the Christian community dependent precisely on the obdurate unbelief of the Jews; it emphasizes sharply, even at the outset, their prior guiltiness (2.23); it bases each advance of the Christian messianic proclamation factually on the guilt of the Jews; . . . it strives vigorously to extricate the issue of the Christians outwardly from that of the Jews, and in this sense it alienates Paul himself from his people. It cannot be intended to have a conciliatory effect on the Jewish Christians.

Overbeck referred in this context to the '*Grundtendenz*' of chs. 1–12, especially to Stephen's speech, and to Paul's experience with Jews during his missionary career and at his trial.[5] (How the *Jewish Christians* fit into Luke's portrayal of the Jews we shall consider below in ch. 4.) It should be clearly noted, incidentally, that Overbeck did not accept as historically accurate the representation of the Jews in Acts but rather referred more strongly than any other modern author to Acts as a 'fiction' (*passim*) that 'is in general unbelievable and has to demonstrate its credibility in each individual instance'.[6]

A short generation later (1908),[7] Loisy wrote, regarding the Lucan version of the trial and crucifixion of Jesus, that 'the Jews did it all';[8]

and he proposed further that one could see this compositional tendency at work, for example, in the embassy that attempted, in the parable of the Pounds, to prevent the throne pretender's ascent to the throne (Luke 19.14), which in fact 'signified nothing other than the incredulity of the Jews towards the word and towards the mission of Jesus, their resistance to the apostolic preaching'.[9] Later (1920), Loisy was almost as emphatic on the point of general Jewish hostility in Acts as Overbeck had been, when he wrote in the introduction to his commentary on Acts that 'all evil comes from the Jews';[10] and he noted that, whenever Christians in Acts experienced unpleasantness in their relations with the Roman authorities, it was 'the Jews' who were 'the perpetual denouncers of the Christians'.[11]

In more recent times, Ernst Haenchen has continued to interpret the role of the Jews in Acts in this way, while at the same time introducing certain refinements into the position. According to Haenchen, the opposition between Judaism and Christianity, which is over the issue of the Christian proclamation of the resurrection,[12] develops as Acts progresses. At first (chs. 3–5), the church expands and enjoys the good will of the people while experiencing the opposition only of the religious leaders.[13] With Stephen, however, the situation changes. Stephen's speech is 'filled' with unmistakable 'aggressiveness and palpitating wrath against the Jewish people', the purpose of which is to distinguish Christianity, as the group in continuity with the Old Testament, from the Jews, whose rejection of Jesus and the gospel shows them to be an 'aberration'.[14] Chapters 8–11 then shift the story-line of Acts from the Jewish mission to the Gentile mission,[15] at the beginning of which the attitude towards the Jewish *people* is completely reversed from that in chs. 3–5, for in 12.3 'the Jews' favour persecution of the Christians. 'Here, therefore, the people are no longer on the side of the Christians, as formerly – according to the Lucan presentation.'[16] From this point on, 'the Jews' oppose Christianity. Paul's first missionary sermon concludes with a rejection of the Jewish mission (Acts 13.46) that, while it refers in the first case only to the Antiochene Jews, has general significance;[17] and after this 'the entire course of the life of the Christian missionary Paul is determined by the arguments with the Jews', the standard synagogue scenes of Paul's ministry being done in 'placard style'.[18] It is the purpose of the Apostolic Council in Acts to be the 'watershed' of this movement from the Jews to the Gentiles.[19] Paul's arrest in Jerusalem provides the opportunity to show him in conflict with

Palestinian Judaism as well,[20] and the final scene, with Paul in Rome, represents for Luke 'a final rejection of Israel and its being replaced with the Gentiles'.[21] Thus Luke expresses 'the theology of Gentile Christianity toward the end of the first century . . .; [this theology] no longer sees any sense or any truth in Israel's election'. 'Luke has written the Jews off.'[22]

Briefly summarized, then, Haenchen's explanation is that, while Luke recognized that the first Christians were Jews and that there was a (successful) Jewish mission in the first days of Christianity, the purpose of Acts is to show how things developed from that stage to the situation in which Luke lived, i.e., a situation in which Christians were Gentiles and in which Jews opposed Christianity. Or, to use Haenchen's own words, 'In reality . . . the historian Luke struggles [in Acts] from the first to the last page with the problem of the *Gentile mission that is free of the Law*.'[23] While Haenchen did not give much attention to the Gospel of Luke in his explanations of Acts, it would not be inconsistent with his position to see the Gospel as also displaying the same tendencies as Acts, inasmuch as the Gospel also begins with a pronounced friendliness towards Jewish religion and then moves from that harmony to conflict and rejection (the passion narrative, of course, but also Jesus' rejection in his home town, Luke 4.16–30), with tips along the way about the Gentile mission coming to a climax with Luke 24.47, '. . . to all the Gentiles'. Haenchen's explanation of the Lucan portrayal of the Jews therefore allows one to see that there is an order to the way in which Luke has portrayed the Jewish people. It is not that they appear *indiscriminately* sometimes as friendly and sometimes as hostile, now the recipients of salvation and now rejected; rather, they fit into these various moulds *according to Luke's plan of historical development*.

As we have noted already, many scholars agree with the position that Luke represents the Jews in general as hostile to the purposes of God and as having rejected his salvation – that is, with the statement that 'Luke has written the Jews off'. Except for the three authors reviewed here, however, virtually everyone adds the qualification that there is always room in Luke's theology for the individual Jew to be converted and be welcomed into Christianity, that Luke's blanket denunciation of 'the Jews' is, as Overbeck indeed named it, a *'nationale Antijudaismus'*, an opposition to 'the Jews' as a group, but not in such a way as to preclude the possibility that any individual Jew could accept God's salvation.

The following positions are especially deserving of notice. Morgenthaler, *Geschichts-schreibung*, vol. 1, pp. 188–9, emphasizes the consistent opposition of the Jews to Jesus and to the church in Luke-Acts. Lohse, 'Lukas als Theologe', p. 79, argues that the Jews uniformly reject Jesus and the gospel in Luke-Acts, and that they are (in Luke-Acts) alone guilty for Jesus' death; and Kränkl, *Knecht*, p. 118, also emphasizes the general Jewish guilt in this regard in Luke-Acts. Via, 'Who Put Jesus to Death?', pp. 129–38, while viewing the people as less guilty than the rulers, nevertheless does see them as participating in the guilt for the death of Jesus. Bihler, 'Stephanusbericht', pp. 265–6, and *Stephanusgeschichte*, pp. 77, 81, emphasizes the uniform Jewish hostility and rejection of the purposes of God in Luke-Acts; and he is closely followed in this by Pesch, *Vision*, pp. 32, 46. O'Neill, *Theology*, pp. 84, 86–7, 98–9, also sees the importance of Jewish opposition to Luke's purpose, and he further emphasizes that the Jews reject their opportunities for salvation. Löning, 'Theologe', p. 219, explains especially clearly the two-sided Jewish rejection – the Jews' rejection of and by God (cf. also Ellis, *Luke*, p. 17). Tolbert, 'Leading Ideas', pp. 445, 447; and Wilson, *Gentiles*, pp. 41, 236–7, 247, lay weight on the way in which Luke's portrayal of the Jews as uniformly hostile to the purposes of God supports, respectively, his apologetic interest (Rome should tolerate Christians and reject Jews) or the Gentile mission as his main interest. Finally, here should also be mentioned the fine essay by Tyson, 'Jewish Public', which appeared too late for further reference in the present work.

The view that only some Jews are incorrigible

The other way of explaining the Lucan portrayal of the Jewish people, that Luke does distinguish among the Jews as a group and that he intends to condemn only those who do not accept the gospel, while it may not be the 'common opinion', is nevertheless the explanation given by some of the better known and esteemed New Testament scholars and may in fact be the view of the majority. This view goes back to Harnack. On the one hand, Harnack could use language quite reminiscent of that of Overbeck to describe the way in which 'the Jews' appear in Acts. Thus he observed that the 'victorious progress' of the Christian mission, as described in Acts,

had a dark side which, to the historian St. Luke, is scarcely less important than the bright side: the Jewish nation . . . had not only rejected their Messiah, but had more and more hardened themselves against the preaching of the Gospel, had everywhere attempted to throw the greatest obstacles in the way of its progress among the Gentiles, and with increasing energy of intrigue had stirred up persecutions against the Christians. Through the malicious machinations of this wretched nation [the narrative of Acts is presented]. Moreover, not only must [Luke] describe these machinations, but he must also show that, in spite of all the ceaseless and sincere attempts of the Apostles – of St. Paul also – to bring the Jews to a better mind, they nevertheless became only more and more hostile.[24]

Thus Harnack did not hesitate to label Acts antisemitic.[25]

Harnack emphasized, however, that Luke distinguished between Jew and Jew. Luke knew the differences among Pharisees, Sadducees, Diaspora Jews, etc., and he did not fail to note that priests were converted to Christianity (Acts 6.7).[26] The reason, then, for his harsh portrayal of the Jews in general was – and Harnack here anticipates Haenchen – that Luke was attempting to answer the question, 'How is it that within the Christian movement, originally Jewish, there arose a mission to the Gentiles?'[27]

Luke therefore conceived, according to Harnack, of a divided Israel, those who rejected Christianity and those who became Christians. This division was necessary because of Luke's view of the fulfilment of prophecy. On the one hand, Israel was a hard-hearted and rebellious people, the divine reaction to whom was the taking of the gospel to the Gentiles; on the other hand, the promises of salvation were to Israel. Both scriptural understandings can be handled if some Jews reject the gospel and some accept. We then have three groups: the Jews, Jewish Christians and Gentile Christians. In other words, in Luke's view 'Christendom stands in two camps . . . first the Jewish people, that is, the pious Israelites who had accepted Jesus as the Lord; secondly, the ἔθνη, who had been afterwards called to the standard.'[28]

More recently, this explanation has been more or less repeated by Conzelmann, George and Jervell. According to Conzelmann, Luke appropriated the concepts 'Israel' (although he never quite used the word in this way) and 'people (of God)' to refer to Christianity. Such usage of course reinforced Luke's notion that Christians and not non-Christian Jews were in the true continuity with the Israelite prophecies.[29] Thus 'the Jews are . . . called to make good their claim to be "Israel". If they fail to do this, then they become "the Jews".'[30] At the same time, of course, according to Luke's epochal understanding of history, 'we can see quite clearly how Luke thinks of the Christians, according to plan, taking over the privileges of the Jews as one epoch is succeeded by the next' at the end of Acts.[31] Since the move from the Jewish epoch to the Christian actually began, however, according to Conzelmann, with the preaching of John the Baptist, the division of the Jewish people into two groups, 'Israel' (or Christians) and 'Jews', actually began with John's baptism,[32] not, as Harnack had explained it, with the Christian preaching.

When one adds to this explanation that the accusations against the Jews placed on the lips of the apostles and Paul are intended to provoke repentance and conversion to Christianity, then one of the two reasons for Luke's 'extreme sharpness of polemic' against the Jews is given,[33] for Luke assumes that the apostles and Paul intended to get as many Jews into 'Israel' as possible. This 'extreme sharpness of polemic', however, manages to avoid 'a summary Christian anti-Semitism'. The other reason for the unfavourable portrait of the Jews drawn by Luke (according to Conzelmann) is that he had his eye on Roman officialdom and its attitude towards Christians. Luke wanted to be sure to point out that, whenever any civil disturbance arose in which Christians were somehow involved, the Jews were at fault.[34]

Considerably more strongly than Conzelmann, A. George argues that the advent of Christianity, according to Luke-Acts, caused a *division within Israel*.[35] 'Many times,' he writes, 'Luke marks the division of the people before the appeal of the Lord.'[36] Like Conzelmann, he sees the division beginning with the ministry of John the Baptist,[37] but he then finds the division to be a constant theme, not a progression. Jesus, who preaches only to his own people,[38] evokes a divided response in each of the three periods of his ministry – initial, on the way to Jerusalem, and in Jerusalem.[39] George finds this division in, e.g., the response to Jesus' preaching in Nazareth,[40] the collection of an expanding group of disciples during the journey to Jerusalem,[41] and the clearly opposite 'disposition' to Jesus during the passion on the part of the people and the leaders.[42] Even the leaders, however, are not 'irreparably' lost, since Luke offers the excuse of ignorance.[43]

It is the same in Acts. The initial period of friendly relationship is followed by hostility,[44] leaving 'two distinct communities' in Palestine;[45] and, as the gospel expands into the Diaspora, there are again Jews who are converted and those who are not.[46] George even goes so far as to write that '*beaucoup de Juifs de la Diaspora*' accept the message of the missionaries.[47] Thus George concludes, rather similarly to Harnack, that, at the conclusion of Acts, there are effectively three groups;[48] there are 'the Jews', who refuse the gospel and who will no longer be the object of evangelistic effort; there is the church, now predominantly and for the future Gentile; and there are and will continue to be Jewish Christians, inasmuch as individual Jews, of course, may be converted at any time. George admits, however,[49] that Luke is rather less interested in the future salvation of Jews than was Paul. 'The Jews' in Luke's view, according to

George, are a foreign people who belong to the past, who have played out their role in the historical drama, and who received their just deserts when Jerusalem was destroyed.[50]

Jacob Jervell has also argued vigorously – and indeed with considerable success – for the 'division among the Jews' theory, but with an interesting shift of emphasis, for Jervell insists that, according to Luke, it is not Jewish rejection of the gospel that ushers in Gentile Christianity, but rather Jewish acceptance! Jervell notes, first of all, that 'the common opinion that Luke describes the Jews as a whole as rejecting the gospel conflicts with the striking remarks in Acts that relate the great success of the Christian mission to Jews',[51] and he cites especially Acts 21.20, 'You see, brother, how many myriads of believers there are among the Jews.' Since these 'myriads' had become Christians *before* the initiation of the Gentile mission, that mission is built on the back of Jewish conversion to, not rejection of, Christianity. Jewish hostility develops only in the Diaspora, after the Gentile mission is under way.[52] Thus the advent of the Christian movement is the advent, as Jervell explains Acts, of the restoration of Israel. When that restoration is virtually complete, i.e., after 'many myriads' of Jews have been converted, then Gentiles begin to be added to the church as 'part of the restoration of Israel'.[53] In other words, 'The conversion of Gentiles is itself a fulfilment of the promises to Israel so that the apostolic mission to Jews turns out indirectly to be the Gentile mission.'[54] Here, what so many authors have taken to be a Lucan hostility to Jews in general is reduced simply to the fact that 'the unrepentant must be excluded from Israel'.[55]

Not only does Jervell, however, shift the explanation of Luke's emphasis within the 'divided Israel' theory from Gentiles to Jews, he also revises Conzelmann's epochal theory by explaining that 'it was clear from the beginning [of Acts] in the preaching to the Jews that the Gentiles should also share in the salvation of Israel'.[56] The fact of Gentile salvation therefore marks no new phase in the Lucan conception of history. The new phase is rather the admission into Christianity of Gentiles as Gentiles – that is, without the requirement of circumcision or of other legal obligations. This change is marked by the Cornelius incident in Acts 10.[57] Along with this explanation, however, goes another revision of the epochal explanation of the Lucan conception of history; for, whereas Conzelmann affirmed that, according to Luke, even at the end of Acts 'for the individual the way of salvation is open, now as always',[58] Jervell understands the judgment at the end of Acts to close, in Luke's thinking, the period of Jewish salvation for ever.[59] Because Gentile Christianity – which in Luke's day had succeeded Jewish Christianity – had come into existence according to divine promise, as *a result of* the restoration of Israel, no further Jewish mission could be undertaken. 'It is . . . settled that there can be no talk about a renewed mission to Jews without misunderstanding the work of the apostles and without calling into question the right of Gentiles to the promises.'[60]

Among those who agree in general with Jervell and his predecessors that, in Luke-Acts, only some Jews are bad are Fitzmyer, *Luke*, vol. 1, p. 191; Tiede, *Prophecy and History*, p. 10; Mussner, 'Stephanusperikope', pp. 289–96; and Juel, *Luke-Acts*, pp. 109–12, who endorse Jervell's position, and Lohfink, *Sammlung Israels*, pp. 51–2, 55, 60, who argues that Jesus and the apostles 'gather' an 'Israel' made up of both Jews and Gentiles. Lohfink's position was also clearly summarized in 'Hat Jesus eine Kirche gestiftet?' and is repeated by Johnson, *Possessions*, pp. 121–4. Radl, *Paulus und Jesus*, p. 323; Dupont, 'La conclusion des Actes', pp. 387–90; Braumann, 'Mittel der Zeit', pp. 136–9; and Gaston, *No Stone*, pp. 244–369, also take positions similar to that of Jervell; and Hare, 'Rejection', pp. 35–8, similarly sees a conflict between Jewish Christians and non-Christian Jews. O'Toole, *Unity*, follows Jervell's position generally but confuses the evidence considerably by trying to show that, in Luke-Acts, 'The Christians are the Pharisees who are the true Jews' (op. cit., p. 17). (For the correct evaluation of the Pharisees, see the next chapter.) Rengstorf, *Lukas*, p. 6, understands Luke to give a positive evaluation of Judaism, and he thus takes a position close to that of Harnack (similarly Jones, 'Hebrews and Lucan Writings', pp. 114–15); and Lake in *Beginnings*, Part I, vol. 5, pp. 113–14, argues that, in Acts, both Jews and Gentiles were brought into the church from the beginning. Lake bases his opinion on a text-critical argument, namely that the word Ἰουδαῖοι in Acts 2.5 is a late addition. Not only is the word not present in MS ℵ, but Acts 2.10 refers to ' "Jews and proselytes" . . . as one of the component parts of the crowd', thus rendering it unlikely that v. 5 intended to describe an audience composed solely of Jews. Burchard, *Dreizehnter Zeuge*, pp. 113, 166–8, has also argued strongly that Paul, in Acts, tries continually to convert both Jews and Gentiles to Christianity. Gnilka, *Verstockung*, agrees in large measure with Conzelmann's position, while emphasizing perhaps more the theme of Jewish 'hard-heartedness', but also proposing that the distinction between people and leaders affords Luke the possibility of distinguishing between 'church' and 'Israel' without 'wounding the Jews' (ibid., p. 151); and Franklin, *Christ the Lord*, pp. 114–15, agrees with Jervell's position; only Franklin thinks that there is still hope for Jewish conversion after the close of Acts. Similarly Buss, *Missionspredigt*, p. 150; Völkel, 'Zur Deutung des "Reiches Gottes" ', pp. 69–70; and Müller, 'Jüdische Entscheidung'. Cassidy, 'Luke's Audience', pp. 150–2, also distinguishes between people and leaders and finds only the Jewish leaders characterized as bad in Luke-Acts. Dupont, 'Les discours missionnaires', p. 141, and Rese, 'Aussagen über Jesu Tod', pp. 344, 346, propose that Luke intends to make only Jerusalemites guilty for Jesus' death. This list is not exhaustive. Talbert, *Reading Luke*, p. 181 (repeated in 'Martyrdom', p. 101), tries to mediate between Jervell and his critics, arguing that it is neither Jewish rejection of the gospel alone nor Jewish acceptance alone that promps the Gentile mission in Acts.

Just to complete our review of the options, we need to note, finally, the opinion of Flender, *St Luke*, pp. 109–17, that Luke's consistent condemnation of the Jews is prototypical, providing examples of the kind of judgment that will fall on anyone who behaves as 'the Jews' in Luke-Acts behave. Ellis, *Luke*, p. 111, maintains a somewhat similar position when he proposes that the bad Pharisees of Luke are to be understood as bad Christians.

Towards a solution

If, now, we want to try to make our way through this thicket of different opinions to a clearer understanding of Luke's attitude towards 'the Jews', towards the Jewish people as a collective entity – or, to put the issue in perhaps a more neutral way, to a satisfactory understanding of Luke's portrayal of the Jewish people, *including* whether he thinks of them as a collective entity – we shall have to pick our way by taking careful notice of the often confusing path markers – that is, of what the Jewish people say and do in Luke-Acts and of what is said about them. At the same time, we shall also want to keep in mind that a successful negotiation of the thicket will be likely to bring us out upon one of two clearings: that which allows us to see that Luke thought that all Jews are perverse, or that which provides a perspective showing that he intended to represent only those who reject Christianity as perverse. We begin with the most obvious 'signposts'.

Distinctions among Jews

One point on which there need be no confusion is whether Luke makes distinctions of any kind among the Jews. Naturally he does. We have already had abundant occasion to note his characterization of the various Jewish religious leaders, and the foregoing references to his treatment of the Pharisees are further indications that he does not just lump all Jews together without distinction. Also, towards the end of Acts, of course, he makes quite a lot out of the differences between Pharisees, who believed in a resurrection from the dead, and Sadducees, who did not. Furthermore, as Jervell has pointed out emphatically, Luke underscores the fact that many Jews were converted to Christianity in its early days in Jerusalem, whereas others were not. Jervell is right; Luke wants his readers to be sure to know that the 3000 in Acts 2.41, the unspecified further number in 2.47, the 5000 men (and additional women?) in 4.4, the multitude in 5.14, the multiplying disciples in 6.1, and the greatly multiplying Christians in 6.7 are Jews – perhaps, in fact, Jerusalem Jews. That he wants to emphasize that point is seen in the last of these summary statements in Acts (21.20), where he has James refer to the 'many myriads of believers . . . among the Jews'. Furthermore, throughout the course of Paul's mission, Luke consistently refers to both Jewish and Gentile response to Paul's preaching, and he sometimes notes that some of the Jews 'believed' (Acts 14.1; 17.11–12; 18.8). Thus, that some Jews became Christians while others did not is one point in Acts that no one could overlook.

The people of God

In the second place, it is also abundantly clear that Luke uses the term 'people of God' or just 'people' (λαὸς θεοῦ, λαός) to mean the church,[61] and that he thinks that the direct line runs from Moses and the Prophets through John the Baptist and Jesus to Christianity, and not in some other direction.[62] It is again on the lips of James that we see this most plainly. In Acts 15.14, as a way of resolving the disagreement in the Apostolic Council, James states that 'Simeon has explained how at first God oversaw taking out of the Gentiles *a people* for his name'; and that Luke knows that he is using a quasi-technical term so to designate Christianity is seen in his considered use of the term 'people of Israel' to designate the Jewish people (Luke 2.32; Acts 4.10; 13.17, 24; and especially 4.27: 'Gentiles and peoples of Israel'). Most significant, however, is the repeated use of the absolute ὁ λαός by the Lucan Paul in Acts 26.17,23. When Paul says here that the Lord confirmed to him that he was 'saving (or choosing) [Paul] from *the people* and from the Gentiles', and when he then affirms that it was according to prophecy that Christ should 'proclaim light to *the people* and to the Gentiles', 'the people' obviously means 'the people of Israel'. But, when the Lord says to Paul in a dream in Acts 18.10, 'I have a numerous *people* (λαός ἐστί μοι πολύς) in this city', he means the church, made up, as vv. 7–8 had explained, of Jews *and* Gentiles. Thus Luke understands that he is shifting the pre-Christian understanding of people of God as people of Israel to the Christian understanding of people of God as Christians.[63] Jervell's proposal, that Luke thinks 'of a people and an associate people',[64] is therefore a misreading of the evidence.[65] 'The Law grew smoothly and naturally into the gospel':[66] and the hostility between Christians and non-Christian Jews is thus to be carried back to the fact that both laid 'claim to continuing Israel's heritage legitimately'.[67]

Along with this continuity theme goes Luke's fairly unconvincing apologetic that the Christian belief in the resurrection (of Jesus) is in reality the familiar Pharisaic belief in the (coming) resurrection. Paul makes this point in Acts 26.6, and it is the rationale for his acquittal in the Sanhedrin, Acts 23.6–10.[68]

Whether it is correct to maintain in this connection, as Conzelmann does,[69] that Luke thinks of the church as 'Israel' is not so certain. Luke never uses such a term, and 'people of Israel' (Acts 13.24) or just 'Israel' (Acts 1.6) always means 'the Jews'. Perhaps, as long as we remind ourselves that what Conzelmann means by 'Israel' is what Luke meant by 'people of God', i.e., the people through whom and to whom God's salvation has come, we may proceed without objecting to such an explanation of the theology of Luke-Acts – so long as we also remind ourselves that Luke used the *term* 'Israel' to refer only to the Jews.[70] The explanation given by Fitzmyer seems to fit the evidence better.[71] According to him, the author of Acts emphasizes that the first Christians were Jews but that they were 'marked off from the Jewish people as such'; and he maintains only that Acts 'vaguely suggests' that the church was the new Israel.[72] When Conzelmann states that in Luke-Acts 'the Church represents the continuity of redemptive history, and to this degree is "Israel"',[73] he also more accurately describes the evidence.

The logical conclusion to be drawn from these two fairly obvious points – that Luke knows one Jew from another and that he thinks of the church and not of the contemporary non-Christian Jews as being in direct continuity with the former holy people of God[74] – is that Luke does, indeed, have a 'divided Israel' theory, according to which the non-Christian Jews, not the Christians, are the aberration. The condemnation announced by Paul and Barnabas in Antioch, 'It was necessary for the word of God to be spoken to you first. Since you reject it and judge yourselves not worthy of eternal life, behold! we turn to the Gentiles' (Acts 13.46), would seem to fit this conclusion well. Alas! however, we cannot finish with the matter so easily; for, in addition to the evidence that exists in support of the 'divided Israel' theory, there exists in Luke-Acts a considerable body of evidence of the 'blanket condemnation' variety, according to which Jews are by nature and congenitally obstreperous and opposed to the will and purposes of God and have been, as a group and as a nation, excluded from God's salvation. Stephen's speech and Paul's last condemnation of the Jews at the end of Acts are ready examples. But this has been the problem all along! The reason that there are two theories about Luke on the Jews is that Luke-Acts makes both kinds of statements, sometimes back to back. Why?[75]

We may dispense briefly with the explanation that Luke's use of different sources accounts for his differing statements about the Jews.[76] Loisy's redaction theory, according to which the anti-Judaic statements in Luke-Acts are the result of redactional activity, was an attempt to deal in those terms with what seems to be Luke's divided attitude towards the Jews. But this putative 'redactor' would be, after all, the person responsible for the final form of Luke-Acts, the work that we have been considering here, so that the question must then be addressed to him. Why does the person responsible for the final form of Luke-Acts seem to hold both the view that the Jews are uniformly bad and a theory of a 'divided Israel' at the same time? Source and redaction theories do not answer our question; they only deal with the process of becoming.[77]

'The Jews' in the speeches in Luke-Acts

The key to the solution of the riddle is to separate speech from narrative in Luke-Acts.[78] When we consider what Luke has his main characters (Jesus, Peter, Stephen,[79] and Paul) say about 'the Jews', apart from any consideration of the story line, and when we then look at how 'the Jews' behave in the narrative, without reference to what the main characters say about them, all the evidence will fall into place.

Acts

Let us consider first the speeches in Acts. Stephen's closing tirade, which gets him lynched, encapsulates the position.

Hard-necked and uncircumcised in hearts and ears, you always thrust against the Holy Spirit; as your fathers, so you. Whom of the prophets did your fathers not persecute? And they killed those who proclaimed beforehand the coming of the Righteous One, whose deliverers and murderers now you have become, you who received the Law in angelic ordinances, and you did not keep it (7.51–53).[80]

These accusations seem to be directed to the Jewish people generally, not merely to the members of the Sanhedrin, who are described as trying him. The descendants of the Jewish ancestors 'always' oppose the divine will, although they are the recipients of the Law.[81] That charge can hardly be limited to the religious leaders,[82] even if the charge of persecuting the prophets may be read to admit the possibility that some Israelites, in any case – namely, the prophets themselves – were not subject to this bent.[83]

Although some recent authors still maintain that the speech of Stephen is different enough from the other speeches in Acts to warrant considering it as something other than a Lucan composition (cf. Scharlemann, *Singular Saint*, p. 52; Selwyn, 'St. Stephen's Place', pp. 312–14), the extensive analysis by Sabbe, 'Son of Man Saying', pp. 251–6 – which concerns the narrative about Stephen as well as his speech – detailing the many correlations between the Stephen episode and the rest of Luke-Acts, renders useless any position that holds that the Stephen episode does not represent Luke's own thinking. Cf. also Kilgallen, *The Stephen Speech*, esp. p. 121. If Sabbe had given as careful an analysis to the rest of Acts as he gave to the Stephen episode, he would not have concluded – primarily on the basis of the fact that, in Acts, the gospel is still preached to Jews after Stephen's martyrdom – that 'the Jews are never excluded from salvation' ('Son of Man Saying', p. 277).

It is not only in Stephen's speech, however, that such accusations occur.[84] Peter, in Acts 2.36, says to 'all the house of Israel', 'You crucified' Jesus;[85] and the statements in Acts 4.10 that 'you crucified' Jesus and in 5.30 that 'you apprehended [him] and hanged him on a tree' – while, according to the verisimilitude of the two scenes, directed at the Sanhedrin – could just as well be intended for 'all the house' or for 'all the people of Israel'. The altering of the proof text from the Psalms immediately following the charge in 4.10, by inserting the word 'you', so that it is quoted to say, 'The stone that was considered of no account by *you* the builders . . .' (v. 11), and the fact that 4.10 makes announcement to 'all the people of Israel' as well as to the Sanhedrin shows that there is not a clear line between people and leaders on this point.[86] Even in the speech to Cornelius, Acts 10.39,[87] Peter cannot omit this charge and says that 'they did away with him' by crucifixion. Since Peter had just referred to 'all that [Jesus] did in the region of the Jews and Jerusalem', there can be little doubt who 'they' are.[88] Especially in this speech to the first truly Gentile convert in Acts, we see how Luke builds up the image of general Jewish guilt in the death of Jesus simply by omitting subjects for the verbs.[89] It would have been easy enough to have written that the Sanhedrin or the chief priests did away with Jesus, but Luke does not do that; so, since he had just written that Jesus worked among the Jews, what is the Gentile reader to think but that 'the Jews' killed Jesus?[90]

But does Luke not alleviate this charge of having killed Jesus, made repeatedly in the speeches in Acts, with an excuse? Does he not twice (3.17; 13.27) say that the Jews acted only out of ignorance? And does he not thereby imply that, if the hearers repent and believe, they may escape their just deserts?[91] These two passages require a little closer scrutiny. Peter's speech in Acts 3, addressed to 'all the people' (v. 11), indeed allows that they 'and [their] rulers' (NB! Both people and rulers are thus indicated as having killed Jesus!) 'acted in ignorance' (v. 17) when they 'killed the Prince of Life' (v. 15). Peter then immediately (v. 19) challenges them to 'repent and turn about'.[92] The second occurrence of the ignorance theme, however – in Paul's first speech – is hardly the same, for the ignorance appears here in the third rather than in the second person. Whereas Peter had challenged the entire Jewish people with their guilt and had, in that connection, offered them the opportunity to repent and be converted, Paul refers his Antiochene hearers back to the Jews in Jerusalem ('those dwelling in Jerusalem and their rulers', 13.27), who are said not to have *acted* in ignorance (as in 3.17), but to have been ignorant of 'him',[93] *although they 'read the voices of the Prophets every Sabbath'* (v. 27). These they then 'fulfilled by condemning' Jesus; yet it is impossible for the reader to escape who is really condemned here. It is those Jerusalem Jews who did not have the sense to understand their own scriptures.[94] After this, Paul moves fairly rapidly toward a pitch for the Antiochene Jews to be converted (vv. 32–41). Surely we are seeing here, therefore, Luke's epochal scheme at work. When the Jerusalem Jews are confronted with their sin and ignorance, they are given the opportunity to be converted.[95] After the Gentile mission begins, Jerusalemite ignorance provides no further opportunity for Jerusalemite conversion but is rather a judgment upon Jerusalem and its inhabitants.[96] This reference back, however, to the condemnation of Jerusalemite Jews for their now inexcusable ignorance provides the incentive for the conversion of Antiochene Jews.[97] I believe that it would be correct to say that, in Luke's opinion, after Paul's sermon in Acts 13, the Antiochene Jews also have no excuse.[98] In a word, the proclamation of the gospel both offers the opportunity for repentance and removes the excuse of ignorance. Thus, if we continue to ignore the story line and concentrate on what Paul says, we see that he is very shortly pronouncing

God's rejection also upon the Antiochene Jews in the first of the three announcements of the turning to the Gentiles: 'To you it was necessary first to speak the word of God. Since you reject it and judge yourselves not worthy of eternal life, behold! we turn to the Gentiles!' (13.46).[99]

After that, Paul does not speak to or about 'the Jews' again until he is in Corinth delivering the second such announcement: 'Your blood be upon your head! I am clean. From now on I will go to the Gentiles'(18.6). Why their own blood? Surely because, by having rejected the gospel, they have sealed their own fate.[100] But 'the Jews' (v. 5) of Corinth had not participated in the death of Jesus; they had only 'opposed' and 'blasphemed' (v. 6).[101] No matter; when Jews in Paul's Diaspora mission reject the gospel they fall under the same condemnation that is pronounced against those in Jerusalem (13.27) who actually carried out the deed.[102] Furthermore 'the Jews' are declared to be regularly hindering Paul's mission (I am referring here only to what Paul says, not to the narrative) when Paul mentions in 20.19, in what is almost an offhand manner, the various Jewish 'counsels (or: plots)' that have brought him 'tears and trials'. After Paul is arrested, while he once explains that it was 'the high priest . . . and all the presbyterium' that gave him his earlier authority to persecute Christians (22.5), still, when the time comes for him to speak before Agrippa, he says simply that he was 'accused by Jews' (26.2; that Paul does not here use the article – 'the' Jews – is rendered irrelevant by the fact that Festus had just said, in introducing Paul to Agrippa, that it was 'the entire multitude of the Jews [ἅπαν τὸ πλῆθος τῶν Ἰουδαίων]' that had been clamouring, 'both in Jerusalem and' in Caesarea, about how Paul 'ought not to live any longer', 25.24).[103] Paul then adds that it was 'Jews' who 'tried to slay [him] in the Temple' (26.21).[104]

Finally, in Paul's last speech, the conclusion and dénouement of Acts, after Paul has again accused 'the Jews' (28.19) for his imprisonment, the Roman Jews are condemned with a scriptural quotation for their intransigent and endemic ignorance,[105] and Paul gives up on them.[106] That this condemnation applies probably to all Jews and not just to Paul's Roman hearers is seen in the existence of the condemnation within scripture, in the address of the scriptural passage to 'this people' (Acts 28.26), and, of course, in the position of the condemnation at the conclusion of Luke-Acts.[107] 'Luke has written the Jews off.'[108]

The witness of the speeches in Acts is, therefore, that the Jews generally are irredeemably resistant to God's will and his offer of salvation, and that they are the murderers of Jesus.[109] When these charges are reduced, in the case of the allowance of the extenuating circumstance of ignorance in Acts 3.17, the purpose is to provide the opportunity for conversion to Christianity; but there seem to be no second chances once such opportunities are past.[110]

The function of the missionary speeches

Having examined what the speeches in Acts say about the Jews, we now need to give some attention to the *role* or *function* of the missionary speeches (all of Peter's sermons and Paul's sermons at Antioch and Athens) within Luke-Acts, as well as to their relation to Stephen's speech, although this discussion will take us briefly away from our analysis of what the leading characters in Luke-Acts *say* about the Jews. Ulrich Wilckens has dealt with this issue at length. According to him, Stephen's speech, which was already in existence before Luke wrote, was adopted by him and became the model for the missionary speeches in Acts, which Luke composed himself.[111] In part, Wilckens depends heavily on a study by Steck, who sought to demonstrate that Stephen's speech was a Christianized version of a widespread genre of Jewish sermon that accused the Israelite people, in the context of a Deuteronomistic view of history, of having persecuted and killed the prophets.[112] That genre of sermon, according to Steck, always included, if only by implication, a call for repentance.[113]

Steck also thought (*Geschick der Propheten*, p. 268) that the origin of Stephen's speech was, to be more precise, '*Hellenistic Jewish Christianity*', and with that assessment Wilckens also agreed; cf. *Missionsreden*, p. 219. G. Schneider, *Apostelgeschichte*, vol. 1, pp. 234–6, also endorses this analysis. The ultimate origin of Stephen's speech is, however, of no immediate interest to the issue at hand, namely how Luke used it. One may also raise some questions about Steck's analysis that do not seem to have occurred to Wilckens, e.g., whether all the passages that Steck cites from Jewish literature indeed attest to the genre, and whether Steck has entirely adequately taken into account the prominent Jewish theology of repentance and forgiveness. That issue is also, of course, beside the point here.

Wilckens concludes, with Steck, that Luke took over Stephen's speech from this Deuteronomistic background, but he then goes further to affirm that Stephen's speech became the model, for Luke, for the other missionary speeches in Acts, and that Luke substituted 'the perfecting of salvation in the history of Jesus, God's Messiah' for the traditional 'invective' of Stephen's speech and its Jewish forebears.[114] The Jews are thus now accused of having killed Jesus instead of the prophets and are for that reason called to repentance.[115] In this way, Luke sets up an '*ordo salutis*' as 'a comprehensive and normative view of repentance generally',[116] i.e., for everyone.

Unfortunately, Wilckens has, in this analysis, failed to deal with three aspects of the issue. One is that Stephen's speech includes no call to repentance,[117] whereas the missionary sermons do. (Is it implied in Stephen's speech?) Another, however, is that the accusation against the Jews is maintained even when there are only Gentiles in the audience (Acts 10.39), a fact that ruins the connection between guilt and repentance and, consequently, the *ordo salutis* pattern.[118] And the third problem overlooked by Wilckens is the response of Jews to these missionary sermons, which is the main issue with which we need to deal at this point. While it is true that many Jews respond favourably to these missionary sermons prior to the Stephen episode, from that point on they do not, and Paul's first missionary sermon, in fact, also becomes the occasion of the first of his three statements of condemnation of the Jews and of turning to the Gentiles (Acts 13.46). Thus the *function* of the missionary speeches in Acts *as regards the Jews* is not to set up an *ordo salutis* (although such a pattern in general terms – that is, regarding the Gentiles – is probably, indeed, very likely part of Luke's purpose); it is rather to show that, after the initial positive response in the first five chapters of Acts, the Jews *reject* the gospel.[119] Since the Stephen episode is the 'watershed' (Haenchen) that comes after the 'Jerusalem springtime' (Lohfink), Stephen's speech neither includes nor implies any call to repentance.

Holtz, 'Stephanusrede', pp. 113–14, proposes that, while the speech is not, in and of itself, 'fundamentally anti-Jewish', Luke has so employed it. F. Keck's study of Luke 21 is also very interesting in this regard. Keck (*Abschiedsrede*, p. 253) has shown that Steck's pattern can be applied to Jesus' 'farewell discourse', but that, whereas according to the standard pattern the 'promise of final salvation' ought to be offered to those among the accused who might repent, Luke has it that the final salvation falls to Jesus' followers, while 'the Jews' are merely condemned and are not offered a chance to repent. This is precisely what is involved in the Stephen episode. It will not do, incidentally, to observe that Stephen's speech contains no call to repentance because he was cut short. Such an explanation takes a too naïvely historical approach. Stephen's speech was cut short not by the Sanhedrin or by the Jewish mob, but by Luke, who thus saw to it that Stephen offered no call to repentance. On the Stephen speech as essentially Lucan, whatever the ultimate origin, cf. again the remarks of Sabbe and Kilgallen, above, p. 51.

'The Jews' in the sayings of Jesus in Luke

We turn now to the Gospel of Luke. What do the sayings of Jesus in the Gospel have to do with 'the Jews'?

When the public ministry opens, we find Jesus prophesying in the synagogue at Nazareth that his audience will one day mock him with the call, 'Physician, heal yourself' (Luke 4.23). Inasmuch as this prophecy is more or less fulfilled in Jerusalem (Luke 23.35) when the *rulers* say, 'He saved others, let him save himself', we may be fairly certain that the prophecy of 4.23 refers more to what 'the Jews' will do than to what Jesus' audience in Nazareth will do – that is, the connection between Jesus' audience in Nazareth and those who fulfil the prophecy made to that audience is that they are Jews, not that they are rulers. In this same speech, then, Jesus goes on to refer pointedly to two of Israel's better-known prophets, Elijah and Elisha, who helped *non-Israelites* in need but not Israelites in similar straits. Since Elijah and Elisha are referred to here in their roles of prophet as physician, the implication is overwhelming that the prophet Jesus, who has just referred to himself as a physician, is also sent to Gentiles and not to Jews.[120] Thus the two-sided Jewish rejection, the Jews' rejection of and by God, is established in this, Jesus' opening address in the Gospel,[121] 'perhaps the most significant passage in Luke-Acts'.[122]

Eltester, convinced of the basic correctness of Jervell's position, nevertheless saw that a consideration of the Gospel of Luke in its current form, especially of the way in which Luke opens Jesus' public ministry (with his rejection in Nazareth, 4.16–30), created a problem for the 'divided Israel' theory ('Israel'), since this opening of the public ministry and the closing of Paul's missionary career (Acts 28.23–28) seem to sandwich all that falls between with statements of total rejection of the Jews. Eltester's resolution of the problem is unsatisfactory and seems to have been accepted by no one else: Luke, some time after completing his two-volume work, in response to increasing rejection of Jewish Christians by synagogues, removed the Nazareth pericope from its original setting, where it paralleled Mark, and placed it where it is now (op. cit., pp. 144–5). Eltester's conclusion regarding the final version thus produced, however, is worth remembering (ibid., pp. 146–7): 'The incident in Nazareth operates within the entire Lucan work like the minus sign before an arithmetic parenthesis. Everything inside the parentheses therefore receives a reversed value.' The modern reader, therefore, cannot ignore 'that minus sign before the parenthesis . . . It points to the beginning of the history of trouble between Jews and Christians' that has had such a 'devastating' effect in recent history.

The next place where Jesus addresses the Jew–Gentile issue in Luke is in a brief remark connected with his having healed someone. Yet the someone and what Jesus says there are closely connected with the explanation that he gave in Nazareth; for the one healed is a Gentile (a centurion's slave), and Jesus declares that he 'has not found such faith in Israel' (7.9).[123] Later, after the travel narrative has begun and the seventy(-two) disciples have been sent out,[124] Jesus closes the books on three Galilean towns, Chorazin, Bethsaida[125] and Capernaum (10.13–15), that had been locales for his now-finished Galilean ministry.[126] Since they did not repent (v. 13) they are doomed;[127] there is no mention of any second chance.

Further, the judgment on 'this generation' in 11.29–32 is probably intended by Luke to be a judgment on 'the Jews'.[128] Luke has, at the beginning of the saying, emphasized that the generation is evil by writing (v. 29), 'This generation is an evil generation', whereas Mark 8.12 and Matt. 12.39 read, respectively, 'Why does this generation seek a sign?' and, 'An evil and adulterous generation seeks a sign.' Luke then moves the conclusion concerning Nineveh to the end of the saying (v. 32; opposite to Matthew, who gives the same conclusion, but earlier in the saying), so that the lack of success in 'this generation' seems to be the point of the Lucan version of the saying. If 'this generation', therefore, is contrasted to the Gentiles, then it must mean 'this *Jewish* generation'.[129] The same is true in Luke 17.25, where the Son of man must be 'rejected by this generation' (Luke only).[130] Further, the saying about 'this generation' worked into the woe upon the 'legists' (11.47–51) obviously has a general application and is not understood as applying only to the legists.[131] Here, Jesus observes that 'you build the tombs of the prophets, but your fathers killed them'; thus 'you consent to the deeds of your fathers, since they killed them and you build' (vv. 47–48). Furthermore, 'The Wisdom of God said, "I will send them prophets and apostles, and they will kill and persecute some of them, so that *the blood of all the prophets* shed from the foundation of the world *may be required of this generation*"' (vv. 49–50).[132] Jesus then underscores this saying by adding, 'Truly I say to you, it will be required of this generation' (v. 51). Thus the condemnations of Stephen's speech and of Paul's telling the Corinthian Jews that their 'blood will be upon [their] head' represent no new perspective in Acts. They are entirely in harmony with the pronouncements of Jesus himself.

Perhaps the warnings in 13.1–5 with the attendant parable of the Barren Fig Tree, vv. 6–9, also belong in this list. Such is, at least, the argument of Egelkraut,[133] who emphasizes that the call to repentance, lest 'you all perish', is given twice (vv. 3, 5), and who proposes that the meaning of the parable is that there is only a brief season for repentance, after which destruction will surely come. 'The emphasis is on ALL . . . The measure of their sin is full, and unless fruit is brought forth shortly all Israel will be cut off, 13.9.'[134]

Another point that we should notice is that Luke adds 'synagogues' to the warning to the disciples about persecution in Luke 12.11 (whereas Matt. 10.19 and Mark 13.11 make no mention of them), thus characterizing the synagogue as the place where Christians are persecuted.[135] This is doubtless in anticipation of Paul's Diaspora mission. Furthermore, those who think that they are in the Kingdom of God but in reality are excluded (Luke 13.23–30) can only be 'the Jews',[136] since the excluded point out in their defence that Jesus 'taught in [their] streets' (v. 26), and since others will come from all directions (v. 29) to enter the Kingdom left vacant by the excluded.[137]

'The Jews' in the parables

As the Gospel approaches its climax, the Lucan Jesus begins increasingly to use parables to voice the condemnation of the Jewish people. Many students of the New Testament will probably be brought up short by that statement, for we are all accustomed to think of the parables of Jesus as the purest, the most noble, the most beautiful, the least obtuse, the most authentic, the most divine, and the most enduring part of Jesus' teaching that has come down to us. Even modern scholarly works that deal with the parables usually abet rather than weaken this impression. But our interest here is in the parables as Luke uses them, not in their original meaning; and Luke uses several parables that appear in the travel narrative – in fact, probably all the better known ones[138] – as further occasions for Jesus to condemn and pronounce judgment on the Jews,[139] just as Jesus has done consistently throughout the Gospel, and just as Peter, Stephen and Paul are to do consistently throughout the Acts, as we have already seen.

The first of these is the parable of the Banquet (Luke 14.16–24). Whether Luke has changed the original invitations in this parable from a series of two to the invited and one to the uninvited (Matthew) to a series of one to the invited and two to the uninvited,[140] or whether Luke has the original whereas it is Matthew who has done the changing, Luke finds a great deal of meaning in the invitations. To begin with, he has tricked the parable out with an elaborate introduction, vv. 7–14, in which the points of the parable are anticipated.[141] Here, after first giving some commonplace sage advice of the kind that one can read in Ben Sira or Phibis or Theognis or Confucius or in any one of numerous such works giving practical advice about getting on in life (vv. 7–11), Luke has Jesus address directly the issues of proper banquet giving. The one who plans such a festivity should invite not 'friends . . ., brothers . . ., relatives . . ., or wealthy neighbours' (v. 12), but rather people who are 'poor, crippled, lame [and] blind' (v. 13). By providing this introduction, Luke seems to have told us how he wants the parable read, i.e. as making a division into two, not into three. Thus while the parable itself readily yields to the interpretation that the originally invited are the religious Jews who exclude themselves because of their self-righteousness (they make the silly excuses in vv. 18–20), that the second group is the outcast Jews (v. 21: the 'poor and cripples and blind and lame', as in v. 13, who are nevertheless to be found in the 'boulevards and streets [πλατεῖαι καὶ ῥύμαι]'), and that the third group is the Gentiles (to be found in the 'country roads and hedgerows [ὁδοὶ καὶ φραγμοί]', v. 23),[142] Luke himself may not have wanted to make anything out of the division into three, since, as we have just noted, this division is not anticipated in the introduction.[143] We may also observe that, whereas the second group in the parable is defined exactly as the second group in the introduction (poor, lame, etc.), the third group in the parable has no definition whatever and is distinguished from the second group only in its location (out of town).

If this interpretation is correct – that is, that Luke sees only two groups in the parable[144] – then two aspects of the parable fall entirely into line with everything else that Jesus, Paul, Peter and Stephen have said on the Jewish issue. The first is the dual Jewish rejection – the Jews' rejection of and then by God.[145] The invited give their silly excuses, they reject the invitation, thus they receive the judgment, 'None of those invited men will taste my supper' (14.24).[146] In the second case, then, our attention is directed to the repeated attempt to get the crippled, etc., to the banquet; they are even finally given an offer that they can't refuse (ἀνάγκασον εἰσελθεῖν, v. 23). It appears that here, as always in the statements made by Luke's main characters, the Jews get only one chance, the Gentiles more than one. The preaching to the Jews is perfunctory; their reponse is a foregone conclusion.

Schottroff and Stegemann, *Jesus von Nazareth*, pp. 129–36, argue that this parable – and the parable of the Rich Man and Lazarus, as well – are not intended allegorically by Luke, but mean just what they say, that God's concern is with the poor. If this were true, it would certainly solve the problems we face in trying to decide what to make of the two groups of originally uninvited in the parable of the Banquet. Schottroff's and Stegemann's interpretation founders, however, when they then propose (op. cit., p. 132) that the poor get into the banquet only because the rich wouldn't come (What kind of gospel to the poor is that?); and still further (ibid., p. 135) that these two parables are warnings to the rich. Well, which is it? Is Luke trying to save the poor or the rich? This attempt to find liberation theology instead of the rejection of the Jews and the salvation of the Gentiles in Luke-Acts, while doubtless proceeding from noble motives, goes quite astray, notwithstanding the statement of Schottroff and Stegemann (op. cit., pp. 129–30) that it is '*verfehlt*' to find a Jew-Gentile contrast in the parable of the Banquet.

The parable of the Rich Man and Lazarus next provides the Lucan Jesus with the opportunity to make a point similar to that which the Lucan Paul later makes in Acts 13.27; for there is no other help possible for the surviving family of the rich man in hell, who are doomed to follow him there if they do not change, inasmuch as they already 'have Moses and the Prophets' (Luke 16.29). As Paul says later, they cannot understand these scriptures even though they read them regularly. 'If they do not hear Moses and the Prophets, they will not be persuaded even if one rise from the dead' (v. 31).[147] Since Luke, of course, knows who rose from the dead, this conclusion to this parable is about as clear a statement as he could give of the Christian opinion that the Jews are intrinsically stubborn, intransigent, and closed-minded.

Here, as with all the parables, most authors are primarily interested in the original parable, not in what Luke makes of it. B. and J. Weiss, *Markus und Lukas*, p. 555; Schlatter, *Lukas*, pp. 373–4; and Harrington, *St Luke*, p. 206, try to decide whether the parable is anti-Pharisaic; and Bundy, *First Three Gospels*, p. 384, thinks that the entire parable may be Jewish. Loisy, *Evangiles synoptiques*, vol. 2, pp. 177–8; Klostermann, *Lukas*, p. 170; Montefiore, *Synoptic Gospels*, vol. 2, p. 540; and Fitzmyer, *Luke*, vol. 2, pp. 1128, 1134, however, see that the present parable is understandable only in terms of the Christian belief in Jesus' resurrection. Loisy's comment is on the mark: the 'five brothers, who have Moses and the Prophets at hand, represent Judaism; they do not hear Moses and the Prophets because they do not know how to find Christ there . . . Thus the parable becomes an allegory that explains the reprobation of the Jews . . . The rich man of the primitive parable has therefore been taken, himself, as a first type of the Jewish incredulity and Lazarus as the type of the Jewish Christian, which they were not originally' (*Evangiles synoptiques*, vol. 2, p. 177). Cf. further Sandmel, *Anti-Semitism*, p. 79; Wilson, *Law*, p. 18. Fitzmyer, *Luke*, vol. 2, p. 1125, interprets the parable as addressed to Pharisees.

An anti-Judaic interest is also found in the parable of the Pounds, which closes the travel narrative and therefore takes on added significance by virtue of its position.[148] This parable is really two parables in one, the parable of the Pounds proper, which is highly similar to although not entirely identical with the Matthaean parable of the Talents (Matt. 25.14–30) and the parable of the Throne Pretender (or Throne Expecter; this part of the parable is variously named), which appears in Luke 19.12, 14, 15a, 27. Whether the Throne Pretender is from an independent source or is Luke's invention, it is with this part of the parable that he makes his point;[149] for, as Jülicher already pointed out, the 'distant region' to which the nobleman travels 'to take possession of a kingdom' before returning (v. 12) is not Italy but heaven.[150] Thus the nobleman is Jesus, his kingdom is the Kingdom of God, those who send an embassy seeking to thwart his accession to dominion over them (v. 14) are the Jews, and the execution of these rebels upon the return of the nobleman now become king (v. 27) is the well-merited destruction of the Jews at the Second Coming.[151]

Could this parable not, however, be understood to refer only to the destruction of Jerusalem instead of to the destruction of all the Jews? There is indeed some evidence that this is the correct interpretation. The parable says that it is the nobleman's 'citizens' (πολῖται, v. 14) who do not want him to rule them; and, almost immediately after the parable, Jesus pronounces the second of his judgments on Jerusalem (19.41–44). Furthermore, the destruction of Jerusalem is, as we saw abundantly in ch. 2, a part of the Lucan theology. The problem of confining the destruction called for in 19.27, however, to Jerusalem is that it is a destruction to take place at the Second Coming.[152] The parable does not leave the time of its conclusion in doubt, since the new king has returned from his journey, having received his kingdom, and has meted out justice to his earthly representatives (vv. 15–25), which judgment is concluded

(v. 26) by one of Jesus' summary apocalyptic judgment statements: 'To everyone who has will be given, but from the one who does not have even what he has will be taken.' Only then does the order to 'slay' the opponents come down. Inasmuch as Luke elsewhere is very careful to distinguish the destruction of Jerusalem, which of course has already happened before he puts pen to papyrus, from the last judgment, which of course lies in the future,[153] the execution of 19.27 is best taken to mean not the destruction of Jerusalem by the Romans, but a final destruction of the Jews at the last judgment.

Probably we should include the parable of the Wicked Tenants, which was associated above in ch. 2 with the destruction of Jerusalem, in this discussion of what Jesus says in Luke about 'the Jews' and relate the dispossessing of the tenants at the climax of that parable to God's final rejection of the Jews.[154] It is true that the conclusion of the parable in 20.16 – 'He will give the vineyard to others' – weighs on the side of interpreting the parable as referring to the destruction of Jerusalem, not of all the Jews;[155] but Luke says (v. 9) that the parable is directed 'to the people'; and he has them respond (v. 16), 'Oh, no (μὴ γένοιτο).' Thus Luke probably thinks of Jews and Jerusalem going down together.

Possible exceptions

A possible, although not very likely exception to the consistent pattern here described is Luke 18.7–8, where Jesus refers to God's reliability in carrying out vengeance on behalf of his 'elect'. Yet nothing in the statement or in the foregoing parable of the Unjust Judge indicates that 'elect' should mean 'Jews', and it would seem more likely that Luke thinks rather of the Christians as those who fall under God's protection. A better candidate for the role of such an exception is the remark of Jesus at the conclusion of his encounter with Zacchaeus: 'Today salvation has come to this house, for he also is a son of Abraham' (19.9). This certainly sounds as if, contrary to everything else that Jesus, Peter, Stephen and Paul say in Luke-Acts on the issue of the salvation of the Jews, the traditional view of election and covenant is here affirmed.[156] If that is the case, then we have a true exception to all that the Lucan Jesus and the leading characters of Acts say on the subject. Two considerations, however, weigh against such a conclusion. For one thing, 'son of Abraham' is Pauline language for 'Christian' (Gal. 3.7), and it could well be that Luke employs that usage at the conclusion of a narrative about the conversion of a toll collector, just as he had, a few verses before, employed Pauline language at the conclusion of a parable in which a toll collector proved himself acceptable to God: 'justified' (Luke 18.14).[157] When Luke then adds to the 'son of Abraham' declaration that 'the Son of man has come to seek and to save what is lost (or: ruined)' (v. 10), he expresses a sentiment that is strongly reminiscent of the attitude displayed in the parable of the Banquet. Thus one may be allowed the suspicion that Luke understands Jesus' statement at the conclusion of the Zacchaeus narrative, like the parable of the Banquet, to be a reference to salvation of outcasts as prototypes of Gentiles.[158] It should not be lost on the reader that Zacchaeus belongs to one of the two groups mentioned in 15.1, the tax collectors (cf. Luke 19.1).

One final saying of Jesus is subject to misinterpretation, his dying prayer that his executioners will be forgiven, 'for they do not know what they are doing' (23.34).[159] This saying, however, only sets the stage for the mission to the Jews in the first chapters of Acts, which mission is, as we have already seen (Acts 3.17), allowed theologically precisely because of the excuse of ignorance in the execution of Jesus.[160]

Thus, with the unlikely exception of Jesus' statement at the conclusion of the Zacchaeus story, Jesus, Peter, Stephen and Paul present in Luke-Acts, *in what they say on the subject*, an entirely, completely, wholly, uniformly consistent attitude towards the Jewish people as a whole.[161] That attitude is that the Jews are and always have been wilfully ignorant of the purposes and plans of God expressed in their familiar scriptures, that they always have rejected and will reject God's offer of salvation, that they executed Jesus and persecute and hinder those who try to advance the gospel, and that they get one chance at salvation, which they will of course reject, bringing God's wrath down upon them, and quite deservedly so.[162] There is not a single saying, story or speech put into the mouths of the four leading speakers in Luke-Acts that contradicts this position, and it is repeated over and over in every way possible *ad nauseam*.[163] Further, we must not forget that Jesus' *first* words at the opening of his public ministry and Paul's *last* words at the close of his are two of the stronger statements of the position. Surely, regarding the *speeches and sayings* in Luke-Acts, Haenchen's judgment is correct without any question: 'The theology [of Luke-Acts] . . . no longer

sees any sense or any truth in Israel's election. . . . Luke has written
the Jews off.'[164] No divided Israel here.

'The Jews' in the narrative of Luke-Acts

When we turn to the role of the Jewish people in the *narrative* of Luke-
Acts, however, we find quite a different situation, for, in the narrative,
the people are often pointedly set apart from their rulers (e.g., Luke
23.35: 'The people stood watching, but the rulers mocked'), they
'hang on [Jesus'] every word' (Luke 19,48); they grant their favour
to the apostles (Acts 2.47) and they both follow Jesus (Luke 12.1)
and later are converted to Christianity (Acts 21.20) by the 'myriads'.
Furthermore, Luke frequently writes that Jesus or the apostles are
attended by 'all the people (πᾶς ὁλαός)' or 'the entire people (ὅ λαὸς
ἄπας)' or 'the whole people (ὅλος ὁλαός).'[165]

Lohfink, *Sammlung Israels*, pp. 43–6, has accurately noted this difference between
sayings and narrative in the Gospel, especially the problems that the contrast creates
in 4.16–30, but he then seeks to resolve the tension by referring the sayings to
sources, whereas the narrative, with its positive attitude toward the Jewish people,
is 'redaction'. As we have now frequently had occasion to observe, such an
explanation answers nothing. To write that 'Luke certainly saw, but took into
account' the tension that this contrast created in the Nazareth pericope (ibid., p. 46)
is also no further help.

Not only is this description of the behaviour of the Jewish people
the exact opposite, however, of what is said about them, but the two
portraits are often juxtaposed (a characteristic of Luke-Acts that has
had a lot to do with the existence of the 'division-in-Israel' theory).
Thus John the Baptist *says* to the 'crowds' that came to him (not just
to Pharisees and Sadducees, as in the Matthaean parallel) that they
are a vile and wicked lot (Luke 3.7–9), but then in the narrative he
baptizes 'the entire people' (v. 21). Likewise, when Jesus begins his
public ministry in Nazareth, '*all* attested to him and were amazed
at the gracious words that came from his mouth' (4.22), yet Jesus
responds with his insult, 'You will say . . . , "Physician, heal
yourself," ' etc., and with his analogy from the prophets showing
that God's salvation has always been intended for the Gentiles
(vv. 23–27). In 11.29, it is 'when the crowds were gathered' that
Jesus gives his 'this evil generation' speech; and, just following the
vicious *saying* of 11.50–51, about the blood of the prophets being
required of 'this generation', we are told in the narrative that 'the

crowd' of 'myriads' was so great that the people were about 'to trample one another' (12.1). Likewise in Acts, all three of the announcements of turning to the Gentiles follow hard on what an impartial observer would surely call descriptions of Paul's considerable success among Diaspora Jews and of reasonably good favour from them. In Acts 13.43, 'many of the Jews and of the devout proselytes followed Paul and Barnabas', and Paul and Barnabas 'persuaded them to abide in God's grace'; but three verses later Paul condemns the Jews and turns to the Gentiles. To be sure, Jewish opposition has arisen in the two verses in between, but does that opposition entirely erase the success of v. 43? This scenario is repeated exactly, if a little more briefly, in 18.4–6; but the final scene in Acts, where Paul denounces the Roman Jews, does not include the element of Jewish opposition to Paul's preaching. Rather, some of Paul's Roman audience is 'persuaded', although others 'disbeliev[e]' (28.24); nevertheless, Paul denounces 'this people' (v. 26) and announces that 'this salvation of God has been sent to the Gentiles' (v. 28).

How can this enigma be explained? Was Luke-Acts written like an opera, with the 'composer' writing the 'score' and some obscure – and, incidentally, antisemitic – 'librettist' writing the speeches to go along with the narrative? Are we, in other words, driven back after all to Loisy's redaction theory to explain the present form of Luke-Acts?[166] The disharmonious juxtaposition just sketched would seem to imply such a necessity; yet a closer examination of *plot development* in the narrative of Luke-Acts will show that only one mind is responsible for the narrative and for the speeches, that the apparent disharmonious juxtaposition of the good Jewish people in the narrative and the bad Jewish people in the speeches is quite deliberate and serves a definite purpose, and that our author finally – and quite skilfully, one might add – brings the two together in a successful resolution.[167]

The Gospel

When Jesus' public ministry begins, while 'all' (4.22) in the synagogue at first respond favourably to him, his further words reverse that situation totally, so that, in v. 28, 'all in the synagogue [are] aroused (ἐπλήσθησαν . . . θυμοῦ)', and seek to lynch him.[168] From this point until the trials before Pilate in ch. 23, the Jewish people collectively follow Jesus and respond entirely favourably to him; they are 'on his side'.[169] Suddenly, however, and without any explanation whatsoever, when Jesus is brought before Pilate the people are put together with the Jewish religious leaders. After Pilate first examines Jesus, he declares Jesus' innocence to 'the chief priests and the crowds' (23.4); yet, when Jesus is then taken to Herod, the people disappear (v. 10: 'the chief priests and the scribes'), only to be brought back by Pilate for the final hearing, pronunciations of innocence, and deliverance to death. In 23.13 Pilate calls 'together the chief priests and the rulers and the people', before whom he twice again pronounces Jesus innocent (vv. 15, 22), but they 'cry out as one multitude (παμπληθεί)' for his death and for the release of Barabbas (vv. 18, 21, 23). Pilate finally acquiesces and delivers 'Jesus to *their* will' (v. 25). Here, although Luke has characteristically avoided writing the subjects for the verbs used in the demands for death – so that we read that '*they* cried out' in v. 18, that '*they* shouted' (v. 21), and that '*they* pleaded with loud voices' (v. 23) – 'they' nevertheless can be only 'the chief priests and the rulers and the people' of v. 13.[170]

Crossan, 'Anti-Semitism', pp. 190–1, has identified four passages in the Gospel where 'the people' or 'the crowd(s)' seem to be opposed to Jesus and where, incidentally, Luke has introduced the reading 'people' or 'crowds', whereas his source in each case had identified some particular group or person. The four episodes are Luke 3.7–9, John's attack on the people; 11.15, where 'some of them', i.e., of 'the crowds', voice the opinion that Jesus is in the service of Beelzebul and others 'try' him by asking for a sign; 11.29–30, the 'this generation is an evil generation' saying; and 12.54–56, where Jesus calls the 'crowds . . . hypocrites' and charges that they cannot interpret signs and times. Crossan proposed that Luke was expressing no antisemitic intent by introducing these changes, but that he simply dropped technical Jewish terms 'like "Scribes, Pharisees, Sadducees"' in favour of the more general 'crowds' for his intended Gentile audience (ibid., p. 192). Now, however, it will be immediately clear that three of Crossan's examples are sayings, and that, whether one wants to label them 'antisemitic' or not, they belong to the categorical denunciations of the Jewish people in the sayings and speeches of Luke-Acts. Only 11.15 therefore appears as an anomaly. Perhaps, then, we have here a second 'tip' in the narrative, in addition to the Nazareth episode, as to how 'the Jews' will eventually behave.

After the scenes before Pilate, just as mysteriously, the people are once again set apart from the religious leaders. In v. 27 'a great multitude of the people [follow] him', and in v. 35 'the people [stand] looking' while 'the rulers [mock]'; furthermore, in v. 48 'the crowds . . . beat their breasts', and later the strolling companions of the resurrected Jesus on the Emmaus Road say (24.20), 'Our chief priests and rulers delivered him and crucified him', thus distancing themselves from the deed. This oddity has led to the conjecture that, originally in Luke, the people were not included among the accusers of Jesus in ch. 23. Rau has argued that 'the entire multitude of them' in 23.1 means only 'the whole Sanhedrin', that the 'crowds' of v. 4 are therefore only the same group, and that v. 13 originally read, . . . τοὺς ἀρχιερεῖς καὶ τοὺς ἄρχοντες τοῦ λαοῦ, 'the chief priests and the rulers *of* the people'.[171] The role of the people in the scenes before Pilate would therefore not be at variance with their role elsewhere in the Gospel. Probably an early antisemitic copyist changed 'of the people' to 'and the people', and the original reading disappeared.

Now, on 23.1 Rau may be correct that what is meant is that the entire Sanhedrin conducted Jesus to Pilate,[172] although Luke's phrasing is rather ambiguous. Regarding the 'crowds' of 23.4, however, Rau is surely wrong.[173] While crowds in Luke, if they are large enough, may include both people and religious leaders (22.47 is a good example), the naming of crowds in addition to chief priests in 23.4 is equivalent to naming 'people', as one can see by the fact that, in 22.2, the religious leaders could not apprehend Jesus because of 'the *people*', just as, in v. 6, 'Judas sought an opportunity to deliver him when the *crowd* was not present'.[174] If the people, however, are present in the crowds of 23.4, then their presence in 23.13 needs no further explanation.[175]

But Rau's question remains. Why do the people appear friendly to Jesus before ch. 23, join the religious leaders in Pilate's presence,[176] and then revert to their friendly status thereafter? To begin with, it is not actually correct that the people revert to their former status after 23.13. Rather, they take a strangely passive and mute role. When Jesus is led away to be crucified he is followed by 'a great multitude of the people and of women' (24.27), but only the women (αἱ) act like mourners,[177] and Jesus' following warning is addressed only to 'daughters of Jerusalem' (vv. 28–31). At the actual crucifixion, while the religious leaders are mocking, 'the people [stand] watching' (v. 35) – not doing anything, not mocking to be sure,[178] but also not mourning, and also not doing anything to prevent the crucifixion, although it is *their* leaders, we must remember, who are carrying out this crucifixion in Luke, not the Romans, and although they had, with their rulers, called for Jesus' crucifixion and had thrice heard Pilate pronounce Jesus innocent (Luke 23.4, 15, 22). Thus Luke seems to want to involve 'the people' in guilt for the execution of Jesus while at the same time maintaining the image of the religious leaders as the primary actors.[179] In this, he keeps the people strictly in Pilate's court, where they hear the three findings of innocence, and he keeps them out of Herod's court. Thus the people join with the rulers at the crucial moment; they call for Jesus' death while learning that he is innocent. Have they, then, any excuse? Their beating of their breasts in 23.48 is probably to be understood as a recognition of their desperate situation.[180]

When, in 24.20, Jesus' interlocutors tell him that '*our* chief priests and rulers' had executed him, it is probably not Luke's intent to absolve 'the people' of guilt.[181] For one thing, in ch. 24 the interest has shifted from crucifixion to resurrection, so that Luke is trying to present a scene here in which people who know that Jesus is dead are astounded to find him alive again – that is, their saying that their rulers had killed Jesus may in the first instance be nothing more than their expression of knowledge that Jesus is dead.[182]

In addition, for Jewish people to admit that 'their' leaders had executed Jesus does not remove them from the taint of guilt any more than their watching while the crucifixion went on; they are left, rather, in the same ambiguous situation. But even more – and this is probably the main reason that Jesus' two companions do not say that they had participated in the crucifixion – Luke apparently intends to designate them as Christians, since he has just been narrating how the women have reported the empty tomb to the apostles, and then he writes that 'two *of them*' were on the road and encountered Jesus.[183] To be sure, the term 'Christian' would be an anachronism here, but Luke is nevertheless describing Jesus' appearances to 'his people'. Such people, of course, did not execute Jesus.[184]

While the issue of just why the Jewish people appear as they do in Luke 23 and 24 must remain not completely resolved until we come to the end of Acts, still their behaviour in Luke is reasonably clear. In the Nazareth episode, the opening of Jesus' public ministry, first *all* in the synagogue respond favourably to Jesus, and then *all* turn against him and seek to kill him. After that, all the people – as opposed to the religious leaders – respond favourably to Jesus up until ch. 23 (with the one exception of 11.15), when they suddenly join with the religious leaders in calling for Jesus' death and in hearing Pilate's acquittals.[185] In the remainder of the Gospel the people only silently observe. One might almost say that they are in limbo.

The recent work of Neyrey, *Passion*, is somewhat puzzling. On the one hand, he has seen more clearly than most the degree to which Luke makes 'the Jews' more culpable in the death of Jesus (and in the trials of Peter, Stephen, and Paul in Acts) than his sources warrant. He repeatedly underscores how the trials in Acts are modelled on Jesus' trials in the Gospel, and he sees, for example, that in Jesus' trial before Pilate 'what is dramatized is Israel's solemn rejection of Jesus as God's prophet' (op. cit., p. 75); further, he sees that, in all the trials, it is really 'the Jews' who are on trial, not Jesus and the leaders of the church (e.g., ibid., p. 83). On the other hand, however, he never evaluates the construction that Luke has put on the material, and he concludes the revised version of his article discussed above in ch. 2 ('Jesus' Address'), which appears as ch. 4 in *Passion*, by noting that Jesus' pronouncement of judgment on Jerusalem 'seems premature or incomplete. Only in Acts do we learn of Israel's repeated and conclusive rejection of Jesus and his witnesses' (ibid., p. 127); and the issue of the Jews is not brought up again in the rest of the book. Thus Neyrey unfortunately gives the impression that he thinks that, by the end of Acts, the condemnation of 'the Jews' is justified. Similarly Kilgallen, *Stephen Speech*, p. 113.

Acts

The behaviour of the Jewish people in Acts runs parallel to that in the Gospel. Parallels are not, however, photocopies, so that the behaviour of 'the Jews' in the Acts is not *exactly* the same as that in the Gospel; nevertheless, there are enough similarities that we can see that Luke was consciously conforming the two narratives to each other in this respect – as, of course, in others. When we have noted carefully how the Jews behave in Acts, then we shall have the whole picture before us, and we shall be able better to understand the puzzling developments at the end of the Gospel.

The 'Jerusalem springtime'

When Acts begins, the Jewish people are, as in the Gospel between the Nazareth episode and the trials before Pilate, uniformly friendly towards and accepting of the apostles. Most obviously, 'myriads' (as Acts 21.20 later reminds us) are converted. The Lucan summary statements tell of 3000 in Acts 2.41, of an unspecified number in 2.47, of 5000 men (implying that there may be women as well) in 4.4, and of a multitude in 5.14. In 6.1, then, we learn that 'the disciples are multiplying' and in v. 7 that 'the number of the disciples in Jerusalem multiplied greatly'.[186] It can hardly be an accident that, of the three places where Luke uses the term 'myriads', one summarizes the number of Judahite converts to Christianity (Acts 21.20) and one refers to the size of Jesus' popular following (Luke 12.1).[187]

Since the last of the summaries, Acts 6.7, refers to converts in Jerusalem, perhaps Luke intends to emphasize the positive response of *Jerusalem*, not that of *the Jews*, to Christianity by writing that myriads have been converted? Inasmuch as, at this stage of the Acts narrative, the gospel has not yet broken out of Jerusalem, of course that is true. But Luke thinks of Jerusalem as the capital of 'the Jews',[188] not as the capital of the Roman province of Judaea, so that it makes no essential difference to him whether there are mass conversions to Christianity 'in Jerusalem' (6.7) or 'among the Jews' (21.20), except that of course in Acts 6.7 there cannot have been any converts outside Jerusalem because there has been no preaching of the gospel outside Jerusalem. Put in other terms, the significance to Luke of the Jerusalem converts mentioned in Acts 21.20 is that they are Jewish, not that they are Jerusalem Jews *as opposed to* Jews elsewhere in 'Jewish country'. Their being *only* in Jerusalem is related to the geographical progression of Acts laid down in 1.8. In any case, Luke went out of his way, in his account of the first Christian sermon, to emphasize that the Jews who responded to the gospel were not just Jerusalemites but Jews from all over. While being 'Jews', they were 'devout men from every people of those under heaven' (2.5), and Peter addressed them as 'Jewish men and residents of Jerusalem' (v. 14).[189] Also, 'those residing in Rome' present at Peter's sermon (v. 10) were 'both Jews and proselytes' (v. 11). The evidence is therefore clear; the significance to Luke of the myriads of converts is that they were Jewish, not that they were residents of Jerusalem.

That they were ἀπὸ παντὸς ἔθνους means that they had come to Jerusalem from other ethnic locales, not, as some think, that they are Gentiles (cf. Koester, *Introduction*, vol. 2, p. 319; Lohse, 'Pfingstbericht', pp. 432–3; Kremer, *Pfingstbericht*, p. 163). There are no Gentiles in Peter's audience; thus correctly Fitzmyer, 'Jewish Christianity', p. 235; Gaston, *No Stone*, pp. 301–2. The view of Cadbury, Lake and Ropes (see p. 46–7 above and *Beginnings*, Part I, vol. 3, p. 12, and vol. 5, pp. 67–8) that MS ℵ, which omits 'Jews' from v. 5, is correct must be rejected for two reasons. First, as Haenchen, *Acts*, pp. 168, 174–5, has pointed out, for the Spirit to pour out its power first on Jews fits Luke's theological plan; but, in the second place, MS ℵ reveals by this omission an 'antisemitic tendency',[190] in keeping with which it also omits ἐν τοῖς Ἰουδαίοις in Acts 21.20. (Munck, *Paul and Salvation*, pp. 240–1, wishes to agree with this omission.) That is, MS ℵ avoids saying that the 'Jews' were 'devout men' and also avoids saying that there are 'myriads' of Christians 'among the Jews'. Loisy, *Actes*, p. 215, thought that Luke had his eye on the eventual world-wide success of the Christian mission (cf. also Dupont, 'Le salut des Gentils', p. 144; 'La première Pentecôte', pp. 498–9 [ET in *The Salvation of the Gentiles*, pp. 35–59, but without notes]), but that aspect seems to play no role in the Pentecost narrative. Luke rather wants to get a representative group of world-wide Jewry involved. So correctly Beck, *Mature Christianity*, pp. 212–13. Wilson, *Gentiles*, p. 219, even thinks that the phrase 'to all those far off' in 2.39 is a reference to Diaspora Jews, not to Gentiles; similarly Jervell, *People of God*, pp. 57–8. Cf. further the address and explanation given in v. 14 (cited immediately above).

In addition to providing the information about mass conversions in his summary statements, Luke has also included other summary statements that simply state in what good favour the early Christians were held by the Jewish people. In Acts 2.47 he states that the Christians had 'favour with the whole people (ὅλος ὁ λαός)'; in 3.11 'all the people (πᾶς ὁ λαός) ran together to' Peter and John; and in 5.13 'the people glorified' the apostles. Thus, in Acts before Stephen's martyrdom, the people behave towards the apostles as they did towards Jesus in the Gospel between the Nazareth episode and the passion narrative.[191] This fact, as Conzelmann has pointed out,[192] shows that there is no 'eternal validity' to 'Judaism . . . Law [,] Temple, [and] Jerusalem', since the church is associated with these Jewish entitites only during the 'initial period'.[193]

After the summary statement of Acts 6.7, of course, Stephen is arrested and killed, a persecution breaks out, and the gospel moves out of Jerusalem on its way to 'the end of the earth' (1.8). And the role of 'the Jews' in Acts changes markedly.[194] In order to grasp the nature of this change clearly, we need to pause for a paragraph to consider the evidence of the concordance under 'the Jews'.

The pejorative use of 'the Jews'

Of the seventy-four occurrences of the plural 'Jews' or 'the Jews' in Luke-Acts,[195] only eight fall before Stephen's martyrdom, of which three occur in the phrase 'king of the Jews' in the passion narrative (Luke 23.3, 37,38). In Luke 7.3 the term is used in a neutral sense to distinguish Jews from Gentiles (the centurion sends 'Jewish elders' to Jesus), and in Luke 23.51 it is merely a geographical designation. The other three occurrences are all in Acts 2, where, as we have just discussed, Luke is emphasizing that the first Christian sermon was addressed to Jews native to Jerusalem as well as from elsewhere (vv. 5, 10, 14). After Stephen's martyrdom, however, while the use to distinguish Jews from Gentiles still occurs (frequently in Paul's mission, e.g., 14.1: 'A great multitude of Jews and Gentiles'), and while the geographical use is still possible (10.39: 'in the region of the Jews'), Luke, however, now uses the term 'the Jews' *in malam partem* with great frequency.[196] Right away, the first occurrence of the term after Stephen's martyrdom is of this type.[197] In 9.22 Paul 'confused the Jews who live in Damascus', and in v. 23, 'The Jews conferred together about how to do away with him.' This kind of use of 'the Jews' continues throughout Acts. In 12.3 Herod's persecution was 'pleasing to the Jews',[198] and shortly after this, following his miraculous escape from prison, Peter explains that he knows that the angel of God 'rescued [him] from Herod's hand and from all the expectations of the Jewish people (τοῦ λαοῦ τῶν Ἰουδαίων)' (v. 11). In Paul's mission, of course, Jewish opposition turns up in different ways, but especially noteworthy for Luke's usage of 'the Jews' is 18.12, 'The Jews with one accord (ὁμοθυμαδόν, one of Luke's favourite words) rose up against Paul.' Finally, in the Pauline passion narrative we may note 23.12, 'the Jews' plotted to ambush and kill Paul, although Luke later relates (v. 13) that it was only something over forty who joined in this plot; and 25.24, where Festus says that 'the entire multitude of the Jews (ἅπαν τὸ πλῆθος τῶν Ἰουδαίων)' has complained to him about Paul. When this kind of use of the term is added to the sheer volume of the number of times the term is used after Stephen's martyrdom, then we see what kind of change has taken place.[199] Even if many of the instances of 'Jews' or 'the Jews' after Stephen's martyrdom are of the distinction-from-the-Gentiles type and thus are perhaps natural in that part of the narrative in which the gospel leaves its Jewish matrix, still such usage cannot obscure the fact that, beginning with Acts 9.22, 'the Jews' are the enemies of Christianity.

Stephen

Having satisfied ourselves on that point, we may now more readily understand how the Jewish people behave in the narrative of Acts following the highly favourable treatment that they give to Christianity in the first five chapters. In Acts 6.9, hard on the heels of the last summary statement (v. 7) of Christianity's great success among the Jewish people, a caucus of Diaspora Jews in Jerusalem becomes aroused and moves against Stephen, provoking his arrest and trial.[200] There can be no doubt that Luke intends to distinguish Diapora Jews from Palestinian Jews, since he lists the main north

African cities (Cyrene and Alexandria) and two Anatolian provinces (Cilicia and Asia) of known Diaspora population.[201] Furthermore, it is again Diaspora Jews from Asia who finally provoke Paul's arrest (21.27). Why does Luke make such a point of this? Is it to distinguish good Palestinian Jews (so friendly to Jesus and the apostles) from bad Diaspora Jews who, between Stephen's and Paul's arrests, cause such problems for Paul's mission? This can hardly be the case, for, in both cases, Luke immediately shows how the entire Jewish people joined in the accusations against Stephen and Paul.[202] In 6.12 it is 'the people and the elders and the scribes' who 'got together (συνεκίνησαν)' to arrest and prosecute Stephen; and, in 21.27–36, it is 'all the crowd (πᾶς ὁ ὄχλος)' that apprehended Paul, and 'the whole city (ἡ πόλις ὅλη)'[203] and 'a convergence of the people (συνδρομὴ τοῦ λαοῦ)' that dragged him outside the Temple. Finally, 'the multitude of the people (τὸ πλῆθος τοῦ λαοῦ)' joined in the cry for Paul's death (cf. also 22.22).[204] Thus the distinction that Luke seems to want to make, in his narrative of both Stephen's and Paul's arrests, is that Diaspora Jews *incite* 'the people' or 'the crowd(s)', i.e. the Jews, who then go along with the mischief.[205] But 'the Jews' are by no means innocent in these matters; they join vigorously in the apprehension of and accusations against our heroes.

While Stephen is tried in the Sanhedrin, Luke probably means his readers to understand that the Jews carried out the lynching. He creates this impression by, again, omitting subjects for his verbs. The only subject that appears in the entire account of Stephen's martyrdom, 7.54–60, is 'the witnesses' (v. 58), who took off their clothes and gave them to Saul (Paul). Thus, as so often in Luke's accounts of opposition to Jesus and to Christianity, we read only that '*they* cried out in a loud voice and shut *their* ears, and *they* rushed him with one accord (ὁμοθυμαδόν), and *they* cast him outside the city and stoned him' (vv. 57–58). Now it is all very well and good to insist that Stephen is in the Sanhedrin (where 'the Jews' could hardly all have been present) and that Luke does not actually write that 'the Jews' lynched Stephen; but has Stephen's long speech not led the reader away from the specific setting of 6.15 towards a more general context?[206] After Stephen is brought into the Sanhedrin, his speech focuses the reader's attention more and more on the Jewish people as a whole throughout their entire history. His conclusion, '[you] who received the Law in angelic ordinances and did not keep it', spoken with all the Jewish people in mind, is followed immediately by all those subjectless third-person verbs that describe his martyrdom: 'When *they* heard these things *they* were cut to the quick (διεπρίοντο ταῖς καρδίαις)', and so on. What is the reader to think?

We also need to note the degree to which Luke has made Stephen's martyrdom run parallel not only to Jesus' martyrdom,[207] but also to his proto-martyrdom in Luke 4.28–29. Just as Jesus is there taken outside the city to be stoned, so is Stephen here;[208] and just as Jesus in the passion narrative asks for the forgiveness of his murderers, because of their ignorance, and 'delivers' his 'spirit' to God (Luke 24.34, 46), so Stephen, when dying, prays that Jesus will 'receive' his 'spirit'; and he likewise calls for forgiveness for his murderers (Acts 7.59–60).[209] Thus in Nazareth all are favourably disposed toward Jesus and then seek to kill him, during Jesus' ministry the people are favourably disposed towards Jesus and then join in condemning him to death in the passion narrative, and in the early church the people are likewise favourably disposed towards the Christians and then martyr Stephen and begin a general persecution. Put otherwise, the narrative of Acts 1–7 runs to this degree parallel to the public career and passion of Jesus, and both narratives follow the pattern already established in the Nazareth episode.[210] In this way Luke builds up the image of all Jews as opposed to Christ and to Christianity.

The transition from Jerusalem to Diaspora

In chs. 8–12 Luke gets us from the Jerusalem mission to Paul's Diaspora mission. The beginning and end of this period – or, probably better, the beginning of this period and the beginning of the next – are marked by persecutions. Stephen's martyrdom is followed immediately by a general persecution (8.1–3), after which the gospel expands into Judaea and Samaria and then to the Gentiles;[211] and likewise James's martyrdom (12.1–2) is followed immediately by further persecutions, after which Paul's mission gets under way. The rather full account of Stephen's martyrdom is followed by a meagre account of the ensuing persecution, and the meagre account of James's martyrdom is followed by a much fuller account of the ensuing persecution (the rest of ch. 12,[212] which also includes the happy dénouement of vv. 20–23).[213] In the course of this narrative, however, we have – what is probably more important for Luke – the account of Paul's conversion and of the fledgling missionary's first attempt at Diaspora synagogue preaching.[214] It can hardly escape our notice that Paul, in this account, makes little if any attempt to convert any of his synagogue audience to Christianity (although their fear, 9.21, that Paul's preaching is a trick and that he only wants to arrest them implies that they think that he wants to convert them) but is happy rather to preach the gospel and to 'confuse' his auditors (9.20, 22). We have already, of course, had occasion to note that those whom Paul confuses are 'Jews' (v. 22).

Paul's mission

Now Paul's mission. The Overbeck-Loisy-Haenchen position leaves one with the impression that Paul had almost no success among Jews in the Diaspora, and that Jewish opposition to Paul's mission was consistent and uniform.[215] Jervell, on the other hand, maintains that nothing has changed and that, now as before, the gospel goes to Jews and Gentiles alike.[216] Burchard has also come down hard on the side of interpreting the Lucan Paul as making every effort to convert Jews throughout his missionary career.[217] Neither position is quite correct.[218]

The truth is that there is a lack of uniformity in the accounts of Paul's attempts to evangelize different cities in Anatolia (including Cyprus) and on the Greek mainland.[219] In Paphos (Acts 13.6), Lystra (14.6–8) and Derbe (14.20–21) he does not go to a synagogue, and in Philippi he finds only a small Jewish group but no true 'congregation' (16.13). Furthermore, he is not always opposed by Jews. No opposition from Jews to his preaching develops in Salamis (13.4–5), Paphos (13.6–12), Derbe (14.20–21), Philippi (16.11–40), or Athens (17.16–34), although in Paphos (and also in Ephesus) he runs up against charismatics (a false prophet in Paphos, 13.6, and exorcists in Ephesus, 19.14) who just happen to be Jewish. Gentiles, however, also attempt to hinder Paul's mission. He is opposed by both Jews and Gentiles (although the Jews are responsible) in Iconium (14.2) and by Gentiles only in Philippi (16.19). Finally, Paul's success in preaching to Diaspora Jews is varied. No Jews respond favourably to the gospel on Cyprus (13.4–12), but at Antioch Paul 'persuades' some Jews (13.43) and at Iconium some 'believe' (14.1).[220] There are again no conversions at Lystra (14.8–20), and, while there are some at Derbe, the brief note does not explain whether they are Jews, Gentiles, or both (14.21a). A God-fearer is baptized at Philippi (16.14–15), in Thessalonica both Jews and Gentiles are 'persuaded' (17.4), in Beroea both Jews and Gentiles 'believe' (17.12), and at Athens only a few Gentiles 'believe' (17.34). At Corinth Paul again 'persuades' both Gentiles and Jews (18.4), and then he has many 'believers' whose race is not specified. At least one is a Jew (18.8). Finally, Paul's success in Ephesus is limited to his re-baptizing some Christians, this time 'in the name of the Lord Jesus' (19.5). Since Priscilla and Aquila, already designated as Jews (18.2), are leading members of the Ephesian church (18.26), it would appear to be a mixed congregation.[221] To this mosaic we also need to add the evidence that some of the Jewish opposition to Paul's mission comes not from Jews in the town where Paul is preaching, but from Jews at an earlier stop on the itinerary. This happens at Lystra, where Jews come from Antioch and Iconium to oppose Paul (14.19),[222] and at Beroea, where Jews from Thessalonica incite the locals (17.13). Some other Gentiles are also converted along the way, but they are not our concern here.[223]

Now, it is clear that Luke has put himself to great effort to show that Paul's Diaspora mission had varied results and that he was hindered from different quarters. These variations in Paul's mission from one city to the next lend credibility to the account.[224] They also, at least in recent times, increase Luke's stock as a 'writer'.

It was Cadbury and Dibelius who started modern authors thinking in such terms, although what Dibelius meant was little different from what Overbeck and Loisy meant when they referred to Acts as a 'fiction'. Cf. Dibelius's remark in his essay on 'The Acts of the Apostles as an Historical Source' that 'the writer's literary ability has a far greater part in the Acts of the Apostles than it had in his Gospel' (*Studies*, p. 103). Cadbury, 'Acts', p. 36, refers more gently to 'the author's . . . capacity to vary style'. But Jervell, *People of God*, p. 62, sees Luke as 'hold[ing] the reader in suspense from scene to scene in order to show the different reactions to the preaching'. Similar sentiments are expressed by others.

To conclude from the evidence of Luke's stylistic variety, however, as some do, that Luke intends to give the impression of a mission directed even-handedly to Jews and Gentiles alike is to miss Luke's point. Rather, he has carefully constructed a progression that is intended to put 'the Jews' in a bad light. Some further observations will perhaps make that point more understandable.

For one thing, Luke has made Paul's first stop (Cyprus) and his last (Ephesus) run parallel to each other. If we view the mission on Cyprus at both Salamis and Paphos as one stop, then it is remarkable how much it is like Paul's stay in Ephesus. First of all, Paul's Ephesian ministry includes an interlude between his two visits there (18.22–28), and this is comparable to his visiting two places on Cyprus,[225] for his mission on Cyprus begins at Salamis (13.5) but ends at Paphos (v. 6), just as his mission at Ephesus is broken into two parts. When Paul comes to Salamis he preaches in synagogues (13.5), but there are no results to this preaching. When he then transfers to Paphos there is no initial preaching, but the results occur (vv. 6–12). Similarly at Ephesus, on Paul's first visit he has only an entrée to the town. When he returns he preaches in the synagogue (19.8), and, when he has no results there, he moves to another location (v. 9). The next step after changing locations is also similar in both places; in Paphos Paul overcomes a Jewish false prophet (13.6–11); in Ephesus he overcomes Jewish exorcists (19.13–16) – in other words, Jewish charismatics in both places.[226] The differences are that some other things happen in Ephesus for which there are no parallels in the Cyprus episode; that at Paphos Paul has a Gentile conversion (13.12), whereas, as we have already noted, he has no conversions at all at Ephesus (although he does give 'some', 19.1, a proper Christian baptism); and that Jewish opposition to the gospel develops only in Ephesus (19.9). Surely, however, Luke has composed these two scenes in conscious parallelism, and we therefore see a tendency of his to make *beginning and end conform* in the Christian mission.[227] We may let this point rest here for the moment, but we shall have to take it up again later when we come to the end of Acts.[228]

In between these two points – the first and last stops on Paul's itinerary – the aforementioned variety exists, but even it is not so varied if we draw a line before ch. 17; for, beginning with the Thessalonian mission, Paul *always* goes first to a synagogue when he arrives in town, and he is *always*, except in Athens, opposed by Jews. Inasmuch as Luke seems primarily concerned to show, in the Athenian episode, in what form the gospel is supposed to be proclaimed when the audience is made up of people with traditional classical educations, perhaps his omission of the theme of Jewish hostility is understandable; but in Thessalonica (17.5), in Beroea (17.13), in Corinth (18.5–6) and in Ephesus (19.9) Paul is opposed by 'the Jews'.[229] Thus, for all that Luke has sketched a variegated portrait of Paul's mission, he has also drawn a picture of *increasing Jewish hostility and opposition to the gospel*.[230] The attitude that Jews in Jerusalem demonstrated *in nuce* in *l'affaire Étienne* is therefore revealed in its fullness in historical development in the course of Paul's ministry. The truth of Jewish opposition to the gospel that is revealed in Stephen's trial and martyrdom is thus borne out in a historical progression in the course of Paul's ministry. The accusations are becoming historical reality.

How little this 'simulacrum of history' (Loisy) is based on any real information about past events is seen in the summary narrative of Acts 14.21b–28. Here Paul goes back over territory where he had earlier experienced such occasionally vigorous opposition from Jews, continuing his preaching (v. 25), and there is not a breath of Jewish hostility anywhere. Others, of course, have commented on this oddity, but none with as much naïve sincerity as Winn, *Acts*, p. 85, who ventures the explanation that, 'either because new magistrates were now in office, or because they worked in secret, they escaped persecution'. For a sober assessment of the narrative, cf. Loisy, *Actes*, p. 560.

It may also be that Luke tries to show that the Jews are 'notorious disturbers of the peace',[231] although this theme is certainly minor compared with that of their guilt in the death of Jesus and in the opposition to the church. Conzelmann calls attention especially to Acts 18.12–17, where Jews accuse Paul before Gallio, and to 24.5–6, where they accuse him before Felix. In both cases they 'are foiled in their intrigues'.[232]

Is it not, however – here we must raise that question again – only *Diaspora* Jews whom Luke portrays as intransigently opposed to the gospel? Luke himself seems to have heard our question; and he answers it by writing now the next long and complex episode, the climax of the Acts of the Apostles, the 'Pauline passion narrative'.[233]

The Pauline passion narrative

The discussion of the 'Pauline passion' provides a convenient opportunity to reply to the essay of Brawley, 'Paul in Acts'. It is Brawley's opinion that Jewish opposition in Acts is directed only at Paul, not at the Gentile mission generally; thus Jervell can be correct, but the reality of Jewish opposition can be somehow accommodated (ibid., *passim*, esp. pp. 129–34, 140–4). Brawley has, however, completely overlooked the following points: 1. Luke has made Paul's passion and Jesus' conform to each other; 2. there *is* no other Gentile mission in Acts after Paul's begins; 3. Jews persecute Stephen, whose martyrdom also exhibits parallels to Jesus'; 4. 'the Jews' approve the martyrdom of James. In Luke's opinion, 'the Jews' oppose Christianity, and no amount of wishing or citing Jervell will alter that fact.

Here I must emphasize what we already had occasion to note in ch. 1, namely that, for all the similarities between Paul's arrest and trials and Jesus' arrest and trials,[234] in Paul's case the Jewish religious leaders are eclipsed by the people.[235] It is 'the Jews' who arrest Paul and who denounce him to the temporal authorities.[236] The announcement of the Pauline passion in 21.11 includes the prophecy that 'the Jews . . . will bind' Paul,[237] something that could not be said of Jesus in the announcements of the passion in the Gospel, although now we probably see at what Luke was hinting in his rewriting of the third such announcement, Luke 18.32–33,[238] where he put the verbs into the passive voice and left the agents unexpressed, just as he so often omits subjects for his verbs when he wants to imply that 'the Jews' are guilty of something but does not quite want to say it. Further, we have already seen that – while Diaspora Jews, as in the case of Stephen, stir up the crowd against Paul – it is 'the whole city' and 'the people' (21.30) who apprehend Paul and the 'multitude of the people' (v. 36) that demands his death. When, then, 'they' again call for Paul to be 'remove[d] from the face of the earth' (22.22),[239] there is no doubt who 'they' are. When Paul is brought before the Sanhedrin, it is because he has been 'accused by the Jews' (22.30), and it is 'the Jews' (23.12) who plot to ambush and kill Paul.

In this last-mentioned narrative Luke shows especially well how little the distinction between *some* Jews and *all* the Jews means to him. While he begins the tale by saying that 'the Jews' vowed 'neither to eat nor to drink until they should kill Paul' (v. 12), he reports immediately in the next verse that it was only 'more than forty' who were involved; and when Paul's nephew tips off the tribune to the mischief afoot,[240] Luke again writes first 'the Jews' (v. 20) and then 'more than forty of them' (v. 21); only now the juxtaposition seems to mean that 'the Jews' have formulated the plot, but that only 'more than forty *of them*', i.e., of those who have done the plotting, will actually carry it out. Luke has, of course, already implicated a wider circle than just the 'more than forty' by having the 'hit men' consult with 'the chief priests and the elders' (v. 14). 'The vague description *the Jews* is made more precise [by the introduction of the forty], but leaves the impression that the action of this group was typical of the attitude of the Jews generally.'[241]

Later, when Festus seeks Herod's advice on what to do with Paul, he tells Herod that 'the entire multitude of the Jews (ἄπαν τὸ πλῆθος τῶν Ἰουδαίων)' (25.24), has been accusing Paul and calling for his death, and when Paul speaks to Herod he says that he has been 'accused by Jews' (26.2), and again that 'Jews . . . tried to slay' him

(v. 21). While the religious leaders can appear, in the Pauline passion narrative, as his accusers and opponents – as just noted in the preceding paragraph and in 25.2, where 'the chief priests and the leaders of the Jews' denounce Paul to Festus – nevertheless they recede quite into the background in comparison with 'the Jews'. Paul is done in not by the religious authorities alone and not by Diaspora Jews alone but by THE JEWS.[242] Jewish opposition to Christianity is now universal and endemic.[243]

The conclusion of Paul's itinerary

When we now turn to Paul's final encounter with Jews at Rome, we shall be able to begin to tie all the threads together. In a sense, Rome is the last stop on Paul's missionary itinerary; it is only that the itinerary has been interrupted by the passion. As regularly during his mission, and always from the beginning of ch. 17 on, Paul looks up the Jewish congregation immediately he arrives in town. In this case, of course, since he is in custody, the Jews must come to him, but the setting is otherwise the same;[244] Paul addresses the local Jewish congregation. After they confirm to him what we already know, that Christianity 'is everywhere spoken against' – by Jews, apparently – Paul preaches to them, just as regularly during his Diaspora mission; and again, as so frequently there, he 'persuades' some, while others 'disbelieve' (28.24).[245] Here, however – and in this way this last stop on the itinerary is different from all the others from the beginning of ch. 17 on – no opposition arises; nevertheless, Paul turns viciously on his auditors, sounding very much like Stephen in quoting Isa. 6.9–10 against them. And then he, for the third and last time, announces that the gospel is going to the Gentiles, 'and they will hear'.[246]

This final scene of Paul's ministry is therefore a reprise of the first scene of Jesus'.[247] (Thus beginning and end again run parallel to each other.) Do we have a synagogue sermon there? So we have here, with the adjustment for verisimilitude that Paul is a prisoner. Is the Book of Isaiah quoted there? So it is here.[248] Is there at first a favourable and then a hostile response there? Similarly here the one response is mixed, part favourable and part unfavourable. And does Jesus there make it clear to his audience that they were never the intended recipients of God's salvation, which is a salvation for the Gentiles?[249] So here as well. The issue was never in doubt.[250]

Solution

Even the casual reader will realize that I have just gone back on my word. I promised to discuss first what the leading characters in Luke-Acts *said* about the Jewish people, then how the Jewish people *behaved* in the narrative, and finally what relation the two complexes – sayings material and narrative – have to each other. In the last paragraph, however, I seem to have obscured the distinction. I plead guilty to this crime, but I offer this in my defence: it was unavoidable, for the distinction has ceased to exist. By the end of the Acts the Jews have *become* what they from the first *were*; for what Jesus, Stephen, Peter and Paul say about the Jews – about their intransigent opposition to the purposes of God, about their hostility toward Jesus and the gospel, about their murder of Jesus – is what Luke understands the Jewish people to be in their essence. The narrative shows how existence comes to conform with essence, the process by which the Jewish people become 'the Jews';[251] yet one should not think that the fact that Luke's narrative shows Jews progressing from an attitude of receptivity to one of hostility provides some hope, from Luke's point of view, for Jews; for what they became was no more nor less than what they always, from the days of their creation as a people, were.[252]

In an article that appeared after the completion of this manuscript ('Israel in Luke-Acts'), Robert Tannehill has argued that Luke portrays the two-sided rejection of the Jews as a tragedy (cf. also Jervell, *Unknown Paul*, p. 135). Like Lohfink, Tannehill points to the incongruity between initial expectation and final reality where the Jews are concerned in Luke-Acts (Tannehill, 'Israel in Luke-Acts', p. 70), but he further correctly sees that the speeches of Jesus, Peter, Stephen and Paul are significant for understanding the author's intent (ibid.); yet he thinks that the accelerating theme of Jewish rejection after Stephen's martyrdom is a tragic turn in the narrative and that the author intended the readers to view the Jews with 'sympathetic pity' (ibid., p. 75; the term is reminiscent of Sandmel's 'residual pity'). I intend to reply to Tannehill's proposal in greater detail elsewhere in the near future, but he must receive at least a brief answer here.

While Tannehill has made a number of correct observations, his interpretation of the observed phenomena – that Luke intends to portray the Jews in a tragic light – is essentially incorrect. This may be seen especially at two points. For one thing, Tannehill has to explain away the evidence of the parable of the Pounds (in a footnote!) by arguing that it only 'seem[s] to conflict with [the] hope' of Israel's salvation (op. cit., p. 84), when what it does, in fact, is to cement the condemnation of the Jews made in all the speeches in Luke-Acts. Further, in one passing allusion – and there only – Tannehill reveals that he actually knows where the real tragedy is in Luke-Acts. He writes (op. cit., p. 74) that 'the author is guiding the readers to experience the story of Israel *and its messiah* (emphasis mine) as a tragic story'. Are we to think that Luke-Acts is a double tragedy? Surely not! The tragedy of the Gospel is the execution of the last great prophet, who journeys through the pages of the Gospel toward his inescapable fate. 'The Jews' are the villains, not the victims.

But how can we attribute such harsh judgment on the Jews to one who quotes the Jewish scripture? It is Franklin's opinion that Luke's use of the Old Testament and of Israelite traditions demonstrates that Luke has not 'written the Jews off' (to use Haenchen's phrase). Luke's 'absorption of the Old Testament,' Franklin writes, 'of its history, promises, and expectations, means that he sees Israel as having some permanent validity within the sphere of God's covenantal people . . . It is scarcely conceivable that one such as Luke who was so immersed in the Old Testament could ever have turned his back upon the nation whose hopes it recorded.'[253] One need only ask, however, what use Luke actually makes of the Jewish scripture to see where Franklin has made his mistake; for the Jewish scripture is quoted, in Luke-Acts, against the Jews. Both in the opening scene of Jesus' ministry and in the closing scene of Paul's the scripture is cited in order to show that God's salvation was *never* intended for the Jews. Stephen's speech, with its lengthy recollection of 'Old Testament' history, makes the same point. Simply to note the fact of the Lucan use of Jewish scripture and to conclude therefrom the existence of some kind of positive attitude towards the Jews, without in this connection analysing *how* the Jewish scripture is used, represents a serious flaw in method.

Of course, Luke does view 'Israel as having some . . . validity' within the divine plan; the question is only whether one may speak of a 'permanent validity'. Precisely the evidence on which Franklin would like to rely, Luke's use of the Jewish scripture, argues against such a notion.[254] One would do better to refer to Luke as giving a 'role' to the Jewish people within the divine plan rather than to his giving them a 'validity', since he imagines that their rejection of the gospel has been prophesied. To show that it has been is one of the main functions of Paul's final speech, quoting Isaiah 6, to the Jews in Rome.[255]

Now the behaviour of the Jewish people during and after the trial and crucifixion of Jesus is understandable, for there they must fit two stereotypes at once. On the one hand, they must so behave that they deserve the later charge of having murdered Jesus; thus they call for Jesus' death and hear Pilate's acquittals. But, on the other hand, they must also so behave that the possibility of mass conversions in Acts 1–5 is a real possibility; thus they follow Jesus mutely to the cross, stand passively at the side while their leaders kill him, and beat their breasts when he dies.[256] By giving the Jewish people such a strange role in the passion, Luke has prepared the way for both necessities in Acts, that of the success of the gospel among 'the Jews' and that of their rejection of the gospel. If Luke had constructed his script so that they entered completely the mode of rejection at the end of the Gospel, then the narrative of Acts would have been anticlimactic,[257] but if they expressed no hostility to the purposes of God during the passion narrative, then the absolute reality expressed in the sayings and speeches from the Nazareth episode on would not be correct. So Luke gives to the Jewish people the ambiguous role in the passion narrative already described. When they then take an active and quite unambiguous role in the Pauline passion narrative, we see better where the passion narrative of the Gospel was heading. The true role of the Jewish people is prefigured in the Nazareth episode, where Jesus' audience turns with one accord against him. 'Luke made it clear that neither Jesus nor his followers had rejected the Jews; they had excluded themselves from the Christian community.'[258] In the passion narrative, then, in the martyrdom of Stephen, and finally in the Pauline passion narrative, they become by stages what the Nazareth episode had already shown us they are.[259] Luke shows by a *historical progression* (Haenchen) the correctness of Jesus' statement that 'the blood of all the prophets' will 'be required of this generation' (Luke 11.50); of Stephen's statement that the Jewish ancestors 'killed those who proclaimed beforehand the coming of the Righteous One, whose deliverers and murderers now [the Jews] have become' (Acts 7.52); and of Paul's statement that the Jews' 'blood' will 'be upon [their] head' (Acts 18.6).[260] The familiar epochal plan of Luke-Acts – which has been recognized, in one form or another, almost since the beginning of critical New Testament scholarship and which Conzelmann has especially emphasized – is but a means to an end. It is Luke's way of describing becoming, becoming culminating in being, being that is already present from the beginning in the sayings and speeches.

4

THE PHARISEES

Our investigation to this point has shown that Luke thinks not merely of the Jewish leaders, and not merely of Jerusalem or of the people of Jerusalem, but rather of all the Jewish people – of 'the Jews' – as being rejected by God because they have rejected him. In this, 'the Jews' fulfil the divine plan prophesied in the Bible. Such a role, maintained constantly throughout Luke-Acts in the speeches of the leading characters, finds its expression in the narrative of Luke-Acts in a process of gradual fulfilment, whereby the power of the gospel even among Jews and the rightful claim of Christianity to be the true and authentic Judaism, incidentally, also come to expression. There is yet one specific group among the Jews, however, that either falls outside this general pattern, which we have so far seen to include all Jews, or fits into it in a strange way, and that is the Pharisees.[1] No thorough study of the Pharisees in Luke-Acts has ever been undertaken before,[2] yet it is essential to have Luke's portrait of the Pharisees clearly before us if we are to have a complete understanding of how he presents the Jews in his two-volume work.

It may be instructive to begin by reminding ourselves of how modern scholars generally characterize the Pharisees in the early Christian period. A few lines from a standard reference work will suffice.

Although [the Pharisees] recognized [Jesus] as a teacher and although they were pleased with his refutation of the Sadducees and his affirmation that God was one and that one should love one's neighbor as oneself, they were hostile to his teaching of doctrines they had not authorized; to his taking the law in his own hand; to his forgiving sins; to his exorcising demons; and, above all, to his affirming, or allowing his disciples to affirm of him, that he was the Son of man, the Messiah. The Pharisees were especially angry over his unwillingness to heed them when they confronted him with his deviations.[3]

However accurate *historically* such a summary may be – and we remind ourselves that our interest here is not a 'quest of the historical Pharisees' – the information on which it relies is drawn primarily from Mark and Matthew and not from Luke-Acts, where the Pharisees take, nevertheless, a significant role. How does *Luke* portray the Pharisees, and why?

Friendly Pharisees

John Reumann begins his introduction to the Facet Book edition of W. D. Davies's *Introduction to Pharisaism* with these words: 'The Pharisees have had "bad press" ever since the first Christian century.'[4] Yet in Luke the situation is otherwise. Perhaps the most striking difference between Luke and his (surviving) predecessors in this matter is that he indicates that some Pharisees were Christians. Not only does he agree with Paul himself that Paul was a Pharisee,[5] he has Paul state the fact twice (more often, therefore, than the real Paul does in his surviving letters) in emphatic terms. Before the Sanhedrin (Acts 23.6) Paul declares that he is a Pharisee from a Pharisaic family, and before Agrippa (26.5) he claims that he has been a Pharisee, which means belonging 'to the very best party' among the Jews. Beyond this, however, Luke even tells us that there were 'some believers from among the party of the Pharisees' (Acts 15.5), so that Paul is by no means represented as unique in his having been a Pharisee before having been converted to Christianity; there were Pharisees among the Christians, Christians among the Pharisees (according to Luke's account).[6] That is quite remarkable in view of the picture of the Pharisees drawn from Mark and Matthew.

But still more. Even those Pharisees who are not Christians are routinely friendly to Christianity.[7] In Acts 5.34–39 it is a Pharisee, Gamaliel,[8] who talks sense to his colleagues in the Sanhedrin and who persuades them not to hinder the nascent Christian movement, since 'if it is from God you will not be able to destroy them' (v. 39). Later, then, when Paul is in the Sanhedrin announcing that he is a Pharisee, he does so deliberately in order to appeal to the sympathies of Pharisees in the Sanhedrin, who pronounce him innocent in the same terms that Pilate had earlier used for Jesus,[9] and who become so vigorous in their defence of his cause that the tribune is forced to intervene and to remove Paul from the tumult for his own safety (Acts 23.10). These two attempts by Pharisees in Acts to save Christians from punishment at the hands of the Jewish authorities surely, then, provide the necessary perspective for interpreting the Pharisaic motive in warning Jesus that Herod wanted to kill him (Luke 13.31).

Some authors have thought that Luke intends his readers to see through this last-mentioned display of Pharisaic friendliness to an underlying hostility or deceit. Thus Loisy writes that

the Pharisees act not in the interest of Jesus, but in that of Herod. The information that they give to the Saviour is something quite different from a witness of sympathy; the advice that they put to him corresponds to a desire that they would not dare express otherwise. Jesus does not give the impression of thinking of them in his response.[10]

Certain aspects of the episode as Luke presents it, however, weigh on the side of realizing that he intends to show the Pharisees attempting to do Jesus a friendly service here.[11] In the first place, this is the obvious meaning of what they say: 'Leave and go elsewhere, for Herod wishes to kill you' (Luke 13.31). This admonition is, on the face of it, a plain warning. While it is possible to interpret this warning as a 'scare tactic', a threat that Herod does not really intend to carry out but that will nevertheless serve the function of restricting Jesus' activity,[12] still, in view of the role that Herod shortly plays in the Lucan passion narrative, such a motivation appears unlikely; but, in any case, however we are to understand Herod's motive here, it is difficult to see how a deceitful motive can be attributed to the Pharisees, since, furthermore – Loisy's remark about Jesus' response to the Pharisees notwithstanding – nothing in his response indicates anything about the Pharisees other than that they are serving the role of neutral and innocent ambassadors and have, in fact, his interest at heart.[13]. Jesus' criticism falls on Herod,[14] not on the Pharisees. When one then brings the evidence of the Pharisees' behaviour in Acts to bear on Luke 13.31, one is left really with only one possible understanding of the Pharisees' motive in warning Jesus. It is sincere.[15]

Luke goes quite beyond this one warning to Jesus, however, in representing the Pharisees as friendly not only to the church but to Jesus as well, for in Luke Jesus is a regular dinner guest of Pharisees.[16] In Luke 7.36 and in 11.37 a Pharisee invites Jesus to dinner (which invitations he accepts), and in 14.1 he is found again going to dine at a Pharisee's house, presumably by invitation. Thus, of the six meals that Jesus takes in others' homes in Luke, half are in the homes of Pharisees! Frequent invitations to dinner are not a sign of hostility. In addition, furthermore, Luke has scrupulously kept the Pharisees out of the passion narrative.[17] Their pronounced appearance at the Triumphal Entry into Jerusalem (Luke 19.39) is their last appearance in Luke-Acts until Acts 5, where Gamaliel plays his aforementioned role. The Pharisees seek to defend the early apostles and Paul, and they have nothing to do with the crucifixion of Jesus. It is therefore not surprising that they also have nothing to do with the martyrdoms of Stephen (Acts 7–8) and of James (Acts 12), the other Christian martyrdoms reported in Acts. Thus the Pharisaic friendliness to Jesus and to the church in Luke-Acts has two sides, an active and a passive. On the active side, they display overt friendliness and attempt to protect Jesus and his followers; on the passive side, they have nothing to do with any of the martyrdoms. No wonder that F. C. Baur could note that Luke 'almost . . . make[s] the Pharisees into Christians'.[18]

Belief in the resurrection

Baur's remark also, of course, had another facet of the Lucan portrayal of the Pharisees in view, one which I have barely avoided mentioning above; that is that the Pharisees, like the Christians, believe in the resurrection.[19] It is this chord that Paul strikes when he is examined in the Sanhedrin in Acts 23; for, not only does he announce (v. 6) that he is a Pharisee, he also plays on the sympathies of the Pharisees in the Sanhedrin by claiming that he is on trial 'concerning the hope and the resurrection of the dead'. When he then tells Herod Agrippa that he is in custody 'because of the hope of the promise to [the Israelite] fathers' (26.6), just after announcing that he is a Pharisee (v. 5), we are apparently to understand that he refers to that shared hope of the resurrection; and the same will be true in Acts 28.20, where he tells the Roman Jews, this time without mentioning his Pharisaic origins, that he is there 'on account of the hope of Israel'. This is to say that, while Paul's language in Acts 26.6 and 28.20 does not specifically include reference to the resurrection and might, in fact, be taken in a broader sense,[20] nevertheless the connection with the resurrection has already been made in 23.6, and the reader will presumably not have forgotten that.[21]

Of course, Luke has quite overstated his case here, since it is obvious that Christians and Pharisees do not really have the same belief in the resurrection, inasmuch as

Christians believe that *Jesus* has risen from the dead (also Vielhauer, 'Paulinism', p. 41). One might even wonder if Luke actually expected his readers to fall for this platitude. The motif of Christianity as the true and authentic Judaism (cf. above in ch. 3), has, however, doubtless overwhelmed all other considerations on this point. So also Maddox, *Purpose*, p. 41, emphatically; similarly Haenchen, *Acts*, p. 102. Roloff, *Apostelgeschichte*, p. 328, says that Luke is 'simplifying' here in representing 'Christians as true Pharisees'. Haenchen, 'Source Material', p. 278, refers the simplification, probably correctly, to Luke's apologetic interest.

Conflict in the Gospel narrative

Of course, it is not the case that the Pharisees are as consistently friendly with Jesus and his followers in Luke-Acts as the episodes just recalled here; there are occasions of conflict. Even the conflict, however, is contained within certain limits. As we have already noted, the Pharisees are kept entirely out of the Lucan passion narrative, and they have nothing whatsoever to do with the Christian martyrdoms in Acts. This is in spite of one appearance of Pharisees in the Marcan passion narrative (Mark 12.13), where the Pharisees are baiting Jesus. Furthermore, Pharisees do not plot against Jesus in Luke as they do in Mark and Matthew. Thus, whereas Mark says plainly at the conclusion of the narrative of Jesus' healing the man with the withered hand on the Sabbath (Mark 3.1–6) that 'the Pharisees immediately took counsel with the Herodians against him about how they could destroy him' (v. 6; similarly Matt. 12.14), Luke moves the Pharisees to the beginning of the narrative, where they become the subject of Mark's subjectless verb 'kept an eye on' (Mark 3.1 par. Luke 6.7), and he does not mention them again at the end of the narrative (as does Mark), where he writes that 'they were quite disorientated and discussed among themselves what they might do to Jesus' (Luke 6.11).[22] To be sure, 'they' here are certainly still the scribes and Pharisees from v. 7, but Luke has reduced their presence at the end of the episode by mentioning them earlier instead of later and by writing only 'they (αὐτοί)' at the end; and he has, furthermore, turned a clear plot against Jesus into something rather more vague. Luke does not want the charge of plotting Jesus' arrest laid at the door of the Pharisees, and Luke-Acts contains no such plot on their part.[23] In what ways, then, is the Pharisaic hostility towards Jesus and his followers portrayed in Luke-Acts?

If we leave aside for the moment, taking a clue from the preceding chapter, what Jesus says to or about the Pharisees and confine our attention to their behaviour in the narrative, we see that, quite strangely, Luke has omitted nearly all the instances of Pharisaic hostility towards Jesus that appear in Mark and Matthew and has substituted his own. In addition to what he has done in Luke 6.7, 11, he has only 'some' claim that Jesus is in league with Beelzebul (Luke 11.15), whereas Mark 3.22 had attributed the charge to the scribes and Matt. 12.24 to the Pharisees; and the introduction to the saying about divorce (Matt. 19.3–8 par. Mark 10.2–10)[24] – which in Matthew, in any case, is a *Streitgespräch* with the Pharisees 'trying him' – simply does not appear in Luke, which includes only the saying *minus* the introduction (Luke 16.18 par. Mark 10.11–12; Matt. 19.9). As we have also noted already, Luke has it that scribes and priests – not Pharisees, as in Mark (Luke 20.20; Mark 12.13) – bait Jesus in the passion narrative on the issue of tribute to Caesar. We also need to note, in addition to these instances of Lucan omission of Pharisaic hostility, one reduction; in Luke 6.2 it is only 'some of the Pharisees' who inquire about the Sabbath behaviour of Jesus' disciples, not, as in Mark and Matthew, 'the Pharisees'.[25]

In spite of these reductions of evidences of Pharisaic hostility,[26] however, Luke has introduced five instances of their opposition that do not appear in Mark or Matthew.[27] In Luke 5.21 it is Pharisees who suggest (cf. Mark 2.7; Matt. 9.3) that Jesus may be blaspheming by forgiving the sins of the paralytic; and Luke introduces his parable ch. 15 by noting that Pharisees and scribes are 'grumbling' because Jesus 'receives sinners and eats with them' (Luke 15.2). After the invective against the Pharisees and 'legists' in ch. 11 (par. Matthew 23), Luke includes the conclusion, which does not appear in Matthew, that 'the scribes and the Pharisees began to have a terrible grudge and to ask him about all kinds of things, lurking to catch him in something that he would say' (Luke 11.53); and in 16.14 he writes that 'the Pharisees, being lovers of money, . . . derided' Jesus. Finally, in 19.39, he writes that 'some of the Pharisees' wanted Jesus to 'scold' his disciples because of their hailing Jesus at the triumphal entry. In addition to these cases, furthermore, the behaviour of Jesus' Pharisaic hosts in chs. 7 and 14 is ambiguous, since, although they invite him to dine, his host in the one case (7.39) questions his prophetic powers and his association with a sinner, while the Pharisees in the other case (14.1) 'were keeping an eye on him'.[28] Surely Luke, by omitting some references to Pharisaic hostility and by introducing others,[29] has sought to present the Pharisees in a particular way. Mere references to a 'special Lucan source' are inadequate to explain his

intent, for the reasons that have already been noted at length in the
previous chapters;[30] Luke intends something. If we now add to our
evidence the other places where, in agreement with Mark and
Matthew, Pharisees figure in Luke's narrative, we shall be able to
gain a reasonably good picture of that intent.

   In Luke 5.30, Luke agrees with Mark 2.16 that 'the Pharisees and
their scribes' (Mark had written 'the scribes of the Pharisees') raised
the question with Jesus' disciples about their eating and drinking
with 'toll collectors and sinners'; in 5.33 par. Mark 2.18, the same
questioners as in 5.30 (again somewhat different from Mark, who
had 'John's disciples and the Pharisees') ask why Jesus does not fast;
in 6.2, 'some of the Pharisees' (Mark 2.24: 'the Pharisees') confront
the disciples with their apparent breaking of the Sabbath by working;
and in 11.37–38 par. Matt. 15.1–2 (cf.also Mark 7.1–5) the Pharisee
who invited Jesus to dinner (this is, of course, the Lucan touch) is
'amazed that he did not first wash before the meal' (similarly Mark
7.5; Matt. 15.2). Thus the only conflict scenes between Jesus and the
Pharisees that Luke has taken over from Mark and from Q or
Matthew are scenes in which the Pharisees are objecting to Jesus'
(or his disciples') breaking the Torah – or, perhaps more precisely,
to Jesus' and his disciples' *peculiar way of following* the Torah, to their
halakah. A particular instance of this variant 'life-style' is Jesus'
association with sinners (Luke 5.30). This theme, then, also governs
two of the five conflict scenes that Luke has added. The Pharisaic
'grumbling' of Luke 15.2 repeats the theme of 5.30 par. Mark 2.16,
where the issue was eating with sinners; and the issue of proper
interpretation of Torah also lies behind 11.53, for, if the Pharisees
are going 'to ask [Jesus] about all kinds of things' in order 'to catch
him out in something that he would say', then it would appear that
they have discussions about Torah interpretation in mind. Naturally,
of course, the preceding invective against the Pharisees and legists
in Luke 11.39–52 has been extremely provocative, so that a motive
of revenge is natural, but both the way in which the hope for
vengeance is put ('ask . . . about all kinds of things'; 'catch him out
in something that he would say') and the content of the invective
lead to the conclusion that the vengeance is to be sought in a
discussion about the Law; for Jesus had said in the invective that the
Pharisaic manner of cleansing was improper (v. 39), that the
Pharisees did not lay sufficient weight on almsgiving (v. 41), that
they tithed improperly (v. 42), and that the scriptural interpretation

of the legists was such as to keep people away from God's salvation rather than to bring them to it (v. 52). Thus even if the rest of the invective is cast in more general terms (e.g., the Pharisees 'love the first seats in synagogues', v. 43), it has indicated disagreement over *halakah* sufficently to make the orientation of the Pharisees' hope for vengeance clear. When they 'hope to catch him out in something that he would say', then they wish to best him in a discussion of Torah.[31] Luke has therefore, so it would appear, gone to considerable lengths to define the Pharisaic opposition to Jesus, over against Mark and Matthew, as being limited to questions of *halakah* or Torah interpretation.[32] That he dines with sinners is mentioned twice (and both times the Pharisees are said to γογγύζειν).

S. G. Wilson thinks that he sees in Jesus' discussions with the Pharisees about Sabbath observance an example of the way in which Luke presented the issue of Christian obligation to the Torah ambiguously in the Gospel.[33] According to Wilson (he refers specifically to Luke 6.1–5), one cannot tell whether Luke meant to show that Jesus and his followers 'remain[ed] under obligation to sabbath law', or whether he intended to show that 'the law . . . is subordinate to Jesus'. He thinks that Luke's interest is primarily 'christological' and that 'Luke nowhere makes the distinction between law and tradition'. Aside from the fact that Wilson has here and elsewhere mistaken practice for tradition, his general point is mistaken; for Luke certainly does want to distinguish between Torah and *halakah*, between divine intent and practice. The argument with the Pharisees about the Sabbath is not about the holiness of the Sabbath but about the way in which one must keep the Sabbath holy. The thirty-nine classes of work are not in the Torah.

All the instances of Pharisaic opposition to Jesus in Luke fall into this category of Torah interpretation except three, all uniquely Lucan. In Luke 5.21, as we recall, Pharisees accuse Jesus of blasphemy when he pronounces someone's sins forgiven, and in 19.39 they encourage him to scold his disciples after the disciples have acclaimed him on the occasion of the triumphal entry into Jerusalem. One possible explanation of both these instances is that Jesus is represented as divine in both, and that Luke shows that Pharisees react against such a notion. Inasmuch as the forgiveness of sins is properly reserved to God, the Pharisees' claim in Luke 5.21 that Jesus is blaspheming would then be understandable.[34] Further, only Luke among the Synoptic Evangelists puts the term 'the King' into the quotation of Ps. 118.26 on the occasion of Jesus' triumphal entry into Jerusalem (Luke 19.38), thus perhaps making understandable the Pharisaic reaction that the disciples who voiced such blasphemy are in need of correction. Still, while such an explanation of these two occasions of Pharisaic opposition to Jesus seems reasonable, other possibilities also suggest themselves. For example, we note that, in the account of the healing of the paralytic, the forgiving of whose sins had provoked the Pharisaic charge of blasphemy, there is a shift in audience attitude at the end of the story. Here the 'amazement [that] took hold of everyone' and the 'fear [with which] they were filled' (Luke 5.26) must have taken hold of and filled the Pharisees along with everyone else, and the Pharisees must have joined in the common statement, 'We have seen something contrary to reason'. But if that is so, if we are to think of the Pharisees as making this statement along with everyone else, then Luke has shown them to have a certain change of mind; for, whereas earlier they did not hesitate to say that Jesus was 'speaking blasphemies', after the healing they are uncertain. Perhaps Luke intended, in a sense, the reader to see both themes: 1. the Pharisees consider Jesus' proposal to forgive sins blasphemy, since such a proposal assumes divine prerogatives, but 2. the ensuing miracle is so impressive that everyone (including the Pharisees) has to wonder about the earlier premise and, in fact, simply does not know what to think.

There is also another possibility for understanding the Pharisees' call for a rebuke of the disciples who have just called Jesus king (Luke 19.38–39), and that is that they are encouraging caution.[35] If in 13.31 they warned Jesus away from Jerusalem, out of fear for his safety, then the same motive might prompt them to encourage Jesus to quiet those who would make such claims for him as to get him into difficulty with the authorities.[36] It seems unwise to make a hard choice among these alternatives, however, inasmuch as Luke's clues in both episodes are a bit soft. If the former uniform explanation is correct, then Luke portrays the Pharisees as hostile to Jesus on two points, his loose interpretation and following of Torah (the major bone of contention) and his implied claims to divinity (not as important as the previous issue).[37] Alternatively, however, it is possible to understand Luke 5.17–26 and 19.38–39 in such ways that Pharisaic hostility seems not to be the real issue in the two passages, in which case we are left only with opposition in the matter of Torah and *halakah*. Certainty here does not seem possible. Finally, the Pharisaic 'deriding' of Jesus in Luke 16.14 lacks a meaningful context and appears groundless. Jesus' preceding saying (v. 13) about human inability to serve two masters could hardly have been objectionable to either real or Lucan Pharisees. Furthermore, Luke's slander that they are φιλάργυροι (lovers of money) is without basis in the Gospel or Acts. We learn from this brief statement, therefore, that Luke has a profound dislike for Pharisees and that he thinks of them as making light of Jesus, but the grounds for both escape us.[38]

G.Schneider, *Lukas*, vol. 2, p. 336, explains that the Pharisees 'laugh at Jesus' because, being lovers of money, they reject Jesus' explanation that one cannot 'serve Mammon' and God at the same time. While this connection with v. 13 is doubtless correct, it still adds little to our understanding of Luke's opinion of the Pharisees, for Luke will have thought in this way: 'I want to introduce Pharisees here again criticizing Jesus; since I just included the saying about not serving "Mammon", I'll make them criticize him for that and explain their critical attitude by pointing out that they are φιλάργυροι.' For us to see that, however, does not help us to understand what it is about the Pharisees that Luke does not like. When Schneider further (ibid.) tries to connect the slander of v. 14 to Jesus' sayings about the Pharisees in v. 15 - and also in 11.39,42,43 – he is in one sense correct, since, as we shall see, those sayings present Luke's opinion of the Pharisees clearly enough; nevertheless, Jesus does not, in those sayings, refer to a Pharisaic greed. Verse 14 is merely a Lucan slander.

In the opinion of Schottroff and Stegemann, *Jesus von Nazareth*, p. 123, the Lucan Jesus here addresses not real Pharisees, but rich people in the church, and that explanation 'does not even need to be justified here again'. That is a blatant dodge.

Distinctions among Pharisees

Before we return to Acts, one other aspect of Luke's portrayal of the Pharisees in the Gospel that has been alluded to before needs to be emphasized, and that is that Luke contradicts Mark and Matthew by distinguishing Pharisee from Pharisee. The singular 'Pharisee' never appears in Mark and occurs in Matthew only in 23.26, where the meaning is not, nevertheless, that an individual is intended. In this case, at the conclusion of the Matthaean version of the invective against the scribes and Pharisees, Jesus employs the vocative singular 'blind Pharisee (Φαρισαῖε τυφλέ)' when he challenges the Pharisees to 'cleanse first the inside of the cup'. Thus the singular here is merely a form of address to Pharisees in general; it does not single out an individual Pharisee. Luke, however, shows at an early stage that he is willing to make distinctions among the Pharisees when in 6.2 he changes Mark's 'the Pharisees' to '*some of* the Pharisees', who inquire about the propriety of the disciples' Sabbath behaviour. Also, Luke's introduction to the invective against the Pharisees and legists in ch. 11 is quite different from Mark and Matthew just in this respect; for, whereas Mark 7.1; Matt. 15.1 had indicated that scribes and Pharisees from Jerusalem were Jesus' interlocutors when the hand-washing question came up (the episode that in Luke forms the introduction to the invective against the Pharisees and legists), Luke puts only one Pharisee – who had, incidentally, invited Jesus to dinner – into the picture and lets him ask the leading question (Luke 11.37–38). Furthermore, two of the Lucan additions to the Synoptic corpus of Pharisaic material also make this distinction. In Luke 7.37–39 it is *the* Pharisee who has invited Jesus to dinner who wonders about Jesus' prophetic ability; and in Luke 19.39 it is '*some of* the Pharisees' who encourage Jesus to scold his disciples. In all these scenes of conflict between Jesus and Pharisees,[39] Luke has seen to it that his readers know that it is only 'some of the Pharisees' or 'a Pharisee' who questions the propriety of Jesus' behaviour. The conclusion seems unavoidable that Luke wants to make it clear that not all Pharisees opposed Jesus, even on the more narrowly defined ground of opposition that Luke presents. This drawing of distinctions regarding Pharisaic opposition is thus the counterpoint to the friendliness of the Pharisees towards Jesus and the church in Luke-Acts, which in the Gospel finds its positive expression in the Pharisaic invitations to dinner and the warning about Herod's plans. If we now return to Acts, other parts of the portrait will come into view.

Pharisees in the narrative of Acts

In Acts, the distinction that Luke makes between Pharisee and Pharisee is different from the distinctions that he made in the Gospel. The distinctions in the Gospel have to do with opposition to Jesus' behaviour; often it is only 'some' Pharisees or 'a' Pharisee who questions his behaviour. The point there seems to be that, while some Pharisees opposed Jesus' *halakah*, not all did, and some were friendly to him. In Acts, while a distinction is made, it is not the same distinction, so that one may not think that Luke reproduced in the Acts the distinctions between Pharisee and Pharisee found in the Gospel. What the Gospel and Acts have in common is that some Pharisees are friendly to Jesus and to the church and that distinctions are to be made among Pharisees; in Acts, however, the Pharisees who are friendly to the church are non-Christians, and the Pharisees who cause the problems are Christian Pharisees![40] Thus all appear-ances of Pharisees in Acts are friendly except for that of the Christian Pharisees in Acts 15.5, who propose the following solution to the problem created by the success of the Gentile mission: 'It is necessary to circumcise [the Gentile Christians] and to admonish them to keep the Law of Moses.'[41] Now, surely every reader of the present work readily recognizes such a proposal as one that Luke, himself, would find unacceptable and even abhorrent.[42] It flies in the face of all that his hero Paul sought to accomplish; and the conclusion of the Apostolic Council (Acts 15.6–29), which is convened to deal with the proposal made by the Christian Pharisees, sets their proposal aside. Luke clearly favours that conclusion. The position of the Christian Pharisees of Acts 15.5, that Gentile converts to Christianity must be at the same time full converts to Judaism, is rendered null and void in the Acts of the Apostles. (We shall return later to the issue of whether the Lucan conclusion to the Apostolic Council is in fact some kind of compromise between the position of the Christian Pharisees and the prior practice of the Gentile mission.)

We see, therefore, that the one appearance of Pharisees in Acts as obstructionist is an appearance of *Christian* Pharisees who disagree with what we might call Luke's *halakah*, i.e., Luke's interpretation of how Gentile Christians ought to live in fidelity or in harmony with the Mosaic Torah. Stated in other terms, the obstructionist Pharisees of Acts 15.5 disagree with Luke on the criteria for Gentiles' being church members. This brief appearance, therefore, provides the clue for understanding the variegated portrait of the Pharisees in the Gospel, for those Pharisees in the Gospel who correspond to the Christian Pharisees in Acts are not the ones who are *friendly* to Jesus but those who *oppose* him because of what they consider his misinterpretation of Torah and his improper associations. This must then be why Luke reduces the Pharisaic opposition in the Gospel almost entirely to this one issue; the Pharisees in the Gospel who oppose Jesus are, for Luke, prototypes of traditionally Jewish Chri-stians (like the Pharisees in Acts 15.5). They 'grumble' because Jesus 'receives sinners and eats with them' (Luke 15.2) or because he eats and drinks with 'toll collectors and sinners' (5.30); they ask why he does not fast (5.33); they question whether some Sabbath behaviour is proper (6.2), and they raise their eyebrows over the fact that he does not wash his hands before dining (15.1–2). These are halachic issues. In fact, therefore, inasmuch as Luke identifies as Pharisees those Jewish Christians in Acts who uphold the strictly (as some people put it today) 'Torathic' Jewish position, we might even go so far as to say that Jesus' Pharisaic opponents in the Gospel *stand for* traditionally Jewish Christians. It thus would appear that, in Luke's opinion, there were those in the early Jewish church who opposed accepting Gentiles who did not become at the same time full proselytes to Judaism, who also opposed other aspects of Jesus' practice and insisted rather on maintaining a stricter *halakah*, and who, perhaps, opposed the claims of Jesus' divinity made by at least some of their fellow Christians. Whether such a 'party' actually existed within early Jewish Christianity and whether, if it did, it was a 'Pharisaic party' is not our purpose to determine here. Its existence is not improbable, and there is certainly evidence from other early Christian literature that at least some of the positions that Luke attributes to his Christian Pharisees did, in fact, exist in early Jewish Christianity. We are not, therefore, dealing with a Lucan distortion here, as was the case with 'the Jews' crucifying Jesus.

There is, furthermore, a certain propriety in Luke's identifying such a group as 'Pharisaic', inasmuch as it was the Pharisees who were primarily interested in *halakah*. Nevertheless, there is good reason for preferring the more general term 'traditional Jews' here as a better description than 'Pharisees' of the group that Luke wishes to characterize by the role that he allots to the Pharisees. While on the one hand, *in Luke's day* (i.e., after the destruction of Jerusalem), the Pharisees were the only one of the earlier parties or groups within Judaism that still had any significant role among the Jewish people, the Sadducees and Essenes having gone into eclipse as a result of the Roman destructions, on the other hand, when Luke has his Christian Pharisees, in Acts 15.5, call for circumcision and obedience to Torah, he attributes to them a position that might well have been upheld by many religious Jews other than Pharisees. (One could hardly, for example, imagine Christians who had come out of Qumran requiring anything less for Gentile converts.) Thus it seems that Luke uses 'Pharisees' to stand for Christian Jews who are religious in the sense of giving strict allegiance to the Law of Moses, and for this reason it seems better to refer to those characterized as being 'Christian Pharisees' as traditionally Jewish Christians. Cf. the remark of Schoeps, *Theologie und Geschichte*, p. 259, that the Christian Pharisees of Acts 15.5 represent the 'extreme Jewish Christian group' in early Christianity, and that they are the true 'ancestors of the later Ebionites'; cf. further the evidence collected by Dunn, *Unity and Diversity*, p. 240.

We have noted that, both in the Gospel and in Acts, Luke has two groups of Pharisees. The distinction is clearer in Acts – where Christian Pharisees who have wrong ideas about Torah observance are distinguished from non-Christian Pharisees, who are quite friendly and helpful to the church – than it is in the Gospel, but the distinction is nevertheless there; and the unfriendly Pharisees in both volumes symbolize the same people – the traditionally Jewish Christians whom Luke does not like. What, however, is the function of the other Pharisees, the friendly but non-Christian ones? Again it is Acts that is clearer. The friendliness demonstrated by the behaviour of the non-Christian Pharisees in Acts, by the fact that Paul was a Pharisee, and by the common belief in the resurrection points, it would seem, to an important moment in Lucan theology that was discussed at length in the last chapter, namely that Christianity is the true and authentic Judaism. The friendly, non-Christian Pharisees in Acts underscore the linkage between Christianity and the ancestral Israelite religion. While they do not themselves become Christians, they and Paul repeatedly score Luke's point that Christianity is not something radically different from the older Israelite religion but is rather just one small step removed from the religion of the 'very best party' in Judaism.[43]

That this is the function of Luke's friendly Pharisees has been exactly seen by F. Keck, *Abschiedsrede*, pp. 26–28. 'The Pharisees', he writes, 'are . . . in Acts demonstrably an element by which Luke exhibits the continuity that exists between church and Judaism' (op. cit., p. 28). Unfortunately, however, Keck has overlooked the role of the Christian Pharisees in Acts 15.5 and of Jesus' frequent rebukes of the Pharisees in the Gospel and thus thinks that Luke presents all Pharisees in the friendly mode. Haenchen, also, who gave some attention to the Pharisees in his commentary, failed to take sufficiently into account the Lucan hostility towards the Pharisees and so also understood them as Luke's way of demonstrating that Christianity shares with Judaism the true belief in the resurrection (*Acts*, pp. 101–2). Haenchen then (ibid., p. 444, n. 6) brought the Christian Pharisees of Acts 15.5 into connection with Paul's statement in 26.5 that they are the 'very best party' in Judaism – that is, the very best Jews support circumcision and Torah observance. Incidentally, one can thus see here how mistaken interpretations can come from considering only Luke or Acts to the exclusion of the other. It is therefore more surprising when Fitzmyer, *Luke*, vol. 1, p. 581, follows this path and asserts that Acts 26.5 gives 'Luke's evaluation of' the Pharisees. Schmithals, *Apostelgeschichte*, p. 11, thinks that Luke wants to emphasize how close Christianity and Pharisaism are because, after the Jewish–Roman wars, Pharisaism was that branch of Judaism that received some Roman approval. There seems to be no evidence for this explanation, however, and it fails to deal with the element of conflict in the portrayal of the Pharisees.

Are these friendly non-Christian Pharisees in Acts, then, identical with those in the Gospel who invite Jesus to dinner and who warn him of Herod's plans (the positive side of the Pharisaic friendliness in the Gospel)? That is not so clear. 'Identical' would, in any case, hardly be the word; 'derivative' perhaps. But it is also possible that the Pharisaic friendliness in the Gospel is related at least as much to Luke's using the Pharisees to represent traditionally Jewish Christians as it is to the issue of continuity. The continuity is not expressed in connection with the friendly Pharisees in the Gospel, as it is in Acts, and it is precisely the friendly Pharisees in the Gospel who receive Jesus' attacks on them (which we are just about to take up in detail). These observations might incline one rather towards the view that *all* the Pharisees in the Gospel represent, in one way or another, the traditionally Jewish Christianity that Luke does not like. On the one hand, they are overtly friendly towards Jesus and certainly have nothing whatsoever to do with his martyrdom (anticipating their eventual conversion), while, on the other hand, Pharisees in the Gospel oppose Jesus' stance with regard to the Torah (anticipating the eventual opposition of traditionally Jewish Christians to Luke's kind of Gentile Christianity). In Acts, while the obstructionist Pharisees continue to represent the traditional Jewish Christianity, the friendly Pharisees are employed in another way than in the Gospel, i.e., to help to make Luke's point about Christianity as the authentic Judaism.

No one makes clearer than Loisy how much the friendliness towards Christianity of these 'authentic Jews' is the product of Luke's 'narrative skill' (i.e., in Loisy's terms, of the redactor's skill in writing fiction). Loisy, ruminating on Gamaliel's advice in Acts 5.34 (*Actes*, pp. 290–1), observes that it is one thing to discuss the 'abstract principle' of letting things work out according to divine plan but something quite different to make a 'rule' of the principle. The thinking behind Gamaliel's reasoning, Loisy concludes, is that such a rule makes perfect sense to Luke, since in his day the Christian preaching was already successful! When Rackham, *Acts*, pp. 73–4, explains Gamaliel's ploy as being 'opportunist' in order to keep the rival Sadducees from doing away with an ally (Christianity), he quite misses the point. Roloff, *Apostelgeschichte*, p. 101, thinks that the Pharisees supported Christianity as long as the Christians kept the Law, and he thus explains the proposal of the Pharisees in Acts 15.5 as a reaction to a change in Christian policy. In this, he has failed adequately to distinguish Christian from non-Christian Pharisees, for the non-Christian Pharisees are still friendly *after* Acts 15.5.

Paul as Pharisee

There is one other facet of the friendly-Pharisee complex in Acts that still has not received adequate explanation, and that is Paul's

Pharisaism. Is not Paul's Pharisaism, which Luke emphasizes, a third type of Pharisaism, a friendly but Christian type? Probably it is, but there are some problems with such a description. Especially we note that Paul's Pharisaism is always mentioned only in his defence.

Thus used, it has nothing to do with his having persecuted the church in his pre-Christian days, as Löning states and as Klein strongly implies (cf. Löning, 'Paulinismus', p. 213; G. Klein, *Zwölf Apostel*, pp. 122–4; cf. further Löning, 'Paulinismus', p. 217, and *Saulustradition*, pp. 166, 170, 175–6). When Paul first persecutes the church (Acts 9) nothing is said about his being a Pharisee; and later, when he recalls that he earlier persecuted the church (Acts 22.4), he also does not mention his Pharisaism, and vice versa (Acts 23.6). Even when the two motifs are juxtaposed (Acts 26.4–12), no connection is made between them, but they are rather two points in his defence: 1. I have been an exemplary Jew, a Pharisee; 2. don't think that I was some kind of 'Christian-lover', for I even persecuted them. His persecution of the church is thus not 'typically' Pharisaic, as Löning and Klein seem to think.

The first time that the Lucan Paul uses the defence (Acts 23.6–9) he does so in connection with belief in the resurrection; he is a Pharisee and believes in the resurrection. As we have already had occasion to note, this theme recurs. To the degree that Luke brings out that Pharisees believe in the resurrection, he shows the straight-line development of Christianity from 'biblical Israel' – that is, Christianity does not represent a break with the tradition, since even non-Christian Pharisees believe, as do Christians, in the resurrection. In this sense, Luke presents a gradation of groups in the development from 'biblical Israel', with the Christians being in direct continuity;[44] the Pharisees, while wrong in not becoming Christians, still partly right in believing in the resurrection; and other Jews being altogether wrong or 'off the track'. That Paul's Pharisaism and his belief in the resurrection are mentioned together is thus a particular case in Luke's theology of the Israelite–Christian continuum.

But we must inquire somewhat more closely into the function of Paul's Pharisaic defence in Acts 23. Luke states that Paul brought up this point in his defence (v. 6) after he 'recognized that one faction [in the Sanhedrin] was Sadducee and the other Pharisaic', and that the result of this ploy was an argument between the factions that quite disrupted the hearing (vv. 9–10). In other words, the function of Paul's Pharisaic defence in Acts 23.6 is not so much to impress upon the reader that Paul believes in the resurrection *as Pharisee* as to show what a disharmonious and confused bunch the Jews are, how easily they can be thrown off the track by Luke's intelligent hero, and how, of course, they are unable to convict Paul of anything. To be sure, the ploy makes sense only if Pharisees believe in the resurrection, and Luke explains that fact in v. 8, but Paul is not affirming in any serious way his Pharisaic beliefs, he is just playing a trick on his audience. One might say that, as in Acts 9.22, Paul 'was confusing' his Jewish audience.

The one other time that Paul's Pharisaism is mentioned is again in a defence, this time before Herod (Acts 26.4–5). Here the defence is serious, i.e. not of the nature of a trick, and what Paul emphasizes is the righteousness of his life – that is, that he has been an exemplary Jew, even a Pharisee (v. 5).[45] How ironic (thus the implication) that so blameless a Jew should be charged with crimes against the state precisely by his fellow Jews! And for what? For nothing more than his Jewish belief in the resurrection (v. 6).[46] The readers are surely not expected to have forgotten the point made earlier that Pharisees believe in the resurrection, but Luke's way of putting together Paul's Pharisaism and his belief in 'the hope of the promise to the [Israelite] fathers' is not such as to emphasize that this belief in the resurrection is something that he holds *as a Pharisee*. Indeed, Luke specifically adds that this hope is one for which *all Israelites* (τὸ δωδεκάφυλον ἡμῶν) yearn; and he has Paul make the same point in his defence before Felix, Acts 24.15. The motifs of being a Pharisee and of believing in the resurrection belong together, rather in the 'Why are they accusing me? I'm such a good Jew' defence. When Paul then adds that he used to persecute Christians (vv. 10–12), the orientation is the same. All these things – his Pharisaism, his belief in the resurrection, and his persecution of the church – are aspects of his defence; they prove that he is a blameless Jew.[47] Thus Paul's Pharisaism is, indeed, different from that of the Pharisaic Christians of Acts 15.5 as well as from that of the non-Christian friendly Pharisees; for Paul is a Pharisee *mutatis mutandis* – that is, he is a Christianized Pharisee, not a Pharisaic Christian.

Let us bring together what we have seen of Pharisaic behaviour in Luke-Acts. In Acts there are, aside from Paul, two groups, the friendly non-Christian Pharisees, who share with Christians the belief in the resurrection and who try to help the Christians out of difficulties with the authorities, and the obstructionist Christian Pharisees, who promote the (for Luke) ridiculous idea that Gentile

Christians ought to be circumcised and ought to follow the Law of Moses. It is probably better to say that, in the Gospel, the Pharisees are viewed under a dual aspect than that they are divided into two groups. On the one hand they are like the friendly non-Christian Pharisees in Acts and thus invite Jesus to dinner and try to keep him out of difficulty with the authorities, but on the other hand they have serious disagreements with him over matters of Torah interpretation, appearing in this respect like the obstructionist Christian Pharisees of Acts. It seems that Luke has portrayed the Pharisees in this strange way in order to let them represent the position within Christianity of traditional Jews, with the added nuance that the friendly Pharisees in Acts help him to demonstrate the continuity between ancient Judaism and Christianity.

The Pharisees in speech – Gospel

Now we must examine what Jesus says to and about the Pharisees in Luke. The way in which the Pharisees are present in speech and in narrative in Luke-Acts is somewhat analogous to the way, as we saw in the last chapter, in which 'the Jews' as a whole appear, although the Pharisees are by no means duplicates of 'the Jews'. Whereas the narrative of Luke-Acts sketched a development on the part of 'the Jews' from friendliness to hostility, no such Pharisaic development takes place in the course of the narrative, although there are certain differences between the Gospel and Acts, as we have seen. In what is said to and about the Pharisees, however, we do have an exact analogy to what is said to and about 'the Jews' in speeches in Luke-Acts, for what Jesus says of the Pharisees in the Gospel undergoes no development or alteration, and it lets us see exactly what Luke thinks of Pharisees.

The invective against 'scribes and Pharisees, hypocrites' in Matthew 23 is certainly among the better known parts of the New Testament, and we may conveniently begin our examination of the Pharisees as they appear in speech in Luke by taking note of what Luke does with this invective.[48] Whether or not Luke has the more original form of this invective is of no moment for the present investigation, since our purpose is to understand Luke's own presentation,[49] but we need to remind ourselves that a great deal of the invective that appears in Matthew does not appear in Luke:[50] Matt. 23.2–3, 'The scribes and the Pharisees sit on Moses' seat', but you are to do what they say, not what they do;[51] Matt. 23.5, 'They do all their deeds to be seen by people, for they broaden their phylacteries and make their fringes bigger'; Matt. 23.8, 'Don't you be called rabbi' (as well as the following advice to the disciples, vv. 8–12); Matt. 23.15, about their seeking proselytes; Matt. 23.16b–22, which has to do with the relation between oath-taking and the Temple and its furnishings; Matt. 23.33, the Pharisees are venomous snakes; and Matt. 23.38, 'Thus on the outside you appear righteous to people, but on the inside you are full of hypocrisy and iniquity.'[52] Because of these differences, we need to exercise due caution when approaching Luke and not let ourselves unwittingly be influenced, while we are reading Luke, by what Matthew says against the Pharisees. To repeat, much of the Matthaean version of the invective does not appear in Luke; Luke has less to say against the Pharisees than does Matthew.[53] In the second place, what Luke does have of the invective of Matthew 23 is not all together in one place,[54] and part of it refers to other persons, not to Pharisees. As far as the location of the sayings goes, the charge of Matt. 23.16 that the scribes and Pharisees are 'blind guides' appears in Luke rather as a general word of advice (not directed to any specific group) in Luke 6.39; and, of course, as we have already noted, Luke places the bulk of the invective that corresponds to Matthew 23 earlier in his Gospel than does Matthew in his, so that Luke does not connect the invective against the Pharisees with the invective against the scribes of Mark 12.27–40. Luke 20.45–47 simply follows Mark 12.27–40, whereas Matthew combines the invective that appears in Luke 11 with the invective against the scribes in Mark 12.27–40 and makes it all refer to Pharisees as well, thus producing the long invective of Matthew 23. Furthermore, in Luke 11, only vv. 39–44 are designated as being against the Pharisees, the rest of the invective (vv. 46–52) being directed only against the 'legists'.[55] Now, whether the Matthaean pattern, according to which all the invective is directed against scribes *and* Pharisees, or the Lucan pattern, in which a brief invective against the Pharisees is followed by a longer one against the legists, is the more original is immaterial for our discussion.[56] Either Luke reproduced from his source the pattern that we find in the Gospel of Luke because he liked it the way it was or he altered the pattern that he found in Matthew or Q to its present form because that was the way that he wanted it. In either case, the polemic against the Pharisees in Luke 11 comprises only six verses and deals mainly with Pharisaic *halakah* (dishwashing, almsgiving, tithing), an aspect of the invective that has been especially well seen by S. G. Wilson,[57] who has observed that it is not 'Pharisaic scrupulosity' as such that is criticized here, but rather 'the neglect of essentials alone'. Thus Luke does not portray the conflict between Jesus and the Pharisees as being over Torah, but as being about *halakah*. Wilson writes, 'Luke apparently saw nothing objectionable in a Pharisaic lifestyle *per se* . . .; he objects only to the neglect of central commands.' Wilson's choice of expression is rather unfortunate, since it is the Pharisaic 'neglect of central commands' that effectively determines the 'Pharisaic lifestyle'; what he means is that Luke objects not to the Pharisaic attempt to do the will of God, expressed in the Torah, but to the Pharisaic *way* of doing that. The invective of Luke 11 concludes with two broadsides (vv. 43–44),[58] that the Pharisees like public acclaim and position and that they are 'like blank gravestones'.[59]

We also note that the Matthaean form of the invective includes the oft-repeated refrain, 'Woe to you, scribes and Pharisees, hypocrites,' which does not appear in Luke. This represents only a formal difference, however,[60] since Luke writes, 'Woe to you,' three times for the Pharisees (vv. 42, 43, 44) and three times for the legists (vv. 46, 47, 52), and since he places at the close of the invective the saying, which Matthew and Mark have elsewhere (Mark 8.15 par. Matt. 16.6), about how one should 'be on guard against the leaven of the Pharisees', to which he then adds, 'Which is hypocrisy' (Luke 12.1).[61] Thus the only meaningful difference between Matthew and Luke on this point is that Luke reserves the charge of hypocrisy for the Pharisees alone.[62] That this is deliberately Lucan is seen in the parallels, for Mark and Matthew agree in placing this saying earlier in their respective Gospels, and neither includes the word 'hypocrisy'. Luke has, therefore, clearly appropriated the saying from another context to make it the conclusion of his invective against the Pharisees and legists, and he has added the word, 'hypocrisy'.[63] The bad leaven of the Pharisees, which works hidden within the dough to spoil the whole, is their hypocrisy.[64]

The legists

Inasmuch as Luke separates the invective against the scribes from that against the Pharisees and calls the scribes not scribes but 'legists', we need to give some attention at this point to this Lucan peculiarity. To begin with, we can be certain that Luke uses 'legist' as another word for 'scribe' and does not think of the legists as a separate group. This becomes obvious at the conclusion of the invective, where (v. 53) it is *scribes* and Pharisees, not legists and Pharisees, who 'began to have a terrible grudge' against Jesus, although the invective had referred to legists, not to scribes. Further, in two of the three places in Luke outside the invective of ch. 11, where legists appear (7.30; 14.3), they are merely the associates of Pharisees, as are the scribes elsewhere. Furthermore, Luke seems to have got the term from Matthew or Q and to have understood it as a variant of 'scribe', as we can see from the way in which the three Synoptic Gospels introduce the Great Commandment. Mark had written that 'one of the scribes' asked Jesus about the commandment (Mark 12.28); but Matthew, shifting the apophthegm to a *Streitgespräch*, first mentions Pharisees and then reports that 'one of them, a legist', put the question to Jesus (Matt. 22.35, the only occurrence of the word νομικός in the Gospels outside Luke). Luke seems to have looked at Mark and Matthew (or Q) together and to have concluded that 'legist' was another term for 'scribe', in so far as scribes are associated with Pharisees and not with priests; and thus he has a 'legist' put the question (Luke 10.25, the remaining occurrence of the term outside ch. 11). Luke seems to have liked this term as an alternative to 'scribe' either as a more understandable term for his Gentile readership or because he thought that it conveyed something that he wanted to convey.[65] Inasmuch as the term 'scribe' predominates in Luke, the former possibility can be ruled out.

What was it, then, that Luke wanted to convey by his occasional use of 'legist' instead of 'scribe'? In part, the term itself answers the question, for its use allows us to see that Luke wants his readers to think of those people associated with Pharisees as being particularly involved with the νόμος, i.e., the Torah. To this degree Luke is abetting his portrayal of the Pharisees as 'Torah maniacs'. Beyond the mere use of the term, however, we have only the invective of ch. 11.

Luke lays three charges on the legists: they 'load people with loads that can hardly be borne' but do not lift a 'finger' to help (11.46). They 'build the tombs of the prophets' (v. 47), which act ties them to the ancestral killing of the prophets (v. 48) and justifies the 'requiring' of 'the blood of all the prophets . . . from this generation' (vv. 50–51). And they 'withhold the keys of knowledge' (v. 52). The first and third charges seem to refer to (first) the unbearable requirements of the Torah according to its Pharisaic interpretation and to (second) the way in which this interpretation locks people out from the true interpretation (i.e., Jesus' interpretation à la Luke). Even though the word βαστάζω is common enough, it seems difficult to avoid the conclusion that Luke wants to make a connection between the legists' loading people up with loads 'that can hardly be borne (δυσβάστακτα)' and Peter's explaining in the Apostolic Council (Acts 15.10) that requiring Gentile converts to Christianity to keep the Torah is 'to put a yoke on the neck of the disciples that neither our fathers nor we have been able to bear (βαστάσαι)'.[66] Since this interpretation of the Torah – that is, Pharisaic *halakah* – is the going one – or, more precisely, is the prime competitor with the Gentile Christian interpretation – it prevents proper knowlege of the Torah, it 'locks up the keys of knowledge'.

These two charges Luke could have laid to the Pharisees, but the middle one, that the legists share complicity in the death of the prophets, he could not. Thus he seems to have employed the legists here, in the one place where he gives them any definition, to accuse the associates of the Pharisees (logically enough) in terms that would have been appropriate for the Pharisees themselves, but also to lay a charge against 'legalistic Judaism' that he would not, in any circumstances, have laid against the Pharisees: killing the prophets. In this way Luke reminds his readers that, while the Pharisees themselves do not share the guilt of 'the Jews', they nevertheless participate with the rest of Judaism in the wrong interpretation of the Torah, which wrong interpretation is tied to the Jewish guilt. Put otherwise, if the Jews could have understood their own scripture they would not always have rejected the purposes of God and killed the prophets, including Jesus. But the Pharisees, who are never said to be guilty, participate in that wrong interpretation of scripture. So where does that leave them?

Other rebukes of the Pharisees by the Lucan Jesus

Luke has made the occasion of the invective in ch. 11 one of Jesus' frequent dinners at a Pharisee's house, and this pattern is also followed on the two other such occasions (Luke 7.36–50; 14.1–6) – that is, every time a Pharisee invites Jesus to dinner Jesus accepts and then takes the opportunity to scold the Pharisees for their incorrect life-style.[67] That is the case not only in Luke 11.37–44, as we have just discussed, but also in 7.36–50. Here also a Pharisee has invited Jesus to dinner;[68] and here also Luke takes the opportunity to have Jesus point out to the Pharisee what is wrong with Pharisaism, for in Luke the sinful woman who anoints Jesus' feet becomes the foil for Jesus' critical dialogue with the Pharisee.[69] The Pharisee thinks, 'If he were a prophet he would have known' the wicked truth about the woman, 'for she is a sinner' (v. 39). The implication seems fairly clear that Jesus is accepting into his company someone whom the Pharisee finds unacceptable. Jesus' response to these thoughts is twofold: first he puts an example (or a parable) to the Pharisee about two debtors whose debts were forgiven, in the one case a large debt and in the other a small, and about their correspondingly large and small gratitude (vv. 40–43), and then he explains in detail how what the woman did for him far surpasses the Pharisee's actions (vv. 44–46).[70] If we draw back a bit from the details of this episode so as to focus on the themes, then we see that Jesus accepts into his company someone whom the Pharisee, who also wishes to be in Jesus' company – he did, after all, invite him to dinner – finds unacceptable because of her sins.[71] Jesus, on the other hand, indicates that the sinner's behaviour toward him (representing contrition?) more than makes up for any absence of traditional righteousness. Thus the issue here is who an acceptable member of Jesus' company is, with Jesus emphasizing attitude (later defined as faith, v. 50), while the Pharisee emphasizes the qualifications of proper behaviour. Perhaps, then, we should see the contrast that Jesus finally draws between the Pharisee and the sinner in vv. 44–46 not as referring to christology,[72] but as referring still to this issue of the proper qualifications for being accepted into Jesus' company. If this interpretation of this episode has anything to commend it, then we see that the Pharisee here is a prototype of those Christian Pharisees in Acts 15.5 who want Gentile Christians to be circumcised and to follow the Law of Moses. The Pharisee Simon, in Luke 7.36–50, also wants only righteous people in Jesus' entourage, not those 'sinners' who get in only on the basis of proper response to Jesus . . . and *belief*; for Jesus concludes this episode extremely pointedly by proclaiming to the sinner that her 'faith has saved' her. It is the criteria for church membership that are under discussion here, not christology.

The term 'church membership' is chosen advisedly in order to do justice to the fact that Luke does not draw a heavy line between *becoming* a Christian and *being* a Christian (as, for example, Paul does). Thus Wilson, *Law*, p. 72, in discussing the Apostolic Decree, observes correctly that 'the issue . . . is . . . not merely post-conversion behaviour but what constitutes true conversion in the first place'.

In Luke 14.1–6 the issue is again *halakah*. A Pharisee – this time one 'of the rulers of the Pharisees' (v. 1)[73] – invites Jesus to dinner on the Sabbath, and Jesus is confronted with a person in need of healing. There follows, then, the halachic discussion: to heal or not to heal on the Sabbath. Jesus bests his Pharisaic opponents (thus the one Pharisee has become in v. 3; legists, too), as we see from the conclusion, 'They were unable to rebut him on these points' (v. 6), and then he carries on with the healing. Thus the opposition has to do again with proper behaviour in view of the Torah.

The brief interchange between Jesus and the Pharisees in Luke 16.14–15 is, as we have already had occasion to note, without sufficient context, so that Luke's description of the Pharisees here (they are 'lovers of money' and 'derid[e]' Jesus) appears as slander.[74] Jesus' response to the Pharisees, however, is quite in line with the theme that has been dominating, as we have been observing, all Jesus' statements to and about the Pharisees – that is, opposition to the insistence of traditionally Jewish Christians that Gentile converts to Christianity must also be converted to Judaism; for here Jesus again addresses briefly the same issue that he had addressed at considerably greater length when he was at the house of the Pharisee Simon (Luke 7.36–50), i.e., the issue of the criteria for church membership. The Pharisees, Jesus says, are 'those who make themselves righteous before people,[75] but God knows [their] hearts'. One might quite justifiably call this saying a capsule summary of the point of Luke 7.36–50. The point of the saying is so obvious that the corollary – that repentance, contrition, and faith in Jesus are, in Jesus' view, the proper path to take in order to be made righteous – does not even need to be expressed.

The Pharisees in parables

Luke also uses several parables to make his point about the Pharisees. Especially noteworthy is the trilogy in Luke 15,[76] which follows the note that the Pharisees and scribes are 'grumbling' because of Jesus' association with 'sinners' (Luke 15.2). Jesus replies with three parables. In the first (vv. 4–7) a shepherd rejoices greatly over a lost sheep that he is able to recover, not over ninety-nine sheep that stayed in the fold. In the second (vv. 8–10) a woman gives a party because she finds a lost drachma, not because of the nine that she did not lose. And in the third (vv. 11–24) a man makes a major social event out of the return home of his prodigal son, not out of the fact (vv. 25–32) that he had another son who never left. The point seems inescapable that the Lucan Jesus is contrasting here God's attitude towards repentant sinners with that towards all those – symbolized by the Pharisees – who stay in the fold, who don't get lost, who pursue the prescribed righteousness.

This last point is particularly obvious in the Prodigal Son, for here the elder son, who had 'never transgressed [his father's] commandment' (15.29), is by virtue of both aspects – temporally prior and commandment-observing – the representative of the observant Jew, whereas the other son is more recent, dwells in 'a distant region' (v. 13), and feeds pigs (v. 15), and is therefore the stand-in for the Gentiles. While in the Lost Sheep and the Lost Coin there is not the slightest intimation that there is anything wrong with what was never lost in the first place, do we not begin to get a whiff of this in the Prodigal Son? Is the portrayal of the older son simply neutral? Or do we not detect in him a certain ungracious and resentful air, brought on by his father's royal treatment of one who has no right to claim anything (as he admits)? When the older son affirms that he 'never transgressed [the father's] commandment' (v. 29), he seems to ally himself with the Christian Pharisees of Acts 15.5, who are resentful over the admission of Gentiles into the church without any obligation to keep Torah.

Cf. my article, 'Tradition and Redaction'. Loisy, who, in *Evangiles synoptiques*, vol. 2, p. 155, stated that the parable did not contain a Jew–Gentile allegory, reversed himself in *Luc*, pp. 37, 402–3 (the years of publication were 1908 and 1924), and proposed that the second part of the parable was added in order to turn the parable into an allegory of saved Gentile and self-rejecting Jew. While a few scholars, e.g., Klostermann, *Lukas*, p. 157, incline toward Loisy's later view, most consider the parable integral, and a great many reject the notion of any allegorizing. Yet cf. Sandmel, *Anti-Semitism*, p. 79, n. 13. Since publishing the article mentioned above, I have inclined towards the later view of Schottroff, 'Gleichnis vom verlorenen Sohn', that Luke composed the entire parable; cf. also van Goudoever, 'Israel in Luke', p. 121, who takes the position that Luke composed the parable out of the raw material of the parable of the Two Sons in Matt. 21.28–32. Although the main points are different, such use seems possible. Aus, 'Luke 15:11–32', overlooks this possibility entirely and attempts rather to find the origin of the parable in a folklore tradition that also turns up in stories about Rabbi Eliezer, but the evidence for that conclusion appears forced (cf. esp. p. 465). Aus's argument (op. cit., pp. 466–7) that the parable is not marked by Lucan language simply will not stand. Fitzmyer, *Luke*, vol. 2, p. 1084, thinks that Luke got the parable from 'L'. In any case, G. Schneider, *Lukas*, vol. 2, p. 324, and others see that the parable refers to the Pharisees.

To propose, therefore, that the parable is *not* 'stamped by the Lucan theology or, as the case may be, soteriology' is simply to turn aside from the obvious.[77] Whatever the parable may have meant in its pre-Lucan form (if there was one), *in Luke* it must be viewed in the overall context of Luke-Acts. It is fully in keeping with that context to disparage those who keep the commandments and who are not sinners in any traditional sense (Pharisees) while approving repentant sinners who 'come home'.

The most effective device, however, that Luke found to make the point that the proper criteria for church membership are repentance and contrition, not following Pharisaic *halakah*, was the parable of the Pharisee and the Toll Collector.[78] The vivid imagery of this parable has conveyed to millions over nineteen centuries a tableau of the starkly contrasting self-righteous Pharisee and the contrite and humble repentant sinner.[79] It is a contrast in black and white, with no grey area between. How perfectly, now terribly righteous the Pharisee of the parable is! He is not a thief, not unjust, not an adulterer, and certainly not, thank God! a toll collector (Luke 18.11); his fasting and tithing, further, leave nothing to be desired (v. 12). The sinner, on the other hand, offers nothing in his own behalf. His only prayer is, 'Bring redemption to me the sinner.' Luke's conclusion to the parable, then, that 'the latter was justified ($\delta\epsilon\delta\iota\kappa\alpha\iota\omega\mu\acute{\epsilon}\nu\circ\varsigma$)', not 'the former',[80] provides the counterpoint to the saying in 16.15, that it is the Pharisees who 'make themselves righteous (οἱ δικαιοῦντες ἑαυτούς) before people'.[81] The Pharisee of the parable, like the Pharisees of Luke 16.15, follows a certain *halakah* and thus manages to appear righteous before people. The Lucan Jesus, however, contends that what is important is rather being righteous in God's sight, for which Pharisaic *halakah* is not effective, but for which true repentance and contrition suffice.

The moral that Luke appends to the parable, then, 'Everyone who exalts himself will be humbled, and the one who humbles himself will be exalted' (v. 14), simply strengthens the conclusion about the sinner's being made righteous. This Pharisee of the parable is therefore hardly to be distinguished from Jesus' Pharisaic host in Luke 7.36–50.[82] Both think that they know the proper way to righteousness: Pharisaic *halakah*; both think that sinners who neglect that *halakah* and offer only their repentance, contrition, and faith, however sincere, are defective in their righteousness. Thus these Pharisees in the Gospel are the prototypes of the Christian Pharisees in Acts 15.5 who likewise advise that those desiring admission to the church should strictly follow the Law of Moses and not rely merely on their 'belief' (Luke 7.50) to get in.[83]

It is against this background, apparently, that we have to understand the summary that Luke has thrown into the midst of Jesus' sayings about John the Baptist, Luke 7.29–30, according to which 'all the people, when they heard [what Jesus had been saying about John], and the toll collectors justified God,[84] since they were baptized in John's baptism; but the Pharisees and the legists set aside the plan of God for themselves, since they were not baptized by him'.[85] The end-result of Pharisaic thinking is thus announced. Reliance on the Law of Moses for salvation rather than on contrition and repentance (which are implied in submitting to John's baptism) – this, as we have seen, is the contrast that Luke consistently draws – spells ultimate doom for the Pharisees.[86] 'Since the will of God set forth in John's ministry was summed up in his "baptism of repentance for the forgiveness of sins" (3.3), for the evangelist to say the Pharisees rejected God's purpose for them is to say they did not repent and did not receive God's forgiveness.'[87] Does this judgment apply even to those who, as in Acts 15.5, are Christians?

The condemnation of Christian Pharisees

We have now arrived at the most difficult question of all; for can it be that Luke intends his readers to understand that even those Pharisees who became Christians are without hope of salvation? Or does he rather understand that, whereas the Pharisaic mentality and life-style (*halakah*) are contradictory to the (Lucan) Christian understanding of salvation, nevertheless, inasmuch as salvation is open to all, some Pharisees were able to bridge the chasm and to 'believe' – for, in Acts 15.5, Luke does, after all, refer to 'Pharisees who have believed'? Perhaps if, with this question in mind, we rethink the evidence that we have examined, we shall be able to reach a satisfactory answer.

The evidence of what Jesus says to and about Pharisees would appear to be uniformly clear; their Torah-strict *halakah* has taken a wrong turn, so that, compared even with toll collectors who repent with true contrition, their situation appears hopeless.[88] They are not 'justified' (Luke 18.14), however often they may invite Jesus to dinner, and even though they had nothing at all to do with the execution of Jesus. Furthermore, when the Lucan Jesus admonishes his followers (i.e., the church) to beware the Pharisaic leaven of hypocrisy (Luke 12.1), he must have in mind the Christian Pharisees, not the non-Christian ones, for what else can this warning mean to the Lucan church? We have seen that the way in which the warning is put is distinctively Lucan. What situation can Luke have in mind in the early Christian church that would justify this warning against the *leaven* of Pharisaic hypocrisy, if it is not the problem of the traditionally Jewish Christians within the church? Leaven works within the dough, not outside it. The hypocrisy of the Pharisees is within the church, not outside it. Thus Luke does not have Jesus rail against the hypocrisy of Pharisaic behaviour in individual cases, as does Matthew; rather, he reserves the charge of hypocrisy for a general statement, one that emphasizes their spoiling activity within the church.

The portrait of the Pharisees in Acts supports this understanding and, indeed, renders it unavoidable; for it is clear that a charge of hypocrisy could scarcely be levelled at the non-Christian Pharisees in Acts, who could hardly behave better towards Christians if they were the church's fairy godmother. No, it is not the non-Christian Pharisees in Acts on whom the label 'hypocrites' is to be attached; it is the Christian Pharisees. Thus now we know exactly wherein the hypocrisy lies. The leaven of hypocrisy is the attempt of traditionally Jewish Christians to get Gentile Christians to follow the Torah. It is the *Christian* Pharisees who are obstructionist; it is *they* who want to be in Jesus' company (thus the dinner invitations) but who want to keep others out who do not follow their pattern of being in that company, their way (*halakah*); it is *they* who object especially to the inclusion of such sinners as prostitutes (Luke 7.36–50) and toll collectors (Luke 18.9–14) on the basis of their contrition and faith alone and who press (Acts 15.5) for all in the church to adhere to the Torah;[89] and it is *they* on whom falls Jesus' summary judgment (Luke 18.14), 'Every one who exalts himself will be humbled, and the one who humbles himself will be exalted.' In that judgment we have it all. That is the statement that makes clear to us exactly why Luke sketched the Pharisees as he did; for he is contending with the traditionally Jewish Christians over the criteria for Gentiles' membership in the church. The way of his opponents he regards as an attempt to exalt themselves, to justify themselves; for they have a prescription, a teaching, a way, and that way is called 'Moses'. In Luke's opinion, however, Jesus had proposed another way into the church, another way into the Kingdom of God, another *halakah* of salvation, if you will; and that way, the way of repentance, contrition and proper response to Jesus, was a much more suitable way for Gentiles to follow in entering into the Kingdom of God than was the halachic way of the traditionally Jewish Christians. Conzelmann observed that Pharisees in Acts are 'inconsistent' if they are not converted, inasmuch as they share the Christian belief in resurrection;[90] but they are, in fact, inconsistent if they are converted, because they bring with them the 'baggage' of Torah fidelity, which is the 'bad yeast' that spoils the dough of the church. Only Paul escapes this double jeopardy by giving up the characteristically Pharisaic insistence that Gentile Christians follow the Law of Moses.

Everything in Luke's portrait of the Pharisees in the Gospel conforms to this pattern, and nothing contradicts it. Only in Acts does a different picture emerge, where there are non-Christian Pharisees who help the church when they can. These Pharisees, however – along with Paul's Pharisaism – help Luke to show the bridge, the link, the continuity between the religion of the 'Old Testament' and Christianity.[91] These non-Christian Pharisees in the Acts are, so to speak, the other side of the coin; for, if Luke uses the Pharisees in the Gospel and the Christian Pharisees in the Acts to show that traditional Torah observance, even in the church, leads into a cul-de-sac of condemnation on the basis of self-exaltation, he uses the non-Christian Pharisees in Acts to help remind his readers that there is more than one road that leads from pre-Christian Judaism into the present time, and that Christianity is surely the right one.

Pharisaism v. belief

In the foregoing discussion, contrition and repentance – and also belief – have been contrasted to the Pharisaic way; yet the role of belief in Luke's understanding of how one is admitted into the church has been more or less overlooked, and we need now to turn to some further clarification of how Luke thinks of belief in relation to the topic in hand. 'Belief' is Luke's normal word for conversion, and the term is often connected with an account or mention of baptism.[92] The first conversions in Acts, after Peter's first sermon, are characterized by baptism (2.41), after which it is said that 'all who believed were together' (v. 44); further, Acts 14.1 refers to Jews and Greeks at Iconium who 'believed'; and the reference to Jewish Christians in

21.20 is to 'those who have believed'. Similarly, the Pharisees of Acts 15.5 are designated as Christians when they are called 'believers (πεπιστευκότες)'; and the concluding statement of Jesus to the sinful woman in Luke 7.50 is that her 'faith (or: belief) has saved' her.

Luke understands this belief, however, to be further defined in two ways. On the one hand, belief involves true contrition and repentance. This point is made both in the narrative to which I have just referred, Luke 7.36–50, and in the parable of the Pharisee and the Toll Collector, and it is also explicit in the first Christian evangelistic sermon in Acts 2, where Peter encourages his hearers to 'repent' (v. 38) and then calls upon them to 'be saved' (v. 40), after which those who respond are called 'believers' (πιστευσάντες, v. 44). On the other hand, however, this belief is not to be encumbered by irrelevant or extraneous additional requirements such as, specifically, requirements from the Mosaic Torah normally applied to Gentiles who were converted to Judaism; and that means especially, to be even more precise, circumcision.

Where does all this, then, leave the Christian Pharisees of Acts 15.5? Of course they have believed, since it is 'believers' that Luke calls them, thereby indicating that they are Christians; but have they believed in true contrition and repentance?[93] That is not so clear. Luke does not discuss the quality of the belief of the Christian Pharisees in Acts 15.5; nevertheless, everything said to and about them in the Gospel argues that Luke thinks of them there, in any case, as not being truly contrite. Pharisaic Torah fidelity and true contrition seem to be mutually exclusive, as Luke regards the matter, since to adhere to the requirements of the Mosaic Torah in addition to belief is to seek to 'justify' oneself or to 'exalt' oneself (Luke 18.14), and to promote such notions in the church is to be, in Luke's thinking, in the precise sense of the term, a 'hypocrite' (Luke 12.1) – that is, one who pretends to be something that one is not. The Christian Pharisees of Acts 15.5 stand, in the view of the author of Luke-Acts, under the charge of hypocrisy (Luke 12.1) because, while seeming to be 'believers', they are in reality promoting self-justification and self-exaltation. Thus the truly contrite sinner 'goes down to his house justified instead of' the Pharisee – yes, instead of even the Christian Pharisee.

It is against the background of this understanding that we can understand why it is the Pharisees to whom Jesus addresses his much discussed saying in Luke 17.21, 'The Kingdom of God is among you';[94] for we again have here, apparently, a contrast between one who responds properly to Jesus and the Pharisees. In this case the person who responds properly is not a Judahite religious outcast like a prostitute or a toll collector; he is a Samaritan (Luke 17.16); what he does is to 'fall on his face at [Jesus'] feet and thank him' (v. 16). Thus Lukk has Jesus say to the thankful Samaritan exactly what he had said earlier to the contrite prostitute, 'Your faith has saved you' (v. 19). With what unmitigated gall do the Pharisees then dare to question 'when the Kingdom of God is coming' (v. 20)! Jesus has just demonstrated amazing spiritual power (he has healed ten lepers), he has provided an object lesson on the nature of true faith, and then the Pharisees ask when the Kingdom is coming. If they had any sensitivity to the issue at all they would have drawn the obvious implication from the preceding episode: it is there among them.[95] They do not see that any more than those who, one page earlier, could not understand the point about eternal refreshment and punishment even though 'they have Moses and the Prophets' (Luke 16.29). Indeed, these Pharisees in Luke 17.20 cannot be distinguished clearly from those Jews in 16.29 who have the Bible. There is something wrong in their perceptual orientation, and we know what it is. It is the *way* in which they understand the Bible. The cloud of doom that hangs over those who, in the parable of the Rich Man and Lazarus, cannot understand the Torah appears also to darken the future of the Christian Pharisees in Acts 15.5. 'Having believed' could have worked for their 'salvation'; but they remained hardened in their traditional interpretation of scripture. They thus become 'hypocrites', not true members of the Christian community.[96]

The Apostolic Council

Now that we have before us the full picture of Luke's description and representation of the Pharisees, we are almost in a position to comment on his attitude towards Jewish Christianity generally, but we need first to examine his report of the Apostolic Council, Acts 15.6–29, for it also impinges on the issue. The degree to which this report differs from that given by Paul in Gal.2.1–10, and which version of the Council is the 'right' one, need not concern us here, for it is the way in which Luke reports on the Council, not what really happened there, that is our concern.[97] We have already had abundant occasion to comment on the fact that it was the proposal of the Christian Pharisees that Gentile Christians should be circumcised and should follow the Torah that prompted the convening of the Council, but now we must focus our attention on the outcome – that is, on what became of the Christian Pharisees' proposal. In a sense, of course, that is well-known; Gentile Christians were to be admonished to 'abstain from sacrifices offered to idols and from blood and from things strangled and from sexual immorality (πορνεία)' (Acts 15.29).[98] While circumcision is conspicuously mising from this list, so that the decree rejects the proposal of the Christian Pharisees on that point, the restrictions do, in fact, come from the Torah. Their choice, furthermore, is by no means accidental or arbitrary, for they are to be found in a section of the Torah that designates them as regulations to be followed not only by Israelites, but by 'sojourners' among the Israelites as well; and they are found there in the same order as in Acts 15.29.[99] Leviticus 17.8–9 requires that all sacrifices offered by sojourners in Israel must be offered to Yahweh: vv. 10–16 prohibit the eating of blood, even by sojourners, and v. 13 specifies birds caught (i.e., in a snare) whose blood is not drained; and Lev. 18.6–23 provides a long list of sexual taboos (no incest, no bestiality, etc.). That these laws are to be followed by sojourners as well as by Israelites is emphasized again in Lev. 18.26.[100]

Wilson has provided a lengthy and detailed discussion of the various possibilities that have been suggested for the origin of the regulations in the Apostolic Decree (*Law*, pp. 84–102). Especially his analysis of the possibility that the Decree was intended to keep Christianity distinct from various pagan cults is helpful and doubtless points to a likely context for understanding the role of the Decree in early Christianity, whether Luke invented it or derived it from some source (ibid., pp. 94–9). But Wilson's argument that the decree cannot stem from Leviticus 17–18 fails to convince, primarily because he seems not to have grasped why the prohibition in the Apostolic Decree against 'things strangled' is related to Leviticus 17–18. Thus he both fails to notice the reference to hunting (with the implication of the use of the snare) in Lev. 17.13 (p. 88) and is puzzled by Philo's once mentioning hunting in connection with dietary laws against eating 'what dies of itself or what is torn by beasts' (terms that appear in Lev. 17.15; Wilson, *Law*, p. 90). But Lev. 17.13–15; Philo, *de Spec. Leg.*, 4.122 (the passage here under discussion); and Acts 15.29 all have this in common, that something killed in the hunt might not be properly drained of blood and might thus not be fitting for an Israelite, or for a Gentile associated with Israel, to eat.

The Apostolic Decree for the Gentiles

Wilson emphasizes that the LXX translates 'sojourner' as 'proselyte' in Leviticus 17–18,[101] a fact that 'would suggest that . . . Luke [probably] would not have seen these demands as relevant to Gentile Christians (except those already fully proselytized before becoming Christians)'. This argument is less than compelling, however, for two reasons. For one thing, as we have yet to discuss,[102] Luke has a high regard for proselytes and regards them as significant in the divine plan for the progression of the gospel. Secondly, inasmuch as Luke thinks of the (Gentile) church as being the proper continuation of 'biblical' Israel, he may very well think of Gentile Christians as being similar to proselytes. Thus the translation of 'sojourner' as 'proselyte' in the LXX may have abetted his sense that these commandments were appropriate rather than working against it.

The orientation of the list of prohibitions in the Apostolic Decree is therefore clear. It is a list of prohibitions that God has specifically given for Gentiles living among his people.[103] Whether Luke took the list from some intermediate source[104] or whether he extrapolated it himself from the Torah,[105] it fits perfectly into his understanding of the relation of Christianity to 'biblical Israel'; for, in Luke's understanding, while the church stands in direct continuity with 'biblical Israel', it is quite distinct from the Judaism that is contemporary with it, which has taken a wrong turn and has divorced itself from continuity with 'biblical Israel'. It is not that 'Luke does not know', as Löning suggests,[106] 'that, according to Jewish understanding, confession to a church made up of circumcised and uncircumcised persons *ipso facto* means a break with Jewish tradition'; it is rather that Luke thinks that said Jewish understanding is wrong. 'Luke therefore solves the problem as to why the Gentile church, in distinction from the primitive church, no longer keeps the Mosaic Torah not as Paul would have, but in terms of church order; the Apostolic Council produces this rule of church order that, of course, now distinguishes two historical phases but preserves the continuity of salvation history.'[107] Thus Luke, by the use of this list, is able to demonstrate the proper fidelity of *Gentile* Christianity to the Law of Moses while at the same time freeing Gentile Christians from any need to be converted to Judaism, especially from any need to be circumcised.

Haenchen, *Acts*, p. 449, refers to the Apostolic Decree as a 'concession' to Gentile Christians; and Lake in *Beginnings*, Part I, vol. 5, p. 204, as a 'minimum . . . in lieu of circumcision'. (Is Schmithals, *Apostelgeschichte*, p. 139, being overly fastidious when he argues that one should not use the word 'concession' here, since Luke is 'not psychologizing', merely 'establishing' a 'fact'?) Jervell, *People of God*, pp. 144–5, is thus correct to the degree that the Gentile mission is not severed from Torah, since, as he affirms, Luke's Gentile Christians are expected to keep those laws intended for them; cf. also id., *Unknown Paul*, p. 121. Nevertheless, Jervell has Luke's theology set on its ear when he thinks that Luke is emphasizing the enduring validity of the entire Torah, Jewish laws for the Jews and Gentile laws for the Gentiles. Juel, *Luke-Acts*, pp. 104–7, also takes this position. That early Jewish Christians were perfectly Torah-observant is not a continuing theme for Luke, but an aspect of his linkage theme. So exactly Schulz, *Stunde*, p. 273. Thus to refer, with Conzelmann, *Theology*, p. 212, and Haenchen, *Acts*, p. 100, to a Gentile mission freed from the Law is more nearly correct than is Jervell's position; cf. further Weiser, 'Apostelkonzil', p. 162. Sandmel, *Anti-Semitism*, p. 90, writes correctly of a 'divinely sanctioned transition from the ceremonial requirements of Judaism to their nullification in Christianity'. Stagg, *Acts*, pp. 12–17, takes this to be the primary purpose of Acts!

More recently, Jervell (*Unknown Paul*, pp. 30–5) has proposed a rather different explanation of the Apostolic Decree – that is, that it was a restricting of an earlier, open situation, in which Gentiles became Christians with *no* Jewish obligations. Thus he refers (op. cit., p. 31) to 'a mission to Gentiles without the demand of circumcision'. He repeatedly refers to Galatians 2 as supporting this interpretation. This makes no sense at all. According to Galatians 2, Paul had the idea that Gentile Christians did not have to be circumcised and that Jewish Christians, at least in the Antioch church, were permitted to eat non-kosher food. Paul explains that Peter concurred in this opinion until others from the Jerusalem church persuaded him away from it. What was, therefore, the position of the Jerusalem church regarding the circumcision of Gentile Christians, according to Galatians 2? Cf. Betz, *Galatians*, p. 85: 'It is . . . clear that for this law-free gospel Paul was not depending upon the authorities in Jerusalem.'

Is the Apostolic Decree a compromise?

Does the Apostolic Decree, therefore, represent a compromise between the position of the traditionally Jewish Christians on Gentile conversion and that of Paul's Gentile churches on the same point, as those positions are represented in Acts?[108] This question cannot receive a completely negative or positive answer. Nevertheless, we must be careful how we understand 'compromise'; for, if by compromise one means some mutual give and take, a sort of fifty-fifty approach to problem-solving that produces a result that leaves all parties feeling that what they gained in the compromise is better than if they had lost out altogether, then there is no compromise here. The essential position of the Christian Phariseess is that all Christians must become Jews, and that is the position that is rejected by the Council. The Gentile Christians continue as just that, as *Gentile* Christians; they do not become proselytes to Judaism. Furthermore, as far as Luke is concerned, the Gentile church could have arrived at the list in Acts 15.29 and elsewhere without attempting to compromise with Jewish Christianity on the issue of which laws were valid.[109] That list is entirely understandable, given Luke's interest in demonstrating the continuity between Christianity and the Israelite religion of the Bible. The (*Gentile*) church has not broken with the true religion instituted by the one God as recorded in the Bible. The church is rather the continuation of that religion; its existence was prophesied there. Inasmuch as God had prophesied the existence of the church as a *Gentile* religion, he also saw fit to include a few laws for that *Gentile* church. By keeping those laws the Gentile church demonstrates its continuity with and fidelity to the Bible. Circumcision is a Jewish affair.[110]

Stolle, *Zeuge*, p. 113, thinks that it is Luke's view that all in the church should be law-abiding, whether they are Jews or Gentiles. Jews should obey the Torah and all citizens the Roman law. While that approach to the problem is not entirely wrong, it obscures Luke's attitude towards the Torah and towards Jewish Christianity. For Luke, 1. God has given certain laws for Jews and a certain few for Gentiles; 2. inasmuch as the gospel has gone to the Gentiles, the Gentile laws of the Torah are Christian laws; 3. Jews and their laws are, after the 'Jerusalem springtime', tolerated within Christianity, but they are a source of trouble. Thus it is manifestly not true that '*Juden und Heiden prinzipiel auf einer Stufe stehen*' (ibid., p. 115; similarly Richard, 'Divine Purpose', pp. 196, 200).

Beyond this, Peter's witness in the Apostolic Council shows that Luke does not think of the outcome of the Council as in some sense accepting the second part of the proposal of the Christian Pharisees, namely that the Gentile Christians be required to keep the Law of Moses; for Peter asks (Acts 15.10), 'Why do you put God to the test by putting a yoke on the neck of the disciples that neither our fathers nor we have been able to bear?' Thus Luke seems to accept the notion of the basic invalidity of the Torah,[111] *as it is obeyed in the* halakah *of traditional Judaism*, as is also the case in ch. 10,[112] where Peter comes to understand, on the basis of the example given him by God in a vision, that Gentiles are acceptable to God;[113] but the example in the vision was that the dietary laws do not coincide with the divine will: 'Do you not defile what God has cleansed' (Acts 10.15)! That is to say, do not set up an evaluative system (a set of laws) that has the effect of rendering unclean what God has purified. That seems a plain statement that the dietary laws disagree with God's will. 'The

Gentile mission was divinely approved as a direct sequel to the abolition of Jewish food laws.'[114] The Apostolic Council, as it is presented in Acts, throws out the position of the Christian Pharisees; it does not attempt to reconcile their position with that of the Gentile church under Paul's leadership. If one wishes to retain the word 'compromise' for such an outcome, that would still be permissible, but the user would have to realize that the basic point of the traditionally Jewish Christian position has disappeared from this compromise.

Wilson's discussion, in *Gentiles*, of Cornelius's conversion and of the Apostolic Council is puzzling. While the discussions of the two episodes appear in a chapter entitled 'Cornelius and the Apostolic Council' (*Gentiles*, pp. 171–95), he explains that the Cornelius episode means 'no circumcision' and no 'food regulations' for Gentiles (ibid., p. 177), but, when he comes to discuss the Apostolic Decree, he thinks that its purpose is to make 'contact possible between Jews and Gentiles' (ibid., p. 189). He has another go at trying to relate the two episodes in *Law*, pp. 71–6, where he observes that the 'issue' of their 'relationship' is 'most perplexing' (p. 71) and concludes that this issue cannot be decided as long as one supposes that the Apostolic Decree represents, for Luke, an attempt to impose certain requirements from the Torah on Gentile Christians. What Wilson now thinks was the purpose of the Decree, in Luke's opinion, is discussed below, p. 125.

The legacy of the Tübingen school, that the Apostolic Council in Acts is conciliatory, is thus still very much with us; but there is precious little conciliation going on, inasmuch as the grounds of the traditionally Jewish Christian position are quarried away by Peter (Acts 15.10). Thus, as Overbeck (*Apostelgeschichte*, p. 224) already pointed out, the traditionally Jewish–Christian position disappears from the deliberations of the Council after it is first put forward in v. 5. It is worth noting, incidentally, that F. C. Baur quite keenly saw the evidence correctly: 1. The real situation (*Paul*, vol. 1, p. 117) was that Jewish Christians must have generally opposed the move to let Gentiles be absolved from the requirements of the Law. 2. In Acts, however, it is converted Pharisees who take this viewpoint (ibid., p. 123), while 3. the Christian Jewish leaders blandly go along with and even support the Pauline position (ibid., pp. 123–4). But Luke does not present this picture in order to reconcile Jewish–Christian and Gentile–Christian factions (as Baur, op. cit., p. 135, maintained), but rather to invalidate the Jewish Christian position. (Baur did not propose, furthermore, that 'table fellowship' was the goal of the 'Apostolic Decree', just conciliation.)

Does the Apostolic Decree promote fellowship?

Some authors maintain that the goal of the regulations in the Apostolic Decree is to permit or to facilitate 'table fellowship' between Jewish Christians and Gentile Christians.[115] According to this view, Luke (or the 'real' Apostolic Decree, or some other source used by

Luke) wants Gentile Christians to abstain from food offered to other gods and from blood, therefore also from the flesh of animals killed by strangling, so that Jewish Christians will have no objection to dining with Gentile Christians – presumably at official or quasi-official Christian gatherings. Now, it is probably (in my opinion) true that a main purpose of the laws of *kashrut* was to keep Jews apart from their Gentile neighbours,[116] and it is also doubtless true that two factions of a movement will split apart and go their own ways if some disagreement over food prohibits their dining together in any circumstances. But the 'table fellowship' explanation of the Apostolic Decree overlooks three things. One is that the four prohibitions in the decree hardly cover the laws of *kashrut*: one need think only of pork, shellfish, and meat with milk.[117] A second is that the dietary laws do not, in fact, prevent Gentiles' and Jews' having a common meal – if the Jews do the cooking. Someone who keeps strict kosher cannot dine at my house, but nothing keeps me from dining at his house if I am invited. Finally, and this seems always to be overlooked in the 'table fellowship' explanation of the Apostolic Decree, it is clear that the Apostolic Council is not convened to deal with the issue of dining together, since it is the position of the Christian Pharisees that, had it prevailed, would have facilitated such table fellowship! If table fellowship had been the real problem, then the Christian Pharisees had the only real solution (among the alternatives presented in Acts). Their position, circumcising the Gentile Christians and bringing them under the complete Law of Moses, would have made Jews of all Christians, and there would have been no problem about table fellowship.[118] The Gentile position is rather the one that continues the separation. It disregards the Jewish position altogether and appropriates for itself only that part of the Law of Moses that it sees as having been designated specifically for Gentiles. If the Jews want to cut off their foreskins and wash their hands before eating, let them have at it. Those are not *Christian* practices.

   If, however, the goal of the regulations in the Apostolic Decree is not *table* fellowship, then perhaps (as some propose) it is just *fellowship*, i.e., going to church together.[119] Yet this suggestion is also built on an insufficient foundation, for who can produce any Jewish regulation in antiquity or now that forbids *associating* with Gentiles?[120] Even if there were such a regulation, would it specify the sojourner requirements of Leviticus as the basis for association? In any case, Luke had already dealt with the issue of association in ch. 10, where he had Peter explain to Cornelius that, although 'it is illegal for a Jewish man to associate with or to approach one of another race', nevertheless (κἀμοί), 'God has indicated to me to call no person common or unclean' (v. 28); therefore Peter's presence in Cornelius's house is divinely permitted.[121] The proper basis for asociation of Jews and Gentiles together in the church is, for Luke, God's abrogation of the Torah (except for those laws intended specifically for Gentiles). If *table* fellowship is not the issue in the Apostolic Decree, then the issue is also not *fellowship*.[122]

The issue of the relation of the Apostolic Decree to then-current Jewish regulations is complicated only if we assume the real existence of the Apostolic Decree and inquire into its purpose. In that case, we are lacking any precise Jewish regulations for this period regarding contact with Gentiles, as Schäfer, 'Aposteldekret', col. 556, emphasizes. All regulations in the Jewish scripture dealing with such contact assume a national Israelite state or something like it, and the rabbinic literature is later. Jews may have been quite restrictive regarding such contact in the Roman period (so the article on 'Gentiles' by the editors, *Encylopaedia Judaica*, vol. 7, pp. 410–11). What regulations there are in the Mishnah are less than conclusive. Gittin 59b allows that 'the poor of the heathen may not be prevented from gathering gleanings, forgotten sheaves, and the corner of the field, in the interests of peace'; and the immediately following *Mishnaic* passage, Git. 61a, deals first with household associations with those who may not be observing a sabbatical year, then with relations between *haberim* and *'amme' ha'ares*, and concludes, 'Heathens may be assisted in the sabbatical year but not Israelites, and greeting may be given to them, in the interests of peace' (Soncino translation). Cf. further Schiffman, 'Relations with Non-Jews', esp. pp. 385–9, who shows that both at Qumran and in early rabbinic literature Jews were forbidden to sell kosher animals to Gentiles only because the Gentiles might sacrifice the animals. Wilson, *Law*, p. 69, refers to passages from Philo, Josephus, the Sibylline Oracles, Dio Cassius, and Tacitus as providing 'ample evidence . . . that many Jews [in the Roman period] believed it necessary to separate themselves from Gentiles'; yet, only the infamous statement of Tacitus is, upon investigation, germane to the point. However, it is hardly to be trusted. Wilson appears not to have read these sources himself, but only to have taken the list from somewhere.

It is just possible that Jewish Christians in Luke's own day had in fact put forward the list of prohibitions – perhaps an early version of the Noachic laws – as an attempt to improve relations between themselves and Gentile Christians. This is the position of Townsend, 'Date', who cites several passages in the *Kerygma Petrou* stratum of the Pseudo-Clementine literature that show striking similarities to the Lucan Apostolic Decree. One may note esp. Hom. 7.8, which lists, as part of the proper Christian worship (θρησκεία), *not* taking part in the 'table of demons', namely 'offerings to idols, corpses, things strangled, θηριάλωτοι (things caught by wild beasts), blood'. The origins and date of this work are too uncertain, however, and the possibility that the author merely quoted from Acts too strong for any hard conclusions to be drawn from the similarities; cf. Schoeps, *Theologie und Geschichte*, p. 39. Schoeps does, however (op. cit., pp. 259–60), think that the regulations in the Apostolic Decree are a version of the Noachic laws. Wilson's assertion that 'the Noachic laws are dissimilar in both number and content to the terms of the decree' (*Law*, p. 74) obscures the fact that there is a significant overlap. Novak's study of the Noachic laws in *Image of the Non-Jew* confirms the opinion that the regulations of Luke's Apostolic Decree are an early version of the Noachic laws, inasmuch as the *terminus a quo* for the seven Noachic laws, formulated as such, appears, according to Novak, to be the time of the Bar Kochba revolt, while the core of the code – the three 'rational' prohibitions against idolatry, illicit sex and blood – will be older (cf. Novak, op. cit., pp. 28–31). That would coincide with Luke's time. Thus Luke probably took this list from Jewish Christianity of his own day. (This is the conclusion of Townsend, 'Date', pp. 55–6.). Weiser, 'Apostelkonzil', p. 152, similarly thinks of an origin within Jewish Christianity *after* the treaty between Paul and the Jerusalem leaders, discussed in Galatians.

If we stay with Luke's meaning, however, whatever his source(s), the matter is much simpler. When James first mentions the regulations in the Apostolic Council (Acts 15.20), he proposes them so as 'not to create difficulties' for the Gentile Christians, whom the Christian Pharisees want to circumcise; and this is in keeping with Peter's call (v. 10) not 'to put a yoke on the neck' of the Gentile Christians. In the official decree, it is again specifically said that the Jerusalem leadership wishes to put no 'weight' (v. 28) on the Gentile Christians other than the necessary four regulations. Finally, when James repeats the list to Paul in 21.25, he cites it as evidence protecting Paul from the charge of promoting antinomianism in the Diaspora. Therefore, every time that this list occurs in Acts, it is said specifically to have to do with which laws are proper for the Gentiles to keep. How Wilson, *Law*, p. 81, can write, therefore, that 'it is one of the oddities of Luke's narrative that he does not tell us precisely what the decree was for' is an oddity itself. Never does Acts give the slightest hint that Jewish–Gentile 'associations' in the church are at stake. For Luke, the issue is the proper laws in the Torah for Gentiles – and that means for his Gentile church (similarly Schille, *Apostelgeschichte*, p. 320).

Löning, 'Paulinismus', pp. 228–9, notes the juxtaposition of Paul's circumcising of Timothy because of Jewish sensitivities in Acts 16.3 and a further reference to the Apostolic Decree in v. 4, and concludes that the purpose of the decree is to assuage those very sensitivities; but that is to overlook what is said about the decree every time that it occurs. Luke seems to want to give, in Acts 16.3–4, an object lesson about the now-clarified role of the Torah in the church: as the apostolic church was Torah-observant in those halcyon days of yesteryear, so the (now-Gentile) church should keep those laws prescribed for it.

That the Lucan Apostolic Council is loaded from the start on the Gentile-Christian side is, finally, further clear from what Peter and James both say in it. Peter observes in v. 7 that it was by divine will that Gentiles began to join the church, and James seconds that position by interpreting it to mean (v. 14) that 'at first God laid plans (ἐπεσκέψατο) to take from the Gentiles a people for his name'.

Finally, James observes further that 'Moses, being read in the synagogues every Sabbath, has people proclaiming him from olden days city by city' (v. 21). The meaning of this last statement seems to be that the laws prescribed for Gentile Christians in the preceding verse are nothing new and that Gentiles being converted to Christianity come under no obligation to obey any additional laws in the Torah that were not already obligatory for them in their pre-Christian state.[123]

The Pharisees as provokers of the Apostolic Council

In order to complete our examination of the way in which Luke's description of the Apostolic Council reveals his attitude towards Jewish Christianity, we need now to return briefly from the conclusion to the convening of the council. Such a consultation is always proposed, of course, by those dissatisfied with the current state of affairs. Since the Gentile mission was flourishing, and since Gentile converts to Christianity were not being circumcised, Gentile Christians would have no reason for calling for the convening of such a council. It is the traditionally Jewish Christians, the ones who think that Christianity should be developing otherwise with regard to Gentiles, who urge the convening of the council. It is thus quite in keeping with what we have seen of Luke's portrayal of the Pharisees in the Gospel that Christian Pharisees call for the council, since Luke lets the Pharisees represent the position within early Christianity (according to his image of it) of the traditional Jews.[124] Luke shows his hand a little more, however, when he prepares for this Pharisaic demand in Acts 15.5 by writing in v. 1 that 'some came down from Judaea' to Antioch and insisted that circumcision was a requirement for salvation – not 'some Christian Pharisees' but 'some from Judaea', i.e., 'some Jews'.[125] Luke does not, in fact, designate these 'some' as Christians, although that would seem to be the implication, even when we resist, as we should, allowing ourselves to be influenced by Paul's account in Galatians, where the 'some' receive more definite contours (cf. also Acts 21.21). But the truth is that, for Luke, it does not really matter whether the 'some' of Acts 15.1 are Christians or not. They are Jews. They represent the Jewish position, whether it is found without or within Christianity. Thus two aspects of Luke's account point in the direction of the conclusion that the position that Luke is opposing in Acts 15 is the one that he considers the essential position of Jewish Christians and not merely that of a 'minority'

(Haenchen). One is that he has two different groups of Jews push the issue; the other is that he states their position in the most general of Jewish terms (circumcision, Moses). Luke therefore does not intend to describe, by his use of Pharisees, an intransigent conservative group among Jewish Christians; rather, he uses the Pharisees to represent the Jewish–Christian position as such, a position that comes down to this: Moses.[126] The 'clincher' in this argument is Acts 21.20–21: The 'myriads of Christians [believers, as in Acts 15.5] among the Jews[127] . . . are all zealots for the Law'[128] and fear that Paul is 'teach[ing] apostasy from Moses'.[129] Pushing the Torah on the Gentiles is not the work of the Pharisees or of some other minority alone; it is the work of *the* Jewish Christians.[130] Thus Schmithals writes that Luke wants to make 'Jewish Christians the advocates of Pharisaism'.[131]

Wilson's analysis of Torah in Luke-Acts

S. G. Wilson has investigated the place of the Torah in Luke-Acts in some detail,[132] and we need at this point to give attention to his analysis. According to Wilson, the Gospel presents one position with regard to the Torah while Acts presents another. In the Gospel, in Wilson's analysis, Jesus affirms some laws, e.g., the love command,[133] while abrogating others, e.g., Sabbath;[134] and he seems to say inconsistent things about keeping and not keeping the Law, as in 16.16–18.[135] These observations lead Wilson to the conclusion that 'the question of Jesus' attitude towards the law was not a problem for Luke and his readers . . . at the time he composed the Gospel'.[136]

Although Wilson's observations about what the Lucan Jesus says about the Torah, and about what he says that may imply some understanding of or attitude toward the Torah, are generally keen, there is one place where he has found differing attitudes towards the Torah expressed where it is likely that no difference exists, and that is in a comparison between Jesus' reply to the question about how to get eternal life in Luke 10.25–28 and his reply to the same question in 18.18–22.[137] As Wilson understands it, the Lucan Jesus accepts the requirements of the Torah as sufficient in the former case, where he cites the love command, but adds a required supplement to the Torah in the latter case ('Yet one thing is lacking to you. Sell everything that you have and distribute it to the poor' [18.22]). It is highly likely, however, that Luke identified love of neighbour with giving to the poor,[138] so that he thought that the addition of the requirement of distributing to the poor to the list of commandments from the Decalogue, cited by the rich young ruler, was a way of adding the love command to them,[139] as in the former case.

In any case, however, Wilson finds the situation in Acts to be markedly different from that in the Gospel. In Acts, the constant emphasis on the church's, especially Paul's Torah fidelity, and the large role that the issue of Paul's Torah fidelity plays in the conclusion of Acts, show that the issue has become a topic of considerable importance by the time Acts was written.[140] Since 'the Jews' at the end of Acts so consistently and heatedly oppose what they take to be Paul's setting aside of the Law, and since Luke emphasizes only one side of Paul's statement in I Cor. 19.20–21 that he 'became as a Jew to the Jews . . . [and] as an iniquitous person to the inquitous [i.e., as a Gentile to Gentiles]' in the pursuit of evangelistic success, that one side being that Paul was always faithful to the Jewish Law,[141] Luke must be attempting to meet criticism from Jews or from Jewish Christians that Paul advocated the overthrow of the Torah.[142] Wilson takes 'an extremist Jewish Christian minority' to be the likely source of such criticism.[143]

The need to deal with that criticism has also led Luke, according to Wilson, to refine in Acts his opinion about the validity of the Torah for Jewish and for Gentile Christians. The presentation of the early church as Torah-observant and the statement in Acts 21.20 that the Jewish Christians are 'zealots for the Law' mean, for Wilson, that 'in general Luke approved of Jewish Christian adherence to the law';[144] but the Apostolic Decree shows that Luke's opinion about the relevance of the Torah for Gentile Christians has not changed since he wrote the Gospel, since here as there Luke maintains that 'the Gentiles were freed from the law . . . and yet at the same time obligated to its central commands', like the love command.[145] As we have already had occasion to note,[146] Wilson thinks (incorrectly) that the regulations of the Apostolic Decree cannot be directly derived from the Torah. They were important, rather, because of their apostolic authority, just as the love command was important because of its dominical authority, although in both cases 'a basis for them could be found in Mosaic law'.[147]

Because Wilson sees the Gospel and Acts as representing somewhat different attitudes toward the Torah, he also emphasizes the difference between the Pharisees in the Gospel and the Pharisees in Acts. Luke's undeveloped ideas about the Torah in the Gospel, according to this explanation, coincide with an 'ambivalent' portrait of the Pharisees in which they are sometimes opposed to Jesus and sometimes hospitable. The portrayal of them in Acts as friendly is therefore motivated by Luke's desire to emphasize Paul's Pharisaism and the consistent harmony that existed between Paul and the best part of Judaism.[148]

While Wilson has made many keen observations about the way in which the Torah is presented in Luke-Acts and about its varied relation to Jewish Christians and to Gentile Christians in the two-volume work, and while he has noticed, at least, most of the relevant statements and episodes in both works, he has, nevertheless, failed to put the evidence together entirely satisfactorily and to reach the correct conclusions. Thus, although Wilson is correct to point to the similarity between the love command in the Gospel and the Apostolic Decree in Acts – both valid for Gentile Christians, both somehow related to the Torah, both given authority for the Gentile church by, respectively, Lord and apostles – he has overlooked that practice is set aside in both books in the same way; for, just as the Pharisees in the Gospel are in regular conflict with Jesus for breaking the Sabbath – or, to be more precise, over how the Sabbath is to be observed – so the setting aside of the regulations regarding circumcision (Acts 15) and diet (Acts 10) arouses the opposition of *Christian* Pharisees in Acts, who demand that Gentile Christians be 'circumcise[d]' and that they 'keep the Law of Moses' (Acts 15.5). Wilson, however, has failed to bring together the insistence of the Pharisees in Acts that Gentile Christians keep the Law – which he does note[149] – with the insistence of the Pharisees in the Gospel that Jesus does not obey the Law correctly, since he views the Pharisees in the Gospel as primarily hostile to Jesus but those in Acts as primarily friendly to the church, as we have noted.

He has also failed to bring together another similarity between the two books regarding the Law, and that is that both books begin with scenes of devout Jewish piety. He correctly describes Luke 1–2 as presenting a strongly positive attitude towards Torah observance,[150] but he subsumes this trait under what he takes to be Luke's disinterested attitude toward Torah observance in the Gospel. When Acts, then, begins in the same way, Wilson seems puzzled by the 'Jerusalem springtime' and thinks that this friendliness between church and Judaism is a part of Luke's attempt to defend Paul against charges of teaching emancipation from the Law,[151] whereby one also sees that Luke thinks it appropriate that Jewish Christians observe the Law.[152] Wilson refers to the 'casual allusions' in the early part of Acts to the church's fidelity to Judaism and asserts that 'it can scarcely be said that they reveal an overriding interest on Luke's part in the early Church as a law-abiding community'.[153] Thus, in trying to show that the Gospel and Acts present different attitudes toward the Torah, Wilson has to ignore or attempt to explain away the fact that both works begin with descriptions of Torah fidelity, that both consider *some* laws from the Torah valid for Gentile Christians, that both set aside the practice of traditionally halachic Jews as improper for Gentile Christians, and that both present the Pharisees as opposing this (to them) deviant *halakah*. Had Wilson given more attention to the Pharisees in Luke-Acts, he might have made better sense out of the evidence, which he has, by and large, observed fairly well.

Whereas Wilson sees, as we have just noted, that it is Pharisees in Acts 15 who demand full obedience to the requirements of the Torah for Gentile Christians, he does not let this observation disturb his judgment that the Pharisees in Acts are generally friendly to the church;[154] yet, in the Gospel, he sees an 'ambivalent' attitude towards the Pharisees,[155] in which they and Jesus argue over details but not over the basic issue of 'scrupulosity',[156] and in which they may even be Jesus' dinner hosts.[157] A more careful analysis of the Pharisees in Luke-Acts would have found this 'ambivalence', also, in both books. When the Pharisees in Luke-Acts are understood, Luke's attitude towards the Torah falls into place.

Wilson could be correct in proposing that it was Jewish–Christian charges against Paul that led Luke to adopt his particular attitude toward the Torah. We shall return to that issue again. But, again, Wilson is mistaken in finding an ambivalent attitude towards the Law in the Gospel but a consistent one in Acts, for he has failed to see the degree to which criticism of Jesus in the Gospel is similar to criticism of Paul in Acts – that is, the prototype of the charges against Paul that he taught the ignoring of the Law is the repeated disapproval of Jesus' improper observance of the Sabbath; and these charges are brought in the one case by Jewish Christians and in the other by Pharisees. Thus, if Jewish–Christian accusations against Paul (and against Pauline Christianity?) have prompted Luke's portrayal of the issue of Torah observance in Acts, then Luke has carried this same portrayal back into the Gospel and has shown that it was a significant issue in Jesus' ministry.

In his conclusion, Wilson comes to one realization about the portrayal of the Law in Luke-Acts that might, had he seen the point earlier, have led him on a truer course. That is that 'the positive side to Luke's view of Judaism, including his view of the law . . ., [is] largely related to the past'.[158] There we have the solution in a nutshell; for Luke is at pains to show how the early church, like the early Jesus, sought a home of piety and devotion in Judaism, but it would not. And so Jesus and the church turned from Judaism and the Jews to the Gentiles, and Christianity became a Gentile religion, and all the Jewish laws in the Torah were rendered null and void, and Torah-observant Jewish Christians became hypocrites.

Luke's opinion of Jewish Christians

Our examination of the way in which Luke portrays the Pharisees has thus, finally, disclosed to us Luke's opinion of the Jewish–Christian position. It is that the position is hypocritical.[159] Luke apparently does not care if those Christians who are Jews continue to be circumcised and to obey the Torah, but Christian Jews can be valid Christians, in Luke's opinion, only to the degree that they are willing to recognize that Christianity is not a part of Judaism, is not Judaism, is in fact a Gentile religion. Any attempt by Jewish Christians to get Gentile converts to Christianity to accept the validity of any more of the Law of Moses than Jesus and the Apostolic Council have deemed valid earns for them the label 'Pharisees', i.e., 'hypocrites'.[160] Looking at Luke's position from a slightly different angle, we see that the choice that he has posed for the Jewish Christians of his own day is, to rephrase a popular modern slogan, 'Gentile Christianity; love it or leave!' In other words, Jewish Christians may escape the epithet 'hypocrites' if they are willing to deny the validity of their own traditional religion, for that is what their affirmation of Gentile Christianity, of Christianity as a Gentile religion will have to involve for them.[161] The 'people' of God are now taken 'from Gentiles' (Acts 15.14). Judaism, circumcision and obeying the Torah have nothing to do with the true religion or with salvation; they are therefore reduced to the status of quaint ethnic practices. 'God has abolished the Law.'[162] Any Jew who is willing to agree with that proposition, to believe in Jesus as the Messiah and to repent in true contrition may become a Christian. Even so, the time when such Jews – like Peter and James – existed, as far as Luke is concerned, is over. Luke envisages no continuing Jewish mission after the conclusion of Acts. In this, both Jervell and Haenchen are correct.[163]

Harnack, one may wish to recall, thought that Luke's attitude toward the Torah was entirely positive (*Acts*, pp. 284–6), so much so that Luke even still ascribed saving power to the Law where Jews were concerned, only with the proviso that Jews needed forgiveness of sins, inasmuch as they had failed to keep the entire Law. To such a view two considerations may be objected. If Luke had entertained such a notion he would thereby have endorsed the normal Jewish view of salvation (i.e., the view that Harnack attributes to Luke is in no way specifically Christian); furthermore, Peter's appeal to his Jewish audience on Pentecost to 'repent and be baptized' (Acts 2.38) and the reference to Jews as 'believers' in 21.20 show how Luke thinks Jews are to be saved. Harnack has been misled by Luke's emphasis on the Torah fidelity of the early Christians; but that chord belongs to the theme of Christianity as the true Judaism; it has nothing to do with Luke's soteriology.

Jervell's opinion that Luke conceives of Christianity as the body of the redeemed in Israel plus some added Gentiles, as 'a people and an associate people',[164] is therefore mistaken. For Jervell has got the relationship between Jewish and Gentile Christians reversed. 'We Gentiles,' thinks Luke, 'are in charge here, and you Jews can just sit down and shut up.' Luke does not imply that Jews *cannot* join his church,[165] although he would have been surprised – shocked, even – if any actually did; but he makes it crystal clear that, if they do, their Judaism becomes merely a matter of personal preference.[166]

A few lines now seem to be in order so that we may be sure that we understand how the evidence that was discussed in the last chapter is related to what we have seen in this chapter. While it may seem to some that Luke has been inconsistent in his treatments of 'the Jews' and of 'the Pharisees', lumping all the Jews together but making distinctions among the Pharisees, there is really no inconsistency if we keep Luke's epochal scheme in mind. Luke, we must remember, has to show two things: 1. that Christianity grew integrally out of its 'Old Testament' background rather than breaking sharply with it and that, in keeping with this development, 'myriads' of devout and Torah-observant Jews became Christians in the early days; and 2. that Christianity became a Gentile religion, which development was in accord with the divine plan. In Luke's day, however, there seem to be Jews who have not been nor are about to be converted to Christianity, and there are also Jews who claim to have the same beliefs as Gentile Christians (that is, they are Jewish Christians), but who still go about circumcising their male children, washing their hands before eating, and such things, and at least implying that all Christians should behave similarly.[167] Luke's problem is to explain the existence of these two types of Jews and why both are in error. (Pluralism was not something that Luke would have understood.) 'The Jews' represent the non-Christian Jews. Through the course of the Gospel and Acts they develop into the monolith that it was known from the first they were; they reject the purposes of God for themselves. But the Jewish Christians are a little trickier, since they appear outwardly to be Christians; nevertheless, at heart (as God knows), they are still Jews, and thus they also reject God's plan for themselves. Still, somehow the transition has to be made smoothly, and the Pharisees help to bridge the gap. On the one hand they are Christians who are not quite Christians ('hypocrites'), but on the other hand they are Jews who are almost Christians (like Gamaliel). Luke's Pharisees can 'go either way' because Luke knows of Jews who try to 'go both ways'. When Christianity comes to be viewed as a religion separate and distinct from Judaism, which is the way Luke viewed it, then someone who tries to be both is, from a dispassionate descriptive point of view, an anomaly, but from a partisan religious viewpoint a hypocrite.

Concerning Luke's purpose

Now, also, we have a further consideration to include in our discussion of Luke's purpose, for Wilson has proposed that Luke describes the Christian relation to the Torah as he does because of Jewish–Christian objections to Pauline Christianity.[168] Up until now, we have been led by the evidence towards agreement with Maddox's theory that Luke portrays the Jews as he does because of an early Christian identity problem, inasmuch as Jewish claims to and interpretation of the common Scripture will have led Christians to question the validity of their own claim to and interpretation of that Scripture. Now, however, we see that Luke paints a dismal picture not only of 'the Jews', but of traditionally Jewish Christians as well – that is, of those Jewish Christians who want to understand Christianity as the true expression of Judaism and who therefore go right on with their observance of halachic regulations;[169] and so we have to ask whether this portrait can also be explained on the identity-problem theory. Perhaps it can. We would thus have to suppose that the traditionally Jewish Christians, with their allegiance to Torah and *halakah*, also caused not all Christians, but especially Gentile Christians, to question the validity of their form of Christianity, of their interpretation, perhaps by making accusations against Paul. As a matter of fact, of course, we know from Galatians that just such a problem existed in Paul's day, since one of the main issues addressed in Galatians is the pressure brought by some Jewish Christians on Gentile Christians to do precisely what Acts 15.5 reports, to be circumcised and to accept the commandments of the Torah; furthermore, given the tenor of Paul's criticism of those Jewish Christians in Gal. 2.11–14; 5.12, it can well be imagined that equally vigorous criticism proceeded in the other direction as well. If this problem were continuing in Luke's own day, then it would surely explain why Luke portrayed the Pharisees and represented the issue of the Law as he did, but perhaps it would help us to understand better the reason behind his entire portrait of the Jews – that is, perhaps it was Luke's disgust with Jewish Christians that led him to view all Jews so unfavourably. Surely, furthermore, there can be no doubt that this problem did still exist in Luke's day, because it is one of the main issues – some would say, the main issue – with which he deals in Acts. The horse that receives such a beating cannot yet be dead.

On the other hand, however, we are not compelled to accept this explanation, inasmuch as a similar but more general setting could well have produced the same result; for, if Luke felt it important to show that Christianity and not Judaism was the proper successor to 'biblical Israel', what better way could he have found to show that than his presentation of the early church, including Paul? The early Jewish Christians, according to Luke, were better Jews than the non-Christian Jews. We see this not only in Paul's defences, but also in 21.20, where the 'myriads . . . of believers [Christians] among the Jews . . . are all zealots for the Law'; and as well in the 'Jerusalem springtime' scenes of the first five chapters of Acts. Later Christians were to go so far as to say that the Christians were the true *Jews*. While Luke does not use that language, it is not inappropriate to his theology.

With these remarks, we had best lay down the discussion of Luke's *purpose* in describing the Jews as he does, to pick it up again at the end, after we have finished examining all the evidence.

5

THE PERIPHERY: OUTCASTS, SAMARITANS, PROSELYTES, GOD-FEARERS

We now have the main information before us that we need in order to have an accurate and adequate picture of how Luke thinks of 'the Jews' in all their variety. We know what he thinks of the Jewish religious leaders, of Jerusalem, of the Jewish people as a collective group, and of Jewish Christians ('Pharisees'). In order to complete our analysis, however, and to be able to see some of the more subtle shades of Luke's portrait of the Jews, we need next to turn our attention to several groups that hover about the periphery of Judaism, none of them truly Jewish yet none properly Gentile either. These groups inhabit a kind of ethnico-religious grey area. Inasmuch as they have some kind of attachment both to the black night of Judaism and to the bright day of the Gentiles (as Luke thinks of the two realms), they of necessity – and, as it turns out, conveniently for Luke – belong to the twilight dawn, to the intermediate and transitional stage of the divine process of *Heilsgeschichte*. These twilight figures in Luke's portrait are the Jewish religious outcasts, the Samaritans, and those Gentiles who have attached themselves, to a greater (proselytes) or lesser (God-fearers) degree, to Judaism.[1]

Toll collectors and sinners

Many authors have noted Luke's seeming interest in '*les misérables*' of Jesus' and the apostles' day.[2] There can be no doubt that Luke has such an interest, and we can see it best if we pay attention to what happens to 'sinners' and 'toll collectors ($\tau\epsilon\lambda\tilde{\omega}\nu\alpha\iota$)' in the Gospel.[3] We have already noted, in ch. 4, that these people are regularly contrasted – favourably – to Pharisees. It is a toll collector who, in the parable of the Pharisee and the Toll Collector (Luke

18.9–14), is 'justified' rather than the Pharisee because he recognizes that he is a 'sinner' and prays only for 'redemption' (vv. 13–14); and it is a 'sinner' who is 'saved' by her 'faith' (7.39,50) when she anoints Jesus, whereas Jesus' Pharisaic host is only critical. Toll collectors even showed their predisposition to respond favourably to God's final prophet when they came to John for baptism (Luke 3.12), whereas the Pharisees did not seek this baptism (7.29–30). In Luke 5.27 a toll collector, Levi, leaves all to follow Jesus, without any question, and two verses later 'a big crowd' of toll collectors is banqueting with Jesus and Levi. The parable chapter 15, we further recall, is introduced with the note that '*all* the toll collectors and sinners were approaching him'.[4]

From the statistical point of view the presence of 'sinners' in Luke's Gospel is remarkable, since the word 'sinner' occurs in Luke seventeen times, much more frequently, therefore, than in Matthew (five times) and Mark (six times) together. In addition to the episodes cited in the preceding paragraph, we may note that Jesus is called (according to his own report) 'a friend of toll collectors and sinners' in 7.34, and that the Pharisees say essentially the same thing about him in 15.2. The closely following parables of the lost then repeatedly make the point that 'there will be more joy in Heaven over one repentant *sinner* than over ninety-nine righteous persons who have no need of repentance' (15.7; cf. also vv. 10, 24),[5] and, furthermore, when Jesus brings Zacchaeus into his circle (the '*Doppelgänger*' of Levi [Wellhausen]), he is said to be associating with a 'sinner man' (Luke 19.7).[6] It is an 'evildoer', finally, who is saved even while dying with Jesus; at least, he seems to be saved, inasmuch as Jesus promises him life in 'Paradise' (Luke 23.43), and inasmuch as this follows the 'evildoer's' humble and contrite confession of his wrongdoing (v. 41) and his plea to Jesus (v. 42), as well as the immediately preceding mockery that Jesus could not 'save himself' (vv. 35, 37).[7]

Finally, we should perhaps consider again the parable of the Banquet with its introduction (Luke 14.7–24). We were led already for two reasons[8] – that there are only two groups in the introduction to this parable and that the third group in the parable is given no distinguishing characteristics – to conclude that Luke probably intended only two groups in the parable, the originally invited and the unfortunates, the latter of whom receive a renewed, even compelling invitation. It seemed reasonably certain, in our earlier discussion, that Luke thought of the first group as 'the Jews', who

receive the first offer of salvation but who turn it down; but who the
originally uninvited are remained less than perfectly clear. They may
be the Gentiles, since Luke thinks of the gospel as going from the
Jews to the Gentiles; but they might also be the Jewish religious
outcasts, who, as we have now had occasion to note in detail, respond
favourably to Jesus and in the proper way to the offer of salvation.
Or perhaps Luke does not have a distinction clearly in mind, thinking
of outcasts and Gentiles as belonging somehow together; or perhaps
he does think after all of two groups among the originally uninvited,
outcasts and Gentiles. We may be able to reach final clarity on this
matter after we have seen what happens to these outcasts, these 'toll
collectors and sinners', in Acts.

Their counterparts in Acts

However many groups there may be in the parable of the Banquet,
and whether the outcasts are intended or not, we do see that Luke's
portrait of the outcasts is consistent. They repent in contrition and
humility and are saved because of their faith. Never do the toll
collectors and sinners appear otherwise in the Gospel.[9] In Acts,
however, they disappear completely, the words 'sinner' and 'toll
collector' occurring not a single time in Acts. While it might be
possible to think that Peter's healing of the lame man in Acts 3.1–10
carries over into Acts the 'interest' in unfortunates present in the
Gospel, there is really little to link this healing narrative with the
portrayal of the toll collectors and sinners in the Gospel. Beyond the
fact that the man healed is described first as 'lame' (v. 2), there are
no connections. He does not repent or show contrition, nor is there
any reference to his sinfulness. He does not believe, and it is not said
that he is saved. His healing, rather, serves to show the power of the
gospel (or of the Spirit) outside the group of the disciples and to
attract a crowd for Peter's second sermon. The healed man is in no
way considered an outcast and is not contrasted to the Pharisees. If
this unfortunate person, however, is not the continuation into Acts
of the unfortunates in the Gospel, then where are they continued?
The place of the toll collectors and sinners in the Gospel is taken in
Acts, rather, by the Gentiles.

To be sure, the Gentiles in Acts are not 'unfortunates', but they
are in the essential aspect like the outcasts of the Gospel. '*They* will
hear' (Acts 28.28). It is the Gentiles who respond favourably to the
gospel, while the Jews reject it, just as, in the Gospel, the outcasts

responded favourably while the religiously proper did not. In Acts 13.46–48, Paul tells the Jews at Antioch that they 'have rejected' the gospel and that he will therefore 'turn to the Gentiles'. When the Gentiles hear this 'they rejoic[e] and glorif[y] the word of the Lord; and those who were determined for eternal life believ[e]'.[10] Similarly, the announcement of the rejection of the Jews and of the turning to the Gentiles in Acts 18.6 is followed immediately (v. 7) by the acceptance of the gospel by a Gentile 'God-worshipper', Titius Iustus. While the theme of humility and contrition does not carry over into Acts, Luke being apparently content to let its presence in the Gospel serve as a model for church membership, the theme of belief does. As toll collectors and sinners are, in the Gospel, contrasted to those religiously devout persons who refrain from following Jesus and are presented as those who *believe*, so the Gentiles are, in Acts, contrasted to the Jews who reject the gospel and are presented as those who believe.

The parable of the Banquet

Thus we are perhaps able to see a little better what Luke was doing in the parable of the Banquet, since the sinners in the Gospel fade into the Gentiles in Acts. The common denominator for Luke is that those who would not normally expect to receive the Israelite God's salvation do receive it; the sinners of the Gospel are therefore prototypes of the Gentiles in Acts. As the 'Pharisaic' Jewish Christians complain about Jesus' association with 'sinners' in the Gospel (Luke 7.39; 15.2), so in Acts the same 'Pharisaic' Jewish Christians complain about letting Gentiles into the church without circumcising them and bringing them under the entire Law of Moses (Acts 15.5; 21.21). So if, in one sense, Luke thinks of only two groups in his introduction to the parable of the Banquet, the Jews who exclude themselves and the non-Jews who are unexpectedly granted salvation, perhaps in the parable itself he allows himself to think of the granting of salvation to non-Jews as being a two-stage process, with Jesus saving outcasts and the church Gentiles. Perhaps we can never be entirely certain about the precise meaning with which Luke intended to endow this parable. If we interpret the parable from the rest of Luke-Acts, however, and not the rest of Luke-Acts from the parable, then we can at least see that the outcasts are, like the Gentiles later, drawn to salvation after Jewish rejection.

The problem with proposing this interpretation, I realize, is that Jervell or someone is going to argue that, if one proposes a two-stage process of salvation in Luke-Acts, then that two-stage process should take account of the massive Jewish conversions to Christianity described in the first five chapters of Acts. The problem is that Luke can hardly think of the 'myriads' of Jews who are converted during the 'Jerusalem springtime' of the church as being the 'poor and cripples and blind and lame' (Luke 14.21) who are offered salvation after those who could have been expected to receive it have rejected it. Yet this seems to be the interpretation given by Gnilka, *Verstockung*, p. 150, who takes the poor, etc., of the parable to be the '*einfache[s] Volk*', who are distinguished from the leaders. Otherwise (op. cit., p. 133) Gnilka seems to propose a three-stage interpretation of the parable similar to that suggested here: 'the hardened part of the people, the despised strata in Israel', and Gentiles; and he correctly sees a 'gradual development' from Jews to Gentiles as an ingredient of Luke's plan. Similarly Fitzmyer, *Luke*, vol. 2, p. 1053, who, however, equates the originally uninvited with the Pharisees and their associates. Cf. also Beck, *Mature Christianity*, pp. 192–3.

Here then, we are able to get a better perspective on the exact nature of Luke's anti-Judaism or antisemitism.[11] It is not exactly a racial hatred in the way in which we think of racial hatred today,[12] and we see here the best evidence for the argument that Luke's 'antisemitism' is related solely to the Jewish religion, for toll collectors and sinners are hardly more 'Jews' in Luke's thinking than are prophets and apostles. 'Jews' adhere to the Law of Moses, whereas sinners are outcasts. Yet this attitude should not be evaluated in isolation from the rest of Luke-Acts.

Returning to the issue of the periphery, we see that, in Luke 5.32, after the toll collector Levi has left all to follow Jesus and Jesus is at the toll collectors' banquet, the Pharisees and scribes complain that he is associating 'with toll collectors and sinners' (v. 30), and Jesus responds by saying that he 'did not come to call righteous persons but sinners to repentance'. While this saying belongs to the triple tradition, it is Luke who has added 'to repentance', so that he has emphatically brought the saying into harmony with his view that it is toll collectors and sinners who repent, whereas the religious Jews do not. If Jesus' ministry, therefore, was to outcasts – people who were not acceptable to 'the righteous', people who were beyond the pale of true Judaism – then the ground is laid for the gospel, in Acts, to go to the Gentiles, who are likewise beyond the pale. Thus Luke creates a transition zone between Jews and Gentiles, for the outcasts belong to that grey area of those who are not truly Jewish and yet are not properly Gentile either but who nevertheless are open to God's salvation, as the Jews are not but as the Gentiles will later be.

Proselytes and God-fearers in Acts

If in the Gospel, however, there are Jews who are not truly Jews and who help to prepare the way for the transfer of God's salvation from the Jews to the Gentiles, the exact counterpart exists on the other side; for in Acts there are Gentiles who have attached themselves to Judaism and so also belong to the grey area between Jews and Gentiles. These are proselytes and those who 'fear' or 'worship' God.[13] Not only do Gentiles in Acts replace outcasts in the Gospel as those who believe; there are even Gentiles who belong in the periphery with the outcasts.

While it is well known what a proselyte is – one who has been converted to Judaism, has been circumcised, and has accepted the rule of the Torah[14] – we must rely on Luke to tell us what a God-fearer is, and that he never quite does. Since he describes the most prominent such person to appear in Acts, Cornelius, as someone who was 'devout and who, with all his household, feared God, who did many charitable things for the people, and who prayed to God all the time' (Acts 10.2), and since he also never says that Cornelius was a proselyte or that he had been circumcised, and since he describes Cornelius as a centurion, apparently quite unusual for a Jew,[15] it is normally thought that Luke means, by the designation of certain Gentiles as those who fear or worship God, that they were quasi-converts of some kind – people who worshipped the Jewish God, sought to live by the Torah, and attended synagogue (as in Acts 13.16,26; 18.7 and elsewhere) – but those who had not submitted to circumcision and thus become full converts.[16] This nearly universal understanding is not without its problems.[17] For one thing, Luke never actually says that the God-fearers *as a group* are uncircumcised (although that is, of course, the obvious implication in the case of Cornelius), and, for another, 'to fear God' is a classic biblical expression for obeying the Torah.[18] Furthermore, Luke uses the term 'worshipping (σεβόμενοι) proselytes' in Acts 13.43; yet the Gentiles who 'worship God' are in no way clearly distinguished from those who 'fear God', as a comparison between Acts 13.16, 26 and 17.17 will make clear. In the former instance Paul addresses, respectively, 'Israelite men and those who fear God' and 'sons of Abraham's race and those among you who fear God' while speaking in the synagogue in Antioch, whereas in the latter case it is said that he 'carried on a discussion . . . in the synagogue with the Jews and the worshippers' in Athens. If, then, we can have (apparently) God-fearers distinguished from Jews in Acts 13.16, 26 and then those same persons (apparently) called 'worshipping proselytes' in v. 43, and if Acts 17.17 then appears ambiguous, with its 'worshippers', because of this confusing use of terms in ch. 13, it will be better if we do not simply follow the tradition of assuming that 'God-fearers' are not proselytes but rather think of them together, keeping our eyes open, nevertheless, for any differences that may emerge.[19] When we come eventually to discuss how all these groups – outcasts, proselytes, God-fearers and Samaritans – fit into the chronological scheme of Acts, we shall see that Luke attempts to distinguish between proselytes and God-fearers; yet even there the distinction is not perfectly plain.

To return, then, to the earlier point: while the Gospel portrays a group of Jews who are not really Jews but outcasts and who respond properly to Jesus' ministry, Acts portrays the Gentile counterpart to that group, Gentiles who have attached themselves to Judaism, i.e., proselytes and those who worship or fear God.[20] Thus, if we could note earlier that the role of the outcasts in the Gospel is taken by the Gentiles in Acts, that equivalency is even more precisely true with regard to the proselytes and God-fearers. On the occasion of the first Christian sermon, at Pentecost, Luke emphasizes that the audience is made up of 'Jews and also proselytes' (Acts 2.10),[21] which possibly implies that proselytes were among the first group of Christian converts (2.41); and then we learn that one of the deacons chosen in ch. 6 is a proselyte (Nicolaus, v. 5).

The presence of Nicolaus among the earliest Christians would appear to be widely overlooked because of a stress that the Gentile mission first begins in ch. 10. Thus Haenchen, *Acts*, p. 171, writes that 'there are no pagans [in the Pentecost audience], for the gentile mission did not (according to Luke) begin until' ch. 10. The explanation thus given by Haenchen (and by many others, at least by implication) is that Nicolaus is a Jew (in Luke's opinion), since the first *Gentile* is converted only in ch. 10. If this were Luke's opinion, however, then he would place proselytes with Jews on one side and God-fearers with Gentiles on the other. Yet we have just seen that the line between proselyte and God-fearer is unclear in Acts. In this respect, Jervell seems to be more nearly correct when he argues that Gentiles are brought into Christianity from the first (cf. *People of God*, p. 43); and his statement (ibid., p. 66) that 'the new thing [in ch. 10] is not the salvation of the Gentiles, but that they are saved simply as Gentiles without . . . first becoming proselytes' is entirely correct. Jews may have considered proselytes to be Jews and no longer Gentiles, but one must be very careful about assigning that position to Luke. The mistake on both sides is the failure to see the role of the periphery in Luke's plan and the relation of proselytes and God-fearers in Acts to outcasts in the Gospel.

In ch. 10, then, the significant conversion of the God-fearer Cornelius is for Luke the occasion of the divine sanction of and inauguration of the carrying of the gospel to the Gentiles. We have already had occasion to discuss Peter's dream and its significance. The dream has, in fact, what one might call an immediate and an extended implication. In the first case, it means that the dietary laws are abrogated – 'Do not defile what God has purified' (Acts 10.15). In the second case, however, the dream is taken to justify the Gentile mission, so that Peter first reports to Cornelius and his other auditors that God has told him to 'call no *person* common or impure' (v. 28), showing that he understands now that it is permitted to associate with Gentiles;[22] and this understanding then leads to the full acceptance of Cornelius and his household as *Gentiles* into the church (Acts 10.44–11.18).[23] Thus, while Cornelius is himself a God-fearer, this episode becomes, for Luke, the divine initiation of the taking of the gospel to those Gentiles who have no association with Judaism.[24] The periphery, like Janus, looks both ways. Cornelius belongs in the periphery along with the proselytes (see the paragraph immediately following), but his conversion is the occasion of the church's realization that the gospel may be taken to the Gentiles as such.

These proselytes and God-fearers continue to be present in the Diaspora mission. In Paul's first sermon, he twice addresses Jews and God-fearers (Acts 13.16, 26), and then he is followed by 'many of the Jews and of the worshipping proselytes' when he leaves the synagogue (v. 43), whom he 'persuade[s] . . . to abide in the grace of God'. Later, after 'the Jews' oppose him and he delivers the first announcement of turning to the Gentiles (vv. 45–47), it is 'the Gentiles' who are converted in considerable numbers. What Gentiles? Surely those who had already been hearing him in the synagogue, i.e., the God-fearers and worshipping proselytes in the congregation. Paul's first converts follow the pattern established in the conversion of Cornelius and come from among this peripheral group. When 'the Jews' then incite the 'worshipping women' (v. 50) against Paul, we can hardly think that the women who are incited come from the group of new converts, especially since the episode closes with Luke's summary remark that 'the disciples were filled with grace and the Holy Spirit'. (v. 52). The women must rather be some of the proselytes (or God-fearers) who were not converted. The intermediate status of this group, in Luke's presentation, is thus underscored.

The class of Gentiles attached in some way to Judaism seems to be mentioned next in Acts 16.14, where Paul converts and, indeed, finds the assistance of a woman who is described as 'worshipping God', a term that would appear to be equivalent to 'fearing God';[25] and the same usage is employed in Acts 17.4, where we are informed that many 'of the worshipping Greek women . . . were persuaded'. In Acts 17.17 Paul speaks 'to Jews and worshippers', as we have noted, and, finally, seeks refuge in the house 'of Titius Iustus, a God-worshipper', from opposition raised by Jews in the synagogue at Corinth.

Proselytes and God-fearers in the Gospel

These proselytes and God-fearers and -worshippers, therefore, seem to take the role in Acts that was assigned to the outcasts in the Gospel; however, whereas there are no Jewish outcasts in Acts, there appears to be one God-fearer in the Gospel, the centurion whose slave is healed on the basis of the centurion's faith (Luke 7.1–10). While this centurion is not said to be a proselyte or God-fearer, there are several things about the narrative that make it seem that Luke wants to present him as one, or at least as almost one.[26] (The similarity between this centurion and the one in Acts 10 has often been noted.)[27] For one thing, the Jews say of him that 'he loves our people and built the synagogue for us himself' (v. 5). Would a Roman centurion go so far as to become the benefactor or perhaps patron of a Jewish town if he were not in some way devoted to the Jewish religion?[28] Further, when he desires a miracle worker he sends for a passing Jewish one (Jesus), which again shows his willingness to accept the validity of Jewish religion. Finally, however, and this is the most telling point, he believes. Jesus in fact declares that he has 'not found such faith in Israel' (v. 9). It is not permissible to think, as we might be inclined to do, that this faith is of a different order from that of the woman who is a 'sinner' in the closely following narrative set in a Pharisee's home (7.36–50), who is 'saved' because of her 'faith'. Not only does Luke make no attempt to distinguish these two faiths, but for us to think that Luke would have expected

his readers to see a difference between one faith and the other would
be to credit early Christians with the ability to distinguish theological
fine points which most modern Christians would not be able to
distinguish.[29] The much more likely assumption is that Luke expected
his readers to *connect* the two instances of faith, inasmuch as they
appear so close together in the Gospel, both attributed by Jesus at
the ends of the two stories to those whom he has helped.[30]

It is possible that Luke also thinks of the centurion who calls the just-deceased Jesus
δίκαιος in Luke 23.47 as displaying an attitude similar to that of that of Cornelius
and the centurion in Luke 7. The problem is that, as we saw in ch. 1, Luke apparently
thinks of the soldiers who crucified Jesus as Jewish soldiers. It would not seem to
be beyond Luke, however, to try to represent two things at once: 1. 'The Jews' killed
Jesus (and so the soldiers who carried out the actual execution are Jewish); 2. the
centurion who approaches Jesus immediately after his death (from Mark 15.39) is
similar to the centurions in Luke 7 and Acts 10 (similarly Walaskay, *We Came To
Rome*, p. 45). How one decides this matter determines how one translates δίκαιος
here. If the centurion belongs in a group with the other two, then he is a 'proto-
Christian' and proclaims Jesus 'righteous'. If, however, he is a soldier on whom the
injustice of Jesus' execution has just dawned, then he blurts out that Jesus is
'innocent'. Luke seems to have wanted to be deliberately vague. Cf. further the
discussion by Matera, 'Death of Jesus', p. 482. Grundmann, 'Lukas', p. 435; Ellis,
Luke, p. 270, and Schmid, *Lukas*, p. 351, emphasize that the centurion is a Gentile
and at least somewhat like the other two centurions. It is also worth noting, further,
that the centurion at the cross is placed close to the 'crowds' (v. 48), who are 'beating
their breasts'. Thus it is possible that Luke wants to show two responses to Jesus'
death (similarly Fitzmyer, *Luke*, vol. 2, p. 1515) – that of the centurion and that of
the crowds – and does not intend his readers to connect the centurion with the
soldiers; cf. further the discussion below in ch. 6.

It seems, then, that, while Luke has kept the outcasts out of Acts
altogether, he has not kept the proselytes and God-fearers entirely
out of the Gospel but has included at least one appearance of a
representative of that peripheral group.[31] This fact perhaps allows
us to understand a little more clearly the oft-repeated statement that
Luke makes a neat temporal separation between Gospel and Acts,
saving the mission to the Gentiles for the church, after Jesus' mission
to Israel.[32] That issue now needs to be put a little differently. While
it is true that Jesus does not, in Luke, *go* to the Gentiles, still we have
this one instance in which someone comes to him and 'believes' in
the Christian way, i.e., not as in Israel;[33] and we have also seen that
this one Gentile in the Gospel looks suspiciously as if he belongs to
the group of proselytes and God-fearers whom we find in Acts in

such profusion. When we remember, in addition to those points, that the proselytes and God-fearers in Acts take over the function of the outcasts in the Gospel and that this one apparent God-fearer in the Gospel appears in very close proximity precisely to one of those outcasts, who is also believing, then we are virtually driven to this conclusion: Luke thinks of God's salvation as passing from the Jews to the Gentiles via a periphery, a penumbra, that is made up of outcasts, proselytes and God-fearers and Samaritans. While he seems to want to refrain from having the gospel go to the Gentiles until after Acts 10, when God inaugurates the Gentile mission, he still cannot think of Jesus as having been entirely divorced from the Gentile mission, so he sets up the category of the Jewish periphery inhabited by outcasts, to whom God's salvation comes in Jesus' ministry, and then he lets the proselytes and God-fearers in Acts take the place of the outcasts as the first to whom the salvation of the Gentiles comes. He underscores this equivalency, furthermore, by placing one God-fearer in the Gospel in close proximity to an outcast and by pointing out that both believe, whereas 'Jews' do not. In Luke 7, therefore, Luke has 'tipped us off' that the proselytes and God-fearers in Acts are equivalent to the outcasts in the Gospel. They both belong to the periphery, to the twilight dawn between Judaism and Gentile Christianity, and they both respond to Jesus or, *mutatis mutandis*, to the gospel in the same way, in faith. We can discuss the degree to which Luke thinks of outcasts, proselytes and God-fearers as dwelling in a *series of concentric zones* subdividing this periphery only after we have examined the role of the Samaritans in Luke-Acts.

Samaritans in the Gospel

If the outcasts who believe in response to Jesus' ministry are kept in the Gospel and the proselytes and God-fearers who believe in response to the preaching of the early apostles and missionaries are kept, with the exception of one prototype (or two), in Acts, such isolation is not true of the third group on the periphery, the Samaritans, who bridge whatever gap exists between the outcasts in the Gospel and the proselytes and God-fearers in Acts, inasmuch as they are present in both and make – usually, in any case – the proper response to Jesus or to the gospel.[34]

Who the Samaritans were and what their relation to Judaism was is as well known as was the case with the proselytes.[35] The descendants of the long-destroyed northern kingdom of Israel, a population probably corrupted, from the strict Jewish point of view, by intermarriage with other peoples settled in the region by the ancient Assyrian destroyers, the Samaritans had incurred the everlasting wrath of the Jewish religious leadership when they sought to unite with the Jews in the building of the Second Temple and in the restoration of the Israelite religion. Rebuffed by the Jewish religious leadership, the Samaritans built their own temple at the ancient holy site of Shechem and adopted, along with the Jews, the Torah as their sacred scripture. From the Jewish side, in any case, the hostility overrode any awareness of Israelite kinship, and the Jews thought of the Samaritans as being 'like Gentiles'.[36] However, to the degree that anyone – Jew or Gentile – thought about the Samaritans, it was clear that Samaritans were not exactly Gentiles like Syrians or Greeks or Romans; but of course it was equally clear that they were not Jews. They belonged to the transitional periphery. Thus it is quite possible that the existence of Samaritans, most likely Samaritan Christians, in Luke's day first gave him the idea of the periphery, in which he then included Jewish religious outcasts and those Gentiles who had formed some kind of attachment to Judaism; but we cannot carry that speculation further here.

The first appearance of Samaritans in Luke-Acts is the one that fits the pattern least well. In Luke 9.52–53, at the outset of the travel narrative, Jesus sends his 'advance people' into a Samaritan village, but the Samaritans repulse them, as Luke says, 'because his person was travelling to Jerusalem'.[37] This act angers some of the disciples, who suggest annihilating the village by means of their superior divine fire power (v. 54), but Jesus 'scold[s] them. And they journe[y] to another village' (vv. 55–56). The action of the Samaritans in this episode and Jesus' response have provoked no little discussion, with by far the majority of authors seeing in the episode a parallel to Jesus' rejection at Nazareth in ch. 4,[38] the two rejections therefore forming the introductions to, respectively, the Galilean and the central portions of Jesus' ministry.[39] Some include still other rejections as additional parallel introductions to other stages of Jesus' ministry.[40] Now, there can hardly be any doubt that the rejection scene in the Samaritan village inaugurates the travel narrative at the end of ch. 9, just as the rejection scene in the Israelite village (Nazareth) inaugurates the Galilean ministry at the end of ch. 4, and that Luke uses these rejections deliberately to introduce the major sections of

Jesus' itinerant ministry; nevertheless, to stop with that observation is to fail to see the differences separating the two rejections and therefore Luke's point.

The differences are not subtle; they are glaring and of great importance. For one thing, Luke provides, in 9.53, a rationale for the Samaritans' rejection of Jesus: he was on his way to Jerusalem. Giving this as a rationale shows that Luke expects his readers to know something of the long-standing hostility between Samaritans and Jews, and perhaps that the Samaritans had a rival temple. The Samaritan reaction to Jesus here is thus provided with a reasonable excuse: they reject him because of his Jewish behaviour and for no other reason.[41] The other difference between this rejection episode and the earlier one set in Nazareth is even more striking: whereas in Nazareth Jesus threw it in the teeth of his Jewish congregation that God's grace had always gone to Gentiles and not to Israelites (Luke 4.24–27), thus angering them so that they would have killed him had he not escaped miraculously, in this second rejection episode Jesus turns the other cheek.[42] He says nothing and calls off those who would attack the Samaritans.[43] To put the matter as bluntly and plainly as possible, no charge is made against the Samaritans who reject Jesus.

Inasmuch as, after this rejection, Jesus proceeds to 'another village' (v. 56), and since the parable of the Good Samaritan and the narrative of the Samaritan leper both fall within the travel narrative, it is possible that Luke wishes his readers to understand that the travel narrative is an account of Jesus' travel through Samaria. This has been especially strongly argued by Enslin, 'Samaritan Ministry', who mentions, in addition to the Samaritan aspects just cited, the sending out of the seventy on Luke 10 as a doublet of the sending out of the Twelve in Luke 9.1–6 (ibid., pp. 30, 32–3) and the omission of the Matthaean prohibition against evangelizing Samaria (Matt. 10.15). Enslin goes so far as to propose that the Lucan introduction to the travel narrative, 'Travelling on, they entered a village of the Samaritans' (Luke 9.52), is a deliberate 'rebuttal' of the Matthaean prohibition (ibid., p. 32). The opinion that the travel narrative is intended as a Samaritan travel narrative has also been endorsed by Lohse, 'Lukas als Theologe', p. 85, and 'Missionarisches Handeln', pp. 8–9; and others. McCown, 'Luke's Central Section' and 'Gospel Geography', p. 15, thinks that Luke intends Samaria but makes a mess of it; and Schmithals, Lukas, p. 119, sees the Samaritan journey as 'the first step into Jewish universalism or into universal Judaism'. Conzelmann, Theology, p. 71, however, thinks that only the introductory section, Luke 9.51–56, can be seen as giving any indication that Luke intends to represent Jesus as travelling through Samaria, and that the emphasis in this narrative falls on rejection. 'All the other observations support the idea of a direct transition from Galilee to Judaea.'

While it would seem to fit well into Luke's plan to have Jesus travel through Samaria at this point, the Gospel thus proceeding according to a geography the reverse of that in Acts, the truth is that Luke has been much too subtle about indicating that, if it was his meaning. Nevertheless, it is also true that all references to Samaritans in the Gospel fall within the travel narrative. It thus seems to me that Luke probably wanted to show that Jesus' *contact* with Samaritans (which he does want to emphasize) falls within that period of his ministry immediately preceding his Jerusalem ministry; but that he was not especially concerned to show that the journey of the travel narrative was through Samaria. Still, the statement of Robinson, 'Context', p. 29, that 'specific locale was of [little or no] concern to Luke' seems to me to be more an attempt to distance his position from Conzelmann's than an accurate description of the role of Samaria and Samaritans in the travel narrative.

After this clumsy entrance of Samaritans in 9.52–54 on to Luke's stage, the Samaritans proceed to turn in a sterling performance in a supporting role. In Luke 10.30–35(36) appears one of the most famous of all characters in Christian literature, the Good Samaritan.[44] Do those prissy priests and Levites keep their ritual hands clean and leave a man dying at the roadside? Not so our unbelievably generous yet self-effacing Samaritan, who turns over his hospital insurance card (or maybe it's his bank card) to the local hospital, promising to pay later 'whatever [the hospital administration] spend[s] in addition' to the down payment that he had already made (v. 35). For our purposes here we must forget whatever point or points Jesus may have intended when he told this marvellous little story and concentrate on Luke's meaning. That meaning will, of course, be found in the Lucan framework, which Crossan has shown includes vv. 25–29 and 37.[45] This Lucan framework begins by asking how to 'inherit eternal life' (v. 25) and concludes with the advice to 'go and do likewise yourself' (v. 37). Like a Samaritan, not like the Jewish religious leaders.[46]

This contrast is as strong as that between Pharisee and toll collector, in the parable of the same name, that occupied us at some length in the preceding chapter.[47] Just as Luke used one of his peripheral characters there (an outcast) as an example of proper Christianity over against the behaviour of one of the Jewish groups that he so dislikes (halachic Jews), so here he uses another character from the periphery, a Samaritan, as an example of true Christian behaviour that is contrasted to that of another despised Jewish group, the religious leadership. Samaritan here, toll collector there; except for the element of verisimilitude that prevents a Samaritan's going to the Jerusalem Temple to pray, they are entirely interchangeable.

A similar sort of correlation exists between the sinner who anoints Jesus in ch. 7 and the Samaritan leper who is healed in 17.11–19.[48] In this latter case, ten lepers have approached Jesus for healing, nine Jews and one Samaritan.[49] While we do not learn of this division until v. 16, Luke prepares the way for such an 'interracial' group by writing in the introduction to the narrative that Jesus is travelling 'through the midst of Samaria and Galilee' (v. 11). When, however, the one healed leper who is grateful is then designated a Samaritan, Jesus emphasizes that he is a 'foreigner (ἀλλογενής)' and says to him exactly what he said in 7.50 to the outcast at the home of the Pharisee Simon, 'Your faith has saved you' (Luke 17.19).[50]

That the phrase 'through the midst of Samaria and Galilee' (Luke 17.11) is geographically impossible is immaterial. On the difficulty of the phrase, cf. esp. Fitzmyer, *Luke*, vol. 2, pp. 1152–3. The significance of this geographical designation has received much discussion since Conzelmann indicated its importance, taking it to mean '*between* Samaria and Galilee' (*Theology*, pp. 69–70; cf. the discussion in Bauer-Arndt-Gingrich, *Greek-English Lexicon*, s.v. μέσος, 2). Bruners, *Reinigung der Aussätzigen*, p. 162, refers almost mysteriously to 'a definite Lucan topographical concept' that allows Samaria to be mentioned before Galilee, and he refers to Acts 9.31 (as did Conzelmann, also, *Theology*, p. 69). We shall best understand the designation 'through the midst of Samaria and Galilee', however, if we ignore the question of what Luke thought a map of Palestine looked like and simply recognize that Luke has created this geographical anomaly because he wanted to make the one healed leper who was thankful a Samaritan in order to contrast Samaritan and Jewish response to Jesus, and that he therefore referred to a place where Jesus might find Jews and Samaritans together, namely while journeying 'through the midst of Samaria and Galilee'. So also Goulder, *Type*, p. 58. The phrase is not merely a 'narrative slip', as Hengel, *Between Jesus and Paul*, p. 100, thinks. Bruners, *Reinigung der Aussätzigen*, has, in my opinion, demonstrated that Luke created this story out of the earlier healing of a leper in Luke 5.12–16 (par. Mark 1.40–45) and certain biblical (i.e., Old Testament) themes. Even persons who are not so convinced, however, will realize that the presence of the Samaritan in the narrative is what Bruners (*Reinigung der Aussätzigen*, p. 243), calls a 'supplemental intensification'.

Discussions about just what 'saved' is supposed to mean in these two cases and about just what the relation is between 'faith' and salvation in either case are beside the point;[51] for the significance for Luke is that both these persons who are said to have faith that saves come from the periphery of Judaism. They are not exactly Jews, but they are not really Gentiles either. They form the transition zone between Judaism and the Gentile church, and their response to Jesus is prototypical of the response of Gentiles to the gospel. Within the periphery, therefore, the equivalencies exist on all sides, and, *as far as Luke's theology is concerned*, it matters not a whit whether the person who anoints Jesus or the leper who is healed or the one who prays for redemption in the Temple is an outcast, a Samaritan, or a proselyte or God-fearer. Their response to Jesus or their exemplary piety is of one piece, and the differences exist only for verisimilitude and for narrative interest. When Luke wants to present a contrast to the halachic Pharisees he uses an outcast, and when he wants a contrast to 'the Jews' he employs a Samaritan or a God-fearer or proselyte; or, when he needs someone in the Temple, he uses an outcast because he knows that Gentiles and Samaritans were not permitted there, and, when Jesus is on his way from Galilee to Jerusalem, Luke uses a Samaritan instead of an outcast or a proselyte or God-fearer because he knows (more or less) where the Samaritans were.[52]

Samaritans in Acts

In Acts the Samaritans continue to appear in the same way. The first group to be evangelized, after the persecution of Christians broke out in Jerusalem on the heels of Stephen's martyrdom (Acts 8.1–3), was the Samaritans. Although Luke states that the Jerusalem Christians 'were scattered throughout the regions of Judaea and Samaria' (8.1), Judaea is then entirely ignored, and we learn that 'Philip . . . preached Christ' in 'the city of Samaria' (v. 5) – presumably the main Samaritan city of Sebaste, the ancient Samaria[53] – and that the citizens responded 'with one accord' (v. 6). Like Jesus' ministry and the earlier apostolic ministry, this ministry was also accompanied by healing miracles (v. 7). When the preaching and the expressions of miraculous power had led to many conversions to Christianity (vv. 11–13), the apostolic leadership of the church bestowed its seal of approval on the inclusion of Samaritans in the church (vv. 14–15) and completed the process by arranging the outpouring of the Spirit on the newly baptized believers (v. 17). Just so that we are not left with the impression that only those Samaritans in 'the city' became Christians, Luke concludes this narrative by informing us that the apostolic delegation returned to Jerusalem 'evangeliz[ing] many Samaritan villages' along the way (Acts 8.25). Apparently, the Samaritans fulfil the promise demonstrated in the Gospel and are converted to Christianity *en masse*.[54]

Samaritans as neither Jews nor Gentiles

It is the peripheral position of the Samaritans in Luke-Acts that has consistently misled so many authors who have tried to understand their role. On the one hand, many have viewed them as Gentiles or as proto-Gentiles,[55] but others have attempted to understand them as some kind of Jews, even as renegade Jews, as 'the lost sheep of the House of Israel', to use Jervell's term.[56] The former mistake is easier to understand and is, in a sense, more nearly correct, for the Samaritans respond favourably to Jesus in the Gospel and are those among whom the first advance of the Gospel away from Judaism is made in Acts 8.[57] On the other hand, Jervell's position regarding the Samaritans, that they are Jews of some kind, is predicated on his belief that the gospel is sent to the Jews and that the Gentiles are saved only as an extension of the salvation of Israel.[58] Jervell's argument is primarily negative – that is, he attempts to show that Luke does not think of the Samaritans as Gentiles. Thus he argues that the conversion of Samaria in Acts 8 'awaken[s] . . . no suspicions . . . in Jerusalem' and that, inasmuch as the Samaritan mission precedes the conversion of Cornelius, the Samaritans cannot be Gentiles.[59] Furthermore, Jervell thinks that the Samaritan rejection of Jesus in Luke 9.51–56 shows that Luke cannot think of the Samaritans as Gentiles, since elsewhere in Luke-Acts only Jews reject Jesus, whereas Gentiles never do.[60] Jervell's positive argument, that the Samaritans are Jews in Luke-Acts, begins with this same narrative, in regard to which he emphasizes (correctly) that the cause of the Samaritan rejection of Jesus is Jesus' Jewish 'orthodoxy', i.e., his journeying to Jerusalem in order to worship.[61] Also, the 'mass conversions' in Samaria in Acts 8 and the apostolic legation of 8.14–17 prove to Jervell that Samaritans are, for Luke, some kind of extension, albeit heterodox, of Israel.[62]

Now, if Jervell had emphasized more the heterodox connection and not so much the kinship, and if he had seen the degree to which Samaritans and proselytes are interchangeable in Luke-Acts, there would not be so much to object to in his presentation. Yet he specifically rules out the possibility 'that Luke saw the Samaritans as a kind of proselytes',[63] and therefore is behoves us to show why Jervell's position is unacceptable as an adequate explanation of the portrait of the Samaritans in Luke-Acts.

The primary problem is the alternative posed: either Gentile or

Jew; but surely the evidence that has been presented above is sufficient to show that the alternative is false and that Luke thinks of the world's population as being divided into three and not into two groups, the three being the Jews, the periphery about Judaism, and the Gentiles. To the degree that Jervell's case rests on showing that Luke does not think of the Samaritans as Gentiles, the realization of the existence of the periphery in Luke's thinking removes the support for Jervell's conclusion, even though his point is correct; the Samaritans are *not* Gentiles.

Jervell's positive argument, that the Samaritans *are* Jews, rests, as we have seen, primarily on his interpretation of two sections of Luke-Acts, the Samaritan rejection of Jesus at the outset of the travel narrative and the Samaritan conversions to Christianity in the first part of Acts 8. Regarding the first point, I can only repeat my earlier observation, namely that the Samaritan rejection of Jesus at the beginning of the travel narrative is not of one piece with the Jewish rejection of Jesus at the beginning of the Galilean ministry, since the Samaritan rejection is excused on the basis of a rationale and since criticism of the Samaritans who reject Jesus is shunted aside. But the Samaritan conversions in Acts also do not prove that the Samaritans are thought to be Jews, for the volume of conversions is precisely what it should be for an intermediate group, large but not quite as large as that of Jewish conversions during the 'Jerusalem springtime', which ran to the 'myriads' (Acts 21.20). Thus the quantity of Samaritan conversions to Christianity in Acts 8 fits the Lucan oddity that, as the gospel progresses from the Jews to the Gentiles, the volume of conversions declines. (Probably this is only a seeming oddity, since, for Luke, the period of Jewish salvation is over, whereas the period of Gentile salvation is just getting under way. Therefore he says of the Gentiles at the conclusion of Acts, 'They *will* hear.')

Beyond this, however, Jervell gets into difficulty when he tries to deal with the evidence that does not, in his opinion, directly support his case. His attempt to explain the narrative of the Samaritan leper who was healed in Luke 17 is instructive. To begin with, the false alternative, Jew or Gentile, gets in his way, so that, while he recognizes that 'an uninformed reader might conclude that the Samaritan was a Gentile', it would nevertheless 'remai[n] unintelligible for the reader how Jesus could send this Gentile along with the nine Jews to the Temple in Jerusalem'.[64] In addition, however, to the fact that, in Luke's thinking, not being a Gentile does not *ipso facto* make the Samaritan a Jew, one would have to ask whether an informed reader would find it any more intelligible that Jesus would send a Samaritan to the Jewish Temple. It is only by realizing that Luke's position does not conform to that of Judaism (if you're not a Jew you're a Gentile) that we can understand the conclusion to the narrative of the healed Samaritan leper. Even beyond this, however, Jervell has to face the fact that Jesus calls the Samaritan an ἀλλογενής, i.e., someone of another race (Luke 17.18). Jervell sees well enough that the term ἀλλόφυλος (Acts 10.28), which ought to be synonymous with ἀλλογενής, means 'Gentile',[65] but then he can only state arbitrarily that ἀλλογενής in Luke 17.18 'does not . . . by itself . . . mean that [the Samaritans] are non-Israelites in a purely ethnic sense, even though this is the usual use of the term in the Septuagint'.[66] That argument can only be labelled a *tour de force*; if Samaritans are ἀλλογενεῖς then they are of another race.[67]

Jervell also has trouble with Luke's labelling the Samaritans in Acts 8.9 a 'people (ἔθνος)' or, as he translates, 'nation'.[68] Of this designation Jervell can only write that 'nothing is mentioned about what kind of nation they are', an observation that completely skirts round the issue at hand – that is, whether the Samaritans are Jews or not. Finally, Jervell gives no discussion of the parable of the Good Samaritan; whereas, as we have seen, this parable is not insignificant for a complete and proper understanding of Luke's portrayal of the Samaritans.

It is Cullmann who has understood the role of the Samaritans most accurately.[69] 'The mission to Samaria,' he writes, 'forms a natural transition towards the mission to the Gentiles.' Luke 'understood that the proclamation of the gospel in Samaria was the decisive step towards the mission to the Gentiles'.[70] And Cullmann also saw that the desire to portray the Samaritans as a 'natural transition' group lay behind Luke's particular emphasis on the Samaritans in the Gospel.[71] As we have seen, the evidence supports that understanding and not an understanding of the Samaritans that makes them either Gentiles or Jews. The Samaritans are, for Luke, a 'natural transition' group between Jews and Gentiles. They belong, with the Jewish outcasts and the Gentile proselytes and God-fearers, on the periphery of Judaism.

Now that we have the periphery completely in view, we see that it is uniform in both the Gospel and Acts, and that the differences among the three groups – outcasts, Samaritans and proselytes and God-fearers[72] – are matters of historical verisimilitude, narrative interest, or *heilsgeschichtliche* progression (outcast Jews in the Gospel replaced by proselytes and God-fearers in Acts); and the function of this periphery within the overall scheme of Luke-Acts seems obvious: to serve as a transition zone as the salvation of God moves from the Jews to the Gentiles. While this statement appears adequately to represent the way in which Luke has portrayed these several groups, there is yet one aspect of his portrayal that seems to involve a distinction, and perhaps even a necessary one. That is the narrative of the progression in Acts 8–11.

A distinction between proselytes and God-fearers

After the gospel is received in Samaria and the Samaritan Christians are approved by the Jerusalem leadership of the church, Philip converts an Ethiopian eunuch (Acts 8.26–39), a man clearly thereby labelled as a Gentile; yet, this conversion precedes the conversion of Cornelius in Acts 10, which is, as is universally recognized, the programmatic inauguration of the Gentile mission. How, then, can we have a Gentile conversion before this event?

There are two possible answers to this question. One is that Luke has not been entirely systematic in following the scheme that he himself laid down in Acts 1.8 (Jerusalem, Judaea and Samaria, the rest of the world) and has only followed it generally, while leaving the story of the conversion of the Ethiopian eunuch in what seems to be its best location, from the point of view of a reasonable historical narrative. The fact that he also took account of a proselyte conversion in Acts 6.5 might also support this answer. The other alternative is that Luke has a definite scheme in mind, and that he thinks of the Ethiopian as a *proselyte*, who is therefore to be distinguished from the *God-fearer* Cornelius.[73] We would then have a definite progression after the persecution of Acts 8.1: Samaritans, proselyte (the Ethiopian), God-fearer (Cornelius), Gentile mission (beginning slowly in Acts 11.19–24, then gaining momentum after ch. 12).[74] This pattern would dovetail with the geographical scheme announced in Acts 1.8, and we note further that Luke does mention 'Judaea and Samaria' in 8.1, just prior to the Samaritan mission, which would seem to show that he is thinking of the pattern of Acts 1.8.[75]

The issue of Luke's intended order of progression becomes considerably more complicated if we try to make sense, as does Sahlin, *Dritter Kapitel*, pp. 122–5, out of who gets baptized and who receives the Spirit, and in what order. According to Sahlin, the Spirit that is bestowed at Pentecost, since it is bestowed on the Twelve, is given symbolically to all Israel; thus, the converts who follow shortly are only baptized, since they have already, symbolically speaking, received the Spirit. The same is then the case with the eunuch, who is not a Gentile but a ritually impure Jew. The Spirit falls on the Samaritans, since they are not symbolically included in the Twelve, indicating the inclusion of all Samaritans in the true Israel of God; and then, of course, the Spirit is bestowed on Cornelius as the representative of all Gentiles. Cornelius's baptism *follows* his receiving the Spirit because the epoch-making event of the inclusion of Gentiles is of such importance that it has forced the bestowing of the Spirit forward, baptism then becoming 'only . . . a necessary consequence' (ibid., p. 124). While this is an ingenious solution to the relation of Spirit to baptism in Acts, there are two apparent problems. One is that Luke does not emphasize that the Spirit fell at Pentecost on the Twelve; rather, his statement (Acts 2.1) that 'all were together', while possibly referring to the reconstituted Twelve at the end of ch. 1, could as well refer to the whole group of the followers (120 according to Acts 1.15; it is normally so taken) or, perhaps better, to the Eleven 'with women and Mary the mother of Jesus' of v. 14. The other problem is that the eunuch is surely a proselyte (see immediately below), someone whom Luke associates with God-fearers and does not quite think of as a ritually impure Jew. In any case, Sahlin's solution does not help us to clarify what order of progression Luke had in mind for the spread of the gospel, since, if he were correct about the eunuch, the eunuch's conversion would seem to fit more appropriately before that of the Samaritans.

It may be that no eunuch was, in fact, a proselyte to Judaism in post-exilic antiquity, inasmuch as Deut. 23.1 (Heb. v. 2) specifically prohibits such people from being members of the 'assembly'. There is a most interesting section of Isaiah, however, that would seem to bear on the situation in Acts. In Isa. 56.4–5 the prophet speaks for God, saying, 'To the eunuchs who keep my Sabbaths . . . I will give in my house and within my walls a monument and a name';[76] and this promise is immediately followed by a direct reference to proselytes, v. 6, where 'the foreigners joined to Yahweh, to minister to him and to love the name of Yahweh, to become his servants, everyone who keeps Sabbath', are mentioned. That would have settled the matter for Luke, whose fondness for the book of Isaiah we recall, whatever the true historical situation may have been regarding the relation of eunuchs to Judaism. The eunuch, *who is reading the book of Isaiah* when Philip approaches him (Acts 8.30), is a proselyte as far as Luke is concerned. Nevertheless, there are still some problems with this answer to the question as to whether Luke makes a clear distinction between proselytes and God-fearers as a part of his explanation of the progression of the gospel from the Jews to the Gentiles. Not the least such problem is the presence, to which we have already referred, of proselytes among the early converts in Acts and, even more, of at least one believing God-fearer in the Gospel. Furthermore, of course, Luke does not label the eunuch either a proselyte or a God-fearer, and we have already noted in detail that, apart from the problem that immediately concerns us, the distinction is hardly clear in the latter part of Acts.[77] This issue will probably never be resolved to everyone's satisfaction, but the following conclusions would seem to be unassailable.

In general, Samaritans, outcasts and proselytes and God-fearers belong, as a group, to the same clearly defined periphery about Judaism through which the salvation of God passes on its way from the Jews to the Gentiles. Further, Luke normally uses the terms 'proselyte, God-fearer' and 'God-worshipper' interchangeably, and he even equates them on occasion. While he keeps the main thrust of the movement of salvation from the Jews to the Gentiles in the latter part of Acts (after ch. 10), he does not uniformly hold Gentiles back from God's salvation prior to that point, as we see from the case of the apparent God-fearer in Luke 7.1–10. Since there seems little doubt that he thinks of the Ethiopian of Acts 8 as a proselyte, he seems to want to show a progression in the advance of the gospel from the Jews to the Gentiles after Acts 8.1 via Samaritans, proselytes and God-fearers. Otherwise, however, the distinction between proselyte and God-fearer is irrelevant to him, inasmuch as all Gentiles who have attached themselves to Judaism in some way belong equally to the periphery, along with Samaritans and outcasts.

This concludes the thematic analysis of the problem. It is time now to take a somewhat different approach in our investigation of Luke's portrayal of the Jews.

Part Two

SYSTEMATIC ANALYSIS

A thematic investigation, like the foregoing one, is a useful way to clarify an issue or issues in a body of literature, and our thematic investigation here has, indeed, proved quite fruitful; for we have been able in this way to gain new insights into Luke's portrait of the Jews in its several aspects. Even so, however, our study cannot stop here; for the thematic investigation needs to be tested against the portrait as it is actually seen – that is to say that we need to proceed directly through Luke-Acts from beginning to end, not skipping around from here to there, in order to be sure that the insights gained in the thematic investigation coincide with the narrative as Luke presents it. Indeed, S. G. Wilson has called attention, in his most recent work on Luke-Acts, to the problems of a thematic investigation. Such an approach 'can result,' he writes, 'in distortion both of the intention of the author, in so far as this is recoverable, and of the impression the narrative would have had on its first readers.' Further, even, 'a thematic approach may also give a false impression of coherence to material which is recorded in a haphazard way' (Wilson, *Law*, p. 12. Wilson's cautions do not faze him, and he goes ahead to follow a 'thematic approach', anyway). It is especially Wilson's latter caution that I take to heart, for we are dealing with a major issue here, the early stages of Christian antisemitism, and I do not want to be unjust to Luke or to make it appear that his work is something that it is not. A mistaken impression must surely be avoided. Primarily for this reason, therefore, we need to proceed now to what I have chosen to call a systematic analysis, a 'commentary-like' study of Luke-Acts, in which we move directly through the Lucan work from the prehistory in Luke 1–2 to the final scene of Acts, where Paul speaks to the Roman Jews, examining those passages that bear on our issue as they come up. Only when we have done this can we be sure that we have got Luke's point(s). We are, in other words, about to test the conclusions reached previously.

There is, furthermore, a more benign kind of distortion that an investigation such as the foregoing can produce, and that is the distortion of particular perspectives. In inquiring first into Luke's portrayal of the Jewish leaders, then of Jerusalem, and so forth, we run the risk of being like the blind persons in the famous Indian fable, each one of whom touched an elephant in a different place. For Luke does not always keep leaders and people, leaders and Pharisees, people and Pharisees in isolation from one another; and the threads of Jerusalem and of the periphery are woven into the tapestry of the whole rather than forming borders or fringes, as it were. If, therefore, we want to step back from the portrait to view it as a whole, to see how the various colours blend or contrast with one another (that is, to see how the individual themes discussed in Part One interact), then there is only one way to gain this perspective, and that is to follow Luke's development of the several themes through in his order, from Luke 1 to Acts 28.

Finally, there is a further, secondary reason for presenting the following systematic analysis, and that is that, try as we might, every relevant and pertinent section of Luke-Acts could not be discussed conveniently in the foregoing thematic investigation. The section with which we begin now, the prehistory, is a prime case in point. In the following systematic analysis it will be possible to examine everything that Luke wrote about the Jews, in the order in which he wrote it, without overlooking even minor touches. When that examination is complete, we will have Luke's entire picture before us, and we can return, in Part Three, to the question of Luke's motivation.

Inasmuch as the thematic investigation has been amply referenced with notes, it has seemed to me appropriate to dispense, by and large, with the use of notes in the following systematic analysis and to employ, rather, the device used in many commentaries and other reference works of presenting a list of the relevant literature at the beginning of the discussion of each section of Luke-Acts.

6

THE GOSPEL OF LUKE

Luke 1.5–25, 57–79   *Annunciation and birth of John the Baptist*
1.26–56   *Annunciation of the birth of Jesus, and the two birth stories brought into contact with each other*
2.1–52   *Jesus' birth and childhood*

Important literature: R.E. **Brown**, *Birth*, pp. 256–496; **Dibelius**, 'Jung-frauensohn und Krippenkind'; **Drury**, *Tradition and Design*, pp. 46–60; **Dupont**, 'Le salut des gentils', pp. 136–8; **Fitzmyer**, *Luke*, vol. 1, pp. 304–447; **Franklin**, *Christ the Lord*, pp. 80–7; **Gnilka**, 'Hymnus des Zacharias'; **Grundmann**, *Lukas*, pp. 45–70; **Kilpatrick**, 'ΛΑΟΙ'; **Kloster-mann**, *Lukas*, pp. 6–29; **Laurentin**, *Structure et théologie*; **Lohfink**, *Sammlung Israels*, pp. 1–32; **Loisy**, *Evangiles synoptiques*, vol. 1, pp. 277–86, 314; **Maddox**, *Purpose*, pp. 11–12; **Mattill**, 'Evans', pp. 22–3; **Minear**, 'Birth Stories'; **Montefiore**, *Synoptic Gospels*, vol. 2, pp. 379–80; **Morgenthaler**, *Geschichtsschreibung*, vol. 1, pp. 178–80; **Oliver**, *Birth Stories*; **Radl**, *Paulus und Jesus*, pp. 73–5; **Sahlin**, *Messias und Gottesvolk*, pp. 331–9; **Sandmel**, *Anti-Semitism*, p. 75; **Vielhauer**, 'Benedictus'; **Wilson**, *Gentiles*, pp. 134–5; **Wink**, *John the Baptist*, pp. 58–82.

The birth stories stand so much apart from the rest of Luke-Acts that they are often explained as coming from a special source, or even as having been added after the original completion of the Gospel. Thus Conzelmann (*Theology*) did not take them into consideration in his analysis, finding their relevance questionable,[1] whereas Sahlin found himself driven, by his study of this part of the Gospel, to support the theory of a Proto-Luke 'translated [from Aramaic or Hebrew] and reworked by Luke'.[2] Even those who do not hold such 'severe' (if we may use that term without prejudice) theories widely hold that 1.5–25, 57–79 come from an earlier story about John that Luke has taken up and brought into contact with the narrative about

Jesus, or that Luke has taken over and used as a model for the stories of Jesus' birth;[3] and still others think that the prehistory belongs to a second edition of Luke, the first edition having begun at what is now 3.1.[4]

Whatever sources Luke may have used for this 'prehistory' – and the case for an origin of the Johannine stories in a Johannine circle seems especially appealing – the final product seems to fit well into his overall plan. Indeed, the very characteristic that has led Sahlin and others to argue for a separate, Semitic, origin for chs. 1 and 2 is, when viewed from a different perspective, the characteristic that fits so well into Luke's plan, and that is the overwhelming Jewishness of this section. That Luke has got some Jewish customs wrong (e.g., the reference to purification in 2.22) does not detract from this overall impression. 'The details [of these chapters] serve to heighten the Jewish and OT colouring of the setting in which the gospel events begin.'[5] Much of the action in these chapters occurs in the Temple in Jerusalem, or on the way to or from it, and two of the three major hymns recorded – the *Benedictus* (1.68–79) and the *Nunc dimittis* (2.29–32) – are sung in the Temple. All three of the hymns, further-more (including the *Magnificat* 1.46–55), are loaded with biblical (i.e., Old Testament) allusions. Nearly every author who has studied the infancy narratives has noted this trait, and Brown observes that the hymns 'have their closest parallel in the Jewish hymns and psalms attested in the literature from 200 BC to AD 100, e.g., in I Maccabees, Judith, *II Baruch*, *IV Ezra*, the Qumran *Hodayoth* (Thanksgiving Psalms), and the Qumran War Scroll'.[6] He then gives the Jewish parallels that he notes for the three hymns.[7] Thus we have, in these two chapters, not only a setting in which much happens in the Temple and in which all is done according to the Torah, but in which the major 'production pieces', the three main hymns of the section, draw heavily on biblical language. The author of Luke 1–2 has spared no effort to show the thorough Jewishness of Jesus' origins. Should we for this reason, therefore, ignore these two chapters in an investigation of the aspects of Luke's theology?

Decidedly not. The setting in the Temple is quite in place; for, as Morgenthaler has shown, both Luke and Acts begin and end with Temple scenes (more or less, as we saw above in ch. 2). This appears to be an aspect of Luke's architectonic parallelizing. Even beyond this structural function, however, the Jerusalem scenes serve a theological purpose, for Luke uses them to mark the major shifts in his *Heilsgeschichte*: Jesus begins enshrouded in Jerusalem Jewishness; he takes his message to Jerusalem and finishes his career there; the early church likewise begins in a 'Jerusalem springtime'; and finally Paul, like Jesus, is brought to trial in Jerusalem. The two parallel endings have their differences, which have occupied our attention in Part One and will do so again; but here I want to fix on the point regarding the beginnings. That both Jesus and the church, in Luke-Acts, begin in a 'Jerusalem springtime' can be no accident. Luke wishes to emphasize a point.

The point is, put most simply, that Jesus and the church did not turn their backs on the Jews; it was the other way round. The 'Jerusalem springtime' of Luke reaches its climax in the closing scene, in which the boy Jesus 'amazes' (2.47) his hearers with 'his understanding and answers' and responds to his distraught parents, 'It is necessary for me to be involved with those matters that are my father's' (v. 49). What a lovely and appealing story! The young innocent, his *Bar mitzvah* (so to speak) just over, so earnestly devoted to his religion, and manfully rebuking his parents for not having realized his manhood and his devotion. How completely *involved* Jesus is in the Jewish religion! What went wrong? What, indeed! Thereby hangs the tale that is Luke-Acts; for this scene of the boy Jesus in the Temple is integrally related to Paul's three statements in Acts that the Jews' rejection of the gospel marks the turning to the Gentiles. In every way possible Luke informs us that Christianity did not seek an exodus out of Judaism but was rather squeezed out by the Jews. The infancy narratives play their part in that pattern, for they show how totally immersed the Christian beginnings were in good Jewish piety.

The pendulum of scholarship, in fact, has swung so far away from the view that Luke 1–2 bears little or no relation to the rest of the Gospel that Lohfink finds in 2.34 – 'Simeon . . . said . . ., "He is set for the fall and rise of many in Israel"' – the clue to the entire theology of Israel in Luke-Acts,[8] with the rising happening in Acts 1–5, the falling taking place in the remainder of Acts. That is to say that Lohfink finds in Luke 2.34 a programmatic statement that is then carried out systematically in Acts. As we were able to see above in Part One, however, Lohfink's explanation emphasizes too much the concept of a division within Israel (people v. leaders, those who respond to Jesus and the gospel v. those who do not) and not enough the temporal shift *from* Israel *to* the Gentiles. That is what an analysis of the role of the Jews in Luke-Acts shows to be the meaning of Luke 2.34: not that Jews take sides, but that the 'Jerusalem springtime' of Jewish salvation has given way to a divinely-willed Gentile church. Lohfink is correct that there is a line between Acts 5 and Acts 6, and he is correct to label the first five chapters an account of Christianity's 'Jerusalem springtime',[9] but he has failed to draw the correct implications from these observations. Even his realization that all the uniformly harsh characterizations of 'the Jews' in the Gospel are in 'direct discourse', i.e., in the words of Jesus,[10] did not lead him to follow up on the difference between speech and narrative throughout Luke-Acts and to reach the correct conclusion.

The Lucan infancy narratives are indeed steeped in Jewishness, and the Lucan Jesus will indeed be the catalyst for the 'fall and rise of many in Israel', but these traits of chs. 1–2 do not support the 'division in Israel' theory; rather, they prepare the way for the reader to feel quite satisfied with the conclusion of Acts. The rejection of the Jews was their own fault.

Luke 3.1–20   John's ministry

Important literature: **Conzelmann**, *Theology*, pp. 18–22; **Fitzmyer**, *Luke*, vol. 1, pp. 450–78; **George**, 'Israël', pp. 488–9; 'La prédication inaugurale'; **Lampe**, 'Luke', p. 826; **Morgenthaler**, *Geschichtsschreibung*, vol. 1, pp. 178–80; **Sahlin**, *Dritter Kapitel*, pp. 38–40; **Walaskay**, *We Came to Rome*, pp. 28–32.

The cosy relationship between Jesus and traditional Judaism is now over, and the difficulties are about to begin. It is probably significant that John's audience is made up of 'crowds' (v. 7), 'toll collectors' (v. 12), and 'soldiers' (v. 14), but none of the priestly leadership or Pharisees, as in the Matthaean parallel (Matt. 3.7). It would be difficult to say with certainty whether Luke has omitted the Pharisees and Sadducees from his source or whether Matthew has added them. If Luke's source did include the reference to an audience made up of Pharisees and Sadducees, then Luke's change of the description of the audience is all the more significant; but that question must remain open.[11]

In any case, the absence of such people and the fact that, apparently, all who come to hear John receive his baptism (vv. 7, 12), make it impossible to agree with George that, '*devant ce message, Israël se divise*'.[12] What does happen, however, is that the crowds both accept John's baptism and are condemned by him, whereas the other two groups baptized, toll collectors and soldiers, seem not to be so criticized. If we skip over John's 'generation of vipers' tirade for a moment, we note two things. One is the way in which the reference to the three groups is constructed in parallel form. 'The crowds come out to be baptized by him' (v. 7); they ask him, 'What then shall we do?' (v. 10), and he replies with moral advice appropriate to their status in life (v. 11). Likewise the toll collectors 'c[o]me . . . to be baptized and sa[y] to him, ". . . What shall we do?"' (v. 12); and he again replies with moral advice appropriate to their status in life (v. 13). When, then, in v. 14 the soldiers ask John, 'What are we also to do?' and when he also replies with moral advice appropriate to their status in life, we are surely to understand that the soldiers have also come to be baptized and that Luke has not mentioned that fact specifically, in the interest of avoiding wooden repetition in his narrative.

Into the account about the crowds, however, Luke has spliced John's condemnation (which Matthew directs towards the Pharisees and Sadducees). The crowds come to John to be baptized, he condemns them as a generation of vipers, and only then do they ask his advice and receive his admonition. Thus Luke has directed the 'generation of vipers' speech pointedly at the crowds alone, *not* at the toll collectors and soldiers. Luke has thereby managed to accomplish several things at once. He has kept the religious leadership and the Pharisees from being baptized by John; he has kept the Pharisees from being condemned by John; he has shown toll collectors and soldiers to be both accepting of John's message and acceptable to John; and he has put the crowds into the kind of ambiguous position that they will again assume at the end of the Gospel, where they both participate in and stay aloof from Jesus' execution.[13] This last point can hardly be emphasized strongly enough. So far from using the narrative of John's ministry to begin a characterization of a 'divided Israel', Luke has skilfully shown that John condemns the crowds, i.e., the 'people', outright *even though they receive his baptism.* Thus what we actually have here is an early warning of the divine rejection of the Jews.

Some question must remain about the soldiers. They are not, as Walaskay thinks, to be identified with the centurions who turn up later in the Gospel and in Acts who are a part of the proselyte/God-fearer group;[14] nevertheless, they are apparently put alongside the toll collectors. As outcasts? Most commentators correctly understand these soldiers to be Jewish, and many think of soldiers in the service of Herod (which is, of course, not said); but they certainly cannot be Gentile soldiers. There is not the slightest hint in Luke's narrative that he intends to place Gentiles in John's audience or to have them receive John's baptism; and, furthermore, even in the passion narrative there are Jewish soldiers, as we saw in Part One. Does Luke then think of Jewish soldiers as outcasts along with toll collectors and sinners? If so, then Walaskay will be at least partially right in designating the Lucan 'proletariat of Palestine' as 'peasants, tax-collectors, and soldiers',[15] although we would have to change 'peasants' to 'sinners' and emphasize that the soldiers are Jewish and not Gentile. (The term 'proletariat' is also out of place here; Luke's interest is in religious outcasts, some of whom [Zacchaeus] may be wealthy.) If, however, it was Luke's desire to class Jewish soldiers with sinners and toll collectors, he might have done us the service of being a little more explicit on the point.

Luke 4.1–15   The temptation

Aside from other aspects of this scene that are related to Luke's christology and other interests, we cannot help but be struck with how properly Jewish Jesus appears here. All his answers to the Devil's temptations are quotations from Deuteronomy. This is, of course, also true of Matthew's account, but we must again remind ourselves that Luke does not hesitate to alter his sources when he wishes to present something different from what he reads in them. The order of the temptations in Luke, in which the second and third temptations appear in reverse order of that found in Matthew, also fits Lucan theological interest, inasmuch as there is a geographical progression from 'the kingdoms of the world' (v. 5) to 'Jerusalem' (v. 9), a progression that coincides with Luke's interest in showing that Jesus travels from the 'outland' to Jerusalem and that the gospel then travels in the opposite direction.

Luke 4.16–30   Jesus' synagogue sermon at Nazareth

Important literature: **Conzelmann**, *Theology*, pp. 31–8; **Dupont**, 'Le salut des gentils', pp. 141–4; **Eltester**, 'Israel', pp. 131–47; **Fitzmyer**, *Luke*, vol. 1, pp. 526–39; **Lampe**, 'Luke', p. 828; **Löning**, 'Theologe', pp. 218–20; **Lohfink**, *Sammlung Israels*, pp. 44–6; **Loisy**, *Evangiles synoptiques*, vol. 1, pp. 839, 849; **Montefiore**, *Synoptic Gospels*, vol. 2, pp. 394–9; **Nolland**,

'Words of Grace', pp. 47–8; **Ó'Fearghail**, 'Rejection', pp. 60–72; **Radl**, *Paulus und Jesus*, pp. 94–100; **Reicke**, 'Jesus in Nazareth'; **Sandmel**, *Anti-Semitism*, pp. 76–7; K. L. **Schmidt**, *Rahmen*, pp. 39–40; **Schürmann**, *Lukas-evangelium*, vol. 1, pp. 225–39; **Tannehill**, 'Mission of Jesus'; **Tolbert**, 'Leading Ideas', pp. 442–3; **Wilson**, *Gentiles*, pp. 40–1.

This scene is 'programmatic' for Luke-Acts, as one grows almost tired of reading in the literature on the passage (the word 'typical', which also occurs with frequency, can be misleading, inasmuch as the intent is not merely to show that Jesus regularly attended or preached in synagogues, cf. Luke 4.44), for it sums up and presents in a dramatic way Luke's theology of the rejection of the gospel by the Jews and of the divine intent to send it to the Gentiles.

Luke begins by writing that Jesus 'entered . . . the synagogue according to his custom' (v. 16; words not found in Matthew or Mark). While this notation, coupled with the summary in 4.44, is doubtless one reason for the frequent designation of this scene as 'typical', we see that something more than mere typical behaviour on the part of Jesus is involved when we read in Acts 17.2, in exactly the same words, that, 'according to Paul's custom, he entered in to them', where 'in to them' refers to 'a synagogue of the Jews' in the preceding verse. These two nearly identical statements of course make the point, on one level, that Jesus and Paul were not remiss in their Jewish piety; they were regular synagogue-goers. Thus no one can accuse Jesus or the early church of having been untrue to Israelite tradition. If Jesus was practically born and reared in the Temple, according to Luke 1–2, and if the early church practically resided in the Temple in Acts 1–5, then Jesus and Paul also, in the adult lives of Jesus and of the church respectively, attended synagogue regularly. To that degree these two parallel statements about Jesus' and Paul's 'custom' emphasize the continuity between 'biblical Israel' and Christianity. On another level, however, a rather different animus motivates these two statements; for it immediately turns out that Jesus and Paul go to synagogue not to worship but to preach (cf. Acts 17.2b), and, just as Paul repeatedly (although not in the scene in Acts 17.1–9) explains that the Jewish rejection of the gospel leads to its being offered to Gentiles, even finally (Acts 28.26–27) explaining that such behaviour was prophesied, so in Jesus' syna-gogue sermon does he announce, by means of a biblical example, that the taking of salvation to Gentiles and *not* to Jews follows the divine will.

Jesus begins by reading from the Bible a prophecy of his mission (vv. 18–19). Since this prophecy contains the word 'anoint ($\chi\rho\iota\omega$)', Luke surely intends his readers to understand the biblical statement as christological in the precise sense. (We need not tarry, as do many commentators, over the issue of what kind of scroll of Isaiah Jesus might have used in Nazareth that would have had statements from different parts of Isaiah together; for we are not dealing here with any real synagogue sermon that the real Jesus preached in the real Nazareth, but rather with a narrative that Luke has constructed for a purpose.[16] As far as Luke is concerned, Jesus' ministry was prophesied in Isaiah. That one would have to roll the scroll a bit and skip a few lines in order to read the prophecy as Luke gives it would have bothered Luke no more than taking the sayings out of context. Neither skipping a few lines nor taking sayings out of context, furthermore, would have troubled any other ancient Christian or Jew. They would not have understood the issue.) Following his reading of the christological prophecy, Jesus explains that it applies to him (v. 21). The immediate Jewish response, however, is less than clear. First, Luke writes that 'all gave witness to him and were amazed at [his] words' (v. 22). While 'giving witness' would appear to be a strange response to a synagogue sermon, and while 'being amazed' is neutral and could conceivably represent either a hostile or a friendly response, the likelihood seems to be that Luke intends to indicate a positive response. That would be the most reasonable way to take 'giving witness', since the 'giving witness' seems to follow from Jesus' self-attestation and must therefore refer either to agreement or to acclaim. Furthermore, the frequency with which the pattern of favourable response followed by rejection occurs in Acts would lead one to expect Luke to follow that pattern here in some way. Which way the following question, 'Is he not Joseph's son?' (v. 22), leans is not clear and is explained variously by different authors. Does it continue the sentiment of favourable amazement ('Wow! This is Joseph's son?') or does it signal the onset of hostility ('Who does he think he is? He's just Joseph's son.')? Inasmuch as Luke places immediately after the question from Jesus' hearers Jesus' foretelling of their later taunt (v. 23), 'Physician, cure yourself' – which neither Matthew nor Mark includes – we are probably to understand their question about his ancestry as marking the shift to hostile response. If, however, that issue must remain less than perfectly clear, we do see, nevertheless, that the initial positive response soon shifts to one of hostility. If the question about Jesus' being Joseph's son does not indicate that hostility, Jesus nevertheless assumes such hostility when he foretells his hearers' taunt about his healing abilities, and Jesus and his audience remain in adversarial positions from that point on.

After the proverb of v. 24, 'No prophet is welcome in his native country (or: home town)', Luke gets down to business, for from this point he departs entirely from the narrative as found in Matthew and Mark and presents an account that is, as is so often noted, 'programmatic' for all Luke-Acts. Here Jesus gives the twin examples of Elijah's miraculous feeding of the Sidonian widow, even though 'there were many widows in Israel in Elijah's days' (v. 25), and of Elisha's healing of the Syrian leper, even though 'there were many lepers in Israel' at that time (v. 27). Nothing is said here about any Israelite rejection of offers of aid. Jesus' analogies seem rather to have an obvious point, which is that divine salvation went to Gentiles even in the days of the prophets. To be sure, the Nazareth scene as Luke sketches it has contained the note of Jewish rejection, if not explicitly (the question about being Joseph's son) then at least indirectly (Jesus' prophecy of their later taunt); yet, Jesus does not reply here as does Paul twice in Acts that salvation will be taken to the Gentiles because of Jewish rejection. What he says rather is that it was God's will even in 'biblical times' to give salvation to Gentiles and not to Jews, and this seems also to be the position that the Lucan Paul expresses at the conclusion of Acts – again, we do not fail to note, in the context of a quotation from Isaiah. If it is therefore true that the gospel is taken to the Gentiles on the back of Jewish rejection, it is also true that the Jews, by rejecting the gospel, are conforming to the divine foreknowledge and will.[17]

Jesus' audience then seeks to kill him, just as Paul's Jewish audience can seek to kill him (Acts 14.19), and just as Stephen's Jewish audience actually does kill him (Acts 7.59). In all three of these cases the victim is taken outside the city and stoned, although not necessarily in that order (Acts 14.19); and all three incidents follow statements either of God's intended salvation for the Gentiles (in the cases of Jesus and of Paul) or of the Jews' endemic refusal of God's salvation (in the case of Stephen). Furthermore, when we put these three executions and attempted executions together with the execution of Jesus and the final attempts to kill Paul, we see plainly that no one group of the Jews is guilty of opposing Jesus and the church; it is simply 'the Jews'. In Nazareth Jesus' fellow citizens seek to kill him, but only after he has already lumped them together with those who will later mock him in Jerusalem (cf. Luke 23.35); in Jerusalem the religious leaders kill Jesus, but with the passive acquiescence of 'the people'; there later the same people kill Stephen, but after Diaspora Jews have provoked the crisis; at Lystra Paul is stoned by Diaspora Jews; and in Jerusalem, finally, everybody gets into the act in trying to get Paul killed.

While many authors have seen the importance of Luke 4.16–30 in one way or another, it would be difficult to state that significance better than Tannehill has done.

It should not be surprising that the scene which Luke places at the beginning of the ministry of Jesus also serves to interpret the development which follows it. It does so by announcing that it is not those who are closest to Jesus but others who will benefit from his work, and by establishing the pattern of rejection by Jesus' own people and moving on to others which will be typical of the mission as a whole. It also does so by interpreting the whole mission of Jesus through the Isaiah quotation. The significance of this quotation is not limited to the particular situation in Nazareth. *It is the title under which Luke places the whole ministry of Jesus* [emphasis mine] and is to be understood as a summary of Jesus' work and message throughout Luke's gospel.[18]

Given the obvious programmatic placing of the Nazareth pericope in Luke's Gospel, it is difficult to escape the conclusion that Luke-Acts is written to show how God's will was carried out in the Jewish rejection of salvation and in the consequent Gentile mission.

Luke 5.17–26   The healing of a paralytic and the first argument with the Pharisees about practice

Important literature: **Fitzmyer**, *Luke*, vol. 1, pp. 577–86; K. L. **Schmidt**, *Rahmen*, p. 81.

Luke has added the Pharisees to this narrative, something that even Matthew did not think of doing (perhaps thinking that the designation of the scribes implied the presence of Pharisees). Not only has he added them to the scribes in v. 21 (par. Mark 2.6), but he has focused attention on them at the beginning of the narrative by writing, 'Pharisees and teachers of the Law were in the audience (ἦσαν καθήμενοι) who had come from every village of Galilee and of Judaea, and Jerusalem' (v. 17), whereas Mark 2.2 had designated the audience only as 'many'. Luke has thus pitted Jesus here against universal Pharisaism. S.G. Wilson is of the opinion that, although the main theme of this narrative is christological (Jesus can cure paralytics), a conflict over the Law is implied; thus he writes that 'Jesus' claim is not presented as a challenge to the law, but in its challenge to one aspect of current belief it was open to the charge of disobedience to the law – even though the charges are not pressed'.[19] This seems to be as judicious an appraisal of Luke's purposes in this episode as can be given, inasmuch as Luke states that the charge of blasphemy (v. 21) is related to claiming to have powers that only God possesses but then follows this charge with the argument between Jesus and the Pharisees over what is 'easier' (v. 23; except for the addition of the Pharisees, following Mark). While Wilson is correct in arguing that a discussion about what is easier is not directly a 'challenge to the law', we nevertheless have here the first of Jesus' arguments with the Pharisees about practice. It is that issue (overlooked by Wilson) that runs through all Jesus' conflicts with the Pharisees and appears to be related to Luke's objections to (Torah-observant) Jewish Christians in his own day. Luke has grasped the first opportunity – Mark's account of an objection by the scribes to an aspect of Jesus' practice – to bring this theme into play. Jesus' arguments with the Pharisees are generally (although not exclusively) concerned with practice, as here. The Lucan Jesus never actually opposes the Torah as such (contrary to the opinion of Wilson),[20] but he frequently defines Christian practice (halakah) over against Pharisaic.

Luke's conclusion of this healing narrative is also significant. Whereas Mark had written that those observing the healing 'were all amazed and glorified God, saying "We never saw anything like this"' (Mark 2.12) and Matthew that 'the crowds were afraid and glorified the God who had given such authority to human beings' (Matt. 9.8), Luke writes at the end (after conflating Mark and Matthew or Q) that the audience said, 'We have seen things that are contrary to reason (παράδοξα)' (v. 26). Does Luke intend to apply the term παράδοξα only to the healing or also to the argument with the Pharisees? Since he has so emphasized the presence of the Pharisees in the audience as to turn the spotlight from the paralytic to them, one is likely to think that Jesus' question about practice also falls under the category 'contrary to reason'. That would mean that Luke wishes to represent the Pharisees, in this first conflict scene, as being unable to subsume Jesus' practice and his justification of it under their traditional rational categories. They are 'amazed' or 'confused' ('taken by ἔκστασις') and realize that they have been confronted by 'paradoxes'. If that is what Luke wants his readers to understand by his conclusion to the narrative, then it means that he conceives of the Pharisaic 'mind set', so to speak, as being unable to grasp Jesus' *halakah*.

Some authors have difficulty believing that Luke really intended to say that 'Pharisees and teachers of the law. . . had come from every village of Galilee and of Judaea, and Jerusalem' (v. 17), preferring to understand that Luke meant that there were some Pharisees and teachers of the Law there, as well as people from every village, etc. Thus Ernst proposes that Luke's desire to mention Pharisees and teachers of the Law right at the outset has led him to formulate a sentence that does not adequately convey his meaning. Ernst explains 'The reading of syr^s, which corrects the text by splicing in "and the people who came" (καὶ ἦσαν ἐλ . . .), might most accurately convey what was actually meant'.[21] Unfortunately, however, there are several problems with such an explanation. For one thing, the Sinaitic Syriac can hardly be cited as an evidence, since, in the photographs,[22] in any case, it is quite illegible (we are dealing with the erased original of a palimpsest). Thus the editors of the Bible Societies' *The Greek New Testament* indicate in their apparatus that the reading of syr^s here is not completely verifiable.[23] Furthermore, if the reading is what it is taken to be, it is not what Ernst thinks it is, since the words that, in the purported reading, follow 'teachers of the Law' are *ūc^{a}d 'etaw min*, 'and when (or: after) they had come from'; but Ernst, in any case, does not propose that the reading of syr^s contains a more original reading, just that it represents a correction of the sort that he proposes to make in order to get the right meaning, so that reference to syr^s provides little help. Finally, however, there is no reason why Luke would have thought it any more likely that people could come from all over Galilee and Judaea than that Pharisees could come from the same places. Luke seems to want to focus on the Pharisees in this narrative, and explaining that those in Jesus' audience are representative of Pharisees everywhere is a good way to do that.

Luke 5.27–32   The call of Levi and the complaint of the Pharisees, with
Jesus' response

Luke, of course, did not invent the theme of Jesus' associations
with outcasts and of the Pharisaic opposition to such association,
since these elements are also the point of the Marcan story (Mark
2.13–17). Thus here we find not only that the Levi who becomes a
disciple of Jesus is a toll collector, but also that, to celebrate his
conversion, he hosted a dinner party for Jesus and for 'many toll
collectors and sinners' (Mark 2.15). Mark also includes the Pharisaic
complaint (v. 16) and Jesus' response, 'I came not to call righteous
persons but sinners' (v. 17). By and large, Luke has just done some
minor rewriting of this episode, e.g., adding drinking to the complaint
about eating (Luke 5.30); but one Lucan change is significant, the
addition of 'to repentance' to Jesus' response about calling sinners.
Repentance, as we saw in detail in Part One, is for Luke one of the
primary virtues of the outcasts, which he puts over against the precise
following of prescribed practice that he attributes to the Pharisees.
While that aspect of Pharisaic existence has not fully emerged at this
point in the Gospel narrative, we are now prepared for the contrast
by the nature and conclusion of the present episode. The Pharisees
criticize Jesus' associations with outcasts, and he replies that his
mission is not to 'righteous persons' (obviously the Pharisees) but to
'sinners' for 'repentance'.

How Luke – and, obviously, already Mark – thinks of this contrast
will perhaps be clearer if we speculate briefly about the possible
original meaning of Jesus' words (assuming that they are authentic),[24]
whether they were originally independent or a part of this narrative,
which we encounter as an apothegm. If we think of the saying's pre-
Synoptic setting, it is possible to conjecture a non-polemical intent
for the saying. 'Righteous' is a perfectly good word in Jewish
tradition, without negative connotations. We can therefore construe
Jesus' meaning as being that he was simply doing what any 'preacher'
does, trying to get sinners to repent, under the assumption that the
righteous do not need to repent. If the saying is, indeed, merely a
secondary variant of the preceding saying about the physician (see
the preceding note) – which in its Lucan form reads, 'The healthy
have no need of a physician, but those who are sick' (v. 31) – then
the more so. The Christian tradition, however, finds the saying to be
polemical, and Luke seems to think in these terms: the *self*-righteous

Pharisees, following their *halakah*, do not understand the mercy of God; Jesus therefore goes to sinners, since they can be called to repentance. In this way the Lucan Jesus begins to present the contrast between the two forms of church membership, that of traditional Jews and that of Gentiles. '*They* will hear' (Acts 28.28).

Luke 5.33   The question about fasting

The first word of v. 33, 'They', apparently refers back to the Pharisees of the preceding narrative, although it is somewhat strange that 'they' then speak of Pharisees in the third person: 'The Pharisees'' disciples fast. Probably this minor anomaly is due to Luke's wanting to keep the Marcan contrast between 'the Pharisees' disciples' and 'your disciples'. One could hardly refer to a conflict between Jesus and the Pharisees in this episode, since they only ask a question to which Jesus replies; but the issue is, in any case, consistent with what has gone before. Whereas the Pharisees earlier objected to Jesus' eating and drinking with sinners, now they question his eating and drinking instead of fasting. The issue is practice, *halakah*; and the Pharisees are consistently shown to be following petty rules, whereas Jesus pays attention to significant issues.

Luke 6.2   Another Pharisaic challenge to Jesus' practice

Jesus' disciples pluck and eat some raw grain on the Sabbath (v. 1) and are immediately challenged by Pharisees, who charge that such activity is 'not allowed' (v. 2). The theme of disagreement over right practice in keeping with God's will therefore continues, but Luke has made an interesting change. Whereas Matthew and Mark have it that 'the Pharisees' bring this challenge (Matt. 12.2; Mark 2.24), Luke writes that it was '*some* of the Pharisees'. Thus, having in the preceding section 5.17–39 established the scope of Jesus' disagreement with the Pharisees – both the geographical extent and the material issue of that disagreement – Luke now begins the move to his friendly-Pharisee theme by offering an olive branch: it was not all the Pharisees in the country (5.17) who kept following Jesus around and questioning his practice, but only 'some'.

Luke 6.6–11   The Pharisees object to Jesus' healing on the Sabbath

The issue continues: Jesus' *halakah*; and this time it is a rather different order of forbidden (according to the Pharisaic objection) Sabbath activity, healing. We thus see the genius of the Marcan order, which Luke is happy to repeat, in this series of stories about opposition from the Pharisees to Jesus' activity, for this last narrative in the series forms the climax of the group. The Pharisees are here shown, by objecting to such an obvious 'doing of good' (v. 9) as healing a man's withered hand, to be absurdly petty and inhuman in their emphasis on *practice*. Luke's Gentile readers can have no sympathy with the Pharisaic perspective after this point, for the Pharisees – that is, those who seek to make the Torah and its interpretation their guide in all aspects of life – are revealed in this narrative to have lost touch with reality.

The Pharisees are said to be just waiting to see if Jesus would respond to the deformed man and heal him on the Sabbath 'so that they could find some charge to bring against him (ἵνα εὕρωσιν κατηγορεῖν αὐτοῦ)' (v. 7, cf. also Mark 3.2; Matt. 12.10). The fact that Luke has repeated the term 'bring a charge against him' from his source should not, however, be taken to mean that Luke thinks of the Pharisees as somehow taking part in the final plot to do away with Jesus, inasmuch as Luke later so carefully excludes the Pharisees from the passion narrative altogether, has them warn Jesus about Herod's hostile intentions (13.31) and, in Acts, portrays them as the helpers of Christians or even as Christians. That the Pharisees sought to 'bring a charge against' Jesus may very well, in the pre-Lucan tradition, have meant that they were involved in the plots against Jesus, but Luke does not so understand the charge. For him, the Pharisees want to charge Jesus with some activity proscribed by their version of religion. Jesus, of course, robs them of the opportunity by shifting the issue from that of proscribed or prescribed to that of 'doing good' or 'doing bad' (Luke 6.9).

Luke 7.1–10   The healing of the centurion's slave

Important literature: **Fitzmyer**, *Luke*, vol. 1, pp. 647–53; **Grundmann**, *Lukas*, p. 158; **Lampe**, 'Luke', p. 830; **Loisy**, *Evangiles synoptiques*, vol. 1, pp. 651–2; **Walaskay**, *We Came to Rome*, pp. 32–5.

With this narrative Luke picks up the other aspect of the theme that he emphasized so strongly and clearly in the episode of Jesus' Nazareth synagogue sermon. If there the emphasis fell on the sending of salvation to the Gentiles (and not to the Jews), here it is on the fact that the Gentiles will receive the offer of salvation (and the Jews will not). That this, no less than the other, is Luke's major interest is seen in the fact that he closes Acts on this theme. Paul will take the gospel to the Gentiles, for 'they will listen'.

While it is not said that this Gentile is a God-fearer or proselyte, that he is such is strongly implied by his described activity with regard to the Jewish religion: 'He loves our people and built the synagogue for us himself' (v. 5). Thus this centurion is a prototype of Cornelius in Acts 10, as many have realized. It is such a person, therefore, who exhibits 'such faith' as cannot even be 'found . . . in Israel' (v. 9). The statement of Jesus presents a contrast, not a comparison. It cannot be taken to mean, as in the opinion of a number of modern authors, that the Lucan Jesus takes for granted Israelite faith and thinks that the centurion's faith exceeds that faith in degree. What Luke has Jesus say, rather, is that such faith as is exhibited by the centurion is not to be found among the Jews. While this statement does not rule out Jewish faith altogether (there were, after all, Jewish Christians), it does show that Jesus finds from the centurion the kind of response for which he is looking, and that he does not find that kind of response among the Jews. This Gentile with some kind of association with Judaism thus joins the toll collectors and sinners of ch. 5 in the periphery around Judaism that responds favourably to Jesus and forms the first stage of the taking of the gospel from the Jews to the Gentiles.

Luke 7.29–30   Toll collectors v. Pharisees

Important literature: **Ernst**, *Lukas*, p. 251; **Fitzmyer**, *Luke*, vol. 1, pp. 670–6; **Hauck**, *Lukas*, p. 100; **Talbert**, *Reading Luke*, p. 85.

'All the people . . . and the toll collectors justified God, since they were baptized in John's baptism; but the Pharisees and the legists set aside the plan of God for themselves, since they were not baptized by him.' This characteristically Lucan summary statement pits, characteristically, the toll collectors (in this case with 'all the people' as well) against the Pharisees (and their allies the scribes, here called 'legists'). Exactly what 'justified God' is supposed to mean is about as clear as 'bore witness to him' in 4.22; obviously we are to understand a positive response of some kind, presumably agreement with the plan of God.

The summary is hardly understandable apart from the rest of the Gospel. The 'people' are present here in keeping with their positive response to Jesus up until the passion narrative, at which time their actions begin to be open to question (thus anticipating the overwhelmingly positive response of the Jewish people to the gospel in the first section of Acts as well as their later rejection of the gospel); the toll collectors are here, as so frequently in Luke, representing the outcasts who consistently accept God's salvation – in this, not surprisingly, contrasted to the Pharisees; and the Pharisees (with their allies, the legists) are here representing the Jewish religious response that, as Luke portrays it, sees no need for repentance but rather follows *halakah* and thus rejects true Christian salvation. While we learn from other aspects of Luke's portrayal of the Pharisees that he uses them to represent traditionally Jewish Christians, one would not guess at that connection from this summary alone, where the Pharisees and legists are simply involved in a characteristic attempt to accomplish their own salvation.

Luke 7.31–35   The analogy of children in the market
   Important literature: **Fitzmyer**, *Luke*, vol. 1, pp. 677–81.

The analogy is applied in two different ways. First Jesus asks to what he should compare 'the people of this generation' (v. 31); and he replies that 'they are like children in the market', who did not 'dance' when 'we played the flute' or 'cry' when 'we wept' (v. 32). Then he applies the analogy to John's and his ministries, which were both, though employing differing *modi operandi*, unsuccessful. (The same discourse appears in Matt. 11.16–19 with minor differences.) Many commentators find the train of thought here confusing and the analogy of the children in the market enigmatic, but the meaning seems straightforward enough.

   The term 'this generation' carries here as elsewhere a pejorative edge; and, coming just after, as it does, the statement about how the Pharisees and legists rejected the plan of God, the phrase would appear to mean this *Jewish* generation. That appearance is strengthened when vv. 33–34 then turn the analogy toward John's and Jesus' lack of success in their ministries. 'This generation', therefore, is hopeless, inasmuch as neither John's procedure nor Jesus' has been effective in eliciting the proper response from it. Occurring as it does between the shortly preceding narrative of the healing of the centurion's slave and the immediately following narrative of the 'sinner' woman who anoints Jesus, in both of which cases the proper response to Jesus *does* occur, the saying about 'this generation' and

John's and Jesus' failure in it becomes vivid in its contrast to the other two narratives. From a God-fearer and from an outcast Jesus receives pure 'Christian' faith; from 'this generation' he does not.

*Luke 7.36–50   Jesus, guest of a Pharisee, is anointed by a 'sinner' and turns
          the occasion into an object lesson of faith*

Important literature: **Fitzmyer**, *Luke*, vol. 1, pp. 684–92; **Lampe**, 'Luke', p. 831; **Wilckens**, 'Vergebung für die Sünderin'.

Here we begin to see the evidence that allows us to realize that, of the several ways in which Luke uses the Pharisees in his two-volume work, one of the most interesting is to let them represent those people who do make at least a superficial response to Jesus, who desire his presence and to be in his presence, but who object to his allowing into his company persons who are not properly righteous in the 'Pharisees'' understanding. This aspect of Luke's portrayal of the Pharisees, which is unique in early Christian tradition and is remarkable in view of the portrayal of the Pharisees in other early Christian literature, is his way of criticizing the Jewish Christians of his own day, who are of the opinion that being Christian does not release one from the obligation to obey the Torah (cf. Acts 15.5; Gal. 2.11–14). Thus the leper Simon of Luke's sources (Mark 14.3; Matt. 26.6) becomes the Pharisee Simon in Luke's account (Luke 7.36, 40), and, whereas Jesus was only unexplainedly 'in the house of Simon the leper' (Mark 14.3) in Luke's sources, Luke has Jesus' Pharisaic host actually *invite Jesus to dine* (Luke 7.36).

After the woman enters and washes (with her tears) and anoints Jesus' feet, the Pharisee is critical of Jesus' allowing this 'sinner' to approach him. At this point, we must not fail to note, Luke departs entirely from his sources, since Mark and Matthew do include a criticism, but of the waste of such valuable things, not of Jesus' allowing the woman into his presence. To be sure, the Pharisee does not give voice to this criticism, but everyone knows what he is thinking. Now, it is true that, as the narrative progresses to the next stage, it is Jesus who addresses these inner thoughts of the Pharisee; but Luke does not bother to explain that Jesus is able to do so because his 'prophetic' powers just maligned allow him to know what the Pharisee is thinking. It is rather Luke who knows what the Pharisee is thinking. That is to say that the Pharisee's thoughts are so in character that it is sufficient simply to state them without any explanation as to how one might know what the Pharisee 'said within himself' (v. 39). It is typical, in Luke, for Pharisees to criticize Jesus' practice and to criticize him for allowing into his presence those whose practice is on all counts condemnable – outcasts. For this reason we are able to know what this Lucan Pharisee thought but did not express.

Jesus responds to the criticism with the parable about two debtors who loved the one who forgave their debts in direct proportion to the amount of the debt forgiven (vv. 41–43), and he then applies the parable to the 'sinner' woman's and to the Pharisee's behaviour towards himself in the Pharisee's house (vv. 44–46). Most commentators are of the opinion that Luke intends to portray the Pharisee as having neglected 'the customary marks of hospitality',[25] but Weiss is of the opinion that we should not see here a criticism by Jesus of the neglect of a host's minimal responsibilities, but rather a contrast between proper and improper response to Jesus,[26] and that is probably correct. The woman's response is finally labelled (like that of the centurion at the beginning of the chapter) 'faith' (v. 50), and that is what the Pharisee Simon, for all his apparent friendliness towards Jesus, does not give. He, the one who normally is so careful to do all that is required, neglects what is in the last analysis the only important thing, believing in true contrition. While Luke will later add to the tints of this picture, the sketch is now clear to the viewer. Pharisees are those who seek to do what is required. They fall short, however, inasmuch as, even though they may seek out Jesus' companionship, they fail to approach him in true contrition and faith; and they even criticize Jesus for allowing into his fellowship those who approach him only on those terms. The Pharisees in this way reject the plan of God for themselves. Jesus came to call sinners to repentance, not righteous people; those who place emphasis on required practice are not wanted in Luke's church.

We may conveniently avoid taking up the often impassioned discussion as to whether Luke intends to maintain, in this narrative, that the *quantity* of one's faith or love is significant in one's salvation, and as to whether some acts which precede faith may lead to salvation. The issues are, in any case, more a matter of Protestant theology than they are of Luke's meaning; but Montefiore's comment is worth preserving (he was responding especially to the recently published work of Johannes Weiss, *Die Schriften des Neuen Testaments*): 'If [those statements had] occurred in the Talmud, how theologians like J. Weiss would have been down on [them]. Is gratitude to be reckoned by the mere size of the service? How Jewish! So much service, so much gratitude. How Rabbinical!'[27]

Luke 9.9   Herod wishes to see Jesus

This brief note is apparently to be taken in a hostile sense. It is reported to Herod that some people think that Jesus is John *redivivus*, Herod knows that he killed John, he wants to see Jesus. While it would be possible in this instance to take Herod's expressed desire to see Jesus in a neutral sense and to think of Luke as portraying him as merely wishing to 'get to the bottom of things', the later explanation in 13.31 that Herod wants to kill Jesus would seem to give content to his desire to see him at this point. In Luke, therefore, the opposition of the Jewish leaders to Jesus that will prove fatal to him begins even before the priestly leadership is brought into the picture. Furthermore, even the fact that this opposition will lead to Jesus' death is indicated at this early stage of the Gospel, so that, before the first announcement of the passion, the deadly opposition of the Jewish leadership is brought into play.

Luke 9.22, 31   The first announcement of the passion, and the prophecy of Jesus' exodus

Important literature: **Fitzmyer**, *Luke*, vol. 1, p. 800; G. **Schneider**, *Lukas*, vol. 1, p. 216.

Shortly after bringing Herod's hostility into his narrative, Luke includes the first announcement of the passion, which designates the 'elders and high priests and scribes' as those who will reject Jesus.[28] Following Mark, Luke keeps the verbs in the passive and does not say who will kill Jesus. Only from the passion narrative itself do we learn exactly what he must be thinking at this point.

The statement about Jesus' 'exodus' is found only in Luke, and its meaning is by no means entirely clear, not the least because it is prophesied to be 'fulfill[ed] in Jerusalem'. One would think that a reference to Jesus' exodus might have in mind his exodus from this earth, but that would not be fulfilled in Jerusalem, but only facilitated, especially in view of Luke's further narrative of the Ascension in Acts 1. What is fulfilled or terminated in Jerusalem is Jesus' way (ὁδός), not his *exodus*, but it is also possible that what Luke means here is 'way' and not 'departure'. The statement about the exodus could, on that view, mean that Jesus' journey is to be terminated in Jerusalem in the sense that he is journeying *out of* Galilee to Jerusalem, whereas this scene of the Transfiguration in which the prophecy of the exodus occurs is still in Galilee. But the majority of commentators think that exodus here means death, or perhaps death + ascension, and that is probably the simplest solution. Jerusalem is thus, of course, thereby indicated as the place where Jesus will 'fulfil' his 'exodus'. Thus, before the initiation of the travel narrative, Herod, the priestly leadership and Jerusalem have all been clearly identified as playing their respective roles in Jesus' death.

It is perhaps worth-while, also, to recall that, during most of the Galilean ministry, Jesus has been heavily involved in arguments with the Pharisees about practice, about how one correctly obeys the will of God, and that, during those arguments, the Jerusalem leadership has been quite out of the picture. Towards the end of the Galilean ministry, however, Luke begins increasingly to bring in hints of Jesus' impending doom (in part, of course, following his sources); and here it is the Pharisees who are out of the picture. That Luke is responsible for this construction can be seen from the parallels with Mark. At Luke 9.9, where Luke mentions Herod's desire to see Jesus, Luke is following the Marcan order, where Mark is recounting the death of John the Baptist (Mark 6.14–29). Between this point in Mark and the conclusion of the Transfiguration narrative (Mark 9.2–10), where Luke places the exodus prophecy, Mark includes three instances of opposition between Jesus and the Pharisees, all of which Luke has moved into the travel narrative. Luke has used two of the cases (the Pharisaic questioning of Jesus' and his disciples' failure to wash their hands before eating, Mark 7.1–5, and the reference to the 'leaven of the Pharisees', Mark 8.15) as the opening and conclusion of the diatribe against the Pharisees and scribes (Luke 11.37–41; 12.1). The other, a reference to the Pharisees' 'seeking a sign from' Jesus (Mark 8.11), Luke has both moved into the travel narrative (Luke 11.16) and cleansed of its reference to Pharisees ('others'). We thus see how systematically Luke has kept the opposition to Jesus from the Jerusalem leadership, which culminates in Jesus' death, separate from the disagreements with the Pharisees over practice, which disagreements do not preclude acts of overt friendliness towards Jesus (and, later on, towards the church) on the part of the Pharisees. It is this kind of distinction that points to the Torah-observing Jewish Christians of Luke's own day as the people whom he wishes to criticize by his portrayal of the Pharisees.

Luke 9.51–56   The outset of the travel narrative and rejection by a Samaritan village

Important literature: **Conzelmann**, *Theology*, pp. 65–6; **Enslin**, 'Samaritan Ministry'; **Ernst**, *Lukas*, p. 317; **Fitzmyer**, *Luke*, vol. 1, pp. 823–30; **Harrington**, *St. Luke*, pp. 145–6; **Jervell**, *People of God*, pp. 119–27; **Lampe**, 'Luke', p. 833; **Loisy**, *Evangiles synoptiques*, vol. 2, p. 102; *Luc*, pp. 284–7; **Radl**, *Paulus und Jesus*, pp. 117–26; **Robinson**, 'Context'; K. L. **Schmidt**, *Rahmen*, p. 267; G. **Schneider**, *Lukas*, vol. 1, pp. 229–30; J. **Schneider**, 'Analyse des Reiseberichtes'; **Talbert**, *Reading Luke*, pp. 111–12; **Wilson**, *Gentiles*, pp. 41–4; **Zingg**, 'Stellung zur Heidenmission', pp. 203–4.

We come now to a major turning point, as is universally recognized. Jesus begins his journey towards Jerusalem with determination; he 'made his countenance firm' (v. 51) to go there. From this point on, even though at times Jesus does not seem to be travelling at all, not to mention anywhere in particular, and even though Luke writes sometimes as if the journey to Jerusalem were only incidental (e.g., Luke 17.11), Jesus is on his fateful 'way' towards Jerusalem and his rendezvous with destiny.

The way from the 'outland' to Jerusalem lies through the periphery; geographically, that means through Samaria. The many scholarly discussions about Luke's geographical knowledge as displayed in the travel narrative sometimes fail to grasp what is of significance here for Luke; for he has a theological geography, and, if it at times coincides accurately with political boundaries and the lay of the land in his day and at times does not, that is the direct outcome of his theological interest. Jesus must pass from the 'outland' through the periphery in order to get to Jerusalem. Since there is an obvious geographical aspect to the periphery – Samaria (there being no obvious geographical unit associated with outcasts or with proselytes and God-fearers) – Jesus passes through Samaria. When Luke later writes that Jesus is 'going through the midst of Samaria and Galilee' (17.11), we need not pore over our maps to discover either where such a journey could have taken place or how Luke could have been misled into writing such a geographically anomalous statement, for his theological interest is again and still dominant (see below).

The reception that the Samaritans accord Jesus is surely to be seen as a parallel to the reception that his fellow citizens gave him in Nazareth in ch. 4; thus a rejection inaugurates both phase one and phase two of Jesus' ministry. And yet, while the Samaritan rejection is *parallel* to the Nazareth rejection, it does not *duplicate* it; for a rationale is given for the Samaritan rejection (Jesus is travelling toward Jerusalem, v. 53), whereas no such excusable explanation of the Nazareth rejection is presented; and Jesus, given the opportunity to destroy the offensive Samaritans (v. 54), not only fails to grasp the opportunity for such destruction, but actually 'scolds' *the disciples* (v. 55). Thus this brief episode at the outset of the travel narrative functions in two ways. On the one hand, it continues the motif of rejection that must, according to Luke, inaugurate every phase of Jesus' ministry; but, on the other hand, it deals gingerly with the Samaritans and carefully avoids the summary judgment upon them that is implied for the Nazarenes in 4.16–30. In this way Samaria is established, as the travel narrative begins, as the geographical designation of that periphery about Judaism where, as Luke will later show, the transition to the Gentile mission will be made.

Luke 10.13–15   Woes on Chorazin, Bethsaida and Capernaum

Important literature: **Enslin**, 'Samaritan Ministry'; **Fitzmyer**, *Luke*, vol. 2, pp. 850–5.

It seems reasonably clear that Luke also wishes to indicate, at the beginning of the travel narrative, that the region of Jesus' prior ministry has had and has rejected its last chance, and that there is no escape for it from the coming destruction. This is, in any case, the construction put on these verses by the majority of commentators, and it seems to coincide best with Luke's other statements and hints about the offer of salvation to the Jews. In a sense, Jesus returns here to the theme of his Nazareth synagogue sermon, for the cities contrasted to the three Jewish towns are Gentile: Tyre and Sidon. If Jesus had ministered in those Gentile cities, they would be set to survive the coming woes, for they would have responded to Jesus in contrition and faith. The Galilean ministry is therefore explained, in this last reference to it, as proving the principle set out in the Nazareth synagogue sermon that God's salvation was always intended for Gentiles and not for Jews. Why is that? Because Gentiles will accept it and Jews will refuse it. The northern Jewish areas of Jesus' ministry (one cannot accurately say 'Galilean', since Bethsaida was not in

Galilee, although Luke may have thought of it that way) belong to 'this generation' (Luke 7.31) that Jesus had earlier likened to unresponsive children, to this 'faithless and perverted generation' (Luke 9.41). They have, as God foreknew and even intended, rejected the last offer of salvation to be made to them. Destruction follows.

But was Jesus' Galilean ministry really entirely without result? Is he not travelling towards Jerusalem with an entourage, the tangible result of his success in Galilee? This question can be answered only when we separate speech from narrative (see again the discussion of this point in Part One). While Jesus' ministry and, later, the church's mission do have some success – could Luke have dared to present the ministry of Jesus and of the early church as being without success? – nothing that Jesus *says* about his life's work indicates such success. Jesus' words, rather, refer consistently to complete Jewish rejection, without distinction. We would never infer, from what the Lucan Jesus says about Jewish salvation, that Jesus has at this point in any way 'gathered' the repentant and believing part of Israel.[29] Thus, in spite of the fact that Luke is surely aware that he has just written an account of Jesus' ministry that included some success, he can now have Jesus pronounce summary doom on the area of his former activity for that area's failure to respond properly to him.

Luke 10.25–37   The Great Commandment and the parable of the Good Samaritan

Important literature: **Crossan**, 'Parable and Example'; **Enslin**, 'Samaritan Ministry', pp. 33–7; **Fitzmyer**, *Luke*, vol. 2, pp. 877–88; **Klostermann**, *Lukas*, p. 119; **Lambrecht**, *Astonished*, pp. 57–80; **Loisy**, *Evangiles synoptiques*, vol. 2, pp. 355–7; *Luc*, p. 309; **Reicke**, 'Barmherziger Samariter'; **Sandmel**, *Anti-Semitism*, p. 77.

The commandment itself, and the different form of it in Luke from that in Matthew and Mark, have little bearing on the issue with which we are concerned here, Luke's portrayal of the Jews. S. G. Wilson is of the opinion that Luke's inclusion of the commandment shows that Luke thought of it as one other law, in addition to those of the Apostolic Decree, binding on the Gentile church.[30] There is no reason to object to this opinion, although one should also remember that Luke could hardly have written a gospel without the Great Commandment (even John is compelled to include it, albeit in even more altered form than Luke's version) and that Luke seems much more interested in using it as a springboard to the parable than in seeking to elicit its implications for the church.

Quite enough has already been written about the way in which the parable supplements or does not supplement the commandment, and about whether the parable shifts emphasis between its opening and closing questions, and, if so, whether that shift of emphasis is intentional or not;[31] so there is no need to add to that discussion here. We must begin by reminding ourselves that our interest here is Luke's purpose, not what the parable may have meant at any stage of transmission prior to Luke's use of it. Thus the setting and the questions belong within our field of interest just as much as any pre-Lucan core of the pericope. When we hold firmly to this tack, we recognize that Luke sees the parable as explaining the commandment. The legist's question (v. 29) is not answered by the parable in any direct sense, inasmuch as Luke plainly indicates that the purpose of the legist's question was 'to justify himself'. Now, it does not take much familiarity with the Gospel of Luke, or much scurrying through the concordance, to discover in what company Luke has thereby put this legist, for in Luke 16.15 it is Pharisees who are said to 'justify [them]selves in front of people', and in 18.14 it is the toll collector, not the Pharisee, who goes home from the Temple 'justified'. The legist, therefore, is one of those Torah-observant Jews, associated with Pharisees, who seek to justify *themselves* – that is, who seek to manage their own salvation, by following a certain *halakah*:[32] '*Having done what* will I inherit eternal life?' The question of v. 29, therefore, seeks a specific clarification so that the commandment can be obeyed precisely, so that the legist may 'justify (read: save) himself'.

Luke's reply, the parable, involves a *metabasis eis allo genos*; by no Jewish prescribed practice, but by behaving like a Samaritan, can salvation be obtained. While the parable succeeds admirably in making Jewish religious leaders (priests and their 'colleagues') appear pedantic, silly and downright immoral in their ritual piety and the Samaritan, to put it mildly, big-hearted, it does not adequately set aside the legist's orientation, which is probably what Luke had in mind, since it is not made clear why the legist could not, by 'going and doing likewise' (v. 37), still 'justify himself'. Luke seems to have been satisfied to see the Jew-Samaritan contrast and to think that this contrast was sufficient to overturn the legist's approach, since Jesus' final words mean not only that the hearer should behave in a certain way, but that the legist should behave like a Samaritan, *not* like the Jewish religious leaders. If we are correct in thinking that the setting of this narrative, for Luke at the time of his writing, was an argument between Gentile Christians and Jewish Christians over obedience to the Torah, then we can understand why Luke thought that he had shown the inadequacy of the legist's approach; for no halachic Jewish Christian would have been likely to agree that Christianity was best typified by a Samaritan, however nice, rather than by the Jerusalem priesthood, however picayune the priests might appear to Gentiles. Thus Loisy observed that, for Luke, 'the Jewish doctor represents Judaism, with which Jewish Christianity is more or less combined, and the Samaritan represents true – that is to say, universal – Christianity'.[33] Luke seems to have thought that the parable rebutted the approach of self-justification or self-salvation taken by the legist, or by Torah-observant Jews or Jewish Christians.

Luke 10.38–42   Martha and Mary

Important literature: **Fitzmyer**, *Luke*, vol. 2, pp. 891–5; **Loisy**, *Luc*, pp. 33, 311.

Loisy thought that the theme of Judaism + Jewish Christianity v. true Christianity was continued into this narrative;[34] but only one other author discussing this passage, to my knowledge, has ever agreed with this opinion.[35] Yet we should avoid the merely reactive response to Loisy's suggestion that replies that such a warmly human story of differing attitudes towards how best to serve Jesus could not possibly have any other meaning than advice about how to be a better Christian, about doing what is 'necessary' or what is 'the good part' (v. 42); for Martha is said to have 'care' and to be 'upset' (v. 41), and the round of activity that disturbs her is contrasted to the one necessary thing: 'Martha, Martha, you have cares and are upset about many things, but there is need of one thing; for Mary has chosen the good part' (vv. 41–42). Is not the moral of this brief narrative, indeed, that Jesus is not properly served by care-producing and upsetting *practice*, by being 'quite occupied with much service' (v. 40), but instead by 'sitting at the feet of the Lord' and hearing 'his word' (v. 39)? If this narrative, in isolation, could have a perfectly benign intention, does it not acquire something of a polemical edge when directly juxtaposed to the parable of the Good Samaritan, where the anti-Jewish point lies right on the surface? Loisy wrote that, as the Samaritan of the parable represents the Gentile believer in perfect Christian form, the two sisters in the account that follows immediately could well typify the two fractions of the primitive Church, Jewish Christian and Hellenistic Christian, according to their character and in their mutual rapport, who were not, in that way, two enemies. It is of little importance that the service of Martha is not a legal observance, since it is a question of a symbol; the sending out of the seventy-two advance people in Samaria [Luke 10.1] nevertheless typifies the evangelizing of the Gentiles.[36]

Luke is too interested in the issue of the wrong (in his opinion) Jewish way of being a Christian for us to rule out this interpretation.

Luke 11.29–32   This evil generation and Jonah

Important literature: **Fitzmyer**, *Luke*, vol. 2, pp. 930–7; **Lampe**, 'Luke', p. 834; **Loisy**, *Evangiles synoptiques*, vol. 1, p. 999; **Mora**, *Le signe de Jonas*, pp. 75–83; **Talbert**, *Reading Luke*, pp. 138–9; **Zahn**, *Lucas*, pp. 467–9.

Again we have a reference to 'this generation', probably meaning 'this Jewish generation' (cf. 7.31; the term is probably also used in that sense in 9.41). Luke has emphasized that the generation is 'evil' more than is the case in the other Gospels. In Mark 8.12 the generation is not even designated as evil but is said only to be 'this generation' that 'seeks a sign'. Matt. 12.39 does include the qualifier, 'evil', for the generation – 'An evil and adulterous generation seeks a sign' – but even this is not as emphatic as Luke's 'This generation is an evil generation' (Luke 11.29). What Luke then does with the analogy of Jonah and the Ninevites is more than passing strange.[37]

Luke's version of the sign-of-Jonah saying (v. 30) is that 'as Jonah was a sign to the Ninevites, so the Son of man will be a sign to this generation'; yet that saying would appear to mean that Luke thinks that 'this generation' will repent, inasmuch as the Ninevites repented when Jonah preached there. Does Luke after all, then, express hope, confidence even, that the Jews will respond in repentance to Jesus' ministry, just as the Ninevites responded to Jonah's ministry by repenting? It would be possible to infer that on the basis of this saying, if we considered the saying in isolation. The problem with such an interpretation of the saying, as it appears in Luke, however, is that the point of the immediately following twin saying about the Queen of the South and about Jonah is again similar to the point of the woes pronounced on the three northern towns in 10.13–15 – that is, that such Gentiles as the Queen of the South and the inhabitants of Nineveh did have the good sense to respond favourably to, respectively, Solomon and Jonah, whereas those at whom the Lucan saying is directed will not follow the lead of the Queen of the South and of Jonah and respond favourably to Jesus. For this reason, 'the men of Nineveh will arise in the judgment with this generation and condemn it' (v. 32). Why will the Ninevites condemn 'this generation'? Because it has *not* repented in response to Jesus' ministry, 'because [the Ninevites] repented when Jonah preached (εἰς τὸ κήρυγμα Ἰωνᾶ), and behold! something more than Jonah is here' (v. 32). Because this is what Luke makes out of the Jonah example, it would seem impossible to read v. 30, about Jesus' being 'a sign . . . to this generation' like Jonah to the Ninevites, as implying hope for salvation for 'this generation'. 'This generation' is to be condemned because, *un*like the Ninevites, it has failed to repond to God's call to repentance in Christ. We are therefore on firm ground in reading 'this generation' in vv. 29–30 as meaning 'this evil Jewish generation', as is the case everywhere else in Luke-Acts where the phrase is used, and Jesus' being a sign in a general sense, not as a direct analogy to Jonah's success.

Luke 11.37–12.1   The woes upon the Pharisees and legists[38]

Important literature: **Egelkraut**, *Jesus' Mission*, pp. 102–3; **Fitzmyer**, *Luke*, vol. 2, pp. 943–55; **Montefiore**, *Synoptic Gospels*, vol. 2, p. 486.

We have now the second of the three occasions, unique to Luke, on which Jesus visits Pharisees in their homes. As before, the Pharisee – who is superficially friendly to Jesus in that he invites him to dine – criticizes Jesus' practice, and Jesus responds with a teaching that harshly criticizes the Pharisees' practice. Jesus' woes pronounced upon the Pharisees are, for the most part, related to their *way* of obeying the Torah, the woes dealing with other matters being by and large separated out and applied only to the legists, not to the Pharisees. Finally, the Pharisaic practice as such is labelled 'hypocrisy'.

After inviting Jesus to dine with him (v. 37), 'the Pharisee . . . was astonished that he did not wash first before supper'. Yet the Pharisee says nothing, just as was the case in the similar situation in 7.39. It is again Luke who knows what the Pharisee was thinking. Does Luke know this because he has, in the past, heard Jewish criticism about Jesus' or the church's practice, or does he know it because he observes

Jewish practice from afar and recognizes that its continuation involves an implicit criticism of the church's practice? In either case, from what quarter comes this criticism, from the synagogue or from Jewish Christians? While the introduction to the invective against the Pharisees and legists does not provide the answer to that question, the conclusion probably does, for there Luke cautions against the hypocrisy of Pharisaic leaven – that is, that which works within the dough. It is this that points towards Torah-observant Jewish Christianity as the source of Luke's irritation.

It should also not escape our notice that, here as before, Jesus' response to the Pharisaic objection is much more heated than the original objection itself. By following that pattern, Luke both continues to allow the Pharisees to be seen as wanting to be friendly with Jesus (albeit preferably on their own terms) and shows how totally wrong their position is and how greatly it displeases the Founder.

Jesus' objections to the Pharisees are, according to Luke, the following. They wash the outsides of dishes, but their own insides are 'full of plunder and iniquity' (v. 39); they tithe certain things but 'pass God's judgment and love by' (v. 44); they 'love the front seat in synagogues and being greeted in public ($\dot{\alpha}\sigma\pi\alpha\sigma\mu\text{o}\grave{\iota}$ $\dot{\epsilon}\nu$ $\tau\text{o}\hat{\iota}\varsigma$ $\dot{\alpha}\gamma\text{o}\rho\alpha\hat{\iota}\varsigma$)' (v. 43); and they are 'like unmarked graves' that people do not notice (v. 44). The 'legists' come in for much harsher criticism. They are the ones (not the Pharisees) who share in the guilt of killing the prophets (vv. 47–51), and it is they who 'have lifted the key of knowledge', neither entering into knowledge nor allowing others to enter (v. 52). At the conclusion of the invective, it is suddenly the scribes, who have been nowhere present in the invective or in its introduction and who are therefore here merely as the traditional allies of the Pharisees, and the Pharisees, who 'lie in wait for him to trap him in something that he might say' (v. 53).

The division that Luke makes between the invective against the Pharisees and that against the legists appears to be a division between his criticism of Jewish Christianity and his criticism of non-Christian Judaism, which is nevertheless similar to Jewish Christianity in its orientation towards the Torah. The Pharisees, aside from being merely slandered – the second two of the four woes upon them – are accused of improper *halakah*, washing and tithing. This is always the nature, in Luke-Acts, of the debate with the Pharisees; and, when we add the ingredient of the repeated Pharisaic friendliness to Jesus and to the church, then we see that it is a debate with Jewish Christianity. Those Jews who come to Jesus, who seek his company, but who nevertheless insist on traditional Torah observance receive their criticism; but it is not the same criticism that falls on the rejecting Jews. For these kill the prophets (and Jesus, and the early Christian martyrs) and do what they can to prevent other Jews from being saved. Thus upon the legists falls the now familiar epithet, 'this generation' (v. 50), which will have to answer for 'the blood of all the prophets' (cf. Acts 18.6: 'Your blood be upon your heads'). The sin of 'the Jews' is rejection; that of the Jewish Christians is improper response to the gospel, the failure to realize that Christianity has replaced Judaism. Yet both sins are tied to Torah observance.

When the Pharisees and scribes, then, at the conclusion of the invective, are said to want to trap Jesus in 'something that he might say', this refers to their attempt to show that their way, and not his, is the true way, not to any attempt on their part to 'do away with' Jesus, as Luke so often puts it; for the Pharisees in Luke are routinely and consistently kept away from any guilt for the death of Jesus.

The correctness of the preceding analysis of the Pharisees in this section is borne out by the conclusion (12.1), which cautions the 'disciples' to 'keep themselves away from the leaven of the Pharisees, which is hypocrisy' (whereas the scribes or legists do not appear in this warning); for leaven works within the dough. These Pharisees, who seek out Jesus' company and even seek to protect him (13.31; cf. Acts 5.34–39), are bad leaven within the dough. They are a problem within the church. Again, it is both aspects of this section of Luke – that the Pharisees are accused only of incorrect practice (along with some very general unpleasant attitudes) and that they are designated as the bad leaven *within* the dough against which the disciples must guard themselves – that allow us to realize that Luke is using the Pharisees to criticize the Jewish Christians of his own day.

Luke 12.11–12   Christians on trial before various authorities
    Important literature: **Fitzmyer**, *Luke*, vol. 2, pp. 962–6.

Luke, apparently, adds to this saying those *before whom* Christians are likely to be tried (cf. Mark 13.11; Matt. 10.19): 'synagogues and rulers and authorities' (v. 11). Synagogues are certainly Jewish, and rulers are likely to be, as can be seen by comparing the term here (ἄρχαί) with Luke 24.20, where chief priests (ἄρχιερεῖς) and rulers (ἄρχοντες) are designated as having 'crucified' Jesus. The 'authorities' are indefinite. Thus the persecution of the nascent church in the first part of Acts by the Jewish authorities in Jerusalem, during the course of the Diaspora mission by synagogues, and at the end of Acts by combined Jewish forces, is here foretold by Jesus. Jesus' experience in the synagogue in Nazareth is carried over on to the church. How much truth is there to this Lucan portrait of Jewish persecution of early Christianity? We shall attempt an answer to that question in Part Three.

Luke 13.1–9   The Jews must repent or be killed

Important literature: **Fitzmyer**, *Luke*, vol. 2, pp. 1004–9; **Lampe**, 'Luke', p. 835; **Loisy**, *Evangiles synoptiques*, vol. 2, pp. 285–6; *Luc*, pp. 359–64; **van Goudoever**, 'Israel in Luke', pp. 117–18; **Walaskay**, *We Came to Rome*, pp. 24–5; **Zahn**, *Lucas*, p. 523.

Whatever historical events may lie behind the reports in vv. 1, 4 (this issue is discussed in most commentaries), they appear here as object lessons for Jesus' hearers. Inasmuch as Jesus' Galilean ministry is closed, one might be tempted to think that Luke sees in the event reported in v. 1 the beginning of the doom pronounced on the Galilean towns in 10.13–15; yet he seems not to make such a connection, inasmuch as he follows the Galilean example with a Jerusalem one, an example from a place that has not been offered its last chance yet. Luke's point seems to be the more general one: Repent or die. While the direct address, 'If *you* do not repent' (vv. 3, 5), has served Christian preachers everywhere well through the centuries, it may be that Luke is here thinking specifically of the coming destruction of Jerusalem as being deserved by the Jews for their failure to repent, for their rejection of Jesus' ministry; but we could know that only from the accumulated evidence of all of Luke-Acts. Such a point is not explicit here.

Luke follows this twin example with the parable of the Fig Tree, apparently turned by him into a parable from the similar narrative in Mark (cf. Mark 11.12–14; Matt. 21.18–19). Following, as it does, the twin threats pronounced on those who do not repent, the parable's reference to fruit not borne is an obvious reference to repentance not done. It would thus seem that this Lucan parable is intended allegorically.[39] The repeated coming of the owner in quest of fruit appears to represent God's repeated sending of the prophets to Israel in search of repentance; but, as Israel has always rejected the prophets (cf. Luke 11.49, and also Acts 7.52), so the fig tree bears no fruit. The doom pronounced upon the fig tree for not having borne fruit is therefore the doom pronounced upon those who do not repent. Yet the doom is postponed for one more 'year' (v. 8) in order to see if a little extra tender loving care will produce the desired fruit/ repentance. To what this postponement refers is not perfectly clear. It may mean that, while Israel already deserved destruction before Jesus, his ministry provides a last merciful chance for the Jews to repent and to escape destruction; but, in view of the narrative in Acts, the extra year of grace may refer rather to the mission of the church.[40] In any case, destruction in the travel narrative would be premature. The examples in 13.1–5 and the parable in vv. 6–9 are a warning, evidently a last one. 'God is preparing a judgment and it matters not whether it comes by sword (13.1) or accident (13.4). The vehicle of destruction is unimportant; what matters is that by her rejection of Jesus [Israel has brought it about that] the doom of the nation is now scheduled on the divine calendar.'[41]

Luke 13.10–17   Jesus heals in a synagogue on the Sabbath

Important literature: **Fitzmyer**, *Luke*, vol. 2, pp. 1010–14; see also 13.1–9.

Here is the second of Luke's three such stories (cf. 6.6–11 and 14.1–6), only the first of which is found in the other Gospels. Jesus' Sabbath healing and the Jewish opposition to it are thus quite an important theme for Luke. On this occasion it is not Pharisees (as on the other two occasions) who oppose Jesus for 'working' on the Sabbath, but the synagogue president (ἀρχισυνάγωγος; v. 14). Nevertheless, when Jesus' response to the president (only this singular opponent has been mentioned), begins 'Hypocrites!' (plur.), we understand that Luke thinks of the argument as being an argument with the Pharisees, inasmuch as, elsewhere in Luke, hypocrites are Pharisees (12.1). Luke thus shows several things in this narrative: 1. that Jesus continues to attend synagogue 'according to his custom' (Luke 4.16) and as Paul also will do later; 2. that Jesus' practice is in opposition to Pharisaic legalism; and 3. that opposition to Jesus identical with that which comes from the Pharisees also comes from the synagogue, as 12.11 had warned and as 4.16–30 had already demonstrated.

Jesus' humanitarian point, that such an act of mercy surely ought to be allowed on the Sabbath (v. 16), reduces his opposition to 'shame' (v. 17), whereas 'the crowd rejoice[s]'. Thus the antithesis between rulers and people, which endures until the passion narrative, seems to be brought into play here. An *Archisynagōgos*, it would appear, belongs in the same basket with *Archiereis* (chief priests) and with *Archontes* and *Archai* (rulers) – and not with the Pharisees. Is, then, the portrayal of the synagogue President's opposition as being of the same nature as that of the Pharisees an attempt to show that the gulf between Jews (represented by the rulers) and Jewish Christians (represented by the Pharisees) is not so great after all? This possibility cannot be ruled out, but if Luke intends such a portrayal, his colours have been rather too subtle. Probably the present scene is related rather to Luke's desire to show Jesus' experience as the forerunner of the church's experience, inasmuch as Paul – who, we remember, like Jesus, regularly attended synagogue – also encounters opposition in the synagogue. The point at issue, healing on the Sabbath, would then be a convenient issue for provoking the opposition; and we recall also that a reference to healing figured in Jesus' first synagogue confrontation (Luke 4.23). The plan of the narrative of the Gospel of Luke, however, requires that the people ('the crowd') not appear here in opposition to Jesus.

Luke 13.23–30   Those who expect to be in the Kingdom of God will not be, and others will take their place

Important literature: **Fitzmyer**, *Luke*, vol. 2, pp. 1020–7; **Lagrange**, *Luc*, pp. 38–9; **Loisy**, *Evangiles synoptiques*, vol. 2, pp. 122–3; *Luc*, pp. 370–3; **Maddox**, *Purpose*, pp. 47–8; **Sandmel**, *Anti-Semitism*, p. 78; **Schmid**, *Lukas*, pp. 23–9.

If there remains some reasonable doubt about just what Luke sought to convey about the opposition to Jesus in the last synagogue Sabbath healing scene, this complex of sayings contains no such doubtful elements. (Matthew contains in part the same and in part similar sayings, but not collected together as in Luke.) The saying in vv. 24–25, about trying to get through the door before it is shut, is in itself unrelated to the Jewish issue, since it is broadly applicable to all seeking salvation; but when those who are locked out complain that they 'ate' and 'drank . . . before' Christ, and that he 'taught in [their] streets' (v. 26), then we have those among whom Jesus' ministry has taken place. And when Jesus says that they will look into the windows of the Kingdom and see not only the patriarchs, but 'all the prophets' (v. 28), the identity of the excluded is further defined, for, in Luke-Acts, it is 'the Jews' who are regularly accused of having rejected and killed 'the prophets'. Finally, vv. 29–30 erase all doubt, for people will come from the four corners of the world to banquet in the Kingdom, whereas those among whom Jesus ministered will be excluded, thus 'there are those who are last who will be first, and there are those who are first who will be last' (v. 30). As is characteristic for the speeches of Luke's leading characters, the Jews are out and the Gentiles in.

Luke 13.31   A Pharisaic warning

Important literature: **Conzelmann**, *Theology*, pp. 65, 132–9; **Denaux**, 'L'hypocrisie des Pharisiens', pp. 261–85; **Egelkraut**, *Jesus' Mission*, pp. 176–9; **Fitzmyer**, *Luke*, vol. 2, pp. 1028–32; **Hauck**, *Lukas*, p. 186; **Maddox**, *Purpose*, pp. 48–9; **Neyrey**, 'Jesus' Address', pp. 79–80, 82–4; **Radl**, *Paulus und Jesus*, pp. 150–5; **Robinson**, *Weg*, pp. 54–5; **Schweizer**, *Luke*, pp. 229–31.

While some authors find in this brief narrative some sort of Pharisaic trick, there is no reason to take the Pharisees' warning at other than face value, and the assumption that it masks some hostility towards Jesus is probably read in from a general perception of the Pharisees gained from Matthew and Mark, or from an imprecise reading of the earlier conflicts between Jesus and the Pharisees in Luke. What the Pharisees say to Jesus here implies, of itself, no deceit and no collusion with Herod, and Jesus' reply (v. 32) likewise fails to evidence any awareness of Pharisaic hostility. The Pharisees, furthermore, are regularly presented in Luke as attempting to be friendly toward Jesus, and they never have anything to do with the plot to kill him. Finally, in Acts it is Pharisees in the Sanhedrin who on two occasions aid the Jerusalem apostles (Acts 5.34–39) or Paul (Acts 23.6–9). That something similar happens in Acts is a compelling argument, inasmuch as Luke-Acts gives abundant evidence of the author's intent to show that what happened to Jesus also happened to the church; thus, if Pharisees assist the church in Acts, then we are obliged to search for places in Luke where Pharisees aid Jesus. This is one of those places.

Luke 13.32–33   Jesus' career continues until his death in Jerusalem
    13.34–35   The first lament over Jerusalem

Important literature: **Fitzmyer**, *Luke*, vol. 2, pp. 1033–7; see also 13.31.

Exactly what is meant by 'today and tomorrow and the third day' (v. 32) and by 'today and tomorrow and the next day' (v. 33) has been discussed in some detail by a number of authors, but we may conveniently pass the issue by here, for it seems unrelated to the topic at hand. It is possible that the first saying arises out of a carrying back of resurrection typology on to the life of Jesus, but something else could be meant, and the resurrection typology seems not to work for v. 33, where the phrase may be no more than a graphic way of saying, 'I have been travelling towards Jerusalem, and I intend to continue travelling in that direction until I get there.'[42]

The conclusion of v. 33, however, clearly refers to Jesus' appointment with destiny in Jerusalem. The prophet Jesus can 'perish' only in Jerusalem, because that is where all the prophets have perished, *at the hands of Jerusalem* (v. 34). This charge of killing the prophets, strange in the light of a cursory perusal of the historical and prophetic books of the Jewish scripture – that is, of what were the 'prophets' in Jesus' day – is nevertheless of Jewish homiletical provenance and occurs first in Ezra 9.11 and Neh. 9.26. This seems, in any case, to have been demonstrated adequately by Steck.[43] Steck's further assumption, however, that vv. 34–35 are, 'in their entirety a late Jewish saying',[44] is open to question. Such an origin could be correct for v. 34, although even there it is remarkable that Jerusalem alone is singled out for the charge of having murdered the prophets, not the Jewish people, who ought to be, according to the form, the ones so charged, in order to bring about their repentance. It is difficult, however, to assume such an origin for v. 35, inasmuch as v. 35a, 'Your house is forsaken', prepares for the later doom sayings in Luke pronounced upon Jerusalem, while v. 35b, '. . . until you say, "Blessed is the one who comes in the name of the Lord"', turns out to be a kind of prophecy that is fulfilled in some sense in 19.38.[45]

In any case, Luke's source is not the Deuteronomistic homiletical tradition, but Q (or Matthew); cf. Matt. 23.37–39, where the saying appears almost verbatim as in Luke. It is the beginning, for Luke, of the building of the case against Jerusalem. Jerusalem is, for Luke, the focal point of the Jewish rejection of Jesus and the gospel, and 13.34–35 is the first hint of that theme.[46]

Luke 14.1–6   Disagreement with a Pharisee while dining at his house

Important literature: **Fitzmyer**, *Luke*, vol. 2, pp. 1038–42; G. **Schneider**, *Lukas*, vol. 2, p. 312.

For the third and last time Jesus dines with a Pharisee. Since this has happened twice before, Luke does not bother to inform us that the Pharisee has invited Jesus, either because he thinks that we should assume that an invitation has been issued or because he is of the opinion that, by now, it is simply customary for Jesus to dine in Pharisees' homes. This last time, however, it is not the home of just any Pharisee, but of 'one of the leading Pharisees' (v. 1).[47] This Pharisee has other leading Pharisees with him, 'and they were observing' Jesus. The opposition of the Pharisees to Jesus has been sufficiently detailed already in the Gospel for us to know why these Pharisees are observing Jesus; it is in order 'to catch him out in something that he might say' (11.53) – or, in a more general sense, to see whether he would propose or do something contrary to their *halakah*. The issue that comes up is, as has been the case twice before (6.6–11; 13.10–17), that of healing on the Sabbath. As Luke represents it, this is the point regarding which Jesus most easily shows the Pharisees to be in error. Not only does Luke present Jesus as healing on the Sabbath on three different occasions and as making the point that 'doing good' on the Sabbath is allowed,[48] but he shows each time that it is a legal issue. In 6.9 Jesus asks whether it 'is permitted on the Sabbath to do good or to do bad'; and in 13.15 he calls his opponents 'hypocrites' and brings up, as in 14.5, the example of the cow in trouble. Here in 14.3, again, the issue is what 'is allowed'. The author of Luke-Acts, it seems, considers Jesus' position on this point so self-evident that it shows the folly of the Pharisees' position: 'Are you people so immersed in your pedantry and so divorced from reality that you do not even allow healing of the sick on the Sabbath?' Thus, on this final occasion of Sabbath healing, the Pharisees 'ke[ep] their peace' (v. 4) and are 'not able to respond with a contrary argument (ἀνταποκριθῆναι)' (v. 6). They are bested.

We need to remind ourselves that this argument that Luke is carrying on with the Pharisees' notion of *halakah* is not an argument with *Judaism* as a separate religion, but with *Christian Judaism*. The nature of the argument even shows that to be true; for what interest could a Gentile Christian of the late first or early second century have had in proving conclusively (for this is surely what Luke thinks that he is doing) that *the Jews'* religious practice was wrong? The question becomes more pronounced when we become aware that those people against whose practice Luke strives so mightily are regularly portrayed as being friendly to Jesus. The argument is with those Christians who try to continue to be Jews, whereas for Luke the only true Christianity is Gentile Christianity.

Luke 14.7–24   The parable of the Great Supper, with introduction

Important literature: **Dodd**, *Parables*, p. 94; **Fitzmyer**, *Luke*, vol. 2, pp. 1043–57; **Funk**, *Language, Hermeneutic, and Word of God*, pp. 163–98; **Gnilka**, *Verstockung*, pp. 132–3, 150–1; **Hahn**, 'Einladung zum Festmahl'; **Jülicher**, *Gleichnisreden*, vol. 2, pp. 416–18; **Klostermann**, *Lukas*, p. 153; **Lampe**, 'Luke', p. 836; **Loisy**, *Evangiles synoptiques*, vol. 2, p. 327; *Luc*, pp. 382–8; **Maddox**, *Purpose*, p. 49; **Montefiore**, *Synoptic Gospels*, vol. 2, p. 512; **Sandmel**, *Anti-Semitism*, pp. 78–9; **Schmid**, *Lukas*, p. 246; G. **Schneider**, *Lukas*, vol. 2, pp. 317–18; **van Goudoever**, 'Israel in Luke', pp. 118–19; **Wilson**, *Gentiles*, p. 34.

While the parable itself is a somewhat different version of the parable that appears in Matt. 22.1–10, the introduction appears in Luke alone, and we shall therefore do well to examine it carefully and to note its implications for understanding the parable. The introduction moves through three stages. To begin with, it picks up on the setting in the home of the 'leading Pharisee' and connects that setting with the slander, already mentioned (11.43), that Pharisees like to get front-row seats at synagogue (14.7). The problem with the connection is that, as far as we know, everyone at the banquet is a Pharisee except Jesus, so that the charge against the Pharisees that they like the best seats appears out of place. Luke, however, seems content so to characterize the Pharisees. The second stage of the introduction, then, is vv. 8–11, in which a saying of Jesus about first and last is put forward as a correction of such 'Pharisaic' behaviour. Whether Luke intends this widespread general advice[49] actually to correct Pharisaic practice (thus implying that he holds out hope that Jewish Christians may be converted to his way of thinking) or whether he merely uses the connection with the Pharisaic love of front-row seats as a means of providing what he takes to be general advice would be difficult to determine. Of one thing, however, we can be sure, and that is that Luke uses this general advice as a transition to the third stage, vv. 12–14, which is the explicit introduction to the parable.

What is significant about this third stage is that it discusses only two groups, whereas the parable itself contains three groups of people invited to the banquet. Here, however, the advice is simple and straightforward: don't invite 'friends or brothers or relatives or rich neighbours' (v. 12), but rather 'poor, cripples, lame, blind' (v. 13). For this one will be 'paid back . . . in the resurrection' (v. 14). Since this final part of the introduction to the parable of the Banquet emphasizes the issue of foregoing present reward in favour of divine reward later on, we would hardly take it to refer to the issue of Jew and Gentile if it were not for the fact that the parable then employs the same language.

In the parable, there are three groups. First there are those originally invited, who make their silly excuses and miss out. Almost all commentators take these to stand, for Luke, for the Jews who reject the gospel, and the point seems so obvious that it needs no further labouring. We may note the conclusion (v. 24), 'None of those invited men . . .'. If Luke had only, then, stopped with the next group, there would be no confusion, for they are identical with the second group of the introduction, 'poor and cripples and blind and lame' (v. 21). This connection between introduction and parable can only be Lucan; and the meaning thus far would appear, again, to be straightforward: the Jews, to whom the gospel first came, turned it down, and so God sent the gospel to others, i.e., to Gentiles. But Luke adds a third group,[50] people who are to be found in 'the highways and hedgerows' (v. 23), and one wonders if their location is significant, in view of the fact that the first group is to be found 'in the streets and alleys of the city' (v. 21). Taken alone, the parable in its Lucan form would seem to set up a three stage plan of salvation: to the proper Jews, to the outcasts (in the city but poor, lame, etc.), and to Gentiles (outside the city), with the first group, of course, turning down the invitation. Either pattern – not the Jews but the Gentiles, or not the 'true' Jews but the periphery and then the Gentiles – would fit Luke's plan.

We must leave this riddle unsolved. Luke has not provided adequate clues for a completely satisfactory solution; perhaps he was content to let both 'outlines' – from the Jews to the Gentiles, and from 'the Jews' to the periphery and then to the Gentiles – come to expression here.

Luke 15.1–32   Parables of the lost

Important literature: **Fitzmyer**, *Luke*, vol. 2, pp. 1071–92; **Hauck**, *Lukas*, p. 199; **Jülicher**, *Gleichnisreden*, vol. 2, pp. 333–9, 357–65; **Klostermann**, *Lukas*, p. 157; **Lambrecht**, *Astonished*, pp. 24–53; **Lampe**, 'Luke', p. 836; **Loisy**, *Luc*, pp. 37, 402–3; **Sanders**, 'Tradition and Redaction'; **Schnider**, *Verlorene Söhne*; **Schottroff**, 'Gleichnis vom verlorenen Sohn'; **van Goudo-ever**, 'Israel in Luke', p. 121.

The saying placed at the end of ch. 14 about throwing out the salt (vv. 34–35) serves at once to reiterate the point about the rejection of the Jews and to make a break with the setting, dining in the home of a Pharisee. Thus, when ch. 15 opens, even though Pharisees are again mentioned, Jesus seems not to be thought of as being in the home of one of the 'leading Pharisees'. Rather, 'all the toll collectors and the sinners' are 'approach[ing] him . . . to listen to him' (v. 1), and this causes 'the Pharisees and the scribes' again to 'grumbl[e]' (cf. 5.30) 'because he receives sinners and eats with them' (v. 2) – hardly the setting of the parable of the Banquet. We are therefore returned to the issue of the outcasts, of Jesus' success with them, and of the Pharisaic opposition to his association with those who are improper (cf. 7.39). We note that Pharisees are again in Jesus' audience and that their only complaint is that he associates with toll collectors and sinners with whom the Pharisees think he should not associate.

The following twin parables, then, the first of which also appears in Matthew (18.12–14), are pointed directly at this issue; for, when the shepherd recovers the lost sheep or when the woman recovers her lost drachma, there is much 'joy' and 'rejoicing' (vv. 5, 6, 7, 9, 10) – because of 'one sinner who repents' (vv. 7 and 10). This connection between the recovery of the lost item and the repentant sinner, not made in the Matthaean version of the Lost Sheep, is Lucan and is in line with the contrast that he regularly draws between Pharisees and sinners. The twin parables of the Lost Sheep and of the Lost Coin therefore serve to justify the taking of the gospel to the periphery by referring to the divine joy thereupon attendant. The point is the same as 5.32: 'I have not come to call righteous persons, but sinners to repentance.' That the gospel goes to the outcasts – and eventually to the Gentiles – is God's will.

Is this then also the theme of the following parable, unique to Luke, of the Prodigal Son? While many, perhaps most commentators so understand this parable, the connection is not as air-tight as it might be. It is true that there are two sons, one of whom may readily be described as lost, and that the return of the lost son produces 'joy' (v. 32), as in the foregoing twin parables. There are also some substantial differences, however. No one goes to seek the prodigal; rather, he comes to his own senses. Furthermore, his life away from home not only is miserable, but is apparently described as being a life among Gentiles, inasmuch as he is feedings *pigs* (v. 15).[51] Then, when the Torah-observant (v. 29) son is put over against the one who feeds pigs, it could well be intended as a Pharisee–Gentile contrast, or as a contrast between Jewish Christians and Gentile Christians. Thus the parable may fall into line with the preceding twin parables and intend Pharisees v. toll collectors and sinners, or v. Gentiles. That it is somehow both at once, with the prodigal son representing the periphery that moves over into the realm of the Gentiles, is difficult to imagine. Still, Luke does think of the periphery as being the transition zone between Jews and Gentiles, and he may well think of this parable as, in the first instance, giving the contrast between Pharisees and sinners, while at the same time adding some tints to the portrait that allow us to see that the mission to the outcasts portends that to the Gentiles.

We now have two parables in a row, more or less, that present something of the same problem: the Banquet and the Prodigal Son. If the question in the former was whether Luke thought of outcasts *and* Gentiles or only of Gentiles, the question in the latter is whether he thinks of outcasts *or* of Gentiles. While we have had some difficulty answering these questions precisely, it is perhaps, nevertheless, not too difficult to follow Luke's thinking in this section of the Gospel. Luke, we recall, thinks of the gospel's moving out from the Jews to the periphery to the Gentiles in a smooth and unbroken development.[52] It is therefore one continuous development and follows the divine plan. If Luke is somewhat imprecise in distinguishing those who represent outcasts from those who represent Gentiles in his parables, it is likely to be because he views those groups not as discrete groups but as stages on a continuum, the former standing in for and representing the latter.

Luke 16.14–15   The Pharisees are reviled

Important literature: **Fitzmyer**, *Luke*, vol. 2, pp. 1111–13.

Without any justification Luke accuses the Pharisees of being 'lovers of money'. He calls them this, however, in order to explain why they 'thumbed their noses at' Jesus (v. 14), and the whole sentence seems related to what immediately precedes, Jesus' saying that it is not possible 'to serve God and Mammon' (v. 13). Luke thus seems to represent the Pharisees as deriding Jesus because he has said that one cannot both be religious and 'serve Mammon', which is taken to be the same as 'lov[ing] money', whereas the Pharisees, being 'lovers of money', are precisely seeking to do both. (Luke does not need to tell us here that Pharisees seek to be religious; he has already told us that enough times.) All that we learn from this statement, therefore, is that Luke dislikes the Pharisees enough to slander them; the statement provides no real information about Luke's portrayal of the Pharisees. Verse 15, however, is another matter, for here the standard charge that the Pharisees seek to 'justify themselves before people', even though such 'arrogance' is in fact 'an abomination before God', is made again. This harsh judgment on Pharisaic practice, which Luke has mentioned before, will receive its fullest expression in the parable of the Pharisee and the Toll Collector, Luke 18.9–14.

Luke 16.16–18   Statements about the Law

Important literature: **Conzelmann**, *Theology*, p. 101; **Fitzmyer**, *Luke*, vol. 2, pp. 1114–23; **Hauck**, *Lukas*, pp. 206–7; **Klostermann**, *Lukas*, p. 167; **Loisy**, *Luc*, pp. 414; **Wilson**, *Law*, pp. 29–31, 43–51.

These three verses present a challenge to interpretation. First (v. 16), Luke seems to say that the Law is abrogated: 'The Law and the Prophets were up until John; since then the Kingdom of God is being preached.' The next statement (v. 17), however, seems to reverse that position, since it appears to say that not the tiniest portion of the Law will be set aside as long as 'heaven and earth' last. The final statement, then, about divorce (v. 18), either is or is not an example of the principle expressed in v. 17. Whether it is or is not depends on whether Luke knew or did not know that such a regulation about divorce would be in fact much more stringent than the divorce laws in the Torah. The whole puzzle is made even more challenging by the realization that it is Luke, himself, who is responsible for the juxtaposition of these several statements. While vv. 16 and 17 may have been attached already in Luke's source,[53] he is the one responsible for bringing up v. 18, which is more like Mark 10.11–12 than it is like Matt. 19.9. Thus it would appear that Luke has attached the Marcan saying (Luke 16.18) to the other two statements about the Law, whereas Matthew has also included the Marcan saying, but in revised form and not associated with the other statements about the Law. Why has Luke created this puzzle? What do these statements mean for him?

S. G. Wilson has gone into this issue at some length and has concluded that Luke had no 'consistent' attitude towards the Torah (in the Gospel), and that 'the ambuguity of Lk. 16.16–18 epitomizes the ambiguity of Luke's Gospel as a whole, in which the law is both upheld and challenged'.[54] He thus proposes that Luke has simply put together three statements 'linked by a common theme but not by a consistent approach to it'.[55] Wilson leans toward the possibilities that v. 17 'expresses the extreme difficulty, rather than the impossibility, of altering the law', that it is a 'hyperbole';[56] but that v. 18 is probably best understood 'as a challenge to the authority' of the Torah.[57] Only someone who had an 'inconsistent' or 'ambiguous' attitude toward the Torah could put three such statements together.

This explanation is unsatisfactory, not least because it moves the scholar's inability to fathom the intent of the author of Luke-Acts on to that author himself and labels it 'inconsistency'. It is one thing to be able to observe that Luke has been deliberately ambiguous at points – as, e.g., in the narrative of Stephen's martyrdom – and we have seen such deliberate ambiguity on several occasions; but it is something else to move from the realization of our lack of understanding at some point to the conclusion that Luke was inconsistent. It is best to confront the puzzle of these verses, therefore, assuming that Luke had some purpose in putting these three statements together, even though we may be unable to determine that purpose with precision.

Heaven and earth are not going to pass away. Even if one were to say, as Luke very well may have done, that heaven and earth *will* pass away when the Lord comes, we would still be faced with the situation that the Lord had not yet come and that not even the most minute particle of the Law had therefore been abrogated (according to v. 17). The passing away of heaven and earth can hardly be understood as hyperbole for the difficult but impossible,[58] since it will have been perfectly clear to Luke that this was an impossibility, at least this side of the Lord's return. On the other hand, however, v. 16, while not explicitly saying that the Law ceased after John, surely means that the 'period' of the Law is over after John. The problem of the relation of v. 17 to v. 16, it seems to me, can be solved if we recall that Luke, like much of early Christianity, viewed the Jewish scripture – the Bible, as we would say, 'the Law and the Prophets' – as being essentially prophetic of Christ (along with other things related to Christ's coming, such as that the gospel was intended for the Gentiles). This understanding of 'the Law and the Prophets' is plainly the operative one when, just a few verses later, the Abraham of Luke's parable tells the rich man in hell that the rich man's relatives can be saved from equal torment if they will just heed 'Moses and the Prophets' (Luke 16.29); and the same understanding is at work later when, in Acts 13.27, Paul accuses those in Jerusalem of not having been able to understand 'the voices of the Prophets that were read every Sabbath'. If, therefore, Luke views the Law and the Prophets here in their prophetic capacity, then Luke 16.16 does not speak of abrogation of the Torah at all, for the Law and the Prophets foretold Christ up until John, but from that time on there was no further need for this prophetic activity, since the gospel was being preached. It is possible that Luke thought of v. 17 as continuing in this same vein and as asserting that all the Law and the Prophets either have been or will be fulfilled; nothing in them will 'fall'. In light of v. 18, however, it is more likely that Luke thought in v. 17 simply of the need to keep the Law. We saw in Part One, in some detail, how Luke's view of the Law is that, whereas the great bulk of the Torah is not relevant for the Gentile church and is not to be followed there, some few laws are intended for the Gentiles (the Apostolic Decree). Probably Luke thinks of the divorce law in v. 18 as being one regulation, like the love commandment and the regulations of the Apostolic Decree, that is universally valid, i.e., not to be kept by Jews only. In this case, therefore, we must assume either that Luke does not realize, contrary to Wilson's conjecture,[59] that v. 18 is a stricter law than is found in the Torah (if Jesus ave it as a requirement, it must be in there somewhere), or that, for reasons that are not altogether clear, he wanted to make it appear that such a law for Gentiles was in the Torah. One notes that both the Marcan (Mark 10.2–12) and the Matthaean (Matt. 19.3–9) context make it clear that Jesus' commandment goes beyond the Torah, whereas Luke has dropped this contrast.

It seems possible, therefore – if we try to think of the Jewish scriptures as Luke did – to see a consistent viewpoint in Luke 16.16–18. All that was foretold in the Law and the Prophets has been taking place since John the Baptist. That the Law and the Prophets are being fulfilled, however, does not mean that the Torah has been summarily set aside, for God still expects the Jews to keep all the Law and the Gentiles some of the laws, like the one against divorce.

Luke 16.19–31   The parable of the Rich Man and Lazarus

Important literature: **Fitzmyer**, *Luke*, vol. 2, pp. 1125–34; **Jülicher**, *Gleichnisreden*, pp. 632–41; **Klostermann**, *Lukas*, p. 170; **Loisy**, *Evangiles synoptiques*, vol. 2, pp. 177–8; **Maddox**, *Purpose*, p. 49; **Montefiore**, *Synoptic Gospels*, vol. 2, p. 540; **van Goudoever**, 'Israel in Luke', pp. 121–2.

Our interest here is not in the ultimate origin of this parable, however interesting that origin may be and although there is a considerable literature on that subject. Rather, it is again the reference to the Law and the Prophets, 'Moses and the Prophets' (v. 29), and what is said about them that are germane to the issue at hand. Here, as in v. 16, the background perspective is fulfilment; what Christ and the church have been doing was proclaimed in the scripture, and people with good sense can recognize that fact. The rich man of the parable wants someone to 'go from the dead' to his family to warn them about the torments of hell so that they will repent (v. 30) – always for Luke the proper response to Jesus and to the gospel. Surely there is a connection here with the resurrection of Jesus, for there is a simple connection between the difficulty posed by Abraham at the end of the parable and the situation of the early church in attempting to convert Jews to Christianity: since the Jews cannot understand their own scriptures, the fact of the resurrection of Jesus will likewise have no effect on them. 'If they do not listen to Moses and the Prophets, they will not be convinced if one should rise from the dead' (v. 31).

A number of commentators, apparently carried away by Luke's slander of the Pharisees as 'money lovers' in v. 14, think that this parable is anti-Pharisaic and that the rich man represents the Pharisees; but there is nothing in the parable of Luke's characterization of the Pharisees. The rich man dies and goes to hell; he is in torment there; when he realizes that there is a heaven he wants someone to warn his relatives about hell. What is Pharisaic about that?

It is statements in Luke-Acts such as the conclusion to this parable that prompt Sandmel's reference to Luke's 'residual pity' for the Jews;[60] yet the pity is more read into Abraham's statement than expressed there. Abraham's statement is in fact without emotion, giving voice to what is for Luke the actual state of affairs: the Jews can't and won't understand. When Luke then elsewhere condemns the Jews for their rejection of the gospel (e.g., in Acts 18.6), it is that sentiment that we should probably hear at the conclusion of the parable of the Rich Man and Lazarus, not pity.

Luke 17.11–19   The healing of ten lepers

Important literature: **Betz**, 'Ten Lepers'; **Bruners**, *Reinigung der Aussätzigen*; **Bundy**, *First Three Gospels*, p. 387; **Conzelmann**, *Theology*, pp. 68–73; **Fitzmyer**, *Luke*, vol. 2, pp. 1149–56; **Jervell**, *People of God*, p. 121; **Lampe**, 'Luke', p. 837; **Loisy**, *Evangiles synoptiques*, vol. 2, p. 181; *Luc*, p. 428; **Montefiore**, *Synoptic Gospels*, vol. 2, pp. 544–5; **Sandmel**, *Anti-Semitism*, p. 80; **Schmid**, *Lukas*, p. 272; **Talbert**, *Reading Luke*, pp. 165–6.

That Luke has created this story out of the narrative of the healing of a leper in Luke 5.12–14 par. and certain biblical (i.e., Old Testament) allusions seems to have been convincingly demonstrated by Bruners,[61] although that issue need not detain us here, since our interest is Luke's use of the narrative, not his source. The narrative begins with the geographical information that Jesus is ministering partially in the periphery; he journeys 'through the midst of Samaria and Galilee' (V. 11). This strange and anomalous designation seems to arise from Luke's need to have Jesus encounter an inter-racial group of Jews and Pharisees. If location, however, arises out of the demands of the story, then it is probably pressing its significance too much to find here, as some authors do, evidence that Luke thought of the whole travel narrative as Jesus' Samaritan ministry. That such a conclusion involves drawing too much from the geographical designation can be seen if we focus on the other term, Galilee; for we know that Jesus is supposed to have left Galilee, apparently for good, since in 9.51 he started out for Jerusalem, then in v. 52 entered Samaria, and finally in 10.13–15 called down doom upon the area of his former ministry. Here, however, he is going through 'the midst of Samaria and *Galilee*'; but one should not press this statement to mean that Jesus has returned to Galilee or that he, in fact, never left, and the same must be true of the other location, Samaria. Jesus is here said to be 'go[ing] through the midst of Samaria and Galilee' because Luke wants to locate him somewhere where he can encounter Jews and Samaritans together, not because of the geographical scheme of the Gospel as a whole.

Following the geographical designation, Luke presents us with a fairly routine healing miracle – routine, that is, until one and only one of the ten former lepers returns to 'thank him' and until this returning one is said to be a Samaritan (v. 16). Now the interest of the story quickens. 'Could no one be found coming back to give glory to God except this foreigner?' (v. 18). Forget that there is no reason why all ten could not have given 'glory to God' in doing just what Jesus had told them to do and what the nine presumably did, 'show[ing] [them]selves to the priests' (v. 14). Luke has no interest in having such logical inconsistencies in his polemical stories pointed out to him. He wants to show that a bunch of Jews did not make the proper response to Jesus when he healed them, but that a Samaritan did. That the response to Jesus, and not 'giving glory to God', is what is really at issue is made plain by Jesus' last words to the Samaritan, 'Your faith has saved you' (v. 19). This conclusion tells us what the narrative is really about. We are not to ask why the Samaritan's faith saved him and the Jews' faith did not save them, when the Samaritan's apparent expression of faith came after the healing and not before, for Luke is interested in contrasting Jewish and Samaritan response to Jesus. Samaritans believe and Jews do not.[62] Just as in the conclusion to the story of the sinner's anointing Jesus (Luke 7.50), so here there are problems in determining exactly where Luke sees the 'faith' in the narrative and, indeed, just what he means by faith. If we rest content, however, to see 'faith' for Luke as the label for the proper response to Jesus, and to see that he has in both these stories drawn a contrast – sinner v. Pharisee, Samaritan v. Jew – then we at least understand that much.

Furthermore, we now have a trio: the sinner in ch. 7, the proselyte or God-fearer in the same chapter whose 'faith' is 'such' as cannot be 'found . . . in Israel' (7.9), and this Samaritan, of whom, it would seem, the very same thing could be said. Thus, while it is surely true that Luke, in this episode, wants to 'anchor the Samaritan mission of Acts already in the life of Jesus itself',[63] and that 'the Samaritan here has exemplary significance' for the later Gentile mission,[64] the portrait that Luke has painted actually has more variegated colours than that; for he has placed representatives of his three peripheral groups, the latter two of whom are important for the progression of the gospel described in Acts, in the Gospel, and he has contrasted their proper response to Jesus to that of the Jews and, in the case of the sinner, to that of the Pharisees.

Luke 17.20–21 The Kingdom of God is among the Pharisees

Important literature: **Conzelmann**, *Theology*, pp. 120–5; **Fitzmyer**, *Luke*, vol. 2, pp. 1157–62; **Montefiore**, *Synoptic Gospels*, vol. 2, pp. 546–50; B. and J. **Weiss**, *Markus und Lukas*, p. 565; **Zahn**, *Lucas*, p. 600.

The saying that 'the Kingdom of God is among you' (v. 21) cannot be considered apart from those to whom it is directly addressed,[65] the Pharisees, and this statement to the Pharisees cannot be understood apart from the preceding narrative about the cured Samaritan leper who had faith when his Jewish counterparts did not. In the face of such a miracle and object lesson, the Pharisees ask, 'When is the Kingdom of God coming?' (v. 20). 'The question of the Pharisees to Jesus, about when the Kingdom of God is coming, which follows immediately on the narrative [of the healing of the lepers] overlooks the fact that the question has already been taken care of by Jesus in view of the cleansing of the lepers: in his person and his saving activity the Kingdom is present there amongst them.'[66] The Pharisees, so interested in prescribed practice that overlooks the really important aspects of God's will, so keen to justify themselves by this practice, so critical of Jesus' associations with outcasts, nevertheless have the Kingdom of God among them but do not know it. Who can these be but the Torah-observant Jewish Christians, viewed from the perspective of Luke's Gentile Christianity? Jewish Christianity, according to the author of Luke-Acts, is so close to the truth but incapable of seeing it. While Jewish Christians 'believe', in a certain sense, still they do not have 'faith' in the way Luke defines it, for their faith relies on practice and not on true contrition and repentance, like that of the sinner at Simon the Pharisee's house or that of this Samaritan who returned to glorify God and to thank Jesus. The Kingdom of God is among these 'hypocrites', but they are unaware of it.

Luke 18.9–14   The parable of the Pharisee and the Toll Collector

Important literature: **Cortés**, 'Greek of Luke 18.14a'; **Fitzmyer**, *Luke*, vol. 2, pp. 1183–9; **Loisy**, *Luc*, p. 444; **Schmid**, *Lukas*, p. 281.

This parable, again unique to Luke and probably written by him,[67] is one of his gems. The Pharisee and the toll collector are outstanding examples of caricatures, their respective essences made stunningly clear by a few simple strokes. Again the Pharisee is contrasted to the outcast on the periphery; again the one seeks to justify himself and the other approaches God in true repentance and contrition; again the Pharisee expresses the two traits that Luke consistently attacks, a distaste for the outcasts and a prescribed practice (fasting and tithing, v. 12); and the conclusion (v. 14a), that the toll collector is justified and the Pharisee not, is but another way of saying what Jesus has said already to outcast, to God-fearer and to Samaritan, 'Your faith has saved you.' Over and over in the Gospel, the author shows us that those on the periphery know how to respond to Jesus whereas the Pharisees do not.

Luke 18.31–34   The third announcement of the passion[68]

Important literature: **Fitzmyer**, *Luke*, vol. 2, pp. 1207–10; **Radl**, *Paulus und Jesus*, pp. 153–5; G. **Schneider**, *Lukas*, vol. 2, p. 373.

A number of commentators are of the opinion that Luke has here sought to reduce the role of the Jews in Jesus' passion by the way he has altered the Marcan form of the announcement (Mark 10.32–34), but that is not the case at all. Luke has, rather, accomplished two things by his changes in this saying. The first is that he has cast those active verbs that in Mark might be taken as describing the action of 'the Gentiles' into the passive, thus making the role of 'the Gentiles' in the 'sporting with and mistreating and spitting upon' Jesus (Luke 18.32) quite unclear; and the second is that he has, by these changes, made the saying well-nigh unamenable to understanding. That this was his intent, that he deliberately rendered the saying unintelligible, is made perfectly clear by the explanation that he has tagged on to the end of the saying: 'And they understood nothing of these things, and this saying was hidden from them, and they had no knowledge of the things said' (v. 34). This closing remark is comical, for Luke has rendered his purpose transparent, openly explaining that he expects his readers not to understand the third announcement of the passion. The saying does not lay culpability at the door of the Gentiles.

Luke 19.1–10   Zacchaeus

Important literature: **Fitzmyer**, *Luke*, vol. 2, pp. 1218–26; **Loisy**, *Luc*, pp. 38, 453–8; **Wellhausen**, *Evangelium Lucae*, p. 104.

Just as, near the beginning of his ministry, the Lucan Jesus saved a toll collector, Levi (Luke 5.27–32), so, near the end of his ministry, he saves another, Zacchaeus. Furthermore, just as Jesus dined with Levi, so he dines with Zacchaeus (19.5); just as the Pharisees and scribes 'grumble' about such an association in the former case, so in the latter 'everyone grumble[s]' (19.7, διαγογγύζω; cf. γογγύζω in 5.30); and, just as Jesus answers the Pharisaic objections by responding in 5.31–32 that 'those who are well do not need a physician, but those who are sick', which he then interprets to mean that he 'did not come to call righteous persons, but sinners to repentance', so he responds in 19.10 to those who object to his association with Zacchaeus that 'the Son of man came to seek and to save the lost'. Small wonder that Wellhausen referred to Zacchaeus as the '*Doppelgänger* of Levi'.[69]

As part of his justification of associating with Zacchaeus, the Lucan Jesus also explains that he has brought 'salvation' to Zacchaeus 'inasmuch as he, himself, is also a son of Abraham' (v. 9). While, on one level, this positive reference to 'son of Abraham' might be taken as evidence contradictory to the view that Luke portrays 'the Jews' as completely rejecting and rejected by God, the statement should not be so read. For one thing, Luke so consistently elsewhere develops the rejection motif that one would have to wonder in this case, indeed, about his consistency, if this statement be taken as representing a contrary opinion. Even more than that, however, such an interest is foreign to the Zacchaeus episode, inasmuch as Jesus' statement about Zacchaeus's being a child of Abraham is linked to his statement about saving the lost and thus has the primary meaning that the detractors are mistaken, for outcasts may take their rightful place in the Kingdom of God. They are no longer disadvantaged by their failure to follow a certain practice, a certain *halakah*. Like the Gentiles after them (who replace them functionally in Acts), '*They* will listen' (Acts 28.28). Put otherwise, when Luke affirms that Zacchaeus is also a son of Abraham, he means that people like Zacchaeus are proper objects of the church's mission, not that Zacchaeus is a 'Jew'.[70] It is among the outcasts, in the periphery, that Jesus finds appropriate response, and this periphery is to be the springboard to the Gentile mission.

Luke 19.11–27   The parable of the Pounds[71]

Important literature: **Egelkraut**, *Jesus' Mission*, pp. 212–13; **Ernst**, *Lukas*, pp. 519–21; **Fitzmyer**, *Luke*, vol. 2, pp. 1228–38; **Grundmann**, *Lukas*, pp. 361–5; **Jülicher**, *Gleichnisreden*, vol. 2, pp. 485–92; **Klostermann**, *Lukas*, p. 186; **Lambrecht**, *Astonished*, pp. 167–80; 187–91; **Loisy**, *Evangiles synoptiques*, vol. 2, pp. 464–81; *Luc*, pp. 458–62; **Maddox**, *Purpose*, pp. 49–50; **Montefiore**, *Synoptic Gospels*, vol. 2, pp. 565–6; **Sanders**, 'Parable of the Pounds'; **van Goudoever**, 'Israel in Luke', pp. 120–1; **Wellhausen**, *Evangelium Lucae*, p. 106.

The Lucan version of what is in Matthew the parable of the Talents (Matt. 25.14–30) has an admixture of further and different information about the man of means who takes a journey, entrusting the management of his affairs to his 'slaves' (v. 13), and it is this admixture that concerns the theme at hand. While many authors think that the admixture was originally a separate parable that either Luke or someone before him has blended together with the Pounds, it is more likely that it is Luke himself who has added these allegorical details, since they fit into his plan so well. But no matter, it is not Luke's sources that interest us here, but what he does with them. The introduction to the parable, v. 11, which relates the parable to the delay-of-the-parousia theme, is actually an introduction only to that part of the parable that is similar to the Matthaean parable of the Talents (what to do till Messiah comes). Luke then uses the occasion of the parable to include the other, anti-Judaic theme, and the introduction appears unrelated to that issue.

The unique aspects of the Lucan version of the parable are that the man of means is someone 'wellborn' who is going to 'receive' a 'kingdom' (v. 12), that 'his citizens hat[e] him and sen[d] an embassy after him', requesting that he not be given the rule over them (v. 14), and that, after he settles up his accounts with his slaves upon his return, he then orders 'those who didn't wish [him] to reign over them' to be 'sla[in] before' him (v. 27). While these details, as commentators never tire of informing us, to a considerable degree mirror Archelaus's relations with Rome and Jerusalem, for Luke they surely take on an allegorical meaning. In fact, the allegory is so clear that it hardly needs explication. The 'wellborn' one who goes away to 'receive' a 'kingdom' must be Jesus, who goes, as Jülicher so aptly observed,[72] not to Italy but to heaven, to return in his royal splendour. 'His citizens' can therefore be only the Jews, who reject his Messiahship; and there is no pity for them, for they have had their chance. They are to be 'sla[in] . . . before' him. This is the climax and conclusion of the travel narrative, the justified slaying of the Jews.

In the next verse Jesus enters Jerusalem, and the juxtaposition of that entry to the order to slay the Jews is pointed. This outcome has been known since Jesus' synagogue sermon in Nazareth. The Jews will now altogether reject his offer of salvation and be rejected – slain, even – in turn, just as those in Galilee earlier rejected him and had doom pronounced upon them.

Luke 19.28–40 The entry into Jerusalem

Important literature: **Ernst**, *Lukas*, p. 527; **Fitzmyer**, *Luke*, vol. 2, pp. 1242–52; **Flender**, *St Luke*, pp. 107–9; **Robinson**, *Weg*, pp. 55–6; **Sandmel**, *Anti-Semitism*, p. 80.

With minor alterations, Luke follows the Marcan narrative of Jesus' triumphal march into the city as far as the acclaim of the crowds, at which point his changes become more significant. He adds the word 'king' to the biblical quotation that the crowd chants, 'Blessed is he who comes in the name of the Lord' (v. 38), thus removing any doubt about Jesus' identity; but then he makes two other changes that are apparently designed to rescue Jesus from the later charges of arousing the populace and of sedition (23.2). According to Luke, it is only the disciples, albeit the 'entire multitude' of them, who acclaim Jesus king (v. 37), instead of the 'many' of Mark 11.8, so that this acclamation loses its character as evidence supporting the charge of arousing the populace; and while Luke does include 'king' in the acclamation, he concludes the acclamation with an unmistakable echo of the song of the angels in 2.14: 'Peace in heaven and glory on high' (19.38), so that the appearance that 'King Jesus' might want Caesar's throne is removed by the indication that Jesus' kingdom is or is to be a heavenly, not an earthly one.

In v. 39 the Pharisees again offer a friendly but mistaken warning. Just as, in 13.31, they warned Jesus to stay away from Jerusalem for his own health but failed to understand his mission, so here they suggest that he quiet the disciples, whose cries of 'king' could get Jesus into trouble. But again they are mistaken, for, if Jesus did quiet the disciples, 'the rocks would cry out' (v. 40). This is the last appearance of Pharisees in the Gospel, and the reason is not in doubt. Luke wants to make sure that they are kept well away from any taint of guilt in the death of Jesus. Thus his portrait of them has been consistent throughout the Gospel. They are friendly toward Jesus, they have nothing to do with his death, but they criticize his associations with outcasts and his lax practice, in return for which he blasts their own practice as an attempt at self-justification (or self-salvation) that ignores the necessary repentance and contrition and that will not result in the desired goal. Surely Luke has portrayed the Pharisees in the Gospel in this way in an attempt to discredit the Jewish Christianity of his own day. But the Jewish Christians cannot yet be entirely written off, because they have an important role to play in Acts; thus, the last appearance of the Pharisees in the Gospel is friendly and without a rebuke from Jesus.

Luke 19.41–44   The ruin of Jerusalem

Important literature: **Fitzmyer**, *Luke*, vol. 2, pp. 1253–9; **Gnilka**, *Verstockung*, p. 138; **Loisy**, *Evangiles synoptiques*, vol. 2, p. 272; **Neyrey**, 'Jesus' Address', pp. 80–4; G. **Schneider**, *Lukas*, vol. 2, pp. 389–91; **Walaskay**, *We Came to Rome*, pp. 45–8.

We now have the second of Jesus' woes pronounced on Jerusalem. If in 13.34 there is a note of sadness in prospect of the coming destruction – 'How often I have wished' – no such element blurs the consistency here of accusation and destruction, destruction and accusation. 'Even you,' Jerusalem, did not 'know . . . what things would bring peace' (v. 42); and, 'You did not know the hour of your visitation' (v. 44). Peace is therefore 'now hidden from your eyes' (v. 42), and destruction, destruction, destruction is coming. There is no lament here, but rather a 'sentence-curse'.[73] Thus the symbolic nature of Jerusalem in Luke-Acts – Jerusalem the capital of the Jews, Jerusalem the focal point of Jewish hostility to Jesus – now begins to come to the fore. As the author of Luke-Acts looks back on the destruction of Jerusalem in the year 70, he sees the justly deserved punishment of the Jews for their rejection of God's salvation.

Luke 19.45–48   The cleansing of the Temple, and opposition

Important literature: **Fitzmyer**, *Luke*, vol. 2, pp. 1260–70; **Morgenthaler**, *Geschichtsschreibung*, vol. 1, pp. 180–4; G. **Schneider**, *Lukas*, vol. 2, p. 393; **Talbert**, *Reading Luke*, pp. 185–8.

Following upon the narrative of the cleansing of the Temple, from which Luke pointedly removes the reference to the Temple as a place of worship 'for all peoples' (v. 46; cf. Mark 11.17), Luke records that it was 'the chief priests and the scribes' (so also Mark 11.18) who sought to 'destroy' Jesus, as well as the 'leading citizens (οἱ πρῶτοι τοῦ λαοῦ)' (v. 47, Luke alone), whereas 'the entire people hung on his every word' (v. 48; similarly Mark 11.18). Thus the separation of people from leaders, with the people favourable to Jesus and the leaders hostile, that has run consistently through the *narrative* of the Gospel, is here emphasized. When Jesus speaks of Jewish rejection and of consequent doom he refers to all, with no distinction between leaders and people, but the narrative makes the difference apparent. The beginning of the resolution to this dichotomy still lies ahead.

Luke 20.1–8   Hostility from the priests and their associates

Important literature: See 19.45–48; further, **Fitzmyer**, *Luke*, vol. 2, pp. 1271–6; **Schmid**, *Lukas*, p. 295.

Finally, the priests think that they can possibly ensnare Jesus on the issue of authority, and so they ask him 'by what authority [he] do[es] these things'. Since in 19.47 the chief priests were associated with scribes and leading citizens, whereas here they are associated with scribes and 'elders' (v. 1), we are apparently to think of the leading citizens as synonymous with the elders. Jesus proves too cagey for his inquisitors, however, by asking them about John, and they are forced to withdraw their question to him.

Luke 20.9–19   The parable of the Wicked Tenants

Important literature: **Ernst**, *Lukas*, p. 538; **Fitzmyer**, *Luke*, vol. 2, pp. 1277–87; **Grundmann**, *Lukas*, p. 372; **Loisy**, *Luc*, p. 480; **Maddox**, *Purpose*, pp. 50–1; **Talbert**, *Reading Luke*, p. 189; **van Goudoever**, 'Israel in Luke', pp. 116–17.

Three different interpretations of this parable, as it is used by the author of Luke-Acts, are possible. It may refer to the overthrow of the religious leadership and to the replacing of the leaders with others, perhaps the apostles; it may refer to the Roman conquest of Jerusalem; and it may refer to the replacing of the Jews with the Gentiles as those to whom God's work on earth is to be entrusted. All three alternatives can be found amply championed in the commentaries, and there is something to be said for each of the three.

In the first place, the context of the parable is the opposition from the priestly leadership to Jesus' ministry. Both before the parable (vv. 1–8) and after (v. 19–26), the chief priests and their cohorts are trying to find grounds for a charge against Jesus. Furthermore, the parable plainly refers to tenant farming (v. 9: 'He let it out to farmers') and to the tenants' being replaced with other tenants (v. 16: 'He will give the vineyard to others'), an aspect that seems to make it applicable only to those in charge. On the other hand, however, the parable is addressed not to the priests and their associates, but to the 'people' (v. 9); and it is then they, and not the priests, who respond, 'Oh, no! (μὴ γένοιτο)' (v. 16). When this immediate introduction and response are emphasized, it would appear that the parable refers not merely to the overthrow of the priesthood, but to the destruction of Jerusalem, and perhaps to the rejection of Israel. Nevertheless, when all is said and done, the priestly leaders 'knew. . .that he spoke this parable directed at them', and they would have liked to arrest him then and there, but 'they feared the people' (v. 19). If, then, the people are here still clearly on the side of Jesus, then the parable must be directed, as v. 19 says, (only) at the priests. Then why is the parable addressed to that same people, and why is it they who respond, 'Oh, no!'?

If we separate speech from narrative, again, the matter becomes somewhat clearer. In the narrative at this point, of course, it is still necessary for Luke to keep people and priestly leadership separate, since it is important for Luke to continue to show Jesus' success with the people, even in Jerusalem. The time has not yet come when they will stand with the priests, leaving Jesus to suffer and die. Thus, for the priests to know that the parable is directed at them but to be incapable of doing anything about Jesus because of his popularity with the people coincides with Luke's narrative interest. But it is Luke who has added the word 'people' to the introduction to the parable (v. 9), and it is he who has 'them' reply, 'Oh, no!' (v. 16). Since these traits are Luke's additions to the Marcan version of the parable, it would appear certain that he wants his readers to see the application of the parable to the people; yet, he follows Mark (cf. Mark 12.12) in having the priests know that the parable was directed at them, and in describing them as fearing the people (Mark: 'crowd'), because this observation coincides with his narrative interest.

Now, while it may seem strange to us, literary analysts that we are, for Luke to let us think at the end of the parable that 'the people' take its point as threatening, and for him then to write, three verses later, that the chief priests saw that the parable was directed at them, Luke has included both these notations because they suit his different interests in speech and narrative. By his additions to the introduction and immediate response to the parable he shows that Jesus here, as everywhere, speaks of the rejection of the Jews in favour of the Gentiles; but, by his retention of what now becomes the secondary response to the parable, Luke continues the narrative plan in which, at this point, priests are hostile and people friendly. The 'others' of v. 16, therefore, to whom the vineyard will be given, are the Gentiles who are soon to replace the Jews as the objects of God's salvation.

Luke 20.20–26   Regarding tribute to Caesar

Important literature: **Derrett**, 'Luke's Perspective'; **Fitzmyer**, *Luke*, vol. 2, pp. 1289–97; **Lampe**, 'Luke', p. 838; **Walaskay**, *We Came to Rome*, pp. 35–6.

That the priests, in v. 19, understood the parable of the Tenants to be directed at them also forms, of course, the transition to the continuation of the narrative, for now as before the parable the priests are seeking grounds on which they can charge Jesus before 'the rule and the authority of the governor' (v. 20). As before, they ask him a question; and, as before, he replies with a question that stumps them, thus ending the matter (for the moment). Again Luke embellishes his source by adding that the priests 'were not able to fasten on to his saying in view of the people' (v. 26), thus keeping the separation of priests from people vividly before us.

Luke 20.27–40   The Sadducees bait Jesus

Important literature: **Fitzmyer**, *Luke*, vol. 2, pp. 1299–1307; **Loisy**, *Evangiles synoptiques*, vol. 2, p. 337; **Morgenthaler**, *Geschichtsschreibung*, vol. 1, pp. 180–4; **Schmid**, *Lukas*, p. 300.

Now the Sadducees, identified as those 'who deny that there is a resurrection' (v. 27), and who are apparently already considered by Mark to be associated with the priests, here join their colleagues, the priests, in asking Jesus a question. While Luke later specifically connects the Sadducees with the priests (cf. Acts 4.1; 5.17), and thus here blithely follows the Marcan order and content in including this story, we note, nevertheless, that the Sadducees' question is different from the preceding questions from the priests about Jesus' authority and about tribute to Caesar, since his answer to this question could hardly lead to his death, however he should answer. Consequently he answers, and even with further clarification: Yes, there is a resurrection, but is is not what you think (Luke 20.34–38). Luke emphasizes even more than Mark that this is the last in a chain of baiting questions put to Jesus, by concluding with the observation that 'they dared no longer ask him anything' (Luke 20.40).

When 'some of the scribes' at the end of this interchange recognize that Jesus has spoken 'well' (v. 39), we probably have an anticipation of Acts 23, where Paul, before Jewish accusers, appeals for support from the Pharisees against the Sadducees on the basis of his and the Pharisee's common belief in the resurrection. Luke would like to make it clear here that Jesus' rejection of the Sadducean position on the resurrection wins friends among another group; but, since he has to keep the Pharisees out of the passion narrative, he is unable to have Pharisees provide the needed response, and so he has 'some of the scribes' – persons earlier associated with the Pharisees – say what is necessary. In doing this, of course, he causes the scribes to step out of character momentarily, for, while they were associated with the Pharisees before the passion narrative, once Jesus comes to Jerusalem they are regularly the associates of the priests (except in 20.46, on which see below).[74]

Luke 20.41–44   From defence to attack

Important literature: see 20.27–40; further, **Fitzmyer**, *Luke*, vol. 2, pp. 1309–15.

By removing the Great Commandment (Mark 12.28–34; cf. Luke 10.25–28) from its place between the preceding interchange with the Sadducees and Jesus' question 'to them' (Luke 20.41), Luke has heightened the contrast between the three questions put to Jesus and Jesus' question put to his inquisitors. The 'they' of v. 41 seems indeterminate. While it could refer to the previously mentioned scribes or to the Sadducees who brought the last question, it probably means 'the opponents'; as 'they' have been baiting Jesus, now he will bait 'them'. The subject, whether or not the Messiah is David's son, is irrelevant for the topic at hand.

Luke 20.45–47   The scribes are reviled

Important literature: **Fitzmyer**, *Luke*, vol. 2, pp. 1316–19.

Luke continues to follow the Marcan order and content, but his introduction gives pause for thought. Whereas Mark 12.37 had indicated that a 'big crowd (πολὺς ὄχλος)' was attending Jesus and that his following words were addressed to them, and whereas Matt. 23.1 had it that 'Jesus spoke to the crowds and to his disciples', Luke conflates strangely and writes, 'When all the people were listening he said to his disciples . . .' (Luke 20.45). Luke apparently wants to show two things by this introduction: one, that 'all the people' are still attending to Jesus and, two, that the following teaching is for the disciples. When we see what the teaching is we have an idea why it is for the disciples, for the charges made against the scribes, which Luke takes from Mark, are included by Matthew in the invective of Matthew 23 against the scribes and Pharisees (Matt. 23.6,14).[75] Yet Luke, in his version of that invective, had already included a portion of these charges, but applied to the Pharisees; and the other charges here laid against the scribes are also to be found elsewhere in Luke, also applied to the Pharisees. Thus the charge that the scribes 'love greetings in public and front row seats in synagogues' (Luke 20.46) is almost verbatim the same (but in reverse order) as Luke 11.43, where it is the Pharisees who 'love front row seats in synagogue and greetings in public'; and the following charge (20.46) that the scribes also love the 'most prominent places at dinners' repeats what was said of the Pharisees in 14.7, that the Pharisees 'chose the most prominent places' (πρωτοκλισίαι in both cases) at a banquet. Further, that the scribes of 20.47 'devour widows' houses' coincides with the charge in 16.14 that the Pharisees were 'lovers of money' who 'thumbed their noses at' Jesus because he had said in the preceding verse that they 'could not serve God and mammon'. Finally, the charge of 20.47 that the scribes 'pray long for appearance' is more than a little reminiscent of the portrayal of the Pharisee and the Toll Collector.

Why has Luke taken these charges against the scribes that appear in 20.46–47, which he has from Mark, and applied them elsewhere to the Pharisees, for which additions he had no sources?[76] Or, perhaps the more germane question is why, having done so, he then follows Mark and includes the accusations against the scribes, which he copies in 20.46–47. Inasmuch as Luke has already let the scribes stand in for the Pharisees in the passion narrative, when in 20.39 they approved Jesus' remarks about the resurrection, it appears that we again have such an instance. Luke has used the Marcan accusations against the scribes that appear in Mark 12.38–40 elsewhere in his Gospel and has applied them to the Pharisees, not to the scribes, because they fit very well the portrait that he wants to draw of the Pharisees: they seek the best seats and greetings in public, but their prayer is for show (seeking to justify themselves before people, not before God), and they are greedy. When Luke comes to the passion narrative, then, he cannot include the Pharisees anywhere, because he wants to keep them away from any taint of guilt in the death of Jesus; but now he comes again to the Marcan accusations against the scribes, and so he includes them as appropriate, inasmuch as the scribes were, before the passion narrative, the associates of the Pharisees. That they become, in the passion narrative, the associates of the priests does not prevent Luke's including these charges against them here, charges which were earlier appropriate when applied to the Pharisees. By the use of the scribes in the passion narrative, therefore, Luke can continue to refer to those people who agree with Jesus about the resurrection but whose practice is misguided and condemnable, without mentioning a single Pharisee in the passion narrative.

That Luke uses the Pharisees – and, here, the scribes when the Pharisees are unavailable – to represent the Jewish Christians probably explains his strange introduction to this saying (20.45), that the people were listening but that Jesus addressed his disciples; for warnings against the Pharisees, like Luke 12.1 – and, in this case, against the scribes – are warnings against Jewish Christianity to the church, i.e., to the disciples.

Luke 21.5–24   The destruction of Jerusalem[77]

Important literature: **Caird**, *Luke*, pp. 231–2; **Conzelmann**, *Theology*, pp. 134–5; **Fitzmyer**, *Luke*, vol. 2, pp. 1323–47; **Flender**, *St Luke*, pp. 112–14; F. **Keck**, *Abschiedsrede*, pp. 95–105, 224–31, 251–61; **Lampe**, 'Luke', p. 837; **Morgenthaler**, *Geschichtsschreibung*, vol. 1, pp. 180–4;

Neyrey, 'Jesus' Address', pp. 80–4; **Robinson**, *Weg*, pp. 46–55, 59–66; G. **Schneider**, *Lukas*, vol. 2, pp. 424–6; **Walaskay**, *We Came to Rome*, pp. 44–8; **Zmijewski**, *Eschatologiereden*, pp. 213–23, 315–16.

The destruction of Jerusalem foretold in vv. 5–6 is, in and of itself, neutral. The prophecy assumes a threatening and judgmental character, however, in view of the sayings that follow.

In v. 12, Luke changes Mark's 'councils and synagogues' (Mark 13.9 par. Matt. 10.17) to 'synagogues and prisons' as the places to which 'they' will 'deliver' the Christians. Aside from the fact that the addition of 'prisons' shows what result the delivering to 'councils and synagogues' will have – the Christians will be delivered both to trial and to incarceration – the Lucan saying also probably anticipates the several times in Acts when the apostles or Paul and his companions are jailed as a result of Jewish denunciations. If all these jailings in Acts do not follow from *synagogue* action, Luke has nevertheless made his point here, which is that synagogues tried early Christians and sent them to jail. Thus the portrait of Jewish persecution of early Christianity is heightened in Luke beyond what is in his sources.

It is in vv. 20–24, however, that Luke has most pointed the Synoptic Apocalypse against Jerusalem and the Jews, and these verses are largely his own and without parallel in Matthew and Mark. That v. 20, with its 'infantry . . . surround[ing] Jerusalem', is a *vaticinium ex eventu* referring to the Roman siege of Jerusalem in 69–70 CE is widely recognized. This siege and consequent destruction are Jerusalem's 'days of vengeance' (v. 22), the time of the outpouring of 'wrath upon this people' (v. 23), at which time 'Jerusalem will be trodden down by Gentiles' (v. 24). Thus Neyrey takes vv. 20–24 to be 'a more descriptive approach' to the judgments that are pronounced on Jerusalem in 13.34–35; 19.41–44; and 23.27–31.[78] 'Now the promises made in the Scripture are fulfilled, for *God's wrathful judgment* has broken in upon his people.'[79] If his judgment upon 'the people' (v. 23) seems unprovoked, closely following, as it does, the statement in 20.45 that 'all the people were listening to him', then we must remind ourselves again of the consistent distinction between speech and narrative. In the narrative, we have not yet reached the point at which 'the people' begin to turn into 'the Jews', not to mention the point at which they have done so completely. In the sayings of Jesus, however, nothing new is introduced here, for the people have been condemned from the first as 'Jews', even if not always in those terms. The presence of 'this people' in 21.23 shows that it is not Jerusalem alone that falls under judgment; Jerusalem is the capital, for Luke, of the entire 'region of the Jews' (cf. Acts 10.39).[80]

It might be possible to interpret v. 24 as holding out a veiled promise of some future hope for Jerusalem by taking the clause *'until the times of the Gentiles are fulfilled'* to imply that, after those times should be finished, Jerusalem would rise again. As Caird has emphasized, however, v. 24 relies heavily on the apocalyptic imagery of Daniel.[81] Now, while it is true that Dan. 8.13–14; 9.26–27; and 12.7 all emphasize that the destruction of Jerusalem and the Temple by the Gentiles will continue until a certain limit has been reached, after which time the rule of the Gentiles will be broken, there are nevertheless two problems with supposing that the author of Luke-Acts, in reliance on Daniel, thought of some future restoration of Jerusalem after Roman rule should have ended. One is that he never elsewhere hints at such a possibility, so that we would be left with only this one veiled allusion. Even more telling, however, is the fact that Daniel, on whom Luke seems to rely here, does not write in those terms. As far as Daniel is concerned, when the 'time, two times, and half a time' (Dan. 12.7), or what Luke calls 'the times of the Gentiles' (Luke 21.24), are completed, comes the resurrection (Dan. 12.1–3). That will surely be what Luke has in mind, not any kind of restoration of Jerusalem, the Jews, and Judaism. First, for Luke, there is the time of Israel, then there is the time of the Gentiles, and then the Lord will return. The destruction of Jerusalem marks the end of Time I.

Some authors follow another tack and note the parallel between Luke 21.24 and Rom. 11.25, where Paul speaks of difficulty with the Jews 'until the fullness of the Gentiles comes in'. But there are in reality many differences, as Zmijewski has shown in his careful analysis,[82] and recognizing the differences helps us to see Luke's intent. Whereas Luke refers to Jerusalem's being 'trodden down', Paul writes rather of the refusal of *some* Jews to become Christians: 'A hardening has partially happened to Israel'; and whereas Luke thinks ahead to the future conclusion of Gentile domination of Jerusalem, à la Daniel, Paul hopes rather for the eventual conversion of all Gentiles to Christianity. Thus there 'exists between Rom. 11.25 and Luke 21.24c . . . a not insignificant difference that may not be overlooked; whereas Paul, in spite of everything, still keeps the attention focused on the final conversion of the Jews, this thought is not expressed by Luke in 21.24c'.[83] The 'times of the Gentiles' will one day, in Luke's thinking, come to an end, but their beginning is already the end of the 'times of the Jews'. Luke has no notion of some future restoration or salvation of the Jews. 'The fall of Jerusalem marks for him the visible sign for the *heilsgeschichtliche* "turning" (especially described in the Stephen narrative) from the Jews to the Gentiles, which had been finally completed in his own time.'[84]

Luke 22.1–2   The Chief Priests and Scribes seek to get rid of Jesus
*   22.3–6   The betrayal by Judas*
    Important literature: **Fitzmyer**, *Luke*, vol. 2, pp. 1359–75.

In the brief summary statement of v. 2, Luke again reminds us that it is 'the chief priests and the scribes' who 'seek . . . to do away with' Jesus, but that they are unable to find opportunity so to do because of Jesus' popularity with 'the people'.

It is thus to 'the chief priests and the captains' (v. 4) – the latter now mentioned for the first time and peculiar to Luke – that Judas betrays Jesus. These 'captains' are, as Part One explained, the Temple police force (as Luke understands it) necessary if the Temple authorities are to go out into the city to arrest someone. The presence of such a 'military unit' under the control of the chief priests will also later allow Luke to make more credible his picture of the Jews killing Jesus.

Luke 22.47–54a   Jesus is arrested
    Important literature: **Bachmann**, *Jerusalem und Tempel*, pp. 187–96; **Fitzmyer**, *Luke*, vol. 2, pp. 1447–52; **Morgenthaler**, *Geschichtsschreibung*, vol. 1, pp. 180–4; **Radl**, *Paulus und Jesus*, pp. 211–12, 297–9; **Talbert**, *Reading Luke*, pp. 185–7; **Via**, 'Who Put Jesus to Death?' pp. 122–33.

Judas carries out his part of the bargain and leads the Temple authorities to Jesus by night (vv. 47, 53). While Luke follows Mark 14.43 in having Judas come at the head of 'a crowd' (v. 47), he later (v. 52, Luke only) gives a more precise description of those who arrest Jesus: the 'chief priests and captains of the Temple, and elders'. Luke is not ready for the people to begin to move over to the priests' side, and so he wants to be certain that his readers understand that the 'crowd' did not come to arrest Jesus, but that it was only the Temple and religious authorities who did it. The captains (στρατηγοί) thus appear here in their proper (for Luke) capacity as those empowered to take someone into custody. It is clear that Luke thinks of the Temple authorities as having this kind of jurisdiction in Jerusalem – that is, they are allowed to go out into the city and arrest people guilty of religious crimes. They are, in his thinking, like the praetors (στρατηγοί) of a Roman provincial city (cf. Acts 16.20–38).

Those who do the arresting conduct Jesus to 'the house of the high priest' (v. 54), not as in Mark 14.53 and Matt. 26.57 merely 'to the high priest'. When Luke here, furthermore, drops the Marcan notation that 'all the chief priests and the elders and the scribes convened', then he clearly wants us to think of a private, perhaps a clandestine proceeding.

Luke 22.63–65   Jesus' captors beat and mock him

Important literature: **Fitzmyer**, *Luke*, vol. 2, pp. 1453–68; **Neyrey**, *Passion*, pp. 69, 71.

Luke continues this portrayal of a nocturnal, clandestine abuse of Jesus by writing, after the interlude of Peter's denial, that 'those who were detaining' Jesus (v. 63) – i.e., the aforementioned captains, chief priests, and elders (or perhaps merely the captains) now at the home of the high priest and presumably in his presence or at least with his consent – abused Jesus and treated him shamefully (vv. 63–65). There is little difference between the details of this episode in Luke's and in Mark's accounts; what is significantly different is that, whereas the episode in Mark took place in the Sanhedrin (Mark 14.53), Luke puts it ahead of the Sanhedrin hearing. Why he has made this change, however, is less than clear. It seems unlikely that he wants to show that the council did not officially mistreat Jesus, as some authors propose, in view of the beating ordered by the council for the apostles in Acts 5.40; and, if Luke wants us to think of some kind of 'mob' action, as is also occasionally proposed, then he should not have designated the perpetrators as 'those who were detaining' Jesus. Does he want to portray the Temple authorities as stooping so low as to abuse Jesus so even before they had held his hearing? Has he just moved the abuse forward so as to make the connection between hearing in the Sanhedrin and trial before Pilate more direct (22.71–23.1)? Is the move merely some kind of stylistic improvement? The next to last possibility, that Luke wants to make a more direct connection between the Sanhedrin hearing and the trial before Pilate, strikes me as likely, but it is impossible to be certain. Most commentators simply note the difference, and a few express wonder at it.

Luke 22.66–71   Jesus in the Sanhedrin

Important literature: see 22.63–65; further, **Conzelmann**, *Theology*, pp. 84–5; **Montefiore**, *Synoptic Gospels*, vol. 2, p. 614; **Morgenthaler**, *Geschichtsschreibung*, vol. 1, pp. 180–4; **Neyrey**, *Passion*, pp. 71–6; **Radl**, *Paulus und Jesus*, pp. 212–13, 297–9; G. **Schneider**, *Lukas*, vol. 2, p. 469; **Via**, 'Who Put Jesus to Death?'; **Walaskay**, *We Came to Rome*, pp. 38–40.

It seems plain from Luke's introduction to the Sanhedrin hearing that he thinks of the Sanhedrin as a place: 'They led him into their Sanhedrin' (v. 66). Why a number of more discerning authors dispute that point is something of a puzzle. Just why Luke thinks of the Sanhedrin as a place and not as a council is not obvious, but that he so thinks is clear not only from this clause, but from the evidence of Acts as well (cf. again the discussion of this point in Part One). The *group* that convened was called, to Luke's way of thinking, the Presbyterium: 'When it was day the presbyterium of the people was convened, both chief priests and scribes, and they led him . . .' (v. 66).

Some authors emphasize that this council does not, in Luke, actually condemn Jesus, thus raising again the possibility that Luke seeks to avoid having an official Jewish body mistreat or condemn Jesus. It is open to question, however, whether Luke actually intends to represent the Presbyterium as not condemning Jesus – that is, as failing to decide whether he is guilty or not. It is true that Luke drops from his account Mark's statement that the Council 'condemned him as deserving of death' (Mark 14.64) and that he omits the word 'blasphemy' from that Marcan charge; but Luke hardly wants to represent the council as finding Jesus innocent! Rather, he wants to show that the council conducts a preliminary hearing and then passes on its findings to Pilate, with the recommendation that Jesus be put to death. At this point, we have only the first act of that drama, with the rest shortly to follow. As Luke presents the hearing (not trial) in the Sanhedrin, Jesus is briefly interrogated on the issue of whether he considers himself to be the Messiah (vv. 67–70), after which 'they' conclude that they 'have [no] further need of testimony, for [they] [them]selves have heard from his own mouth' (v. 71). Then they immediately (23.1) get up and rush him to Pilate with their charges against him (23.2). That these charges are political explains why Luke has dropped the charge of blasphemy from the Marcan account; he wants to show the Jewish religious leadership as presenting patently false political charges against Jesus and not as themselves finding him guilty on religious grounds. Because Luke wants to lay all emphasis on the falsity of the Jewish political charges against Jesus before Pilate, he also omits the religious accusation. The council, according to Luke, interrogates Jesus in order to bring charges against him to the temporal authorities, who are sure to find him innocent of those charges.

Luke 23.1–5   The accusations before Pilate

Important literature: **Fitzmyer**, *Luke*, vol. 2, pp. 1471–6; **Hauck**, *Lukas*, p. 277; **Morgenthaler**, *Geschichtsschreibung*, vol. 1, pp. 180–4; **Neyrey**, *Passion*, pp. 76–7; **Radl**, *Paulus und Jesus*, pp. 213–17; D. **Schmidt**, 'Luke's "Innocent" Jesus', pp. 111–21; **Schmithals**, *Lukas*, p. 220; **Schweizer**, *Luke*, pp. 350–1; **Via**, 'Who Put Jesus to Death?'; **Walaskay**, *We Came to Rome*, pp. 40–2.

As soon as the Presbyterium has heard enough, it conducts Jesus straight to the procurator. According to Luke, 'the entire multitude' (v. 1) saw to this transfer (not, e.g., only the captains). This label, apparently Luke's revision of Mark's 'the whole Sanhedrin' (Mark 15.1), emphasizes the complete participation of the council in denouncing Jesus to Pilate. It may also be, however, that Luke wants his readers to think of a wider participation than just that of the council, since in v. 4, when Pilate reports his verdict after interrogating Jesus, he addresses 'the crowds'. With v. 4, therefore, Luke begins the shift of the people away from Jesus to the side of the priests that will characterize their behaviour throughout the trials before Pilate; it is 'the chief priests and the crowds' who hear Pilate's innocent verdict. Perhaps Luke realized that the sudden appearance of the people associated with the priests here would be jarring on his readers (it is) and sought to soften the harshness of the transition by writing that 'the entire multitude', not just the presbyterium, took Jesus to Pilate.

The indictment contains three counts, all political (v. 2, Luke only). They are that Jesus disturbed the peace ('our race'), that he 'forb[ade]' paying 'tribute to Caesar', and that he claimed to be a 'king'. The Jewish leadership is therefore represented as presenting quite serious charges against Jesus, all of which make him out to be a threat to the state. If Jesus were to be found guilty of these charges, the procurator would have to 'do away with' him, which was what the priests wanted. It may well be that Luke includes just these charges because they fit his conception of charges brought before Gentile authorities by Jews in the Diaspora against Christians. Thus, both in Acts 16.20 and in 17.6–7 Paul falls victim to similar charges. Especially the latter case is significant, since here Jews in Thessalonica accuse Christians before the 'civil authorities' of having 'rous[ed] up the inhabited world', of 'behav[ing] contrary to the decrees of Caesar', and of 'saying that Jesus is another king'. Whether that Lucan conception of Christian–Jewish hostility in Asia Minor is correct we cannot adequately test. It may be true, but Luke's narratives have quite a bit of the caricature about them. Furthermore, even his own report in Acts 16.20 raises doubts about the uniform character of such Jewish denunciations, since here he shows that Gentiles were not free of the taint of denouncing Christians for disturbing the peace. However, while Luke is not above letting us see that some of the hostility to Christians came from Gentiles, what he wants us to focus on is the Jewish hostility, and that (for Luke) *typical* hostility is seen in the indictment against Jesus brought before Pilate.

Luke has, of course, been at pains to show in advance that the charges are without adequate foundation. The charge that Jesus counseled non-payment of taxes is directly refuted by the earlier episode in Luke 20.20–25, where Jesus orders, 'Pay to Caesar the things that are Caesar's' (v. 25); and the Lucan version of the triumphal entry into Jerusalem seems to have been pointed, as we have already seen, in the direction of refuting the later charges, for there it is only the disciples (not the general populace) who make an uproar in acclaiming Jesus; and their acclamation that he is a king, which Luke adds to his sources, is surrounded by vivid heavenly colours (Luke 19.37–38). Thus all these charges are unfounded, just as are those in Acts 17.6–7. The Jewish religious authorities accuse Jesus falsely, and 'the Jews' accuse Christians falsely. Fortunately, the Roman authorities are on to their act.

The interrogation of Jesus by Pilate (Luke 23.3) is all too brief, and one wonders why it would have convinced Pilate of Jesus' innocence; but Luke has omitted nothing material from the Marcan account (Mark 15.2–5). Luke adds to the Marcan account, however, that Pilate pronounced Jesus innocent (Luke 23.4): 'I find no cause (i.e., no grounds for prosecution) in this person.' The Jews – and now we must use that designation, for Pilate has addressed 'the chief priests and the crowds' – reply by reasserting the charge of disturbing the peace (v. 5). In the course of doing so they mention Galilee, and so Pilate sends Jesus to Herod, whose responsibility Galilee was (23.6–7).

Luke 23.6–12   The trial (or hearing) before Herod (Luke only)

Important literature: **Buck**, 'Jesus Before Herod', pp. 166–9; **Dibelius**, 'Herodes und Pilatus'; **Morgenthaler**, *Geschichtsschreibung*, vol. 1, pp. 180–4; **Fitzmyer**, *Luke*, vol. 2, pp. 1478–82; **Neyrey**, *Passion*, pp. 77–80; **Radl**, *Paulus und Jesus*, pp. 217–20; **Walaskay**, *We Came to Rome*, pp. 42–4.

Luke has not forgotten that he earlier wrote that Herod wanted 'to see' Jesus (9.9). Oddly, though, whereas there the context implied that Herod wanted to get his hands on Jesus since it was said that Jesus was John *redivivus*, here (23.8) Luke attributes to Herod a benign desire to see Jesus: 'He had been wanting to see him for a long time because of his reputation, and he hoped to see some sign done by him.' This theme is not followed up, however, and Herod immediately turns to interrogating Jesus (v. 9), not to trying to coax him to 'do a sign'. Luke seems to have thought something along these lines: Herod the Jewish temporal authority, who put John to death, wanted to do the same to Jesus. But Herod is also a ruler, like Pilate, under the authority of the Romans. Now Herod must play the Roman governor, not the Jew, and so he must find Jesus innocent. How can he do that, when he had earlier expressed a desire to kill Jesus? Simple; a little 'revisionist historical writing' will show that his desire to see Jesus is, after all, a friendly wish, not a hostile one.

After the interrogation (v. 9), which Luke does not essay to 'record', Herod also pronounces Jesus not guilty. Now 'the chief priests and the scribes . . . accus[e]' Jesus (v. 10). That they are the accusers continues the theme that the Jewish religious authorities were responsible for Jesus' death. That they accuse him after the hearing and not before seems to be related to the facts that Luke would have had difficulty working the accusation smoothly into the account of Herod's seeing Jesus, that the accusation and the accusers are in any case understood, and that the accusations must be repeated after the innocent verdict is pronounced, as in the case of the preceding hearing before Pilate. When Herod and his soldiers then mistreat and abuse Jesus (v. 11) we are left without explanation. Why so treat an innocent person? Because Herod, after having shown his Roman side, reverts to being a Jew? Perhaps; but the concluding statement (v. 12), that 'Herod and Pilate became friends', surely refers again to the solidarity of the temporal authorities, who in every case find Jesus and the Christians innocent.

Luke 23.13–25   Jesus again before Pilate

Important literature: **Conzelmann**, *Theology*, pp. 86–7, 140; **Dibelius**, 'Herodes und Pilatus'; **Ernst**, *Lukas*, p. 627; **Fitzmyer**, *Luke*, vol. 2, pp. 1483–92; **Franklin**, *Christ the Lord*, pp. 92–5; **Gnilka**, *Verstockung*, p. 139; **Hauck**, *Lukas*, pp. 278–81; **Klostermann**, *Lukas*, p. 221; **Lampe**, 'Luke', p. 841; **Lohfink**, *Sammlung Israels*, pp. 41–3; 'Hat Jesus eine Kirche gestiftet?', pp. 87–8; **Loisy**, *Evangiles synoptiques*, vol. 2, pp. 651–2; **Montefiore**, *Synoptic Gospels*, vol. 2, p. 622; **Morgenthaler**, *Geschichtsschreibung*, vol. 1, pp. 180–4; **Neyrey**, *Passion*, pp. 80–4; **Radl**, *Paulus und Jesus*, pp. 213–17, 297–307; **Rau**, 'Das Volk'; **Schmid**, *Lukas*, p. 345; D. **Schmidt**, 'Luke's "Innocent" Jesus'; G. **Schneider**, *Lukas*, vol. 2, p. 477; **Surkau**, *Martyrien*, p. 95; **Via**, 'Who Put Jesus to Death?'; **Walaskay**, *We Came to Rome*, pp. 44–5.

'Pilate convened the chief priests and the rulers and the people' (v. 13) to repeat the verdict of innocent.[85] For 'the people' to join in the accusation of Jesus (vv. 5, 18, 21, 23) and to hear the innocent verdicts (vv. 4, 13–15, 20, 22) is important to Luke for two reasons. In the first case, their presence here justifies the blanket charges made in the speeches in Acts that 'you' Jews killed Jesus. Beyond this, however, the narrative of Luke-Acts is now moving more rapidly toward the point of agreement with what is said about 'the Jews' from the first in speech. If the speeches of Jesus and of the important characters in Acts reveal the Jews as they are (in Luke's thinking), the narrative shows how they got to be that way. Thus the people, only recently portrayed as being so solidly behind Jesus that the religious authorities would not dare to move against him, now join with those authorities in calling for his death. That Pilate on this occasion three times (vv. 14, 20, 22) declares Jesus innocent and seeks to release him emphasizes Pilate's good and the Jews' evil will, and at the end the death knell sounds: 'Their voices prevailed' (v. 23). Pilate's brave gambit has failed, and so he 'deliver[s] Jesus to their will' (v. 25).

Luke 23.26   Jesus is taken to be crucified

Important literature: see 23.13–25; further, **Klostermann**, *Lukas*, p. 225; **Loisy**, *Luc*, p. 552.

Luke omits Mark's account (Mark 15.16–20) of the Roman soldiers' mistreatment of Jesus – Roman soldiers do not, in Luke's way of thinking, do such things, although it is all right for Herod's soldiers to do them – and moves directly from Pilate's delivering Jesus to *their* will (v. 25) to the statement that '*they* led him away' (v. 26). In this way he gives the distinct impression that it was the Jews who took Jesus away to be crucified, while avoiding saying so explicitly.

Luke 23.27–31   Jesus' last oracle of doom

Important literature: **Fitzmyer**, *Luke*, vol. 2, pp. 1494–9; **Franklin**, *Christ the Lord*, pp. 89–91; **Klostermann**, *Lukas*, p. 227; **Neyrey**, 'Jesus' Address', pp. 74–86; **Schweizer**, *Luke*, pp. 357–8; **Walaskay**, *We Came to Rome*, pp. 44–8.

Women mourners, 'daughters of Jerusalem' (v. 28), follow Jesus on the way to the cross, and he counsels them not to 'cry over him' but 'over [them]selves and over [their] children' because of the coming destruction of Jerusalem. 'If they do these things when the wood is green, what will happen when it is dry?' (v. 31). While Jerusalem's guilt is not mentioned here, Jesus' pronouncement of this 'prophetic oracle of judgment' (Neyrey) while on his way to the gallows dramatically brings that guilt into view.

Luke 23.32–38   The crucifixion

Important literature: **Conzelmann**, *Theology*, pp. 89–94; **Fitzmyer**, *Luke*, vol. 2, pp. 1500–6; **Kränkl**, *Knecht*, p. 106; **Loisy**, *Luc*, p. 556; **Morgenthaler**, *Geschichtsschreibung*, vol. 1, pp. 180–4; **Schmid**, *Lukas*, pp. 348–9; **Schmithals**, *Lukas*, p. 226; G. **Schneider**, *Lukas*, vol. 2, p. 483; **Surkau**, *Martyrien*, p. 97.

The Jews crucify Jesus, and he prays for God to forgive them (vv.

32–34). In Matthew and Mark, of course, it is not actually the Jews who carry out the crucifixion, but here it is. In Luke there is no break in the continuity of Jewish action after Pilate acquiesces, for Pilate 'delivered Jesus to *their* will' (v. 25), '*they* led him away' (v. 26), and '*they* crucified him' (v. 33). The realization that it is the Jews who do the crucifying probably explains the omission of v. 34 from several important early manuscripts; for, as antisemitic sentiment increased in the early church, some person or persons apparently preferred not to have Jesus ask for forgiveness for his Jewish executioners and so dropped Jesus' prayer that they be forgiven. Had the early church thought that the prayer was for the forgiveness of Romans, it would surely not have been left out. That the prayer for forgiveness is original is seen in the parallel with Stephen's prayer for leniency toward his Jewish executioners (Acts 7.60) and in the further parallel between Acts 7.59 and Jesus' other Lucan 'last word' in Luke 23.46.

Now the people and religious leaders are again separated, after their brief collusion in Pilate's court, but things are not quite as they were before; for, whereas before Jesus' arrest the people were so strongly behind him that the priests were afraid to move against him (20.19; 22.2), now the people 'observe' while 'the rulers thum[b] their noses' (v. 35). The rulers have not changed, but the people are strangely quiet and passive. Formerly the rulers could not even have apprehended Jesus because of the people, but now they crucify him while the people only look on. The people's participation in calling for Jesus' death – which Luke never adequately explains – has changed them, and they make no move to halt the crucifixion that their leaders are performing. Their guilt is increasing.

The soldiers who mistreat the dying Jesus (v. 36) are Jewish soldiers. If Luke does not actually say that they are, he leads us, in any case, to think so. Of course he knows that, in his sources, it is Roman soldiers who carry out the act of crucifixion, but he has built up the evidence that leads us to think that they are Jewish soldiers in two ways. Not only has he doctored the passion narrative so that it is plain that Jews crucify Christ, but he has also sprinkled his narrative with Jewish military personnel from the beginning. There are soldiers who respond to John's baptism (Luke 3.14) and soldiers in Herod's service (23.11), and the Temple has captains (22.4), who have authority to go out into the city and arrest people (22.52). While Luke probably does not think of the captains (στρατηγοί) as themselves bearing arms, his analogy will be the praetor (στρατηγός) of a provincial city, who certainly had the authority to administer corporal punishment (cf. Acts 16.20–38). There is therefore no problem with taking the soldiers of 23.36 as Jewish soldiers, and Luke has, in fact, given us every reason so to take them.

But is it not odd that Jewish soldiers would mock Jesus with the words, 'If you are *the King of the Jews*, save yourself!' (v. 37)? Would not Jewish soldiers have said, 'If you are our (or: the) Christ . . .'? Luke has heard our question and answers with v. 38: '*For* there was (ἦν δὲ καί) an inscription on him: "This is the King of the Jews".'[86] The Jewish soldiers taunt Jesus with a charge that is odd for them, *because it was on a sign hanging around Jesus' neck*.

Luke 23.47–48   Responses to Jesus' death

Important literature: **Fitzmyer**, *Luke*, vol. 2, pp. 1512–20; **Grundmann**, *Lukas*, p. 435; **Kilpatrick**, 'Lucan Passion Story'; **Schmid**, *Lukas*, p. 351.

'*The* centurion' judges Jesus to have been *dikaios* (v. 47). What centurion, a Jewish or a Roman one? There is no consensus of opinion in the scholarly literature on this point. The likelihood, however, is that Luke thinks of him as a Roman centurion. There are no other Jewish centurions in Luke-Acts, but a number of Roman ones, all of them friendly to Jesus and Christianity, and two of them important figures in Luke's portrayal of God-fearers and proselytes as part of the periphery on the way from the Jews to the Gentiles (Luke 7.1–10; Acts 10). Furthermore, while our immediate response, because we know the story from Mark and Matthew, is to associate the centurion with the soldiers who crucify Jesus, Luke may not have made that association. The centurion (from Mark 15.39) is paired rather with the people (Luke only) as responding to Jesus' death, not with the soldiers as causing it; and Luke lets the article ('the') from Mark stand, although he goes to the trouble to translate 'centurion' into Greek. Does he want us to think of *the* centurion. . . from ch. 7? In any case, that this centurion calls Jesus 'righteous' or 'innocent (δίκαιος)'' seems to throw him into the camp of the periphery, to make him a Gentile. This does not, however, alter the impression that Luke has given throughout the trials and crucifixion of Jesus that the Jews did it all.

Another puzzle follows. Why do 'the crowds . . . retur[n] beating their breasts' (v. 48)? Are they sorrowing for Jesus or for themselves? If the latter, is it because they are sorry for what they have done or because they are worried about their future? Is this Luke's way of opening the possibility of later repentance, to take place in Acts?

It seems possible that Luke has sought to characterize here two types of response to Jesus, that of the periphery and that of the Jews.

Luke 23.50–51   A 'good' Jew

Important literature: **Fitzmyer**, *Luke*, vol. 2, pp. 1523–7; **Hauck**, *Lukas*, p. 287.

Luke is, naturally, constrained to report the entombment of Jesus. But Mark had written that this was carried out by one Joseph, who was 'an honourable councillor' (Mark 15.43), and this was not enough for Luke, for it implied that there may have been someone on the council that put Jesus to death who was nevertheless honourable enough to bury Jesus; so Luke expands on Mark's phrase. Joseph was a 'councillor' (Luke 23.50) all right, but he was, furthermore, 'a good and righteous man', and 'he was not present (οὐκ ἦν συγκατατιθειμένος)' when the presbyterium condemned and executed (τῇ βουλῇ καὶ τῇ πράξει) Jesus (v. 51). Thus Luke solves the problem that, on the one hand, the council condemned and executed Jesus and that, on the other, Joseph was a member of the council by a *tour de force*.

Luke 24.20   The guilt of the priestly leadership

Important literature: **Fitzmyer**, *Luke*, vol. 2, pp. 1557–60, 1564; **Hauck**, *Lukas*, p. 293; Loisy, *Luc*, p. 576; **Wanke**, *Emmauserzählung*.

The risen Jesus has encountered 'two of them' on the Emmaus Road (v. 13) – two of his followers, that is; and when they do not recognize him, he asks them to tell him about himself (v. 19). Their brief narration, which does not otherwise concern the present study, includes the charge that the Jewish 'chief priests and rulers . . . delivered him to death and crucified him' (v. 20). If there was any doubt in the passion narrative about whether Romans or Jews killed Jesus, that doubt has now been removed. 'Our Chief Priests and rulers' are fingered as the perpetrators. The 'rulers' cannot be taken in such an inclusive sense here as to include the Roman authorities, for Luke has consistently used 'rulers' throughout his Gospel to mean the Jerusalem rulers (cf. 23.13, 35), and their connection here with the 'chief priests', as well as their being called 'our rulers', show that

Luke means the *Jewish* rulers. Luke has therefore gone beyond his sources in making the Jewish religious leadership guilty of the actual act of crucifying Jesus, and he has been at some pains to portray the context in which they could have done that, for he has made a point of showing us that there are Jewish soldiers and that the Temple had its own police force.

At this point in the narrative, therefore, the development has only partially caught up with the 'final reality' expressed in speech throughout Luke-Acts from the beginning, that 'the Jews' are guilty of the execution of Jesus. The Galileans have had their chance and are doomed (10.13–15. NB! There is no Galilean mission in Acts, despite the reference in Acts 9.31); and now the priestly leadership in Jerusalem is added to the list of the guilty. Finally it will be all 'the Jews', but that point has not yet been reached. Nevertheless, there is little doubt that these 'chief priests and rulers' are the arch villains in Luke.

Luke 24.47–49   The Lucan 'Great Commission'

Important literature: **Bundy**, *First Three Gospels*, p. 572; **Caird**, *Luke*, p. 261; **Fitzmyer**, *Luke*, vol. 2, pp. 1578–82, 1584–5; **Grundmann**, *Lukas*, p. 453; **Hauck**, *Lukas*, pp. 297–8; **Klostermann**, *Lukas*, p. 242; B. and J. **Weiss**, *Markus und Lukas*, p. 690.

The verse presents us with a textual problem which, when solved, presents us with a punctuation problem and a consequent problem of meaning. Most modern editors agree that ἀρξάμενοι ('beginning') must be read, and not ἀρξαμένων, ἀρξάμενον, or ἀρξάμενος; and they are surely correct in their judgment. ἀρξαμένων would have to be taken with either ἁμαρτιῶν or τούτων, presumably with τούτων, since it would make little sense with ἁμαρτιῶν; but the syntax, while not impossible, would be more than passing strange for Luke. This alternative appears to be a characteristic attempt by the Western tradition to solve a problem, but which problem? The weakly attested ἀρξάμενος is grammatically impossible, but the much better attested ἀρξάμενον would have to pick up 'Christ' in v. 46, something that would be most difficult syntactically in view of the intervening accusatives 'repentance' and 'forgiveness' (v. 47), both of which are feminine. ἀρξαμένων must, therefore, be a correction for ἀρξάμενοι, which makes perfectly good sense if we just punctuate correctly.

Most editors insist on punctuating vv. 47–48 so that they read '. . .

repentance and forgiveness of sins to all the Gentiles – beginning from Jerusalem; you [are] witnesses of these things',[87] but this punctuation makes a hash of the only connection possible for ἀρξάμενοι, ὑμεῖς. However, if one punctuates so as to read '. . . repentance and forgiveness of sins to all the Gentiles. Beginning from Jerusalem, you [are] witnesses of these things',[88] two things are accomplished. The masculine plural ἀρξάμενοι is connected with the masculine plural ὑμεῖς, which is where it belongs, and vv. 47–48 can be a statement that leads directly into v. 49; for there the disciples are told, 'You sit in the city until you are clothed with power from on high.' The meaning of vv. 47–49, then, beginning with the word ἀρξάμενοι, is that the disciples are to remain in Jerusalem until they receive power, after which they are to start out from Jerusalem being witnesses to the Gentiles of the suffering and resurrection of Christ and of the repentance and forgiveness of sins in his name (vv. 46–47a). Does this sound like a summary of Acts? Indeed it does, for the Acts of the Apostles, to which we now turn, tells the story of how the disciples stayed in Jerusalem after the ascension, received power from on high, and started out from Jerusalem witnessing to the death and resurrection of Christ, and of the repentance and forgiveness that that death and resurrection have ushered in.

Is there an interlude? Do some people other than Gentiles receive the disciples' preaching? Does the summary of Luke 24.47–49 undergo a slight revision in Acts 1–8? So be it. Should we therefore translate πάντα τὰ ἔθνη here as 'all peoples' and not as 'all the Gentiles'? No; for Luke has given us his meaning here; Acts is to show how the gospel begins in Jerusalem and goes to all the Gentiles. The Jews along the way are an interlude, albeit necessary; for the preaching of the gospel to the Jews in Acts is the author's way of getting that preaching out to the Gentiles. Thus we turn next to a systematic analysis of the way in which the Jews, in all their variety, are portrayed in the Acts of the Apostles.

7

THE ACTS OF THE APOSTLES

Acts 2.1–13   The outpouring of the Spirit on the church

Important literature: **Beck**, *Mature Christianity*, pp. 212–13; *Beginnings*, Part I, vol. 3, p. 12; vol. 5, pp. 67–8, 113–14; **Dupont**, 'La première Pentecôte', pp. 498–9; **Haenchen**, *Acts*, pp. 167–75.

The stage is set for this event by v. 5: 'There were Jews dwelling in Jerusalem, reverent men from every people of those under heaven.' This 'dispersion over the whole world . . . probably . . . made [these Jews] symbolic of the future worldwide Church'[1] – at least, that seems to be the best opinion. The authors and editors of the *Beginnings of Christianity*, however, were less than convinced by such arguments and omitted the word 'Jews' from v. 5, following MS א.[2] Their argument was based more on internal evidence than on the witness of א (although they probably would not have decided to omit 'Jews' if א had not led the way). 'The desire of the writer,' Lake wrote, 'was . . . to show that from the beginning the Gentiles heard and the Jews refused the testimony of the spirit.'[3] Thus, according to him, the author of Acts included a representative universal Gentile audience in v. 5 and then added 'Jews and proselytes' to the list in vv. 10–11. How the presence of 'Jews and proselytes' in the latter list, however, signals the opposition of the Jews is less than clear; and, furthermore, this is not the only verse of Acts from which א omits the word 'Jews', which fact also did not escape the notice of the editors of the *Beginnings of Christianity*. Their explanation of this second omission, however (21.20), was that the omission was 'probably an accident'.[4] Accident, indeed! In Acts 2.5 MS B refers to 'Jews' who are 'reverent men' and א omits the word 'Jews'; and in Acts 21.20 B states that there are 'many myriads of believers among the Jews' and א omits the word 'Jews'. What we have uncovered here, therefore, is an antisemitic tendency in **א**, whose scribe did not want to write that Jews were either 'reverent' or 'believers' and so simply omitted the word 'Jews' in both cases.

This leaves us with 'Jews' as original in 2.5 and with Lampe's explanation – which, though not without certain problems, remains the best and also the most widely suggested. At the outset of the narrative of Acts, Luke cannot yet have a truly Gentile audience (Jervell notwithstanding), since the gospel has not yet gone to the Gentiles; but what he can do is to signal, by his description of the Pentecost audience, the eventual world-wide hearing of the gospel. In any case, the more different native speakers there are in the audience, the greater is the miracle of hearing in the native languages. The primary reason, however, for Luke's including representatives of *world-wide Jewry* at Pentecost is not to hint at the universal gospel and not to heighten the miracle of hearing in native languages, but to attest to the universal Jewish guilt in the death of Jesus. That will become clear in the following explanation.

Acts 2.14–36   Peter's first sermon
   2.37–42   Repentance and baptism

Important literature: **Beck**, *Mature Christianity*, pp. 212–13; **Dupont**, 'Le salut des Gentils', pp. 144–6; **Haenchen**, *Acts*, pp. 180, 183; **Kränkl**, *Knecht*, pp. 102–3; **Lampe**, 'Acts', p. 889; **Loisy**, *Actes*, pp. 197–205; **Overbeck**, *Apostelgeschichte*, p. 39; **Rese**, 'Aussagen über Jesu Tod', pp. 344–7; **Roloff**, *Apostelgeschichte*, pp. 50–1; G. **Schneider**, *Apostelgeschichte*, vol. 1, p. 271; **Wilch**, 'Jüdische Schuld', pp. 238–43; **Wilckens**, *Missionsreden*, pp. 32–7; **Wilson**, *Gentiles*, p. 219.

After his long quotation from scripture, Peter gets down to business in v. 22 (repetition of address): '*Israelite men*, hear these words! Jesus the Nazarene, a man attested by God to *you* by mighty deeds and wonders and signs that God did through him *in your midst*, as *you yourselves* know. . . .' Clearly this is an address neither to Gentiles nor to Jerusalemites, and certainly not just to the priestly leadership. It is an address to the assembled Jews, representatives, as we recall (2.5), of world-wide Jewry. Theology predominates here over historical verisimilitude; this first Christian sermon addresses, in representative fashion, all the Jews in the world! In Luke's theology, the mighty deeds of God done in Jesus were done before all Jews. The consequences of that fact follow presently. Not only is Peter's representative audience said to have witnessed Jesus' ministry, but Peter next announces (v. 23), '*You* laid hands on him and did away with him' (ἀναιρέω, Luke's standard term for 'killing' Jesus). The point must be made again, even at the risk of a charge of repetitiousness: it is not the priestly leadership, nor Jerusalemites, nor even Judahites or Palestinian Jews alone whom Peter accuses of 'doing away with' Jesus; it is a representative group of Jews from all over the world.

Two other phrases in v. 23 have occasioned no little comment and are sometimes taken to provide an escape from this charge of inexorable Jewish guilt. One is that Jesus' death was by the 'ordained will and foreknowledge of God'; the other is that the Jews killed him 'by the hand of lawless (or: iniquitous) persons'. The divine plan, of course, is a major element of Lucan theology, and everything of any significance that happens in Luke-Acts is a part of that plan. This is especially true in the case of the death of Jesus and in the spread of the gospel to the Gentiles. This divine plan, however – as many authors note – does not excuse the Jews of their guilt, neither in the case of the rejection of the gospel nor in the case of the death of Jesus. One may say that Luke presents two causes for the important developments in his two-volume work, a theological and a historical. Jesus was killed in accordance with the divine plan, but the Jews did it.

The statement 'You did away with [Jesus] by the hand of lawless persons', also seems straightforward enough, although a number of authors take this to be a statement of Roman guilt in the death of Jesus. Ἄνομοι, however, means the Romans, likely enough, but says nothing about their guilt. They are said only to be the instruments used by the Jews in their heinous crime. Verse 23 is, in fact, quite a good summary of the Lucan passion narrative, according to which the Jews used the procurator in order to 'do away with' Jesus. In the passion *narrative*, of course, the high priests were the culprits, with the people in an ambiguous role as hangers on. Now that the gospel is being preached, however, such distinctions are no longer made, and world-wide Jewry is accused of killing Jesus. Following more quotations from scripture and additional explanations by Peter, Luke repeats the charge in v. 36: 'All the house of Israel' is to understand that they ('you') 'crucified . . . Jesus (Ἰησοῦν . . . ἐσταυρώσατε)'.

The response to this charge is quite strange, inasmuch as no one objects that he is not guilty. The representatives of world-wide Jewry accept the charge of guilt in the death of Jesus! And 'about 3000' of them (v. 41) 'accepted what [Peter] said [about repenting and being baptized, v. 38, and about being saved, v. 40] and were baptized' (v. 41). Thus this first Christian sermon, with its charge to all the Jews (representatively) that they killed Jesus, provokes neither defensiveness nor hostility from them; rather, several thousand of them are converted to Christianity on the spot – a good start towards the 'myriads' of such converts eventually claimed in Acts 21.20. At this point, Jervell's and Lohfink's analyses could well seem correct; we do seem to be seeing the 'gathering of Israel'; but this is not the whole story. Here, in the beginning of Acts, Luke must show the great success of the gospel among its native people.

Finally, we must not overlook that from which Peter encourages his audience to be saved, 'this crooked generation' (v. 40). This term is the carry-over into Acts of the term so frequent in the Gospel to designate the Jews, 'this generation', as we saw in ch. 3 (cf. again Luke 11.29–32, 50–51), here designated 'crooked' instead of 'evil'. 'Save yourselves from these wicked Jews!' is Peter's appeal. The Jews do not become an evil entity by virtue of their rejection of the gospel; rather some, by grasping their chance on the occasion of Peter's sermon, escape their natural fate. We do not have to do with 'holy remnant' theology here, however, but rather with Luke's need to show that Christianity is firmly rooted in its Jewish past.

Acts 2.43–47   An idealized summary of Christian beginnings

Important literature: **Lampe**, 'Acts', p. 889; **Lohfink**, *Sammlung Israels*, pp. 47–9; **Loisy**, *Actes*, pp. 221–2.

Luke has given here a portrait of the harmonious, selfless, 'Christian' existence of the nascent church that Christianity has tried for 2000 years to regain. Our interest lies especially in v. 47, where Luke claims that the Christians found 'favour with the whole people', and that the number of converts was increasing 'daily'. The last, of course, continues the theme struck in connection with the first conversions – that is, that the gospel was successful in its earliest, Jewish phase. Luke seems to intend us to think of the recurrence of scenes like that in Acts 2, which he does not recount individually but merely summarizes.

Claiming that the church found 'favour with the whole people' raises problems. 'The people' here obviously means the Jews,[5] but one must wonder, on the one hand, why the Jews regarded the Christians so kindly inasmuch as they had killed the founder and were daily being accused of that heinous crime; and, on the other hand, why they were not simply converted instead of merely holding the Christians in good favour. Luke's summary, however, is entirely understandable in the light of his historical theology; for he must argue for the veracity of Christianity in terms of its ancient origins, and that means showing how it grew harmoniously out of its Jewish roots. When we realize that the 'argument from antiquity' is paramount in Luke's thinking, then we see why he must claim 'myriads' of converts among the Jews and also why the unconverted Jews bestowed 'favour' on the church. In a sense, Luke probably would like to claim that everyone was converted to Christianity; but that, of course, he knows to be untrue; so he settles for 'myriads' of converts and 'favour' from everyone else.

In Acts 2 we thus have a clear picture of the tension between speech and narrative in Luke-Acts where the Jews are concerned. Peter's sermon has made it clear who the Jews *are*: Christ-killers; but the narrative must show a development, in the course of which the church will break away from its Jewish context, and the requirements of this theology of development dictate that an early, harmonious stage be the matrix from which the church emerges as distinct from Judaism.

Acts 3.12–26   Peter's second sermon

Important literature: **Beck**, *Mature Christianity*, p. 215; **Gnilka**, *Verstockung*, pp. 141–4; **Haenchen**, *Acts*, pp. 205–7, 211–12; **Jervell**, *People of God*, pp. 58–60; **Kränkl**, *Knecht*, pp. 103–8; **Loisy**, *Actes*, pp. 230–3; **Overbeck**, *Apostelgeschichte*, p. 52; **Rackham**, *Acts*, p. 51; **Rese**, 'Aussagen über Jesu Tod', pp. 339–47; G. **Schneider**, *Apostelgeschichte*, vol. 1, pp. 318–19; **Wilckens**, *Missionsreden*, pp. 37–44, 220–1; **Wilson**, *Gentiles*, pp. 219–22; **Zehnle**, *Pentecost Discourse*, pp. 133–5.

A Jesus-like healing miracle accomplished by Peter and John (3.1–11) affords Peter the opportunity for another sermon. Peter's audience is again 'all the people' (v. 11), not here designated specifically as being representative of world-wide Jewry, but nevertheless labelled with a universal term; Peter speaks here to all the Jews. As before, he tells them that they 'delivered' and 'denied' Jesus

(v. 13), that they 'denied' him and 'sought' the release of another (v. 14), and that they 'killed the Prince of Life' (v. 15). On this occasion, however, Peter adds an important explanation that was not a component of his first sermon, namely that what the Jews did they 'did in ignorance, and [their] rulers as well' (v. 17). Here, then, is the reasonable excuse that makes their conversion possible. While Luke never formulates explicitly the notion that the Jews who killed Jesus were only instruments of the divine will, he comes close to such a position. The Jews killed Jesus, but Jesus' death was according to God's will. The Jews therefore acted in ignorance and are given the opportunity to repent; and they grasp this opportunity by the myriads. *Down to this point*, therefore, Acts portrays a co-operative relationship between Judaism and the Christianity that is coming to birth within it. Unfortunately, Acts is more than three chapters long, and the initial stage is about to draw to a close.

Before we turn to the rising conflict, however, we need to reflect briefly on the portrait of the relationship between Christianity and Judaism that Luke has drawn in Acts 2–3. Many writers, by no means Jervell and Lohfink alone, see Luke as expressing a positive attitude toward the Jews in these chapters, even if that positive attitude is sometimes seen to be a grudging one. Does not Luke demonstrate in these chapters his desire to convert Jews,[6] even a warm feeling towards Jews, in view of which any claim that he is antisemitic or hates Jews or has no interest in Jews will have to be mistaken? Those who express this opinion seem to be carried away by Luke's narrative skill; for, as we have seen, the appeal to Jews to be converted rests entirely on the assumption that they are all guilty of Jesus' death, a notion that Luke himself could have accepted only if he more or less wilfully avoided asking the obvious question, 'Is that true?' Such an avoidance can arise only out of a prior commitment to a position, namely, that the Jews are vile. That Luke includes the excuse of ignorance in Peter's second sermon, in fact, shows that he is vaguely aware of the problem, and that he sees that his blanket charge of having killed Jesus does not provide sufficient motivation to the recipients of the charge for them to repent.

There are no real Jews in Acts 2–3, only puppets on Luke's stage, who do not question the accusation of universal guilt and who respond almost mindlessly to Luke's various commands. Be guilty of the death of Jesus! Grant favour to the church! Be converted by the myriads! It was no mean feat for Luke to hold two principles

together in these two chapters, the guilt of the Jews in the death of
Jesus and their positive reception of the church and of the gospel
during the church's initial phase. How well he accomplished his task
can be seen by the numbers of scholarly students of Acts who have
found here a positive or receptive attitude towards Jews.

Acts 4.1–4   *The arrest of the apostles, and more conversions*

Our old friends from the passion narrative of the Gospel, the
priests and 'the captain of the Temple', arrest Peter and John (vv.
1–2), primarily (v. 2) because they are 'announc[ing] that the
resurrection from the dead is by Jesus (or: in Jesus)'. (We may
conveniently avoid concern with the exact meaning of ἐν τῷ Ἰησοῦ,
since it is not important to the issue at hand.) The emphasis in the
cause for arrest lies on the term 'resurrection' as we see from Luke's
inclusion here of the Sadducees among the arresting party (v. 1),
apparently thereby setting up the later conflict (ch. 23) between
them and the Pharisees over the issue of the resurrection. Further,
inasmuch as the Sadducees are designated as allying themselves with
the arresting priests and captain, the Pharisees are consciously
omitted. Luke wants his readers to be sure to understand that the
Pharisees play no part in the arrest of the apostles, although they
later turn up in the Sanhedrin (chs. 5 and 23), where, nevertheless,
in both cases they assist the Christians. Two important MSS, B and
C, write 'chief priests' in v. 1 instead of 'priests', which is what we
would expect, but the obvious explanation of this is that the scribes
of B and C have been influenced by the passion narratives to
those same expectations and have corrected, either deliberately or
inadvertently, in line with them. Luke apparently had the priests,
here, and not only the chief priests, come with the Temple 'police
chief' and the Sadducess to arrest Peter and John.

In v. 4 we have still more Jewish conversions, this time 5000 men
(implying still more women?). The number of Jewish conversions is
growing in an arithmetic progression toward the myriads of 21.20.

Acts 4.5–22   *The trial of Peter and John, and Peter's third sermon*

Important literature: **Bauernfeind**, *Apostelgeschichte*, pp. 73–4; **Dupont**,
'La conversion', p. 464; **Gnilka**, *Verstockung*, p. 139; **Haenchen**, *Acts*,
pp. 217, 223–4; **Kränkl**, *Knecht*, p. 108; **Lampe**, 'Acts', p. 891; **Neyrey**,
Passion, pp. 89–93; **Rese**, 'Aussagen über Jesu Tod', pp. 344–7; **Wilckens**,
Missionsreden, pp. 44–5.

The trial court is composed (v. 5) of the 'rulers', the 'elders', and the 'scribes' (here in association with the priests, not with the Pharisees) and is, of course, held in the Sanhedrin (see v. 15). This is what we would expect from the passion narrative. It is also in keeping with the Lucan passion narrative that Peter immediately accuses his hearers of 'crucif[ying]' Jesus (v. 10) and of 'set[ting him] at naught' (v. 11). But, while Peter's address is plainly to the 'rulers of the people and elders' (v. 8), Luke does not allow his readers to forget the charge that the entire people is guilty of Jesus' death, for he includes in Peter's address that the charge is to be 'known . . . to all the people of Israel' (v. 10) as well as to his auditors. Thus the person who would like to think that Luke intends really to accuse only the rulers of Jesus' death is prevented from doing so. While Peter speaks here only to the rulers, Luke makes it clear that the accusation of guilt remains applicable to all Jews.

In this narrative no martyrdom follows from the arrest, but only a mild substitute: the apostles are forbidden to continue preaching (vv. 17–18). Naturally, they reject this command, and then Luke tells us a second time, this time by reporting the thinking of the rulers (v. 21), that the people favour the Christians. Luke thus repeats here the theme from the passion narrative (Luke 19.48; 20.19), that the rulers are unable to move against the church because the people are on the church's side, by explaining (v. 21) that the rulers were unable to 'chastize' the apostles 'because of the people, for they were all glorifying God' as a result of the miracle wrought by Peter and John. As far as the *narrative* of Luke-Acts goes, therefore, the people are, in this opening stage of Acts, firmly in their pre-passion narrative mode of siding with Jesus and the church. Their solidarity with the rulers, which they began only confusedly to display in the passion narrative, has not yet risen to the surface.

Acts 4.23–31   The prayer of the church on the release of the apostles

Important literature: **Dibelius**, 'Herodes und Pilatus', pp. 289–91; **Gnilka**, *Verstockung*, p. 139; **Haenchen**, *Acts*, pp. 227–8; **Kränkl**, *Knecht*, pp. 109–11; **Lampe**, 'Acts', pp. 891–2; **O'Neill**, *Theology*, p. 84; **Rese**, 'Aussagen über Jesu Tod', pp. 39–44; G. **Schneider**, *Apostelgeschichte*, vol. 1, pp. 357–8.

The meaning here of Ps. 2.1–2, quoted in vv. 25–26, and of the interpretative comments in v. 27 was discussed in detail in ch. 1, and that discussion will not be repeated here. According to v. 27 Herod, Pilate, the Gentiles, and the 'peoples of Israel . . . were convened . . . against (or: at) . . . Jesus' in order to carry out the divine plan (v. 28). For our purposes here, we need only note the following: 1. Since Jesus' death was God's plan, the four entities 'convened' were merely instruments in that plan, as Peter's earlier sermons have made clear. 2. In no sense does v. 27 reduce Jewish guilt in the death of Jesus, since 2.23 has already explained the relation between Jews and Gentiles in the matter of Jesus' execution. If God used all four entities, nevertheless the Jews used the Gentiles.

Acts 5.12–16   Another idealized summary

Important literature: **Haenchen**, *Acts*, pp. 242, 245; **Loisy**, *Actes*, p. 272; **Stählin**, *Apostelgeschichte*, p. 87.

Now 'the people' begin their withdrawal from the Christians, as could be expected after the onset of persecution in ch. 4. While 'the people' still 'magnif[y]' the church, 'no one dare[s] join them' (v. 13); the wedge has been driven in between. Having established that fact, however, Luke then seizes the opportunity of a summary to report further conversions! 'No one dared join them'; nevertheless, 'believers were added to the Lord, multitudes of men and also of women' (v. 14). The paradox exists only in our minds, not in Luke's, for these two statements, appearing anomalously side by side, are entirely understandable given the sketch of the birth of Christianity that Luke wants to present. On the one hand, the hearing in the Sanhedrin signals the beginning of the rejection that had begun to rear its head as early as the passion narrative; and so the people do not join the church. On the other hand, however, the church is still in its Jewish period, and so the success of the gospel must be reported, except that Luke abandons his mathematical progression for a generality. Probably the readers are expected to let their imaginations soar; we had 3000 in 2.41, an unspecified number of 'daily additions' in 2.47, 5000 men alone in 4.4, and now 'multitudes'. At this rate, the 'myriads' finally reported in 21.20 will be accounted for before the umbilical cord is actually severed.

Luke concludes his summary (vv. 15–16) by reporting how many sick are brought to the Christians for healing, and from how far away they come. This report shows both the high esteem in which the Jews hold the Christians and the power of the gospel. But now the break is at hand.

Acts 5.17–42   A second arrest of the apostles, and Peter's fourth sermon

Important literature: **Beck**, *Mature Christianity*, p. 218; **Haenchen**, *Acts*, pp. 251, 255; **Loisy**, *Actes*, pp. 275–92; **Neyrey**, *Passion*, pp. 89–93; **Rese**, 'Aussagen über Jesu Tod', pp. 344–7; **Wilckens**, *Missionsreden*, p. 45.

Once again, those who arrest the apostles and bring them to trial are the same villains as in the passion narrative, but this time Luke is more precise in their identification than he was in 4.1,5. The responsible parties in v. 17 are 'the high priest and all his colleagues, namely the party of the Sadducees', and v. 18 reports, if we take it literally, that this entire group arrested the apostles (cf.Luke 22.52). Those who convene for the hearing, then (v. 21), are 'the high priest and his colleagues', with 'the Sanhedrin and all the senate of the sons of Israel' (Luke departs here from his normal usage of 'Sanhedrin' as the place of meeting to use the term to mean – apparently – one of the groups in the plenary session). In the Gospel, as we discussed in detail in ch. 1, Luke calls the Temple police force 'captains of the Temple', whereas in Acts there is only one 'captain', who has 'sergeants (ὑπηρέται)'. Inasmuch as the usage in Acts is more nearly correct, it may be that someone explained to Luke, after he published his Gospel but before he finished Acts, that the Temple had only one captain. However that may be, after the miraculous escape of the apostles (vv. 19,23) it is 'the captain with the sergeants' who go to apprehend the apostles yet again (v. 26). In v. 27 Luke returns to his normal use of 'Sanhedrin' as the place of hearing, and 'the high priest' begins the proceedings.

Peter's speech is rather short, but he manages to reiterate the Jewish guilt for the death of Jesus. Again it is perfectly plain who the agents of Jesus' death are: 'You laid hands on [him] and hanged [him] on a tree' (v. 30). Inasmuch as this speech is addressed only to the trial court, we could think, if we did not have the earlier speeches in Acts, that Luke did intend, after all, to accuse only the priestly leadership of killing Jesus. Since we have already had the other speeches, however, and since Luke has made it plain in the narrative contexts that surround them that the charge applies to *all* Jews from all over the world, we cannot view Acts 5.30 in isolation. Of course, Luke does think of the priestly leadership as being primarily culpable; but the people in no wise escape culpability. When we then read this charge of guilt addressed to the priestly leadership, after the earlier similar charges in Acts, we come to see that the charge is always applicable to a Jewish audience, from whatever class of Jewish society and from wherever in Jewry it comes.

Peter next claims (v. 31) that 'God raised [Jesus] . . . to give repentance to Israel and forgiveness of sins'. (This is the word-order, but we are surely to understand that both repentance and forgiveness are to be given to Israel.) This statement is fully in keeping with the reports of thousands of Jewish conversions to Christianity in response to Peter's earlier preaching in Acts, and thus we may agree in the main with Jervell and Lohfink in their explanation of the mission to the Jews in the early part of Acts. 'In the period of the first apostolic preaching, the true Israel is gathered out of the Jewish people'[7] – so to speak. And Jervell is, of course, further correct when he sees that Luke intends no further mission to the Jews after the conclusion of Acts.[8] The disagreement with Jervell's and Lohfink's position has to do primarily with their explanation of the relation of the Gentile mission to the Jewish, for it is incorrect to say with Lohfink that 'the true Israel is only really achieved when the Gentiles have been brought into the community of the people of God'.[9] That issue will be discussed below as it arises in the course of Acts; but here we cannot escape noticing what Haenchen, especially, has also seen in the narrative here under discussion[10] – that is, that Peter's reference to 'repentance' and 'forgiveness' provokes hostility. The members of the trial court 'gnas[h their teeth]' and 'wis[h] to do away with them' (v. 33). The Jewish leadership, in any case, is having nothing to do with the gospel; soon they will be joined in their hardness by the people. The end of the period of Jewish salvation is at hand.

Now, however, re-enter the Pharisees. No less than the famous Gamaliel, also named as the teacher of Paul (Acts 22.3), speaks on behalf of the church. Possibly, he suggests, the Christian movement is actually divinely led (v. 39); if it is not, it will play itself out and amount to nothing (v. 38). Here we have the first appearance in Acts of the friendly non-Christian Pharisee; the godfather, so to speak, of Christianity.[11] When non-Christian Pharisees appear in Acts, they always take the part of the church; it is only when they become Christians (except in the case of Paul) that they cause problems. That is to say that, in Acts, when Pharisees are seen as Jews they are viewed as a very special and almost separate part of Judaism, 'the very best party of the [Jewish] religion', as the Lucan Paul is later to say (26.5). They do not receive that designation merely because they believe, as do the Christians, in the resurrection, as most authors today seem to think; Luke's positive evaluation of non-Christian Pharisees in Acts goes quite beyond that belief, although it certainly includes it. We see this in the present scene. Although the resurrection has been mentioned, and although Luke probably expects his readers to know that Pharisees and Sadducees argued over whether such a thing would occur, Gamaliel makes no reference to resurrection in his defence of granting latitude to the Christians; rather, he appeals to historical precedent (vv. 36–37).[12] That the Pharisees are 'the very best party' in Judaism, therefore, has to do with their generally friendly attitude towards the church, with their support of the apostles and of Paul in their trials. By this tactic Luke highlights the point that Christianity is related to Judaism, that it is not some 'Johnny-come-lately' movement, but that it is the authentic continuation of Israelite or 'biblical' religion. One is helped to understand that point when one sees that 'the very best party' in Judaism is quite close to Christianity in belief and in support of the apostles. These friendly Pharisees in Acts are not Christians, but *as Jews* they are not so very far removed from Christianity.

Acts 6.7 *More conversions, especially of priests*

Important literature: **Lampe**, 'Acts', p. 894; **Preuschen**, *Apostelgeschichte*, p. 37.

The martyrdom of Stephen, which follows immediately, brings the 'Jerusalem springtime' of the church – which, as we have seen, is itself not unmarked by opposition – to an end. Thereafter the gospel will spread out from Jerusalem, but the church will never again lead the idyllic existence that has characterized its initial period in Jerusalem; and, especially, it will never again experience the conversion of 'myriads'. Thus, in order to prepare adequately for that sum, not to be mentioned explicitly for several chapters yet (21.20), Luke now explains that the church 'grew, and the number of disciples in Jerusalem was multiplied considerably' (6.7). The two numbers that have been given are 3000 (2.41) and 5000 (4.4), and all the other reports of conversions have mentioned only multiplication (except for 2.47, which refers to daily additions). Since Luke says here that what grew was 'the gospel' (literally, 'the word of God'; cf.

4.31; 8.14, and throughout Acts), it appears that his emphasis on such astounding numbers in the church's earliest phase is an attempt to impress his readers with the gospel's success at that time. To the indefinite summary in v. 7, Luke then adds that 'a large crowd of priests' was converted.

Just what this note is doing here is not perfectly clear. The explanation that Luke is following a source is inadequate, as we have noted so often before; but there is little consensus among authors who attempt to fathom Luke's intent. Probably he adds priests to his last report of conversions in Jerusalem to demonstrate again the success of the gospel, since he shows us in this way that the gospel was so effective that it reached even into that group from which the greatest hostility towards Jesus and the church had come.

Acts 6.8–15   The arrest of Stephen

Important literature: **Bauernfeind**, *Apostelgeschichte*, p. 109; **Beck**, *Mature Christianity*, pp. 220–1; **Bihler**, 'Stephanusbericht'; *Stephanusgeschichte*; **Haenchen**, *Acts*, pp. 271, 273; **Preuschen**, *Apostelgeschichte*, pp. 37–8; **Simon**, *St Stephen*, pp. 20–6; **Surkau**, *Martyrien*, pp. 109–19; **Wilson**, *Gentiles*, pp. 130–8.

We come now to the episode that nearly every author calls the 'turning point' in the narrative of Acts – the arrest and martyrdom of Stephen. We may omit here a discussion of the first six verses of the chapter, which explain how Stephen came to be a deacon, since the situation and events described there seem to have no bearing on our issue. (Verse 7 was discussed in the preceding section.) In v. 8, however, Stephen is doing what Peter and John had earlier been doing, performing 'great wonders and signs among the people'. Something about Stephen must have been different, however, although we are not given any such information; for whereas, when Peter and John performed miracles 'the people' held them in highest esteem (4.21), when Stephen does the same thing 'the people' put him to death. The reason, of course, why this happens actually has nothing to do with Stephen himself, but has everything to do with Luke's episodic progression, because at the end of ch. 6 the time of Jewish conversions in Acts is over and the time of Christianity's separation from Judaism and of eternal enmity between the two religions has arrived. Thus now 'the people', who have stood solidly behind Jesus and the church – except for their strange behaviour in the passion narrative and except for their increasing reserve towards the Christians after the arrest of the apostles in Acts 4 – become uniformly hostile. Not only are 'the people' given an active role in the opposition to Stephen in v. 12, they are put at the head of the list! Those who are 'excited' by the accusations against Stephen are the 'people and the elders and the scribes'.

The accusers, however, are Diaspora Jews. Later, it will be Diaspora Jews who are responsible for Paul's arrest (21.27), so that there is no doubt that Luke wants to stress this point. Those who 'rose up . . . and disputed with Stephen', according to v. 9, were, if we read literally what the list says, 'some people from the synagogue named "Of the Libertines and Cyrenians and Alexandrians"', and some from Cilicia and Asia'. This verse is much discussed in the commentaries, especially the meaning of 'Libertines' and how many synagogues Luke had in mind. Those questions aside, however, we remind ourselves that Alexandria and Cyrene were major Jewish population centres along the south-eastern Mediterranean and that the Roman provinces of Cilicia and Asia were home to many Jews in the north-eastern Mediterranean region. Thus we again have something of an impression of world-wide Jewry, now not receptive of the gospel as in Acts 2, but hostile to it and in active opposition against it. To be sure, these Diaspora Jews do not represent Jews throughout the entire world, as did the Pentecost audience in Acts 2, since they are designated as coming from those areas in the direction of which the gospel will travel as it moves west from Jerusalem. (Luke routinely ignores both the eastern Diaspora and eastern Christianity.) While we must continue to postpone until a concluding chapter a detailed discussion of Luke's reasoning in portraying the Jews as he does, still the apparent – I should even say 'obvious' – motive for giving Diaspora Jews such a villainous role in Acts can be noted. Surely Luke makes Diaspora Jews the chief villains in the martyrdom of Stephen and in Paul's arrest because the Jews whom he has most cause to hate are Diaspora Jews; Luke's experience with Judaism is with Diaspora Judaism.

These Diaspora Jews 'dispute' unsuccessfully with Stephen (vv. 9–10) and then 'put forward men' (apparently from among their own number) who accuse Stephen of 'blasphemy against Moses [sc. the Torah] and God' (v. 11). Having thus 'excited the people and the elders and the scribes', the Diaspora Jews apprehend Stephen and 'le[a]d him into the Sanhedrin' (v. 12). Here for the first time, therefore, we have a new type of arrest of Christians. Jesus and the earlier apostles had been arrested only by the Temple authorities (with their associates), but now Luke describes a citizens' arrest by Diaspora Jews. Except in the case of the martyrdom of James at the beginning of Acts 12, all succeeding arrests of Christians in Acts will be either carried out or provoked by Diaspora Jews. This is the guilt that Luke wants to attribute to Diaspora Jews; the significance of that attribution will become clearer as we proceed through Acts.

The Diaspora Jews next put forward 'false witnesses' against Stephen in the Sanhedrin, who accused Stephen of speaking against Temple and Torah (v. 13). Specifically, these false witnesses claimed (v. 14) that Jesus, as reported by Stephen, would 'destroy' the Temple and 'alter the customs that Moses delivered'. That false witnesses make a similar charge against Jesus in Mark 14.56–58 but not in the Lucan passion narrative is everywhere noted, but the explanation widely offered, that Luke deliberately omitted the account from the passion narrative in order to include it here, is doubtful. Luke is, rather, at pains to make Stephen's martyrdom look very much like Jesus', as we see especially in Stephen's 'last words', vv. 59–60. Probably Luke does think of the presence of false witnesses in Stephen's trial as being parallel to the passion narrative. Then why do they not appear in the Lucan passion narrative? It may be that Luke wanted to include the charges somewhere but did not want to dilute the political charges made in Luke 23.2, 5 with these religious accusations; but certainty does not seem possible on this point.

While the witnesses may be false, their testimony is, on analysis, true; or, at least, it is in keeping with Stephen's following speech and Luke's general attitude toward Mosaic customs. Stephen, in his speech, certainly opposes the validity of the Temple (vv. 48–50); and of course Luke is quite opposed to Mosaic customs in the church, as we saw in detail in ch. 4. The term 'customs ($\tau\grave{\alpha}$ ἔθη)' more or less renders *halakah* and is quite to the point. It is over practice that Luke and Jewish Christianity – and, to a considerable degree, non-Christian Judaism – part company. The church that was inaugurated in consequence of Jesus' death and resurrection is to be, essentially, a Gentile church, and it owes no loyalty to Mosaic customs, like circumcision. It thus appears that all Luke's arguments against Jews, whether Christian or non-Christian, coincide here at the end of ch. 6: 1. the Jews persecute the church; 2. Jews have quaint and objectionable customs that they try to foist on the church.

Acts 7.1–53 *Stephen's sermon*

Important literature: **Bauernfeind**, *Apostelgeschichte*, pp. 110–13; **Bihler**, *Stephanusgeschichte*; **Franklin**, *Christ the Lord*, pp. 99–108; **Gnilka**, *Verstockung*, pp. 144–5; **Haenchen**, *Acts*, pp. 289–90; **Kilgallen**, *The Stephen Speech*; **Kränkl**, *Knecht*, pp. 112–13; **Lampe**, 'Acts', pp. 894–6; **Loisy**, *Actes*, pp. 318–21, 345–7; **Maddox**, *Purpose*, pp. 51–4; **Mussner**, 'Stephanusperi-kope', pp. 289–97; **Neyrey**, *Passion*, pp. 94–8; **O'Neill**, *Theology*, pp. 78–89; **Overbeck**, *Apostelgeschichte*, pp. 94, 110; **Rese**, 'Aussagen über Jesu Tod', pp. 39–44; **Schmithals**, *Apostelgeschichte*, pp. 72–3; **Wilckens**, *Missionsreden*, pp. 208–19; **Wilson**, *Gentiles*, pp. 130–8.

Most commentators are of the opinion that Stephen's long speech does not address the charges. That is by and large true, inasmuch as the bulk of the speech, down through v. 47, is a recitation of certain important events in Israel's religious history; the best opinion seems to be that Luke included all this material because it came from a source, which source then in fact became the model for all the missionary speeches in Acts.[13] That is possible and may explain the presence of vv. 1–47 in Stephen's speech. Luke is unlikely to have included such a long passage, however, simply because it was in a source and led up to the attack on the Temple in which he was interested. Interest in a Moses typology has been proposed.[14] What-ever Luke's reason for including the bulk of the speech, however, he comes at the end to the issue of the Temple. 'The Most High does not dwell in something handmade' (v. 48); and he quotes Isa. 66.1–2 to prove it. If Stephen had not been reporting that Jesus would destroy the Temple, as the 'false witnesses' who accused him had maintained, he now at least implies sympathy with that prospect.

From opposition to the Temple Stephen moves directly to the charge that the Jews (we must remember that everyone, including 'the people', was involved in Stephen's arrest, vv. 8–12) 'always thrust against the Holy Spirit' (v. 51), that they 'became the murderers . . . of the Righteous One', i.e., Jesus (v. 52), and that they 'received the Law in ordinances from angels[15] but . . . did not keep it' (v. 53). Thus, again, 'the Jews' are accused of killing Jesus, and their consistent opposition to the divine will – one of Luke's main themes – is repeated. They are also said, however, not to have 'kept' the Law. Is this not the other side of the coin, the former side of which is that Jesus would change 'the customs that Moses delivered to' the Israelites? It would appear that Luke wants to distinguish between divine Law and 'the customs' from Moses (like circumcision). The Law came from God – through angels – but it has been perverted into Mosaic 'custom', i.e. *halakah*. When the Christian Pharisees in Acts 15.5 want the Gentile Christians to be circumcised and to keep the Law of Moses, Luke objects. The true, divine Law is something different. Luke may be on soft ground here, but what he has in mind is the Torah as interpreted by Gentile Christianity. 'Mosaic custom' is the Torah interpreted by the Pharisees, and that interpretation is something that Jesus, according to Luke, is going to change. It may be a twentieth-century theologian who believes that the Law was fulfilled in the New Testament and not in the Talmud, but Luke could hardly express that position better than he has done. The *Jews* did not keep the Law, because they followed 'Mosaic customs'; Christians, however, will keep the Law and are enabled to do so because they are *not* encumbered by Mosaic customs.

That is Stephen's (Luke's) reply to the charges brought by the 'false witnesses'. The witnesses are 'false' only in a *pro forma* sense (since they accuse Stephen, they must be false witnesses); Luke has no objection to their accusations. Stephen and, indeed, all Christianity à la Luke oppose the Temple and Mosaic custom. Stephen's sermon in the Sanhedrin allows Luke to express his objections to Judaism and to put clearly before his readers the nature of the rift between Judaism and Christianity. We must note, as have so many others, that Luke's Christians are innocent in the matter of the rift; it is all the Jews' fault.

Acts 7.54–60   The martyrdom of Stephen

Important literature: **Baur**, *Paul*, vol. 1, pp. 56–60; **Bihler**, 'Stephanus-bericht'; *Stephanusgeschichte*; **Haenchen**, *Acts*, p. 296; **Holtzmann**, *Apostelge-schichte*, pp. 61–3; **Lampe**, 'Acts', p. 896; **Neyrey**, *Passion*, pp. 94–8; **Pesch**, *Vision*; **Roloff**, *Apostelgeschichte*, p. 128; **Sabbe**, 'Son of Man Saying'; **Simon**, *St Stephen*, pp. 20–6; **Surkau**, *Martyrien*, pp. 109–19; **Talbert**, *Reading Luke*, p. 213; **Wilson**, *Gentiles*, pp. 130–8.

Now Stephen is killed. The aspects of his martyrdom that are parallel to Jesus' are numerous and remarkable, and Luke doubtless meant to show that the Jews martyred the church just as they did Jesus. That it is 'the Jews' who kill Stephen and not merely the priestly rulers is beyond all reasonable question. Luke has told us in Acts 6.12 that 'the people' are involved, along with everyone else in sight, in the arrest of Stephen; the long speech, concluding with round denunciations of all Jews, has focused attention away from the priestly leadership on to the people as a whole; and, in the stoning scene, Luke has called up his best 'narrative skill' and has written not a single subject for all his plural verbs in the stoning scene, except 'the witnesses' in v. 58, who 'put off their clothes at . . . Saul's . . . feet'.[16] Thus, after Stephen's highly generalizing denunciation of 'you and your fathers' (v. 51), it is 'they' who are enraged (v. 54), 'they' who 'cry out' and 'cover their ears', 'they' who 'rush at him all together' (v. 57), 'they' who cast Stephen 'out of the city', and 'they' who 'stone' him (v. 58). Surely Luke does not intend us to think that 'they' are limited to the ruling priesthood. 'The Jews' have done it.

Many commentators have broken their heads here over the theory of two sources, one of an official execution and one of a lynching, to no avail. The entire scene is rather the product of what so many authors today delicately call Luke's 'narrative skill', or what Helmut Koester more bluntly calls his 'gift of invention'. It is a 're-hash' of the martyrdom of Jesus and of the attempt at killing him in Luke 4.29. As in Luke 4.28–29, 'When they heard these things, . . . they cast [him] out of the city' (Acts 7.54,58). The only differences in phrasing between these two parallels are ἐξέβαλον in Luke 4.29 and ἐκβαλόντες in Acts 7.58 – a mere shift from finite verb to participle – and the presence of the pronoun αὐτόν in Luke 4.29, whereas it is implied in Acts 7.58. As 'the Jews' sought to stone Jesus to death at the beginning of the Galilean ministry, so they suceed in stoning the first Christian martyr to death at the conclusion of the 'Jerusalem springtime' of the church. Furthermore, Stephen's last words in Acts 7.59–60 – 'Lord Jesus, receive my spirit', and 'Lord, do not hold this sin against them' – are surely expected to bring to the reader's mind Jesus' last words according to the Gospel of Luke – 'Father, forgive them, for they do not know what they are doing', and 'Father, into your hands I deposit my spirit' (Luke 23.34,46). Stephen's martyrdom is supposed to awaken in the person who has already read Luke a sense of *déja vu*. What the Jews had always done, ignoring the will of God and killing the prophets, they continue doing to Jesus and to the church. Nothing is new, the Jews are a hopeless lot, the behaviour of the Jews in the narrative is moving towards coincidence with the charges made against them in the speeches.

Acts 8.3–8   The conversion of Samaria

Important literature: **Haenchen**, *Acts*, p. 298; **Jervell**, *People of God*, pp. 117–19, 122–3; **Munck**, *Acts*, p. 73; **Overbeck**, *Apostelgeschichte*, pp. 118–19; **Schmithals**, *Apostelgeschichte*, p. 80; **Simon**, *St Stephen*, pp. 26–38.

Now Philip takes up the task of preaching the gospel. Since he is mentioned second in the list in Acts 6.5, and since he takes up the cause after Stephen's demise, Luke obviously thinks of him as Stephen's successor. Philip's preaching, however, is not to Jews strictly speaking, but to two of the groups that we were able to define in ch. 5 as being on the periphery, as lying between Jews and Gentiles – Samaritans and proselytes (the only two of the three peripheral groups in Acts). The martyrdom of Stephen has closed for ever the period of Jewish salvation, and the gospel now begins to make its way outwards towards its Gentile destiny. Thus, while the *Gentile* mission is, it is true, only inaugurated by Peter in Acts 10, the movement in that direction begins as soon as the Jerusalem period closes, and the movement in the direction of the Gentiles passes through the Samaritans and the proselytes.

There will, of course, be other conversions of individual Jews in the course of the narrative of Acts, but their existence in the narrative rests not on Luke's attempt to show that the period of Jewish salvation continues, that the *entire* spread of the gospel is the 'gathering of Israel', to which Gentile salvation is incidental. The later accounts of conversions of individual Jews exist because of three other aspects of Lucan thinking. For one thing, Luke wants to show, in the remainder of the narrative, how the Christian preachers sought to bring salvation to Diaspora Jews but met with rejection. Even so, however, the gospel cannot be powerless, and so a few Jews are saved along the way. In the second place, Luke probably would agree with many of his modern interpreters that, although the *period* of Jewish salvation is over, individual Jews may still be saved at any time, if they repent and believe (although this will increasingly become an oddity). Finally, of course, Luke knows of Diaspora Jewish Christians in his own day. He may not like the ones whom he knows, but he cannot ignore their existence and make it appear that the gospel, in the context of the Diaspora, was received only by Gentiles. Jewish salvation after the martyrdom of Stephen, however, is incidental to the Gentile mission and to the theme of Jewish rejection; it is not the principal motif, as Jervell, Lohfink and their followers maintain. The 'great persecution' that 'scattered' the Christians into 'the region of Judaea and Samaria' (Acts 8.1) marks the end of the Jerusalem period, as the similarity of phrasing with 1.8 shows.

Luke describes Philip, then, as going 'to the city of Samaria' (Acts 8.5). Either Luke intends to designate, by this term, Sebaste, the main city in the region of Samaria, or he has no definite information about any Samaritan *poleis* and assumes that Samaria includes some city that is the equivalent of Jerusalem in Judaea;[17] but 'the city' designates a definite place. How different the reception of the gospel here from that in Jerusalem! Not only do these Samaritans 'cleave to' Philip's preaching (v. 6) and offer up their possessed and ill readily to the healing power of the gospel (v. 7), so that there is 'much joy in that city' (v. 8), but nobody opposes the gospel! (The theme of the power of the gospel is continued in the following story of Simon Magus, vv. 9–24.) When Philip and Peter leave 'the city', then, to return to Jerusalem, they 'evangeliz[e] many villages of the Samaritans' (v. 25). The second component of Luke's geographical outline given in Acts 1.8, Judaea and Samaria, is disposed of quickly in the narrative; all Samaria has now been evangelized, and we have the impression of many conversions and no opposition. Opposition to the gospel, in Acts, comes almost exclusively from Jews.

Acts 8.14–24   The embassage of Peter

Peter now comes from Jerusalem to the Samaritan city to administer the bestowing of the Holy Spirit on the Samaritan Christians. While this narrative reveals a number of things about Luke's ecclesiology, two points are especially significant for our interest here. One is that the bestowing of the Spirit on the Samaritan Christians shows that they are full and proper Christians in every sense of the word. They do not belong to any second order of Christianity, and they do not have to be converted to Judaism. The path to Gentile conversion is thus opened. The other point worth noting in connection with this narrative is that Luke in this way shows the legitimacy of Samaritan Christianity and, by extension, of Gentile Christianity. The apostles did not carry out the Samaritan mission, but it is not thereby some sucker growing of itself from the roots of the main tree; it is a new fruit-bearing branch of the tree itself.

Acts 8.26–40   The conversion of a proselyte

A Gentile eunuch reading Isaiah (Luke's favourite book of Scripture) is a proselyte to Judaism. When that very same book of Isaiah refers to 'eunuchs who keep my Sabbaths' and two sentences later to 'foreigners joined to Yahweh' (Isa. 56.4, 6), that will have been enough for Luke, whatever synagogue regulations in his day were. The scholar, therefore, who knows that eunuchs were not allowed to be proselytes, who nevertheless sees that Luke's plan of expansion calls for a proselyte at this point, and who thus proposes that a eunuch was not a eunuch has simply overlooked the significance of Isaiah for Luke (or the content of Isa. 56.4, 6).[18] While it is true that there were proselytes in Peter's Pentecost audience (Acts 2.11), and while one of the seven deacons, of whom Stephen and Philip were the first, was a proselyte (Nicolaus), still Luke has not specifically recounted a proselyte conversion, and it is important for him to do so at this point.

Why he mentioned the proselytes earlier is something of a puzzle. Perhaps he included proselytes in 2.11 because he wanted as inclusive a group as possible in Peter's audience. Still, he does not note that any of those who were converted to Christianity was a proselyte (cf. 2.41). Nicolaus may be designated a proselyte because of an early Christian tradition, but such an assumption is speculative. What we can be more certain of is that Luke does not mind informing his readers as early as ch. 6 that some of the first Christians were proselytes, not Jews by birth. In spite of the fact, however, that we learn from Acts 6.5 that at least one early Christian had earlier been a proselyte to Judaism, Luke does not recount any conversions of proselytes until he comes to Philip's conversion of the Ethiopian in 8.27. This is where proselytes fit into Luke's plan: the gospel begins in Jerusalem, proceeds into the periphery (called Judaea and Samaria in 1.8 and, apparently, 8.1, although Judaea is actually passed over in the narrative in favour of the Ethiopian) of Samaria and the realm of the proselytes, and then to the God-fearers, which stage becomes at the same time the opening of the Gentile mission.

At the conclusion of the narrative of proselyte conversion Luke has appended a missionary summary comparable to the one that he attached to the end of the narrative of Samaritan conversions. Just as, in Acts 8.25, Philip and Peter 'evangelized many villages of the Samaritans', so in 8.40 Philip 'evangelized all the cities [from Azotus] until he came to Caesarea'. Does this summary not mean that Philip has carried the gospel through 'proselyte land' up to Caesarea, the place where, two chapters later, the first truly Gentile conversion to Christianity so designated will take place? This appears to be Luke's meaning. The events of ch. 8 take us, as well as Philip, up to Caesarea. The *geographical* plan of the expansion of the gospel in the first eight chapters of Acts may be Jerusalem first, then Judaea and Samaria, but the *theological* plan is Jews first, then Samaritans and proselytes. Luke has skilfully taken us through both the geographical and the theological territories at once, and we are therefore prepared for the conversion of Saul-to-become-Paul, the missionary *par excellence* to the Gentiles, and for the beginning of Gentile conversions.

Acts 9.1–22   Saul's conversion

Important literature: **Haenchen**, *Acts*, pp. 319–20; **Loisy**, *Actes*, p. 416.

Since our purpose here is not to analyse the Gentile mission, only certain details of this narrative which bear directly on Luke's portrait of the Jews are of interest. In the first place, Luke once again designates the high priest (v. 1) as the authority behind the Jewish persecution of Christians, thus maintaining his emphasis that the priestly authorities in Jerusalem are those most vigorously and consistently opposing Jesus and the church. (Whether there actually was such a persecution will be the subject of our reflection in Part Three.) After Saul's conversion in Damascus, then, he preaches to his fellow Jews (Acts 9.20–22), *yet he makes no attempt to convert them*; rather, he *confuses* (συγχύνω) them. Why does Paul, who will later preach in just such synagogues as this and attempt to convert Jews, not attempt to convert the Damascus Jews? Their response to his preaching (v. 21) shows that they think that he wants to convert them, and that he wants to do so in order to entrap them into becoming Christians, so that he may arrest them and take them to Jerusalem for persecution. Yet Paul makes no such attempt but 'confuses' them instead. This is a puzzling narrative; but is the puzzle not solved when we realize that the period of Jewish salvation came to a close on the occasion of the martyrdom of Stephen, and that the real purpose of Paul's preaching to Diaspora Jews is to provoke the rejection that Luke knows will come? Luke, in other words, thinks of Paul's Diaspora mission in these terms: the gospel was taken to the Jews in the Diaspora, just as it was taken to the Jews in Jerusalem. The preachers of the gospel, naturally, had no ulterior motives and earnestly sought Jewish conversions. The period of Jewish conversion, however, had ended at the end of Acts 6, and so the response of Jews to the gospel from that point on, with precious few exceptions, was rejection.

Thus it is not surprising when, in response to Paul's 'confusing' preaching, 'the Jews plotted to do away with him' (v. 23). Here is quintessentially Lucan language. These 'plots' by 'the Jews' will dog Paul to the end and will prove at least partially successful; and when Luke writes that the Jews wanted to 'do away with' Paul, he uses his characteristic term for what it is that the Jews do or try to do to Jesus and to the other leaders of the church.

Furthermore, we need to pause to note the degree to which Luke has deliberately perverted – there is no other word for it – the account of this episode in Paul's life; for, from Paul himself, we learn what really happened at Damascus in connection with his being got out of the city in a basket. Paul explains in II Cor. 11.32–33 that 'the ethnarch of Aretas the king' was waiting to apprehend him outside Damascus, and so he 'was let down in a basket through the wall'. We cannot take up here the issues of the identity of King Aretas and of why he may have been after Paul; but we must note that Luke's retelling of the event shows enough verbal similarities to Paul's account to warrant our thinking that Luke had read Paul's account (or had heard it read and remembered it) and had rewritten it to his own satisfaction (διὰ τοῦ τείχους and χαλάω in both cases). Now let us suppose, for the sake of argument, that King Aretas and his ethnarch were Jewish. This is not likely, since he was most probably a Nabataean,[19] but let us suppose that Luke and Paul, in any case, could have considered him a Jew. Even if that were the case, however, Luke would still have altered Paul's account; for Paul (assuming even that Paul would have said that King Aretas was a Jew) found no significance in King Aretas' race. It was not because he was a Jew that King Aretas sought to apprehend Paul, but, as far as Paul was concerned, for some other reason. In Luke's thinking, however (we are still trying to give Luke the benefit of the doubt and imagine some line of thinking on his part that will allow him to escape the charge of deliberate distortion), the significance of King Aretas would have been his Jewishness; 'the Jews' sought to persecute Paul.

Thus, even if we bend over backwards to attribute as much innocence to Luke as possible, still he cannot escape the charge of distortion, since, even if he thought of King Aretas as a Jew, the fact that he drops the varietal name for the generic 'Jews' shows that he has introduced a significance into Paul's account that greatly alters Paul's meaning. It did not occur to Paul that 'the Jews' were after him in Damascus, but that is the way that Luke presents the account.

Acts 9.29–30   A further attempt on Paul's life and his escape

Important literature: **Loisy**, *Actes*, p. 425; G. **Schneider**, *Apostelgeschichte*, vol. 1, p. 408.

In Jerusalem, in response to Paul's preaching to them, 'the Hellenists' – here obviously Diaspora Jews in Jerusalem, whatever the term means in Acts 6.1 – seek 'to do away with' Paul, but 'the brothers' get him out of the city and to Caesarea, and thence on to Tarsus. (Of course, Paul has to be far from Caesarea before Peter's encounter with Cornelius there in the following chapter.) This attempt on Paul's life in Jerusalem is, therefore, exactly a repeat of the plot against him in Damascus, with only minor differences. We certainly want to note, however, that Luke fingers Diaspora Jews (instead of just 'the Jews') again as those in Jerusalem who agitate against Luke's main characters. They succeeded in getting Stephen killed, and they will eventually succeed in getting Paul arrested and nearly killed. Luke views Diaspora Jews as especially dangerous.

Acts 10.1–48   The conversion of Cornelius

Important literature: **Dupont**, 'Le salut des Gentils', pp. 146–9; **Haenchen**, *Acts*, pp. 346–62; 'Judentum und Christentum', pp. 167–9; **Jervell**, *People of God*, pp. 57–8; **Kraabel**, 'Disappearance'; **Loisy**, *Actes*, pp. 432–51; **Overbeck**, *Apostelgeschichte*, pp. 151–9; **Rese**, 'Aussagen über Jesu Tod', pp. 344–7; G. **Schneider**, *Apostelgeschichte*, vol. 2, pp. 65–74; **Wilckens**, *Missionsreden*, pp. 46–50; **Wilcox**, 'God-Fearers', pp. 104–6; **Wilson**, *Gentiles*, pp. 171–7; *Law*, pp. 68–71.

Luke makes it abundantly clear in this fairly lengthy narrative that Cornelius is the first truly Gentile (not a proselyte) convert to Christianity. Cornelius is labelled a 'God-fearer' in vv. 2 and 22, and Peter addresses him in v. 28 as an 'ἀλλόφυλος (of another race)'. Even more specifically, Peter's companions, who are 'of circumcision', express surprise that 'the gift of the Holy Spirit has been poured out on Gentiles also' (v. 45), and the court of inquiry in Jerusalem that later investigates Peter's extra-halachic contact with Cornelius concludes that 'also to the Gentiles God has given repentance unto life' (11.18). After this narrative, Luke seems to make no distinction between proselytes and God-fearers in the rest of Acts, and indeed there may be no historical basis for Luke's categories. (See again the discussion of this issue in ch. 5.) In Acts 8 and 10, however, Luke does seem to want to distinguish these two groups, bringing the class of the proselytes (the Ethiopian) into Christianity before the God-fearers, who are the first of the Gentiles. Since both proselytes and God-fearers belong on the periphery, and since both lie on the path between Jews and Gentiles, there is really no need for Luke to try and maintain the distinction that he has made in chs. 8 and 10 later in Acts. In ch. 10, it is clear, a God-fearer is a Gentile who reveres the Jewish God but has not been converted to Judaism. He is not circumcised and is not Jewish. He is a Gentile.

What most catches our attention in this episode, however, is not how Luke sketches the periphery around Judaism through which the gospel passes on its way to the Gentiles, but how the Lucan Peter cannot preach to Gentiles without accusing 'the Jews' of killing Jesus. On Peter's statement in Acts 10.39 shatters every attempt to hold on to the belief that the motif of the guilt of the Jews is present in Acts in order to provoke Jewish repentance and conversion to Christianity. Announcing to Cornelius that the Jews killed Jesus has nothing to do with anyone's repentance; Jewish guilt is rather a fixed and unalterable part of the gospel. To be sure, Luke does not actually write here, 'The Jews killed Jesus', but that is nevertheless plainly his meaning. For Peter first refers, in v. 39, to 'all that [Jesus] did in the region of the Jews and Jerusalem', and then he adds, 'Whom they did away with, hanging [him] on a tree'. Luke has resorted here, as so frequently, to the device of omitted subjects, but there can be only one subject for 'did away with', and that is the immediately preceding 'Jews'. This theme never varies in the speeches of Luke's main characters in both Gospel and Acts. In Luke's Gentile Christianity the epithet thrown at Jews has its roots: 'Christ-killers'.

Acts 11.1–18   The Jerusalem church accepts the Gentile mission

Important literature: **Beyer**, *Apostelgeschichte*, p. 70; **Lampe**, 'Acts', pp. 900–1.

When Peter returns to Jerusalem, he is 'called on the carpet' about his improper behaviour in the presence of Gentiles, and he defends his actions by recounting his dream and audition, and then how Cornelius believed and how he received the Holy Spirit. His inquirers are satisfied by this explanation and conclude that Gentiles are also to be allowed to become Christians (v. 18).

Peter had told Cornelius in 10.28 'how illegal it is for a Jewish man to be joined to or approach one of another race', and it is his 'collusion' with Gentiles that leads to the inquiry when he returns to Jerusalem, for those 'of circumcision' there (apparently not the same persons 'of circumcision' who had already seen the point in 10.45) accuse him in these terms; 'You entered in to (εἰσέρχομαι πρός, cf. προσέρχομαι in 10.28) men who have foreskin and ate with them' (11.3). Thus we see plainly what Luke thinks the Jewish rules about association with Gentiles were in the early days of Christianity, whatever they were in fact. According to Luke, there were Jewish rules absolutely forbidding associations with Gentiles. It may have been a later shunning of Christians practised by synagogues, not pre-Christian Jewish rules, that led Luke to this opinion; but that he has the opinion is important to remember, for the issue will concern us again in the discussion on Acts 15.

Acts 11.19–25   The early expansion of the Gentile mission

Important literature: **Haenchen**, *Acts*, pp. 365–6, 370.

Now Luke tells us that those Christians who had to flee Jerusalem because of the persecution in Acts 8.1 have also been converting Gentiles, albeit accidentally. Luke seems apologetic about this fact, because it would appear that this Gentile conversion was already going on before Peter visited Cornelius. Thus Luke reports (literally), 'To no one they spoke the word except only to Jews' (v. 19). He seems to protest too much; but then he adds, 'But there were some men of them, Cyprians and Cyrenians', NB! *not* Jerusalem expatriates, 'who went to Antioch and spoke also to the Greeks' (v. 20), and so there were some Gentile conversions up there (v. 21). It seems that Luke actually thinks that these Gentile conversions may have taken place before Cornelius's conversion, but that he had to postpone telling about them until after the Cornelius episode, because that was the theological beginning of the Gentile mission. To look at the matter another way, more directly in line with our interests here, we see that Luke includes an account of the spread of the gospel to the Gentiles that oversteps the intermediate approach to the periphery. He therefore places the account later in his narrative than it would seem properly to fall chronologically, in order to make it appear that the gospel, when it went out from Jerusalem, went to the Gentiles by way of the periphery (Acts 8).

Acts 12.1–19   Further persecutions of the Jerusalem church

Important literature: **Haenchen**, *Acts*, pp. 382–4; **Jacquier**, *Actes*, p. 360; **Lampe**, 'Acts', p. 902; G. **Schneider**, *Apostelgeschichte*, vol. 2, p. 105.

In the Gospel of Luke, as we recall, it was primarily the priestly authorities who sought and brought about Jesus' death. Herod, however, also played a role, but an apparently vacillating one; for, early on in the Gospel, he arrested John the Baptist (Luke 3.20) and wanted to kill Jesus (Luke 13.31); but, in Luke 23.9, he concurred in Pilate's acquittal of Jesus and (v. 12) allied himself with Pilate. This strange behaviour, as we discussed in ch. 1, seems related to Luke's attempt to portray Herod first as *Jew* and then as *temporal authority*. While we deal with different Herods in Acts, that pattern is again followed, and here in Acts 12 Herod persecutes the church, just as Herod persecuted John in the Gospel. Later, Herod will ally himself with the procurator in acquitting Paul, just as Herod allied himself with the procurator Pilate in acquitting Jesus in the Gospel.

Herod, therefore, 'd[oes] away with . . . James the brother of John' (Acts 12.2). Further, he seeks to 'do away with' Peter, when he observes how the martyrdom of James was 'pleasing to the Jews' (v. 3)! This is now the new element that could not have been present in the Gospel; for, since the martyrdom of Stephen, 'the Jews', all the Jewish people, oppose Christianity. Later individual exceptions in Acts to that general rule will be just that, individual exceptions to the general rule. Luke hammers home the point of general Jewish opposition to the Christians, then, by reporting that, after Peter's arrest and ensuing miraculous escape from jail, Peter thanks God for rescuing him 'from the hand of Herod *and from all the expectation of the Jewish people*' (v. 11). The Lucan Peter no longer thinks of himself as truly Jewish, for 'the Jews' seek his death. Christianity is now distinct from Judaism.

Acts 13.1–12   The beginning of Saul's (Paul's) mission

Important literature: **Beyer**, *Apostelgeschichte*, p. 80; **Lampe**, 'Acts', p. 903; **Loisy**, *Actes*, pp. 509–18; **Overbeck**, *Apostelgeschichte*, pp. 194–5.

Saul and Barnabas are now sent out on the first truly foreign mission – to Cyprus (v. 4). Nevertheless, they take the gospel first to 'the synagogues' (v. 5), as will regularly be the case throughout Paul's career. On Cyprus no opposition from Jews generally to the gospel develops, but the missionaries encounter an evil Jew – 'a certain magician, a Jewish false prophet' – at Paphos (v. 6) who attempts to hinder the conversion of the proconsul, Sergius Paulus (v. 8). For that Paul blinds him, calling him a 'son of the devil' (vv. 10–11). Then the proconsul 'believe[s]' (v. 12). Thus, while Luke has not shown synagogue opposition to the gospel here, he has had Paul preach in synagogues, has had an evil Jew oppose Gentile conversion, has shown the power of the gospel over the evil Jew (who is explicitly associated with the devil), and has recounted the conversion of an important Gentile. If the reader turns from that account with any view other than that the missionaries take the gospel to Jews, who oppose it, and that the missionaries then preach successfully to Gentiles, it will not be for want of Luke's 'narrative skill', for he has highlighted these themes well. Furthermore, this is the general pattern that he will present numerous times in the course of Paul's ministry, but with enough variety in his accounts that the pattern does not become boring.

Acts 13.13–52   Paul at Antioch

Important literature: **Buss**, *Missionspredigt*; **Dupont**, 'La conclusion des Actes', pp. 384–5; **Epp**, 'Ignorance Motif', pp. 57–8; **Haenchen**, *Acts*, pp. 410–18; **Jervell**, *People of God*, pp. 60–2; **Kränkl**, *Knecht*, pp. 116–17; **Loisy**, *Actes*, pp. 523–41; **O'Neill**, *Theology*, pp. 86–7; **Overbeck**, *Apostelgeschichte*, pp. 189–210; **Radl**, *Paulus und Jesus*, pp. 82–100; **Rese**, 'Aussagen über Jesu Tod', pp. 344–7; **Schille**, *Apostelgeschichte*, pp. 291–8; **Wilckens**, *Missionsreden*, pp. 50–4, 221–2; **Wilcox**, 'God-Fearers', pp. 108–10; **Wilson**, *Gentiles*, pp. 222–4; **Zehnle**, *Pentecost Discourse*, p. 132.

Luke has managed to report two sermons by Paul in Jewish

synagogues in the Diaspora – at Damascus and at Salamis – without 'quoting' Paul exactly (13.5 had said that Paul 'announced the gospel' and 9.20 that he was saying that Jesus was 'the Son of God'). Now, however, for the first time we have Paul's words. Having gone to the mainland of Asia Minor from Cyprus and having made his way to Antioch and to the synagogue there, Paul is asked by the '*archisynagogi*' (v. 15) to speak. He responds (vv. 16–41) with his first sermon in Acts. In general, this is a Christian evangelistic sermon, giving the Israelite salvation-history background of Jesus and then the significance of Jesus, and encouraging the hearers to accept the truth of the content of the sermon. Jesus is said to be a 'saviour' (v. 23), and then 'forgiveness of sins' and 'justification' are said to be 'through him' (vv. 38–39). There is, therefore, nothing remarkable for our interest here – except for v. 27, where Luke brings up the ignorance theme again. We recall that, in Peter's second sermon (Acts 3.17), Luke had acknowledged that the Jewish murderers of Jesus had acted out of ignorance, and that Luke seemed to introduce that element into the sermon in order to make room for conversion. Here, however, the way in which Paul refers to ignorance does not give the impression that the reference is for the purpose of opening the door to conversion. For one thing, Paul's audience in this scene did not kill Jesus; it was rather the Jerusalemites, as Paul says. And, indeed, in keeping with the way in which 'the Jews' are portrayed in Acts after Stephen's martyrdom, it was *all* the Jerusalemites. Paul says that 'those dwelling in Jerusalem and their rulers . . . asked Pilate for [Jesus] to be done away with' (vv. 27–28). This continues the impression that 'the Jews' – at least, those in Jerusalem – were responsible.

In the second place, furthermore, Paul refers to the Jerusalemites' guilt in an accusatory, not in an excusatory manner. The Jerusalemites were 'ignorant even of the voices of the prophets that are read every Sabbath'; thus, 'condemning' Jesus, they 'fulfilled' the prophecies (v. 27). To this Paul adds that the Jews called for Jesus' death even though they 'found no cause for death', i.e., they found Jesus guilty of no crime deserving capital punishment. That the Lucan Paul does not mean to imply that 'the Jews' – and not Pilate – actually crucified Jesus is ruled out by v. 29: 'As they finished everything that had been written about him . . .' The Jews in Jerusalem fulfilled the prophecies about Jesus; they killed Jesus.

One might expect that the Lucan Paul would move from this

accusation to an appeal: 'Please, Antiochene Jews, do not follow the footsteps of your Palestinian relatives and join in the condemnation of Jesus. Accept, rather, the truth of what I am saying and believe in him.' Only the latter theme occurs, however, and in a somewhat unusual setting. Paul follows his condemnation of the Jerusalem Jews with verification of the resurrection (vv. 30–37), then he explains the meaning of the resurrection for his hearers (vv. 38–39): 'Through this one the forgiveness of sins is proclaimed to you; and from everything from which you were not able to be justified by the law of Moses, by this one everyone who believes is justified.' One might, then, expect some encouragement to believe from the preacher, but this does not occur. Instead, a threat follows: 'Watch out, therefore, lest what is said in the prophets come to pass' (v. 40), and then Paul quotes Hab. 1.5, the last line of which declares that God is doing something 'that you will not at all believe, even if someone explain it to you'. The choice before the Lucan Jews in Antioch of Pisidia, therefore, is whether to behave like Jews or to show good sense and be converted.

Their response is not straightforward. First of all, 'they' (v. 42), apparently 'the Jews' in Paul's audience, ask to hear more 'next Sabbath'. Then, furthermore, as people are leaving the synagogue, 'many of the Jews and of the worshipping proselytes follo[w] Paul and Barnabas, who addre[ss] them and persuad[e] them to abide in the grace of God' (v. 43). Why do Paul and Barnabas pass up their chance? They have 'many' of their audience following them through the streets of Antioch, so eager are they to hear the gospel (and to believe?), but Paul and Barnabas let pass this opportunity for conversions and settle for encouraging their hearers to remain fixed in their accustomed religious development; for 'abide in the grace of God' means just that (προσμένω + dat. = 'remain attached to'). Why do the Christian preachers, who seemed shortly before to appeal for belief, not now open the opportunity for it, ask their followers if they believe, and call for baptism? We must imagine that, if we were among those so excited by Paul's words that we were chasing him along the street, we would surely feel rebuffed by this response. Has Paul not just preached a new way of salvation, one that offers justification superior to that of the Law of Moses (vv. 38–39)? Of course he has. And have we not eagerly pursued him out of the synagogue precisely because of that superior justification, and are we not therefore eager to believe? Surely it would seem so. Why then does Paul now tell us to 'remain attached to' our old religion? Does he wish to *prevent* our salvation?

While Luke may not have posed the questions for himself quite so sharply, something like that is what he had in mind. To be sure, Luke would not be willing to admit that the Christian preachers were insincere in their preaching to Diaspora Jews; it is important to his theme of Jewish rejection of the gospel that Paul offer the gospel to Jews and that they reject it. But Luke's desire for variety in that theme within his narrative in the latter part of Acts has got him into a jam he is having difficulty getting out of. He wants to show some positive response from the Jews, but not too much; and, indeed, the theme of initially favourable Jewish response to the gospel followed by rejection is one of his favourite ways of handling the issue, as we can see from Jesus' Nazareth sermon, from Paul's last sermon in Rome, and from the current instance. But he has sketched the initially positive response so vividly that he then has to present his heroes in the embarrassing situation of calming the potentially Christian zeal of the Jewish audience and of 'persuading' them to 'stay good Jews' – which persuasion he then phrases in such a way that the rebuff is not immediately obvious. After he has carried that off, however, Luke proceeds to the theme of Jewish rejection and Gentile acceptance of the gospel.

'The coming Sabbath,' as Luke explains (v. 44), 'nearly all the city' came to hear Paul preach. Naturally, since the Jews did not make up the vast majority of the population of Antioch, Gentiles were crowded into the synagogue; so (v. 45), 'when the Jews saw the crowds they were filled with jealousy and disputed the things said by Paul.' To be sure that we ᴄo not miss the significance of what it meant to dispute Paul, Luke adds, 'They were blaspheming.' Now the expected opposition from 'the Jews' is forceful and thoroughgoing; and Paul responds with the first of his three announcements in Acts of taking the gospel to the Gentiles because the Jews oppose it. This first such announcement occurs in Asia Minor, to be followed, geographically significantly, by similar announcements in Greece and in Rome, as Dibelius so accurately noted.[20] According to Paul and Barnabas (v. 46), 'It was necessary for the gospel to be spoken first to' the Jews; and in this 'necessary' we are doubtless to hear that it was God's will. 'Since,' however, the Jews 'reject it and consider [them]selves not worthy of eternal life, behold,' Paul and Barnabas will 'turn to the Gentiles'. We are not told exactly what the Jews had said, but, inasmuch as they had 'disputed' Paul's preaching of 'the gospel (ὁ λόγος τοῦ κυρίου)' and had 'blaspheme[d]', they had said quite enough for a Christian to conclude that they were 'rejecting . . . eternal life'. They have therefore behaved like good puppets in response to Luke's string-play and have rejected the gospel, providing Luke with an opportunity to announce that the gospel is for the Gentiles and to quote a prophecy, furthermore, that proves that fact (v. 47). All this is straightforward enough and should demonstrate the impossibility of agreeing with Jervell that 'the addition of Gentiles is part of the restoration of Israel'[21] – unless one should follow Lohfink's path and declare the speeches in Acts mere sources that do not express Luke's true meaning.[22]

When many Gentile conversions then occur, 'the Jews' (v. 50) precipitate a 'persecution against Paul and Barnabas, and they expel[1] them from their borders'. While it would be straining Luke's verisimilitude to the breaking point to think that he meant that all the Jews in the world persecuted Paul and Barnabas in Antioch, nevertheless his repeated reference to 'the Jews' as opposing Jesus and the church now gives that impression. That is to say that these Jews in Antioch behave typically and are an example of the general rule that 'the Jews' persecute Christianity.

Acts 14.1–7   Paul at Iconium

Important literature: **Haenchen**, *Acts*, pp. 419–23; **Stählin**, *Apostelge-schichte*, pp. 188–9.

Immediately Paul arrives in Iconium he goes to the synagogue and starts preaching the gospel. Some authors, especially Franklin,[23] see this pattern of going again to a Jewish audience after Jewish persecution as meaning that God does not reject the Jews; that, however often the gospel encounters Jewish opposition, it is taken again and again to Jews. In this view, the narrative of Acts is therefore cyclical and not progressive. But such a cylical interpretation of Luke-Acts sets aside all the insights of scholarly investigation of Luke-Acts in the last century, a constant realization of which has been that Luke does, indeed, intend to present a progression. And he does. Everything about the plan of Luke-Acts shows that Luke thinks of forward movement – from Galilee through Samaria to Jerusalem, and thence back out, à la Acts 1.8, through Samaria and the periphery to 'the end of the earth'; and from the Jews to the

Gentiles. That the theme 'from the Jews to the Gentiles' is repeated does not mean that we are involved in a circle. It means, rather, that Luke finds the theme important enough to repeat.

Furthermore, however, even if one thinks of circular narration, one cannot overlook the beginning and end point of each episode; for each episode begins with preaching to the Jews and concludes with Jewish rejection (with the variations for narrative effect that were noted in ch. 3 and will crop up again as we continue through this analysis). Since Jervell has correctly seen that, at the conclusion of Acts, the salvation of the Jews is over,[24] it is a pity that others who would like to agree with him that Luke is primarily interested in the salvation of Israel do not also see that the salvation of Israel comes to an end in Acts. The Iconium episode does not show that the gospel always goes again to Jews; *au contraire*, each such episode presents a specific example of the general truth that the Jews reject the gospel.

And what, in any case, of the Jews back in Antioch? Does the gospel go to *them* again? Never; their chance at salvation has come and gone. They receive only one chance, which they miss, as God had always known they would. Perhaps that opinion of Luke's will become even more obvious if we juxtapose it to his attitude toward Gentile rejection of the gospel. Never is any such thing said in Luke-Acts of Gentile rejection of the gospel as Paul says to his Jewish opponents in Antioch and elsewhere.

Iconium is one of the few places on Paul's itinerary where there are Jewish conversions. In v. 1 'a great number of Jews and also of Greeks believed'. As we have already had occasion to observe, Luke has to show some Jewish conversions in Asia Minor, because in his day there were Jewish Christians there. Perhaps he knew, especially, of a mixed Jewish and Gentile congregation at Iconium; but, in any case, throwing in a few Jewish conversions now and then keeps his narrative from looking wooden. This variation does not unseat the general principle of Jewish rejection, and, in any case, 'the Jews' do not become monolithic in their opposition to Christianity in the *narrative* until the end of Acts.

As both Jews and Gentiles are converted in Iconium, so both Gentiles and Jews seek to persecute the missionaries (v. 5). Even so, however, we see to what degree Luke connects persecution of Christianity with 'the Jews' when we read in v. 4 that 'the one group [of the divided city] was with *the Jews* and the other with the apostles'. Apostles are not Jews, and Jews are not Christians. Can there be any better proof that Luke thinks of 'the Jews' as the enemies of (Gentile) Christianity?

Acts 14.8–21a   Paul at Lystra and Derbe

Important literature: **Haenchen**, *Acts*, pp. 429–38; **Loisy**, *Actes*, pp. 557–9.

Connected with Lystra we have the story of a miracle wrought by Paul and Barnabas and of their near apotheosis. The missionaries prevent the crowds' sacrificing to them by a little preaching, but not of the gospel. (There is one true god, not the ones you worship, and there are those things in your lives that attest to him, vv. 15–17.) Then, however, in spite of the fact that Paul and Barnabas have not gone to a synagogue, that they have not preached the gospel, and that there have been no conversions, 'Jews c[o]me to town from Antioch and Iconium, and, having persuaded the crowds' (of what?) 'and having stoned Paul, they dra[g] him outside the city, thinking him dead' (v. 19). Two aspects of this brief account are significant. First, we see that Jewish hostility and persecution follow on Paul's preaching even in towns where there are no Jews and where there have been no conversions. Luke in this way keeps the consistency of Jewish hostility before our eyes, while varying the narrative enough to make it believable and interesting. Secondly, we note that now Paul, just as earlier Jesus and Stephen, is taken outside the city to be stoned by Jews. Of course Luke varies the accounts. Jesus was taken outside the city to be stoned, but he escaped; Stephen was taken outside the city and stoned; and Paul was stoned first, then 'dragged' outside the city; but Luke nevertheless shows us here the degree to which Paul, like Stephen, shares Jesus' fate.

In vv. 20–21 Paul and Barnabas move on to Derbe, where they 'evangelize that city and make disciples of enough', but we are given no more detail about the Derbe mission: whether Paul preached in a synagogue or whether there were any Jews among the new disciples. Apparently, Luke intends his readers to have the impression that no Jewish opposition arose.

Acts 14.21b–28   Retracing the steps of the first missionary journey

Important literature: **Loisy**, *Actes*, p. 560.

Paul and Barnabas return towards Jerusalem through Lystra,

Iconium and Antioch, but their activity is much different from what it was when they first came through these cities. For some strange reason, on this retrograde journey, they make no attempt to win new converts – and they experience no Jewish hostility whatsoever. Paul and Barnabas 'provide strength to the souls of the disciples', they 'counsel [them] to abide in faith', and they tell the disciples 'that through many tribulations it is necessary for [them] to enter into the Kingdom of God' (v. 22); but there is not a breath of Jewish opposition blowing anywhere. The reason is not hard to find; the mission to the interior of Asia Minor is over. After the approaching Apostolic Council (ch. 15), Paul will scurry quickly back through Asia Minor, have his dream of the beckoning Macedonian (16.9), and be off to Philippi, where the mission will pick up again as before. We therefore have only generalities here of 'strengthening' the church; and, in any case, a different kind of Jewish opposition is about to arise, that of Jewish Christianity to the Gentile mission.

Acts 15.1–35   The Apostolic Council

Important literature: **Baur**, *Paul*, vol. 1, pp. 121–50; **Conzelmann**, *Primitive Christianity*, pp. 88–90; **Franklin**, *Christ the Lord*, pp. 124–6; **Haenchen**, *Acts*, pp. 449–72; **Jervell**, *People of God*, pp. 51–3, 64–7, 133–51, 188–93; **Lake** in *Beginnings*, Part I, vol. 5, p. 204; **Loisy**, *Actes*, pp. 587–94; **Nolland**, 'Acts 15.10'; **Novak**, *Image of the Non-Jew*, pp. 28–31; **Overbeck**, *Apostelgeschichte*, pp. 224–33; **Perrot**, 'Les décisions de l'assemblée'; **Richard**, 'Divine Purpose', pp. 189–92, 194–7; **Sandmel**, *Anti-Semitism*, pp. 89–90; **Schäfer**, 'Aposteldekret', pp. 556–7; **Schmithals**, *Apostelgeschichte*, pp. 138–41; *Paul and James*, pp. 97–102; G. **Schneider**, *Apostelgeschichte*, vol. 2, pp. 183–7; **Simon**, 'Apostolic Decree'; **Townsend**, 'Date', pp. 49–52; **Weiser**, 'Apostelkonzil'; **Wilson**, *Gentiles*, pp. 189–93, 224–5; *Law*, pp. 71–102.

In the first five verses of this chapter, Luke tells us twice that it is Jewish Christians who want the Gentile converts to be brought within the sphere of normative Jewish practice, specifically to be circumcised and to follow 'Moses', in other words to become converts, proselytes to Judaism. In v. 1, 'some . . . from Judaea t[each] the brothers, "If you are not circumcised in the custom of Moses, you are unable to be saved"'; and in v. 5 it is Christian Pharisees, 'some believers of those from the party of the Pharisees', who assert that 'it is necessary to circumcise them and to admonish them to keep the Law of Moses'. Thus Luke has twice put 'Moses' and 'circumcision' together here, just as in 6.14 he put Temple and Moses together in the charges against Stephen. We saw there that the charges were correct, that Lucan Christianity does see itself in opposition to those who follow 'Moses', and the same motif is present here at the beginning of ch. 15. For Luke 'Moses' means *halakah*, what he calls in both 6.14 and 15.1 (obliquely in the latter case) 'the customs (τὰ ἔθη) of Moses'. In a general sense, Luke considers the Torah to be the word of God, along with the Prophets. When Jewish Christians, however, interpret Torah to mean that Gentile Christians must be circumcised, then they have turned the word of God into 'the customs of Moses', a perversion of God's will.

Now, it is true that Luke makes it clear that those Jewish Christians who want to have the Gentile Christians circumcised are Judaeans, not from the Diaspora; but in Acts the *only* Jewish Christianity is in Judaea. (We shall see this again at 21.20.) In spite of a few Jewish conversions in Paul's mission, there is never really anything outside Judaea, in Acts, that one could call 'Jewish Christianity'. That portrait may conform, more or less, to reality; but in Acts 21.28 the Diaspora Jews who bring about Paul's arrest claim that he has been 'teaching . . . against the people and the Law and this place', i.e., the Temple. If Diaspora Jews, therefore, who are apparently not Christians, line up with Jewish Christians from Judaea on the issue of faithfulness to the Law of Moses, how deep a trench can there be between Jewish Christianity in Judaea and Jews elsewhere (as far as Acts is concerned)?

Peter's speech in favour of allowing Gentiles to become Christians without having to shoulder the 'impossible burden' (v. 10) of the Mosaic law and Paul's and Barnabas's report on the success of the gospel among Gentiles (v. 12) decide the matter, and James offers the solution, which the Jerusalem church then accepts (vv. 22–29). There is no need to repeat here the lengthy discussion of the Apostolic Decree from ch. 4, and we may therefore summarize. The Jerusalem church agrees that Gentiles do not have to be converted to Judaism – to circumcision and the customs of Moses – when they become Christians. These Gentile Christians do, however, have the obligation to obey those requirements that God has given for Gentiles: 'to keep away from things offered to idols and from blood and from things strangled and from sexual immorality' (v. 29) – regulations that are apparently an early version or forerunner of the later Noachic laws discussed in Judaism, i.e., the minimum divine requirements for Gentiles. Nothing is said in Luke's account of the Apostolic Council about table fellowship between Jewish Christians and Gentile Christians, or about any kind of compromise between pro-Jewish and pro-Gentile factions. As Luke sees it, Jewish Christians tried to force Gentiles who became Christians also to be converted to Judaism, but the church (naturally) recognized that the Mosaic Law was a burden and that Gentiles needed only to keep those laws that God had given for them. Luke's only interest, therefore, is what laws God had given for Gentiles. Circumcision and various other unnamed 'customs'? No! Only those laws designated for *Gentiles*, namely those in the Apostolic Decree. The church, therefore, agreed with God and not with Judaism about requirements for Gentile Christians. Luke seems to imply, furthermore, that there is really hardly any need for the decree, since Gentiles should know these laws already; for 'Moses, being read in the synagogues every Sabbath, has people proclaiming him from olden days city by city' (v. 21).

Jervell lays great weight on the scripture quotation in James's conclusion to the Apostolic Council, vv. 16–17.[25] According to him, Luke's quoting the prophecy about God's 'build[ing] up again the fallen tent of David' 'seems to mean that God will first rebuild and restore Israel, and then, as a result of this event, the Gentiles will seek the Lord'.[26] Now, it is true that the just quoted prophecy is given a purpose: 'So that the remainder of people may seek the Lord' (v. 17); and it is clear that Luke takes the divine rebuilding of David's fallen tent to be for the purpose of the Gentile mission. But there are two problems with the association that Jervell makes. For one thing, the prophecy of rebuilding, interpreted according to Jervell, would be entirely out of harmony with the theology of the rest of Luke-Acts regarding the Jew–Gentile issue, as we saw in ch. 3. If the rest of Luke-Acts supported the idea that Luke thought that the Gentiles could be converted only as a result of the restoration of Israel, then, of course, we should have to interpret this quotation in James's speech in that way. But the rest of Luke-Acts does not support that interpretation, and therefore we had best look for another meaning here. In the second place, however, Luke does not explain what he takes 'build up again the fallen tent of David' to mean. Jervell has only inferred that it means to 'rebuild and restore Israel'. This is, of course, what Jervell (and Lohfink, and their followers) wants the quotation to mean, but Luke does not say that. Is it not likely that he thinks that the existence of the Jerusalem church – of Jewish Christianity – fulfils the prophecy?

To a degree, Jervell and Lohfink would agree with that suggestion; but they go further to assert that the existence of Jewish Christianity is the divine 'gathering of Israel', and that those Gentiles who become Christians are then part of Israel; whereas, what Luke means appears rather to be that the Jerusalem church must first exist in order to facilitate the Gentile mission. The primary divine purpose, in other words, is, according to Luke, Gentile Christianity; and the Jerusalem church is a means to that end. Luke does not think that the Jerusalem church is the goal, and that Gentile Christians are merely an extension of it, that the church is made up of 'a people and an associate people'.[27]

Acts 16.1–4 · The circumcision of Timothy and the propagation of the Apostolic Decree

Important literature: **Loisy**, *Actes*, p. 618; **Overbeck**, *Apostelgeschichte*, pp. 248–52; G. **Schneider**, *Apostelgeschichte*, vol. 2, p. 201.

Since Timothy's mother was Jewish, Jews would regard Timothy as Jewish, also. Thus Luke seems to want to show that Paul, while being the leading missionary of the Gentile mission, is nevertheless scrupulous in his own observance of the 'customs of Moses', inasmuch as he himself is Jewish. Later (21.21), Luke will report that just this is charged against Paul by Jews in Jerusalem, that he 'teach[es]' Diaspora 'Jews . . . not to circumcise their children'. Since it then becomes a strong part of the Lucan Paul's defence that he has been an observant Jew (23.1; 26.5), Luke shows us already here in ch. 16 how baseless is the charge that Paul promotes non-observance among Jews. Luke therefore clearly thinks it proper for Jewish Christians to adhere to the customs of Moses; where he parts company with them is at their insistence that Gentile Christians should also adhere to those customs. Therefore he juxtaposes the two notes here; Paul circumcises Timothy, who can be considered a Jew, so that he will not be a non-observant Jew (16.3). Then, however, he spreads the news about the Apostolic Decree (v. 4). For Jews Moses, for Gentiles the decree.

Luke also shows us, however, that he considers the circumcision of Timothy a nuisance and much ado about nothing; for Paul circumcises Timothy 'because of the Jews who were in those parts'.

That Luke includes a story about Paul's circumcising Timothy, whereas Paul himself tells us (Gal. 2.3) that he did not circumcise Titus, who was a Gentile (and never mentions any circumcising of Timothy), is worth noting but has no further bearing on our discussion of Luke's theology of the Jews.

Acts 16.9   The vision of the Macedonian

Here we have an excellent opportunity to clear up some confusion that exists in the current scholarly discussion about Paul's mission, the Jews and the Gentiles. Jervell, Lohfink, and others – as we have had now perhaps too many occasions to note – think that the purpose of the spread of the gospel in Acts is the salvation of Israel, and that the salvation of Gentiles is a part of the salvation of Israel. Burchard, further, has emphasized that Paul tries to save Jews right through to the end of his career. This vision that Paul receives, however, and to which he responds, tells us exactly where *Luke* thinks the emphases lie; for the person appearing to Paul in his dream in Troy is 'a Macedonian man', and his appeal is, 'Come over to Macedonia and help us.' Can we think that this 'Macedonian man' is Jewish, or that his appeal to 'help us' has Macedonian Jews in mind? Utterly absurd! There are no Jews in the picture or on the horizon in this vision; and we therefore see clearly what Luke thinks the purpose of Paul's mission is: to 'help' Gentiles, in this case Macedonians. How is Paul to 'help' these Gentiles? By mending tents? Certainly not! The help that Paul is to provide is 'to evangelize them' (v. 10).

Acts 16.11–40   Paul at Philippi

Important literature: **Haenchen**, *Acts*, pp. 494–9; **Loisy**, *Actes*, p. 633; **Munck**, *Acts*, p. 161; **Overbeck**, *Apostelgeschichte*, p. 259; **Schwartz**, 'Accusation and Accusers'; **Stählin**, *Apostelgeschichte*, pp. 217–23; **Wilcox**, 'God-Fearers', pp. 110–11.

Arriving here, Paul seeks out the Jewish congregation (v. 13). Is his behaviour out of harmony with the preceding dream? It may appear so to the casual observer, but everything makes sense when we understand Luke's theology of Jews and Gentiles. The *purpose* of Paul's mission, for Luke, is to carry the gospel to the Gentiles. At the same time, however, an effort must be made to reach Jews, so that the theme of rejection can be carried forward; although, in this case, Jews virtually disappear from the picture. Thus it is interesting that, in Philippi, there are no Jewish conversions and no Jewish persecution, even though Paul goes first to the synagogue (v. 13). The converts are Lydia, one who 'worships God' and is therefore apparently a God-fearer or proselyte, 'and her house' (vv. 14–15). The first Macedonians helped by Paul's mission belong to the periphery and are originally, at least, Gentiles. (We remind ourselves that Luke does not seem to consider proselytes Jews, contrary to normal Jewish custom.)

There are apparently insufficient Jews in town to persecute Paul for his activity (v. 13 implies that the congregation is small and entirely female), and he is too far removed from Asia Minor for Jews in his former sphere of activity to play the role of 'outside agitators' (although Luke has not forgotten this stylistic device and will use it again), so the necessary persecution must arise from among the Gentiles (vv. 16–40). This episode, while interesting, has nothing to do with the Jews, except for one aspect. Those who 'conduct' Paul 'to the magistrates' attempt to prejudice the case against him by pointing out that he is a Jew who is trying to spread Jewish 'customs (ἔθη)' among the 'Roman' populace (vv. 20–21). While this approach succeeds in getting Paul thrown into jail temporarily, and while we certainly do see here that Luke can present an example of pagan antisemitism (and this is not the last), we have to be careful about leaping to the conclusion that Luke wishes in this way to criticize such antisemitism. For is the reader not expected to see that the charge is false, that Paul is certainly not, so soon after the Apostolic Council, trying to push Jewish 'customs' à la Moses on to Gentiles? Are the reader's sympathies not expected to go, in other words, with Paul, not with 'the Jews'? Luke expects us to think at this point, so it seems, that Paul's Gentile accusers have gone *slanderously* astray in associating Paul with 'Jewish customs'. After all, Luke has already told us in 14.4 that, in the case of such civil strife, apostles are one thing and Jews another. Luke is not seeking here to create in the hearts of his readers some sympathy for Diaspora Jews, who regularly experienced such antisemitism; rather, he wants his readers to agree that the charge of promoting Jewish propaganda is false. As Sandmel points out,[28] Paul was jailed as a Jew but released as a Roman (vv. 37–39); Luke saves Paul by distancing him from the Jews, not by appealing for justice for Jews.[29]

We may note in passing that there are praetors (or magistrates, στρατηγοί, v. 22) in charge in Philippi, who have lictors (ῥαβδοῦχοι,

v. 35) under their command, just as Luke thinks of there being Temple στρατηγοί or a στρατηγός in Jerusalem who has sergeants (ὑπηρέται) under his control. In this way Luke can lead his Gentile readers to think – and perhaps he thinks himself – that the Temple possessed the authority and the means to inflict corporal, even capital punishment, as if Jerusalem or the Temple state were a Roman provincial town.

Acts 17.1–9   Paul at Thessalonica

Important literature: **Bauernfeind**, *Apostelgeschichte*, p. 212; **Haenchen**, *Acts*, pp. 507–10; **Loisy**, *Actes*, p. 653; **Rese**, 'Aussagen über Jesu Tod', pp. 39–44; **Wilcox**, 'God-Fearers', pp. 111–12.

In Thessalonica, in Beroea, and in Corinth – that is, in all the remaining stops on Paul's itinerary except Athens, which is a special case, and Ephesus, Paul's last stop, where Luke returns to the themes of his first stop on Cyprus – the fixed pattern obtains: Paul goes first to a synagogue, he either converts or 'persuades' both Jews and Gentiles, and then Jewish persecution breaks out. So, here, Paul goes to the synagogue in Thessalonica (v. 1), where 'some of them were persuaded and became attached to Paul and Silas' (v. 4); but then Luke adds, 'also of the worshipping Greeks [i.e., proselytes or God-fearers] a great number and of the leading women not a few'. The statement does not make it perfectly clear to what degree these 'persuaded' persons are Jews or Gentiles. 'Some of them' obviously refers to those in the synagogue, and, since Luke then mentions Gentiles immediately, we do not know to what degree Luke intends us to think of 'them' as Jews or as a mixture of Jews and Gentiles. It is possible that the Gentiles and women mentioned after 'them' are epexegetical, defining 'them', in which case we should have the impression of a congregation predominantly Gentile (as in Philippi, apparently). It is further unclear whether the 'leading women' do their leading in the synagogue or in the city, but even having that issue clear would not tell us whether they were Jews or Gentiles. It appears, however, that Luke intends us to have the general impression of at least predominantly Gentile adherents of Paul, since immediately 'the Jews are jealous' (v. 5). It is the conversion or 'persuasion' of Gentiles that regularly arouses the ire of Diaspora Jews in Acts against Paul.

We should recall that, as we saw in 13.43, 'persuasion' is not necessarily the same thing as conversion.

The jealous Thessalonian Jews then engage in a skilful bit of rabble rousing. 'Getting together some wicked men of those who frequent the market' – we might say, 'of those who hang around downtown' – 'they created a crowd and caused an uproar in the city' (v. 5). Paul seems to have slipped away from the melée (like Jesus in Luke 4.30), but not his host Jason (a Greek name, but one that could also be that of a Diaspora Jew), who is 'dragged' by the mob to the authorities (v. 6), where charges are made against the Christians that are highly reminiscent of those made by the Jewish leadership in Jerusalem against Jesus before Pilate. The charges against Jesus in Luke 23.2 were that Jesus disturbed the peace ('our race'), that he 'forb[ade]' paying 'tribute to Caesar', and that he claimed to be a 'king'. Here Paul is accused of having 'rous[ed] up the inhabited world', of 'behav[ing] contrary to the decrees of Caesar', and of 'saying that Jesus is another king' (Acts 17.6–7). While the third charge could probably reasonably be connected with what Paul had been saying – although we are given no Thessalonican sermon of Paul's – inasmuch as he probably would have been explaining that Jesus was the Messiah, the only basis for the former two charges is that they appear in the indictment of Jesus in Luke 23.2, and in that order. 'The Jews' behave toward Paul in Thessalonica in the same way as did the priestly leadership in Jerusalem toward Jesus. There is no difference. The role of the priestly leadership in 'doing away' with Jesus is merely the prime example of generic Jewish behaviour, according to Luke, not a unique episode from which the rest of world-wide Jewry is to be kept separate. It is 'the Jews' who are guilty, in Luke-Acts, of persecuting Jesus and the church, so that what one group of Jews did to the Founder 'the Jews' do to Christians.

The authorities respond mildly to the charges, 'taking bail from Jason and the others' and 'let[ting] them go' (v. 9).

Acts 17.10–15   Paul at Beroea

Important literature: **Haenchen**, *Acts*, pp. 508–9; **Loisy**, *Actes*, p. 657; **Overbeck**, *Apostelgeschichte*, pp. 271–2.

Paul and Silas are spirited away from the Thessalonian difficulties and go immediately to the synagogue in Beroea (v. 10). Here, after some days of teaching the Christian interpretation of the Jewish scriptures (v. 11), they receive large numbers of converts, apparently both of Jews and of Gentiles (v. 12). That Luke writes that 'many . . . believed' instead of 'many were persuaded' makes it clear that he intends his readers to understand that these people became Christians.[30] Similarly to the summary about Thessalonica (cf.v. 4), Luke reports that 'of women . . . and of men' who were Gentiles there were 'not a few', only here he adds that these Gentiles were 'from the better classes' (εὐσχήμονες). Again, whether Luke intends us to understand that the converts were predominantly Gentile is not clear, but the Gentile converts are certainly the ones in whom Luke is most interested and of whom he is proudest.

Now, as in Lystra (Acts 14.19), Luke imports Jews from Paul's previous stop to cause the persecution. Unlike Lystra, however (and also unlike Philippi, where Luke had not placed enough Jews to make Jewish persecution believable), there are Jews in Beroea who could have instigated the persecution; but Luke nevertheless imports his agitators. By this device of having the Jewish persecutors come occasionally from the place where Paul had previously preached, Luke makes the pattern of Jewish persecution less boring and more believable. So 'the Jews from Thessalonica' came to Beroea to hinder Paul's mission 'when they heard . . . that the gospel was being proclaimed by Paul in Beroea, too' (v. 13). Paul, however, escapes to Athens (vv. 14–15).

Acts 17.16–21   Paul at Athens

Important literature: **Lampe**, 'Acts', p. 912; **Overbeck**, *Apostelgeschichte*, p. 275.

This section of Acts, containing Paul's second sermon, is of great importance for Luke's theology of the Gentiles but has little of interest for our present investigation. Paul goes to the synagogue in Athens, where he 'discuss[es] . . . with the Jews and with the worshippers' (v. 17), the latter here obviously meaning the group of the proselytes and God-fearers. No further contact with Jews in Athens is reported, however, and Paul removes immediately to the public market (v. 17). There are finally a few converts (v. 34), but the theme of Jewish hostility to the gospel and persecution of the missionaries does not develop. It would appear that Luke is so interested in painting an ideal scene of Paul in the intellectual centre of the classical world that he does not want to distract from the impression of the scene by introducing the contrasting colours of Jewish opposition. That theme, however, comes strongly to the fore in the following episode.

Acts 18.1–17   Paul at Corinth

Important literature: **Beck**, *Mature Christianity*, pp. 229–31; **Dupont**, 'La conclusion des Actes', pp. 385–6; **Haenchen**, *Acts*, pp. 539–40; **Lampe**, 'Acts', pp. 914–15; **Loisy**, *Actes*, pp. 691–703; **Overbeck**, *Apostelgeschichte*, pp. 289–95; **Wilson**, *Gentiles*, pp. 225–6.

Here Paul first encounters the prominent Corinthian Jewish Christians, whom Luke knows either from Paul's letters or from early Christian tradition or from both, Aquila and Priscilla (in Paul's letters always 'Prisca', cf. I Cor. 16.19), and he 'lodge[s]' with them (v. 2). Luke manages almost to give the impression that Aquila and Priscilla were Christians before Paul's arrival, but that they were is not confirmed by anything in Paul's Corinthian correspondence, and Luke does not quite say that they are Christians already. Perhaps he is influenced by the tale that he includes a few verses later, of Priscilla's and Aquila's correcting of Apollos's preaching, where Priscilla and Aquila are in Ephesus when Apollos arrives.

'But Paul was discussing in the synagogue every Sabbath, and he persuaded Jews and Greeks' (v. 4). The standard opening gambit, therefore, that Luke first employed in the episode of Jesus' Nazareth sermon and has utilized so frequently in his account of Paul's career is again used here; Paul preaches in the synagogue and receives an initial positive response. Again, it is not clear that the 'persuasion' of Jews and Gentiles in the congregation means that they were converted, especially because we later (vv. 7–8) have an account of definite conversions. The 'persuasion', rather, is Luke's way of presenting some kind of equivalent to the initial positive response of Jews in the Nazareth synagogue to Jesus' first sermon (Luke 4.22). Shortly, however, 'the Jews' (v. 5) 'oppos[e] . . . and blasphem[e]' (v. 6). Since opposing Paul would be, for Luke, blasphemy, we may think of a sort of hendiadys here; opposing Paul = blasphemy (exactly as in Acts 13.45). According to this account, it is apparently Paul's Christian preaching of Jesus as the Messiah (v. 5), not the salvation of Gentiles, that provokes the Jewish opposition. We must remember, however, that these two points were not clearly distinguished in Luke's thinking – that is, for Luke, the meaning of

Jesus' Messiahship was that God had brought salvation to the Gentiles.

This Jewish opposition to the gospel provides Luke with the second opportunity, now on the Greek mainland, to have Paul announce the turning of the gospel to the Gentiles. 'Your blood be upon your head!' he declares (v. 6); 'I am clean [i.e., innocent of blood guilt]. From now on I will go to the Gentiles.' The reference to blood and to Paul's innocence regarding it is a reference to the death of the Jews, presumably by violence (bloodshed). By opposing the gospel they merit their own destruction, of which Paul is innocent because he has sought to convert them. According to Luke, the early Christian missionaries, after the 'Jerusalem springtime', continued to make every effort to convert Jews everywhere to Christianity, but the Jews everywhere rejected their own salvation (cf. Acts 13.46), as was foretold in their own scriptures, which they were always reading but were unable to understand. For this reason they are condemned.

Of course, almost in the next breath, we have the account of the conversion of no less than the synagogue president (ἀρχισυνάγωγος, v. 8), so that this second announcement of turning to the Gentiles, which of course occurs in speech, does not mean that the narrative immediately conforms to the principle of Paul's declaration. There is more to the story; the Jews must continue becoming what they are. The announcements of turning to the Gentiles establish the timeless truth that Jewish rejection of the gospel leads to the salvation of the Gentiles and to God's rejection of the Jews; but the narrative must show how that occurs, and, as well, how Christianity is innocent of the Jewish destruction, inasmuch as the Christian missionaries spared no effort in the attempt to convert Jews. There were, as here in Corinth, some successes in that attempt.

After his confrontation with 'the Jews' in vv. 5–6, Paul removes from the synagogue to the house of one who dwells on the periphery, a God-fearer (or proselyte), 'a God-worshipper' (v. 7). From this base the aforementioned conversion of the synagogue president is effected, as well as that of 'many of the Corinthians' (v. 8), apparently but not certainly Gentiles.

The account of these conversions is followed by one of a divine audition; 'the Lord' tells Paul that he has 'a numerous people . . . in' Corinth (v. 10). It would seem to be no accident that this language is employed shortly after the announcement of turning to the Gentiles, for here the term 'people' is clearly used to mean the Christians, the church, whereas Luke earlier showed that he knew very well that the word was a quasi-technical term for the *Jewish* people (cf. Luke 23.13).[31] In Corinth, therefore, several things follow in logical order: an announcement of turning to the Gentiles, numerous Gentile conversions, and the use of the term 'people' to mean not the Jews, but the church. The Jews are no longer the people of God, the (Gentile) church is. The Jews are well on their way to becoming what they are.

'The Jews' then bring Paul before the proconsul Gallio (v. 12), 'saying' (v. 13) that 'he is persuading people to worship God against the law'. What Luke apparently expects his readers to understand by this formulation is that 'the Jews' were offended by Paul's teaching, which they took to be contrary to their Torah, but that they then brought this religious quarrel before the state and translated Torah into νόμος, law, in order *deliberately ambiguously* to try to get Gallio to think that Paul was doing something against the *law*, i.e., against the Roman law.[32] Gallio, of course, is as smart as Luke's readers and sees through this ruse, telling the Jews to take care of their own religious matters (v. 15). Verse 17 then gives a brief notice about which no consensus has been reached:[33] 'All' – are they Jews or Gentiles? – 'beat Sosthenes, the synagogue president', before the tribunal. Is Sosthenes another name for Crispus (v. 8), or is he Crispus's successor? Why would either the Jews or the Gentiles beat him because of the brief hearing before Gallio? The final note of Luke's account, however, is plain enough: 'None of these things concerned Gallio.' Roman proconsuls cannot be bothered if a mob beats a synagogue president in front of the Roman judicial seat, and neither can Christians. The Jews reject the gospel and persecute the messengers of God; they get what they deserve.

Acts 18.18–21   Paul at Ephesus, scene 1

Important literature: **Overbeck**, *Apostelgeschichte*, p. 296; **Roloff**, *Apostelgeschichte*, p. 275.

This is the last stop on Paul's itinerary before his arrest in Jerusalem, and, like his first stop in ch. 13, on Cyprus, it is divided into two parts.[34] It would appear that Luke intends, by this stylistic device, to emphasize the beginning and the end of Paul's career. In this brief account, we have only the first part of the standard pattern, for Paul goes to the synagogue, 'discusses with the Jews' (v. 21), is asked by them to stay (v. 20 – that is, he receives a positive response from them), but leaves (vv. 21–22). This is very much like the account in Acts 13.5, where Paul, 'in Salamis, announced the gospel in the synagogues of the Jews' and then left town (v. 6); and his return to Ephesus, to which we are coming presently, is like the continuation of his Cypriot ministry, in Paphos, for in both cases Paul bests evil Jewish magicians. It would appear that Luke thought that, by spreading out Paul's ministry into two stages on the first and last of his missionary attempts, he was heightening the importance of these two episodes. In any case, Paul's activity in Ephesus is interrupted by his departure, and into the interstice is placed Apollos.

Acts 18.24–28   Apollos

This episode contains several puzzles, not the least of which is how someone who 'had been taught the way of the Lord', Luke's term for Christianity, could 'kno[w] only the baptism of John' (v. 25). The only parts of the sketch that are of interest to our theme, however, are the facts that Apollos is a Hellenistic Jew (v. 24) and that, after his Ephesian 'correction', he goes to Achaia and 'thoroughly confute[s] the Jews' (v. 28). If we ignore for a moment the identity of this Hellenistic Jewish missionary of the gospel who visits both Corinth (cf. 19.1) and Ephesus (in reverse of Paul's order) and refutes 'the Jews', then we see that his function in Acts is to conclude the portrait of Paul's Corinthian ministry with what is, for Luke, a brighter tone, proving that 'the Jews' are wrong. Another way to describe Apollos's function is to say that he is the *Doppelgänger* of Paul, who completes Paul's job in Achaia, proving that the Jews do not understand their own scriptures, 'pointing out by the scriptures that Jesus is the Christ' (v. 28; cf. Acts 17.2–3).

Modern authors attempting to understand this episode have routinely occupied themselves with trying to probe behind the Lucan narrative to understand something of the early church, and such attempts are certainly worth-while. Even when the issue of Luke's purpose has been raised, however,[35] other aspects of the episode than Apollos's refuting the Jews in Achaia have been emphasized. This is entirely understandable, for, by the end of Acts 18, there is hardly anything novel in the Lucan note that a Christian missionary shows the Jews the truth of Christianity from their own scriptures. Precisely. It is the ordinariness of the theme that we need to emphasize here. By this point in Acts the reader knows without any doubt how inflexible and how wrong the Jewish view is, how hopeless the situation of the Jews is, and that there is no need any longer to try to convert them. Apollos, therefore, behaves in Achaia as did Paul in Damascus. He does not attempt to convert Jews, he just shows them the error of their ways. In Ephesus, after Paul has returned to Asia Minor from the Greek mainland, the mission to the Jews is concluded. Apollos's behaviour in Achaia signals that the end is at hand.

Acts 19.1–41   Paul at Ephesus, scene 2

Important literature: **Haenchen**, *Acts*, pp. 574–5; **Lampe**, 'Acts', p. 917; **Overbeck**, *Apostelgeschichte*, pp. 313–16, 325–8; **Wikenhauser**, *Apostelgeschichte*, p. 223.

Only Paul, of course, can make the final effort. After making the Ephesian church orthodox in vv. 1–8, Paul returns to the synagogue. Luke does not actually write that Paul *returns* to the Ephesian synagogue, and, as a matter of fact, if we had not already read 18.19, we would think that 19.8 described his first visit there. The similarity of language that Luke uses, however, to describe Paul's two visits to the Ephesian synagogue shows that he is, in the second instance, picking up the thread of the first; or, to use the language of the source critics, we see in 18.19 and in 19.8 the tell-tale overlapping cloth of a seam. Luke had written in 18.19, 'He entered the synagogue and discussed with the Jews'; and he now writes in 19.8, 'He entered the synagogue and spoke out boldly for three months, discussing . . .' Going forward from the seam, Luke adds that Paul was 'persuading about the Kingdom of God'. Luke's language here is very carefully chosen. The last attempt to convert Jews must be a vigorous one, and so Luke makes sure that his readers know that Paul 'spoke out boldly', as he had done previously in various Diaspora synagogues (cf., e.g., 13.46). This bold speaking, however, does not lead to any conversions. No one believes and no one is baptized; we are told only that Paul 'was persuading'. While 'persuade' can at times in Acts refer to conversion, as in 26.28, it is also Luke's term of choice when he wants to indicate a positive response from Jews that falls short of conversion, as in 13.43. When he wants to make it clear that someone becomes a Christian, his language is 'believe' and 'baptize', as in 2.41 and 13.48; thus the choice of 'persuade' in 19.8 is deliberately ambiguous. Finally, we are not told that anyone was persuaded, only that Paul 'was persuading'. No numbers are given, nor is it said that there were additions to the church.

The only response that Luke reports to Paul's 'persuading' is that of hostile opposition. 'Some were hardened and disbelieved' (v. 9; we shall encounter the antithesis of 'persuasion' and 'disbelief' again), and they 'defamed the way before the multitude'. This falls short of persecution, of course, but it succeeds in getting Paul out of the synagogue; he finds another hall and 'bound[s] off the disciples'.[36] *Finis* to the mission to the Jews; the 'dividing wall', as Eph. 2.14 calls it, probably about the time that Acts was written, has been erected. Paul has 'bounded off the disciples' from Judaism.

Luke's concluding summary (v. 10) returns to the theme of the 'speaking out boldly' of v. 8, for he now affirms that 'everyone dwelling in [the Roman province of] Asia heard the gospel, both Jews and Greeks'. Paul's final missionary effort is one of saturation; no conversions are mentioned.

In vv. 11–20 Luke shows us once again that the 'power of the gospel' (v. 20) is not limited to conversions but is also to be seen in miracles and wonders, and with this stroke he returns us again to the theme of Paul's first missionary stop, on Cyprus, where the second part of the mission to Cyprus, at Paphos, was similarly characterized (cf. Acts 13.11). Here, as there, Paul is opposed by Jewish magicians; and this second time they are a group, not merely one, as before. Furthermore, they are a group of seven, a quintessentially Jewish number, and they are even said to be the sons of a high priest (v. 14)! Luke has therefore given us this further indication of solidarity between Diaspora Jews and the Jerusalem priestly leadership; and he strengthens in this way the impression of uniform Jewish hostility to Christianity.

Whereas at Paphos the power of the gospel was made manifest in the blinding of the opposing Jewish magician (13.11), here the seven Jewish magicians attempt to use 'the name of the Lord Jesus' in an exorcism (v. 13), and this stupid and presumptuous act backfires on them. The evil spirit that they are attempting to exorcize replies to them, 'Jesus I am acquainted with, and Paul I know; but who are you?' (v. 15); and then the possessed gives them a thorough thrashing, so that they must flee 'naked and wounded' (v. 16). In this way, therefore, are the evil Jewish opponents of Christianity held up to ridicule.

With these two stories of the power of the gospel (in Paul's hands) over Jewish magicians, Luke has formed the framework of Paul's career. As it began, so it ends, with spiritual warfare between the evil magic of Judaism and the power of the gospel. 'But, surely,' someone suggests, 'Luke doesn't intend to stain all of Judaism with this dark colour'; to which I can only reply, 'Oh, doesn't he?' Why else are the magicians here said to be seven and the sons of a high priest? Why else are the only magicians with whom Paul does battle said to be Jewish? Why else do these episodes form the framework of Paul's career? Is it reasonable to think that, after Luke has gone to so much effort to emphasize these two events and the Jewishness of the magicians, he wants us *not* to think that the kind of behaviour exhibited in the two incidents is endemic to Judaism? The burden of proof must lie with the doubter. Produce a better explanation for these two scenes dealing with magicians; but don't try to ignore that the magicians in both cases are Jews or that Paul's career begins and ends with these episodes.

Luke now presents a story that shows that the spread of the gospel is cutting into Gentile religion (vv. 21–40). Devotees of Artemis are upset by the success of the gospel (vv. 24–27) and create a civil disturbance. 'The Jews', then, 'put forward' one 'Alexander' (v. 33), although why the Jews do this is not clear. This Alexander then attempts 'to make a defence', although, again, whether he is attempting to defend Paul or the Jews is less than certain. When the crowd, in any case, observes that Alexander 'is a Jew' (v. 34), it refuses to let him speak (v. 34). Finally, a civic official calms the crowd (v. 35), and they all go home (v. 40). What all this means for Luke's view of the Jews is much less than certain, and different commentators suggest different possibilities. Perhaps we have here a story of what Cadbury calls 'mob Jew-baiting', which, he suggests, Luke may 'tell . . . with a little malicious glee'.[37] Other than that possibility, there seems to be no connection between this scene and Luke's portrait of the Jews.

Acts 20.1–6   Paul revisits the Greek mainland

Important literature: **Loisy**, *Actes*, p. 758; **Radl**, *Paulus und Jesus*, pp. 133–58; **Schille**, *Apostelgeschichte*, p. 395.

As before, when his ministry in the interior of Asia Minor was completed, Paul revisited the earlier sites of his missionary activity, so now he returns to Macedonia and Greece (vv. 1–2). When that pattern was followed formerly (14.21–28), as we noted, the standard Jewish opposition failed to develop. By the time that Paul leaves Ephesus, however, Luke seems to have noted the oddity that we noted regarding 14.21–28, and so he tosses off as an aside that 'there were designs on him (or: plots against him) by the Jews' (v. 3) during his time revisiting the Greek mainland. Nothing more is said than that, but it is enough to remind us of the general Jewish hostility to Paul – and to alert us to the dark events upcoming.

Acts 20.18b–35   Paul's sermon at Miletus

Important literature: **Loisy**, *Actes*, p. 771; **Overbeck**, *Apostelgeschichte*, p. 342; **Radl**, *Paulus und Jesus*, pp. 133–58.

This third speech of Paul's is important for a general understanding of Acts and for an understanding of Jesus–Paul parallels, but it has little to do with our theme. In v. 19, however, Paul reminds his Ephesian audience of his ministry among them, which was 'with all humility and tears and trials that happened to me by the schemes (or: plots) of the Jews'. He does not elaborate, but the note of Jewish 'plots' that was struck in v. 3 is in this way kept alive.

Acts 21.10–14   Agabus's prophecy and Paul's response

Important literature: **Haenchen**, *Acts*, p. 605; **Loisy**, *Actes*, pp. 786–7; **Overbeck**, *Apostelgeschichte*, pp. 361–2; **Radl**, *Paulus und Jesus*, pp. 133–58; **Roloff**, *Apostelgeschichte*, p. 310.

Now on his final trip to Jerusalem, Paul is greeted in Caesarea by a prophet from Jerusalem, one Agabus, who adds considerably more detail and colour to the earlier vague references to Jewish plots. This prophet takes off Paul's belt and ties Paul up and then reports, 'Thus says the Holy Spirit: the man whose belt this is the Jews will likewise bind in Jerusalem; and they will deliver him into the hands of Gentiles' (v. 11). This is thus the announcement of the Pauline passion, comparable to the three announcements of Jesus' passion in the Gospel. (It seems most like the Lucan form of the third, Luke 18.31–32.) Paul, even, appears to subscribe to this understanding, for he responds to the alarm of his friends by saying (v. 13), 'I am ready not only to be bound but also to die for the name of the Lord Jesus.' Fateful words, indeed. Luke has therefore set the stage for the end of Acts to be parallel to that of the Gospel.

Acts 21.17–26   Paul's arrival in Jerusalem

Important literature: **Haenchen**, *Acts*, pp. 608–9; **Holtzmann**, *Apostelge-schichte*, p. 131; **Jervell**, *People of God*, pp. 44–7, 193–9; **Lampe**, 'Acts', pp. 908, 920; **Loisy**, *Actes*, p. 799; **Sanders**, 'Salvation of the Jews', pp. 109–12; **Schmithals**, *Paul and James*, pp. 87–92.

Arriving at Christian headquarters in Jerusalem, Paul is told by James and 'the Elders' (v. 18) that he can see 'how many myriads of believers there are among the Jews, and [that] all are zealots for the law' (v. 20). Here we have again, as in Acts 15, Luke's characterization of Jewish Christianity and of the conflict produced by Paul's success 'among the Gentiles' (v. 19). The problem is that, Paul's circumcision of Timothy notwithstanding (Acts 16.3), the Jewish Christians 'have been instructed concerning [Paul] that [he] teach[es] apostasy from Moses to all the Jews among the Gentiles, saying for them not to circumcise their children nor to walk in the customs' (v. 21). We need to comment on several aspects of this speech to Paul in order.

First of all, the reference to 'myriads' of Jewish Christians refers to those Jews in Jerusalem and Judaea converted to Christianity during the 'Jerusalem springtime'. We see this plainly when James and the elders distinguish these Jewish Christians from Diaspora Jews in reporting what the 'myriads' have heard about Paul's teaching to Diaspora Jews.[38] It distorts the text to read it as referring to a continuing successful Jewish mission.[39] The primary Jewish mission, that in Jerusalem, was the most successful. Paul's mission had only a little success among the Jews, and Luke does not want us to think of continuing Jewish conversions to Christianity in Jerusalem after Acts 7.

The charge that the Jewish Christians have brought against Paul, that he 't[aught] apostasy . . . to all the Jews in the Diaspora', may, in fact, accurately describe the behaviour of the real Paul (cf. Gal. 2.11–14). Luke, however, sees the matter otherwise; for him, it is against just such charges that Paul must be defended. As the analysis of the Tübingen school originally pointed out, Luke is likely to be representing here the conflict of his own day between Jewish Christianity and Gentile Christianity – that is, it is Jewish Christians who make the charge against Gentile Christianity that it is 'apostate'. Such a charge may or may not have been made in terms of Paul, but in the light of Galatians 2 there seems to be no reason why it could not have been. It is not harmony between the two factions that Luke wants to produce, however, but rather the vindication of Gentile Christianity. At this point he wants to show that the original Jewish missionaries to Gentiles (Paul) were themselves kosher Jews. Gentile Christianity did not come into existence because of some renegade bunch of Jews; rather, the early Jewish Christians were 'daily . . . in the Temple' (Acts 2.46), and the one of them primarily responsible for the existence of Gentile Christianity comes from 'the very best party' in Judaism (26.5). He certainly has not been 'teach[ing] apostasy'.

Finally, inasmuch as Luke has prepared for this scene by recounting how Paul circumcised Timothy (Acts 16.3), he wants us to see how baseless and, indeed, devious the charge of the Jewish Christians is. There is no basis for their charge, but they are involved in a 'scheme' to get rid of Paul. Jewish Christians, therefore, are here little to be distinguished from non-Christian Jews. Both are hostile to Gentile Christianity, to what is for Luke proper Christianity, and both bring absurd charges against Paul.

The elders then advise Paul in the following way (vv. 23–24): he is to join some other men in the carrying out of a vow that they have made and in this way purify himself, so that 'all will know that there is nothing to what they have been instructed about you, but that you are proper yourself in keeping the Law'. Both the elders (the leaders of the Jerusalem church) and Paul, of course, are to be distinguished from the entity of Jewish Christianity, as the episode makes clear, since the elders do not associate themselves with those who are 'zealots for the Law' (v. 20). For Luke, furthermore, Paul and the Jerusalem elders belong to a bygone day, whereas Jewish Christianity is still about accusing Gentile Christianity of being improper. Because Luke wants to take this opportunity to set the record entirely straight about how the Torah is to be kept in the church, he has the elders remind Paul of the Apostolic Decree (v. 25).

This strikes many commentators as odd, for Gentile obedience to the Torah is not under discussion, and Paul certainly knows what was in the Apostolic Decree. The reminder is for the readers of Acts, however, and not for Paul. Inasmuch as Paul's fidelity even to ritual Torah is now being underscored, Luke does not want any readers to become confused and to get the idea that perhaps Christians should, after all, follow the 'customs of Moses'; and so he reminds them of which laws are applicable to Gentiles, especially to Gentile Christians. And then Paul performs the ritual acts (v. 26).

Acts 21.27–40   Paul's arrest

Important literature: **Lampe**, 'Acts', p. 920; **Neyrey**, *Passion*, pp. 98–107; **Radl**, *Paulus und Jesus*, pp. 211–12; **Stählin**, *Apostelgeschichte*, pp. 279–81.

The period of Paul's purification over, he is fingered by 'the Jews from [the Roman province of] Asia', where Ephesus was (v. 27), as being 'the person who teaches everyone everywhere against the people and the Law and this place; and furthermore he even brought a Greek into the Temple and profaned this holy place' (v. 28). Does Luke mean us to understand that it is Jewish Christians who thus accuse Paul? We have just seen how it is Jewish Christians who are upset because they have been 'instructed' that Paul was teaching 'apostasy'. This seems not to be Luke's point, however; these Jews who accuse Paul are more likely the ones who have been 'instructing' Jewish Christians amiss.

We should not miss the point that these Jews come from Asia, the last area of Paul's missionary activity, of which area Luke had noted pointedly, 'Everyone dwelling in Asia heard the gospel, Jews and also Greeks' (19.10). These Jews from Asia who accuse Paul, therefore, are guilty of deliberately presenting false witness, just as false witnesses earlier accused Stephen. Whereas the accusation of those false witnesses against Stephen, however, seemed in fact to be justified, the same charges brought by the Jews from Asia against Paul are patently false, for nothing that the Lucan Paul has done or said lends any credence to the charges of teaching against the Jewish people or against the Torah or against the Temple. Luke has in fact shown the absurdity of these charges before they are made. Only in the matter of taking a Gentile into the Temple, therefore, does he feel called upon to offer an explanation: the Asian Jews had seen an Ephesian with Paul, 'whom they supposed that Paul took into the Temple' (v. 29). Naturally, the ritually pure Paul did no such thing. The Asian Jews are on the one hand lying, on the other mistaken.

That Luke calls Paul's accusers 'the Jews' and at the same time labels them as being Diaspora Jews is an interesting twist (οἱ ἀπὸ τῆς Ἀσίας Ἰουδαῖοι, v. 27). That they are designated as being Diaspora Jews, of course, falls into line with Luke's particular polemic against

Jews in the Diaspora – where Luke lives and where the real conflict between Christianity and Judaism is taking place. It was Diaspora Jews who got Stephen arrested (Acts 6.9), and it is Diaspora Jews here who get Paul arrested. Luke clearly portrays *Diaspora Jews* as the opponents of the church, just as he portrayed Jerusalem Jews as the murderers of Jesus (Acts 13.27). Surely the reason for this is ready to hand. Jesus, Jerusalem and the Jerusalem priesthood all lie in the past for Luke; when he writes, they are gone. But he does know Jews in the Diaspora, and them he regards as the enemies of the church; thus he writes this enmity back into stories of Jewish persecution of the early church. This perceived enmity of Diaspora Jews is why Luke can also call them here 'the Jews', as if all the Jews in Asia were in Jerusalem to accuse Paul. Of course, Luke does not really intend to give the impression that all the hundreds or perhaps thousands of Jews in the Roman province of Asia were in Jerusalem to accuse Paul; he only wants to tar Paul's accusers with the pitch of his standard *nomen opprobriosum*; Paul's accusers are, in addition to being Diaspora Jews, *the* Jews.

As was also the case with Stephen, however, the other Jews readily respond to the instigation of the Diaspora Jews, so that 'the *whole city* was moved and . . . took [Paul] out of the Temple' (v. 30). All Jerusalem is now against Paul, as it had earlier been against Jesus, and tries 'to kill' Paul (v. 31). Does Luke really mean 'all Jerusalem'? He has heard our question and immediately confirms the phrase by having it reported to the Tribune that 'the whole of Jerusalem is in confusion' (v. 31). As 'the Jews' and 'Jerusalem' did away with Jesus, so they are going to try to do away with Paul; and 'the multitude of the people crie[s] out, "Take him away!"' (v. 36), as in the Gospel 'the chief priests and the rulers and the people . . . cried out as one multitude saying, "Take him away!"' (Luke 23.13, 18). As the narrative of Luke-Acts progresses, 'the Jews' become more and more what the speeches have said from the first they are.

Acts 22.1–21   Paul's fourth speech

Important literature: **Haenchen**, *Acts*, p. 628; *Apostelgeschichte*, pp. 601–4; **Löning**, *Saulustradition*, pp. 173–6; **Loisy**, *Actes*, p. 820; **Neyrey**, *Passion*, pp. 98–107; **Overbeck**, *Apostelgeschichte*, p. 394; **Roloff**, *Apostelgeschichte*, p. 324; **Stählin**, *Apostelgeschichte*, pp. 284–6; **Stolle**, *Zeuge*, pp. 105–15; **Walaskay**, *We Came to Rome*, pp. 53–4; **Wendt**, *Apostelgeschichte*, p. 309; **Wikenhauser**, *Apostelgeschichte*, p. 246.

Now begins the series of Paul's defence speeches. The theme that the Lucan Paul most hammers home in these speeches is his true and devout Jewishness, and on that note he begins. He is a 'Jew', who was 'trained at the feet of Gamaliel according to the strictness of the traditional Law, a zealot for God', just like all the other Jews in his audience (v. 3). Gamaliel seems to be the most famous Pharisee of whom Luke knows, and we have not forgotten that it was he who assisted the apostles earlier in Acts (Paul, of course, in his surviving letters, never mentions Gamaliel). Paul's credentials as a Torah-observant Jew are therefore unimpeachable. Furthermore (point two), Paul 'persecuted Christianity (literally: this way) unto death, binding and delivering to jail both men and women' (v. 4); and he was doing these things under the auspices of the 'high priest . . . and . . . the presbyterium' (v. 5). Thus he informs his audience not only that he was a Torah-observant Jew, but that his credentials as a Christian-hater are also unimpeachable, since he was active in persecuting the church 'unto death'. While this phrase appears to coincide with Paul's own statement in Gal. 1.13 that he 'sought to destroy' the church, we need to remember that there is a certain over-statement in the way Acts portrays Paul's earlier persecution of Christianity, since, in Acts 9, he is said to be going to Damascus with arrest warrants for Christians. That the Jerusalem Temple, however, possessed the authority under Roman rule to reach as far as Syria in arresting and executing heretics is preposterous,[40] but that is the picture that Acts paints for us in the present passage and in Acts 9. To return to Paul's defence as it stands here, however, we see that Luke is emphasizing to his readers Paul's Torah fidelity and his earlier hatred of Christianity. His conversion, then, which Luke recounts next, is all the more dramatic by contrast.

Luke is really making two points here at once. The first is that Paul is innocent of the charges against him, but the second is not unimportant; and that is that Christianity is in direct continuity with the former Judaism. This second theme comes more to the fore when Paul tells his audience, and reminds Luke's readers, of the role of Ananias in his conversion, for he emphasizes here that Ananias was 'a devout man according to the Law, attested to by all the Jews dwelling' in Damascus (v. 12). Christianity is not a perversion of Judaism but is rather the 'way' followed by the most deeply religious Jews. This does not mean, however, 'walking in the customs of Moses', terms which are notable by their absence here.

After his account of his conversion, Paul describes an event of which we have not heard before. 'While [he] was praying in the Temple' (v. 17), he fell 'into ecstasy' and had a conversation with 'him', apparently with Jesus (cf. v. 16), at the end of which ecstasy Jesus told him, 'Go, for I will send you far off to the Gentiles' (v. 21). Again, therefore, we have both the theme of continuity and that of blamelessness at once. Paul's command to be the missionary to the *Gentiles* is above reproach, since it came to him while he was praying in the Temple; and, since it was given in the *Temple* in the form of a divine vision, it arose within the core of Judaism, not on the fringe.

Up to this point Paul's Jewish audience has listened politely (cf. v. 2: 'They kept their peace'); but the theme of the gospel to the Gentiles arouses, as regularly, the anticipated hostility, and the crowd clamours, 'Take him away from the earth, for it is not fitting for him to live' (v. 22). Jerusalem and the Jews will never change; they refuse to hear and understand.

Acts 22.30–23.10   Paul before Jewish rulers

Important literature: **Haenchen**, *Acts*, pp. 639–42; **Holtzmann**, *Apostelgeschichte*, pp. 137–8; **Loisy**, *Actes*, pp. 829–30; **Neyrey**, *Passion*, pp. 98–107; **Overbeck**, *Apostelgeschichte*, pp. 398–9; **Radl**, *Paulus und Jesus*, pp. 212–13; **Walaskay**, *We Came to Rome*, pp. 53–4.

Now Paul, like Jesus and Stephen before him, must appear before the Jewish priestly rulers for a formal hearing. This hearing is arranged by the tribune, who is trying to get to the bottom of things (22.30). We must note that Luke writes that the tribune wants to find out 'what is charged by the Jews', again the general and inclusive term. When Paul in the council opens by affirming again his scrupulous Torah observance (23.1), the high priest 'order[s] those standing by him to strike him on the mouth' (v. 2), to which Paul replies, 'God is going to strike you, whitewashed wall. Do you sit judging me according to the Law, and then transgress and command me to be struck?' Luke is playing to the galleries here, and we can hear the cheers going up from Gentile Christians everywhere. Bravo for Paul! He has given the Jews just what they deserve.

Now, however, Luke must backtrack. He has been pointing out so emphatically how pious a Jew Paul is, and then he has us cheering when Paul insults the high priest. What of Paul's reputation as pious Jew? Luke escapes this pickle by having Paul profess ignorance of the identity of the person whom he has just insulted. Thus the discussions in many commentaries about whether Paul could conceivably have been ignorant of the high priest's identity quite miss the point, for the reason that Paul is ignorant of the high priest's identity is that Luke is in this way able to have Paul give the high priest his 'come-uppance' and still remain a devout Jew. And so, when it is pointed out to Paul that it is the high priest whom he has just called a 'whitewashed wall', Paul replies in sombre piety, 'I did not know, brothers, that he is the high priest; for it is written, "You shall not speak evil of a ruler of the people."'

Before the hearing can actually begin, Paul cleverly notices that some of the Jewish officials present are Sadducees and some Pharisees (v. 6). This is the first time that we have heard of Pharisees since the Christian Pharisees in Acts 15.5 pressed to have Gentile Christians circumcised and brought under 'Moses', and it is the first that we have seen of friendly, non-Christian Pharisees since Gamaliel rescued the apostles in ch. 5. Paul, then, avoids having to endure the hearing by 'exclaim[ing] in the Sanhedrin, "Brother men, I am a Pharisee, son of Pharisees; concerning the hope and the resurrection of the dead I am being judged"' (v. 6). This ploy of Paul's is in the nature of a trick that he plays on the Sanhedrin, as we saw in ch. 4; Paul makes no serious attempt to have his Pharisaism or his beliefs discussed. Saying in the Sanhedrin that he is a Pharisee is therefore like telling his Philippian jailers that he is a Roman (Acts 16.37); it is just a way of getting out of trouble. On cue, the Pharisees create an uproar (v. 7), which becomes sufficiently boisterous for the tribune to have to break up the meeting in order to secure Paul's safety (v. 10; the tribune does nothing to stop the uproar, leaving the troublesome Jews, apparently, to bloody one another's noses until they tire of the fight). In the course of the melée, however, the Pharisees take it on themselves to acquit Paul, sounding strangely like Pilate acquitting Jesus: 'We find nothing bad in this person' (v. 9), to which we may compare Luke 23.4, where Pilate says, 'I find no cause [for punishment] in this person.' That the Pharisees pronounce this acquittal and not the procurator, or at least the tribune, is worth noting. Paul will later be more or less acquitted by Herod and the procurator, but that judgment comes after Paul's appeal to Rome, at which time there is nothing that the procurator can do (Acts 26.30–32). Luke seems to be trying to tell us that not only the Roman authorities, but also the 'nearly correct' Jews have no quarrel with Christianity. Thus the friendly Pharisees at Paul's Sanhedrin hearing fall into the same pattern as the friendly Pharisee Gamaliel at Peter's Sanhedrin hearing in Acts 5 (where is Gamaliel here, by the way?) and try to prevent the persecution of Christianity. In this way Luke continues to show that Christianity is the product of the best of Jewish traditions, since the best party in Judaism (cf. Acts 26.5) has no quarrel with the Christians.

Except for Paul's later reference to his Pharisaism, this show of partisanship here in ch. 23 is the last reference to Pharisees in Acts, and we may therefore pause to remind ourselves how clear and unambiguous the role of the Pharisees in Acts is (aside from Paul, who is a special case). When Pharisees are not Christians, they are those Jews most like Christians, and they favour Christianity. Like Christians, they believe in the resurrection, and they help to protect the early church from the designs of the priestly leadership. Luke thus presents us with a kind of gradation among the descendants of the older Judaism, of 'biblical' Israel. The true and proper descendants are the Christians; the perverse descendants, who oppose and reject the plans of God, are 'the Jews'; and somewhere in between are the Pharisees, who function to show how Christianity is not something distinct from 'biblical' Israel. When Christian Pharisees appear in Acts, however, they represent Jewish Christians, who want to bring Gentile Christianity under the sway of 'Moses', i.e., *halakah*. While Luke does not criticize these Christian Pharisees in Acts as roundly as he does their counterparts in the Gospel, it is plain that he rejects their position; and we cannot forget that, in Luke 12.1, he has Jesus warn the church against their 'leaven' – that is, against their 'hypocrisy'.

Acts 23.12–35   The Jewish plot on Paul's life and his transfer to Caesarea

Important literature: **Haenchen**, *Acts*, p. 650; **Loisy**, *Actes*, pp. 837–8; **Schille**, *Apostelgeschichte*, p. 428; **Schmithals**, *Apostelgeschichte*, p. 209.

Now 'the Jews' plot to ambush and kill Paul. While in the course of the ensuing narrative we learn that the 'hit men' are not *all* the Jews but only 'more than forty' (vv. 13, 21), Luke nevertheless shows in two ways that he is serious in claiming that 'the Jews' sought to kill Paul. In the first place, that is the way the narrative begins: 'The Jews' agreed to 'mak[e] themselves anathema, saying that they would neither eat nor drink until they should kill Paul' (v. 12). Then, when Luke has given the limited number, he has the conspirators present their plan to 'the chief priests and the elders' and elicit the cooperation of this official body (vv. 14–15). The fact that those who are actually to do the ambushing are only 'more than forty' does not prevent the guilt's falling on 'the Jews'.

The plot is unsuccessful. We have paused earlier to be amused (in ch. 3) at the way Luke uses his famous 'narrative skill' to rescue Paul, but that does not need to be discussed again here, being, as it is, irrelevant to the issue at hand. The upshot of the narrative is that the tribune rescues Paul and gets him away from Jerusalem to Caesarea (v. 23), where Paul is placed under the custody of the procurator, Felix. In his letter of transmittal accompanying Paul, the tribune explains that Paul is in custody because 'the Jews [had] apprehended [him] and [were] about to d[o] away with' him (v. 27). The tribune does not indicate that a particular group among the Jews, like 'more than forty', was responsible, even when he mentions the plot (v. 30). As far as the tribune, Felix, Luke and (Luke hopes) his readers are concerned, 'the Jews' tried to 'do away with' Paul.

Acts 24.1–23   Paul's trial before Felix

Important literature: **Loisy**, *Actes*, pp. 858–9; **Neyrey**, *Passion*, pp. 98–107; **Radl**, *Paulus und Jesus*, pp. 213–17; **Stählin**, *Apostelgeschichte*, p. 296; **Stolle**, *Zeuge*, pp. 115–19; **Walaskay**, *We Came to Rome*, pp. 54–5.

Just as Jesus was questioned in the Sanhedrin and then accused before the procurator by the Jewish leaders, so these same things must happen to Paul, and in the same order. The manner in which Paul is transferred from the Sanhedrin to the procuratorial judgment seat is rather different, but nevertheless, now that the Sanhedrin hearing is over, Paul is accused before the procurator by the Jewish religious leaders. 'The high priest Ananias with some of the elders' come to Caesarea to present their formal charges against Paul, and they use a spokesman, one Tertullus (v. 1). The charges are, of course, familiar. The first count of the indictment is the same that was charged against Jesus in Luke 23.2 and against Paul in Acts 17.6, that of 'provoking unrest' (v. 5); and the third count picks up again the theme of earlier accusations against both Stephen and Paul (Acts 6.13; 21.28), that they oppose the Temple, as well as the charge of Acts 21.28 that Paul 'sought to profane the Temple' (v. 6).

The second charge is something new; Paul is accused of being 'a head of the party of the Nazarenes' (v. 5). In this way Luke shows us that, in the opinion of the Jewish religious leadership, being a Christian ought to be considered a crime against the state (and he also, incidentally, here introduces a new term for Christianity). It is therefore clear that, according to Luke, 'the Jews' are out to suppress Christianity and to use the power of Roman authority to do it, since they make being a Christian part of their indictment of Paul before Felix.

After Tertullus's opening statement, '*the Jews* also agreed, saying that these things were so' (v. 9), Luke could very well have written 'the high priest and the elders', but he chose to write 'the Jews' instead. It does not really matter which group of Jews is opposing Christianity at the moment; they do so as Jews. Opposition to Christianity is, in Luke's thinking, a part of being Jewish.

In vv. 10–21 Paul makes his defence, his fifth speech in Acts. In vv. 12–13 he briefly rejects and in part refutes the charges brought against him, and then he gives a confession of faith in vv. 14–15. Since the confession is one with which Luke would be in total agreement, we might even say that we have Luke's credo here. Paul says, 'I confess this to you: I worship the traditional (πατρῷος) God according to the way that they call a party, believing in everything that is written in the Law and the Prophets [i.e., in the Bible], having hope in God – which [hope] they also admit, themselves – that resurrection is going to come to both the just and the unjust.' In this way Luke shows, again, that Christian belief is the true Jewish belief, and that it is the Jews who are wrong to accuse the Christians.[41] Of course, the two beliefs in a resurrection are not the same, since the Jewish belief is in a coming resurrection, much as the Lucan Paul expresses it here, whereas the cornerstone of the Christian belief is that Jesus has been raised from the dead. This difference Luke glosses over, in the interest of emphasizing the propriety of Christianity as the true Judaism. To this confession Paul adds (v. 16) that his 'conscience give[s] no offence'.

In the remaining portion of his defence speech, vv. 17–21, Paul further refutes the charges brought against him, concluding with a reiteration of the point about the resurrection: 'Concerning the resurrection of the dead I am on trial today before you.' The procurator postpones a decision but keeps Paul in custody (vv. 22–23).

Acts 24.27   Paul's continued detention
Important literature: **Overbeck**, *Apostelgeschichte*, p. 423.

At the time of procuratorial succession, according to Luke, Felix, the outgoing procurator, kept Paul jailed, 'wishing to gain favour with the Jews'. Luke realizes that he has portrayed Felix as being of the opinion that there are no substantial charges against Paul, and yet he is faced with the problem of keeping him in jail, so that he can be sent to Rome. Why would a procurator step down to receive another assignment and leave an innocent prisoner locked up?[42] The answer lies close at hand, of course: *the Jews* are responsible. Here they do nothing, but their will is known, and thus they influence the authorities to act against the Christians simply by their known hostility. It would seem that we have here a parallel to Acts 12.3, where Herod expands his persecution of the church when he observes that the execution of James 'is pleasing to the Jews'.

Acts 25.1–7   Renewed plots and charges against Paul
Important literature: **Beyer**, *Apostelgeschichte*, p. 144; **Loisy**, *Actes*, pp. 871–2; **Radl**, *Paulus und Jesus*, pp. 219–21; **Stählin**, *Apostelgeschichte*, pp. 299–300; **Walaskay**, *We Came to Rome*, pp. 55–6.

Now Festus is the new procurator, and the Jews think that they will try to rehabilitate their plot from ch. 23 to ambush Paul; so 'the chief priests and the leaders of the Jews' ask Festus to return Paul to Jerusalem so that they may 'do away with him along the way' (vv. 2–3). Doubtless we are not to think that this was the reason that they gave to Festus; rather, their motive is transparent to Luke. Here nothing is said of the 'more than forty' who were to be the actual assassins before, but whether Luke really means us to think that the chief priests and leaders are planning to plunge the knives, or whether we are still to think of lackeys, is not clear. The distinction is, in any case, immaterial, since both here and in ch. 23 we have plots of 'the Jews' against Paul, so that it really matters little which individuals of 'the Jews' are going to pull the trigger.

Luckily for Paul, Festus does not agree to the request of the Jews but invites them to present their charges before him in Caesarea (vv. 4–5). Since Luke has already given us the charges in 24.5–6, he does not repeat them here and reports only that 'the Jews who came down from Jerusalem . . . press[ed] many and grave accusations, which they were not able to demonstrate' (v. 7). That Luke does not think of some vague charges here but rather of those already, and repeatedly, brought is clear from what follows.

Acts 25.8–12   Paul's defence and his appeal to Caesar

Paul's defence is brief (v. 8), but it shows us what charges Luke had in mind: 'Neither against the Law of the Jews nor against the Temple nor against Caesar have I sinned.' And then, following a brief inquiry from Festus, he appeals to Caesar (v. 11).

Acts 25.13–27   Paul transferred to Herod

Important literature: **Haenchen**, *Acts*, pp. 676–7; **Radl**, *Paulus und Jesus*, pp. 219–21; **Stählin**, *Apostelgeschichte*, pp. 305–6; **Walaskay**, *We Came to Rome*, pp. 55–6; **Wikenhauser**, *Apostelgeschichte*, p. 269.

Luke calls this Herod 'Agrippa', thus avoiding any confusion between him and the Herod who tried Jesus (cf. again the discussion in ch. 1). Nevertheless, just as Jesus appeared twice before the procurator and once before the Jewish temporal ruler, so Paul must appear before two procurators and once before the Jewish temporal ruler (although the sequence is different). In asking Agrippa to hear Paul's case, Festus says that Paul is the man 'concerning whom *the entire multitude of the Jews* has besought (ἐντυγχάνω) me both in Jerusalem and here, shouting that he ought not to live any longer' (v. 24). This statement by the procurator makes it official, in a sense, that it is not only some of the Jews who want to 'do away with' Paul, it is 'the entire multitude of' them. In transferring Paul to Agrippa, Festus – like Pilate in the case of Jesus – declares that the prisoner has 'done nothing deserving. . . of death' (v. 25).

Acts 26.1–23   Paul's last defence speech

Important literature: **Burchard**, *Dreizehnter Zeuge*, p. 113; **Haenchen**, *Acts*, pp. 683–93; **Löning**, *Saulustradition*, pp. 176–80; **Loisy**, *Actes*, pp. 891–9; **Munck**, *Acts*, p. 240; **Neyrey**, *Passion*, pp. 98–107; **Overbeck**, *Apostelgeschichte*, p. 443; **Rese**, 'Aussagen über Jesu Tod', pp. 39–44; **Stolle**, *Zeuge*, pp. 124–36; **Walaskay**, *We Came to Rome*, pp. 57–8.

The Lucan Paul, in his sixth speech, sums up the purpose of his career and the role of Jewish opposition to that career and to him. In v. 2, in opening his defence, he acknowledges that he has 'been charged by Jews', but we may not understand the omission of the article here to mean that Luke intends to say only that Paul has been accused by *some* Jews, as some authors would do; for too much has been said previously about how 'the Jews' want to 'do away with' Paul, and Festus has just made it crystal clear: 'The entire multitude of the Jews' (25.24), not just some of the Jews, has accused Paul. Against these charges of the Jews (not reiterated here; but Luke is coming to stating the rationale behind them at the end of Paul's speech) Paul emphasizes that he has been a strict Pharisee, i.e., that he has 'lived as a Pharisee according to the very best party of our religion' (v. 5). Here two points are made at once: one, that the Pharisees are that party in Judaism closest to Christianity and, two, that Paul's Jewish righteousness is impeccable. The latter is primary. Paul is giving a defence here, we must recall, and, although the charges have not been repeated, we know what the real issue is, namely that he has been promoting laxness toward the Torah, and even non-observance.

The first point of his defence, therefore, is to insist that he has been an exemplary religious Jew, that he has followed his religion 'according to the very best party' in it, that he has been a Pharisee. There is no interest here in his having persecuted the church, and he does not go immediately to that point. Paul's persecution of the church, in Acts, is in no way connected with his being a Pharisee, and his Pharisaism is always mentioned as a defence – here, to demonstrate what a good Jew he has been, in the religious sense.

Lying behind the designation of the Pharisaic movement as the 'very best party' in Judaism, of course, is, for the reader, the memory that Paul is a Pharisee and that Pharisees otherwise (when they are not Christians) help the church. From the Christian point of view, in other words, the Pharisees (as Luke presents them) are not such a bad lot. The reader will also remember that Pharisees believe in the resurrection. Thus Pharisees, while they may be Jews, are closer to Christianity than are other Jews. Christianity is in continuity with Judaism. It is interesting, however, that, while Luke does mention the resurrection next, he refers to it not as a Pharisaic belief, but as the hope of all Jews. Paul claims that, although he is a righteous Pharisee, he has been accused because of his belief in the resurrection; but this belief was 'in hope of the promise made to our fathers by God' (v. 6; explicit reference to the resurrection appears in v. 8), and 'into [it] our twelve tribes hope to come' (v. 7). Thus the Lucan Paul stretches a point. Luke has already informed us that it is the Pharisees among the Jews who believe in the resurrection; but now Paul is making a defence, and he argues that he is being accused for nothing more than something in which all the Jews believe. How senseless, therefore, and false are the accusations.

In vv. 9–11 Paul recalls his early persecution of the church. This theme in part adds to his defence that he was a good Jew and in part prepares for the miracle of his conversion, recounted in the following verses, inasmuch as it serves to show that he did not have some kind of inclination towards Christianity before his conversion. As he continues his brief biographical statement of defence – one might say, his *apologia pro vita sua* – Paul comes to recount his missionary career briefly (v. 20). What he says here is hardly justified by the account of his life in Acts, however, for he claims in v. 20 to have sought to convert persons (since Gentiles are mentioned later, he apparently means Jews) 'in Damascus, and also Jerusalemites, and all the country of Judaea, and the Gentiles'.[43] Yet, Acts 9.22 had said that Paul only 'confused' the Jews in Damascus, not that he sought to convert them (which is what they thought, 9.21); and the brief note in 9.28–29 is the only evidence offered in Acts to support the claim of evangelizing Jerusalem and Judaea. Nevertheless, Paul is defending his career here, and so he makes a blanket claim for world-wide evangelism.

And that is the real bone of contention. 'On account of these things,' adds Paul (v. 21), 'Jews took me into custody in the Temple and attempted to slay me.' 'On account of these things' – that is, on account of the things done in Paul's career, his preaching the gospel, especially to Gentiles. It is the taking of the gospel to the Gentiles, the making of Christianity into a Gentile religion, that 'the Jews' especially oppose; and that opposition underlies the other charges: apostasy, profaning the Temple, and the rest. At the end of his career, the Lucan Paul indicts the Jews for their opposition to Gentile Christianity. The concluding words of his defence speech are, 'to the people and to the Gentiles' (v. 23).

Acts 28.17–28   Paul in Rome

Important literature: **Dupont**, 'Le salut des Gentiles', pp. 136–8; 'La conclusion des Actes'; **Franklin**, *Christ the Lord*, pp. 113–15; **Gnilka**, *Verstockung*, pp. 152–4; **Haenchen**, *Acts*, pp. 723–9; 'Judentum und Christentum', pp. 183–6; **Jervell**, *People of God*, pp. 62–4; **Lampe**, 'Acts', p. 925; **Loisy**, *Actes*, pp. 932–9; **Overbeck**, *Apostelgeschichte*, pp. 474–80; **Radl**,

Paulus und Jesus, pp. 252–65; **Sanders**, 'Salvation of the Jews'; G. **Schneider**, *Apostelgeschichte*, vol. 2, pp. 417–20; **Wilson**, *Gentiles*, pp. 226–7.

The account of Paul in Rome follows the same pattern as the accounts of his stops during his missionary career, with the modification for the sake of verisimilitude that the Jews come to him rather than his going to the synagogue. 'Three days' after his arrival in Rome he 'call[ed] together the prominent members of the Jewish community (οἱ ὄντες τῶν Ἰουδαίων πρῶτοι)' (v. 17) in order to explain his plight to them. He is a victim. He has 'done nothing against the Law or the customs of the fathers' (v. 17), and the Romans 'wanted to release' him (v. 18). Why, then, is he a prisoner in Rome? 'The Jews' did it. The Lucan Paul says, 'When *the Jews* contradicted me, I found it necessary to appeal to Caesar' (v. 19). Now, this statement does not quite fit even the account that Luke gave in Acts 25.8–11, since there Paul appealed to Caesar because he did not like the suggestion of Festus that he be tried in Jerusalem, not because the Jews 'contradicted' him, which is what got him imprisoned, in a sense, in the first place. But 'the Jews' must be the evil characters of our melodrama, and so Paul says here that it was Jewish opposition that forced him to appeal to Caesar.

Paul then explains (v. 20) that it is for no reason other than 'the hope of Israel' that he is a prisoner, which we must surely understand to mean his belief in the resurrection, inasmuch as Acts 26.6–8 had defined the resurrection in those terms. By continuing to emphasize this point, Luke underscores the notion that Christianity is nothing more than the proper Judaism. 'The resurrection is something for which all Jews hope. Why are the Jews, then, singling out me for destruction merely because I hold that belief?' Luke is apparently serious in his apologetic, here, but he has moved belief in the resurrection from the Pharisees to all the Jews – a situation that will have been more or less correct in Luke's day but not in Paul's – and then he asserts that, because Christians and Jews both believe in the resurrection, it is strange that 'the Jews' oppose Christianity. This line of reasoning, of course, buries the difference that Jews believe in the coming resurrection, whereas Christians believe that Jesus has already been raised from the dead. Christianity and Judaism are not the same religion, for all that Luke wants to make it appear that Christianity is simply the true Judaism. It is over the word 'true' that Christians and Jews parted company in Luke's day, and still do so; but Luke is writing apologetic here, and so Christianity is portrayed as, really, nothing more than Judaism.

Now, however, the apologetic theme of similarity gives way to the polemical themes of opposition and rejection. When Paul preaches the gospel to the Roman Jews (v. 23), some are 'persuaded', but others 'disbeliev[e]' (v. 24). Luke thus characterizes this Jewish response to the gospel in exactly the same way in which he has characterized nearly all synagogue responses from Luke 4 on: there is a divided response. Furthermore, as so often, he is careful not to report that any believed, only that some were persuaded, which, as we have seen (Acts 13.43), does not necessarily mean that they were converted. Following the narrative thus far, one might think that Paul had made a fairly good inroad among the Roman Jews; he has 'persuaded' some, so surely there is some hope for them. Perhaps they will come to believe. Alas! This is not Luke's thinking. Since Paul's entire Jewish audience did not clamour for immediate baptism, 'the Jews' are rejected. Paul quotes against the Roman Jews the words of Isa. 6.9–10, which, when applied in this way, must refer not only to Jews in Rome but to all Jews:

Go to this people and say,
  'With hearing you will hear, and you will not understand,
    and, seeing, you will see, and you will not perceive;
  For the heart of this people has become dulled,
    and with ears they have ill heard,
      and their eyes they have closed,
      lest they perceive with eyes
    and with ears hear
  and understand in heart and turn about,
    and I will heal them'

(vv. 26–27).

To this Paul adds his own conclusion, which can be nothing other than the Lucan interpretation of the Isaiah passage: 'Let it then be known to you that to the Gentiles has been sent this salvation of God; and they will hear' (v. 28).

Luke does not have Paul say here that he will never any more seek to convert Jews, and he does not say it himself editorially; and in this fact some modern authors find hope. These interpreters see that the same themes are present in this concluding speech as in Paul's earlier statements of turning to the Gentiles, in the episodes in Antioch and in Corinth, and they prefer to think of Luke as having created an alternating pattern of rejection and mission, a circle of going repeatedly to the Jews. But the Book of Acts is here at an end, and so is the cycle. Jervell has seen this plainly, and it is regrettable that others who would like to ally themselves to his position have not been so clear-sighted. Luke, in fact, has prepared for this final scene in many ways: with the Nazareth pericope, structurally so similar to Paul's many visits to synagogues and to this last scene, and with the earlier statements of rejection in Antioch and Corinth. Luke has saved his principal proof text, however, for the end. Both the preaching to the Jews and their rejection of the gospel have been foretold; what Jesus said in Nazareth and Paul has reiterated for now the third time was known by God all along and was foretold by him (by 'the Holy Spirit') 'through Isaiah the prophet' (Acts 28.25). This Jewish essence, foretold by God through the prophet, is the Lucan truth about 'the Jews'. The narrative development of Luke-Acts has justified the prophecy.

Part Three

CONCLUDING EVALUATION

In the foregoing investigation and analysis we have been able to gain a clear view of Luke's portrait of the Jews. We have seen that, while Luke is probably willing to allow the admissibility into Christianity of an occasional Jew, in general 'the Jews' are roundly condemned for the crucifixion of Jesus and for similar hostile acts against the church. Whether Luke considers it possible for any Jew to be converted to Christianity after the end of Acts is, furthermore, open to serious question; for the note on which Luke closes is the exclamation point to his two-volume proof that Jews are inherently unable to understand their own scriptures and are routinely hostile to the purposes of God.

Jewish Christians belong in a somewhat different category, since they have, after all, believed; but even they, like their non-Christian kin, prefer following Moses to repenting and believing in true contrition and so fall into the category of hypocritical bad leaven within the dough of the church. They therefore share, so it would appear, in the doomed condition of 'the Jews', even though they were once part of the 'Jerusalem springtime' of the nascent church (Acts 21.20). Excepted are the apostles and Paul. Naturally, the power of the gospel had to be manifested during that springtime, and it is shown to be manifest both in the miraculous deeds attending the nascent church and in the 'myriads' of conversions during the springtime.

We have also seen, however, abundant evidence that Luke creates his monolithic anti-Judaism out of source material that is by no means so uniform, that he categorizes and caricatures; and thus we have come to suspect, with many other authors, that some particular animus gives life to Luke's opinion of Jews, and that such animus is probably related *as much as (or more)* to something going on in Luke's day *as to* anything in his sources. While we have engaged in some discussion of this issue, especially in ch. 1, and we have by no means given it the attention that it deserves. Now we are in a position to give the question our undivided attention.

Why does Luke portray the Jews as he does?

8

LUKE'S MOTIVES

Now that Luke's portrait of the Jews is clearly in view, it is time to see what can be said about his motives for portraying them as he does that will take us beyond the few brief forays that we have made into this subject earlier. We had best begin by surveying the alternatives.

Suggested alternatives

Overbeck accused Luke of a '*nationale Antijudaismus*', i.e., an 'antagonism against the Jews as a nation' and added that 'nothing c[ould] be much more evident than that Acts sacrifices Jewish Christianity as such'. It was, for Overbeck, Luke's Gentile-Christian position that allowed him to maintain this united front against all Jews, whether non-Christians or not.[1] While I have to express some sympathy for this view, still it must be said that it is overly general, especially in view of our foregoing study. More precision is needed than this. What is correct about Overbeck's position, however, is its rectifying of the earlier explanation of the Tübingen school, which was that the purpose of Acts was to reconcile Jewish-Christian and Gentile-Christian factions contemporary with the writing of Acts. Overbeck saw through that explanation precisely: no Jewish Christian would have been likely to think that Acts was conciliatory, inasmuch as Acts (and the Gospel of Luke, as well) routinely opposes and discredits all Jewish positions, Christian or otherwise. Far from being conciliatory, Luke-Acts is polemical. This insight has been substantiated in the foregoing chapters. But the explanation of 'national anti-Judaism', while in a sense accurate as a description, does not go far in explaining the rationales for Luke's attitude toward Jews as a group.

If the *recognition* of the polemical character of Luke-Acts does not *explain* that polemical character, then perhaps the polemic against the Jews is to be explained as arising from and as part of Luke's apologetic interest.[2] According to this apologetic theory, Luke was led to cast the Jews as the sole villains in *les affaires Jésus et Paul* in order to let the Roman authorities appear to be favourably disposed towards Jesus and towards the church.[3] The two issues do not hang together integrally, however, as one sees as soon as one looks at the behaviour of the Jews elsewhere in Luke-Acts than in the passion narratives, for the opposition of the Jews is not always the foil for Roman justice. Alternately, it is insufficient to suggest, as an explanation of the portrayal of the Jews in Luke-Acts, that the Jewish hostility towards Christianity expressed in Luke-Acts grows out of Luke's desire to show that Christians are not to be identified with those bad people whom the Romans just wiped out in Jerusalem.[4] The many protestations of the innocence of Jesus and of the early Christians (e.g., Luke 23.14; Acts 18.6) would have sufficed for that.

Further, while Luke's portrayal of the Jews certainly assisted him in presenting the Romans as favourably disposed towards Christianity, that portrayal is too far-reaching to have arisen only on the basis of the function of currying favour with the Roman authorities. Plümacher takes a similar view and concludes his survey of the apologetic theory by emphasizing its limited focus:[5] the 'only correct' view of Luke's apologetic interest is 'probably' to see Luke as attempting to rescue Christianity from the charge of being 'seditious and insurrectionist'. Ruether, further,[6] keenly notes that the blame for the death of Jesus is shifted in early Christianity from Roman *political* to Jewish *religious* authority, and that the 'shift was [therefore] not merely one of apologetics towards the Gentiles, but one, first of all, of polemic towards the Jewish religious tradition'. That is exactly correct for Luke-Acts. The polemic against the Jews and the apologetic toward the Romans may not be entirely separate and distinct, for the polemic does assist the apologetic; but the apologetic motif is insufficient to stand as the rationale for the pervasive polemic against the Jews – and against the Jewish Christians.

A third suggestion, which likewise deals only with the portrayal of Jewish hostility and not with the portrayal of the Jewish Christians, is that Luke's portrayal of Jewish hostility toward Jesus and the church is a reflection of the situation in his own time, which was that, wherever out in the Diaspora Luke was, Jewish leaders chastized

Christians in synagogues and brought trumped-up charges against them before Roman authorities. Thus Gerhard Schneider writes, 'The Lucan work probably has in view the oppressions that threatened the Hellenistic congregations from the synagogue quarter, brought about by Jewish accusation of Christians before pagan authorities.'[7] A variation on this theme refers not to persecution but only to opposition. So Winter lays down the axiom that *'the actual opponents of Christianity, coeval with a particular evangelist, are cited as adversaries of Jesus'.*[8] The problem, however, with taking Jewish *persecution* of Christianity (we shall consider the persecution theme first, then that of opposition) as the clue to Luke's portrayal of the Jews is that precious little evidence of such persecution *that may be contemporary with the writing of Luke-Acts* exists outside Luke-Acts itself.

A setting of Jewish persecution?

From Paul's letters, of course, we know both that he persecuted Christians before his conversion (Gal.1.13, 23; I Cor.15.9; Phil.3.6) and that he was, as an apostle, subject to Jewish persecution (II Cor.11.24). Paul never explains, however, of what his persecutions of Christians consisted; he says that he 'persecuted' them, a word which is subject to a variety of interpretations, and once that he 'ravaged' the church (Gal.1.13). According to the last-mentioned statement, furthermore, this persecution and ravaging were done 'excessively (καθ' ὑπερβολήν)'. Since Paul does tell what persecutions he received from Jews, as a Christian missionary, we may perhaps assume that the persecution that he meted out earlier was similar to what he later received. Just that, however, is not perfectly clear. That he 'received five times from Jews forty save one [stripes]' (II Cor.11.24) is plain enough; but how far into the following list (v. 25) does he intend the phrase 'from Jews' to apply? Surely not to the 'shipwreck'; but stoning looks as if it might be something that Jews would have done. The problem is that being 'thrashed' (with a rod: ῥαβδίζω) intervenes between receiving the stripes and being stoned, and that thrashing appears to be a Gentile custom – that is, it is something done by ῥαβδοῦχοι = lictors;[9] thus Paul may be emphasizing only that he received stripes from Jews, while the deliverers of the following punishments in II Cor.11.24–25 would be indefinite. Luke obviously took the stoning to have been done by Jews, and so he reports such an incident (Acts 14.19);[10] but, does Luke report the incident of Paul's being stoned simply because he read an allusion to such an incident in II Corinthians, or does he report it because he knows of Jewish stoning of Christian missionaries in his own day? I would suspect the former; but the report in Acts 14 is not sufficient evidence, in any case, of what was going on in Luke's time.

With Matthew, however, we are much closer to Luke's time, if not contemporary with it, and Matthew refers clearly to Jewish persecution of Christians (as does Mark 13; but Mark is earlier, and his allusion is borrowed and reworked by Matthew, so that we deal with Mark's allusion to Jewish persecution of Christians when discussing Matthew). Douglas Hare has examined these Matthaean references in detail, and we may follow his analysis. Probably the most striking such statement in Matthew is 23.34, 'I will send prophets and sages and scribes to you. You will kill and crucify some of them, and some of them you will flog in your synagogues and harry from city to city.'[11] Hare takes 'crucify', however, to be a later addition to Matthew, primarily because it is 'redundant' after 'kill'.[12] He is less than entirely clear in providing an explanation of 'kill', but he does finally conclude that this and other 'references to violent death . . . are sufficiently vague that a large number of martyrs need not be implied'.[13] All the other 'references to violent death', however (10.21, 28; 22.6; 23.37), are in fact sufficiently vague that they do not even seem to apply specifically to Jewish persecution, so that nothing about Jewish persecution of Christians can be concluded from them. It may, furthermore, very well be that Matthew thought of the killing and crucifying (the text-critical grounds for omitting the crucifying are weak) as having occurred already, since he has just mentioned prophets (v. 31), and that the impression that he intends to give is that the Jews killed the prophets, crucified Jesus, and flogged and harried Christians.

Matt. 10.16–33 takes up the reference to persecution in Mark 13. Matthew writes here of 'people' (vv. 17–18) that they 'will deliver you to Sanhedrins (or: to councils), and in their synagogues they will flog you; and before governors and kings you will be led on account of me, as a witness to them and to the Gentiles'. Hare argues that the reference to 'governors and kings' is a reference to Gentile persecution of Christian missionaries retained here by Matthew,[14] but that Matthew's primary interest is to show the danger of synagogue persecution for such missionaries.[15] Thus the Matthaean Jesus advises a few verses later, 'When they persecute you in this city, flee to another' (v. 23), seeming in this way to have in mind a 'harrying' of Christian missionaries from one place to another.[16] Hare thus thinks that Matt. 10.17, 23 show that Matthew 'is concerned primarily with Jewish persecution, not persecution in general; . . . that the synagogue has become for him an alien institution'; and, furthermore, 'that the era of persecution in the synagogues is largely past'.[17] The first two points seem evident enough, but whether we can, on the basis of Matthew 10, conclude that Matthew thinks of Jewish persecution of Christian missionaries as being over is less than certain.

The last two beatitudes and the conclusion to the beatitudes (Matt. 5.10–12) present a similar picture, in Hare's analysis.[18] Matthew writes here that 'those who are persecuted on account of righteousness' are 'fortunate', and he adds, 'You are fortunate when they reproach and persecute you and lie and say all bad things against you on my account.' We may agree with Hare at this point. That Matthew intends these statements as referring to Jewish and not to general persecution is seen in his conclusion: 'Thus they persecuted the prophets who were before you.'

Hare is probably correct that the two sets of servants who invite people to the banquet in the Matthaean version of the parable of the Royal Banquet (Matt. 22.3–6) refer to the prophets of old and to the Christian missionaries.[19] Here, again, Matthew refers to 'killing' the missionaries (v. 6), and Hare argues again that 'the number of martyrs implied must not be exaggerated'.[20] That may be true, but we nevertheless have here an unambiguous allusion by Matthew to Jewish persecution of Christians that includes 'killing'.

When Matthew, in 5.44, encourages Christians to 'pray for those who persecute' them, Hare is doubtless correct in concluding that 'Matthew, who elsewhere in his gospel is concerned primarily with Jewish persecution, understood the injunction as applying primarily to the conflict between the Church and the synagogue'.[21] Hare investigates other possible Matthaean allusions to Jewish persecutions of Christians and concludes that they are too general or too lacking in the necessary indicators to be included as allusions to such persecutions.

Hare's primary conclusions, on the basis of his investigation, are that Matthew refers to a persecution of missionaries only, that he refers to persecution that took place before the destruction of Jerusalem, and that he refers to persecution in the Diaspora, not in

Judah.[22] The first conclusion seems clear enough (the 'harrying'), but I am less than convinced by the other two. Matthew nowhere says that he thinks of persecution in the Diaspora; and 10.23, where persecution is linked with the mission to Israel, would seem to locate such persecution in Judah (unless by 'Israel' Matthew meant to *include* the Diaspora). Also, Hare's argument that the position of the woe pronounced on Jerusalem (23.37–39), coming as it does after the prophecy of persecution in v. 34, shows that the foretold persecution is understood to occur before the destruction of Jerusalem could use a little more support.[23] We seem therefore left with the witness of the Gospel of Matthew, at a time more or less contemporary with Luke-Acts (following the destruction of Jerusalem and before 150), that synagogue persecution – 'harrying' from city to city, flogging, and at least under some circumstances killing – can at least be *expected*. Matthew seems to locate such persecution in Judah.

Luke-Acts and the persecution alluded to in Matthew

There are now two questions. We have to ask, first, to what degree this picture of persecution in Matthew corresponds to that in Luke-Acts, and then we have to ask whether such persecution as envisaged by Matthew would explain the black portrait of 'the Jews' painted by Luke. Correspondence exists, but it is not complete. Matthew refers to floggings in synagogues, to 'harrying' (persecuting) from one place to another, and to killing; he thinks only or primarily of persecution of missionaries; and he seems to anticipate such difficulties for his readers. Luke also represents Jewish persecution of missionaries and describes what might well be called 'harrying' of Paul, but killing plays a much larger role in Luke-Acts than it does in the Matthaean allusions. What the Jews always want, in Luke-Acts, is to 'do away with' Jesus and the missionaries. Luke, further, clearly sees a particular problem with Diaspora Jews, since he not only describes persecutions of Paul in the Diaspora but makes Diaspora Jews the moving forces in the martyrdom of Stephen and in the near-martyrdom of Paul.

Hare's conclusion that Matthew has a similar situation in mind is, as we have seen, open to question. It is Luke, however, and not Matthew who describes such persecution as happening to the early missionaries and seems to have no interest in warning his readers of such persecutions to come. The Lucan version of the 'killing the prophets' saying (Luke 11.49) refers to killing 'prophets and apostles';

and the Lucan version of the parable of the Great Supper (Luke 14.16–24) does not mention killing. Further, the Lucan version of the admonition to pray for one's persecutors (Luke 6.28) does not employ the word 'persecute', and is much more general in its scope than is the Matthaean version; and the Lucan version of the last Beatitude (Luke 6.22) warns against the hatred of 'people', not against persecution. Finally, Luke emphasizes that Jewish persecution involves turning Christians over to Roman authorities, a theme that seems not to be present in Matthew. Luke 12.11 (par. Matt. 10.17–18) warns, 'When they conduct you before synagogues and rulers and authorities . . .', whereas Matthew's 'Before governors and kings you will be led' (Matt. 10.18) by no means necessarily implies that Jews will do the leading; and Luke 21.12, which does refer to 'persecution', says that the persecutors will 'deliver you to synagogues and jails' and will 'turn you over to kings and governors'. These prophecies are, of course, fulfilled in the narrative in Acts. It would therefore appear that Luke represents a Jewish persecution of the apostles and early missionaries of the church that involved harrying, killing, and denouncing the missionaries to Roman authorities. He seems to think primarily of Diaspora Jews. While this portrait shows some similarities to Matthew's allusions to Jewish persecution, Matthew's allusions corroborate Luke's portrait only in the matter of harrying, and even here the locale appears to be different.

This result would also seem to answer the question as to whether the persecution envisaged by Matthew explains the Lucan hostility to 'the Jews'. It could hardly do so. Denouncing Christians to Roman authorities was the backbone of that possibility, and that is the thing that seems to be missing both in Paul and in Matthew. Paul and Matthew stand closer together in their presentation of Jewish persecution of Christians. Both witness to flogging – and perhaps to occasional stoning or killing – of Jewish Christian missionaries in synagogues, let us assume both in Judah and in the Diaspora. Such practice may have continued into Luke's day; but Luke's Gentile Christians could not have experienced such persecutions, inasmuch as Gentiles were not subject to synagogue discipline. It is possible that Luke knows of synagogue persecutions of Jewish Christians, and that his hatred of Jews is thereby enhanced, and he surely knows of Paul's accounts, but such persecutions and information probably cannot explain the entirety of Luke's portrait of 'the Jews'.[24] Something more is needed. What we learn of Jewish persecution of

Christians from Paul and from Matthew does not seem adequate to explain Luke's hostility towards Jews generally.

Extra-canonical evidence

Evidence outside the New Testament for Jewish persecutions of Christians is sparse. Outside the New Testament, the only Jewish persecutions of which we have direct knowledge are the martyrdom of James the brother of Jesus[25] and Bar Kochba's martyrdom of Christians during the second Jewish revolt (c. 135 CE).[26] The martyrdom of James is especially ill-suited to qualify as 'persecution', since it was an isolated Christian martyrdom, since other people in Jerusalem who were (presumably) not Christians were martyred at the same time, and since the martyrdoms created such a reaction that the High Priest responsible was removed from office shortly thereafter.[27] This martyrdom, however, could explain Matthew's two references to killing. Even if Luke-Acts was written, however, so late as to follow the Bar Kochba revolt, the persecution that occurred there does not seem to be what Luke has in mind.[28] Thus synagogue persecution – flogging, 'harrying', and perhaps occasional killing, like that of James the brother of Jesus – of *Jewish* Christian missionaries, perhaps into Luke's time, is believable, likely, and supported by at least some evidence. Such persecution, however, does not coincide with the picture of Jewish persecution that Luke paints (more killing, denunciation of Christians to Roman authorities, widespread persecution in the Diaspora), and so some more general context is needed to explain Luke's blanket hatred of the Jews as a group.

The birkat ha-minim

The role of the *birkat ha-minim*, the curse against 'heretics' in one version of the Eighteen Benedictions (a standard synagogue prayer), in this complex of possibilities needs to be discussed at this point. In this version of the prayer, the twelfth benediction reads,

> For the apostates let there be no hope,
> And let the arrogant government be speedily uprooted in our days.
> Let the Nazarenes and the heretics (*minim*) be destroyed in a moment,
> And let them be blotted out of the Book of Life and not be inscribed together with the righteous.
> Blessed art Thou, O Lord, Who humblest the arrogant.[29]

Did such a prayer have any effect on the church?

Martyn has argued that the three occurrences in the Gospel of John of the term ἀποσυνάγωγος (John 9.22: 'The Jews had already agreed that if anyone should confess him to be Messiah, he would become an excommunicate from the synagogue [ἀποσυνάγωγος]'; 16.2: 'They will cause you to be excommunicated from the synagogue'; and 12.42: '. . . lest they be excluded from the synagogue [ἀποσυνάγωγος]'),[30] show that John knows of synagogue expulsions of Christians, and, further, that 'the formal separation between church and synagogue has been accomplished in John's *milieu* by means closely related to the Jewish Benediction Against Heretics'.[31] Martyn proposes that the 'four key points in John 9.22' all fit the use of this prayer. Those four points are '(1) a formal decision, (2) made by Jewish authorities, (3) to bring against Christian Jews, (4) the drastic measure of excommunication from the synagogue'.[32] Martyn's position has been supported by Kimelman,[33] who is at pains to show that the prayer was not generally anti-*Christian*, but who concludes that it was likely that the version under consideration was directed against *Jewish* Christians[34] (which was also Martyn's point). Katz has argued, against this position, that the prayer was never intended to be directed against Christians at all,[35] but his argument rests primarily on discrediting the importance of the version of the prayer that includes the word 'Nazarenes'. This version, he maintains, 'has no special status, except that which comes from having survived', whereas 'other ancient and medieval forms of the malediction exist, none of which includes the term *Notzrim*', i.e., Nazarenes.[36] Katz could be correct that the version cursing Christians was not the official version of the prayer, but we must bear in mind that 'official' does not have the meaning for ancient Judaism that it has for, e.g., traditional Catholicism. That the version of the prayer cursing Christians was not official means only that a small group of rabbis in Yavneh (Jamnia) did not propose or sanction it. It does not mean that it did not exist or have currency; for we have, after all, the surviving fragment. What we do not know is the extent of its currency. If the curse against Jewish Christians was in effect somewhere in John's day, then John's use of the term ἀποσυνάγωγος is made more understandable.

Very well. What has this curse against Christians, however broadly it was circulated or not circulated, to do with Luke's account of Jewish persecution of Christianity, or with Luke's own situation, that could help to explain his portrait of the Jews? I suspect, nothing. Martyn, in fact, presents cogent arguments that Acts does not reflect the same situation as does John.[37] He notes, among other things, that the Jewish harrying of Paul in the Diaspora that is recounted in Acts, while 'serious discipline', gives 'no hint of excommunication'.[38] And he correctly distinguishes Paul's 'bounding off' of the Christians from the synagogue in Acts 19.9 from their being excommunicated from the synagogue.[39] Evidence for Jewish persecution of Christians *in Luke's day*, therefore, is rather slim and coincides with Luke's portrait of that persecution only to a minor degree. There is no evidence outside Luke-Acts that Jews persecuted Diaspora Christians, perhaps even Gentile Christians, by denouncing them to the Roman authorities.

Jewish persecution and Roman persecution

There is another aspect of this discussion about the possible Jewish persecution of Christianity as the background for Luke's adverse portrayal of the Jewish leaders that is more than passing strange, and that is that, even if Luke and Acts were written shortly after the fall of Jerusalem, the Neronian persecution of Christians in Rome would have occurred already; and Luke-Acts may be late enough to follow the persecutions under Domitian and Trajan, which were more widespread.[40] Yet one gets not the slightest hint in Luke-Acts that Christianity faced any difficulty from the Roman authorities. If, therefore, Luke and Acts are so unreliable in presenting us with an accurate image of the relation of *Roman* authorities to Christianity in the time when Luke-Acts was written, then why should we assume that these works are more reliable in presenting us with an accurate image of the relation of *Jewish* authorities to Christianity in that same time? And if we can be reasonably certain that there is a theological reason – not a historical one – for Luke's portrayal of the Roman authorities,[41] then surely we had best look for a theological reason – not a historical one – for his portrayal of the Jewish authorities;[42] and so we return from the question of Jewish persecution of Christianity as a possible backdrop for Luke's portrayal of the Jews to the issue of Jewish *opposition*.

A Gentile-Christian identity crisis

Maddox proposes that Luke's characterization is a response to an identity problem within Gentile Christianity.[43] Briefly put, the problem faced by Gentile Christians, according to Maddox, was that Christianity was supposed to be the inheritor of the Jewish promises, but that Jews increasingly rejected Christianity and increasingly put forward a solid and united front against it. There may have been 'considerable . . . pressure on the faith of Christians', even if there were no overt acts of persecution.[44] 'If once the charismatic testimony of the Spirit grew dim,' Maddox suggests, 'the onset of persecution, or even of sustained psychological pressure from the Jews through dispute' over main points of Christian theology 'will have shaken many people's confidence in their faith'. According to this theory, therefore, the key to Luke's portrayal of the Jews is *opposition* of Jews to Christianity, not necessarily persecution. Such a situation would have posed the question that Luke's portrayal of the Jews was supposed to answer, namely, 'How could non-Jews hope to find any value in something which has its roots in Judaism, yet seems to be repudiated by the leaders of the Jews?'[45] Luke answers the question, in Luke-Acts, with a 'directly historical argument' – that is, that 'the leaders of Judaism have in repeated instances, and in spite of every opportunity to hear the gospel, excluded themselves from the Kingdom of God'.[46]

This view is somewhat similar to the earlier approach of Jervell, who formulated the problem in this way: 'Because the promises that were fulfilled in Christ belong to Israel, and because Luke knows only one Israel, i.e., the Jewish people, the Gentile mission forms a difficult problem for him.'[47] Jervell's peculiar treatment of Luke's view of Israel, namely that Luke intends to present no real division between Israel and Christianity, has of course been shown to be incorrect, but his view of Luke's presentation of the Gentile mission focuses on the problem somewhat as Maddox sees it. Luke's characterization of the Gentile mission, according to Jervell, allows Luke to be 'able to explain why there still is an Israel alongside and unrelated to the Christian church, to which the church is not obligated'.[48] Both writers have therefore proposed that Luke's characterization of the Jews indeed grows out of Luke's own ecclesiastical situation, but that Luke's ecclesiastical situation, rather than being one marked by the kind of persecution that Luke-Acts describes for an earlier time,[49] is in fact one in which it appears necessary to define Christianity over against Judaism while holding on to the reality of the promises made to Israel. Somewhat similarly, Loisy had earlier tried to follow the reasoning of the 'redactor' of Acts: he 'imagine[d] retrospectively how the Jews became more and more hostile to the Christian movement', and he understood 'well that the Jews disowned their Christ . . ., just as they disown Christianity'.[50]

There is much to be said for this theory of Jewish opposition to (not persecution of) Christianity as the key both to Luke's polemic and to his apologetic. The uniformly hostile portrait of the Jews, which hostility takes a variety of forms, and Luke's belabouring of the continuity issue, including the lengthy discussion about which laws it is proper for Gentiles to keep, could well both be explained on the basis of the identity problem.[51] Furthermore, we may now have reached the point that will allow us to make better sense out of Luke's portrayal both of non-Christian Jews and of Jewish Christians; for, if Luke knows of *Jewish* opposition to *Christianity*, he also knows of Jewish-*Christian* opposition to *Gentile* Christianity. This possibility must now be explored in more detail.

Crisis over the inclusion of Gentiles

With this issue, the discussion of the setting that provoked the writing of Luke-Acts has come full circle, for this is what the Tübingen school proposed, that Luke sought to settle a dispute between Jewish Christians and Gentile Christians.[52] It is, further, a part of the Tübingen position that 'the chief aim of' Acts was an 'apology for the Apostle Paul'.[53] Trocmé has, in more recent times, proposed a modernized version of this theory as an explanation of what it was that provoked Luke to write, and his views merit our consideration. It is Trocmé's thesis that Luke was 'endeavouring to defend the churches that he represented – their teaching and their founder Paul – against the dangerous attacks to which some other Christians, partisans of James, were submitting them'.[54] Thus opposition from Jewish Christians is described in Acts 11, where the Jerusalem church objects to the acceptance of Cornelius; in Acts 15, where the Jerusalem church proposes circumcising Gentile Christians; and in Acts 21, where some Jewish Christians, at least, report that Paul is promoting apostasy in the Diaspora.[55] The role of James, to the contrary, is almost played out of Acts entirely.[56] These aspects of Acts show that Luke's Christianity is under attack by '*une grande Eglise judéo-chrétienne*'.[57] In order to triumph over such an onslaught, Luke fires, as we Americans would say, shotgun blasts at his opponents and hits a rather wide target. In this counter-attack all the Jews are attacked, and Acts '13–28 . . . are therefore the trial of Israel, in particular of its *Diaspora*'.[58]

Now, Trocmé has probably misconstrued the role of James in Acts, inasmuch as Jervell seems correctly to have shown that the older Tübingen position is more nearly correct than Trocmé has realized on this point – that is, that James in Acts is 'the defender of Paul' rather than Paul's opponent.[59] Trocmé, however, may well have laid his finger on the issue that gives coherence to Luke's hostility towards both non-Christian Jews and Jewish Christians; for is not, in fact, the Jewish opposition to and hostility toward Christianity and Jesus, as Luke presents the matter, from first to last over the issue of the inclusion of Gentiles? In Jesus' Nazareth sermon, Jesus' explanation of the sending of salvation to Gentiles and not to Jews provokes the first hostility (Luke 4.25–28); when Paul's mission begins, it is Gentile interest in the gospel that provokes synagogue hostility (Acts 13.45); and when Paul is apprehended for the last time, the charge is not only apostasy, but also the inclusion of a Gentile (Acts 21.28).[60] Throughout Luke-Acts, therefore, the hostility of non-Christian Jews towards Christianity and of Jewish Christians towards Gentile Christianity is provoked by the inclusion of Gentiles.[61] (The arrest of Jesus, with its accompanying secular accusations, is no exception, since the Jesus arrested in Luke 22 is the same Jesus who announced the turning to the Gentiles in ch. 4. Paul, further, the missionary to the Gentiles *par excellence*, is painted with Jesus colours.) To this telling observation we may add the further one, already partly detailed in the earlier part of this chapter,[62] that the Jewish persecution of Christianity that Luke narrates lies in the past, whereas he seems to regard the argument between Jewish Christians and Gentile Christians as ongoing. As we saw, Luke's description of the Jewish persecution of Christianity concerns Jesus and the early church and finds little external support. His allusions to the arguments between Jewish Christians and Gentile Christians, however, concern his own time, inasmuch as he has Jesus warn the church against the 'leaven' of 'hypocrisy' that is the Jewish Christian position. Inasmuch as the saying about the leaven of hypocrisy is a warning to the church, not a description of something that went on in former times, surely the warning against hypocritical leaven is one that Luke relates to his own day, not merely to the past.[63]

In Luke's opinion, there is little difference between Jewish Christians and other Jews. While the former have 'believed', it is true, they have not done so in true contrition and repentance but seek rather, in their belief, to 'justify themselves' on the basis of their 'Moses'. When they, then, seek to foist 'Moses' upon the Gentile church, they show that they are cut from the same cloth as are their non-Christian kin, who also oppose the notion that the gospel was destined from the beginning for Gentiles. Inasmuch as Luke knows of Jewish Christians in his own day who want to 'Judaize' Christianity and receives at the same time the Christian tradition that the Jewish leaders and Jerusalem killed Jesus – which may already have become in Luke's tradition that 'the Jews' killed Jesus – he comes to the opinion that all Jews are equally, in principle at least, perverse; and he turns his attack on all together, without distinction.

In Luke's opinion, the world will be much better off when 'the Jews' get what they deserve and the world is rid of them. 'Protect yourselves from the leaven of the Pharisees, which is hypocrisy' (Luke 12.1); 'Lead here those enemies of mine who do not wish me to reign over them and slaughter them before me' (Luke 19.27); 'Your blood be upon your heads; I am clean. From now on I will go to the Gentiles' (Acts 18.6). The modern reader of Luke-Acts is now forced to ask whether Luke's polemic against 'Jews' has not become the leaven within Christianity – and within Western society – against which we must all and eternally be on guard.

Bibliography

Texts, editions and lexica

Aland, Kurt (ed.), *Synopsis quattuor Evangeliorum*, Stuttgart: Deutsche Bibel-gesellschaft [12]1982.

Bauer, Walter, *A Greek–English Lexicon of the New Testament and Other Early Christian Literature*, trans., rev. and augmented by W. F. Arndt and F. W. Gingrich, Chicago: University of Chicago Press [4]1957.

Corpus inscriptionum judaicarum, 2 vols., Sussidi allo studio delle antichità Cristiane 1,3, ed. J.-B. Frey, Città del Vaticano: Pontificio Istituto di Archeologia Cristiana 1936–1952.

Greek New Testament, The, ed. K. Aland, *et al.*, United Bible Societies [3]1983.

Liddell, Henry George, and Robert Scott, *A Greek–English Lexicon*, new ed. rev. and augmented by H. S. Jones, *et al.*, Oxford: Clarendon Press 1940.

Syrus Sinaiticus, ed. A. Hjelt, Helsingfors: no publ. 1930.

Commentaries

Bauernfeind, Otto, *Die Apostelgeschichte*, THKNT 5, Leipzig: A. Deichert 1939.

Beginnings, *see* Jackson and Lake.

Betz, Hans-Dieter, *Galatians. A Commentary on Paul's Letter to the Churches in Galatia*, Hermeneia, Philadelphia: Fortress Press 1979.

Beyer, Hermann Wolfgang, *Die Apostelgeschichte*, NTD 5, Göttingen: Vandenhoeck & Ruprecht, [5]1949.

Black, Matthew, and H. H. Rowley (eds.), *Peake's Commentary on the Bible*, London: Thomas Nelson and Sons, Ltd 1962.

Bruce, F. F., *Commentary on the Book of the Acts*, NICNT, London: Tyndale Press and Grand Rapids: Eerdmans 1954.

Bundy, Walter E., *Jesus and the First Three Gospels*, Cambridge, Mass.: Harvard University Press 1955.

Cadbury, *see* Jackson and Lake.

Caird, G. B., *Saint Luke*, Pelican Commentaries, Harmondsworth: Penguin

Books 1963, reissued London: SCM Press and Philadelphia: Westminster Press 1977.

Conzelmann, Hans, *Die Apostelgeschichte*, HNT 7, Tübingen: Mohr (Siebeck) 1963.

DeWette, W. M. L., *Kurze Erklärung der Apostelgeschichte*, rev. and greatly expanded by Franz Overbeck, Leipzig: Hirzel [4]1870.

Easton, Burton Scott, *The Gospel According to St. Luke*, New York: Scribner's 1926.

Ellis, E. Earle, *The Gospel of Luke*, The Century Bible, new ed. London: Thomas Nelson and Greenwood, SC: Attic Press 1966.

Ernst, Josef, *Das Evangelium nach Lukas*, RNT, Regensburg: Pustet [5]1977.

Fitzmyer, Joseph A., *The Gospel According to Luke (I–IX)*, and *The Gospel According to Luke (X–XXIV)*, AB 28, 28A, Garden City, NY: Doubleday 1981, 1985.

Gilmour, S. MacLean, 'The Gospel According to Luke, Introduction and Exegesis', *IB*, vol. 8, pp. 1–434.

Grant, Frederick C., *Nelson's Bible Commentary*, Vol. 6: *New Testament, Matthew-Acts*, New York, etc.: Nelson 1962.

Grundmann, Walter, *Das Evangelium nach Lukas*, THKNT 3, Berlin: Evangelische Verlagsanstalt [7]1974.

Haenchen, Ernst, *The Acts of the Apostles. A Commentary*, Oxford: B. H. Blackwell and Philadelphia: Westminster Press 1971.

——, *Die Apostelgeschichte*, MeyerK 3, Göttingen: Vandenhoeck & Ruprecht [7(16)]1977.

Harrington, Wilfrid J., *The Gospel According to St Luke*, New York etc.: Newman Press 1967.

Hauck, Friedrich, *Das Evangelium des Lukas*, THKNT 3, Leipzig: Deichert 1934.

Holtzmann, H. J., *Die Apostelgeschichte*, HKNT 1,2, Tübingen and Leipzig: Mohr (Siebeck) [3]1901.

Jackson, F. J. Foakes, and Kirsopp Lake (eds.), *The Acts of the Apostles* (earlier editions also known as *The Beginnings of Christianity*, Part I), 5 vols, reprint ed., Grand Rapids: Baker Book House 1979 (contains articles by H. J. Cadbury, J. H. Ropes and K. Lake).

Jacquier, E., *Les Actes des Apôtres*, EBib, Paris: Gabalda [2]1926.

Kealy, Sean, *The Gospel of Luke* (also John P. Kealy, *Luke's Gospel Today*), Denville, NJ: Dimension Books 1979.

Klostermann, Erich, *Das Lukasevangelium*, HNT 5, Tübingen: Mohr (Siebeck) [2]1929.

Knox, Wilfred L., *The Acts of the Apostles*, Cambridge: University Press 1948.

Lagrange, M.-J., *Evangile selon Saint Luc*, EBib, Paris: Gabalda [7]1948.

Lake, *see* Jackson and Lake.

Lampe, G. W. H., 'Acts', in *Peake's Commentary on the Bible* (*see* Black and Rowley), pp. 882–926.

——, 'Luke', in *Peake's Commentary on the Bible* (*see* Black and Rowley), pp. 820–43.

Leaney, A. R. C., *A Commentary on the Gospel According to St. Luke*, BNTC, London: A. & C. Black = HNTC, New York: Harper & Row ²1966.

Lietzmann, Hans, *An die Korinther I & II*, HNT 9, Tübingen: Mohr (Siebeck) ⁴1949.

Loisy, Alfred, *Les Actes des Apôtres*, Paris: Nourry 1920.

——, *L'Evangile selon Luc*, Paris: Nourry 1924.

——, *Les Evangiles synoptiques*, 2 vols, Ceffonds, près Montier-en-Der (Haute-Marne): publ. by author 1907–8.

Macgregor, G. H. C., 'The Acts of the Apostles, Introduction and Exegesis', *IB*, vol. 9, pp. 3–352.

Manson, William, *The Gospel of Luke*, MNTC, New York: Harper & Brothers and London: Hodder & Stoughton, no date [1930].

Marshall, I. Howard, *The Acts of the Apostles*, London: Inter-Varsity Press and Grand Rapids: Eerdmans 1980.

——, *The Gospel of Luke. A Commentary on the Greek Text*, New International Greek Testament Commentary, Exeter: Paternoster Press and Grand Rapids: Eerdmans 1978.

Montefiore, C. G., *The Synoptic Gospels*, 2 vols, London: Macmillan ²1927.

Munck, Johannes, *The Acts of the Apostles*, AB, rev. W. F. Albright and C. S. Mann, Garden City, NY: Doubleday 1967.

Overbeck, *see* DeWette.

Plummer, Alfred, *A Critical and Exegetical Commentary on the Gospel According to S. Luke*, ICC, Edinburgh: T. & T. Clark ⁴1910.

Preuschen, Erwin, *Die Apostelgeschichte*, HNT 4,1, Tübingen: Mohr (Siebeck) 1912.

Rackham, Richard Belward, *The Acts of the Apostles. An Exposition*, London: Methuen 1901.

Rengstorf, Karl Heinrich, *Das Evangelium nach Lukas*, NTD 3, Göttingen: Vandenhoeck & Ruprecht ⁹1962.

Roloff, Jürgen, *Die Apostelgeschichte*, NTD 5, Göttingen: Vandenhoeck & Ruprecht ¹⁷1981.

Ropes, *see* Jackson and Lake.

Schille, Gottfried, *Die Apostelgeschichte des Lukas*, Berlin: Evangelische Verlagsanstalt 1983.

Schlatter, Adolf, *Die Apostelgeschichte*, Stuttgart: Calwer 1962.

——, *Das Evangelium des Lukas. Aus seinen Quellen erklärt*, Stuttgart: Calwer ²1960.

Schmid, Josef, *Das Evangelium nach Lukas*, RNT 3, Regensburg: Pustet ⁴1960.

Schmithals, Walter, *Die Apostelgeschichte des Lukas*, Zürcher Bibelkommentare, Zurich: Theologischer Verlag 1982.

——, *Das Evangelium nach Lukas*, Zürcher Bibelkommentare, Zurich: Theologischer Verlag 1980.

Schneider, Gerhard, *Die Apostelgeschichte*, 2 vols, HTKNT 5, Freiburg etc.: Herder 1980–82.

——, *Das Evangelium nach Lukas*, 2 vols, ÖTNT 3, Gütersloh: Mohn and Würzburg: Echter Verlag 1977.

Schürmann, Heinz, *Das Lukasevangelium*, vol. 1, HTKNT 3, Freiburg etc.: Herder 1969.

Schweizer, Eduard, *The Good News According to Luke*, Atlanta: John Knox and London: SPCK 1984.

Spinetoli, Ortensio da, *Luca*, Assisi: Cittadella editrice 1982.

Stählin, Gustav, *Die Apostelgeschichte*, NTD 5, Göttingen: Vandenhoeck & Ruprecht 1962.

Stagg, Frank, *The Book of Acts. The Early Struggle for an Unhindered Gospel*, Nashville: Broadman 1955.

Talbert, Charles H., *Reading Luke. A Literary and Theological Commentary*, New York: Crossroad 1982.

Valensin, Albert, and Joseph Huby, *Evangile selon Saint Luc*, VS 3, Paris: Beauchesne 1952.

Weiser, Alfons, *Die Apostelgeschichte*, vol. 1, ÖTNT 5, Gütersloh: Mohn 1981.

Weiss, Bernhard (with J. Weiss), *Die Evangelien des Markus und Lukas*, MeyerK 1,2, Göttingen: Vandenhoeck & Ruprecht [9]1901.

Wellhausen, J., *Das Evangelium Lucae*, Berlin: Georg Reimer 1904.

Wendt, Hans Hinrich, *Die Apostelgeschichte*, MeyerK 3, Göttingen: Vandenhoeck & Ruprecht [9]1913.

Wikenhauser, Alfred, *Die Apostelgeschichte*, RNT, Regensburg: Pustet [3]1956.

Williams, C. S. C., *A Commentary on the Acts of the Apostles*, BNTC, London: A. & C. Black = HNTC, New York: Harper and Row 1957.

Winn, Albert C., *The Acts of the Apostles*, The Layman's Bible Commentary 20, Richmond: John Knox 1960.

Zahn, Theodor, *Das Evangelium des Lucas*, KNT 3, Leipzig and Erlangen: Deichert [3,4]1920.

Other scholarly works and articles

Albertz, Rainer, 'Die "Antrittspredigt" Jesu im Lukasevangelium auf ihrem alttestamentlichen Hintergrund', *ZNW* 74, 1983, pp. 182–206.

Aus, Roger David, 'Luke 15.11–32 and R. Eliezer ben Hyrcanus's Rise to Fame', *JBL* 104, 1985, pp. 443–69.

Baarlink, H., 'Friede im Himmel. Die lukanische Redaction von Lk 19,38 und ihre Deutung', *ZNW* 76, 1985, pp. 170–86.

Bachmann, Michael, *Jerusalem und der Tempel*, BWANT 6,9, Stuttgart, etc.: Kohlhammer 1980.

Balz, Horst, and Siegfried Schulz (eds), *Das Wort und die Wörter*. *Festschrift Gerhard Friedrich*, Stuttgart, etc.: Kohlhammer 1973.

Baron, Salo Wittmayer, *A Social and Religious History of the Jews*, vol. 2, New York: Columbia University Press ²1952.

Bartsch, Hans-Werner, *Wachet aber zu jeder Zeit*, Hamburg-Bergstedt: Herbert Reich – Evangelischer Verlag 1963.

Batdorf, I. W., 'Benefactors', *IDB*, vol. 1, p. 381.

Baur, Ferdinand Christian, *Paul the Apostle*, 2 vols, ed. E. Zeller, London and Edinburgh: Williams and Norgate 1873–75.

Beck, Norman A., *Mature Christianity. The Recognition and Repudiation of the Anti-Jewish Polemic of the New Testament*, Selingsgrove: Susquehanna University Press; London and Toronto: Associated University Presses 1985.

Betz, Hans Dieter, 'The Cleansing of the Ten Lepers (Luke 17.11–19)', *JBL* 90, 1971, pp. 314–28.

Bihler, Johann, 'Der Stephanusbericht (Apg 6,8–15 und 7,54–8,2)', *BZ*, NF 3, 1959, pp. 252–70.

——, *Die Stephanusgeschichte im Zusammenhang der Apostelgeschichte*, Münchener theologische Studien 1,16, Munich: Hueber 1963.

Blinzler, Josef, *Der Prozess Jesu*, Regensburg: Pustet ⁴1969.

Böcher, Otto, and Klaus Haacker (eds.), *Verborum Veritas. Festschrift für Gustav Stählin*, Wuppertal: Brockhaus 1970.

Boismard, M. E., 'Le martyre d'Etienne', *RSR* 69, 1981, pp. 181–94.

Bornkamm, Günther, *Paul*, New York and Evanston: Harper & Row and London: Hodder & Stoughton 1971.

Bouwman, Gilbert, *Das dritte Evangelium*, Düsseldorf: Patmos 1968.

Bovon, François, 'Israel, die Kirche und die Völker im lukanischen Doppelwerk', *TLZ* 108, 1983, pp. 403–14.

——, '"Schön hat der heilige Geist durch den Propheten Jesaja zu euren Vätern gesprochen" (Act 28:25)', *ZNW* 75, 1984, pp. 226–32.

Bowman, John, *The Samaritan Problem*, PTMS 4, Pittsburgh: Pickwick Press 1975.

Braumann, Georg (ed.), *Das Lukas-Evangelium*, Wege der Forschung 280, Darmstadt: Wissenschaftliche Buchgesellschaft 1974.

——, 'Das Mittel der Zeit', *ZNW* 54, 1963, pp. 117–45.

Brawley, Robert L., 'Paul in Acts: Lucan Apology and Conciliation', in *Luke-Acts. New Perspectives* (*see* Talbert), pp. 129–47.

Brown, Raymond E., *The Birth of the Messiah*, Garden City, NY: Doubleday and London: Geoffrey Chapman 1977.

Brown, Schuyler, *Apostasy and Perseverance in the Theology of Luke*, AnBib 36, Rome: Pontifical Biblical Institute 1969.

Bruners, Wilhelm, *Die Reinigung der zehn Aussätzigen und die Heilung des Samariters Luk 17,11–19*, Forschung zur Bibel 23, Stuttgart: Verlag Katholisches Bibelwerk 1977.

Buck, Erwin, 'The Function of the Pericope "Jesus Before Herod" in the Passion Narrative of Luke', in *Wort in der Zeit* (*see* Haubeck and Bachmann), pp. 165–78.

Bultmann, Rudolf, *The History of the Synoptic Tradition*, Oxford: B. H. Blackwell 1968.

Burchard, Christoph, *Der dreizehnte Zeuge. Traditions- und kompositionsgeschichtliche Untersuchungen zu Lukas' Darstellung der Frühzeit des Paulus*, FRLANT 103, Göttingen: Vandenhoeck & Ruprecht 1970.

Buss, Matthäus Franz-Josef, *Die Missionspredigt des Apostels Paulus im Pisidischen Antiochien*, Forschung zur Bibel 38, Stuttgart: Verlag Katholisches Bibelwerk 1980.

Busse, Ulrich, *Das Nazareth-Manifest Jesu*, SBS 91, Stuttgart: Verlag Katholisches Bibelwerk 1977.

Cadbury, H. J., 'Acts of the Apostles'. *IDB*, vol. 1, pp. 28–42.

——, *The Book of Acts in History*, New York: Harper and Brothers and London: A. & C. Black 1955.

——, *The Making of Luke-Acts*, London: SPCK ²1958.

Cassidy, Richard J., 'Luke's Audience, the Chief Priests, and the Motive for Jesus' Death', in *Political Issues in Luke-Acts* (see the following entry), pp. 146–67.

Cassidy, R. J., and Philip J. Scharper (ed.), *Political Issues in Luke-Acts*, Maryknoll, NY: Orbis Books 1983.

Catchpole, D. R., 'Trial of Jesus', *IDB*, Supplementary vol., pp. 917–19.

——, *The Trial of Jesus*, SPB 18, Leiden: Brill 1971.

Cerfaux, Lucien, 'La composition de la première partie du Livre des Actes', in *Recueil Lucien Cerfaux*, vol. 2, pp. 63–91, BETL 7, Gembloux: Duculot 1954.

Conzelmann, Hans, *Heiden – Juden – Christen*, BHT 62, Tübingen: Mohr (Siebeck) 1981.

——, *History of Primitive Christianity*, Nashville and New York: Abingdon Press and London: Darton, Longman and Todd 1973.

——, *The Theology of St Luke*, New York: Harper & Brothers 1960, reissued London: SCM Press 1982.

——, 'Zur Lukasanalyse', in *Das Lukas-Evangelium* (*see* Braumann), pp. 43–63.

Cortés, Juan B., 'The Greek Text of Luke 18:14a', *CBQ* 46, 1984, pp. 255–73.

Crossan, Dominic M., 'Anti-Semitism and the Gospel', *TS* 26, 1965, pp. 189–214.

Crossan, John Dominic, 'Parable and Example in the Teaching of Jesus', *NTS* 18, 1972, pp. 285–307.

Cullmann, Oscar, *The Early Church*, ed. A. J. B. Higgins, London: SCM Press and Philadelphia: Westminster Press 1956.

——, *The Johannine Circle*, London: SCM Press and Philadelphia: Westminster Press 1976.

Dahl, Nils Alstrup, *Jesus in the Memory of the Early Church*, Minneapolis: Augsburg Publishing House 1976.

——, 'A People for His Name', *NTS* 4, 1957–58, pp. 319–27.

——, 'The Story of Abraham in Luke-Acts', in *Studies in Luke-Acts* (*see* Keck and Martyn), pp. 139–58.

Danker, Frederick W., *Benefactor*, St. Louis: Clayton 1982.

Davies, Alan T. (ed.), *AntiSemitism and the Foundations of Christianity*, New York etc.: Paulist Press 1979.

Davies, W. D., *The Gospel and the Land*, Berkeley, Los Angeles and London: University of California Press 1974.

——, *Introduction to Pharisaism*, FBBS 16, Philadelphia: Fortress Press 1967.

Dehandschutter, B., 'La persécution des chrétiens dans les Actes des Apôtres', in *Les Actes des Apôtres* (*see* Kremer), pp. 541–6.

De la Potterie, I., 'Les deux noms de Jérusalem dans les Actes des Apôtres', *Bib* 63, 1982, pp. 153–87.

——, 'Les deux noms de Jérusalem dans l'Evangile de Luc', *RSR* 69, 1981, pp. 57–70.

Denaux, A., 'L'hypocrisie des Pharisiens et le dessein de Dieu. Analyse de *Lc.*, XIII, 31–33', in *L'Evangile de Luc* (*see* Neirynck), pp. 245–85.

Derrett, J. Duncan M., 'Luke's Perspective on Tribute to Caesar', in *Political Issues in Luke-Acts* (*see* Cassidy and Scharper), pp. 38–48.

Dibelius, Martin, *Botschaft und Geschichte. Gesammelte Aufsätze I*, ed. G. Bornkamm and H. Kraft, Tübingen: Mohr (Siebeck) 1953.

——, *From Tradition to Gospel*, Cambridge: James Clarke and Greenwood, SC: Attic 1971.

——, 'Herodes und Pilatus', in *Botschaft und Geschichte* (see above), vol. 1, pp. 278–92.

——, 'Jungfrauensohn und Krippenkind. Untersuchungen zur Geburtsgeschichte Jesu im Lukas-Evangelium'. in *Botschaft und Geschichte* (see above), vol. 1, pp. 1–78.

——, *Studies in the Acts of the Apostles*, ed. H. Greeven, London: SCM Press 1956.

Dodd, C. H., *The Parables of the Kingdom*. rev. ed., London: Hodder & Stoughton and New York: Scribner's 1961.

Donaldson, T. L., 'Moses Typology and the Sectarian Nature of Early Christian Anti-Judaism', *JSNT* 12, 1981, pp. 27–52.

Drury, John, *Tradition and Design in Luke's Gospel*. London: SPCK and Atlanta: John Knox Press 1976.

Dunn, James D. G., *Unity and Diversity in the New Testament*, London: SCM Press and Philadelphia: Westminster Press 1977.

Dupont, J., 'La conclusion des Actes et son rapport à l'ensemble de l'ouvrage de Luc', in *Les Actes des Apôtres* (*see* Kremer), pp. 359–404.

——, 'La conversion dans les Actes des Apôtres', in *Etudes sur les Actes des Apôtres* (see below), pp. 459–76.

——, 'Les discours de Pierre dans les Actes et le chapitre XXIV de l'évangile de Luc', in *L'Evangile de Luc* (*see* Neirynck), pp. 329–74.

——, 'Les discours missionnaires', in *Etudes sur les Actes des Apôtres* (see the following entry), pp. 133–55.

——, *Études sur les Actes des Apôtres*, LD 45, Paris: Editions du Cerf 1967.

——, 'La première Pentecôte', in *Etudes sur les Actes des Apôtres* (see the preceding entry), pp. 481–502.

——, 'Le salut des gentils et la signification theologique du livre des Actes'. *NTS* 6, 1959–60, pp. 132–55.

——, *The Salvation of the Gentiles. Essays on the Acts of the Apostles*, New York etc.: Paulist Press 1979.

——, 'Un peuple d'entre les nations (Actes 15.14)', *NTS* 31, 1985, pp. 321–35.

Easton, Burton Scott, *Early Christianity. The Purpose of Acts and Other Papers*, ed. F. C. Grant, Greenwich, Conn.: Seabury Press 1954.

Egelkraut, Helmuth L., *Jesus' Mission to Jerusalem. A Redaction Critical Study of the Travel Narrative in the Gospel of Luke, Lk 9:51–19:48*, Europäische Hochschulschriften, Reihe 23, Theologie 80, Frankfurt: Peter Lang; Bern: Herbert Lang 1976.

Eltester, Walther, 'Israel im lukanischen Werk und die Nazarethperikope', in *Jesus in Nazareth* (*see* Grässer), pp. 76–147.

The editors, 'Gentile', *EncJud*, vol. 7, pp. 410–11.

Enslin, Morton S., 'The Samaritan Ministry and Mission', *HUCA* 51, 1980, pp. 29–38.

Epp, Eldon Jay, 'The "Ignorance Motif" in Acts and Anti-Judaic Tendencies in Codex Bezae', *HTR* 55, 1962, pp. 51–62.

——, *The Theological Tendency of Codex Bezae Cantabrigiensis in Acts*, SNTSMS 3, Cambridge: University Press 1966.

Farmer, William R. (ed.), *New Synoptic Studies*, Macon, Ga.: Mercer University Press 1983.

Finn, Thomas M., 'The God-fearers Reconsidered', *CBQ* 47, 1985, pp. 75–83.

Fitzmyer, Joseph A., 'Crucifixion in Ancient Palestine, Qumran Literature, and the New Testament', *CBQ* 40, 1978, pp. 493–513.

——, 'Jewish Christianity in Acts in Light of the Qumran Scrolls', in *Studies in Luke-Acts* (*see* Keck and Martyn), pp. 233–57.

326 BIBLIOGRAPHY

Flender, Helmut, *St Luke. Theologian of Redemptive History*, London: SPCK and Philadelphia: Fortress Press 1967.

Ford, J. Massyngbaerde, 'Reconciliation and Forgiveness in Luke's Gospel', in *Political Issues in Luke-Acts* (*see* Cassidy and Scharper), pp. 80–98.

Franklin, Eric, *Christ the Lord. A Study in the Purpose and Theology of Luke-Acts*, London: SPCK and Philadelphia: Westminster 1975.

Funk, Robert W., *Language, Hermeneutic, and Word of God*. New York etc.: Harper & Row 1966.

Gager, John G., *The Origins of Anti-Semitism*, New York and Oxford: Oxford University Press 1983.

García del Moral, A., 'Un posible aspecto de la tesis y unidad del libro de los Hechos', *EstBib* 23, 1964, pp. 41–92.

Gasque, W. Ward, and Ralph P. Martin (eds.), *Apostolic History and the Gospel. Biblical and Historical Essays Presented to F. F. Bruce*, Exeter: Paternoster Press and Grand Rapids: Eerdmans 1970.

Gaster, T. H., 'Samaritans', *IDB*, vol. 4, pp. 190–7.

Gaston, Lloyd, *No Stone on Another*, NovTSup 23, Leiden: Brill 1970.

Gealy, Fred D., 'Captain of the Temple', *IDB*, vol. 1, pp. 535–6.

George, Augustin, *Etudes sur l'oeuvre de Luc*, SB, Paris: Gabalda 1978.

——, 'Israël dans l'oeuvre de Luc', *RB* 75, 1968, pp. 481–525.

——, 'La prédication inaugurale de Jésus dans la synagogue de Nazareth', *BVC* 59, 1964, pp. 17–29.

Gill, David, 'Observations on the Lukan Travel Narrative and Some Related Passages', *HTR* 63, 1970, pp. 199–221.

Girard, Louis, *L'Evangile des voyages de Jésus ou la section 9,51–18,14 de Saint Luc*, Paris: Gabalda 1951.

Gnilka, Joachim, 'Der Hymnus des Zacharias', *BZ* 6, 1962, pp. 215–38.

——, *Die Verstockung Israels. Isaias 6, 9–10 in der Theologie der Synoptiker*, SANT 3, Munich: Kösel 1961.

Goulder, M. D., *Type and History in Acts*, London: SPCK 1964.

Grässer, Erich, *et al.*, *Jesus in Nazareth*, BZNW 40, Berlin and New York: de Gruyter 1972.

Grant, Robert M., *Early Christianity and Society*, San Francisco, etc.: Harper & Row 1977.

Groh, Dennis E., and Robert Jewett (eds.), *The Living Text. Essays in Honor of Ernest W. Saunders*, Lanham, New York, and London: University Press of America 1985.

Grundmann, W., 'Der Pfingstbericht der Apostelgeschichte in seinem theologischen Sinn', in *Studia Evangelica*, vol. 2 (q.v.), pp. 584–94.

Gutbrod, Walter, 'Ἰουδαῖος, Ἰσραήλ, Ἑβραῖος in the New Testament', *TDNT*, vol. 3, pp. 375–91.

Haacker, Klaus, 'Das Bekenntnis des Paulus zur Hoffnung Israels nach der Apostelgeschichte des Lukas', *NTS* 31, 1985, pp. 437–51.

Haenchen, E., 'Apostelgeschichte', *RGG*,[3] Vol. 1, cols. 501–7.

——, 'The Book of Acts as Source Material for the History of Early Christianity', in *Studies in Luke-Acts* (*see* Keck and Martyn), pp. 258–78.

——, 'Historie und Verkündigung bei Markus und Lukas', in *Das Lukas-Evangelium* (*see* Braumann), pp. 287–316.

——, 'Judentum und Christentum in der Apostelgeschichte', *ZNW* 54, 1963, pp. 155–89.

Hahn, Ferdinand, 'Das Gleichnis von der Einladung zum Festmahl', in *Verborum Veritas* (*see* Böcher and Haacker), pp. 51–82.

Hanfmann, George M. A., *et al.*, *Sardis from Prehistoric to Roman Times*, Cambridge, Mass., and London: Harvard University Press 1983.

Hare, Douglas R. A., 'The Rejection of the Jews in the Synoptic Gospels and Acts', in *AntiSemitism and the Foundations of Christianity* (*see* A. T. Davies), pp. 27–47.

——, *The Theme of Jewish Persecution of Christians in the Gospel According to St Matthew*, SNTSMS 6, Cambridge: University Press 1967.

Harnack, Adolf, *The Acts of the Apostles*. (New Testament Studies 3). Crown Theological Library 27, New York: Putnam's 1909.

Hastings, Adrian, *Prophet and Witness in Jerusalem*, London, New York, and Toronto: Longmans, Green 1958.

Haubeck, Wilfrid, and Michael Bachmann (ed.), *Wort in der Zeit; Festgabe für Karl Heinrich Rengstorf*, Leiden: Brill 1980.

Hengel, Martin, *Acts and the History of Earliest Christianity*, London: SCM Press and Philadelphia: Fortress Press 1979.

——, *Between Jesus and Paul*, London: SCM Press and Philadelphia: Fortress Press 1983.

——, 'Die Ursprünge der christlichen Mission', *NTS* 18, 1971, pp. 15–38.

Hoffmann, Paul (ed.), *Orientierung an Jesus. Zur Theologie der Synoptiker. Für Josef Schmid*, Freiburg, Basel, and Vienna: Herder 1973.

Holtz, Traugott, 'Beobachtungen zur Stephanusrede Acta 7', in *Kirche – Theologie – Frömmigkeit* (q.v.), pp. 102–14.

Jeremias, Joachim, *The Parables of Jesus*, rev. ed., London: SCM Press and New York: Scribner's 1963.

——, 'Σαμάρεια, κτλ.', *TDNT*, vol. 7, pp. 88–94.

Jervell, Jacob, *Luke and the People of God*, Minneapolis: Augsburg Publishing House 1972.

——, 'Paul in the Acts of the Apostles. Tradition, History, Theology', in *Les Actes des Apôtres* (*see* Kremer), pp. 297–306. Reprinted in *Unknown Paul*, pp. 68–76, but cited here throughout according to the original.

——, *The Unknown Paul. Essays on Luke-Acts and Early Christian History*, Minneapolis: Augsburg Publishing House 1984.

Johnson, Luke Timothy, *The Literary Function of Possessions in Luke-Acts*,

SBLDS 39, Missoula, Mont.: Scholars Press (for the Society of Biblical Literature) 1977.

——, 'The Lukan Kingship Parable (Lk. 19:11–27)', *NovT* 24, 1982, pp. 139–59.

Jones, C. P. M., 'The Epistle to the Hebrews and the Lucan Writings', in *Studies in the Gospels (see* Nineham), pp. 113–43.

Juel, Donald, *Luke-Acts. The Promise of History*, Atlanta: John Knox and London: SCM Press 1983.

Jülicher, Adolf, *Die Gleichnisreden Jesu*, 2 vols, reprint ed., Darmstadt: Wissenschaftliche Buchgesellschaft 1963.

Katz, Steven T., 'Issues in the Separation of Judaism and Christianity after 70 C.E.', *JBL* 103, 1984, pp. 43–76.

Kaye, B. N., 'Acts' Portrait of Silas', *NovT* 21, 1979, pp. 13–26.

Keck, Fridolin, *Die öffentliche Abschiedsrede Jesu in Lk 20,45–21,36*, Forschung zur Bibel 25, Stuttgart: Verlag Katholisches Bibelwerk 1976.

Keck, Leander E., and J. Louis Martyn (eds.), *Studies in Luke-Acts*, Philadelphia: Fortress Press and London: SPCK 1966.

Kertelge, Karl (ed.), *Paulus in den neutestamentlichen Spätschriften*, Quaestiones disputatae 89, Freiburg, Basel, and Vienna: Herder 1981.

Kilgallen, John, *The Stephen Speech. A Literary and Redactional Study of Acts 7,2–53*, AnBib 67, Rome: Biblical Institute Press 1976.

Kilpatrick, G. D., 'ΛΑΟΙ at Luke II. 31 and Acts IV. 25, 27', *JTS* NS 16, 1965, p. 127.

——, 'A Theme of the Lucan Passion Story and Luke xxiii. 47', *JTS* 43, 1942, pp. 34–6.

Kimelman, Reuven, '*Birkat Ha-Minim* and the Lack of Evidence for an Anti-Christian Jewish Prayer in Late Antiquity', in *Jewish and Christian Self-Definition*, vol. 2 (*see* E. P. Sanders), pp. 226–44.

King, N. Q., 'The "Universalism" of the Third Gospel', in *Studia Evangelica* (q.v.), pp. 199–205.

Kirche – Theologie – Frömmigkeit. Festgabe für Gottfried Holtz, Berlin: Evangelische Verlagsanstalt 1965.

Klein, Günter, *Die zwölf Apostel. Ursprung und Gehalt einer Idee*, FRLANT NF 59, Göttingen: Vandenhoeck & Ruprecht 1961.

Klein, Hans, 'Die lukanisch-johanneische Passionstradition', *ZNW* 67, 1976, pp. 155–86.

Kodell, Jerome, 'Luke's Use of *Laos*, "People", Especially in the Jerusalem Narrative', *CBQ* 31, 1969, pp. 327–43.

Koenig, John, *Jews and Christians in Dialogue*, Philadelphia: Westminster Press 1979.

Köster, Helmut, *Einführung in das Neue Testament*, Berlin and New York: de Gruyter 1980.

——, *Introduction to the New Testament*, 2 vols, Hermeneia Foundations & Facets, Philadelphia: Fortress Press 1982.

Kraabel, A. T., 'The Disappearance of the "God-Fearers"', *Numen* 23, 1981, pp. 113–26.

Kränkl, Emmeram, *Jesus der Knecht Gottes*, Münchener Universitäts-Schriften, Katholisch-Theologische Fakultät, Regensburg: Pustet 1972.

Kremer, J. (ed.), *Les Actes des Apôtres. Traditions, rédaction, théologie*, BETL 48, Gembloux: Editions Duculot; Louvain: University Press 1979.

——, *Pfingstbericht und Pfingstgeschehen*, SBS 63 and 64, Stuttgart: Katholisches Bibelwerk 1973.

Kümmel, Werner Georg, *Introduction to the New Testament*, rev. ed. Nashville and New York: Abingdon Press and London: SCM Press 1975.

——, 'Das Urchristentum', *TRu* NF 22, 1954, pp. 138–70, 191–211.

Lambrecht, Jan, *Once More Astonished. The Parables of Jesus*, New York: Crossroad 1981.

Lampe, G. W. H., 'The Holy Spirit in the Writings of St Luke', in *Studies in the Gospels* (*see* Nineham), pp. 159–200.

——, 'The Lucan Portrait of Christ', *NTS* 2, 1955–56, pp. 160–75.

Laurentin, René, *Structure et théologies de Luc I–II*, EBib, Paris: Gabalda 1957.

Levenson, Jon D., 'Is There a Counterpart in the Hebrew Bible to New Testament Antisemitism?', *JES* 22, 1985, pp. 242–60.

Löning, Karl, 'Lukas – Theologe der von Gott geführten Heilsgeschichte (Lk, Apg)', in *Gestalt und Anspruch des Neuen Testaments* (*see* Schreiner), pp. 200–28.

——, 'Paulinismus in der Apostelgeschichte', in *Paulus in den neutestamentlichen Spätschriften* (see Kertelge), pp. 202–34.

——, *Die Saulustradition in der Apostelgeschichte*, NTAbh 9, Münster: Aschendorff 1973.

Lohfink, Gerhard, 'Hat Jesus eine Kirche gestiftet?', *TQ* 161, 1981, pp. 81–97.

——, *Die Sammlung Israels. Eine Untersuchung zur lukanischen Ekklesiologie*, SANT 39, Munich: Kösel, 1975.

Lohse, Eduard, 'Die Bedeutung des Pfingstberichtes im Rahmen des lukanischen Geschichtswerkes', *EvT* 13, 1953, pp. 422–36.

——, 'Lukas als Theologe der Heilsgeschichte', in *Das Lukas-Evangelium* (*see* Braumann), pp. 64–90.

——, 'Missionarisches Handeln Jesu nach dem Evangelium des Lukas', *TZ* 10, 1954, pp. 1–13.

Lowry, Richard, 'The Rejected-Suitor Syndrome: Human Sources of New Testament "Antisemitism"', *JES* 14, 1977, pp. 219–32.

Lüdemann, Gerd, *Paulus, Der Heidenapostel*, Vol. 2: *Antipaulinismus im frühen Christentum*, FRLANT 130, Göttingen: Vandenhoeck & Ruprecht 1983.

McCown, C. C., 'The Geography of Luke's Central Section', *JBL* 57, 1938, pp. 51–66.

——, 'Gospel Geography. Fiction, Fact, and Truth', *JBL* 60, 1941, pp. 1–25.

Maddox, Robert, *The Purpose of Luke-Acts*, FRLANT 126, Göttingen: Vandenhoeck & Ruprecht 1982.

Manson, T. W., 'The Life of Jesus: A Survey of the Available Material. (3) The Work of St Luke', *BJRL* 28, 1944, pp. 382–403.

Mantel, Hugo, 'Sanhedrin', *IDB*, Supplementary vol., pp. 784–6.

Martyn, J. Louis, *History and Theology in the Fourth Gospel*, Nashville: Abingdon Press ²1979.

Matera, Frank J., 'The Death of Jesus According to Luke: A Question of Sources', *CBQ* 47, 1985, pp. 469–85.

Mather, P. Boyd, 'The Search for the Living Text of the Lucan Infancy Narrative', in *The Living Text* (*see* Groh and Jewett), pp. 123–40.

Mattill, A. J., Jr, 'The Jesus-Paul Parallels and the Purpose of Luke-Acts: H. H. Evans Reconsidered', *NovT* 17, 1975, pp. 15–46.

——, *Luke and the Last Things*, Dillsboro, NC: Western North Carolina Press 1979.

——, 'The Purpose of Acts: Schneckenburger Reconsidered', in *Apostolic History and the Gospel* (*see* Gasque and Martin), pp. 108–22.

Menezes, Franklin, 'The Mission of Jesus According to Lk 4:16–30', *Biblebhashyam* 6, 1980, pp. 249–64.

Michel, O., 'ναός', *TDNT*, vol. 4, pp. 880–90.

Minear, Paul S., 'Luke's Use of Birth Stories', in *Studies in Luke-Acts* (*see* Keck and Martyn), pp. 111–30.

Miyoshi, Michi, *Der Anfang des Reiseberichts. Lk 9,51–10,24*, AnBib 60, Rome: Biblical Institute Press 1974.

Moessner, David P., 'Luke 9:1–50: Luke's Preview of the Journey of the Prophet Like Moses of Deuteronomy', *JBL* 102, 1983, pp. 575–605.

Momigliano, Arnaldo, 'Patronus', *OCD*, p. 791.

Moore, George Foot, *Judaism in the First Centuries of the Christian Era*, 2 vols, reprint ed., New York: Schocken 1971.

Mora, Vincent, *Le signe de Jonas*, Paris: Editions du Cerf 1983.

Morales Gómez, Gonzalo, 'Jerusalén – Jerosólima en el vocabulario y la geografía de Lucas', *Revista Catalana de Teologia* 7, 1982, pp. 131–86.

Morgenthaler, Robert, *Die lukanische Geschichtsschreibung als Zeugnis*, 2 vols, Zurich: Zwingli Verlag 1949.

Müller, P.-G., 'Die jüdische Entscheidung gegen Jesus nach der Apostelgeschichte', in *Les Actes des Apôtres* (*see* Kremer), pp. 523–31.

Muhlack, Gudrun, *Die Parallelen von Lukas-Evangelium und Apostelgeschichte*, Theologie und Wirklichkeit 8, Frankfurt am Main etc.: Peter Lang 1979.

Munck, Johannes, *Paul and the Salvation of Mankind*, London: SCM Press and Atlanta: John Knox Press 1959.

Mussner, Franz, *Tractate on the Jews. The Significance of Judaism for Christian Faith*, Philadelphia: Fortress Press and London: SPCK 1984.

——, 'Wohnung Gottes und Menschensohn nach der Stephanusperikope (Apg 6,8–8,2)', in *Jesus und der Menschensohn. Für Anton Vögtle* (*see* Pesch), pp. 283–99.

Neirynck, F. (ed.), *L'Evangile de Luc. Problèmes littéraires et théologiques. Mémorial Lucien Cerfaux*, BETL 32, Gembloux: Duculot 1973.

Neyrey, Jerome H., 'Jesus' Address to the Women of Jerusalem (Lk. 23. 27–31) – A Prophetic Judgment Oracle', *NTS* 29, 1983, pp. 74–86.

——, *The Passion According to Luke*, New York and Mahwah: Paulist Press 1985.

Nineham, D. E. (ed.), *Studies in the Gospels. Essays in Memory of R. H. Lightfoot*, Oxford: B. H. Blackwell 1955.

Nolland, John, 'A Fresh Look at Acts 15.10', *NTS* 27, 1980, pp. 105–15.

——, 'Words of Grace (Luke 4,22)', *Bib* 65, 1984, pp. 44–60.

Novak, David, *The Image of the Non-Jew in Judaism*, Toronto Studies in Theology 14, New York and Toronto: Edwin Mellen Press 1983.

O'Connor, Edward D., *Faith in the Synoptic Gospels*, South Bend, Ind.: University of Notre Dame Press 1961.

Ó Fearghail, Fearghus, 'Rejection in Nazareth: Lk 4.22', *ZNW* 75, 1984, pp. 60–52.

Oliver, H. H., 'The Lucan Birth Stories and the Purpose of Luke-Acts', *NTS* 10, 1963–64, pp. 202–26.

O'Neill, J. C., *The Theology of Acts in Its Historical Setting*, London: SPCK ²1970.

O'Toole, Robert F., *The Unity of Luke's Theology*, Good News Studies 9, Wilmington, Del.: Glazier 1984.

Parker, Pierson, 'Lawyer', *IDB*, vol. 3, p. 102.

Perrin, Norman, and Dennis C. Duling, *The New Testament. An Introduction*, New York etc.: Harcourt Brace Jovanovich ²1982.

Perrot, Charles, 'Les décisions de l'assemblée de Jérusalem', *RSR* 69, 1981, pp. 195–208.

Pesch, Rudolf, *et al.* (eds.), *Jesus und der Menschensohn. Für Anton Vögtle*, Freiburg etc.: Herder 1975.

Pesch, Rudolf, *Die Vision des Stephanus. Apg 7,55–56 im Rahmen der Apostelgeschichte*, SBS 12, Stuttgart: Katholisches Bibelwerk, no date [1966].

Plümacher, Eckhard, 'Acta-Forschung 1974–1982', *TRu* 48, 1983, pp. 1–56.

Pope, M. H., '"Am Ha'arez', *IDB*, vol. 1, pp. 106–7.

Prete, Benedetto, 'L'arrivo di Paolo a Roma e il suo significato secondo *Atti* 28,16–31', *RivB* 31, 1983, pp. 147–87.

Purvis, J. D., 'Samaritans', *IDB*, Supplementary vol., pp. 776–7.

Radl, Walter, *Paulus und Jesus im lukanischen Doppelwerk*, Europäische Hochschulschriften, Reihe 23, Theologie 49, Bern: Herbert Lang; Frankfurt am Main: Peter Lang 1975.

Rau, Gottfried, 'Das Volk in der lukanischen Passionsgeschichte. Eine Konjektur zu Lk 23:13', *ZNW* 56, 1965, pp. 41–51.

Reicke, Bo, 'Der Barmherzige Samariter', in *Verborum Veritas* (*see* Böcher and Haacker), pp. 103–9.

——, *The Gospel of Luke*, Richmond: John Knox Press 1964.

——, 'Instruction and Discussion in the Travel Narrative', in *Studia Evangelica* (q. v.), pp. 206–16.

——, 'Jesus in Nazareth', in *Das Wort und die Wörter* (*see* Balz and Schulz), pp. 47–55.

Rese, Martin, 'Die Aussagen über Jesu Tod und Auferstehung in der Apostelgeschichte', *NTS* 30, 1984, pp. 335–53.

Richard, Earl, 'The Divine Purpose: The Jews and the Gentile Mission (Acts 15)', in *Luke-Acts. New Perspectives* (*see* Talbert), pp. 188–209.

Richardson, Neil, *The Panorama of Luke*, London: Epworth Press 1982.

Rivkin, E., 'Pharisees', *IDB*, Supplementary vol., pp. 657–63.

Robinson, W. C., Jr, 'The Theological Context for Interpreting Luke's Travel Narrative', *JBL* 79, 1960, pp. 20–31.

——, *Der Weg des Herrn. Studien zur Geschichte und Eschatologie im Lukas-Evangelium*, TF 36, Hamburg-Bergstedt: Herbert Reich 1964.

Roetzel, Calvin J., 'Jewish Christian – Gentile Christian Relations. A Discussion of Ephesians 2:15a', *ZNW* 74, 1983, pp. 81–9.

Rolland, Philippe, 'L'organisation du Livre des Actes et de l'ensemble de l'oeuvre de Luc', *Bib* 65, 1984, pp. 81–6.

Roloff, Jürgen, 'Die Paulus-Darstellung des Lukas', *EvT* 39, 1979, pp. 510–31.

Ruether, Rosemary Radford, *Faith and Fratricide. The Theological Roots of Anti-Semitism*, Crossroad Books, New York: Seabury Press 1974.

Sabbe, M., 'The Son of Man Saying in Acts 7,56', in *Les Actes des Apôtres* (*see* Kremer), pp. 241–79.

Sahlin, Harald, *Der Messias und das Gottesvolk. Studien zur protolukanischen Theologie*, ASNU 12, Uppsala: Almqvist & Wiksell 1945.

——, *Studien zum dritten Kapitel des Lukasevangeliums*, UUÅ 1949:2, Uppsala: A.-B. Lundequistska, no date [1949].

Sanders, E. P., *et al.*, (eds.), *Jewish and Christian Self-Definition*, Vol. 2: *Aspects of Judaism in the Graeco-Roman Period*, London: SCM Press and Philadelphia: Fortress Press 1981.

Sanders, Jack T., *Ethics in the New Testament: Change and Development*, Philadelphia: Fortress Press and London: SCM Press 1975, reissued SCM Press 1986.

——, *The New Testament Christological Hymns. Their Historical Religious Background*, SNTSMS 15, Cambridge: University Press 1971.

——, 'The Parable of the Pounds and Lucan Anti-Semitism', *TS* 42, 1981, pp. 660–8.

——, 'Paul's "Autobiographical" Statements in Galatians 1–2', *JBL* 85, 1966, pp. 335–43.

——, 'The Prophetic Use of the Scriptures in Luke-Acts', in Evans, C. A., and W. F. Stinespring (ed.), *Early Jewish and Christian Exegesis. Studies in Memory of William Hugh Brownlee*, Decatur, Ga.: Scholars Press, forthcoming.

——, 'The Salvation of the Jews in Luke-Acts', in *Luke-Acts. New Perspectives* (*see* Talbert), pp. 104–28.

——, 'Tradition and Redaction in Luke XV. 11–32', *NTS* 15, 1969, pp. 433–8.

Sandmel, Samuel, *Anti-Semitism in the New Testament?*, Philadelphia: Fortress Press 1978.

——, 'Felix, Antonius', *IDB*, vol. 2, p. 264.

Sauvagnat, Bernard, 'Se repentir, être baptisé, recevoir l'Esprit: Actes 2, 37ss', *Foi et Vie* 80, 1981, pp. 77–89.

Schäfer, K. T., 'Aposteldekret', *RAC*, vol. 1, cols. 555–8.

Scharlemann, Martin H., *Stephen: A Singular Saint*, AnBib 34, Rome: Pontifical Biblical Institute 1968.

Schiffman, Lawrence H., 'At the Crossroads: Tannaitic Perspectives on the Jewish-Christian Schism', in *Jewish and Christian Self-Definition* (*see* E. P. Sanders), vol. 2, pp. 115–56.

——, 'Legislation Concerning Relations with Non-Jews in the *Zadokite Fragments* and in Tannaitic Literature', *RevQ* 11, 1983, pp. 379–89.

Schmid, J., and A. Vögtle (eds.), *Synoptische Studien. Alfred Wikenhauser zum 70. Geburtstag*, Munich: Zink 1953.

Schmidt, Daryl, 'Luke's "Innocent" Jesus: A Scriptural Apologetic', in *Political Issues in Luke-Acts* (*see* Cassidy and Scharper), pp. 111–21.

Schmidt, Karl Ludwig, *Der Rahmen der Geschichte Jesu*, reprint ed., Darmstadt: Wissenschaftliche Buchgesellschaft 1964.

Schmithals, Walter, 'Die Berichte der Apostelgeschichte über die Bekehrung des Paulus', *TV* 14, 1977–78, pp. 145–65.

——, *Paul and James*, SBT 46, London: SCM Press and Naperville, Ill.: Allenson 1963.

Schneider, Gerhard, *Verleugnung, Verspottung und Verhör Jesu nach Lukas 22, 54–71*, SANT 22, Munich: Kösel 1969.

——, 'Der Zweck des lukanischen Doppelwerks', *BZ* 21, 1977, pp. 45–66.

Schneider, Johannes, 'Zur Analyse des lukanischen Reiseberichtes', in *Synoptische Studien. Alfred Wikenhauser* (*see* Schmid and Vögtle), pp. 207–29.

Schnider, Franz, *Die verlorenen Söhne*, OBO 17, Freiburg, Switzerland: Universitätsverlag; Göttingen: Vandenhoeck & Ruprecht 1977.

Schoeps, Hans Joachim, *Theologie und Geschichte des Judenchristentums*, Tübingen: Mohr (Siebeck) 1949.

Schottroff, Luise, 'Das Gleichnis vom verlorenen Sohn', *ZTK* 68, 1971, pp. 27–52.

—— and Wolfgang Stegemann, *Jesus von Nazareth – Hoffnung der Armen*, Stuttgart etc.: Kohlhammer 1978.

Schreiner, Josef (ed.), *Gestalt und Anspruch des Neuen Testaments*, Würzburg: Echter-Verlag 1969.

Schütz, Frieder, *Der leidende Christus*, BWANT 89 (5,9), Stuttgart etc.: Kohlhammer 1969.

Schulz, Siegfried, *Die Stunde der Botschaft. Einführung in die Theologie der vier Evangelisten*, Hamburg: Furche; Zurich: Zwingli ²1970.

Schwartz, Daniel R., 'The Accusation and the Accusers at Philippi (Acts 16,20–21)', *Bib* 65, 1984, pp. 357–63.

Selwyn, E. G., 'St. Stephen's Place in Christian Origins', *Theology* 5, 1922, pp. 306–16.

Sevenster, J. N., *The Roots of Pagan Anti-Semitism in the Ancient World*, NovTSup 41, Leiden: Brill 1975.

Simon, Marcel, 'The Apostolic Decree and Its Setting in the Ancient Church', in *Le Christianisme antique et son contexte religieux* (see the following entry), vol. 2, pp. 414–37.

——, *Le Christianisme antique et son contexte religieux. Scripta Varia*, 2 vols, WUNT 23, Tübingen: Mohr (Siebeck) 1981.

——, *St Stephen and the Hellenists in the Primitive Church*, London etc.: Longmans, Green 1958.

——, 'Saint Stephen and the Jerusalem Temple', in *Le Christianisme antique et son contexte religieux* (see above), vol. 1, pp. 153–68.

——, *Verus Israel*, Paris: de Boccard 1964.

Soards, Marion L., 'Tradition, Composition, and Theology in Luke's Account of Jesus Before Herod Antipas', *Bib* 66, 1985, pp. 344–63.

Steck, Odil Hannes, *Israel und das gewaltsame Geschick der Propheten*, WMANT 23, Neukirchen-Vluyn: Neukirchener Verlag 1967.

Stolle, Volker, *Der Zeuge als Angeklagter*, BWANT 102 (6, 2), Stuttgart, etc.: Kohlhammer 1973.

Strobel, August, *Die Stunde der Wahrheit*, WUNT 21, Tübingen: Mohr (Siebeck) 1980.

Studia Evangelica, ed. K. Aland, *et al.*, TU 73, Berlin: Akademie-Verlag 1959.

Studia Evangelica, vol. 2, ed. F. L. Cross, TU 87, Berlin: Akademie-Verlag 1964.

Surkau, Hans Werner, *Martyrien in jüdischer und frühchristlicher Zeit*, FRLANT NF 36, Göttingen: Vandenhoeck & Ruprecht 1938.

Swaim, J. C., 'Aretas', *IDB*, vol. 1, pp. 217–18.

Sylva, Dennis D., 'Ierousalēm and Hierosoluma in Luke-Acts', *ZNW* 74, 1983, pp. 207–21.

Talbert, Charles H., *Literary Patterns, Theological Themes, and the Genre of Luke-Acts*, SBLMS 20, Missoula, Mont.: Society of Biblical Literature and Scholars Press 1974.

—— (ed.), *Luke-Acts. New Perspectives from the Society of Biblical Literature Seminar*, New York: Crossroad 1984.

——, 'Martyrdom in Luke-Acts and the Lucan Social Ethic', in *Political Issues in Luke-Acts* (*see* Cassidy and Scharper), pp. 99–110.

——, 'Promise and Fulfillment in Lucan Theology', in *Luke-Acts. New Perspectives* (see above), pp. 91–103.

——, Review of *Kreuzweg and Kreuzigung Jesu* by F. G. Untergassmair, *JBL* 102, 1983, pp. 342–3.

——, *What Is a Gospel? The Genre of the Canonical Gospels*, Philadelphia: Fortress Press 1977.

Tannehill, Robert C., 'Israel in Luke-Acts: A Tragic Story', *JBL* 104, 1985, pp. 69–85.

——, 'The Mission of Jesus According to Luke IV 16–30', in *Jesus in Nazareth* (*see* Grässer), pp. 51–75.

Taylor, Vincent, *Behind the Third Gospel*, Oxford: Clarendon Press 1926.

Theissen, Gerd, *Studien zur Soziologie des Urchristentums*. WUNT 19, Tübingen: Mohr (Siebeck) 1979.

Tiede, David L., *Prophecy and History in Luke-Acts*, Philadelphia: Fortress Press 1980.

Tolbert, Malcolm, 'Leading Ideas of the Gospel of Luke', *RevExp* 64, 1967, pp. 441–51.

Townsend, John T., 'The Date of Luke-Acts', in *Luke-Acts. New Perspectives* (*see* Talbert), pp. 47–62.

Trocmé, Etienne, *Le 'Livre des Actes' et l'histoire*, Études d'histoire et de philosophie religieuses 45, Paris: Presses Universitaires de France 1957.

Tyson, Joseph B., 'Conflict As a Literary Theme in the Gospel of Luke', in *New Synoptic Studies* (see Farmer), pp. 303–27.

——, 'The Jewish Public in Luke-Acts', *NTS* 30, 1984, pp. 574–83.

——, 'The Lukan Version of the Trial of Jesus', *NovT* 3, 1959, pp. 249–58.

——, 'The Opposition to Jesus in the Gospel of Luke', *Perspectives in Religious Studies* 5, 1978, pp. 144–50.

van Goudoever, J., 'The Place of Israel in Luke's Gospel', *NovT* 8, 1966, pp. 111–23.

Via, E. Jane, 'According to Luke, Who Put Jesus to Death?', in *Political Issues in Luke-Acts* (*see* Cassidy and Scharper), pp. 122–45.

——, 'An Interpretation of Acts 7.35–37', *Perspectives in Religious Studies* 6, 1979, pp. 190–207.

Vielhauer, Philipp, 'Das Benedictus des Zacharias (Luk. 1, 68–79)', in

Aufsätze zum Neuen Testament, pp. 28–46, TBü 31, Munich: Christian Kaiser 1965.

——, 'On the "Paulinism" of Acts', in *Studies in Luke-Acts* (*see* Keck and Martyn), pp. 33–50.

Völkel, Martin, 'Zur Deutung des "Reiches Gottes" bei Lukas', *ZNW* 65, 1974, pp. 57–70.

Wainwright, Arthur W., 'Luke and the Restoration of the Kingdom to Israel', *ExpTim* 89, 1977–78, pp. 76–9.

Waitz, H., 'Das Problem des sogenannten Aposteldekrets', *ZKG* 55, 1936, pp. 227–63.

Walaskay, Paul W., *'And So We Came to Rome.' The Political Perspective of St Luke*, SNTSMS 49, Cambridge, etc.: Cambridge University Press 1983.

Wanke, Joachim, *Die Emmauserzählung*, Erfurter theologische Studien 31, Leipzig: St Benno 1973.

Weinert, Francis D., 'Luke, the Temple and Jesus' Saying About Jerusalem's Abandoned House (Luke 13:34–35)', *CBQ* 44, 1982, pp. 68–76.

Weiser, Alfons, 'Das "Apostelkonzil" (Apg 15, 1–35)', *BZ* 28, 1984, pp. 145–67.

Weiss, Hans-Friedrich, 'Φαρισαῖος', *TWNT*, vol. 9, pp. 36–51.

Weiss, Johannes, *Earliest Christianity*, 2 vols, New York: Harper & Brothers 1939.

Wellhausen, J., *Einleitung in die drei ersten Evangelien*. Berlin: Reimer 1905.

Wilch, John R., 'Jüdische Schuld am Tode Jesu – Antijudaismus in der Apostelgeschichte?', in *Wort in der Zeit* (*see* Haubeck and Bachmann), pp. 236–49.

Wilckens, Ulrich, *Die Missionsreden der Apostelgeschichte*, WMANT 5, Neukirchen-Vluyn: Neukirchener Verlag ³1974.

——, 'ὑποκρίνομαι, κτλ.', *TWNT*, vol. 8, pp. 558–71.

——, 'Vergebung für die Sünderin (Lk 7,36–50)', in *Orientierung an Jesus* (see Hoffmann), pp. 394–424.

Wilcox, Max, 'The "God-Fearers" in Acts – A Reconsideration', *JSNT* 13, 1981, pp. 102–22.

Wild, Robert A., 'The Encounter Between Pharisaic and Christian Judaism: Some Early Gospel Evidence', *NovT* 27, 1985, pp. 105–24.

Wilken, Robert L., *The Christians As the Romans Saw Them*, New Haven and London: Yale University Press 1984.

Wilson, Stephen G., *The Gentiles and the Gentile Mission in Luke-Acts*, SNTSMS 23, Cambridge: University Press 1973.

——, *Luke and the Law*, SNTSMS 50, Cambridge, etc.: Cambridge University Press 1983.

Wink, Walter, *John the Baptist in the Gospel Tradition*, SNTSMS 7, Cambridge: University Press 1968.

Winn, Albert C., 'Elusive Mystery: The Purpose of Acts', *Int* 13, 1959, pp. 144–56.

Winter, Paul, 'The Treatment of His Sources by the Third Evangelist in Luke XXI–XXIV', *ST* 8, 1954, pp. 138–72.

——, *On the Trial of Jesus*, rev. and ed. T. A. Burkill and G. Vermes, Studia Judaica 1, Berlin and New York: de Gruyter ²1974.

Zehnle, Richard F., *Peter's Pentecost Discourse*, SBLMS 15, Nashville and New York: Abingdon Press 1971.

Ziesler, J. A., 'Luke and the Pharisees', *NTS* 25, 1979, pp. 146–57.

Zingg, Paul, 'Die Stellung des Lukas zur Heidenmission', *Neue Zeitschrift für Missionswissenschaft/Nouvelle revue de science missionnaire* 29, 1973, pp. 200–9.

Zmijewski, Josef, *Die Eschatologiereden des Lukas-Evangeliums*, BBB 40, Bonn: Hanstein 1972.

Notes

1. The Jewish Leaders

1. Here and throughout the author of Luke-Acts will be called 'Luke', according to normal convention. That does not mean that I identify the author with any known person in antiquity.

2. Since these captains, who appear only in Luke and not in Mark or Matthew, are associated with the chief priests, they must be thought of as captains of the Temple, certainly not as Roman military officers. On this point, cf. Gealy, 'Captain of the Temple'. Luke's further references to these captains show, as will become progressively clear, that he thinks of a Temple police force.

3. Wellhausen, *Evangelium Lucae*, pp. 129–30; Klostermann, *Lukas*, p. 220; Hauck, *Lukas*, p. 275.

4. B. and J. Weiss, *Markus und Lukas*, p. 657.

5. Grundmann, *Lukas*, p. 419. Also Zahn, *Lucas*, p. 639.

6. Montefiore, *Synoptic Gospels*, vol. 2, p. 614.

7. B. and J. Weiss, *Markus und Lucas*, p. 657.

8. Klostermann, *Lukas*, p. 220. Fitzmyer, *Luke*, vol. 2, p. 1466, sees that this is, however, Luke's meaning.

9. Also Marshall, *Gospel of Luke*, p. 101.

10. Also Winter, *Trial*, p. 28.

11. Cf. Conzelmann, *Theology*, p. 41, n. 1, and pp. 68–73, where Luke's confusion about Palestinian geography is detailed (although we shall eventually below have to modify Conzelmann's explanation of Luke's view of Samaria). Cf. also Goulder, *Type*, p. 59: 'The geography of Luke is a muddle because symbolism has taken too large a hand.' Cf. further McCown, 'Luke's Central Section', and 'Gospel Geography', p. 15.

12. Inasmuch as Matt. 22.1–2, the Matthaean parallel to Mark 15.1, also includes the readings 'elders of the people' and 'they led him (ἀπάγω, as in Luke) away', it appears likely that Luke was here conflating Mark and Q (or Matthew, however that may be). Luke's use in Acts, then, of ἄγω and κατάγω as the verbs of choice for getting Christians into the Sanhedrin will be derived from this occurrence.

13. On the puzzling nature of the Lucan account, cf. further Winter, *Trial*, p. 67.

14. On this count, cf. R. M. Grant, *Early Christianity and Society*, pp. 46–7. Fitzmyer, *Luke*, vol. 2, p. 1473, considers the charge of disturbing the peace not to be part of the indictment.

15. So also Walaskay, *We Came to Rome*, pp. 88–9, n. 8; similarly Fitzmyer, *Luke*, vol. 2, p. 1473.

16. Cf., in addition to many commentaries, Conzelmann, *Theology*, p. 140.

17. So also Conzelmann, op. cit., p. 139.

18. So also Conzelmann, op. cit., p. 140.

19. Montefiore, *Synoptic Gospels*, vol. 2, pp. 617–18, thinks that Luke may have hit on historical accuracy by chance in an attempt to rationalize the trial before Pilate; but Luke's purpose is not rationalistic, it is theological.

20. D. Schmidt, 'Luke's "Innocent" Jesus'.

21. Ibid., p. 112.

22. Ibid., pp. 113–14.

23. Ibid., p. 115.

24. Ibid., p. 116.

25. Ibid., p. 117.

26. Ibid., p. 118.

27. Ibid., pp. 118–19.

28. Ibid., p. 119.

29. Cf. Fitzmyer, *Luke*, vol. 1, pp. 213–15.

30. See below, pp. 16–19.

31. Whether or not Luke relies directly on Isa. 53.11 in repeatedly calling Jesus 'innocent' is an issue that does not need to be debated here. One may wish to note Kilpatrick, 'Lucan Passion Story'.

32. G. Schneider, *Verleugnung*, p. 196, sees the matter correctly and cites additional evidence that Schmidt has overlooked: 'The Jews therefore slanderously accuse Jesus of insurrection. In reality, it is they who sanction (23.18–19, 25) and instigate (Acts 13.50; 14.19; 17.5–8; 17.13; 18.12–17; 21.27) the rioting.'

33. Winter, *Trial*; Blinzler, *Prozess*; Catchpole, *Trial*, and 'Trial of Jesus'; Strobel, *Stunde der Wahrheit*. While setting the historical issue aside, we may nevertheless note that there seems little reason to doubt that the Jewish Temple leadership was in fact behind Jesus' execution.

34. Gnilka, *Verstockung*, p. 139, sees Acts 2.23 as referring to this manipulation. Walaskay, *We Came to Rome*, pp. 38–40, argues that Luke intends to show that the 'trial' before the Sanhedrin is no proper hearing at all but rather a kangaroo court.

35. Cf. also Tyson, 'Trial of Jesus', p. 257.

36. There has been a great deal of discussion as to whether Luke has done this as a part of an apologetic to Roman authorities of his own day in an attempt to produce a favourable attitude towards Christianity. One may note especially the studies of Dupont, 'Le salut des gentils' (ET, without notes, in *The Salvation of the Gentiles*, pp. 11–33), and Wilson, *Gentiles*. That issue, which we may think of as the obverse side of the coin of discussion about guilt for Jesus' death, does not directly concern us here. What does concern us is the reverse side, the role of the Jews.

37. Cf. Schmid, *Lukas*, p. 345; Lampe, 'Luke', p. 841.

38. The remark of Bauernfeind, *Apostelgeschichte*, p. 73, *apud* Acts 4.10 is worthy of note: 'The Jewish authorities belong for Luke to the most outspoken opponents of Christianity'; cf. also ibid., p. 92.

39. Cf. Wellhausen, *Einleitung*, p. 65; Conzelmann, *Theology*, p. 87; G. Schneider, *Verleugnung*, p. 195. Fitzmyer, *Luke*, vol. 2, p. 1492, argues that Pilate's delivering Jesus to the executioners 'involves Pilate' in Jesus' death. Well, involvement maybe, but guilt no. Fitzmyer, ibid., p. 1496, is nevertheless perfectly clear about who it is in Luke who conducts Jesus to his death.

40. E.g., Goulder, *Type*, p. 143; Rengstorf, *Lukas*, p. 266; Schütz, *Leidender Christus*, p. 127.

41. Lagrange, *Luc*, p. 584; Wellhausen, *Evangelium Lucae*, p. 133.

42. Grundmann, *Lukas*, pp. 429, 433; Hauck, *Lukas*, pp. 282, 284; Gilmour, 'Luke', p. 403; Ernst, *Lukas*, p. 630; Klostermann, *Lukas*, p. 225.

43. Loisy, *Luc*, pp. 552, 557.

44. Schmid, *Lukas*, p. 346; Caird, *Luke*, p. 249; Leaney, *Luke*, p. 281; Harrington, *St. Luke*, p. 263; Rengstorf, *Lukas*, p. 268; Bundy, *First Three Gospels*, pp. 534, 540; Talbert, *Reading Luke*, pp. 212–13.

45. G. Schneider, *Lukas*, vol. 2, p. 481; similarly Ellis, *Luke*, p. 264.

46. *Synoptic Gospels*, vol. 2, p. 622.

47. Cf., for example, Cassidy, 'Luke's Audience', pp. 147–8; Schütz, *Leidender Christus*, p. 127.

48. While a few of the authors just cited as affirming that the Romans carry out the crucifixion in Luke refer vaguely to the crucifixion scene (Luke 23.33–49) in support of their position, most offer no evidence whatsoever, thus leading me to suspect that they have let what really happened and Luke's narrative become confused in their thinking.

49. Cf. Wanke, *Emmauserzählung*, p. 64; Beck, *Mature Christianity*, pp. 198–9.

50. Schütz, *Leidender Christus*, p. 128, gets deeper and deeper into his trap of trying to make Pilate, not the Jewish religious authorities, Jesus' executioner, then tries to get out by claiming that Luke was trying to show that Pilate was not a true representative of Roman jurisprudence. What Schütz in fact demonstrates is the lengths to which some people will go to avoid the obvious. Ernst, *Lukas*, p. 660 – who also cannot accept the fact that, in Luke, it is the Jews who kill Jesus – proposes that Luke 24.20 is merely a traditional saying that Luke repeats. That answers nothing. What does the saying say? Why does Luke repeat it? Fitzmyer, *Luke*, vol. 2, p. 1564, gets it right.

51. Cf. Loisy, *Actes*, p. 205; Lake and Cadbury in *Beginnings*, Part I, vol. 4, p. 23; Haenchen, *Acts*, p. 180; Jacquier, *Actes*, p. 65; G. Schneider, *Apostelgeschichte*, vol. 1, p. 271; Lampe, 'Acts', p. 889; *et al.* The view is not, however, universal. Kränkl, *Knecht*, p. 102, sees only Jews involved. Conzelmann, *Theology*, pp. 91–2, sees this as an example of the way in which Luke presents a one-sided emphasis on the guilt of the Jews 'and thus produces obvious discrepancies' between his sources and the final narrative. Thus, while ἄνομοι ought to refer to the Romans, 'Acts ii, 23 . . . in its present sense applies to the Jews'; cf. also ibid., p. 161. Marshall, *Acts*, p. 75, takes a similar position.

52. Grundmann, *Lukas*, p. 427, emphasizes the relation of this verse to Luke 23.24–25. Cf. further Lampe, 'Acts', p. 890; Haenchen, *Acts*, pp. 206–7.

53. Fitzmyer, 'Crucifixion', esp. pp. 498–501, 509–10. The phrase 'hang on a tree' refers to Jewish crucifixion in 1QpNah frgs. 3–4, col. i, ll. 1–11.

54. Cf. Bundy, *First Three Gospels*, p. 540; Easton, *Luke*, p. 346; Ernst, *Lukas*, p. 635.

55. So correctly Schmithals, *Lukas*, p. 226; G. Schneider, *Verleugnung*, p. 195; Walaskay, *We Came to Rome*, p. 45; Rese, 'Aussagen über Jesu Tod', p. 344–5. Schneider also takes the centurion of Luke 23.47 to be intended as a Jew. Walaskay, *We Came to Rome*, p. 45, refers rather to 'the lone Roman centurion' as providing a contrast to the Jewish soldiers, and that may come closest to defining Luke's purpose. Fitzmyer, *Luke*, vol. 2, p. 1505, thinks that the soldiers are Roman. On the centurion, cf. further below in ch. 5.

56. Cf. above, p. 3.

57. Gealy, 'Captain of the Temple', p. 536.

58. Tyson, 'Opposition', p. 147, has noted this but has explained it only in terms of the general theme of opposition.

59. ὑπηρέται (RSV: 'officers'). 'Sergeant', itself a corruption of 'servant', is the precise term when it designates somebody under a captain; cf. Liddell and Scott, *Greek-English Lexicon*, s.v. ὑπηρέτης, II.2 and 3.

60. This would agree with Conzelmann's opinion that Luke thinks of Jerusalem or of the Temple or of both as comparable to a free provincial city; cf. *Theology*, p. 70.

61. Herod also has soldiers, στρατεύματα: Luke 23.11. O'Toole, *Unity*, p. 163, declares, on the basis of no apparent evidence, that 'the Jewish officials had police authority in Jerusalem'.

62. Fitzmyer, *Luke*, vol. 1, p. 470, emphasizes that they cannot be Roman soldiers; he takes them to be Herod's. Cf. esp. the discussion by Sahlin, *Dritter Kapitel*, pp. 39–40.

63. Buck, 'Jesus Before Herod', p. 169, points out that only in Luke are both mistreatments of Jesus by 'guards' done by Jews.

64. This seems to be overlooked by Schütz, *Leidender Christus*, p. 130, who explains that Luke has omitted the mocking entirely.

65. So also Gnilka, *Verstockung*, p. 151. Winter, *Trial*, p. 149, assumes that they are 'Pilate's soldiers'. Bundy, *First Three Gospels*, p. 542, observes that this taunting is not characteristic of Roman soldiers; but then, because he knows that the Romans did the crucifying, he wants to delete v. 36 as a later addition! Bachmann, *Jerusalem und Tempel*, pp. 193–6, sees that the captains are important to Luke's understanding of the Temple, but he fails to make the connection to the crucifixion. Schütz, *Leidender Christus*, p. 131, sees that the affiliation of the soldiers is unclear, but he confidently affirms that this lack of clarity should not be attributed to Luke; it must have been in his source.

66. The only exception to this function allotted the soldiers in Acts is really only a variance, i.e., providing safe conduct; cf. Acts 10.7; 22.23, 31.

67. This saying in Mark is in fact ambiguous as to who is to mistreat and kill Jesus, but this is not the place to discuss Mark's meaning, only what Luke wanted the reader to understand. Matt. 20.19, it may be noted, removes the Marcan ambiguity and makes it clear who does the mistreating and killing. Wilckens, *Missionsreden*, pp. 113–17, and Winter, *Trial*, p. 41, explain the Lucan differences as due to a separate source.

68. Rengstorf, *Lukas*, p. 211, mistakenly states that 'only the Romans could be meant', and Ellis, *Luke*, p. 219, and Cassidy, 'Luke's Audience', p. 150, think that Luke has actually, in this passage, reduced the level of Jewish participation below what it was in Mark. Schweizer, *Luke*, p. 288, and G. Schneider, *Lukas*, vol. 2, p. 373, think that God is the implied agent of the passives. Franklin, *Christ the Lord*, p. 93, goes so far as to state that, 'in Luke, the Romans alone actually condemn Jesus and the final responsibility is very definitely stated to be theirs (23.24–25, . . . 18.32–33 . . .)'. Franklin has, however, failed to note that Luke 23.25 is an explanation of v. 24, so that Luke avoids saying that Pilate gave sentence that Jesus be put to death. Cf. Grundmann, *Lukas*, p. 427; Hauck, *Lukas*, p. 281; Montefiore, *Synoptic Gospels*, vol. 2, p. 622; *et al.* Franklin's meaning is, in any case, less than clear since he then goes on to observe (*Christ the Lord*, p. 93) that 'the Jews are presented as being wholly responsible for the crucifixion'.

69. G. Schneider, *Lukas*, vol. 2, p. 373: the statement 'leaves open who will kill Jesus after the flogging'. Fitzmyer, *Luke*, vol. 2, p. 1207, notes the differences between

Luke and Mark, but then, p. 1208, he affirms that 'Jesus speaks quite plainly in vv. 32–33'.

70. Beyond this, the quotation and interpretation of the psalm here have provoked a variety of interpretations. It was the view of Dibelius, 'Herodes und Pilatus', pp. 289–91, that Luke was doing his best here to make something sensible out of confusing pieces of early Christian tradition, and many authors have agreed with that judgment; cf. Kränkl, *Knecht*, pp. 109–11; Haenchen, *Acts*, pp. 226–7; Lampe, 'Acts', pp. 891–2; Roloff, *Apostelgeschichte*, pp. 85–6. Some, however, think that the interpretation in Acts 4.27 fits the quotation, at least reasonably well (e.g., Loisy, *Actes*, pp. 254–5; Jacquier, *Actes*, p. 140), whereas others emphasize discrepancies between quotation and interpretation (e.g., Dibelius, 'Herodes und Pilatus', pp. 289–91; Haenchen, *Acts*, pp. 226–9). On the other hand, whereas many regard the (in my opinion ambiguous) designation of Pilate here as culpable in the death of Jesus as being out of harmony with Luke's normal position (e.g., Kränkl, *Knecht*, pp. 109–11; Lampe, 'Acts', pp. 891–2), others seem to find a connection (e.g., G. Schneider, *Apostelgeschichte*, vol. 1, pp. 357–8). The connection proposed by Talbert, *Reading Luke*, p. 217 – that Pilate and Herod are treated favourably in Luke but unfavourably in Acts – is, unfortunately, mistaken, as the discussion of Herod, below, will make clear. Dibelius, 'Herodes und Pilatus', p. 291, regarded the psalm quotation as the ultimate origin of the narrative of the hearing before Herod in Luke 23.6–11. This is disputed by Fitzmyer, *Luke*, vol. 2, pp. 1478–9, who, however, comes to no definite conclusion.

71. G. Schneider, *Apostelgeschichte*, vol. 1, p. 358, n. 38. Cf. also Bauer-Arndt-Gingrich, *Greek–English Lexicon*, s.v. ἐπὶ, III. 1. a. ϵ.

72. *Pace* Goulder, *Type*, p. 143. The statement of Maddox, *Purpose*, p. 95, that 'Luke makes no bones about naming Pilate as a conspirator in the murder of Jesus' here is also too strong; similarly Rese, 'Aussagen über Jesu Tod', p. 339; and it is certainly not true, as O'Neill, *Theology*, p. 84, maintains, that this passage shows that 'Luke is always at pains to emphasize' mutual Roman and Jewish guilt for Jesus' death.

73. Talbert, *Reading Luke*, p. 185, regarding the passion narrative: 'Throughout there is a pro-Roman and an anti-Sanhedrin thrust.' The view is frequent; cf. only Conzelmann, *Theology*, pp. 90–3; Loisy, *Evangiles synoptiques*, vol. 2, pp. 651–2; Montefiore, *Synoptic Gospels*, vol. 2, p. 618; G. Schneider, *Lukas*, vol. 2, p. 477.

74. Via, 'Who Put Jesus to Death?', pp. 126–38, 140, maintains that everyone in sight was guilty of executing Jesus, 'the scribes, the elders, the Sanhedrin, Roman Pilate, half-Jewish Herod, . . . and soldiers' (p. 140), in spite of the fact that she has given quite a good analysis of the accusatory statements in Acts (pp. 133–5), not a single one of which says anything about Roman culpability. (Via thinks that Acts 4.25–27 names Pilate as sharing guilt for Jesus' death, but cf. above, pp. 13f.) Acts 16.16–17; 19.24–28 cannot be made parallel to Jesus' trial, as Via has it (p. 137), since they do not show how Roman authorities martyred Christians; and how Acts 23.16–33 is supposed to make this point escapes me. When Via concludes the sentence partially quoted at the first of the note with the words, 'all of whom Luke refers to as "rulers" in 23.13 and 23.25', she is simply guilty of a considerable misunderstanding. Her view that the Jewish people are considered equally guilty will be considered below in ch. 3.

75. Above, pp. 9f. Similarly Kealy, *Luke*, pp. 427, 431; Beck, *Mature Christianity*, p. 178.

76. While the commentators routinely take the centurion to be a Roman, G. Schneider, *Verleugnung*, p. 195, thinks that Luke intends him to be a Jew.

77. Winter, *Trial*, p. 79: 'The language is deliberately ambiguous.' Conzelmann, *Theology*, p. 88, and Walaskay, *We Came to Rome*, p. 45, make a similar point about the soldiers.

78. Cf. especially Taylor, *Behind the Third Gospel*; also Winter, *Trial*, pp. 28–32, and 'Treatment of Sources', pp. 170–1.

79. *Theology*. One may note especially Haenchen, *Acts*, pp. 81–90, and the works, cited below in n. 87, that deal with Luke-Acts parallels. Cf. also Bultmann, *Synoptic Tradition*, pp. 271–80.

80. Cf. the discussion in G. Schneider, *Verleugnung*, pp. 132–9, and the conclusion, 'It is possible that the non-Marcan special source of Luke belonged to a non-Marcan passion narrative' (p. 137). Cf. further Strobel, *Stunde der Wahrheit*, pp. 14–18, and H. Klein, 'Lukanisch-johanneische Passionstradition'. It is possible, of course, to find both a special source and redactional activity in the Lucan passion narrative; cf. Bultmann, *Synoptic Tradition*, pp. 271–3; Dibelius, *From Tradition to Gospel*, pp. 199–203.

81. Conzelmann, *Theology*, pp. 32–5, *et passim*; cf., e.g., the emphatic statement by Wilson, *Law*, p. 13.

82. Many authors fail to see any motive other than naïve reporting behind Luke's composition, e.g., Cadbury, 'Acts', p. 38. Such a position has been untenable, however, since the time of the Tübingen hypothesis.

83. See the discussion in Kümmel, *Introduction*, pp. 131–5; and, regarding Acts, pp. 174–85.

84. *Actes*, p. 787.

85. This conformity is found *in nuce* in Luke 21.12: '. . . delivering you to synagogues and jails, leading you before kings and governors'.

86. The term is Talbert's; cf. *Patterns*, p. 5, *et passim*. Cf. also Radl, *Paulus und Jesus*, p. 212. Morgenthaler, *Geschichtsschreibung*, vol. 1, p. 190, had used the noun '*Architektonik* (architectural principle)' in a different sense.

87. Morgenthaler, *Geschichtsschreibung*; Goulder, *Type*; Talbert, *Patterns*; Muhlack, *Parallelen*; Radl, *Paulus und Jesus*.

88. Cf. also Mattill, 'Evans'.

89. Here, then, is further evidence that Luke thinks of the priests, the captains, and their colleagues as ruling Jerusalem in the manner of a Roman provincial city. Bachmann, *Jerusalem und Tempel*, pp. 260–1, reaches the opposite conclusion.

90. Radl, *Paulus und Jesus*, pp. 94–100, details the parallel between Luke 4.16–30 and Acts 13.14–52. That is of course also correct.

91. Cf. Bihler, 'Stephanusbericht', p. 254 and nn. 4, 6.

92. Whereas Loisy, *Actes*, pp. 350–1, proposed that the 'source' told of a juridical execution, that the 'narrator . . . suppressed' that conclusion, and that the 'redactor' brought in the crowd to carry out the stoning, Conzelmann, *Apostelgeschichte*, p. 53, and Haenchen, *Acts*, pp. 295–6, turn the guess around and propose that the lynching belongs to a source, the official trial to Luke. While I have some sympathy with this latter view, the issue of source and redaction here is sufficiently complicated that we had best ignore it and stay, as elsewhere, with the final version.

93. This distinction is more or less overlooked by Walaskay, *We Came to Rome*, p. 53, who emphasizes rather the 'chaotic' nature of the Jewish trials.

94. Winter's long discussion in *Trial*, pp. 112–26, about the true nature of Paul's trial is rendered relative by the awareness of the parallels. Talbert (*Patterns*, p. 22)

thinks that the Lucan passion narrative is modelled on the account of Paul's trial (similarly Mattill, 'Evans', pp. 39–40); but Conzelmann, *Theology*, p. 140, n. 1, is probably more nearly correct: Luke has 'taken the kerygmatic formulae', which he then also uses in Acts, and has 'turned them into narrative' in the passion narrative.

95. So Roloff, *Apostelgeschichte*, p. 342. Talbert, *Patterns*, pp. 17, 22, points out that even the high priestly slapping of Jesus in Luke 22.63–64 is paralleled for Paul in Acts 23.2.

96. Cf. also Tyson, 'Opposition', p. 147.

97. To be sure, while this high priest does not persecute Christians, he is certainly cast in a bad light, since his exorcist sons seek – improperly – to exorcise in the name of Jesus and are bested by their demon-possessed patient. Wikenhauser, *Apostelgeschichte*, p. 223, is probably correct in the assumption that Sceva is intended by Luke to be a member of the Jerusalem high priesthood.

98. Cf. Zahn, *Lucas*, p. 640; Talbert, *Reading Luke*, p. 189; Schweizer, *Luke*, p. 304; G. Schneider, *Lukas*, vol. 2, p. 398. It is possible that Luke intended this parable to be multi-directed; cf. further the discussion below in ch. 2, p. 32.

99. Joseph of Arimathaea is not an exception. The pre-Lucan tradition had already found a title for him that removed him from the circle of the Jewish leaders, 'counsellor' (Mark 15.43). On top of this term, Luke throws in the phrase, 'A good and just man' (Luke 23.50), and adds that 'he was not a participant in their counsel and their deed' (v. 51).

100. See ch. 4. Luke sometimes called the scribes 'legists'. This oddity can best be discussed after we have examined his portrayal of the Pharisees, in ch. 4.

101. Similarly Tyson, 'Opposition', pp. 147–8.

102. Loisy, *Evangiles synoptiques*, vol. 2, p. 652.

103. Fitzmyer, *Luke*, vol. 1, p. 759, takes Luke 9.9 to refer 'only' to Herodian 'curiosity'.

104. Cf. the opinion of Dibelius (above, n. 70) that Ps. 2.1–2 is the source of the story of Jesus' hearing before Herod, Luke 23.6–16. Bultmann, *Synoptic Tradition*, pp. 273, 281, agrees. Juel, *Luke-Acts*, p. 53, thinks that 'Herod and Pilate unite in their opposition to Jesus' in the Lucan passion narrative – by acquitting him?

105. On the parallels in the acquittal narratives cf. Radl, *Paulus und Jesus*, pp. 217–20. Soards, 'Tradition, Composition, and Theology', pp. 358–63, has not discovered this structure and so presents a confusing explanation of Herod's role in Luke 23.

106. The distinction is well seen by Loisy, *Evangiles synoptiques*, vol. 2, p. 652.

107. *Theology*, p. 87. I do not find convincing the explanation of this episode by Fitzmyer, *Luke*, vol. 2, p. 1480 – that Luke 'insinuat[es] an effect of the Christ-event by reconciling Pilate and Herod'.

108. Cf. also Tyson, 'Trial of Jesus', p. 258.

109. Via, 'Who Put Jesus to Death?', p. 136, has overlooked all the distinctions and has lumped Herod together both with the Jewish leaders and with Roman political opposition (à la Pilate).

110. It is also possible that Luke has something more than this in mind when he writes of Herod's desire to see and of his seeing, namely that, while Herod may have had hostile intentions when he first expressed a desire to see Jesus, once he actually saw Jesus he was 'converted'; his attitude was transformed. Such an explanation does not seem to me, however, to fall within Luke's theological scheme in any way. Fitzmyer, *Luke*, vol. 2, p. 1029, finds an unexplained curiosity about Jesus in Luke 9.9c, an unmasked curiosity in 13.31–33, and an explained curiosity in 23.8.

111. Cf. Walaskay, *We Came to Rome*, p. 35: 'Most of [Luke's] changes were designed to heighten the treachery of the Jewish leaders'; similarly, Rese, 'Aussagen über Jesu Tod', p. 347.

112. G. Schneider, *Verleugnung*, p. 194.

113. Maddox, *Purpose*, pp. 183–5.

2. Jerusalem

1. Conzelmann, *Theology*, p. 77. Cf. also Harnack, *Acts*, p. 275.

2. Conzelmann, *Theology*, p. 74.

3. Ibid., p. 212.

4. Conzelmann routinely left Luke 1–2 out of discussion, on the grounds that the Lucan prehistory did not agree theologically with the rest of the two-volume work; cf. ibid., p. 22, n. 2.

5. Morgenthaler, *Geschichtsschreibung*.

6. Cf. esp. ibid., pp. 178–86. Cf. also Talbert, *Patterns*, p. 58; Bachmann, *Jerusalem und Tempel*, pp. 155–7, 170.

7. Cf. the review by Kümmel, 'Urchristentum', pp. 197–200, esp. p. 198.

8. Morgenthaler, *Geschichtsschreibung*, vol. 1, pp. 179, 181, 184. When one reflects on the matter, the fact that, in a sense, both Jesus' ministry (Luke 2.41–52) and that of the church (Acts 2.46) 'incubate' in the Temple, so to speak, is quite remarkable and must surely be laid to Luke's architectonic paralleling. Bachmann also agrees with this assessment of Morgenthaler's analysis (Bachmann, *Jerusalem und Tempel*, pp. 140–2, 149–52, 155–7) and, in fact, contributes a considerable further discussion of the relation between Temple and city; cf. below, p. 33.

9. Morgenthaler, *Geschichtsschreibung*, vol. 1, p. 184. Cf. also Bachmann, *Jerusalem und Tempel*, p. 157, n. 79.

10. This statement of course represents no new insight, and the understanding is, indeed, almost universally recognized. Cf. Roloff, 'Paulus-Darstellung', p. 526: '*Symbol der Kontinuität*'.

11. Cf. also Dupont, 'Le salut des gentils', pp. 139–41; Wilson, *Gentiles*, p. 91.

12. There is, of course, the much debated problem of punctuating 'beginning from Jerusalem'. One may consult the commentaries. I have taken the most obvious course: ἀρξάμενοι agrees with ὑμεῖς μάρτυρες and not with a single word in the sentence preceding. Cf. Gnilka, *Verstockung*, p. 142, and the discussion in Part Two, below.

13. Goulder, *Type*, p. 69.

14. Cf. Schlatter, *Lukas*, p. 332: 'The conversion of Jerusalem is impossible, and . . . it must kill Jesus'; and the guilt for Jesus' murder falls not on Pilate but on Jerusalem. Gnilka, *Verstockung*, p. 139: '*Stadt des Messiasmordes*'. Cf. further Conzelmann, *Theology*, p. 133.

15. Cf. Radl, *Paulus und Jesus*, pp. 295, 299, 304; Gnilka, *Verstockung*, pp. 139–40. This dual aspect was also clearly seen by Perrin; cf. Perrin-Duling, *Introduction*, pp. 297–8; similarly G. Schneider, *Lukas*, vol. 2, pp. 389–91.

16. O'Neill, *Theology*, pp. 72–3; similarly, Flender, *St Luke*, pp. 107–9, describes Jerusalem as 'the place of salvation and judgement'; cf. also Hastings, *Prophet and Witness*, p. 106.

17. O'Neill, *Theology*, pp. 61–76.

18. Ibid., pp. 85–6. Cf. also Grundmann, *Lukas*, p. 31; Flender, *St Luke*, p. 114; Gnilka, *Verstockung*, pp. 144–5.

19. Morgenthaler, *Geschichtsschreibung*, vol. 1, p. 188. Cf. also Dupont, 'Le salut

des gentils'. Trocmé, *Le 'Livre des Actes'*, p. 86, in agreeing with Morgenthaler's analysis, refers to 'a vast symmetrical composition, where the Jewish capital and its temple have become the symbols of Israel elected and rejected'.

20. Cf. Stolle, *Zeuge*, p. 259.

21. This discussion should not be taken to imply that there is any reason to doubt that Paul was arrested in Jerusalem and sent to Rome; but our purpose is to determine how Luke sees Jerusalem as fitting into his theology.

22. As Morgenthaler, *Geschichtsschreibung*, vol. 1, p. 188, proposes.

23. Above, pp. 26f.

24. Cf. Stählin, *Apostelgeschichte*, p. 279; Bruce, *Commentary on the Book of the Acts*, pp. 435–6. Wendt, *Apostelgeschichte*, p. 306, takes 'entire city' to be some kind of mistake, thus falling into the trap of thinking that Acts presents a straightforward historically accurate narrative.

25. Talbert, *Reading Luke*, p. 185, observes that Luke has significantly reduced the role of Jesus' Temple *cleansing* and has played up the role of his *teaching* 'by inserting vs. 47' into ch. 19 and by omitting the charge that Jesus threatened the destruction of the Temple. Cf. also Tiede, *Prophecy and History*, pp. 87–8.

26. N.B.! Luke avoids writing 'chief priests' or 'scribes' or any of his terms for the Jewish leaders in 2.46. If there is no hostility toward Jesus, then the enemies cannot be there.

27. One should also note Acts 13.27 (in Paul's first sermon): 'Those dwelling in Jerusalem and their leaders' are guilty of Jesus' execution. Cf. the discussion in Buss, *Missionspredigt*, pp. 66–9. Overbeck, *Apostelgeschichte*, pp. 200–1; Loisy, *Actes*, p. 523; Haenchen, *Acts*, p. 410, and others take the reference to 'ignorance' in 13.27 to excuse the Jews of guilt; but, differently from Acts 3.17, where Jewish ignorance provides the opportunity for conversion to Christianity, here it is a charge hurled across several hundred miles at people who had every reason to know better ('they read the voices of the Prophets every Sabbath'). Jacquier, *Actes*, p. 400; Wikenhauser, *Apostelgeschichte*, p. 155; Franklin, *Christ the Lord*, p. 95, have seen the point correctly.

28. Radl, *Paulus and Jesus*, *passim*, esp. pp. 68–345; Goulder, *Type*, *passim*, esp. pp. 22–5, 40–3, 61; cf. also Baur, *Paul*, vol. 1, pp. 57–62. Talbert, *Reading Luke*, p. 213, observes that 'the deaths of both Jesus and Stephen are portrayed as martyrdoms in Luke-Acts, the former being the model for the latter'. This statement summarizes a scholarly discussion that goes back to Surkau, *Martyrien*, pp. 115–18, and is widely repeated.

29. With Acts 7.59 cf. Luke 23.46; with Acts 7.60 cf. Luke 23.34.

30. Cf. again the discussion in ch. 1; also Stählin, *Apostelgeschichte*, p. 279. Mattill, 'Evans', pp. 30–7, has laid out the parallels between Jesus' and Paul's passions in Jerusalem very well in a brief space, but he has omitted a discussion of Stephen. The Jesus–Stephen parallels are noted especially clearly by Pesch, *Vision*, pp. 45–6; cf. also Simon, *St Stephen and the Hellenists*, pp. 20–2.

31. Conzelmann, *Theology*, pp. 209–13. That Stephen's martyrdom marks a significant transition in Luke-Acts is, of course, widely recognized; cf. Baur, *Paul*, vol. 1, pp. 57–62; Overbeck, *Apostelgeschichte*, p. 116; Bihler, 'Stephanusbericht', p. 270, and *Stephanusgeschichte*, p. 169; and many others.

32. Goulder, *Type*, *passim*, esp. pp. 65–6.

33. Ibid., p. 16.

34. Goulder recognizes the many parallels among the martyrdoms of Jesus and Stephen and the near-martyrdom of Paul, and that these belong in a class by themselves; cf. ibid., pp. 40–2. Cf. further Cadbury, *Making of Luke-Acts*, pp. 231–2.

35. This has been better seen by Franklin, *Christ the Lord*, p. 97, who emphasizes that the Twelve pass out of the picture when 'the centre of interest passes into the Gentile world'. However, Franklin draws the wrong conclusion from this observation; cf. the discussion below in ch. 3, n. 221.

36. In chs. 3 and 4 we shall return to the issue of those in Jerusalem who are not represented as hostile to Jesus and the church.

37. He gets as close to saying this as he can, since Satan's re-entry into the Gospel narrative in Luke 22.3 occurs in Jerusalem, and since the third – and climactic – temptation before his exit from the narrative in 3.13 is related to the Jerusalem Temple (3.9–12). Cf. Roloff, 'Paulus-Darstellung', p. 526: '*Vom Ort des Heils zum Unheilsbereich*'. On Jerusalem in the Lucan Temptation cf. esp. Loisy, *Evangiles synoptiques*, vol. 1, p. 424.

38. It is distressing to read comments by Christian authors who take this statement and the rest of Luke's portrayal of the Jews at face value and argue for historical accuracy. Thus W. Manson, *Luke*, p. 169, writes that 'Jesus based his prognostication on the facts of history'; but then, ibid., p. 170, has to propose that Jesus was in Jerusalem on several occasions (in order for the 'How often' to be authentic). But if Luke is authentic in one regard, why not in the other? The answer is that Luke does not presuppose any earlier ministry of Jesus in Jerusalem, and that the 'How often' is related rather to the theological scheme. This has been especially well argued by Gnilka, *Verstockung*, pp. 138–40. Rengstorf takes the same attitude as Manson. Regarding 19.41–44 he writes (*Lukas*, p. 220), 'One may not object that Jesus could not have spoken thus. He had before him not only the fate of ancient Jerusalem, which fell to its enemies as a sacrifice because of its disobedience to God,' but also the obviously doomed autonomy movements. Caird, *Luke*, p. 217, expresses a closely similar view. Beck, *Mature Christianity*, p. 182, considers Luke 13.34–35 an example of 'vicious anti-Judaism'.

39. Walaskay, *We Came to Rome*, p. 24.

40. Schweizer, *Luke*, p. 232; cf. pp. 231–2.

41. Ibid., p. 357. Cf. further, on 19.41–44, ibid., p. 301; similarly Weinert, 'Luke, the Temple', p. 76; Grundmann, 'Pfingstbericht', p. 588.

42. G. Schneider, *Lukas*, vol. 2, p. 309. Cf. further, on 19.41–44, ibid., pp. 389–91. The phrase, 'not only in, but by' Jerusalem, is originally Conzelmann's (*Theology*, pp. 90, 133) and is repeated by a number of later authors. That Luke emphasizes the role of Jerusalem in the death of Jesus more than do the other Gospels is also seen by Via, 'Who Put Jesus to Death?' pp. 133, 135.

43. G. Schneider, *Lukas*, vol. 2, p. 481.

44. Neyrey, 'Jesus' Address'.

45. Ibid., p. 75.

46. Ibid., p. 76.

47. Neyrey, ibid., n. 21, cites other authors who maintain this view.

48. Neyrey, ibid., p. 76. στρέφω is a good Lucan word and is probably used in Luke 23.28 in a neutral sense, cf. Luke 7.9. But Neyrey's point is valid; the turning 'is not *necessarily* a call to repentance' (emphasis mine), since in Acts 7.42 turning indicates judgment.

49. Neyrey, 'Jesus' Address', p. 77.

50. Ernst, *Lukas*, p. 631, finds a call to repentance here instead of a judgment.

51. Neyrey, 'Jesus' Address', p. 79. Similarly Egelkraut, *Jesus' Mission*, p. 178.

52. Neyrey, 'Jesus' Address', p. 80. Cf. Tiede, *Prophecy and History*, p. 80: 'A straightforward and searing oracle of doom'. Tiede's further point (ibid., pp. 81–6,

88–96) that the judgments pronounced on Jerusalem in Luke-Acts are merely instances of time-honoured intra-Jewish prophetic judgment – which I consider quite incorrect – will occupy our attention again in ch. 3 (cf. pp. 57–8, 61–2.) The key word in v. 44 is 'visitation'. That this 'visitation' is not a friendly visit but a time of judgment was emphasized by Morgenthaler and also by Robinson, *Weg*, pp. 50–9. Cf. also Zahn, *Lucas*, p. 636.

53. Loisy, *Evangiles synoptiques*, vol. 2, p. 272, and *Luc*, p. 471, may be correct in connecting the preceding parable of the Pounds, Luke 19.11–27, to this judgment on Jerusalem and understanding the parable to refer to Jerusalem. Yet it seems likely that the parable has a wider reference, cf. my 'Parable of the Pounds'. But Jerusalem itself may stand, in a sense, for the entire Jewish people. We cannot finish with this issue until ch. 3 (cf. pp. 61–2). On the relation of the parable to Jerusalem; cf. further Grundmann, *Lukas*, p. 363.

54. Neyrey, 'Jesus' Address', p. 82. Neyrey has also included formal analyses of these sayings, which he thinks support his conclusion. Whether or not the observations regarding form are correct, his observations regarding the uniform meaning of these several passages seems sufficient to carry the case.

55. Cf. Conzelmann, *Theology*, p. 133: 'The journey, the Passion, the guilt of the Jews and the resulting fate of the city form a closely linked chain.' Cf. further F. Keck, *Abschiedsrede*, p. 254; Löning, 'Theologe', p. 222. Fitzmyer, *Luke*, vol. 2, p. 1257, takes the pronouncements of judgment rather as laments and thinks that Luke regrets the destruction of Jerusalem.

56. Loisy, *Evangiles synoptiques*, vol. 2, p. 272, and *Luc*, p. 471, argues for the close relation of this judgment saying to the parable of the Pounds; cf. further Schmid, *Lukas*, p. 294.

57. Cf. Grundmann, *Lukas*, p. 372; Caird, *Luke*, pp. 220–1. Talbert, *Reading Luke*, p. 189; Ernst, *Lukas*, p. 538; Tyson, 'Conflict', p. 322; and Schweizer, *Luke*, p. 304, take the parable to refer to the religious leaders only. Most commentators understand it as being directed against the people or only the people of Jerusalem, but whether they think of the original or the Lucan meaning is not always clear. Luke may have intended the parable to be directed at several groups at once, since not only does he have the religious leaders respond at the end (20.19; cf. above, p. 19), but he introduces the parable (v. 9, contrast Matt. 21.33; Mark 12.1) by writing that Jesus 'began to tell this parable to the people'.

58. Cf. Robinson, *Weg*, pp. 50–1. Walaskay's point (*We Came to Rome*, p. 48), that Luke in ch. 21 'leaves the eschatological question open' regarding the destruction of Jerusalem, is well taken.

59. It is therefore not quite correct to say with Zmijewski, *Eschatologiereden*, p. 221, that Jerusalem is destroyed because it has lost its '*heilsgeschichtliche Stellung*'. The only *heilsgeschichtliche Stellung* that Jerusalem has in Luke-Acts is to kill the prophets and to stone the divine emissaries. Wainwright, 'Luke and the Restoration', thinks that Luke hopes for the eventual 'restoration' of Jerusalem; and he thus finds hope in the words 'Until the times of the Gentiles be fulfilled' (Luke 21.24); i.e., Jerusalem's destruction will be *only* until then (ibid., p. 77). But where is there one word in all of Luke-Acts promising a future rescue for Jerusalem? For the correct sense, cf. Fitzmyer, *Luke*, vol. 2, pp. 1343, 1347.

60. Conzelmann, *Theology*, p. 133, correctly saw both aspects of Luke's portrayal of Jerusalem but reversed the relationship: the 'description of Jerusalem as the necessary place of enmity' was 'necessary . . . from the point of view of redemptive history'. Gnilka, *Verstockung*, pp. 139–40, supports this position.

61. It is correct that, as Franklin, *Christ the Lord*, p. 130, states, 'the destruction of Jerusalem . . . has no significance in God's plans for salvation'; but that is because the destruction is viewed as just punishment for the opposition to those plans. The role of Jerusalem *in* God's plans, like the role of being punished by being destroyed, relies on the notion of opposition.

62. Cf. Conzelmann, *Theology*, p. 134. F. Keck, *Abschiedsrede*, pp. 256–7, thinks that the fact of the destruction of Jerusalem and the Christian identity-problem in Luke's own time are sufficient to explain the existence of the Lucan judgments on Jerusalem.

63. Cf.Bachmann, *Jerusalem und Tempel*, pp. 155, 170. The view of Gaston, *No Stone*, p. 366, that Luke makes some kind of distinction between 'temple (ναός)' and 'temple mount' (ἱερόν)' is ridiculous. Was Jesus, in Luke 20.1, 'teaching inside the Temple Mount'? O.Michel, 'ναός', p. 885, to whom Gaston appeals, refers only to occasional distinctions between 'whole temple' and 'actual house'.

64. Cf. 21.37–38; Conzelmann, 'Zur Lukasanalyse', p. 57; *Theology*, pp. 77, 164.

65. Franklin, *Christ the Lord*, pp. 88–91, emphasizes that Jesus in Luke is not hostile towards the Temple. That is, of course, correct. This observation is apparently what prompted R. E. Brown, *Birth*, p. 237, to write that Luke's view of the Temple is dominated by 'nostalgia', not by 'hostility'. Bachmann, who discusses the subject of the relation between city and Temple for an entire chapter (*Jerusalem und Tempel*, pp. 132–70), nevertheless fails to note the way in which Jerusalem and the Temple are involved in Christian martyrdoms.

66. Almost all commentators note this 'Jewish connection'; cf., e.g., Klostermann, *Lukas*, pp. 4–29.

67. Lohfink, *Sammlung Israels*, p. 55.

68. Cf. Fitzmyer, *Luke*, vol. 1, pp. 316, 376, 419, and esp. p. 438. Lohfink, *Sammlung Israels*, p. 47, refers to Jerusalem as a '*Kontinuitätssymbol*'.

69. Franklin, *Christ the Lord*, p. 89, makes a similar statement about Jerusalem, although Franklin's attempt to show that only the religious leaders in Jerusalem are portrayed as guilty (ibid., pp. 88–9) makes it unclear exactly what his assessment of the issue is. The same confusion exists when he tries to explain (ibid., pp. 99–108) the Stephen episode. On who rejected whom, cf. further Jervell, *People of God*, p. 41.

70. Bihler, *Stephanusgeschichte*, pp. 162–78.

71. Ibid., p. 162.

72. Ibid., p. 163. Consequently, references to the Temple as a place of *sacrifice* and *criticisms* of the Temple that appear in Mark and Matthew are omitted from Luke.

73. Bihler, *Stephanusgeschichte*, p. 168.

74. Ibid., pp. 168–70.

75. Ibid., p. 176. Cf. further F. Keck, *Abschiedsrede*, p. 26. Conzelmann, *Theology*, p. 165, had provided a similar analysis: the anti-Temple charges of Acts 7.48 and 17.24 blend together with the view that, since Jesus' occupation of the Temple, the Jews are improper tenants whose possession of the Temple profanes it; thus it falls under judgment. These two themes 'coincide in the fact that they provide justification for Christian worship apart from the Temple'. Cf. also ibid., p. 78.

76. On the possibility of a connection between Stephen and Samaria cf. Cullmann, *Early Church*, pp. 190–1; *Johannine Circle*, pp. 47–8.

77. There is really hardly a need to suggest a Samaritan background for the Christian argument that the true Temple is not handmade, since the idea appears in such diverse parts of the New Testament; cf. II Cor. 5.1; Mark 14.58; Heb. 9.11, 24, as well as the two places in Acts. Unless, of course, the entire first generation of

Christians was Samaritan! – a suggestion which I suspect most readers would consider preposterous. Even Cullmann's theory (cf. the preceding note) of a Samaritan place in the development of early Christianity would hardly explain the Pauline use of the term. What is distinctively Lucan in the use of the term is that it abets Luke's judgment on the Temple and on Jerusalem as perverse and deserving destruction. Cf. also Kilgallen, *The Stephen Speech*, p. 96.

78. W. Manson, *Luke*, pp. 218–19, emphasized this omission, but he completely misunderstood Luke's purpose.

79. Cf. again n. 36 in ch. 1.

80. Bachmann, *Jerusalem und Tempel*, p. 170, adds the interesting observation that Luke probably found the name Ἱερο-Σόλυμα appropriate for Jerualem because of the degree to which he identified the Temple, τὸ ἱερόν, with the city.

81. The suggestion of Sylva, 'Ierousalēm and Hierosoluma', that Luke kept shifting the terms in order to keep his readers thinking about them so that they would remain reminded of the '"holy Salem" etymology of *Ierousalēm*' (ibid., p. 220) is unconvincing. For Luke's Greek-reading audience, 'Hierosolyma' would have provided its own analogy.

82. De la Potterie, 'Luc' and 'Actes', *passim*, esp. 'Luc', p. 70. The same explanation has also been proposed by Morales Gómez, 'Jerusalén-Jerosólima', with slightly different analysis.

83. De la Potterie, 'Luc', p. 69.

84. Ibid., pp. 155–6.

85. Bachmann, *Jerusalem und Tempel*, pp. 36–8.

86. Ibid., p. 38.

87. Ibid., p. 45; cf. also again above, n. 80.

88. Bachmann, *Jerusalem und Tempel*, p. 52. What 'Judaism as Judaism' is remains unexplained, but Dr Bachmann does have a tendency to use rather fulsome sentences.

89. Ibid., p. 53.

3. The Jewish People

1. Jervell, *People of God*, p. 44.

2. The phrase is Haenchen's; cf. 'Source Material', p. 278.

3. Cf., e.g., Baur, *Paul*, vol. 1, p. 6.

4. Overbeck, *Apostelgeschichte*, p. xxx.

5. Ibid., pp. xxx–xxxi.

6. Ibid., p. lx.

7. The year of Loisy's excommunication.

8. Loisy, *Evangiles synoptiques*, vol. 2, p. 652.

9. Ibid., p. 469.

10. Loisy, *Actes*, p. 118. Similar statements appear throughout the commentary wherever Jewish hostility to the Christian mission occurs.

11. Ibid., p. 119. Loisy was – like Overbeck and, indeed, the Tübingen school (cf. Baur, *Paul*, vol. 1, p. 5) – certain that this scheme was more theological than historical. Unlike the others, however, he attributed the falsification (or tendentious rewriting, if one prefers) not to the original author of Luke-Acts but to a redactor. Cf. his lengthy discussion in the introduction to *Actes*, pp. 50–121. Here, as with Overbeck, the word 'fiction' appears; cf. ibid., p. 51, *et passim*. As far as I can tell, this word almost disappeared from scholarly works on Luke-Acts after Loisy. Ernst,

NOTES TO PAGES 40-44

Lukas, p. 426, refers to the 'fiction of a Jerusalem journey' in the travel narrative, but that is not the same thing.

12. Haenchen, 'Judentum und Christentum', p. 157.

13. Ibid., p. 164.

14. Ibid., pp. 165–6.

15. Ibid., pp. 166–71.

16. Ibid., p. 171.

17. Ibid., p. 173; cf. also Haenchen, *Acts*, pp. 414, 417–18.

18. 'Judentum und Christentum', p. 175.

19. Ibid., pp. 174–5.

20. Ibid., p. 182.

21. Ibid., p. 185.

22. Haenchen, 'Source Material', pp. 266, 278.

23. Haenchen, *Apostelgeschichte*, p. 111 (emphasis his); cf. *Acts*, p. 100.

24. Harnack, *Acts*, p. xxiii. The German original was published in 1908, the same year in which Loisy's *Evangiles synoptiques* was published.

25. *Acts*, p. xxv, n. 1. Acts was, on Harnack's view, only the first stage of developing early Christian antisemitism. The second stage was John, the third the Apologists, the fourth the Epistle of Barnabas, and the fifth and last Marcion.

26. Ibid., p. xxiv. It is not without significance that, whereas Overbeck and Loisy, who had not emphasized such distinctions in the Lucan work, insisted that Luke-Acts (or Acts, in any case) is a fiction, Harnack saw the existence of these distinctions as verifications of the historical accuracy of Acts. 'Where St. Luke knows anything more favourable,' he wrote, 'concerning particular sections or persons among the Jews he does not keep silence, and so sacrifice truth to his theology of history' (ibid., p. xxiv).

27. Ibid., p. xxvii; cf. also pp. 283–6, where the need to free Gentile Christianity from the Torah is discussed.

28. Ibid., p. 287.

29. Conzelmann, *Theology*, pp. 162–3. That Christianity is the proper continuation of 'Old Testament' religion in Luke-Acts is of course widely recognized and is not a point of contention between the alternative approaches being sketched here. Cf., e.g., Loisy, *Actes*, pp. 830, 858; cf. also the further discussion below, pp. 48–9.

30. Conzelmann, *Theology*, p. 145. Beck, *Mature Christianity*, p. 207, finds here 'the essence of anti-Jewish polemic in Acts, which is the most devastating and the most destructive of Judaism in all of the New Testament documents'.

31. Conzelmann, *Theology*, p. 163.

32. Ibid., p. 146.

33. Ibid., pp. 145–6.

34. Ibid., p. 145.

35. George, 'Israël'; the essay is reprinted in George, *Études*, pp. 87–125. Citations throughout the present work are from the earlier publication.

36. 'Israël', p. 485.

37. Ibid., pp. 488–9.

38. Ibid., pp. 491–2.

39. Ibid., pp. 492–506.

40. Ibid., p. 493.

41. Ibid., p. 496.

42. Ibid., p. 501.

43. Ibid., pp. 504–6.

44. Ibid., pp. 506–12.

45. Ibid., p. 512.

46. Ibid., pp. 512–20.

47. Ibid., p. 514.

48. Ibid., pp. 522–3.

49. Ibid., p. 525.

50. Ibid., pp. 524–5.

51. Jervell, *People of God*, p. 44; cf. also id., *Unknown Paul*, pp. 15–16.

52. Jervell, *People of God*, pp. 48–9.

53. Ibid., p. 60.

54. Ibid., p. 68.

55. Ibid., p. 62.

56. Ibid., p. 64; cf. also id., *Unknown Paul*, p. 23.

57. Jervell, *People of God*, pp. 64–5.

58. Conzelmann, *Theology*, p. 145.

59. Similarly Dahl, 'Abraham', p. 151.

60. Jervell, *People of God*, p. 69.

61. Contra Dahl, 'Abraham', p. 151, and 'People', pp. 324–6; Harnack, *Acts*, pp. 50–1. Cf. Dupont, 'Peuple', p. 325.

62. As Loisy, *Actes*, p. 830, says, Luke wants to show that Christianity is 'the sane interpretation of the most authentic Judaism'. Cf. also many others. A very good summary of this aspect of Luke-Acts is given by Talbert, 'Promise and Fulfillment'. Talbert states that 'it was a cultural commonplace in the Hellenistic age for a people to try to trace its origins back to remotest antiquity' (op. cit., p. 100), and he cites Hellenic and Jewish authors and Tertullian as sharing this 'argument from antiquity' (ibid., p. 92) with Luke (ibid., p. 100). Somewhat after Luke's time, Celsus found the Christian break with Judaism to be primary evidence against the legitimacy of Christianity (cf. Wilken, *Christians as Romans Saw Them*, pp. 114–17).

63. Thus correctly Lohfink, *Sammlung Israels*, p. 60. When Dupont, 'Peuple', p. 326, however, argues on the basis of this evidence that the use of the term 'this people' in Acts 28.26–27 implicitly excludes those who have become Christians, he is technically correct but has thereby shifted Luke's emphasis.

64. Jervell, *People of God*, p. 143. When he then in another context (ibid., p. 187) refers to 'Christianity as authentic Judaism', his phrasing, at least, is correct. Bovon, 'Israel, die Kirche und die Völker', p. 408, also overstates the matter when he proposes 'that Luke saw in the promitive congregation not only the legitimate continuity of the people of Israel but also a new creation of God in the midst of the fallen people'.

65. As Eltester, 'Israel', p. 123, points out.

66. Sandmel, *Anti-Semitism*, p. 73.

67. Löning, *Saulustradition*, p. 166.

68. Cf. Loisy, *Actes*, p. 892. Mattill, 'Evans', p. 23, also sees the connection between the continuity theme and the resurrection motif.

69. Cf. also F. Keck, *Abschiedsrede*, pp. 251–2; O'Neill, *Theology*, p. 178. Roloff, 'Paulus-Darstellung', p. 528, goes so far as to use the term 'true Israel'; also Lohfink, 'Hat Jesus eine Kirche gestiftet?', p. 86.

70. So also Dahl, 'People', p. 324.

71. Fitzmyer, 'Jewish Christianity', pp. 235–6.

72. Jervell, *People of God*, p. 135, who of course insists on the division-in-Israel

theory, rejects the possibility that even the 'idea' of a new Israel is present in Luke-Acts.

73. Conzelmann, *Theology*, p. 146; cf. also ibid., p. 213: 'The idea of the "true" Israel has not yet been developed.'

74. Both sides of the coin are important. 'Whereas the continuity of the *Heilsgemeinde* is emphasized, so the fact that the new people of God is not "Israel" is safeguarded' (Egelkraut, *Jesus' Mission*, p. 231).

75. One unsuccessful attempt to sort this out is that of Gaston, *No Stone*, p. 330, who proposes that only the Jewish leaders are designated in the Gospel as being responsible for Jesus' death, since in this way Luke demonstrates 'solidarity with the mass of the people', whereas Acts accuses all in order to lay the ground for repentance.

76. Cf. the remarks of Eltester, 'Israel', p. 135.

77. This is also true, of course, if the theory of H. Klein, 'Lukanisch-johanneische Passionstradition' – that a single non-Marcan passion narrative lies behind Luke and John – should turn out to be correct. Inasmuch, however, as Klein must build on the foundation of complete Johannine ignorance of Luke (op. cit., p. 167), his thesis must remain in doubt. Cf. the discussion in G. Schneider, *Verleugnung*, pp. 70–2.

78. We recall that we have already seen that such a separation is the key to understanding Luke's variant spellings of the word 'Jerusalem'.

79. Stephen is, of course, more important for the development of the narrative in Acts than the space alloted him would indicate, since his martrydom is the 'watershed' (Haenchen) in the geographical progression of the gospel. Also, his importance is greater than might be indicated by the fact that he has only one speech, whereas Jesus, Peter and Paul speak frequently (cf. Harnack, *Acts*, p. 120). When Stephen did start speaking, he produced the longest speech in Acts, and it was hard to get him to stop.

80. Cerfaux, 'La composition', p. 80: '. . . the most anti-Jewish [attitude] in all the New Testament'. I do not understand how Via, 'Acts 7.35–37', pp. 206–7, can think that the main point of Stephen's speech is Jesus' 'salvific significance, in spite of his crucifixion, an obstacle' overcome à la Moses. Kilgallen, *The Stephen Speech*, pp. 63–87, is much better on the Moses typology. Kilgallen sees that Luke has constructed the Moses section of the speech so that the reader will associate Jesus with Moses, who faced 'incomprehension' from 'his fellow-Jews' (ibid., p. 69).

81. Kränkl, *Knecht*, p. 112, observes that Jewish guilt is a 'red thread' in Stephen's speech. (Calling one of Luke's themes a 'red thread' is a tradition unto itself in New Testament scholarship.) Cf. further esp. the discussions in Bihler, *Stephanusgeschichte*, pp. 41–81, and in Kilgallen, *The Stephen Speech*, pp. 97–104.

82. As Easton, *Purpose*, p. 118, proposes. Cf. also F. Keck, *Abschiedsrede*, pp. 198–321.

83. It is also possible, however, that the prophets are not thought of as being Jews (or Israelites). They may be, rather, the messengers of God. The same would be true of the apostles and, of course, of Jesus. Neyrey, 'Jesus' Address', p. 76, comes close to this position, as does Johnson, *Possessions*, p. 77.

84. Conzelmann, *Theology*, p. 91, considers the guilt issue to belong to the early Christian proclamation before Luke, but that Luke 'seems to develop it with a one-sided emphasis on the guilt of the Jews'; cf. further op. cit., p. 140, n. 1.

85. When, e.g., Schille, *Apostelgeschichte*, p. 114, feels called upon to explain that this statement is not antisemitic but represents the 'peak' of 'the preaching of

repentance', one must wonder whether the very protestation does not reveal what it seeks to deny.

86. On 4.10, cf. the statements by Gnilka, *Verstockung*, p. 139, and Schmithals, *Apostelgeschichte*, pp. 49–50. The lack of consensus among commentators on whether 5.30 is directed towards the rulers (e.g., Jacquier, *Actes*, p. 172) or towards the people generally (e.g., Stagg, *Acts*, p. 87) also points up the Lucan ambiguity here. On the form of the charge in 5.30, cf. esp. Fitzmyer, 'Crucifixion', pp. 498–510, who shows that it was possible for the term 'hang on a tree' to refer to *Jewish* crucifixion (through interpretation of Deut. 21.22–23).

87. How Gaston, *No Stone*, p. 306, can think that the 'emphasis' of this speech is that 'salvation has come for Israel, and therefore also to the Gentiles' is beyond me. Schille, *Apostelgeschichte*, p. 249, conveniently overlooks the reference to Jewish guilt in this sermon to Gentiles.

88. Repetition of language here from 5.30: κρεμάσαντες ἐπὶ ξύλου, cf. the discussion of this point by Kränkl, *Knecht*, pp. 111–12. It is therefore foolish for Schütz, *Leidender Christus*, p. 135, to grasp at the straw of the absent subject in Acts 10.39 as a support for his argument that Luke-Acts does not represent the Jews as being guilty of Jesus' execution.

89. Via, 'Who Put Jesus to Death?', p. 131: 'Luke implies . . .'; on Acts 10.39 in particular, cf. further ibid., p. 134.

90. This point is correctly seen by Franklin, *Christ the Lord*, pp. 92–5. George, 'Israël', p. 504, thinks that the accusations against the Jewish people in the speeches in Acts come from Luke's sources and do not represent his point of view. Lohfink, *Sammlung Israels*, pp. 43–6, is of the same opinion. Wilch, 'Jüdische Schuld', pp. 238–43, tries to show that *all* the references in Acts to Jewish guilt in the death of Jesus, save 4.27, involve calls to repentance, and that therefore, '*Wann immer der Tod Jesu in der Apostelgeschichte erwähnt wird, ist kein Antijudaismus damit verbunden*' (op. cit., p. 249). Even Acts 10.39? Yes. Even Acts 7.52? Yes. This is a *tour de force*. I also wish that Luke had not provided us with this blanket condemnation of the Jews, but wishing won't make it so. Beck, *Mature Christianity*, p. 207, views the function of the speeches correctly.

91. As F. Keck, *Abschiedsrede*, p. 256, proposes; similarly Mussner, *Tractate*, pp. 192–205. George, 'Israël', p. 492, further, finds these two references to ignorance 'an excellent commentary on Rom. 1.16'. Cf. also Wilson, *Law*, p. 115.

92. That the statement of ignorance opens the way for repentance is, of course, widely recognized. Wilckens, *Missionsreden*, has, it seems to me, misunderstood this point. On the one hand (op. cit., pp. 97, 120–1), he sees that the speeches in Acts make all the Jews guilty; but, on the other, he thinks that the purpose of these guilt statements is to lead to repentance, and that Luke sets up a universal *ordo salutis* (ibid., pp. 97, 182). Thus both occurrences of the ignorance theme (ibid., pp. 134–5) do not refer to moral guilt but to 'the Jews'' failure to understand the divine plan. Similarly also Gnilka, *Verstockung*, pp. 141–2. The proposal of Zehnle, *Pentecost Discourse*, esp. pp. 59–60, 136, that the speech in Acts 3 presents us with a *bona fide* early example of Christian preaching to Jews, is not convincing; the speech fits into Luke's epochal outline too well.

93. It is unclear exactly to what τοῦτον refers. The near antecedent is 'the message (λόγος) of this salvation' (v. 26), and that may be what Luke intended instead of 'him', i.e., the Jerusalem Jews could kill Jesus because they were ignorant of the message of salvation that was contained in the sacred scripture that they heard weekly.

94. This is correctly seen by a number of authors but is widely misunderstood. Cf. Overbeck, *Apostelgeschichte*, p. 189; Loisy, *Actes*, p. 529; Haenchen, *Acts*, p. 410; Surkau, *Martyrien*, p. 97, n. 78; Gnilka, *Verstockung*, p. 141; and Buss, *Missionspredigt*, p. 68. Bihler, 'Stephanusbericht', p. 266, n. 40, emphasizes that Stephen's speech contains no 'call for repentance'; and, *Stephanusgeschichte*, p. 18, astutely observes that the ignorance theme of Luke 23.34 is missing from its parallel in Acts 7.60; cf. further ibid., pp. 28–9, 81, 92. The Stephen episode is the turning point, and the two statements of ignorance, which fall on opposite sides of Stephen, take on their respective nuances accordingly.

95. Grundmann, 'Pfingstbericht', p. 588, correctly states that '*das Pfingstgeschehen enthält . . . die grosse Chance für Jerusalem*'; nevertheless, he tries to tie this observation to a distinction between rulers (whose chance was missed at the crucifixion) and people, who have their 'big chance' for salvation at Pentecost. That Luke does not make such a connection is seen in the fact that, during the early chapters of Acts when so many Jews are becoming Christians, even priests are converted (Acts 6.7).

96. This is quite accurately explained by Wanke, *Emmauserzählung*, p. 119.

97. Similarly Schmithals, *Apostelgeschichte*, p. 128.

98. J. Weiss, *Earliest Christianity*, vol. 2, p. 666, observes 'the impression gained from the Book of Acts . . . that the attempt of Paul to win over his people was never again repeated'; similarly Marshall, *Acts*, p. 225. This attitude should not be called an '*ordo salutis*' for Jews (Wilckens). Cf. Conzelmann, *Theology*, p. 90: 'After the resurrection . . . unbelief becomes inexcusable'; also ibid., p. 93. Similarly Gnilka, *Verstockung*, pp. 143–4. O'Neill, *Theology*, p. 95, notes the same phenomenon regarding Jerusalem after Stephen's martrydom.

99. It was Dibelius who first pointed out that the three announcements – here, in 18.6 and in 28.28 – occur, geographically significantly, in Asia Minor, on the Greek mainland, and in Rome (*Studies*, pp. 149–50). Haenchen's point (*Acts*, pp. 414, 417–18) that the rejection of the Antiochene Jews has implications for world-wide Jewry is therefore surely justified. Wilson, *Gentiles*, p. 223, correctly claims that Jervell misinterprets Acts 13.46 when he makes it support his contention that it was Jewish acceptance, not rejection of the gospel that led to the Gentile mission. Jervell repeats the position in *Unknown Paul*, pp. 16, 133.

100. While that certainly seems to be the logical assumption, Sandmel, *Anti-Semitism*, p. 91, is correct in pointing out that no reason is given here 'either for the curse on the Jews or for [Paul's] statement of innocence'.

101. Gnilka, *Verstockung*, p. 147, emphasizes the way in which Luke's verbs evoke the pattern of Jewish opposition in the three key episodes in Antioch, Corinth and Rome: ἀντιλέγειν, ἀντιτάσσεσθαι, ἀπιστεῖν.

102. Dupont, 'Les discourses missionaires', p. 141, and Rese, 'Aussagen über Jesu Tod', pp. 344, 346, have argued that Luke intended to make only the inhabitants of Jerusalem guilty, not all Jews everywhere, since Paul in Acts 13.27 referred only to Jerusalem Jews. They seem, however, to have overlooked this blood-guilt saying in 18.6. Löning, 'Theologe', p. 219, expresses the function of the preaching exactly.

103. Luke's 'creative writing' here is especially well underscored by Loisy, *Actes*, p. 887. Köster, *Einführung*, p. 755, refers in general to Luke's '*Erfindungsgabe*', but the term is bleached out in the ET; and Haenchen, 'Apostelgeschichte', p. 503, refers to Luke's '*Erzählergabe*'. Schille, *Apostelgeschichte*, p. 447, takes refuge against a blanket denunciation of all Jews in the absence of the article; but cf. the following note.

104. Munck, *Acts*, p. 240, relates the absence of the article to Attic legal usage, in which one's opponents are always anarthrous.

105. Thus Gnilka, *Verstockung*, p. 148, points out that the Jewish response to Paul's mission should have been no surprise, since 'it finds its ultimate foundation in the logic of Israel's history'.

106. So correctly Maddox, *Purpose*, pp. 43–4. Maddox further (ibid.) finds a 'progressive intensification' in Paul's three announcements of rejecting the Jews: 'At the end of Paul's mission the opportunity offered [to the Jews] at its beginning has been lost'.

107. Gager, *Origins*, pp. 150–1, reaches a similar conclusion. Cf. the apt phrase of Dupont, 'La conclusion des Actes', p. 376, that the Roman Jews of Paul's audience are 'qualified representatives of the people of Israel'.

108. Haenchen, 'Source Material', p. 278; cf. further id., *Acts*, p. 693.

109. So also Gnilka, *Verstockung*, p. 139.

110. Buss, *Missionspredigt*, p. 123, thinks that the statements of turning to the Gentiles are only a 'constant warning' to the Jews. Such a conclusion is reached by letting the narrative of Acts interpret the speeches; cf. op. cit., p. 136; further, p. 144, where Buss argues that the interest of Acts is in the response of individual Jews.

111. Wilckens, *Missionsreden*, esp. pp. 202–22.

112. Donaldson, 'Moses Typology', pp. 29–44, maintains a similar position but observes the difference between original function and function as employed by Luke in Acts.

113. Steck, *Geschick der Propheten*; on Stephen's speech, cf. esp. pp. 266–8.

114. Wilckens, *Missionsreden*, pp. 222–3.

115. Ibid., pp. 178–86.

116. Ibid., p. 182.

117. Emphasized also by Bihler, *Stephanusgeschichte*, pp. 81, 92. Weiser, *Apostelgeschichte*, vol. 1, p. 181, somehow finds the Deuteronomistic call to repentance in Acts 7.39–42a; cf. also ibid., pp. 187–8.

118. This realization, it seems to me, also reveals the mistake of Tiede's argument that the judgment sayings against Jerusalem in the Gospel 'derive from *within* the Jewish scriptural heritage' (*Prophecy and History*, p. 81; emphasis his), thus placing Luke within the prophetic tradition. That the Lucan Peter accuses the Jews to Cornelius, however, explodes the notion that Luke belongs within the prophetic tradition (whatever the source[s] of his accusatory language). For Luke, the Jews are 'other'.

119. Cf. O'Neill, *Theology*, p. 84: 'Luke's primary theological interest . . . is to show how the Jews rejected each opportunity to repent.'

120. Cf. esp. Haenchen, 'Historie und Verkündigung', pp. 299–300; Dupont, 'Le salut des Gentils', p. 144; Fitzmyer, *Luke*, vol. 1, p. 537; and Beck, *Mature Christianity*, p. 168. None of these notes, however, that Elijah, Elisha, and Jesus all appear here in their healing capacity. Gaston, *No Stone*, pp. 284, 313, thinks that the Elijah and Elisha examples have nothing to do with an eventual Gentile church but only emphasize the threat of not recognizing the prophet Jesus in his own native land; but where is there any indication in the text that Elijah and Elisha were not recognized?

121. Cf. almost all the commentaries. For Franklin, *Christ the Lord*, p. 143, to propose that 'the reference to these prophets cannot imply' that Jesus 'was turning aside from his own' is thus to fly in the face of both considerable evidence and the overwhelming weight of scholarly opinion. Reicke, *Luke*, p. 65, also misunderstands

the point when he emphasizes that the Elijah and Elisha examples show only that God 'at times' helped Gentiles and not Jews. The attempt by Albertz, 'Antrittspredigt', to explain the narrative as Luke's way of sending a message to affluent Christians to help unfortunate people (because of the Isaiah quotation) overlooks every connection to the main lines of Luke's theology. Wilson, *Gentiles*, p. 40, observes that 'the prime motif of this section is the rejection by the Jews'.

122. Tolbert, 'Leading Ideas', p. 442.

123. That a *centurion's faith* is emphasized here apparently prefigures the Cornelius episode in Acts 10 (so Loisy, *Évangiles synoptiques*, vol. 1, pp. 651–2; Talbert, *Reading Luke*, p. 79). Most commentators, however, find a comparison in the narrative rather than a contrast, i.e., that Jesus' saying means that, whereas there is faith – even great faith (so Schmithals, *Lukas*, p. 91) – among the Jews, this Gentile faith is even greater. But that is not what Jesus says here. To say that Jesus here 'indirectly' begins 'the Gentile mission . . . by himself' (Kealy, *Luke*, p. 227) is perhaps to overstate the situation.

124. The manuscript evidence leaves it uncertain how many disciples the original of Luke intended. The issue is irrelevant for our discussion. Egelkraut, *Jesus' Mission*, pp. 2–3, correctly emphasizes the 'key importance' of the travel narrative 'for the understanding of Lukan theology'.

125. Bethsaida was not, strictly speaking, in Galilee, since it lay just east of the Jordan, but it was nevertheless a Judahite town in the vicinity of the other two.

126. Similarly Ernst, *Lukas*, p. 335.

127. Loisy, *Évangiles synoptiques*, vol. 1, p. 298; Zahn, *Lucas*, p. 417; Ellis, *Luke*, p. 155; and even Lagrange, *Luc*, p. 299, understand the condemnation of the three Galilean towns to represent the condemnation of the Jews. Caird, *Luke*, p. 143, correctly refers to judgment for want of a 'corporate . . . response'; cf. also Ruether, *Faith and Fratricide*, p. 84.

128. So also Mora, *Le signe de Jonas*, pp. 75–7. Cf. also Luke 7.31–34, where 'the people of this generation' respond neither to the Baptist nor to Jesus. Cf. further the thorough discussion of Luke 7.31–34 by Fitzmyer, *Luke*, vol. 1, p. 679, who agrees that 'this generation' is 'the Palestinian contemporaries of John and Jesus'; cf. further id., *Luke*, vol. 2, pp. 930–2, on the redaction history of 11.29–32.

129. Well seen, as usual, by Loisy, *Évangiles synoptiques*, vol. 1, p. 999.

130. Underscored by G. Schneider, *Verleugnung*, p. 175.

131. The saying is highly similar to Matt. 23.29–36 and therefore comes from Luke's source more or less in the form in which he repeats it. Luke has, however, two references to 'this generation' to Matthew's one (Matt. 23.36); and Luke apparently has the Acts in mind when he has Jesus say, 'I will send them prophets and apostles' (Luke 11.49), whereas Matthew (23.34) had listed 'prophets and sages and scribes'.

132. Bihler, *Stephanusgeschichte*, p. 80, emphasizes the similarity between this saying and that of Stephen in Acts 7.52.

133. Egelkraut, *Jesus' Mission*, pp. 206–7; similarly Walaskay, *We Came to Rome*, p. 24.

134. Egelkraut, *Jesus' Mission*, p. 206. Ernst, *Lukas*, p. 420, also sees that a 'last chance to repent' is given here. Van Goudoever, 'Israel in Luke', p. 118, thinks that the parable shows a Luke sympathetic with the Jewish dilemma who 'did not accept the responsibility to cut down Israel'; and King, 'Universalism', pp. 204–5, thinks that the parable emphasizes the granting of another chance; similarly Fitzmyer, *Luke*, vol. 2, pp. 1005–6.

135. Cf. also 21.12, where Matthew and Mark, however, also refer to synagogues.

136. So most commentators. G. Schneider, *Lukas*, vol. 2, p. 307, proposes that, while the excluded are in the first instance Palestinian Jews, the saying intends a wider application. Fitzmyer, *Luke*, vol. 2, p. 1023, affirms that the Jews and Gentiles who enter the Kingdom 'belong to reconstituted Israel'.

137. These two parts of the Lucan saying do not appear together in Matthew. Gill, 'Travel Narrative', pp. 206–7, gives a good analysis of the Lucan passage in view of the Matthaean parallel but then concludes, oddly, that the saying refers to 'the link between the Jerusalem journey and the Gentile mission'.

138. The parables of the Good Samaritan, of the Prodigal Son, and of the Pharisee and the Toll Collector also have significance here but will be discussed below in chs. 4 and 5, where they have primary relevance.

139. Cf. also Sandmel, *Anti-Semitism*, pp. 78–80; Lampe, 'Lucan Portrait', p. 174.

140. Cf. the discussion in Funk, *Language, Hermeneutic, and Word of God*, pp. 164–6, 172–5, 182–6; and Gnilka, *Verstockung*, pp. 132–3.

141. Also especially emphasized by Funk, *Language, Hermeneutic, and Word of God*, pp. 172–3.

142. This interpretation can be found, for example, in Fitzmyer, *Luke*, vol. 2, p. 1053; Loisy, *Evangiles synoptiques*, vol. 2, p. 327, who interprets the second group as representing Jewish Christians; as well as numerous others. There is no uniformity in the scholarly literature, however, on this point. Gaston, *No Stone*, pp. 327–8, thinks that the emphasis of the parable is on the offering of salvation to the Jews (the originally invited ones of the parable). That is a strange understanding of the parable indeed. Hahn, 'Einladung zum Festmahl', p. 73, thinks that the Lucan version of the parable underscores the need for repeated missionary endeavour, without references to the objects of the mission.

143. Schmithals, *Lukas*, p. 160, thinks that Luke intends only two groups in the parable, although for the wrong reason, i.e., that finding three groups would have been 'inadmissible allegorizing'; but Luke would not have objected to allegorizing. The clue, I maintain, is the introduction.

144. Certainty, however, seems elusive; cf. the further discussion below in ch. 5.

145. Hastings, *Prophet and Witness*, p. 133, thus correctly connects this parable with Luke 13.28–29 (cf. above, p. 58).

146. Thus G. Schneider, *Lukas*, vol. 2, p. 318, correctly connects this saying of the Lucan Jesus to Paul's concluding denunciation at the end of Acts. Franklin's argument (*Christ the Lord*, p. 142) that the rejection is only of 'those who refused the original invitation', not of 'the Jewish nation as a whole', robs the parable of its most obvious point. Similarly van Goudoever, 'Israel in Luke', p. 119. Schweizer, *Luke*, pp. 237–40, interprets the parable as referring, in Luke, only to Jews and Gentiles. Cf. further Sandmel, *Anti-Semitism*, p. 79.

147. So also Maddox, *Purpose*, p. 49; van Goudoever, 'Israel in Luke', p. 112.

148. Cf. my article 'Parable of the Pounds', where other modern literature is also cited.

149. Lambrecht, *Astonished*, p. 176, thinks that Luke 'enriched the parable'. Fitzmyer, *Luke*, vol. 2, p. 1231, reviews the evidence for and against taking the Throne Pretender as Luke's invention and concludes that the 'obvious allegorizing' points to 'Lucan redaction'.

150. Jülicher, *Gleichnisreden*, vol. 2, p. 486.

151. The parable does not serve primarily – as especially Jeremias, *Parables*, pp. 48, 77, maintains – to correct the misunderstanding expressed in v. 11, that the

Kingdom might be about to appear. Cf. my discussion of this point in 'Parable of the Pounds', pp. 665–6. W. D. Davies, *Gospel and Land*, p. 256, has seen the point. Similarly Bartsch, *Wachet aber*, p. 110. Fitzmyer, *Luke*, vol. 2, p. 1233, holds determinedly here to the theory of the reconstituted Israel, because 'the good servants cannot be understood as Gentiles who become Christians'. Why not? Doesn't Luke think of the faithful servants simply as Christians?

152. Ernst, *Lukas*, pp. 519, 521, seems to have seen the point exactly: v. 14 means that 'Judaism rejects the Messiah Jesus'; and the relation of the destruction of Jerusalem in 70 to the slaughter of the opponents in v. 27 is that of an example. Johnson, 'Kingship Parable', p. 158, gets most of the allegory right but then writes that 'one cannot push the "slaughtering"'. Why not?

153. This is most clearly seen in the discourse of ch. 21, where reference is made to the destruction of Jerusalem by the Romans down through v. 24, and to the coming apocalyptic destruction from v. 25 on. The literature on this point is considerable; cf., e.g., Montefiore, *Synoptic Gospels*, vol. 2, pp. 580–1; Conzelmann, *Theology*, p. 130. Zmijewski, *Eschatologiereden*, p. 219, refers to unity as opposed to separation, but he nevertheless sees the difference.

154. So Lohse, 'Lukas als Theologe', p. 80; similarly van Goudoever, 'Israel in Luke', p. 117.

155. So Grundmann, *Lukas*, p. 372. Talbert's position, *Reading Luke*, p. 189, is unusual: 'This is not a reference to the destruction of Jerusalem and to the shift of the good news to the Gentiles. It is an attack on the religious bureaucracy' that says that the apostles will be set up in the place of the bureaucrats. Rau, 'Das Volk', p. 44, understands the parable to refer to the overthrow of Jerusalem but to be directed against the Jewish leaders. Fitzmyer, *Luke*, vol. 2, p. 1281, finds Jews and Gentiles among the respondents and thus sees the parable as referring to 'the reconstituted Israel'.

Zmijewski, *Eschatologiereden*, pp. 214–23, argues strongly that the eschatological discourse of Luke 21 (cf. above in ch. 2) should be understood as directed towards 'the Jews' and not merely towards Jerusalem; that is also likely.

156. Schmid, *Lukas*, p. 287, emphasizes that Zacchaeus is a Jew.

157. Van Goudoever, 'Israel in Luke', p. 123, proposes that Zacchaeus became a 'son of Abraham . . . only after [he] offered his good [*sic*] to the poor'. Fitzmyer, *Luke*, vol. 2, p. 1221, denies any connection with Gal. 3.7.

158. This is the approach taken by Loisy, *Evangiles synoptiques*, vol. 2, p. 253, who argues that the two tax collectors, Zacchaeus and Levi (5.29), are types of pagan converts. The blind man who is healed and then follows Jesus just before the Zacchaeus episode (18.35–43) is then (id., *Luc*, p. 38) a type of the Jewish sinner who is converted. Cf. further Wellhausen, *Evangelium Lucae*, p. 104: Zacchaeus is a '*Doppelgänger*' of Levi'.

159. While the manuscript evidence for the originality of this verse is weak, it must surely be original, since it and the saying in v. 46 about entrusting himself to God's care are the prototypes for Stephen's last words in Acts 7.59–60 (cf. Baur, *Paul*, vol. 1, p. 57; Kränkl, *Knecht*, p. 106; G. Schneider, *Lukas*, vol. 2, p. 483). The alternative, of course, is that Luke 23.34 has been added at some later date by someone who wanted to make Jesus' dying words conform to those of Stephen in Acts; but the more likely explanation of the manuscript evidence is that early Christian copyists, in the second century becoming more and more antisemitic, omitted the saying from Luke so as to prevent Jesus' seeming to excuse his Jewish executioners. So, e.g., Bihler, 'Stephanusbericht', p. 261, n. 22. The authenticity of

the saying is also supported by Schweizer, *Luke*, pp. 359–60. Others, however – e.g., Klostermann, *Lukas*, p. 226, and B. and J. Weiss, *Markus und Lukas*, p. 668, argue that v. 34 is a later addition. Fitzmyer, *Luke*, vol. 2, pp. 1502–3, leans in the same direction.

160. So Loisy, *Luc*, p. 556; Kränkl, *Knecht*, p. 106; Grundmann, *Lukas*, pp. 432–3.

161. Cf. Munck, *Paul and Salvation*, p. 225; O'Neill, *Theology*, pp. 83–4; Egelkraut, *Jesus' Mission*, pp. 132–3.

162. Cf. the judgment of Egelkraut, *Jesus' Mission*, p. 213: 'The overarching theme that dominates the [travel narrative] from the beginning to the end is the confrontation between Jesus and the Jewish people as well as the concomitant conflict in which the fate of Israel as God's people is decided.'

163. Dupont, 'Les discours de Pierre', pp. 337–9, has seen this aspect of the speech material in Luke-Acts as well, although he takes all such charges to be directed only against Jerusalem Jews.

164. Cf. above, p. 4. Indeed, few today would agree with the assessment of Easton, *Purpose*, pp. 56–7, that, 'in the "Way"', according to Luke-Acts, 'Gentile converts or semi-converts were kept strictly under the supervision and control of responsible Jews'.

165. For example, Luke 3.21; 19.48; 24.19; Acts 2.47; 3.11; 13.24. The situation is similar with the 'crowd' or 'crowds'; cf. Luke 6.19, 'All the crowd sought to touch him'.

166. The redaction theory is still just that, even if one names, as does Boismard, 'Le martyre d'Etienne', pp. 190–3, the redactor Luke.

167. Unfortunately successful, as we shall eventually have occasion to note.

168. The suggestion of Miyoshi, *Anfang*, p. 17, that Jesus' audience rejects him because it sees 'only his human aspect' is quite wide of the mark; and the view of Menezes, 'Mission', pp. 250–63, that Luke wishes to play down the theme of Jewish rejection in this episode in favour of his universalist theme is even farther afield. Better is the suggestion of Busse, *Nazareth-Manifest*, p. 53, that Jesus' fellow countrymen attempt to lynch him in ch. 4 and finally bring it off in ch. 23. While that also is not quite correct, it recognizes the connection. Ó Fearghail, 'Rejection', sees that the point of the episode is Jewish rejection, although his attempt to show that the episode contains only rejection, not a favourable response followed by rejection, is not quite successful. Beck, *Mature Christianity*, p. 167, oddly finds the attempted lynching inadequately motivated.

169. Cf. the discussion in Radl, *Paulus und Jesus*, pp. 299–301; the phrase '*auf Jesu Seite [stehend]*' occurs on p. 302; also Lohfink, *Sammlung Israels*, p. 37.

170. Cf. Conzelmann, *Theology*, p. 87; Kealy, *Luke*, p. 429. The role of the people before Pilate is apparently overlooked by George, 'Israël', p. 501, who refers to a distinction between people and leaders throughout the passion narrative; cf. also ibid., p. 504. Similarly Gaston, *No Stone*, p. 331.

171. Rau, 'Das Volk', esp. pp. 43, 48–50. Rau has taken up a conjecture made by Winter, *Trial*, p. 141, n. 23; but one must remember that Winter was much more interested in discovering who really crucified Jesus than he was in understanding the perspectives of the individual evangelists, and his conjecture has to be seen in that light. The idea was not new. Easton, *Luke*, p. 343, found the variant reading 'very tempting'.

172. Cf. also Loisy, *Luc*, p. 542.

173. Lohfink, *Sammlung Israels*, pp. 37, 43, finds the possibility proposed by Rau

'a manner of expression that would be quite unusual and that also would occur nowhere else'. G. Schneider, *Lukas*, vol. 2, p. 477, agrees.

174. That 'people' and 'crowd' may be, and often are, synonymous is also correctly seen by Kodell, 'Luke's Use of *Laos*', p. 327. Kodell's further argument, however – that the use of the term 'people' in Luke-Acts reveals a church setting in which 'Jew and Gentile are received on an equal basis' (op. cit., p. 339) – is just so much wishful thinking. The tortured argument of H.Klien, 'Lukanisch-johanneische Passionstradition', p. 161, that πλῆθος, ὄχλος and λαός are used in a variety of ways in Luke 23.1–16, with which argument he supports his source theory, is quite unnecessary to explain the passage.

175. Hare, 'Rejection', p. 36, sees clearly that Luke intends to make the people guilty along with the rulers. He then, unfortunately, misunderstands Luke's purpose and thinks that Luke goes on to show that the gospel created a schism in Israel (op. cit., pp. 36–7). For the correct view, cf. Montefiore, *Synoptic Gospels*, vol. 2, pp. 617–18, 622, and others. Loisy, *Evangiles synoptiques*, vol. 2, p. 652: '*Ce sont les Juifs qui ont tout fait*'; but some disagree. The position of Schmithals, *Lukas*, pp. 222–3, that the people are present solely to witness the declarations of innocence and do not share guilt with the rulers, cannot be reconciled, as he maintains, with the statements in Acts. Fitzmyer, *Luke*, vol. 2, p. 1476, also sees that 'the "crowds" are here associated with the authorities', but he argues that this does not mean that the people concur in the accusation.

176. The opinion of Cassidy, 'Luke's Audience', p. 151, and of Fitzmyer, *Luke*, vol. 2, p. 1484, that Luke has Pilate call in the people in order to reduce the pressure from the priests finds no support in the text.

177. This is overlooked by Wellhausen, *Einleitung*, p. 65, who regards the crowd as 'sympathetic' and as providing a 'mourners' escort'. Correctly, however, Neyrey, 'Jesus' Address', p. 75. T. W. Manson, 'Life of Jesus 3', p. 396, also sees the point about the women. Unfortunately, however, Manson (op. cit., pp. 396–7) continues by announcing that the 'long series of incidents both in Palestine and in the synagogues of the Dispersion', which he correctly recognizes as intended 'to show . . . the breach between Jesus and' the Jews, are recorded because they were 'fact'.

178. Rau, 'Das Volk', p. 45, of course, takes this to mean that the people are kept innocent.

179. Klostermann, *Lukas*, p. 227, views the crowd as curious but not sympathetic, and Harrington, *St. Luke*, p. 264, as 'morbidly curious'. Radl's phrase is apt (*Paulus und Jesus*, p. 295): the people are 'the loud-volume gallery at the trial'; cf. also his further comments on this point, ibid., pp. 303–4. The explanation of Gaston, *No Stone*, pp. 331–3, that a 'mob' joined the religious leaders in bringing about Jesus' death but that the 'people' remain innocent is, well, unique.

180. G. Schneider, *Verleugnung*, p. 193, takes the action to indicate remorse; and Fitzmyer, *Luke*, vol. 2, p. 1520, tries to decide between guilt and mourning. Lohfink, 'Hat Jesus eine Kirche gestiftet?' p. 88, sees in it attestation for his claim that Luke 'represents the relation of people to Jesus more positively than [does] Mark'.

181. Although nearly all the commentators take the statement to designate only the rulers as guilty. Ellis, *Luke*, p. 266, sees 'religious Judaism' as the guilty party.

182. Wanke, *Emmauserzählung*, p. 66, suggests that the primary motif in the disciples' statement of disappointment is that Jesus, having been killed, could not be the Messiah, as they had hoped.

183. Since 'apostles' is the near antecedent, it might look as if Luke meant that the two were apostles, but this could hardly be the case, since Luke had designated

the Twelve as apostles in 6.13, whereas the one on the Emmaus Road who is named, Cleopas, is not one of the Twelve. Luke probably means 'of them' in a more general sense, i.e., one of those who were among the followers of Jesus and vitally concerned with his death. Thus Wanke, *Emmauserzählung*, p. 115, writes that 'Luke sees in this "circle of brethren" (cf. Acts 1.15), whose centre the "Eleven" form (cf. Acts 1.13ff.; 2.14), the core of the young church'.

184. Schütz, *Leidender Christus*, p. 135, also argues that the emphasis of the scene is not a treatment of the question of guilt, but for the wrong reasons, since he has tried to show (op. cit., pp. 127–8) that Pilate should be awarded the primary responsibility for Jesus' execution. There is some merit, however, to Schütz's proposal (ibid., p. 135) that the emphasis of the scene is the disciples' disappointment at Jesus' death; cf. above, n. 182.

185. This is apparently overlooked by Johnson, *Possessions*, p. 124, who finds the 'ordinary people . . . positive and accepting both of Jesus and the Apostles'.

186. Marshall, *Acts*, p. 343, has also seen that the sum of the numbers of converts given in these summaries is 'myriads'. When Marshall further identifies the myriads with the Christian Pharisees of Acts 15.5, he is more correct than he realizes; cf. ch. 4.

187. The other place is Acts 19.19, a monetary reference. '*Kaum als Zufall [zu] betrachten*' (Lohfink, *Sammlung Israels*, p. 54). There is no shortage of different opinions in the scholarly literature as to whether Acts 21.20 refers to devout Jews or to Jewish Christians and, if the latter, whether or not some or all of them have become Christians since the martyrdom of Stephen, and whether or not only Palestinian Jewish Christians are intended. For a review of the literature and a fuller discussion of these points, cf. my article, 'Salvation of the Jews', p. 475.

188. Bachmann, *Jerusalem und Tempel*, p. 131; Lohfink, *Sammlung Israels*, p. 37; similarly Kealy, *Luke*, p. 320. Cf. the observation of Gutbrod, ' Ἰσραήλ', p. 379, that Ἰουδαῖοι in Acts means Jews in the Diaspora as well as in Judaea.

189. The role of Diaspora Jews in the arrests of Stephen and Paul is another matter, on which see further below.

190. One will, of course, want to recall the fine work by Epp, *Theological Tendency*, in relation to MS D.

191. Stählin, *Apostelgeschichte*, p. 58, correctly points out that the Jewish *people*, not the Jewish *leaders*, hold the Christians in good favour. When Jervell, *People of God*, p. 94, however, assumes on the basis of this same observation that 'Israel as a people is not rejected along with her leaders', he has gone far out on an uncertain limb. How often, on the issue of the Jews in Luke-Acts, the wish seems to be father to the thought. Bihler, *Stephanusgeschichte*, p. 176, is much more accurate.

192. Conzelmann, *Theology*, p. 212. Schille, *Apostelgeschichte*, p. 36, similarly relates Luke's portrayal of the Jerusalem church to the fact that it belongs, for Luke, to a bygone past.

193. Failure to understand this point leads to idealizing the relation of church to Temple in these early chapters of Acts, as is the case with, e.g., George, 'Israël', p. 509. Cf. also again the discussion above, pp. 33–4.

194. Cf. Bihler, 'Stephanusbericht', p. 255, and *Stephanusgeschichte*, p. 12; Pesch, *Vision*, pp. 32, 46; similarly Gnilka, *Verstockung*, p. 145. It is nearly universally recognized, of course, that the Stephen episode is the great turning point in Acts, the 'watershed' (Haenchen), in the scheme, from the Jews to the Gentiles. This change is denied by Jervell, *Unknown Paul*, pp. 15, 21–2, who thinks that Jewish conversions continue unabated throughout Acts.

195. Harnack, *Acts*, p. 53, counted 'about eighty-two'. The difference, of course, has to do with variant readings. It is prudent in a discussion such as this, however, not to rely on questionable evidence and to err, if at all, on the side of caution.

196. Also Conzelmann, *Theology*, p. 145, n. 2.

197. Gnilka, *Verstockung*, p. 146, has noted this change in Luke's use of the term.

198. G. Schneider, *Apostelgeschichte*, vol. 2, p. 105, correctly emphasizes that this means that 'the people of the Jews' are 'God's opponents'.

199. Harnack, *Acts*, p. 54, also makes this point, but then on p. 286 he takes it back. How Haacker, 'Bekenntnis', p. 441, can write that Luke almost always designates the 'responsible persons or groups', and that Luke is 'extremely cautious with blanket accusations against the Jewish people' I simply do not understand.

200. Luke's phrasing is such that one cannot be certain to how many synagogues these Diaspora Jews belonged, and the identity of one named group is also in doubt (freedmen [RSV], libertines, Libyans?). Interesting as they are, those issues are immaterial for our discussion. Nearly all the commentaries seek some solution. Cf. the discussion in Williams, *Acts*, p. 99.

201. Cf. Koester, *Introduction*, vol. 1, p. 223. Throughout Luke-Acts, of course, the author remains totally oblivious both to the eastern Diaspora and to the eastern Christian mission.

202. Seen precisely by Beck, *Mature Christianity*, pp. 220–1. The way in which all 'the Jewish people of Palestine' join with their leaders in accusing Stephen and Paul is overlooked by Trocmé, *Le 'Livre des Actes'*, p. 71, who finds 'an idealized tableau of rapports with Palestinian Jews' put over against 'a very black image of relations with Jews of Greek culture'.

203. The remarks of Wendt, *Apostelgeschichte*, p. 306, and Jacquier, *Actes*, p. 640, that this phrase is a mistake or an exaggeration miss Luke's point.

204. On the Stephen–Paul parallels, cf. further Morgenthaler, *Geschichtsschreibung*, vol. 1, pp. 175–7; Preuschen, *Apostelgeschichte*, p. 39.

205. Lampe, 'Acts', p. 920, endows the account of Paul's arrest with too much historical veracity when he observes that Diaspora Jews had more reason than Jerusalem Jews to fear Stephen and Paul, since it was more important to keep Torah in the Diaspora (because doing so was a mark of identity in a pagan setting) than it was in Jerusalem. The reason for Luke's portrayal of Diaspora Jews is rather to be sought in his own *Sitz im Leben*; Diaspora Jews were more of a problem for Luke than were Jerusalem Jews.

206. Rese, 'Aussagen über Jesu Tod', p. 340, thinks of Stephen as addressing only the Sanhedrin. Cf. again the discussion above, pp. 17–18.

207. Bihler, *Stephanusgeschichte*, p. 12, n. 1, oddly seems to want to play down the extent of the parallels; although, op. cit., pp. 18–19, he then affirms them.

208. Cf. Radl, *Paulus und Jesus*, p. 237; Lampe, 'Lucan Portrait', p. 167.

209. Cf. the earlier discussion of these parallels, above, p. 63. G. Schneider, *Apostelgeschichte*, vol. 1, p. 433, provides a helpful list of parallels in Jesus' and Stephen's martyrdoms, but the brief discussion in Holtzmann, *Apostelgeschichte*, pp. 61–3, is probably the most complete. Cf. also Talbert, *Reading Luke*, p. 213; id., *Patterns*, p. 97. Many other authors note the parallels.

210. Goulder, *Type*, pp. 41–51, 55, has discussed this compositional trait of Luke-Acts in some detail. Lohfink, *Sammlung Israels*, p. 55, explains that the Jewish people change from being friendly to being hostile at Stephen's martyrdom because now all those Jews who are going to be 'gathered' have been gathered. Other Jews thus become – and Lohfink pointedly uses Conzelmann's term – 'Judaism'. He attempts

by this terminology and by, further (ibid., n. 131), rejecting Jervell's notion of 'Israel and associate Israel', to distance his own position from that of Jervell, but the distance is not great.

211. Whether Luke intends to keep the rigid order Jerusalem-Judaea-Samaria-Gentiles is not clear, since Cornelius's conversion (ch. 10) is followed by preaching 'only to Jews' in the near Diaspora (11.19); but what is clear is that Luke intends to show in chs. 8–11 how the gospel got from Jerusalem out into Judaea and Samaria and into the beginning of the Gentile mission. (Cf. the discussion by Bihler, *Stephanusgeschichte*, pp. 183–4.) In this way Paul's mission is prepared. Luke seems really to have had very little interest in the Judaean and Samaritan part of the expansion. There are good discussions of the transition in Haenchen, *Acts*, pp. 298–9, and in Overbeck, *Apostelgeschichte*, pp. 171–2.

212. Even Jacquier, *Actes*, p. 360, and Lampe, 'Acts', p. 902 – both of whom generally do their best to show that not *all* 'the Jews' oppose Christianity in Acts – have to admit that v. 3 means just that. Beck, *Mature Christianity*, p. 224: 'Perhaps the most blatant and vicious anti-Jewish polemic in all of the New Testament.'

213. By such stylistic variations Luke means to lend greater credibility to his account. We shall see more of this sort of thing.

214. Franklin, *Christ the Lord*, p. 97, pursuing the explanation that Acts describes the renewal, not the rejection of Israel, writes that 'the Twelve' pass off the stage at this point because 'the centre of interest passes into the Gentile world', but that they 'are the foundations of the re-made Israel – which is always wider than they'. I am unable, however, to find any support in Acts for this assertion.

215. This is not to say that these authors have given overly simplified analyses. Overbeck, *Apostelgeschichte*, pp. 207–9, presents quite a good analysis of the variations of the pattern that occur in the different episodes of Paul's Diaspora mission. Bihler, 'Stephanusbericht', pp. 265–6 and n. 39, while correctly again emphasizing the programmatic shift in the role of the Jewish people at Stephen's martyrdom, then oversimplifies by finding the 'same scheme' in Paul's mission.

216. In fact, Jervell refers (*People of God*, pp. 158–9) to 'the activity of Paul among the Jews of the Greek diaspora, as a result of which numerous congregations of repentant Jews have arisen with which Gentiles have become associated', thus forcing one to wonder what version of Acts he was reading. Cf. further id., *Unknown Paul*, pp. 15–16. He is followed closely by Juel, *Luke-Acts*, p. 110. Cf. the criticism of this position by Richard, 'Divine Purpose', pp. 198–9.

217. Burchard, *Dreizehnter Zeuge*, p. 113; others take a similar position. The view of the Tübingen school, however, is also worth remembering (cf. Baur, *Paul*, vol. 1, p. 7), that Paul's seeking out of Jews in his missionary endeavours is one more example of his fidelity to Judaism.

218. Löning, *Saulustradition*, pp. 160–2, has provided a necessary correction to Burchard's position: Paul does seek out the Jews, but so that they will reject the gospel, not accept it – as we shall see in the following paragraphs.

219. Jacquier, whose task was to 'correct' the 'errors' of the heretic Loisy, denies that there is any pattern created by Luke for Paul's mission; cf. *Actes*, pp. 411–12. It is, further, equally incorrect to claim that 'Paul repeatedly turns from Jews to Gentiles, yet continues to preach to Jews' (Mattill, *Last Things*, p. 145). Such a statement, in any case, overlooks the epochal plan of Luke-Acts.

220. Whether the 'persuasion' of Jews in Paul's mission is the same, as a number of authors think, as 'conversion' is doubtful; cf. Buss, *Missionspredigt*, p. 134, and my

'Salvation of the Jews', pp. 470–2. Loisy, *Actes*, p. 539, calls these 'persuasions' 'demi-conversions'.

221. Whether George, 'Israël', p. 514, is justified in stating that '*beacoup de Juifs de la Diaspora*' were converted is another matter.

222. Jacquier, *Actes*, p. 431, would like to know what arguments the outside Jews used to persuade the Lystran mob to attack Paul. Indeed! So would we! When Jacquier follows his question with the speculation that the Antiochene Jews' 'Lystran compatriots . . . were probably the first to be aroused against the Apostles', a guess in support of which there is not the least evidence in the text, he merely reveals the degree to which he has fallen into the Lucan way of thinking.

223. Nor are the stories of 'mob Jew-baiting' in Acts 18.17 and 19.34, which are told – as Cadbury, *Acts in History*, p. 94, observes – 'with a little malicious glee'.

224. Talbert, *Patterns*, p. 79, emphasizes 'the aversion to perfect symmetry' on the part of ancient writers.

225. This architectonic parallelism is thus at least a formal answer to the question of Preuschen, *Apostelgeschichte*, p. 113, as to why Paul suddenly breaks off his stay in Ephesus in order to travel somewhere, when he was doing so well in Ephesus. Luke's need to splice in the Apollos episode somewhere is, of course, also a part of the answer.

226. Cf. Also Stählin, *Apostelgeschichte*, p. 256. Radl, *Paulus und Jesus*, p. 308: '*Kein Zufall*'; Löning, 'Paulinismus', p. 207: '*Konkurrierende Karikaturen des Judentums*'.

227. Radl, *Paulus und Jesus*, p. 93, on the rejection of the Jews at Antioch: '*So macht Lukas das Ende schon im Anfang sichtbar.*' Munck, *Acts*, p. 122, also correctly notes parallels between Paul's visits to synagogues – especially his first visit – and Jesus' visit to a synagogue in Luke 4; cf. also Loisy, *Actes*, p. 523.

228. Loisy, *Actes*, p. 518, calls the Barjesus episode of Acts 13 the 'frontispiece' for the story of Paul in Luke's 'simulacrum of history'. Cf. also the remark of Lampe, 'Acts', p. 903.

229. They are called only 'some' in 19.9, but, since they are in the synagogue and oppose 'the way', they can only be Jews.

230. Eltester, 'Israel', p. 130: '*Es ist hoffnungslos mit diesen Juden.*' Morgenthaler, *Geschichtsschreibung*, vol. 1, p. 189: '*Das Heil verlässt Israel.*'

231. Conzelmann, *Theology*, p. 145.

232. Ibid., pp. 142–4.

232. On the appropriateness of this term, cf. Radl, *Paulus und Jesus*, pp. 68–267.

234. Talbert, *Patterns*, p. 22, has it that Luke modelled the trial of Jesus on that of Paul. Cadbury, *Making of Luke-Acts*, p. 231, had leaned in the same direction. The issue makes little difference for the present analysis. The similarities between the two Passions are so obvious and so extensive that the argument of Dehandschutter, 'La persécution des chrétiens' – that persecution of the disciples in Acts is not the imitation of anything in the Gospel, because no disciples are persecuted in the Gospel – gives one pause.

235. Sandmel, *Anti-Semitism*, p. 95, emphasizes that no 'official Jewish body' ever 'condemns Paul'. The position of George, 'Israël', p. 511, on this point is somewhat puzzling. While he notes how often, in the Pauline passion, the accusers are 'the Jews' or 'the people', and that once (24.19) 'it is a question of Jews from Asia', he still thinks that the 'impassioned hostility' is expressed towards Paul only by 'the people of Jerusalem and their leaders'.

236. It should also not escape our notice that the accusations brought against Paul by the Jewish mob in Acts 17.7–8 are essentially the same as those brought

against Jesus in Luke 23.2, as especially Schmithals, *Apostelgeschichte*, p. 157, emphasizes.

237. That the function of Agabus's prophecy is to be such an announcement is seen by Stählin, *Apostelgeschichte*, p. 275, and Roloff, *Apostelgeschichte*, p. 310. Radl, *Paulus und Jesus*, pp. 133–58, so designates both Agabus's prophecy and Paul's words of anticipation in Acts 20.22–25. Cf. also Cadbury, *Making of Luke-Acts*, p. 231.

238. Cf. above, p. 13.

239. I.e., again there is no subject for 'lifted up their voices'.

240. Luke would have done well as a writer for a Hollywood studio known for its production of children's adventure films. A bright young lad listens in at just the right moment to a highly secret plot to destroy the hero. The boy runs immediately to the military authority with his news, where he is received like an important messenger and his report is accepted without any doubt or question. The plot is then foiled and the would-be evildoers are made to look like fools. Loisy, *Actes*, pp. 837–8, refers to 'the lack of logic and the audacious awkwardness' of the narrative; and Schmithals, *Apostelgeschichte*, p. 209, labels the tale 'an original narrative of the writer Luke'. Cf. also Beck, *Mature Christianity*, p. 237. Winn, *Acts*, p. 120, gets caught up in the drama and proposes that the 'more than forty' were Sicarii.

241. Marshall, *Acts*, p. 367. This is not, of course, the only plot of 'the Jews' to do away with Paul; cf. also Acts 9.23; 20.3, 19; 25.1–3. Loisy, *Actes*, p. 417, notes, regarding 9.23, '*Le complot des Juifs est un expédient que notre hagiographe emploiera souvent dans la suite.*'

242. The point that Diaspora Jews are more successful in rousing other Jews up against Paul than they were earlier in Acts in inciting Gentiles against him is not lost on Stählin, *Apostelgeschichte*, p. 279.

243. Koester, *Introduction*, vol. 2, p. 320, still finds opposition only from the Jewish authorities, even in Acts 13.27! But cf. Kilgallen, *The Stephen Speech*, p. 102: 'There is always at the root of the problem a lack of comprehension on Israel's part.'

244. Cf. also Marshall, *Acts*, p. 423; Beck, *Mature Christianity*, p. 241.

245. Gnilka, *Verstockung*, p. 147, n. 91, correctly notes that Paul does not here bring some of his audience to belief; cf. also my 'Salvation of the Jews', pp. 470–2, and the other authors referred to there, as well as G. Schneider, *Apostelgeschichte*, vol. 2, p. 417, and n. 220 above. George, 'Israël', p. 522, mistakenly refers to '[les] *derniers convertis de Rome*'; and Prete, 'L'arrivo di Paolo', pp. 166–9, finds the division in Israel proclaimed right through the last scene in Acts.

246. αὐτοὶ καὶ ἀκούσονται cannot mean 'They also will hear', thus holding out some hope of further Jewish conversions. While such a sense is grammatically possible, the immediately preceding quotation of the Isaiah passage, with its 'hearing but not understanding', its 'being hard of hearing', and its 'lest . . . they hear with their ears', rules such a meaning out entirely. Hastings, *Prophet and Witness*, p. 130, grasps the meaning in his translation: 'They, at least, will listen to it'. What he then means, however, when he says (ibid., n. 1) that Luke's anti-Judaism is only 'of a very theological nature' is less than clear.

247. Cf. also Munck, *Acts*, p. 259; Maddox, *Purpose*, p. 44; Radl, *Paulus und Jesus*, p. 318. Radl further, op. cit., pp. 94–100, shows parallels between Luke 4.16–30 and Acts 13.14–52, the scene of the first rejection of the Jews in Paul's mission; cf. also Tannehill, 'Mission of Jesus', p. 68. Cf. the remark of Dupont, 'La conclusion des Actes', p. 401, that 'Nazareth, Antioch of Pisidia, Rome [are] three landmarks of the same history, three situations permitting variations on the same theme';

also id., 'Le salut des Gentils', pp. 145–6. Cadbury, *Making of Luke-Acts*, p. 188, emphasizes the similarity between Jesus' Nazareth sermon and the 'self-defence' speeches in Acts. Tolbert, 'Leading Ideas', p. 442, calls Luke 4.16–30 'almost a stereotype of other key incidents in Luke-Acts and . . . in fact a microcosm of the whole work'.

248. Preuschen, *Apostelgeschichte*, p. 158, observes that Isa. 6.9–10 was 'a *locus communis* of anti-Judaic polemic' in early Christianity.

249. On the relevance of the parallels to this point, cf. also esp. Mattill, 'Evans', pp. 29–30. Mattill (op. cit., p. 37) writes that Luke has 'personif[ied] his theological program in the life and work of Jesus and Paul'.

250. Many authors have noted that Luke 4.16–30, with its summary judgment on the Jews, is 'programmatic' for Luke-Acts; cf., e.g., Perrin-Duling, *Introduction*, p. 312; Fitzmyer, *Luke*, vol. 1, pp. 526–9. Loisy, *Evangiles synoptiques*, vol. 1, p. 839: 'All that Luke will narrate in his two books is condensed in this single tableau.' Montefiore, *Synoptic Gospels*, vol. 2, p. 395: Luke's 'aim is to symbolize the rejection of the gospel and the Christ by the Jews, and their acceptance by the Gentiles'.

251. Bihler has glimpsed this point when he concludes (*Stephanusgeschichte*, p. 182) that what 'is proclaimed programmatically in the speeches' in Acts is then 'brought to expression by the composition (chs. 2–5: Jewish mission; chs. 8–14: mission among non-Jews)'; cf. further Egelkraut, *Jesus' Mission*, p. 225: 'The rejection of Israel prophesied at Nazareth and effected in the [travel narrative] is actualized in Acts.' Of course, it has long and widely been recognized that Luke-Acts describes the steady and gradual progress of the maxim, 'From the Jews to the Gentiles.' Sandmel, *Anti-Semitism*, p. 100, concludes his discussion of Luke-Acts with these questions: 'Are the Jews of Acts real people or puppets of the author? Is Acts an account of what really happened or is it, with respect to the Jews, a series of vilifications?'

252. On this point, Jervell is more correct than all those who emphasize that the individual Jew can always be converted, when he writes that 'Luke has excluded the possibility of a further mission to Jews for the Church of his time because the judgment by and on the Jews has been irrevocably passed' (*People of God*, p. 64). He is followed closely by Juel, *Luke-Acts*, p. 119. Similarly, Lohfink, *Sammlung Israels*, p. 61, observes that Acts 2–5 carries out the second part of the prophecy of Luke 2.43, that Jesus 'is set for the fall and rise of many in Israel', while Acts 6–28 carries out the first part of the prophecy.

253. Franklin, *Christ the Lord*, p. 79.

254. Eltester, 'Israel', p. 124, has observed correctly that Luke's attitude towards the Bible is that it is the Christians' book, not the Jews'.

255. This point is widely recognized. Cf., e.g., Haenchen, *Acts*, p. 724, and 'Apostelgeschichte', p. 505; Lohfink, *Sammlung Israels*, pp. 30, 62; Gnilka, *Verstockung*, pp. 152–4. The discussion of 'The Fullfillment of Prophecy in Luke-Acts', in Talbert, *Reading Luke*, pp. 234–40, while it does not refer explicitly to the theme of the rejection of the Jews, is nevertheless quite instructive. Cf. my forthcoming article, 'Prophetic Use of Scriptures'. Cf. further Fitzmyer, *Luke*, vol. 1, pp. 179–80.

256. George, 'Israël', p. 501, correctly emphasizes that, in spite of 'this sympathy', none of the people in the passion narrative 'really believed in Jesus'.

257. Lohfink, *Sammlung Israels*, pp. 42–3, has seen this but has misunderstood it, inasmuch as he thinks that the general Jewish guilt demonstrated in Luke 23 prepares the way for later Jewish repentance.

258. The words are those of Tolbert, 'Leading Ideas', p. 445; but the sentiment is repeated by many other authors.

259. This realization should allow us to lay to rest those explanations – such as that of Gnilka, *Verstockung*, p. 151 – of the role of the Jews in Luke-Acts that capitalize on the distinction between leaders and people and thus make Luke appear less antisemitic than he is. Gnilka even goes so far as to say that the way in which Luke uses the distinction avoids 'wounding . . . Jews' (ibid., p. 151). Whether he asked any Jew to read Luke-Acts and to corroborate that opinion he does not say. But to reiterate: the distinction does not occur in the *speeches* of Jesus, Peter, Stephen and Paul, and it disappears in the *narrative* in the Pauline passion.

260. Cf. O'Neill, *Theology*, p. 87: Paul's concluding remarks in Acts '[sum] up the verdict of God on all the Jews, a verdict painfully discovered by the Church throughout the whole of Acts'.

4. The Pharisees

1. Goulder, *Type*, pp. 59–60, unfortunately sees the Pharisees in the Gospel as only specific representatives of the Jews.

2. The short article by Ziesler, 'Luke and the Pharisees', briefly recites the evidence and then moves directly to questions about the relation of Pharisees to Jesus. The *TDNT* article on the Pharisees, altogether too brief on Acts (H.-F. Weiss, 'Φαρισαῖος'), notes simply that, whereas in the Gospels the Pharisees were enemies of Jesus, in Acts they are not (ibid., p. 47) – thus revealing how superficially the author has read both Luke and Acts.

3. Rivkin, 'Pharisees', p. 662. The article is, in general, of course, a good discussion of the *historical* Pharisees. On that issue, cf. also the bibliography there given.

4. Davies, *Introduction to Pharisaism*, p. v.

5. Cf. Phil. 3.5.

6. Munck, *Acts*, p. 49, thinks of 'former Pharisees'.

7. This Pharisaic friendliness, however, is not the same thing as accepting the gospel, as George, 'Israël', pp. 507–8, understands it.

8. Luke was surely aware that he had chosen a particularly famous Pharisee for this role, since he also has Paul claim, in Acts 22.3, that he himself had been a pupil of Gamaliel. Loisy, *Actes*, p. 284, writes that 'for a little one could make of [Gamaliel] the grandfather of Christianity'.

9. Acts 23.9: 'We find no guilt (nothing bad) in this person'; Luke 23.4: 'I find no cause [sc., for a guilty verdict] in this person.' On this point cf. Lampe, 'Acts', p. 921.

10. Loisy, *Evangiles synoptiques*, vol. 2, p. 126. Cf. also Caird, *Luke*, p. 173, and others. Fitzmyer, *Luke*, vol. 2, p. 1030, rejects the possibility of Herodian duplicity in this scene.

11. So also Ziesler, 'Luke and the Pharisees', p. 150; Fitzmyer, *Luke*, vol. 2, p. 1030.

12. E.g., Lagrange, *Luc*, pp. 392–3.

13. So also Grundmann, *Lukas*, p. 288; Gilmour, 'Luke', p. 248; G. Schneider, *Lukas*, vol. 2, p. 309; and Beck, *Mature Christianity*, p. 191. Beck here almost uncovers the true role of the Pharisees in Luke-Acts.

14. Cf. also Buck, 'Jesus Before Herod', p. 177. Whatever 'fox' means to Luke, it is clear that it is not intended to be a complimentary term. Fitzmyer, *Luke*, vol. 2, p. 1031, gives evidence from ancient writers for the meaning 'crafty or sly'; but G. Schneider, *Lukas*, vol. 2, pp. 309–10, attests different meanings.

15. When Hauck, *Lukas*, p. 186, suggests that the story referred originally only to messengers from Herod, not to Pharisees, his interest, of course, is historical, not redactional; but he may well have inadvertently uncovered the true origin of this narrative, for are these Lucan Pharisees from Herod not, indeed, what has become in Luke of the Pharisees and Herodians of Mark 3.6? Schweizer, *Luke*, p. 229, hints at this connection. Hauck, *Lukas*, p. 236, quite consistently suspects the Pharisees who scold the disciples in 19.39 of being equally secondary.

16. This remarkable trait is hardly to be explained as a part of Luke's universalism, as if *'Tischgemeinschaft'* represented *'Lebensgemeinschaft'*, for Pharisees as for all (so Schmid, *Lukas*, p. 147); nor are we to think that the *purpose* of the Pharisaic invitations is to 'test' Jesus (so Kealy, *Luke*, p. 237; similarly Moessner, 'Luke 9.1–50', p. 603). Nevertheless, there is a certain two-sidedness to the repeated Pharisaic hospitality, so that Denaux, 'L'hypocrisie des Pharisiens', p. 262, observes that the Pharisees *'acceptent [Jésus] froidement, ils l'observent, ils le jugent sévèrement'*. Cf. further below, pp. 89–90.

17. Cf. Conzelmann, *Theology*, p. 78.

18. Baur, *Paul*, vol. 1, p. 217.

19. This is not, however, why they are 'the very best party' among the Jews, as, e.g., Löning, *Saulustradition*, p. 169, states; cf. further below, p. 97.

20. It is certainly not above Luke to produce such an ambiguity deliberately; we recall all his subjectless verbs in the matter of the execution of Jesus. More precisely, while Luke probably intends to have Paul say in Acts 26.6 and 28.20, in the first instance, that it is because of his (Jewish) belief in the resurrection that he has been imprisoned, he would not mind if his readers also thought something more general, e.g., that Paul was imprisoned simply because he was a religious Jew.

21. So also Vielhauer, 'Paulinism', p. 41.

22. K. L. Schmidt, *Rahmen*, p. 92, considers the change irrelevant; Fitzmyer, *Luke*, vol. 1, p. 608, notes it but offers no explanation.

23. Löning (*Saulustradition*, p. 170; 'Paulinismus', p. 213) and G. Klein (*Zwölf Apostel*, pp. 124–5) are thus wrong to imply that the pre-Christian Paul persecuted the church *as a Pharisee*. When Paul's persecuting activity is mentioned, nothing is said of his being a Pharisee, and when Paul emphasizes that he is a Pharisee it is to underscore his Torah fidelity and belief in the resurrection; cf. Acts 22.3–4 and 23.6.

24. Part of the 'Little Omission', to use Fitzmyer's term.

25. George, 'Israël', p. 497, thinks that removing the Pharisees from these several conflict scenes is part of Luke's way of showing that 'an important part of Israel . . . now refuses Jesus'.

26. Ziesler, 'Luke and the Pharisees', p. 152, is willing to explain the differences between Luke and Mark in this regard by supposing that Luke may have been lazy!

27. Since Luke introduces Pharisees into this Gospel for a Gentile readership, whereas they were not in his sources at these points, his writing out of Pharisees in other cases could not be a matter of sensitivity to Gentile confusion about Jewish technical terms, as Crossan, 'Anti-Semitism', p. 192, suggests.

28. On the behaviour of the Pharisaic host in 11.38, cf. below, p. 90.

29. The word 'Pharisee' occurs twenty-seven times in Luke; in only nine of those places does the word also appear in the Marcan or Matthaean parallel.

30. My own suspicion is that the additional references to the Pharisees are the product of Luke's 'gift of invention' (Koester); similarly Beck, *Mature Christianity*, p. 168. But the ultimate origin of his extra Pharisees is irrelevant for the discussion at hand.

31. This is thus the nearest that Luke gets to the notion of a Pharisaic plot against Jesus.

32. So also Ziesler, 'Luke and the Pharisees', p. 151. Tyson, 'Opposition', pp. 148–9, and 'Conflict', pp. 318–19, has also seen this point. He writes ('Conflict', p. 326), 'Luke associates the early and less malevolent conflicts with Pharisees and with issues of Torah observance [but] the very bitter conflicts, which resulted in Jesus' death, with priests, Jerusalem, and the temple.' It is unfortunate that Tyson seems to think ('Conflict', p. 318) that the Pharisees can be Jesus' opponents in Luke only to the degree that they are 'leaders'. Mussner, *Tractate*, pp. 169–72, sees the Lucan hostility to the Pharisees as hostility towards Jews and overlooks the friendly aspect of the Pharisees.

33. Wilson, *Law*, p. 35; cf. also ibid., pp. 35–9. Cf. further below, pp. 124–8.

34. Loisy, *Evangiles synoptiques*, vol. 1, p. 471, who thinks that Luke is just 'enlarging the audience' by introducing Pharisees here while at the same time anticipating the conflict coming up at the beginning of Mark 3, and Schmithals, *Lukas*, p. 71, who proposes that Luke is representing Jesus here as a great teacher who draws other teachers from all over to his audience, have missed the theological implications.

35. So Grundmann, *Lukas*, p. 367.

36. F. Keck, *Abschiedsrede*, pp. 26–7, is quite certain that this is the proper understanding; similarly also Schweizer, *Luke*, pp. 299–300; Ernst, *Lukas*, p. 527.

37. Loisy, *Luc*, p. 470, thinks that the Pharisaic scolding of the disciples in 19.39 is an expression of '*la jalousie et l'impuissance de judaïsme devant le succès chrétien*'; similarly Valensin et Huby, *Luc*, p. 368. K. L. Schmidt, *Rahmen*, pp. 278–9, sees Luke as playing up the hostility to Jesus of his opponents versus the 'praise of the people'. The most unique explanation of the Pharisaic rebuke is that of Ellis, *Luke*, p. 225, who finds here a rejection of Jesus' ministry at its conclusion, parallel to that in Luke 9.51 at its beginning.

38. Schweizer, *Luke*, p. 229, has fairly adequately, albeit briefly, noted the Lucan peculiarities in regard to the Pharisees that we have just discussed; but he does not follow this up and moves instead to the historical question of who the real enemies of Jesus were who caused his death.

39. If that is in fact what 19.39 is, as we were just discussing.

40. Koenig, *Jews and Christians*, p. 118, has seen this point correctly.

41. When Wikenhauser, *Apostelgeschichte*, p. 170, then calls them 'former Pharisees', he has not clearly analysed their attitude (similarly Marshall, *Acts*, p. 249). These Christians in Acts 15.5 who want Gentile Christians to be circumcised are 'Pharisees'. Cf. Lampe, 'Acts', p. 908: 'The legalist party at Jerusalem consists of converted Pharisees'. Bruce, *Commentary on the Book of the Acts*, p. 305, also gets it right. Schmithals, *Apostelgeschichte*, pp. 135–6, interprets from Galatians 2 and thinks that those demanding circumcision, including the Pharisees, are neither true Jews nor true Christians; but then, op. cit., p. 137, he correctly identifies the Pharisees as 'Christian Pharisees' who are somehow supposed to represent Judaism and Christianity together! That is precisely the point. Wild, 'Encounter', p. 114, sees the entire Pharisee issue in Luke-Acts as having to do with the problem of Pharisees in the church. Schille, *Apostelgeschichte*, p. 315, replays his refrain about how Acts is not antisemitic.

42. We need recall only the well-known statement of Haenchen, *Apostelgeschichte*, pp. 110–11 (cf. *Acts*, p. 100), that 'the historian Luke contends from the first to the last page with the problem of the *Gentile mission that is free from the Law*' (emphasis his). Ziesler, 'Luke and the Pharisees', p. 148, asserts that the Pharisees of Acts 15.5

are not to be contrasted to Pharisees elsewhere in Acts. That he actually dimly glimpses Luke's meaning, however, is seen when he then qualifies that proposal by writing that the Pharisees in Acts are consistently "'political'', if not always the theological, friends of the Church'.

43. Cf. Loisy, *Actes*, p. 284: Gamaliel is *'un vrai juif*, and one whose opinion counts more than that of all the Sadducees combined', inasmuch as Gamaliel is *'docteur de la Loi* . . . Authentic Judaism comes from his mouth.' Loisy does not, then, make the mistake of trying to bring the position of the Christian Pharisees in Acts 15.5 into harmony with that of the friendly Pharisees; cf. op. cit., pp. 570–1.

44. So Loisy, *Actes*, p. 830, understands Paul's appeal to the Pharisees for help; cf. also ibid., p. 855, on Acts 24.14–16; p. 892, on Acts 26.6; and pp. 932–3, on Acts 28.17–22. Cf. also Mattill, 'Evans', pp. 22–3. Roloff, *Apostelgeschichte*, p. 328, thinks that 'Luke simplifies here and gives an image of Christians as true Pharisees'. Cf. further ibid., pp. 337–8.

45. Similarly Jervell, 'Paul in the Acts', p. 300.

46. Similarly Juel, *Luke-Acts*, p. 85.

47. Stählin, *Apostelgeschichte*, p. 296, writes of Paul's defence in Acts 24, 'The accenting of what causes him to be recognized as a good Jew, what therefore connects him with his opponents, moves through the entire speech from v. 11 to v. 21.' Stählin further observes (ibid.), however, what the difference is, i.e., Paul believes the same scripture, but in the Christian way; he believes in the same resurrection, but the Christian version; he takes pains to be scrupulously religious, but from a Christian perspective. If Luke finds opportunity to emphasize, in different places, now one, now the other side of that coin, in Acts 24.14–16 he manages to show both at once. Cf. further the remarks of Haenchen, *Acts*, p. 729 (on Paul's final encounter with Jews in Rome), regarding how, for Luke, Christianity must be both Jewish and opposed by Jews.

48. This statement should not be taken to mean that I intend to take a position on the issue of whether Luke had Matthew or Q for a source. If he used Q, then he either followed it more or less accurately or he changed it around considerably, but in either case he used it to say what he wanted it to say. If he used Matthew, then he changed it around considerably, using it to say what he wanted to say. As Talbert has recently warned, it 'is necessary [to give] a negative answer' to the question, 'Can one simply assume the two-source theory today?' (review of *Kreuzweg und Kreuzigung Jesu* by Franz Georg Untergassmair, p. 343).

49. Cf. again the preceding note. There are surely, of course, signs in Matthew of embellishment, since Matthew everywhere betrays a vicious hatred of the Pharisees. Ziesler, 'Luke and the Pharisees', pp. 153–4, also refers to this problem. The reader may wish to consult Bultmann, *Synoptic Tradition*, pp. 113–14, on the issue of Luke's and Matthew's alterations of their common source.

50. Cf. also Ziesler, 'Luke and the Pharisees', p. 154.

51. If this saying was in Luke's source, his omission of it would be entirely understandable, since he would hardly have wanted to allow it to be said that Pharisees actually occupied a place of authority in the interpretation of the Torah, inasmuch as that is precisely what is at issue for Luke; for Luke, it is Christianity that properly 'sits in Moses' seat'.

52. While Luke would probably not have been interested in some of these sayings – if they were, in fact, in his source – e.g., the liturgically related admonitions in Matt. 23.16b–22 – I can see no reason why he would have gone out of his way to avoid Matt. 23.5, about the superficial character of Pharisaic righteousness, since he

elsewhere includes this theme, e.g., Luke 11.42. Such an observation might lead one to the assumption that Luke and Matthew had a sayings source in common for this invective, and that each embellished or reduced it according to the dictates of his own interests. But I digress.

53. Luke also (11.37–38), as does Matthew, omits the explanation about Pharisaic handwashing that appears in Mark 7.2–5. I am unable to perceive any particular animus in this omission. Enslin, 'Samaritan Ministry', p. 31, also notes the milder form of the invective in Luke, but he seems to overstate the case when he has the Lucan Jesus display 'an attitude of regretful sorrow' towards the Pharisees in response to their failure to accept his message.

54. It is often, of course, noted that Matthew gathers sayings material into several more or less unified discourses. In this instance, however, such an observation should not be used to help to solve the Synoptic problem in favour of the existence of Q, since Luke would have a very good reason for putting the bulk of the invective into the travel narrative and not into the passion narrative, where it would be if he were following Matthew, since, as we have already seen, he keeps the Pharisees out of the passion narrative. (Matthew 23 agrees with Luke 20 in order.)

55. Translating νομικοί as 'lawyers' is ill-advised, since that term implies to Americans people who deal with the law professionally – those who are called in England either 'barristers' or 'solicitors'. Luke, however, has in mind those who are sticklers for the Torah (νόμος); cf.Parker, 'Lawyer', p. 102.

56. By applying all the invective after v. 44 to the legists, Luke avoids charging the Pharisees with complicity in the murder of the prophets (vv. 47–51; cf. Matt. 23.29–32, 34–36), and he avoids saying that they have the 'keys' (v. 52; cf. Matt. 23.13). Inasmuch as the Lucan versions of these sayings therefore reflect Lucan interest, one should avoid assuming that Luke necessarily has the more original form of the invective, as does Gaston, *No Stone*, pp. 320–1.

57. Wilson, *Law*, pp. 18–19.

58. F. Keck, *Abschiedsrede*, pp. 94–5, sees only these slanderous denunciations in the invective, not the halachic argument, and therefore takes the intention of the invective to be a warning against 'greed'.

59. Ellis, *Luke*, consistently reinterprets the Pharisees as problem 'church members' – that is, he gives a homiletical interpretation to the Pharisees in Luke: 'The churchmen observe only the forms of religion' (ibid., p. 69; cf. also Bouwman, *Drittes Evangelium*, pp. 147, 151–61; Hastings, *Prophet and Witness*, p. 109). While this approach has the value of shifting the interest of the reader away from those bad Jews to Christian self-criticism, it is historically misleading and has the effect of leaving Luke's antisemitism lying there like an undetonated bomb waiting to be tripped over by a less generous interpreter. Fitzmyer, *Luke*, vol. 2, p. 1040, argues against Ellis on this point.

60. Also Schweizer, *Luke*, pp. 200–3; cf. Fitzmyer's discussion of the redaction history of this passage in *Luke*, vol. 2, pp. 943–4.

61. Cf. also Tyson, 'Opposition', p. 149. Luke does not 'avoid' (Grundmann, *Lukas*, p. 246; similarly Koenig, *Jews and Christians*, p. 117) calling the Pharisees hypocrites.

62. Lagrange, *Luc*, p. 352, sees that the 'hypocrisy' of Luke 12.1 is a summary of the several references to that trait in Matthew. Schmid, *Lukas*, p. 214, explains that the saying represents an 'ethical value judgment about' the leaven, not a 'designation of [its] content', and that it does not warn the disciples 'to be on guard . . . against the Pharisees', but rather 'not to imitate them'. Thus he leans towards the position

also taken by Ellis and Bouwman (cf. n. 59). Beck, *Mature Christianity*, p. 172, thinks of a gloss.

63. Cf. Egelkraut, *Jesus' Mission*, p. 103. This realization inclines one naturally towards the view that at least that aspect of the Matthaean form of the invective that includes 'hypocrites' with the repeated 'woes' is the more original form, and that Luke has taken the hypocrisy out of the repeated woes to place it in his concluding statement, which he applies only to Pharisees (so Ernst, *Lukas*, p. 393; Wilckens, 'ὑποκρίνομαι, κτλ.', p. 566). Ziesler, 'Luke and the Pharisees', p. 152, cannot tell if Luke intends to be more or less critical of the Pharisees here than his sources are. Cf. the perceptive comment by Fitzmyer, *Luke*, vol. 2, pp. 953–4.

64. The Lucan Pharisees should not, therefore, be called 'leaders' (as, e.g., by Fitzmyer, *Luke*, vol. 2, p. 1038, and Schmithals, *Lukas*, p. 141), inasmuch as the role of leaven is not that of leadership. Moessner, 'Luke 9:1–50', p. 603, apparently thinks of the leaven's 'rising' characteristic and declares that, 'as the crowds increase . . ., so does the "leaven of the Pharisees"'; but this increase is rather hard to find in Luke 12.1.

65. Parker, 'Lawyer', p. 102, opts for the former alternative. Fitzmyer, *Luke*, vol. 1, p. 676, finds *nomikos* 'probably only a synonym for *grammateus*'.

66. Schweizer, *Luke*, pp. 200–1, also makes this connection.

67. Cf. Gilmour, 'Luke', p. 142. Ziesler, 'Luke and the Pharisees', p. 150, has noted this odd juxtaposition but admits that he cannot explain it. O'Neill, *Theology*, p. 71, finds in the three dinners with Pharisees 'a development in the relationship between Jesus and the Pharisees of increasing antagonism'. Why there is more antagonism in 14.1–6 than in 11.37–44 + 12.1 is not, however, clear.

68. Mark 14.3–9 and Matt. 26.6–13 include what is more or less the same story, but without designating Jesus' host a Pharisee and without the scolding of the host. These are Lucan elements.

69. Wilckens, 'Vergebung für die Sünderin', p. 418, sees it the other way round: the Pharisee is the foil for the Christian lesson. In Mark and Matthew the woman anointed Jesus' head. John 12.1–8 also has her anointing his feet, but it is a different woman, and there is no Pharisee about.

70. B. and J. Weiss, *Markus und Lukas*, p. 395, note that the contrast does not mean that Jesus' Pharisaic host has neglected *normal* politeness, only that the woman's behaviour is of a different order from his. That appears to be correct.

71. These two aspects of this Pharisee are clearly noted by Grundmann, *Lukas*, pp. 171, 173.

72. Ziesler, 'Luke and the Pharisees', p. 151, thinks that the narrative 'concerns both attitudes to the Law, and Christology'.

73. It is possible to translate the phrase as 'one of the Pharisees who was a ruler', especially if, as in a few important manuscripts, the article before Φαρισαίων is missing. So Zahn, *Lucas*, p. 544, prefers to read. In view, however, of the way in which Luke otherwise keeps the Pharisees neatly separate from the religious authorities, I would regard such a translation as impossible, even if the article is not orignal. Cf. the discussion in G.Schneider, *Lukas*, vol. 2, p. 312.

74. Löning, *Saulustradition*, p. 168, mistakenly thinks that 'greed' is Luke's primary criticism of the Pharisees. Ernst, *Lukas*, p. 470, thinks that the reference to greed brings in the issue of idolatry. Fitzmyer, *Luke*, vol. 2, pp. 1112–13, appears to accept the slander.

75. An attitude that is then labelled 'abomination', as Egelkraut, *Jesus' Mission*, p. 132, emphasizes.

76. Cf. especially the discussion by Lambrecht, *Astonished*, pp. 33–52, who proposes – almost correctly – that Luke intended to relate these parables to the issue of 'rigorous' and 'tepid' Christians in his own day.

77. Schnider, *Verlorene Söhne*, p. 87.

78. This is Fitzmyer's translation (Luke, vol. 1, p. 140) of τελώνης. While it may make one think mistakenly of someone in a booth on a highway, it is more suitable than the less wieldy 'customs tax collector'.

79. That the Pharisee in the parable is supposed to appear 'odious' (Montefiore, *Synoptic Gospels*, vol. 2, p. 557) and the toll collector winsome is, of course, universally recognized. And, of course, it is precisely the Pharisee's Jewish halachic righteousness that makes him so objectionable to Luke (Schmid, *Lukas*, p. 281). It is my assumption that Luke is the author of the parable, but who first told it is irrelevant for our consideration here. The points are, in any case, all Lucan.

80. Cortés, 'Greek of Luke 18:14a', gives a good discussion of the textual problems and opts for the reading of A as the original. However that may be, Cortés is certainly correct in finding (op. cit., 270) an adversative and not a relational meaning in the comparison. The narrative demands such an understanding. Fitzmyer, *Luke*, vol. 2, p. 1188, prefers the παρ' ἐκεῖνον of ℵ, B and others.

81. While Paul is likely to be the originator of the Christian use of the verb δικαιοῦμαι to mean something more or less synonymous with 'to be saved' (an examination of the concordance alone will confirm that likelihood), and while Luke to that degree also uses the word in the same way, still Luke attaches his own meaning to the verb, inasmuch as he lays emphasis on the righteousness that comes through contrition and repentance as opposed to that which comes through 'behaving righteously'. Jeremias, of course (*Parables*, p. 141), thinks that 'our passage shows . . . that the Pauline doctrine of justification has its roots in the teaching of Jesus'. Via Luke's Gospel? Fitzmyer, *Luke*, vol. 2, p. 1185, takes a middle position: the justification here goes back to Jesus in a 'generic' way.

82. So also Lampe, 'Luke', p. 831. Koenig, *Jews and Christians*, p. 115, is overcome by the occasional friendliness of the Lucan Pharisees and thus thinks that the Pharisee of the parable does not represent all Pharisees. Cf. also Ziesler, 'Luke and the Pharisees', p. 151.

83. The parable, of course, is intended to have a wider application – that is, to refer to the argument with Jewish Christians over criteria for church membership. To see the Pharisee, however, as 'represent[ing] unbelieving Jews' (Loisy, *Luc*, p. 444) is to miss the point.

84. What, exactly, Luke meant by 'justifying God' is less than clear. Fitzmyer, *Luke*, vol. 1, p. 676, seems correctly to understand it to mean that they 'acknowledged God as righteous', but the reason, then, for translating 'acknowledged . . . God's claims on them' (ibid., pp. 670, 676) seems to be more interpretation that strict meaning. It will surely not fail to strike the reader that the key terms in this little summary are 'toll collectors', 'Pharisees' and 'justify' – in other words the same key terms that appear in the parable of the Pharisee and the Toll Collector. Fitzmyer, op. cit., pp. 673, 675–6, has overlooked that connection and is thus puzzled by the summary statement. Talbert (*Reading Luke*, p. 85) is probably correct in proposing that 'to justify God was to acknowledge the rightness of his call in John and Jesus and to repent and be forgiven'.

85. The absence of the Pharisees from Luke 3.7, whereas they appear in the parallel, Matt. 3.7, is therefore possibly a deliberate Lucan device; Luke may remove the Pharisees from John's audience in anticipation of the statement in Luke 7.30.

In this case, however, it must be considered equally likely that Matthew could be responsible for the presence of the Pharisees and Sadducees in his version (Matt. 3.7).

86. The Pharisees are not here representatives of 'official Judaism' (Lampe, 'Luke', p. 831) or 'authorities in Israel' (Fitzmyer, *Luke*, vol. 1, p. 673); similarly Hauck, *Lukas*, p. 100. The Pharisees are never that in Luke-Acts.

87. Talbert, *Reading Luke*, p. 85.

88. Thus in no circumstances do the Pharisees in Luke, as Flender, *St Luke*, p. 108, thinks, 'represent that group among the Jewish leaders which is receptive to the Christian message'.

89. Tyson, 'Opposition', p. 149, correctly sees that the 'demand' of the Christian Pharisees of Acts 15.5 'for the circumcision of Gentile converts is consistent with the role [the Pharisees] play in the Gospel'; but Tyson fails to find the opposition here and thinks that Luke views these Pharisees as friendly, 'though of a more conservative stripe than Luke's heroes'.

90. Conzelmann, *Theology*, p. 148.

91. F. Keck, *Abschiedsrede*, pp. 27–8, has seen this side of Luke's portrait of the Pharisees, but to the exclusion of the other side of the portrait.

92. Cf. the similar explanations given by Wilckens, *Missionsreden*, pp. 182–3, and Sauvagnat, 'Se repentir', pp. 78–86; cf. also Conzelmann, *Theology*, p. 229; S. Brown, *Apostasy and Perseverance*, pp. 46–7; and Nolland, 'Acts 15.10', pp. 112–13.

93. We do not need to ask whether they have sought to add Mosaic requirements to the criterion of belief, because that, of course, is what Luke says about them and is precisely the point in contention.

94. Some authors, of course, have not seen the presence of Pharisees in this scene as being of any importance. Thus Hauck, *Lukas*, p. 215, sees them as representatives of the Jews and, indeed, of the human race; and Schweizer, *Luke*, p. 273, also thinks of humanity generally. Similar interpretations are given by others. Some emphasize suddenness or unexpectedness in the Kingdom's appearance; cf., e.g., Schmid, *Lukas*, p. 274: and, of course, the text is the backbone of 'realized eschatology', as in, e.g., Dodd, *Parables*, p. 84, n. 1. Yet the saying, in Luke, is addressed to *Pharisees*, as, e.g., Montefiore, *Synoptic Gospels*, vol. 2, pp. 546–50, has seen. Our interest here is not what ἐντὸς ὑμῶν is supposed to mean, but what it means that the saying is addressed to Pharisees.

95. Zmijewski, *Eschatologiereden*, p. 394, and Bruners, *Reinigung der Aussätzigen*, p. 327, think that the Pharisees represent Christians contemporary with Luke who misunderstand the Kingdom; and Bruners adds, further, that they likewise misunderstand Jesus. But there is no direct reference to christology here. Thus I do not quite see why the Pharisees, with their question, are put into the same position as that of the nine who did not offer thanks (Bruners, op. cit., p. 335). Bruners later (op. cit., p. 353) presents what seems a more balanced statement. On the presence of the Kingdom in Jesus' ministry cf. Conzelmann, *Theology*, pp. 122–3.

96. It should also be stated that, much as Luke dislikes the Christian Pharisees, i.e., the traditionally Jewish Christians, even to the point of slandering them (Luke 16.14), he does not attribute ulterior motives to those who (Acts 15.5) prompt the Apostolic Council, as does Jacquier, *Actes*, p. 445, who claims that 'the Pharisees' – not distinguished as Christian and non-Christian – 'wished by means of Christianity to make Gentiles Jews'.

97. In any case, we shall never discover exactly what happened there, for both

Luke and Paul have their own good reasons for reporting the outcome of the Council as they do. On this point cf. my article, 'Paul's "Autobiographical" Statements'.

98. The same list is more or less repeated in Acts 15.20, when the decree is first proposed in the Council, and later in 21.25. There are insignificant textual variants, so that there remains some reasonable question about the exact form and order of the list in each case; but that Luke presents these four restrictions on Gentile Christian behaviour as the concluding decision of the Apostolic Council is not in doubt. For details one may consult the commentaries and Wilson, *Gentiles*, p. 188.

99. This was first pointed out by Waitz, 'Aposteldekret', p. 227; cf. further Haenchen, *Acts*, p. 469. Many other authors have since pointed to the connection.

100. That the requirements come from the Torah renders moot the discussions about whether there may be, in reality, only three prohibitions in the Acts lists (so Loisy, *Actes*, p. 587; Preuschen, *Apostelgeschichte*, p. 95), or even only two (Beyer, *Apostelgeschichte*, p. 95).

101. Wilson, *Law*, p. 86.

102. In ch. 5.

103. Similarly Haenchen, *Acts*, p. 469, and 'Apostelgeschichte', p. 506; Schmithals, *Paul and James*, p. 98.

104. So Haenchen, *Acts*, p. 470; similarly Schmithals, *Apostelgeschichte*, p. 141.

105. As Loisy, *Actes*, p. 116, affirms.

106. Löning, *Saulustradition*, p. 200. Löning otherwise (op. cit., p. 206) accurately expresses Luke's theology of the church as the inheritor of Israelite tradition; cf. again the discussion in the previous chapter.

107. Schulz, *Stunde*, p. 273.

108. Declaring themselves for the opinion that there is a compromise here are, e.g.: Schoeps, *Theologie und Geschichte*, p. 259; G. Schneider, *Apostelgeschichte*, vol. 2, pp. 183-4; Marshall, *Acts*, p. 243; Schille, *Apostelgeschichte*, p. 326.

109. This point is well made by Haenchen, *Acts*, pp. 471-2. Haenchen, however, suggests a different reason for the origin of the laws, 'a horror of the flesh of pagan sacrifices'. If such a horror is in Luke's mind in Acts 15, he covers it up well.

110. So also Loisy, *Actes*, p. 116, and, apparently, G. Schneider, *Apostelgeschichte*, vol. 2, p. 184.

111. Not just of 'the (ceremonial) law', as Hengel, 'Ursprünge', p. 28, thinks; nor can I agree with the proposal of Nolland, 'Acts 15.10', pp. 108-12 – that the Lucan Peter does not mean that the Law is 'offensive', but rather that it is irrelevant for salvation and has never been, in any case, 'fulfilled'. In Luke's opinion the kind of law that the Pharisees promote is a burden. Marshall, *Acts*, p. 255, finds the Decree a 'burden' that is 'necessary for Gentiles' in order for there to be 'harmony' in the church. Wilson, *Law*, p. 60, agrees with Nolland. Yet cf. Haenchen, 'Apostelgeschichte', p. 505: 'Presupposed here is the Gentile-Christian view of the law as an endless number of commands and prohibitions, which no person can carry out.' Cf. further the observation of Schiffman, 'Tannaitic Perspectives', p. 117, from the reverse point of view, that it was 'halakah which ultimately determined the expulsion of the Christians from the Jewish Community'.

112. Haenchen, *Acts*, p. 461, refers to the 'closest affinities' between chs. 5 and 10; cf. also the cogent remarks of Weiser, 'Apostelkonzil', p. 160, on the Gentile–Christian setting of Peter's position.

113. Marshall, *Acts*, p. 186, emphasizes that the vision deals only with dietary laws, not with the Gentiles' acceptability to God, and then, p. 188, that Peter realized that Gentiles were acceptable. But surely Peter drew the proper conclusion?!

114. Sandmel, *Anti-Semitism*, p. 88; similarly G. Schneider, *Apostelgeschichte*, vol. 2, p. 68; Marshall, *Acts*, p. 181. Wilson, *Law*, p. 69, thinks that Luke is not really interested in the laws of *kashrut* here, but only in the 'parabolic' significance of the vision, i.e., that 'the distinction between clean and unclean people . . . had been overturned'; but Schille, *Apostelgeschichte*, p. 248, is more accurate in seeing that the one abolition 'tends towards' the other.

115. Cf., e.g., Lake in *Beginnings*, Part I, vol. 5, pp. 204–5; Lampe, 'Acts', p. 907; Macgregor, 'Acts', p. 204; Conzelmann, *Primitive Christianity*, p. 89; Townsend, 'Date', p. 56; G. Schneider, *Apostelgeschichte*, vol. 2, p. 187; Weiser, 'Apostelkonzil', p. 159. Wendt, *Apostelgeschichte*, p. 234, refers rather to '*Kultgemeinschaft*' (similarly Wilson, *Gentiles*, pp. 188–9, and Schäfer, 'Aposteldekret', cols. 556–7) and Simon, 'Apostolic Decree', p. 415, to 'religious fellowship' – although Simon means the *historical* Apostolic Decree and correctly sees that, in Acts, the issue is 'what rule of life . . . the Gentile Christians . . . have to obey in order to be saved'. Haenchen, *Acts*, p. 468, provides a longer list.

116. Some of these regulations, of course, relate specifically to cleanliness; but the explanation often given popularly, that the ancient Israelites abstained, e.g., from pork because pork insufficiently cooked can produce a fatal disease – that is, the medical explanation for the dietary laws – represents nothing more than an idealization of origins. Why not just a law about how to cook pork? And what possible physical harm could come from eating broccoli with a cheese sauce on it on the same plate with lamb chops?

117. Wilson, *Gentiles*, pp. 188–9, has also seen this problem; cf. also Schäfer, 'Aposteldekret', cols. 556–7. It is thus absurd for Juel, *Luke-Acts*, p. 106, to write that 'Gentiles who [believe] must keep kosher if they are to eat with Jewish Christians'.

118. W. L. Knox, *Acts*, pp. 49–50, states that 'James, the leading *Pharisee*, proposes a *compromise* which abandons the Torah, and . . . issue[s] a warning against the *sins conventionally ascribed to the Gentiles* by Jewish writers' so as to 'make it possible for *Jewish* converts to attend the *common meals* of the Church' (emphases mine). While the point about abandoning the Torah is correct, this statement is otherwise remarkable for its collection of errors of interpretation.

119. Cf. again n. 115 above.

120. So also Overbeck, *Apostelgeschichte*, p. 159. I agree that Luke doubtless thought that such a regulation or regulations existed, as Acts 10.28 shows; so also Wilson, *Law*, p. 70. That Luke had such a notion, however, still does not explain the Apostolic Decree, inasmuch as Acts 15.10, 19–20, 28; 21.24 all explain that what lies behind the Decree is the issue of which laws apply to Gentiles.

121. Similarly Franklin, *Christ the Lord*, p. 125.

122. Löning, 'Paulinismus', p. 229, n. 66, notes that Luke never indicates what effect the decree had in the churches.

123. O'Neill, *Theology*, pp. 82–3, takes the pre-Christian relevance to Gentiles of part of the Law to mean that Gentile Christians should follow the 'universal morality' of the Law. Yet the sense of the requirements as they are used in Acts is: *only* these; and it seems quite a jump from a prohibition against eating blood to universal morality. O'Neill was not, of course, the first to propose such an interpretation; cf. Harnack, *Acts*, pp. 248–63. Schille, *Apostelgeschichte*, p. 322, probably correctly observes that the note about universal reading of the Torah means that the conflict between Jewish Christianity and Gentile Christianity is universal. Jervell, *Unknown Paul*, p. 23, sees the Apostolic Decree as *restricting* Gentile Christians.

124. The issue is clearly that of traditional Judaism within Christianity, not, as Weiser, 'Apostelkonzil', p. 150, thinks, of 'that and how the church is connected to Israel'.

125. That two groups push the issue of circumcision is therefore not a 'minor difficult[y]' that Luke 'accepts without hesitation' (Haenchen, *Acts*, p. 458) – as if Luke were making sense out of his sources – it is rather part and parcel of Luke's portrayal of Judaism.

126. Wilson, *Law*, p. 71, has almost seen this point but does not quite know what to do with the evidence. Thus he writes that 'the effect of [Peter's] vision [in Acts 10] is . . . that Peter abandons his conservative (Palestinian?) position for a more liberal (diaspora Jewish and Christian?) stance'. Wilson has here inadvertently pointed to the fact that, for Luke, there is only one properly *Christian* position. The 'conservative' position is that of all Torah-observant Jews, whether Christians or not. While Luke knows that he cannot go to the limit of saying that such Jewish Christians are not Christians, he does portray them as improper Christians, as bad yeast that ruins the whole loaf.

127. Since these Jews are πεπιστευκότες, just like the Pharisees in Acts 15.5, they cannot be non-Christian Jews, as Munck, *Acts*, pp. 209, 211, proposes. Cf. the discussion above, pp. 112–13. Lohfink, *Sammlung Israels*, pp. 51–4, interprets Acts 15.5 from 21.20 and explains that the reason that some Pharisees are said to be Christians is that Luke wants to show the degree to which the full number of Jews who are going to respond to the gospel are 'gathered'. That some Pharisees become Christians, however, and that their hostility to Jesus in the Gospel is reduced (ibid., p. 51), is only part of the picture.

128. Opinions differ as to whether Luke intends to refer here to all Jewish Christians or only to those in Jerusalem or Judaea. Cf. the discussion of this point above, ch. 3, n. 187.

129. To be sure, what Paul is told that these Jewish Christians fear is that he is teaching Diaspora Jews to abandon the Law. Nevertheless, that Luke's hero Paul must humbly submit to a public display of Torah fidelity shows what kind of pressure Luke thinks of these Jewish Christians as exerting within the church.

130. While I should like to avoid entering, in this work, into the 'early Catholicism' debate, it is worth pointing out that the author of Ephesians takes the next logical step in dealing with the 'problem' of Jewish Christians when he appeals (Eph. 2.15a) for unity in the church on the basis of rejection of the Torah (cf. my *Christological Hymns*, pp. 88–92). Roetzel, 'Relations', p. 88, has remarked that the theological position of the author of Ephesians 'barred the way to the acceptance of Jewish Christians *qua* Jewish Christians in a predominantly gentile [*sic*] church'. Luke-Acts is moving in that direction. Thus I cannot agree with Jervell, *People of God*, pp. 140–1, that Acts 21.20 'demonstrate[s]' the 'permanent validity' of the Law. Its validity was rather pronouncedly temporary.

131. Schmithals, *Paul and James*, p. 90.

132. Wilson, *Law*.

133. Ibid., pp. 14–18.

134. Ibid., p. 33.

135. Ibid., pp. 43–51.

136. Ibid., p. 57.

137. Ibid., pp. 28–9.

138. On this point cf. esp. Theissen, *Studien zur Soziologie*, pp. 180–3.

139. NB! Matt. 19.19 does just that. Further to the issue of the background of this connection, cf. my *Ethics in the New Testament*, pp. 51–2.

140. Wilson, *Law*, pp. 59–102.

141. Ibid., pp. 67–8.

142. Ibid., pp. 68–102.

143. Ibid., p. 107.

144. Ibid., p. 105; cf. also pp. 61–8. Wilson's discussion in this earlier section is clouded by the fact that he does not keep the Lucan Paul distinct from Paul. Wilson, op. cit., p. 105, solves the problem that Peter seems to overthrow the Law in Acts 10 by suggesting that 'Jewish-Christian adherence to the law . . . was an issue of no immediate concern to [Luke] or to the communities for whom he wrote', which were, of course, Gentile.

145. Ibid., p. 107. Cadbury, 'Acts', p. 34, similarly describes the way the author of Acts portrays the significance of the Torah for Jewish and for Gentile Christians.

146. Above, p. 115.

147. Wilson, *Law*, p. 101. Wilson also discusses the Lucan notion of the validity for Christianity in general of the Torah as prophecy (op. cit., p. 26). In that, of course, he is quite correct; but we are interested here only in the issue of obeying the Law's requirements. Cf. also Cadbury, 'Acts', p. 34.

148. Wilson, *Law*, p. 112.

149. Ibid., p. 73.

150. Ibid., pp. 20–3.

151. Ibid., pp. 61–8.

152. Ibid., p. 105.

153. Ibid., p. 61.

154. Ibid., p. 112.

155. Ibid.

156. Ibid., p. 18; cf. also pp. 19, 40–3.

157. Ibid., p. 112.

158. Ibid., p. 115.

159. Thus Haenchen, 'Judentum und Christentum', pp. 168–9, did not go far enough in his analysis when he wrote that, although 'Jewish Christianity would also become suspect along with Judaism', nevertheless 'Luke did not draw this consequence'.

160. It thus would appear that Luke is critical of the theology of the vast majority of Jewish Christians – of *the* Jewish-Christian theology – of his own day, not just of a minority, as Haenchen, *Acts*, pp. 457–8, seems to imply.

161. Thus Stolle, *Zeuge*, p. 114, correctly refers to a 'relativizing of the Law' in Christianity, but for the wrong reasons (cf. p. 118, above).

162. Maddox, *Purpose*, p. 37; cf. also p. 42. Maddox does not, however, see that the problem posed by the Pharisees is a problem *within* Christianity.

163. Cf. above, pp. 40–1, 45–6.

164. Jervell, *People of God*, p. 143. Jervell, op. cit., pp. 143–4, and Perrot, 'Les décisions de l'assemblée', think that the Apostolic Decree supports this notion of Jervell's. But this would mean that, for Luke, the privilege lies in being circumcised!

165. I hereby take the opportunity to repent of having overstated the position in this regard in an earlier article.

166. While it is in a sense true, as Hare has stated, that 'there is not the slightest hint that Luke believes that Jews must become gentiles [sic] in order to be fully acceptable members of the Church' ('Rejection', p. 37), there is also a very strong

hint that these Jews are not to seek to make Jews out of Gentile Christians. Judaism and Christianity are distinct. This being the case, one will also have to wonder if Jewish Christians are really '*fully* acceptable' to Luke.

167. The implication would not necessarily even have had to be overt, since the mere existence of Torah-observant Jewish Christians would itself have been sufficient to be taken by Gentile Christians as an implicit challenge.

168. This was, of course, essentially the view of the Tübingen school; cf. Baur, *Paul*, vol. 1, pp. 1–252, esp. pp. 12, 132–3, 251–2. Among more recent authors one may note, e.g., Trocmé, *Le 'Livre des Actes'*, *passim*, esp. p. 59; and Jervell, *People of God*, pp. 153–83, esp. pp. 175–7.

169. Gaston, *No Stone*, p. 315, offers a unique explanation of the fact that Luke has Jesus criticize friendly Pharisees, namely that the church in Luke's day was sufficiently friendly with Jews to try to convert them but sufficiently inept not to succeed. It is seeing the form of the Lucan portrait of the Pharisees without recognizing its content that has led to such a conclusion.

5. *The Periphery: Outcasts, Samaritans, Proselytes, God-fearers*

1. Cf. Lake's description of God-fearers as a 'fringe . . . surround[ing]' Diaspora 'synagogues' (*Beginnings*, Part I, vol. 5, p. 77).

2. E.g., Dodd, *Parables*, pp. 91–2, and others. Franklin, *Christ the Lord*, p. 141, thinks that this interest has to do only with Luke's desire to show a division within Israel. As we are about to see, he is on the right track.

3. Later rabbinic literature was to label such people with the term '*'amme' ha-ares*, people of the land', meaning thereby that they were 'immoral, irreligious, and ignorant of the law' (Pope, "Am ha' arez', p. 107); and one often sees that term in the literature on Luke-Acts; but we shall be truer to Luke himself if we call them simply 'sinners' or outcasts. On this point cf. Fitzmyer, *Luke*, vol. 2, p. 1075.

4. Walaskay, *We Came to Rome*, pp. 29–31, seems a bit confused about the role of the toll collectors in Luke. On the one hand, he seeks to distinguish them clearly from 'sinners' (p. 81, n. 78), and he calls them 'a middle link in the chain of lower social classes in Palestine' (p. 29), a classification that is not elsewhere explained adequately. Then, however, he sees that they are classified with sinners and that Zacchaeus is, 'in the eyes of' his countrymen, a sinner (p. 30). Walaskay thus seems to have seen the evidence correctly but not to have created an adequate conceptual framework for explaining it. Cf. further n. 72 below.

5. We saw above in ch. 4 that the behaviour of the prodigal son made him a forerunner of the Gentiles; yet, the implication of the statements in vv. 7 and 10, which surely bear on the following parable as well, is that he is an outcast; cf. also Dodd, *Parables*, pp. 91–2, and others. Thus we see how the outcasts in the Gospel prepare the way for the Gentiles in Acts. Lampe, 'Luke', p. 831, correctly compares the parable of the Prodigal Son with the narrative of the 'sinner' who anoints Jesus in Luke 7.36–50.

6. Ernst, *Lukas*, p. 512, makes the keen observation that Zacchaeus is an example of the principle put forward in the parable of the Pharisee and the Toll Collector, which comes shortly beforehand. Schottroff and Stegemann, *Jesus von Nazareth*, pp. 137–8, connect the Zacchaeus narrative with the Lucan version of John the Baptist's repentance preaching (Luke 3.10–14) and argue that Luke is actually proposing that rich Christians give half their possessions to the poor. While this may be good social policy, it is miserable exegesis, because Schottroff and Stegemann overlook the obvious parallel between Zacchaeus and Levi, as well as the regular

association of toll collectors and sinners, and refer to other toll collectors as *'kleine Leute'* (p. 139), as if Zacchaeus were wealthy and the other toll collectors in Luke poor.

7. Winn, 'Elusive Mystery', p. 153, includes the thief in a list of others in the Gospel who belong to the periphery.

8. Cf. above, pp. 58–60. Fitzmyer, *Luke*, vol. 2, p. 1053, sees the first group of the originally uninvited as Jewish outcasts and the second group as Gentiles. His opinion that Luke wishes here to emphasize that some Jews *were* converted misses the point, as the further analysis of this chapter will show.

9. Goulder, *Type*, p. 60, labels Luke 14–18 'the gospel of the outcast'.

10. Whether Luke has some theology of 'predestination' we cannot take up here; cf., e.g., the opposing statements of Loisy, *Actes*, p. 542, and of Conzelmann, *Apostelgeschichte*, p. 78. Such a notion seems to have nothing to do elsewhere with his ideas about which *individuals* are saved and which not. Probably he means only that it was foreordained by God that the Gentiles would accept the gospel after the Jews had had their chance and had rejected it.

11. See again the discussion in the preface.

12. There apparently was no such thing in the ancient world. Cf. Simon, *Verus Israel*, pp. 243–4; Sevenster, *Roots*, pp. 36–56; Sandmel, *Anti-Semitism*, p. 4; Gager, *Origins*, pp. 102–12.

13. Recent studies by Wilcox, 'God-Fearers', and Kraabel, 'Disappearance', have cast grave doubts on the historicity of Luke's 'God-fearers' as a group separate from proselytes, raising the possibility that they exist in Acts only as the result of Luke's 'gift of invention' (to use Koester's term); cf. further the reservations expressed by Finn, 'God-fearers Reconsidered'. Jervell, *Unknown Paul*, p. 15, continues to accept the existence of God-fearers. This issue need not concern us here, however, inasmuch as our goal is to understand Luke-Acts, not to evaluate archaeological evidence.

14. Cf. the discussion by Lake in *Beginnings*, Part I, vol. 5, pp. 77–84.

15. CIJ 920 refers to a 'Benjamin the Centurion of Parembolé'. Inasmuch as Parembolé was the site of a Roman garrison on the Nile (cf. the explanation by the editor, *ad loc.*), and since Jewish mercenaries had been in Egypt for many years before the Romans came, the presence of a Jewish centurion there is probably not unusual. But there seems to be no direct attestation of any Jewish centurions in Palestine, and with good reason; to place one of the occupied in a position of command in an occupying army calls into uuestion the army's ability to act in local matters. All this is unrelated, of course, to Luke's presentation; in Acts, Cornelius is a Gentile.

16. Cf. Moore, *Judaism*, vol. 1, p. 325, and nearly all the commentaries.

17. Cf. the discussion of this issue by Lake in *Beginnings*, Part I, vol. 5, pp. 74–88. Lake concludes (op. cit., p. 88) that there were such Gentiles and that the terms 'God-fearer' and 'God-worshipper' are probably appropriate for them, but that the terms are used imprecisely in Acts, and that they are best applied to a 'vague class', not to a 'specific group with a definite place in organized Judaism'.

18. The idiom stems from Deut. 6.2 and elsewhere in the prologue of the Central Discourse and was normal well before Luke's time; cf., e.g., Sir. 1.11–30. Cf. Lake in *Beginnings*, Part I, vol. 5, p. 85.

19. Wilcox, 'God-Fearers', pp. 109, 115, raises similar doubts about just what Luke means by 'God-fearers' and 'God-worshippers'. Other authors, however, e.g., G. Schneider, *Apostelgeschichte*, vol. 2, p. 65, n. 45, seem oblivious to the problems and go right on describing proselytes and God-fearers as distinct groups.

20. Dahl, *Memory*, p. 97, thinks that this Gentile periphery may even have been the intended audience of Luke-Acts.

21. Lake in *Beginnings*, Part I, vol. 5, pp. 113–14, also thinks that Acts 2.10 means that there were proselytes throughout the audience (not just among the group from Rome); cf. also Haenchen, *Acts*, p. 171. Lake finds more Gentiles in the Pentecost audience, however, than seems allowable; cf. above, p. 70.

22. Cf. also G. Schneider, *Apostelgeschichte*, vol. 2, pp. 73–4.

23. Overbeck, *Apostelgeschichte*, p. 153, over-emphasized this point and declared that Cornelius is a total Gentile, not a God-fearer; but Luke calls him a God-fearer in Acts 10.2.

24. Even so, Luke moves gingerly, since Paul continues to approach both Jews and Gentiles.

25. It seems reasonable to assume that Luke means us to understand that Lydia is one of these peripheral Gentiles; so Munck, *Acts*, p. 161; Stählin, *Apostelgeschichte*, p. 217; and others; nevertheless, since he does not say that she is not a Jew, the possibility that he thinks of her as one cannot be ruled out entirely. Her name and city of origin, also, do not prove that she is a Gentile; still, that appears to be Luke's meaning.

26. So also Lampe, 'Luke', p. 830; and others. Walaskay, *We Came to Rome*, p. 32, thinks that the centurion is not intended to be 'a God-fearer or proselyte, for when such a title is applicable [Luke] uses it'; but that is to overlook Luke's penchant for ambiguity. Walaskay does, however, see that the centurion's response to Jesus 'prefigures' that of Cornelius to the apostles (op. cit., p. 34); and he further (op. cit., p. 84, n. 107) leaves open the possibility that the difference between this centurion and Cornelius is related to Luke's epochal scheme as defined by Conzelmann.

27. Cf. Loisy, *Evangiles synoptiques*, vol. 1, pp. 651–2; Talbert, *Reading Luke*, p. 79; and others.

28. While benefaction is not Luke's point, that would appear to be the position for which the centurion is striving or which he has attained. This is also the conclusion reached by Danker, *Benefactor*, p. 406. The town elders obviously feel that they owe him something. On patronage in the Roman world, cf. further Batdorf, 'Benefactors'; Momigliano, 'Patronus'; and the bibliographies in both places. Walaskay, *We Came to Rome*, p. 33, proposes a connection rather with 'the Augustan religious restoration'.

29. Modern theologians can, of course, make these and even finer distinctions; but do modern theologians not also belong to a periphery? There is a good discussion of different 'types' of faith that one may find in Luke in O'Connor, *Faith*, esp. pp. 71–4, 78–80, 84–7, 108–10. O'Connor sees the faith of the centurion and that of the sinner who is 'saved' as being of the same general type. Cf. also Fitzmyer, *Luke*, vol. 1, pp. 582–3.

30. Many authors think that the faith of the centurion is not to be contrasted with Jewish unbelief, in spite of the fact that this is the plain meaning of v. 9, and in spite of the fact that the same point is made again in 17.18–19; cf. esp. Lagrange, *Luc*, p. 208. Fitzmyer, *Luke*, vol. 1, p. 653, explains that 'the centurion thus becomes in Luke a symbol of Gentile belief over against the general reaction of Israel'. Others make similar statements. Walaskay, *We Came to Rome*, p. 34, refers to 'piety that transcends even the highest of earthly authorities'; but that has missed the point altogether.

31. That the centurions in the Gospel, even so, do not encounter Jesus directly is apparently considered and is intended to preserve a certain distance, which is

overcome only in Acts. Thus W. Manson, *Luke*, p. 76, observes that 'Jesus came to the Jews in person; to the Gentiles he comes only through the preaching of the word'. Similarly Conzelmann, *Theology*, p. 189. It may of course be that Luke keeps Jesus out of the centurion's house in Luke 7 because he thinks that to go there would have violated the Law, as Walaskay, *We Came to Rome*, p. 34, proposes; cf. also Juel, *Luke-Acts*, pp. 103–4.

32. Of course, the seventy or seventy-two 'advance people' who are sent out at the beginning of the travel narrative (Luke 10.1) and who return shortly with an account of great success (vv. 17–20) probably represent the Gentile mission, as Lampe, 'Luke', p. 833, and many others propose. (Zingg, 'Stellung zur Heidenmission', p. 204, doubts that Luke intends this connection.) Yet one must then observe that *Jesus* does not participate in the mission; it is the apostles- and church-to-be.

33. Cf. Grundmann, *Lukas*, p. 158.

34. Lohse, 'Missionarisches Handeln', pp. 11–12, almost has it right when he sees the Samaritans and the centurion in the Gospel as being the 'foundation for the missionary commission' to take the gospel to the Gentiles.

35. Cf. the two articles entitled 'Samaritans', by Gaster and Purvis. The latter provides a corrected view on the date of the Samaritan temple.

36. 'From the standpoint of the Jews, the Samaritans were of Gentile extraction' (Sandmel, *Anti-Semitism*, p. 104, n. 6; cf. also ibid., p. 80). Gaster, 'Samaritans', p. 191, is perhaps more accurate: 'At best, . . . one degree nearer than Gentiles, but still not. . . full-fledged members of the house of Israel.' Cf. also Jeremias, 'Σαμάρεια, κτλ.', p. 91: 'On the same level as the Gentiles'.

37. Franklin, *Christ the Lord*, pp. 141–2, interprets all appearances of Samaritans in Luke-Acts from this narrative and thinks that the Samaritans point up the theme of rejection. Perhaps unconsciously realizing how weak such a position is, he attempts to shore it up by writing that the Samaritan rejection is 'one of the most brutal rejections of Jesus'. Why the Samaritan rejection is brutal at all is not, however, explained. Wilson, *Gentiles*, p. 43, calls it 'brusque'. I am not sure that it is even that. Luke's narrative is brief, but it is not clear that he wishes thereby to portray the Samaritans as being curt.

38. Cf. Fitzmyer, *Luke*, vol. 1, p. 189. Enslin, 'Samaritan Ministry', p. 32, thinks that Luke's primary purpose at this point is to bring Samaritans into the picture, and that the rejection is due only to the need to make the episode parallel to the Nazareth episode.

39. Thus especially Conzelmann, *Theology*, pp. 65–6.

40. E.g., Conzelmann, *Theology*, pp. 64, 197; Robinson, *Weg*, p. 24.

41. K. L. Schmidt, *Rahmen*, pp. 267–8, emphasizes that Luke wishes in this way to show that the Samaritan reaction to Jesus was different from that of the Jews, although, regarding the form of the Gospel, the two rejections introduce the two main sections. Lagrange, *Luc*, p. 286, writes that the Samaritan rejection is not 'personal'. Gill, 'Travel Narrative', p. 203, thinks that Luke wants his readers to see that the Samaritans rejected Jesus 'because they could neither understand nor accept the fact that he had to die'. This explanation, however, is not only overly subtle but would fail to explain why the disciples then want to destroy the Samaritans. Gill's explanation that *they* didn't understand, either (ibid.), is just too subtle.

42. Bowman, *Samaritan Problem*, p. 69, correctly emphasizes that those who are 'scolded' are not the Samaritans but the disciples.

43. Similarly Spinetoli, *Luca*, p. 357. Valensin et Huby, *Luc*, pp. 196–7, think that Jesus forbids the chastisement because he is opposed to violence.

44. Lambrecht, *Astonished*, p. 78, points out that 'one cannot avoid the impression that Luke did not place the story of the Good Samaritan in such close proximity to . . . 9:52b–56 . . . by mere chance'.

45. Crossan, 'Parable and Example', pp. 287–96.

46. Cf., e.g., Loisy, *Luc*, p. 309; Beck, *Mature Christianity*, p. 188. Schmid, *Lukas*, p. 192, considers the specific reference to the Samaritan insignificant; and Wilson, *Law*, pp. 15–16, thinks that the presence of a Samaritan is 'probably a shock tactic' that is, at best, only 'peripherally' related to 'the Samaritan and Gentile missions'. Fitzmyer, *Luke*, vol. 2, p. 885, rejects the Jew-Samaritan contrast as an allegorization of the 'Lucan' parable; but this is to confuse the setting of the parable in the life of Jesus – where allegorizing is a problem – with the Lucan setting.

47. The similarity between these two Lucan parables is accurately seen by Sandmel, *Anti-Semitism*, p. 80, and by Klostermann, *Lukas*, p. 119.

48. So also Lohse, 'Lukas als Theologe', p. 80.

49. Lagrange, *Luc*, p. 458, thinks that Luke deliberately avoids writing that the nine are Jews 'in order to avoid an appearance of hostility'; but what is the reader to think? Fitzmyer, *Luke*, vol. 2, pp. 1155–6, drives home the point.

50. Fitzmyer, op. cit., vol. 1, p. 189, understands both the Good Samaritan and the Samaritan leper as merely 'foils for the Jews to whom [Jesus'] message has been mainly addressed'. Similarly Cadbury, *Making of Luke-Acts*, pp. 258–9. While there is certainly that aspect to both narratives, we cannot overlook the fact that the Samaritan leper is 'saved by faith'. The salvation of God has, in Luke's understanding, come to the Samaritans. Bruners, *Reinigung der Aussätzigen*, p. 198, gives a balanced statement.

51. As in, e.g., Schweizer, *Luke*, pp. 268–9; cf. again the discussion above, n. 30, and also Fitzmyer, *Luke*, vol. 1, pp. 236–7.

52. Some mention needs to be made of the essay by Ford, 'Reconciliation and Forgiveness', pp. 80–98. Ford has correctly put outcasts and Samaritans into one basket together, but it is quite the wrong basket: 'Jesus' ministry . . . of forgiveness and reconciliation' (op. cit., p. 97). Such an explanation may make good homiletics, but it has nothing to do with Luke's intention.

53. The location of this 'city' must remain uncertain; cf. the discussion of the possibilities in *Beginnings*, Part I, vol. 4, p. 89. Hengel, *Between Jesus and Paul*, pp. 123–6, argues at length against the identification with Sebaste and concludes (p. 126), very likely correctly, that Luke assumed that Samaria had a capital city just as did Judaea.

54. After this, however, there are no more Samaritan conversions in Acts; thus there is no reason to think, as does Gaston, *No Stone*, p. 317, that Luke's interest in Samaritans is related to an on-going Samaritan mission in his own day. (Similarly Reicke, 'Instruction and Discussion', p. 211.) For Luke the Samaritan mission, like the Jewish, is a thing of the past. K. L. Schmidt, *Rahmen*, p. 268, had also referred to '*Missionspolitik*' as the motive for having Jesus go to another Samaritan village after being rejected in 9.53; and Conzelmann, *Theology*, p. 72, implies something of the same. Easton, *Luke*, p. 154, thought that Luke's favourable references to Samaritans implied the existence of an accepted Samaritan church in Luke's day.

55. Jervell, *People of God*, p. 129, n. 18, provides a list.

56. Ibid., pp. 113–32. Tiede, *Prophecy and History*, p. 62, writes that they are 'no better nor worse than the Jews'; and he labels them 'para-Jewish' (ibid., p. 56).

57. Furthermore, Jews regarded them as Gentiles. See again n. 36, above.

58. As we have discussed in detail above, pp. 45–9, 128–9. Cf. Jervell's statement

that this is his line of reasoning regarding the Samaritans in *People of God*, p. 114. Fitzmyer, *Luke*, vol. 1, p. 189, takes a similar position, but less emphatically.

59. Jervell, *People of God*, p. 118.

60. Ibid., p. 121.

61. Ibid., p. 124. Similarly Schmithals, *Lukas*, p. 119.

62. Jervell, *People of God*, pp. 125–6.

63. Ibid., p. 124.

64. Ibid., p. 116.

65. Ibid., p. 117.

66. Ibid., p. 124.

67. Cf. Cadbury, *Making of Luke-Acts*, p. 228, and others.

68. Jervell, *People of God*, p. 116. I do not mean to imply that there is anything incorrect in Jervell's translation.

69. Cf. esp. Cullmann, *Early Church*, pp. 185–91, and *Johannine Circle*, pp. 47–8. Cullmann also thought that the reason for Luke's description of the Samaritans as those who were converted first as the gospel moved out from the Jews towards the Gentiles was that this was actually the historical situation. For his view he also produced other evidence from other early Christian works (similarly also Bowman, *Samaritan Problem*, but with less scholarly acumen). That is indeed an intriguing possibility, but it is an issue which we must pass over here. Our purpose is to understand Luke-Acts.

70. Cullmann, *Johannine Circle*, pp. 47–8; cf. also *Early Church*. p. 191. Similarly Schmithals, *Lukas*, p. 119: the Samaritan mission ensures that 'the Gentile mission grows *bruchlos* out of the preaching to the Jews'. The transition is widely recognized; cf. e.g. Jeremias, 'Σαμάρεια, κτλ.', p. 93: 'This first crossing of the frontiers of Israel was the transition to the Gentile mission.'

71. Cullmann, *Early Church*, pp. 185–6. Grundmann, *Lukas*, pp. 31–2, also sees that Samaritans 'lie between' Jews and Gentiles in Luke-Acts. Nevertheless, he sees the Good Samaritan and the Samaritan leper only as examples for Christian 'love of enemies' and 'praising faith'; and he thinks that the mission to the Samaritans in Acts 8 'overcome[s] . . . the enmity between Jews and Samaritans'. In view of the evidence supporting the 'transition group' explanation of Luke's portrayal of the Jews, it is hard to see how Rengstorf, *Lukas*, p. 130, can state that the Samaritan contact in Luke 9.51–56 is not in some way preparing for the Samaritan mission of Acts 8. King, 'Universalism', pp. 201–2, takes the same position and argues further that there is no emphasis on Samaritans in the parable of the Good Samaritan or in the narrative of the healing of the ten lepers. Rather, according to him, love of neighbour is emphasized in the one case and faith in the other. Bruners, *Reinigung der Aussätzigen*, p. 152, states the connection correctly. Wilson, *Law*, p. 17, has seen the specific point well (although not the general principle): 'The appearance of the Samaritan [in the parable of the Good Samaritan] challenges Jewish prerogatives not because he knows and does the law, which does not come into play here any more than in Lk. 17.11f.; but because as one who is technically a non-Jew, or some form of hybrid, he responds to the divine will more readily than those who claim direct and unique knowledge of it.'

72. Walaskay, *We Came to Rome*, pp. 28–32, has made a stab at defining this group but has not got it quite correct. He takes the group to be composed of 'the Jewish proletariat and the representatives of Rome' and thus omits the Samaritans while including 'the crowds' and 'the soldiers'. We have already seen, however, that the crowds, i.e., the Jewish people, in the last analysis move to the side of their religious

leaders (ch. 3); and that the soldiers, except for the centurions (who are correctly included here), are an extension of the authority of the religious leaders (ch. 1). Walaskay attempts no analysis of the role of the Samaritans in Luke-Acts. On Luke's schematizing, cf. Finn, 'God-fearers Reconsidered', p. 83.

73. This is the position of Wilson, *Gentiles*, p. 171, who discounts the eunuch's label as simply 'refer[ring] to the man's high office'. One of the more interesting aspects of the scholarly interpretation of Luke's scheme in Acts 8–11 is that some scholars find a man called an 'Ethiopian, a eunuch', not to be a eunuch, and others find him not to be a Gentile, e.g., Haenchen, *Acts*, p. 314; cf. further the following excursus, pp. 151–2.

74. Conzelmann, *Apostelgeschichte*, p. 56, offers a source explanation for the confusion about the order; but Wilson, *Gentiles*, p. 172, correctly observes that Luke could have placed the narrative of the eunuch's conversion elsewhere had he thought that a problem existed.

75. Similarly J. Weiss, *Earliest Christianity*, vol. 1, p. 8.

76. Wilson, *Gentiles*, p. 171, has also noted this promise in Isaiah but thinks it improbable that Luke has relied on it in this connection.

77. Fitzmyer, *Luke*, vol. 1, p. 191, sees the progression 'Jews in Jerusalem . . . diaspora-Jews among them . . . Samaritans . . . an Ethiopian "worshiper" . . . Jews' outside Jerusalem but still in the Levant, 'and eventually to Gentiles, beginning with . . . Cornelius'. This pattern, however, while not incorrect, overlooks the proselyte(s) in the early part of Acts and fails to identify Cornelius as a God-fearer, thus leaving obscured one of the main problems in determining just what kind of progression Luke had in mind.

6. The Gospel of Luke

1. Conzelmann, *Theology*, p. 18, n. 1.
2. Sahlin, *Messias und Gottesvolk*, p. VI.
3. Esp. Vielhauer, 'Benedictus'.
4. Cf. Fitzmyer, *Luke*, vol. 1, p. 311.
5. Lampe, 'Luke', p. 824.
6. R. E. Brown, *Birth*, p. 349.
7. Ibid., pp. 358–60, 386–89, 458. Similar comparisons abound.
8. Lohfink, *Sammlung Israels*, *passim*, esp. pp. 30, 55; cf. also Mather, 'Lucan Infancy Narrative', p. 138. Beck, *Mature Christianity*, p. 187, puts the passage into a different light: it is 'an ominous prophetic woe'.
9. Ibid., p. 55.
10. Ibid., p. 44.
11. Walaskay, *We Came to Rome*, p. 29, refers bluntly to Luke's 'deviating from his source to have John the Baptist address himself not to the Pharisees and Sadducees, but to the crowds'. I also suspect that such an assessment is correct, but I do not think that certainty is attainable.
12. George, 'Israël', p. 487.
13. This assessment of Luke 3.7–14 is in large part justified by 7.29–30; see below.
14. Walaskay, *We Came to Rome*, p. 31.
15. Ibid., p. 32.
16. Luke built, of course, on the Synoptic tradition.
17. Cf. also Jervell, *Unknown Paul*, p. 130.
18. Tannehill, 'Mission of Jesus', p. 68.
19. Wilson, *Law*, p. 41.

20. Ibid., pp. 27–43.

21. Ernst, *Lukas*, p. 192.

22. Printed in *Syrus Sinaiticus*.

23. *The Greek New Testament, ad loc.*

24. Bultmann, *Synoptic Tradition*, p. 92, takes the saying not to be authentic, but to be a 'secondary explanation of the image of the physician' in Mark 2.17a par. Luke 5.31a. For argument's sake, however, I should like to assume the authenticity of the saying – whether it is really authentic or not – in order to speculate about what such a saying could have meant apart from its current polemical setting, in that way better to understand the saying in its present setting.

25. Cf. Fitzmyer, *Luke*, vol. 1, p. 685.

26. B. and J. Weiss, *Markus und Lukas*, p. 395.

27. Montefiore, *Synoptic Gospels*, vol. 2, p. 431.

28. For Luke's use of ἀπὸ instead of ὑπὸ with the agent of the passive, cf., e.g., Luke 1.26; 7.35.

29. It is the view of Lohfink that the 'gathering of Israel' does not occur until Acts, but that Jesus, in Luke, prepares for this 'gathering' by addressing, symbolically, all Israel, and by being killed by the Jews, so that the motif of the preaching of repentance in Acts is set up; cf. Lohfink, *Sammlung Israels*, pp. 40–6. Lohfink seems, however – although he tries in these pages to deal with the 'tension' between speech and narrative – not to have taken seriously enough Jesus' pronouncements of doom.

30. Wilson, *Law*, pp. 13–15.

31. Reference to the fine essay by Crossan, 'Parable and Example', will surely be sufficient at this point.

32. Cf. again the discussion in Part One.

33. Loisy, *Evangiles synoptiques*, vol. 2, p. 357.

34. Loisy, *Luc*, pp. 33, 311.

35. Lampe, 'Luke', p. 833.

36. Loisy, *Luc*, pp. 310–11.

37. I see no reason to consider Matthew's version of this complex of sayings more original than Luke's. Nothing can be made of the fact that Matthew has the order Jonah / Queen of the South in 12.41–42 whereas Luke has the reverse order in vv. 31–32, since the connection between this twin saying and the preceding saying about the sign of Jonah is difficult in both cases; thus the fact that Matthew has the two Jonah sayings together says nothing about his relative originality. He may have created the connection himself by using the three-day analogy as a way of tying the two sayings together.

38. The differences and similarities between the Lucan and Matthaean forms of this invective and the relation of the place of the invective in the Gospel of Luke to the Marcan order were discussed at some length in Part One, and that discussion will not be repeated here.

39. Objections about allegorizing parables are irrelevant here. We are not dealing with a parable of Jesus, but with a parable that Luke has created from a narrative in his sources in order to illustrate further the point just made about repentance and doom.

40. The proposal of van Goudoever, 'Israel in Luke', p. 118, that we are to see Luke himself masquerading behind the vine-dresser who pleads for the extra time, and that we may thus see that Luke 'did not accept the responsibility to cut down

Israel', represents a considerable misreading of Luke-Acts. Luke can do lots of cutting down when the time is right.

41. Walaskay, *We Came to Rome*, p. 24; cf. also Maddox, *Purpose*, p. 47: 'In 13.1–9 this theme is unmistakable: unless you (the Jewish people) repent, you will be butchered by the Romans even within the Temple courts; unless you repent, the towers of Jerusalem will fall on you; unless Judaism becomes a fruitful tree, she is to be chopped down.'

42. Conzelmann's view (*Theology*, p. 65), that the three days are a reference to the tripartite structure of Jesus' ministry, is well known. While such a meaning is possible for Luke, it would have helped if Luke had been a little less cryptic.

43. Steck, *Geschick der Propheten*. The homiletical purpose was to provoke repentance.

44. Ibid., p. 57.

45. Robinson, *Weg*, pp. 54–5, is correct in emphasizing that 19.38 does not really fulfil 13.35, because, to mention only the most obvious difference, it is not Jerusalem but the disciples who quote the psalm calling Jesus blessed. Even so, 13.35 nevertheless anticipates 19.38. Where there are differences, they are to the point.

46. Luke 9.31 refers only to Jesus' fate, not to the role of Jerusalem in rejecting and being rejected by God.

47. τὶς τῶν ἀρχόντων τῶν Φαρισαίων = 'a certain one of the rulers of the Pharisees'. The article is missing before Φαρισαίων in B, ℵ and a few other less important MSS, giving the reading 'a certain one of the ruling Pharisees'. It is possible to read the text with the article in that way, although unlikely; and it is possible to read the text without the article in the other way, although equally unlikely. But Luke cannot mean to describe a Pharisee as being one of the *Archontes*, because he so carefully keeps those two groups apart everywhere else in the Gospel. He has rather given us a Pharisee here who is a fitting climax for the string of Jesus' three Pharisaic dinner hosts – a 'leading Pharisee'.

48. The Pharisees are not the opponents in 13.10–17, but the issue is the same, and the opponents are called 'hypocrites' (v. 15).

49. Cf., e.g., Sir. 13.10.

50. This grouping, of course, may have been original. On this point cf. Funk, *Language, Hermeneutic, and Word of God*, pp. 164–5. Still, the connection between the second group of the introduction and the second group of the parable is Lucan.

51. Since he is Jewish, this task is more distasteful than if he were a modern urbanite 'slopping hogs'.

52. Cf. again the several discussions of this point in Part One.

53. That they appear in separate places in Matthew does not prove that Luke's source did not have them together, for Matthew may have separated them.

54. Wilson, *Law*, p. 51.

55. Ibid.

56. Ibid., p. 45.

57. Ibid., p. 47.

58. As if Luke were a Seabee: 'The difficult we do immediately; the impossible takes a little longer.'

59. Wilson, *Law*, pp. 45–7.

60. Sandmel, *Anti-Semitism*, p. 73. The theme is also elaborated by Zingg, 'Stellung zur Heidenmission', pp. 205–8.

61. Bruners, *Reinigung der Aussätzigen*, passim. Betz, 'Ten Lepers', pp. 314–23, argues rather for a pre-Lucan narrative not greatly different from the canonical

pericope; but Fitzmyer, *Luke*, vol. 2, p. 1151, calls Betz's recreation of the pre-Lucan tradition 'highly speculative'. Fitzmyer (op. cit., p. 1149) correctly sees, at the least, 'pronounced . . . Lucan redaction'.

62. Cf. Bruners, *Reinigung der Aussätzigen*, pp. 198, 353.

63. Ibid., p. 152.

64. Ibid., p. 272.

65. There is now a widespread consensus that ἐντὸς ὑμῶν means 'among you' (plural). Further linguistic considerations, which others will of course still wish to carry on debating and which will probably never cease, are unrelated to our issue at hand.

66. Bruners, *Reinigung der Aussätzigen*, pp. 334–5.

67. Cf. again the discussion of this point in Part One. We may perhaps recall, in summary, that every single trait of the parable fits perfectly into Luke's overall plan.

68. The second announcement of the passion, Luke 9.44, is irrelevant for our interest, inasmuch as Luke mentions only 'people' as those who will harm Jesus.

69. Wellhausen, *Evangelium Lucae*, p. 104.

70. Cf. Paul's use of the phrase 'sons of Abraham' in Gal. 3.7 to mean Christians. That Luke can make use of Paul's terminology is seen in Luke 18.14.

71. English-speaking people on the American side of the Atlantic have stayed with this British translation of *minae*, apparently because 'dollar' seems too small an amount to fit the story; but the pound isn't worth all that much these days, either. 'Century notes' would be too slangy, however, so pounds it is.

72. Jülicher, *Gleichnisreden*, vol. 2, p. 486.

73. Neyrey, 'Jesus' Address', p. 80.

74. The other apparent exception to this distinction is Luke 9.22, where the scribes are connected with elders and chief priests. This is, however, the first announcement of the passion and therefore anticipates the regular pattern to be observed within the passion narrative.

75. Matthew may not have included the second saying; there is a question about the textual transmission of v. 14.

76. The possible exception is Luke 11.43 par. Matt. 23.6–7. If, indeed, Luke read Matthew, then Luke 11.43 is a conflation of Matt. 23.6–7 and Mark 12.39. I very much doubt this, however, since Matt. 23.6–7 includes the 'most prominent places at dinners' found in Mark 12.39 par. Luke 20.46. If Luke was copying Matthew in Luke 11.43, then we have to assume that he omitted the 'most prominent places at dinners' – to what purpose? He puts the charge to the Pharisees in 14.7 and to the scribes in 20.46 (following Mark); why not to the Pharisees in 11.43? It seems more likely that both Matt. 23.6–7 and Luke 11.43 rely on Mark. 12.39.

77. The following portion of the Lucan version of the Synoptic Apocalypse, vv. 25–36, treats of the return of the Son of man and of the divine conclusion to be brought to the world order and does not concern us here.

78. Neyrey, 'Jesus' Address', p. 82.

79. Zmijewski, *Eschatologiereden*, p. 215 (emphasis his).

80. Cf. Bachmann, *Jerusalem und Tempel*, p. 131.

81. Caird, *Luke*, pp. 231–2. Others have also seen the connection.

82. Zmijewski, *Eschatologiereden*, pp. 218–20.

83. Ibid., p. 219.

84. Ibid., p. 220.

85. That 'the people' is correct here, and that we should not read '. . . rulers *of* the people', was established at length in Part One.

86. On the explanatory use of δέ cf. Liddell-Scott, *Greek–English Lexicon*, s.v. δέ A. II. 2. a.

87. Plummer, *S. Luke*, p. 563, calls the construction 'a rather violent anacoluthon'.

88. Proposed by Klostermann, *Lukas*, p. 242, as one of two possible readings; cf. also the third edition of the Bible Societies' *Greek New Testament* and the twelfth edition of Aland's *Synopsis Quattuor Evangeliorum*. Fitzmyer, *Luke*, vol. 2, p. 1584, considers this a possibility but prefers to see the phrase as an unattached participial phrase.

7. The Acts of the Apostles

1. Lampe, 'Acts', p. 888.
2. Cf. *Beginnings*, Part I, Vol. 3, p. 12; Vol. 5, pp. 67–8, 113–14.
3. Ibid., Part I, Vol. 5, p. 114.
4. Ropes, op. cit., Part I, Vol. 3, p. 204.
5. Cf. again the discussion of this point in ch. 3.
6. Cf., e.g., Franklin, *Christ the Lord*, pp. 101–2.
7. Lohfink, *Sammlung Israels*, p. 55.
8. Jervell, *People of God*, p. 68.
9. Lohfink, *Sammlung Israels*, p. 60.
10. Cf. Haenchen, *Acts*, p. 251.
11. Cf. Loisy, *Actes*, p. 284.
12. That these historical precedents involve Luke in an anachronism (cf. the commentaries) is of no moment for our consideration here, since our purpose is to understand how Luke thinks of the Jews – in this case, specifically of the Pharisees – not to discover the correct historical order for Jesus, Theudas and Judas the Galilean.
13. Cf. Steck, *Geschick der Propheten*, p. 268; Wilckens, *Missionsreden*, pp. 187–224.
14. Cf. Via, 'Acts 7.35–37'.
15. We have to do with a Semitism here and perhaps should translate 'angelic ordinances'; Luke, however, may take the genitive literally.
16. Luke has got it wrong who takes off his clothes at a Jewish stoning, but never mind.
17. So Hengel, *Between Jesus and Paul*, p. 126.
18. So Wilson, *Gentiles*, p. 171.
19. Cf. Swaim, 'Aretas'.
20. Dibelius, *Studies*, p. 150.
21. Jervell, *People of God*, p. 60.
22. Lohfink, *Sammlung Israels*, pp. 43–4.
23. Franklin, *Christ the Lord*, pp. 108–15.
24. Jervell, *People of God*, p. 68.
25. Jervell, *People of God*, pp. 51–3.
26. Ibid., p. 51.
27. Ibid., p. 143.
28. Sandmel, *Anti-Semitism*, p. 91.
29. Schwartz, 'Accusation and Accusers', wants to understand Paul's oppponents in this episode as Jews and not as Gentiles, who charge that Paul and his companions, although Jews, are teaching Christian customs to other Jews who, being Roman citizens, consider the new customs illegal. This interpretation is possible, since the opposition arises because of events that occurred as the missionaries were 'going to (or: into) the synagogue (εἰς τὴν προσευχήν)'. It is only a designated few who bring

the charges, however, and it seems prudent to stay here with the more normal interpretation, that the accusers are Gentile.

30. Cf. again the discussion in ch. 3.

31. Cf. again the discussion of this point in ch. 3.

32. So also, e.g., Conzelmann, *Apostelgeschichte*, p. 107.

33. See the commentaries.

34. Cf. again the discussion of this point in ch. 3.

35. By, e.g., Haenchen, *Acts*, p. 557.

36. ἀφορίζω. The RSV translation 'taking the disciples with him' is misleading, since it implies that there were disciples in the synagogue. Acts does not say that, and disciples were specifically mentioned in 19.1, before Paul's entry into the synagogue.

37. Cadbury, *Acts in History*, p. 94.

38. Correctly seen by Jervell, *People of God*, p. 46.

39. Which Jervell also seems to intend; cf. his reference to 'mass conversions of Jews', with support running through Acts from 2.41 to 21.20, *People of God*, p. 44.

40. Cf. the discussion of this point in Conzelmann, *Apostelgeschichte*, p. 57.

41. Haacker, 'Bekenntnis', p. 440, argues that the 'juristic aspect' of Paul's trial before Felix could not belong to Luke's time, thereby overlooking the degree to which the Pauline passion is a literary plot.

42. The question is Luke's and not mine and reflects his wilful or naive portrayal of the benevolent Roman governor. In reality, Felix was a rather unsavoury character and might very well have left Jewish prisoners in jail for no reason; cf. Sandmel, 'Felix'.

43. At least, that seems to be the best sense that can be made out of the sentence as it stands. 'All the country of Judaea' is in the accusative case, however, and the other three entities are in the dative. The meaning is not clear, and the text may be corrupt. Cf. the discussion in Haenchen, *Acts*, pp. 686–7.

8. Luke's Motives

1. Overbeck, *Apostelgeschichte*, pp. xxx–xxxi.

2. G. Schneider, *Verleugnung*, pp. 193–5; cf. also id., 'Zweck', pp. 60–1; and, further, the summary in Plümacher, 'Acta-Forschung', pp. 52–3.

3. So also Conzelmann, *Theology*, p. 85; *Heiden–Juden–Christen*, p. 235; Grundmann, *Lukas*, p. 31. Cf. further Winter, *Trial*, pp. 70–89, esp. pp. 79–85, and 164.

4. Such a suggestion is made by T. W. Manson, 'Life of Jesus 3', pp. 397–8.

5. Plümacher, 'Acta-Forschung', p. 53.

6. Ruether, *Faith and Fratricide*, pp. 88–9.

7. G. Schneider, *Verleugnung*, p. 194. Cf. also Haenchen, *Acts*, pp. 289–90.

8. Winter, *Trial*, p. 170, emphasis his. Kränkl, *Knecht*, p. 118, and Gager, *Origins*, pp. 135–6, 149–51, also refer to mutual enmity, not to persecution.

9. Cf. the note in Lietzmann, *An die Korinther*, p. 151.

10. So also Loisy, *Actes*, p. 557.

11. Hare, *Jewish Persecution*, pp. 80–96. The translation of διώκω by 'harry' is Hare's (op. cit., pp. 92,119) and, I think, especially fortunate, since it includes both meanings of διώκω, 'pursue' and 'persecute'.

12. Ibid., p. 91.

13. Ibid., pp. 125–6.

14. Ibid., p. 106.

15. Ibid., pp. 99–106.

16. Ibid., pp. 110–11. Matthew follows that statement immediately with the one about 'finish[ing] the cities of Israel', but Hare argues that this second part of the verse does not belong originally with the first part and thus interprets the saying about fleeing to another city as referring to the situation in Matthew's day in the Diaspora. But didn't Matthew put the two sayings together?

17. Hare, *Jewish Persecution*, p. 113.

18. Ibid., pp. 114–21.

19. Ibid., pp. 121–2.

20. Ibid., p. 122.

21. Ibid., p. 123.

22. Ibid., pp. 127–8.

23. Ibid., p. 127.

24. The persecutions referred to by Paul and alluded to by Matthew can only have been of Christians who continued to associate themselves with the synagogue. Cf. Hare, *Jewish Persecution*, pp. 127–8.

25. Josephus, *AJ* 20.9.1, and Hegesippus quoted in Eusebius *Hist. Eccl.* 2.23.4–18.

26. Justin Martyr, *Apol.* 1.31.

27. Hare, *Jewish Persecution*, pp. 32–4; Baron, *Social and Religious History*, vol. 2, p. 131. Cf. also Schiffman, 'Tannaitic Perspectives', p. 155.

28. Scholars who have discussed Bar Kochba's persecution of Christians in detail in recent years (Hare, *Jewish Persecution*, p. 28; Baron, *Social and Religious History*, vol. 2, p. 132) have routinely concluded that Bar Kochba's persecution of (Jewish) Christians was at least as much political as religious, since Bar Kochba was considered to be the Messiah, so that a belief in someone else's Messiahship would imply treason. Nevertheless, a writer like Luke would probably hardly have been interested in Bar Kochba's motives.

29. The translation is after Kimelman, '*Birkat Ha-Minim*', p. 226. The 'standard' version of the prayer does not contain the third and fourth lines of the version here given.

30. The translations are from Martyn, *History and Theology*, pp. 38–40.

31. Ibid., p. 50.

32. Martyn, ibid.

33. Kimelman, '*Birkat Ha-Minim*'.

34. Ibid., p. 244; similarly Schiffman, 'Tannaitic Perspectives', pp. 149–52.

35. Katz, 'Separation'.

36. Ibid., p. 74. Schiffman, 'Tannaitic Perspectives', pp. 149–52, takes it that the curse against the *minim* was originally against Jewish Christians and for the function of preventing such Christians' serving as 'precentors in the synagogue' (p. 149), but that 'Nazarenes' was later added to the curse so that it would include all Christians.

37. Martyn, *History and Theology*, pp. 45–50.

38. Ibid., p. 47.

39. Ibid., p. 49.

40. While most recent scholars date Luke-Acts within a decade or two after the fall of Jerusalem, O'Neill, *Theology*, cites many similarities between Luke-Acts and the works of Justin Martyr and argues for a mid-second century authorship. That is the latest date possible, and I have tried to present the above argument in such a way that it is valid whenever Luke-Acts was written. I make no attempt in this work to date Luke-Acts more closely.

41. Cf. above, p. 22.

42. While addressing a different issue, whether or not Luke was a Jew, Plümacher,

'Acta-Forschung', p. 50, has provided a telling criticism that would seem also to apply to the assumption that Luke knew of Jewish persecution of Christianity in his own day. 'It was not Luke but [the primitive congregation and Paul] who were at home in Judaism.' The same applies to the persecution issue.

43. Maddox, *Purpose*, pp. 183–5. Cf. the discussion of this issue in Plümacher, 'Acta-Forschung', pp. 46–51. The idea already appears in Conzelmann, *Theology*, pp. 146, 209–13. When Conzelmann later (*Heiden–Juden–Christen*, p. 234) states that the Jews in the Diaspora were the 'externally superior' group, he has probably gone too far. Cf. the evidence of Pliny's correspondence with Trajan (Plin. *Epp. X [ad Traj.]*, xcvi) that by *c*. 112 most of Bithynia was Christian. Even the evidence from Sardis, where existed (after 300 CE) the largest known synagogue in the Roman world, does not prove Jews to have been 'externally superior' to Christians – at least not for any appreciable length of time. Cf. the cautious discussion by A. Thomas Kraabel in *Sardis*, pp. 186–8. Cf. also Dahl, *Memory*, pp. 95–7. Maddox's view may be regarded as a variant of that of Harnack, *Acts*, p. xxvii, that Luke was prompted to write Acts in order to answer the question of the origin of the Gentile mission within Judaism. Wilson, *Gentiles*, pp. 246–7, expresses a similar view.

44. Maddox, *Purpose*, p. 184. Similarly Loisy, *Actes*, p. 425.

45. Maddox, *Purpose*, p. 184.

46. Ibid., p. 185. Wilckens, *Missionsreden*, pp. 120–1, relates the accusations in the speeches in Acts to this Gentile-Christian setting.

47. Jervell, *People of God*, p. 68. Cf. further the views of Franklin, *Christ the Lord*, pp. 116–44, and the survey of this position given by Plümacher, 'Acta-Forschung', p. 46.

48. Jervell, *People of God*, p. 68. Wilson, *Gentiles*, p. 248, is in essential agreement. Cf. also Schmithals, *Lukas*, p. 224; and Winn, 'Elusive Mystery', p. 152: 'The rejection of the gospel by Israel according to the flesh posed a major theological problem.'

49. This is only partially true for Maddox.

50. Loisy, *Actes*, pp. 212–13; cf. also p. 425. Similarly Dibelius, *Studies*, p. 134. Wilken, *Christians As Romans Saw Them*, pp. 114–17 and 184–5, has presented conclusive evidence that one of Celsus's primary objections to Christianity, and the Emperor Julian's primary objection, was 'the Christian repudiation of its origin' (ibid., p. 116). Would thinking pagans not already have seen that problem in Luke's time?

51. The psychologist Richard Lowry, 'Rejected-Suitor Syndrome', has proposed that Luke faced a rather different kind of identity problem, that of the suitor who has been rejected. Similarly Levenson, 'Counterpart', p. 245. While such a suggestion may explain, in part, the development of early Christian antisemitism, Luke-Acts seems to present no direct evidence of such an attitude.

52. Cf. only Baur, *Paul*, vol. 1, p. 7.

53. Ibid., p. 9. Mattill, 'Purpose of Acts', p. 115, proposes that the many parallels between Paul and Jesus in Luke-Acts are a part of this apologetic purpose, i.e., to show how much like Jesus Paul was. That 'anti-Paulinism' was, in fact, a major element in early Christianity has recently been argued forcefully and generally persuasively by Lüdemann, *Antipaulinismus*. Cf. Lüdemann's statement, op. cit., p. 165, that an 'anti-Pauline orientation' had existed 'since the Corinthian and the Galatian crisis', and that this orientation involved 'the opposition of a nomistically oriented Christianity against the christologically founded religion of Paul'. Lüdemann, unfortunately, skips over Luke-Acts.

54. Trocmé, *Le 'Livre des Actes'*, p. 70; cf. also Gager, *Origins*, p. 185.

55. Trocmé, *Le 'Livre des Actes'*, p. 58.

56. Ibid., p. 67.

57. Ibid., p. 62. Wilson, *Law*, pp. 109–11, discusses the evidence for considering non-Christian Jews to be the opponents against whom Luke defends Paul, and that for considering Jewish Christians to be those opponents, without deciding. He concludes (ibid., p. 111) that 'Jewish or Jewish-Christian attacks on Paul . . . provide the best explanation for Luke's account of Paul and the law'.

58. Trocmé, *Le 'Livre des Actes'*, p. 118; cf. further the summary explanation, ibid., pp. 117–18.

59. Jervell, *People of God*, pp. 185–207, esp. pp. 187–93, 198.

60. Loisy, *Evangiles synoptiques*, vol. 2, p. 357, would include the parable of the Good Samaritan here, for it contrasts the attitude of 'Judaeo-Christianity' to the inclusiveness of 'true Christianity'.

61. Luke's polemic against Jewish Christianity is overlooked by Kränkl, *Knecht*, who suggests that the polemic against 'the Jews' could only have been effective at a time when Jewish Christianity had become an insignificant part of the church (ibid., p. 118).

62. Cf. above, p. 310.

63. The observation made by Talbert, *What Is a Gospel?*, p. 108, that the Gospel of Luke belongs to a sub-genre of Hellenistic biography that 'arise[s] out of . . . a struggle over where the true tradition is to be found in the present', is thus entirely justified (although Talbert did not have Jewish Christianity in mind as the object of Luke's polemic).

Index of Scripture Passages

Index of Other Ancient Authors

PAGAN

JEWISH

CHRISTIAN

Index of Modern Authors